THE LURE OF THE

Why did the Romans turn out in their tens of thousands to watch brutal gladiatorial games? Previous studies have tried to explain the attraction of the arena by theorizing its cultural function in Roman society. The games have been seen as celebrations of the violence of empire or of Rome's martial heritage, or as manifestations of the emperor's power. The desire to watch has therefore been limited to the Roman context and rendered alien to modern sensibilities. Yet the historical record reveals that people living in quite different times and circumstances (including our own) have regularly come out in large numbers to watch public rituals of violence such as executions, floggings, animal-baiting, cudgeling, pugilism, and so on. Appreciating the social-psychological dynamics at work in attracting people to watch such events not only deepens our understanding of the spectator at the Roman games but also suggests something important about ourselves.

GARRETT G. FAGAN is Associate Professor of Classics and Ancient Mediterranean Studies and History at Pennsylvania State University where he teaches courses in Roman and Greek history, Latin, and ancient warfare. He is the author, co-author, or editor of four books including *Bathing in Public in the Roman World* (1999), *Archaeological Fantasies* (2006), and *New Perspectives on Ancient Warfare* (2010), as well as numerous scholarly articles.

THE LURE OF THE ARENA

Social Psychology and the Crowd at the Roman Games

BY

GARRETT G. FAGAN

CAMBRIDGE
UNIVERSITY PRESS

CAMBRIDGE UNIVERSITY PRESS
Cambridge, New York, Melbourne, Madrid, Cape Town,
Singapore, São Paulo, Delhi, Tokyo, Mexico City

Cambridge University Press
The Edinburgh Building, Cambridge CB2 8RU, UK

Published in the United States of America by Cambridge University Press, New York

www.cambridge.org
Information on this title: www.cambridge.org/9780521185967

First published 2011

Printed in the United Kingdom at the University Press, Cambridge

A catalogue record for this publication is available from the British Library

Library of Congress Cataloguing in Publication data
Fagan, Garrett G., 1963–
The lure of the arena : social psychology and the crowd at the Roman games / Garrett G. Fagan.
p. cm.
Includes bibliographical references and index.
ISBN 978-0-521-19616-1
1. Executions and executioners – History.   2. Gladiators – History.   3. Violence – History.
4. Social psychology – History.   I. Title.
HV8551.F34   2011
937 – dc22   2010042929

ISBN 978-0-521-19616-1 hardback
ISBN 978-0-521-18596-7 paperback

To George and Emmet, gladiators in the making

Contents

Figures

Preface

Large trees start as small seeds. Such is the case in this instance. The central contention of this book – that psychological matters played a key role in luring spectators to Roman arena spectacles – was presented as a twenty minute paper at the AIA/APA Joint Annual Meeting in 2001. I had intended to write it up as an article but when I found that the article had become irredeemably long, I decided it was necessary to extend the treatment to book length. Here is that book, born of the simplest question "Why did they go and watch?"

My first debt of gratitude goes to the Alexander von Humboldt Foundation for its generous support during a Research Fellowship at the Institut für Altertumskunde in the University of Cologne in 2003–4. The bulk of the manuscript was produced during a wonderful year there. Prof. Werner Eck was a model sponsor in Cologne – warmly welcoming and always ready to help. He also offered many useful comments about my project as it progressed. Conversations with other colleagues in Cologne and elsewhere were also very useful: Peter Eich, Rudolf Haensch, and Luke Lavan all contributed ideas and comments. As the book was nearing completion, further financial support was provided by the Institute for the Arts and Humanities at Penn State. I thank the director and my colleagues there for their help and support.

Other colleagues have read parts or all of the manuscript: David Potter, Paul Friedland, Phil Baldi, Christopher Francese, C. W. Marshall, and two anonymous readers for Cambridge University Press. I thank all of them for their input. Erin O'Brien kindly reviewed my notes and caught errors and inconsistencies there. Andrea Gatzke helped in checking the proofs.

Given my social-psychological approach, and the fact that I am untrained in that discipline, it was essential for me not to risk dilettantism and have the appropriate parts of the work vetted by professionals. Several very kindly answered my requests for assistance: Steve Reicher (on crowds), John Duckitt (on prejudice), and Dolf Zillmann (on the attraction of violence as entertainment). I thank them all for putting me straight on various social-psychological matters and advising me in other ways.

The book has been some ten years in the making, and I have presented various parts of it at professional meetings and as invited lectures at different times and places. Audience input has been uniformly useful and thoughtful on those occasions, and while I cannot remember everyone who commented or critiqued, I thank them all here for their feedback. In the end, of course, I take full responsibility for what is presented here and none of the above ought to be tarnished by the stains of errors and infelicities that remain.

Throughout the book, abbreviations for ancient sources follow those laid out in the *OCD*³, while abbreviations for modern journals follow the format of the *AJA*, available at the journal's website (www.ajaonline.org/index.php). Where an *AJA* format was not available, the abbreviations are those used in *L'Année Philologique*.

Introduction: Alypius in the stands

I wondered, and still wonder what it was like to be there.

K. Hopkins, *Death and Renewal* (1983)[1]

During a visit to Rome from his native North Africa, Augustine's friend Alypius was reluctantly dragged along to a spectacle in the Colosseum by some fellow law students. Protesting that such things were beneath him, Alypius first kept his eyes firmly shut. But the roars of the crowd piqued his curiosity, and he sneaked a glimpse at the proceedings. Instantly he was, as Augustine puts it,

> . . . struck with a more serious wound in his soul than was he, whom he wanted to see, in his body . . . For when he saw the blood, he drank in the savagery and did not turn away but fixed his gaze on it. Unaware of what he was doing, he devoured the mayhem and was delighted by the wicked contest and drunk on its cruel pleasure . . . He looked, he shouted, he was fired up, and he carried away with him the madness that would goad him to return.[2]

The strikingly immediate nature of this account raises justifiable suspicions that Augustine is here describing his own experiences rather than someone else's. He admits elsewhere in his writings that he had once entertained a passion for spectacles, although he is vague about the details.[3] If Augustine is

---

[1] K. Hopkins, *Death and Renewal: Sociological Studies in Roman History II* (Cambridge, 1983), 203.

[2] August. *Conf.* 6.13 = T.3 (in Appendix). To avoid needless repetition, pertinent *testimonia* that merit repeated analysis are assembled in the Appendix and are hereafter designated by the appropriate entry numbers for ease of reference. "T" denotes a literary text (Appendix, Section A) and "I" an inscription (Appendix, Section B).

[3] On Augustine's passion for spectacles, see August. *De civ. D.* 2.4 and *En. Ps.* 147.7 = *PL* 36–7, 1918–19: "Watching closely the spectacles that please them, let them look at themselves from time to time and be displeased. For I take pleasure in doing just this in the midst of the crowd – I myself once sat there too, and raged. How many future Christians or even bishops do I think sit there now?" (*et multum intenti in illa spectacula, quae illis placent, aliquando et se spectent, sibique displiceant. in multis enim iam factum gaudemus, et aliquando nos quoque ibi sedimus, et insanivimus: et quam multos putamus ibi nunc sedere, futuros non solum christianos sed etiam episcopos?*). Augustine spent time in Rome in

indeed here speaking from personal experience, even if dimly remembered, then he provides a uniquely first-hand account of the effect that watching the games had on a Roman spectator's mental state.

The passage challenges us to confront a very basic question about the arena: what drew the Romans, in their thousands, to watch brutal gladiatorial spectacles? How and why did they derive pleasure from watching people and animals pitted against each other and slaughtered?[4] What, in short, was the lure of the arena? The argument of this book is that, to be convincing, any answer to this question requires due consideration of human psychology, once it is properly set against the Romans' historical context.

Arena spectacles have been much studied in recent years and many theories promulgated to explain their popularity. These explanations have overwhelmingly employed symbolic, religious, political, sociological, or anthropological lines of argument (see below, chapter 1). All such approaches are culture-specific, in that their analysis fixes the games firmly in the cultural and historical space the Romans inhabited. This is an entirely valid approach: watching violent spectacles obviously has powerful socio-cultural components, and the arena, as a peculiarly Roman phenomenon, was not reproduced elsewhere as such. Yet a corollary of such culturally rooted analyses is an overemphasis on the historical specificity of the Roman fascination with violent spectacle. The historical record makes it depressingly clear that the Romans were by no means alone in finding the sight of people and animals tormented and killed both intriguing and appealing (see below, chapter 2). The central contentions of this book are, on the one hand, that an explanation for the transcultural and transhistorical appeal of violent spectacle must be sought in human psychology and, on the other, that appreciation of the psychology in turn deepens our understanding of the Roman experience.

While it is hardly to be doubted that spectatorship at the arena had powerful psychological components, scholars to date have treated those components only in the most perfunctory manner, if at all. "The human psyche appears susceptible to the thrill of vicarious pain," suggests Kathleen Coleman, while Keith Hopkins proposes that

---

the summer of AD 383 before moving on to Milan the following year; see P. Brown, *Augustine of Hippo: A Biography*, 2nd edn. (Berkeley, 2000), 57–61. Alypius' experience in the arena is not unlike Augustine's own, when, as an adolescent, he particpated in robbing a pear-tree under pressure from his friends; see *Conf.* 2.15.

[4] That the Romans enjoyed watching the games is perhaps so glaringly obvious as to require no documentation, but do note esp. Livy 41.20.11–13 = T.9, Salv. *Gub. Dei* 6.10 = T.18, Tert. *Spect.* 1 and other sources discussed in C. Edwards, *Death in Ancient Rome* (New Haven, 2007), 63–8.

Part of the answer [for the spectators' enjoyment of the games] may lie in the social psychology of the crowd, which helps relieve the individual of responsibility, and in the psychological mechanisms by which some spectators identify more readily with the victory of the aggressor than with the sufferings of the vanquished... At the psychological level, the gladiatorial shows provided a stage (as television news does for modern viewers) for shared violence and tragedy.[5]

The elucidation of these and other psychological processes, and how they were manifested at the Roman arena, is the central focus of this book.

Social psychology offers the most promising tool for the inquiry that follows, since it stands at the intersection of consciousness and context, where situation meets behavior. Given that any sociocultural environment is a product of particular sets of historical conditions, the question arises as to whether social-psychological analyses can legitimately cut across historical boundaries.[6] It was argued over thirty years ago that social psychology, as currently practiced, is firmly presentist. At the same time, the possibility of psychological continuity with the past was left open as a potentially productive line of inquiry.[7] While this potential has not been enthusiastically exploited by social psychologists, at least one study has taken up the challenge and demonstrated historical continuity in the sphere of interpersonal relationships.[8] More recently, the leading crowd

---

[5] See K. M. Coleman, "'The Contagion of the Throng': Absorbing Violence in the Roman World," *European Review* 5 (1997), 401–17 = *Hermathena* 164 (1998), 65–88 (quote at 80); and Hopkins, *Death and Renewal*, 1–30 (quotes at 27 and 30 respectively). For comparable (and comparably vague) observations, see, e.g., K. M. Coleman, "Entertaining Rome," in J. Coulston and H. Dodge (eds.), *Ancient Rome: Archaeology of the Eternal City* (Oxford, 2000), 216; A. Hönle and A. Henze, *Römische Amphitheater und Stadien: Gladiatorenkämpfe und Circusspiele* (Zurich, 1981), 75; D. Kyle, *Sport and Spectacle in the Ancient World* (Oxford, 2007), 126; R. Lane Fox, *The Classical World: An Epic History from Homer to Hadrian* (New York, 2006), 442; K. Nossov, *Gladiator: Rome's Bloody Spectacle* (Oxford, 2009), 168–9; B. D. Shaw, "Among the Believers," *EchCl* 28 (1984), 453–79, esp. 472–9; G. Ville, *La gladiature en Occident des origines à la mort de Domitien*, BEFAR 245 (Rome, 1981), 457–72. David Potter puts it this way – "it was precisely in order to become lost in the emotions of the moment that they went"; see D. S. Potter, "Spectacle," in D. S. Potter (ed.), *The Blackwell Companion to the Roman World* (Oxford, 2006), 385–408 (quote at 386).

[6] Social psychologists are acutely aware of this issue; see M. H. Bond (ed.), *The Cross-Cultural Challenge to Social Psychology* (Newbury Park, 1988); P. B. Smith and M. H. Bond, *Social Psychology across Cultures: Analysis and Perspectives*, 2nd edn. (Boston, MA, 1999). An entire periodical, the *Journal of Cross-Cultural Psychology*, is devoted to this line of analysis.

[7] K. J. Gergen, "Social Psychology as History," *Journal of Personality and Social Psychology* 26 (1973), 309–20, esp. 318 on the historical durability of at least some psychological processes. Social-psychological insights, especially about prejudice and stereotyping, have been applied to real-world conflict situations, and such analysis can include a historical dimension; see, e.g., D. Bar-Tal and Y. Teichman, *Stereotypes and Prejudice in Conflict: Representations of Arabs in Israeli Jewish Society* (Cambridge, 2005); J. L. Chin (ed.), *The Psychology of Prejudice and Discrimination*, 4 vols. (Westport, 2004).

[8] J. Adamopoulos and R. Bontempo, "Diachronic Universals in Interpersonal Structures: Evidence from Literary Sources," *Journal of Cross-Cultural Psychology* 17 (1986), 169–89.

psychologist Stephen Reicher stresses "the necessity of developing a historical and interactive set of methods and of concepts if we are to understand
social understanding and social action."[9] These trends within the discipline of social-psychology dovetail with the historical questions addressed
in this book. On the broadest perspective, our shared humanity with the
people of the past means that any insistence that populations divided by
culture and history do *not* share basic mental processes requires detailed
demonstration, rather than the more reasonable assumption that they do
(as argued in more detail below, chapter 1).

Is it possible that people are somehow inherently inclined – by fear of
death, or morbid fascination – to watch unpleasantness? Certainly, enough
distressing comparanda are at hand from the annals of history (see below,
chapter 2), and some students of the arena have taken it as a given that
basic elements in human psychology were at work among the spectators.[10]
Even if this is so, it is also the case that cultural context governs spectators' attitudes about what is acceptable for any given spectacle. Divergent
historical circumstances account for the marked variations in form, intent,
degree, and scale of spectacular brutality, from Aztec human sacrifice to
American Ultimate Fighting. So the contention here is not that all spectacular and violent rituals are essentially alike. Procedures vary widely, as
do the historical circumstances that give rise to them.

What remains incontestable, however, is that whenever violence of whatever brand is staged in public, people can be found who are more than willing to turn up and watch, often in large numbers. They will watch violent
events that vary considerably in their nature, their form, and the objectives
of their organizers. Similar variety characterizes the manner in which the
political, symbolic, or religious timbres of such spectacles synchronize with
the cultural rhythms of a specific context. In this sense, spectatorship at

---

[9] S. Reicher, "The Psychology of Crowd Dynamics," in M. A. Hogg and R. S. Tindale (eds.), *Blackwell
     Handbook of Social Psychology: Group Processes* (Oxford, 2001), 202–3 (quote at 203); see also the
     similar comments of R. Brown, *Group Processes: Dynamics Within and Between Groups*, 2nd edn.
     (Oxford, 2000), 357–8. Reicher's recent work makes ample use of historical evidence to elucidate the
     psychological processes that are his primary interest; see S. D. Reicher et al., "Saving Bulgaria's Jews:
     An Analysis of Social Identity and the Mobilisation of Social Solidarity," *European Journal of Social
     Psychology* 36 (2006), 49–72; S. Reicher et al., "Making a Virtue of Evil: A Five-Step Social Identity
     Model of the Development of Collective Hate," *Social and Personality Psychology Compass* 2/3 (2008),
     1313–44; S. Reicher, *The Crowd* (Cambridge, forthcoming), ch. 1. (My thanks to Professor Reicher
     for providing me with pre-publication manuscripts of the latter two items.) Social psychology has
     also been profitably applied in Biblical Studies; see, e.g., P. A. Holloway, *Coping with Prejudice: 1
     Peter in Social Psychological Perspective* (Tübingen, 2009).
[10] See Coleman, "Contagion." See also her comments in "They, Too, Enjoyed Watching Violence
     And Death," *New York Times* (July 7, 2001), B9.

any given spectacle can be conceived as a symbiosis between intertwined contextual and psychological factors. While the latter are the focus of this study, context shapes spectator expectations and lends spectacular violence its cultural meaning(s), and those meaning(s) in turn shape the psychological experience of the spectator. Psychology and culture are not readily separable categories. They are in fact flipsides of the same coin. Therefore, in what follows, both cultural and psychological analysis go hand-in-hand to elucidate as fully as possible the experience of watching at the Roman arena.

Violent spectacles can be divided, broadly speaking, into three categories: agonistic/ludic (e.g., boxing, wrestling, cudgeling, animal baiting); punitive/retributive (e.g., public executions, corporal punishment, lynchings); and religious (e.g., human sacrifice, ritual mutilation). These categories are not mutually exclusive and can overlap, as when criminals were condemned to fight as gladiators (which conflated the ludic and punitive categories), or when in later ages religious heretics were burned at the stake as punishment for their thought-crimes. The "conglomerate spectacles" of the Roman arena managed to combine the ludic and punitive categories into a single, complex event suffused with religious symbolism, and thus fashioned an unholy trinity that merged all three forms into one.[11]

Charting the course of a "typical" day at the arena (if there was such a thing as a "typical" arena spectacle) is a difficult task, since the primary sources are scattered and patchy. The format that emerges as common, however, is roughly as follows.[12] The morning show featured exhibitions of animals, the more exotic the better. This phase usually ended in the slaughter of the beasts (*venatio*).[13] The hunt could overlap with the next

---

[11] The religious significance of arena spectacles is a matter we are poorly informed about, but the dressing up of some attendants in religious garb (Tert. *Apol.* 15.4–5) makes the religious aspect self-evident. See also A. Futrell, *Blood in the Arena: The Spectacle of Roman Power* (Austin, 1997); M. B. Hornum, *Nemesis, the Roman State, and the Games* (Leiden, 1993).

[12] The daily format is suggested by Commodus' appearances in the arena, described by Dio from personal observation at 73(72).19.1–2 (hunts, lunch, and then gladiators). Lucian (*Tox.* 59) delineates the same format (hunts, executions, gladiators). Suetonius (*Claud.* 21.1) distinguishes gladiatorial games put on "without the hunt and stage equipment" (*sine venatione apparatuque*) from the more "regular and usual kind" (*iustum atque legitimum*), which presumably means the full, tripartite spectacle. For summaries of proceedings with ample citation of pertinent ancient evidence, see A. Futrell, *The Roman Games: A Sourcebook*, Historical Sources in Translation (Oxford, 2006), 84–119; D. G. Kyle, *Spectacles of Death in Ancient Rome* (London, 1998), 34–127; M. G. Mosci Sassi, *Il linguaggio gladiatorio* (Bologna, 1992), 55–62; T. Wiedemann, *Emperors and Gladiators* (London, 1992), 55–101; Ville, *Gladiature*, 345–445. For the phases of spectacle traced through inscriptions, see M. Fora, *I Munera Gladiatoria in Italia: Considerazioni sulla loro documentazione epigrafica* (Naples, 1996), 41–53.

[13] Note, e.g., *CIL* 9.2350 = *ILS* 5059 = *EAOR* 3.26 (Allifae; second half of first century AD) for mention of a "hunt of African beasts" (*venationem | bestiarum Africanar(um)*), where their African origin is clearly a matter of pride for the sponsor. Animal displays were not always violent; see

stage, the public execution of criminals at midday (*summa supplicia*), since one of the more common modes of execution was exposure to wild beasts (*damnatio ad bestias*). One inscription from Italy includes notice of the execution victims among the categories of animals displayed, which suggests they could be classed as part and parcel of the animal displays.[14] A terracotta plaque from Rome shows man-and-beast hunts in progress in the Circus Maximus, and just below a lunging lion lies a prostrate naked figure – likely a person who had been condemned to the beasts. The two events (hunt and execution) are here represented simultaneously.[15] The lunch break and early afternoon could be occupied with more executions, including exposure to beasts, burning alive, forced combats, or straight butchery of unarmed prisoners. In a bizarre twist, some executions were staged as enactments of myths: a convict garbed as "Icarus" pushed off a tower, or an "Orpheus" failing disastrously to charm wild bears. After these preliminaries, the gladiators made their appearance as the headline event (*gladiatorum paria*). Highly trained and skilled, variously equipped, they fought in pairs announced in advance.[16]

---

below, ch. 7, pp. 247–8. For the ancient terminology of the arena, see C. Mann, "Gladiators in the Greek East: A Case Study in Romanization," *International Journal of the History of Sport* 26 (2009), 272–97, esp. 281–3; Mosci Sassi, *Linguaggio gladiatorio*. Note the existence of the "Morning Training School" (*Ludus Matutinus*) near the Colosseum in Rome, reserved for the performers in this phase of the spectacle; see *LTUR*, vol. iii, 195–8, s.v. "Ludus" (D. Palombi and C. Pavolini). See also M. MacKinnon, "Supplying Exotic Animals for the Roman Amphitheatre Games: New Reconstructions Combining Archaeological, Ancient Textual, Historical, and Ethnographic Data," *Museion* 6 (2006), 137–61.

[14] See *AE* 1899.207 = *ILS* 5063a = *EAOR* 3.42 (Beneventum; second century AD): "He produced as an embellishment for Beneventum a four-day show that featured four wild animals, sixteen bears, four convicts, and the rest herbivores" (*edente Be|neventi exornato | munere diebus IIII | feris n. IIII, ursis XVI | noxeis IIII et ceteris herbariis*). Were the convicts disposed of one per day (although it is possible that *noxii* here means "dangerous/harmful animals")? Note also *CIL* 9.3437 = *ILS* 5063 = *EAOR* 3.35 (Caporciano, near L'Aquila; mid-second century AD) which mentions a three-day spectacle featuring four *noxii* and *CIL* 4.9983a = P. Sabbatini Tumolesi, *Gladiatorum Paria: Annunci di spettacoli gladiatorii a Pompei* (Rome, 1980), 107 (no. 79) for mention of *cruciarii* ("crucifixion victims"), hunts, and the awning in an advertisement for games. A relief from Apri in Asia Minor, as well as the Zliten mosaic from Libya, appear to show executions occurring concurrently with beast hunts, although the possibility that a series of events is being depicted in the same image cannot be ruled out; see S. Aurigemma, *I mosaici di Zliten*, Africa italiana 2 (Rome, 1926), 129–201, esp. 178–94; L. Robert, *Les gladiateurs dans l'Orient grec* (Paris, 1940; repr. Amsterdam, 1971), 90–1 (no. 27) and plate 24. For the term *meridiani* ("midday performers"), see Sen. *Ep.* 7.3 = T.20; Suet. *Claud.* 34.2 = T.23; Tert. *Spect.* 19.2 = T.28 and *Apol.* 15.4.

[15] D. Augenti, *Spettacoli del Colosseo nelle cronache degli antichi* (Rome, 2001), 68–9. When the mob at Smyrna demanded that a lion be loosed on the martyr Polycarp, they were told it was not allowed, since the days of the animal shows were over; see *Pass. Polyc.* 12.3 = H. Musurillo, *The Acts of the Christian Martyrs: Introduction, Texts and Translations* (Oxford, 1972), 10–12. In all likelihood, considerable variation characterized the phasing of spectacles in different parts of the empire.

[16] An advertisement for games at Pompeii (*CIL* 4.2508 = Sabbatini Tumolesi, *Gladiatorum Paria*, 71–4 [no. 32] = Fora, *Munera Gladiatoria*, 128 [no. 57] = I.3) includes the names of the combatants

Each phase of the spectacle had its own prior history. The *venatio*, first held at Rome in 186 BC, could trace its ancestry back through the Greek world to the traditions of royal zoos and *paradeisoi* (safari parks that doubled as hunting estates) of the ancient Near East.[17] Public executions long predated arena events and had been conducted outside cities or in town squares for centuries, and these venues continued to be used even during the era of the arena's popularity.[18] The origins of gladiators are not entirely clear, but they were likely an Italic development, and the closest antecedents have been identified among the funerary rites of the Lucanians in south-central Italy in the fourth century BC. But it remains far from certain whether these combats were the sole ancestors of gladiatorial *munera* and whether other sources of influence remain as yet undetected. Whatever the case, gladiators first appeared at Rome in 264 BC, in a funerary context.[19] The fully developed, conglomerate arena spectacle was thus a

along with their fight records up to that point (see below, ch. 6, pp. 209–13, for discussion). Later, the results were noted by a different hand; see J. P. V. D. Balsdon, *Life and Leisure in Ancient Rome* (London, 1969), 337–8.

[17] Livy 39.22.2 (186 BC). On the precursors to the *venatio*, see J. K. Anderson, *Hunting in the Ancient World* (Berkeley, 1985); J. Aymard, *Les chasses romaines des origines à la fin du siècle des Antonins* (Paris, 1951), 25–85; J. M. Barringer, *The Hunt in Ancient Greece* (Baltimore, 2001); K. M. Coleman, "Ptolemy Philadelphus and the Roman Amphitheater," in W. J. Slater (ed.), *Roman Theater and Society* (Ann Arbor, 1996), 49–68; M. Giebel, *Tiere in der Antike: Von Fabelwesen, Opfertieren, und treuen Begleitern* (Darmstadt, 2003), esp. 184–97.

[18] Plato (*Rep.* 439e–440a) locates an execution ground somewhere outside Athens on the way to the Piraeus, and the Tarpeian Rock in Rome or the hill of Calvary outside Jerusalem need no introduction. The Forum (for convicts of status), outside the Colline Gate (for lapsed Vestal Virgins), and the Campus Martius and the Esquiline hill (for commoners) are all attested as places of execution in Rome; see F. Hinard, "Spectacle des exécutions et espace urbain," in *L'urbs: espace urbain et histoire* (Paris, 1984), 111–75, esp. 113–17; and several esssays in *Du châtiment dans la cité: supplices corporels et peine de mort dans le monde antique*, CEFR 79 (Paris, 1984). Cicero describes a flogging and searing with hot plates in the marketplace of Messana (Cic. *Verr.* 2.5.162–4) and notes that crucifixions were usually staged on the Pompeian Road behind the town (ibid. 2.5.169). In the *Acts of the Christian Martyrs* vague phrases like "place of martyrdom" or "place of execution" or "the usual place" appear frequently. The martyrdom of Marian and James in the third century AD took place in a river valley near the Numidian town of Cirta. The valley had high banks that functioned as a sort of natural theater; see *Pass. Mar. et Iacob.* 9–12 (= Musurillo, *Acts of the Christian Martyrs*, 206–11). Similarly, Potamiaena was martyred in some public place in Alexandria where the crowd had direct access to her person and had to be beaten back by the soldier Basilides; see *Pass. Pot. et Basil.* 3–4 (= Musurillo, *Acts of the Christian Martyrs*, 132–3). Cyprian was beheaded before witnesses on the grounds of a private citizen's estate; see *Pass. Cypr.* 5 (= Musurillo, *Acts of the Christian Martyrs*, 174–5). Conon was killed in the streets and agora of Magydos; see *Pass. Con.* 6 (= Musurillo, *Acts of the Christian Martyrs*, 192–3). Seven female martyrs at Saloniki in Macedonia were burned alive at "a high place"; see *Pass. Agap. et al.* 7 (= Musurillo, *Acts of the Christian Martyrs*, 292–3). Irenaeus was beheaded on a bridge at Sirmium; see *Pass. Iren.* 5 (= Musurillo, *Acts of the Christian Martyrs*, 298–9).

[19] Livy, *Per.* 16 (264 BC). Much has been written on the origins of gladiators. For contrasting proposi-tions, see, e.g., Futrell, *Blood in the Arena*, 9–51 (favors Etruria); J. Mouratidis, "On the Origin of the Gladiatorial Games," *Nikephoros* 9 (1996), 111–34 (suggests a Greek connection); Ville, *Gladiature*,

hybrid, a synthesis of several originally distinct types of event combined into a single show, often spread over several days.[20] The very complexity of the games ensures that any social-psychological analysis of spectatorship there will have to be multifaceted.

THE STRENGTHS AND LIMITATIONS OF SOCIAL PSYCHOLOGY

Social psychology studies the mental mechanics of social interaction and the influence of situation on behavior. As such, it combines the insights of individual psychology (how a person thinks) with an appreciation of the sorts of issues that normally occupy the attention of the sociologist or cultural anthropologist (patterns of behavior). What might be termed "external" contextual concerns are united with "internal" psychological considerations in formulating explanations. The chief advantage of this approach is that it raises fundamental and important questions about Roman arena spectators: why did they watch? What were they thinking or feeling as they made their way to the arena and took their seats? In what ways did the brutal games give them pleasure? What were the attractions of the arena?

Prior explanations infer the popularity of the games by theorizing their cultural function. Therefore, their explanations are both subliminal and historically localized. These were lures not consciously experienced by the spectators. Nobody argues, for example, that Romans en route to the arena actively thought they were setting out to neutralize socially threatening forces by witnessing them staged under controlled conditions, or fulfilling a conscious need to be reminded of their martial heritage, or thinking it was about time the emperor's power over nature was reiterated in their presence.[21] Appreciation of the crowd's psychological state(s) may alert us to the more immediate attractions of the arena, to the consciously experienced feelings, emotions, and attitudes that stemmed from (and

1–56 (argues for an Oscan origin). Kyle (*Spectacles of Death*, 34–75; reiterated in his *Sport and Spectacle*, 270–3) adopts a sensible attitude toward the question of origins: blood rituals in the form of sports, combats, and sacrifices were so prevalent in Iron Age Italy that a simple linear transmission to Rome from any single source seems unlikely. Analogous agnosticism is expressed by K. E. Welch, *The Roman Amphitheatre from its Origins to the Colosseum* (Cambridge, 2007), 11–18.

[20] Kyle (*Spectacles of Death*, 34–127) charts this process clearly.

[21] Histories of collective *mentalités* posit behavior driven precisely from unconscious cultural flotsam such as this, embedded in rituals and collective memories that were not willfully recognized by those sharing in them; "[their] object is that which escapes historical individuals because it reveals the impersonal content of their thought"; see J. Le Goff, "Mentalities: A History of Ambiguities," in J. Le Goff and P. Nora (eds.), *Constructing the Past: Essays in Historical Methodology* (Cambridge, 1985), 166–80 (quote at 169).

drove) attendance. Indeed, the mental processes charted in what follows offer a bridge between the unconsciously appreciated meanings of the games in Roman culture and the lived experience of the spectator in the stands.

For this reason, the psychological analysis adopted here does not supersede or disqualify the culture-specific approaches that have dominated arena scholarship to date. The psychological processes at the heart of this study must be understood as operating in close conjunction with the historical and cultural environment the Romans had created, even if the precise valence of this interaction cannot be charted in a linear fashion. So there is no claim here to uncover the ultimate, let alone the only explanation for the Roman attachment to spectacular violence. Rather, an appreciation of the mental processes operative among arena spectators enriches and complements the other explanatory models (though it may question or clash with some of them). It adds another tessera to our mosaic of understanding.

What follows is therefore an interdisciplinary study that draws heavily on comparative history and social psychology. As with any vibrant modern social science, propositions in social psychology undergo revision with a rapidity that, from the perspective of the humanist, is nothing short of harrowing. Work considered groundbreaking in one decade can be deemed passé in the next (though there are seminal "classics" that continue to earn the respect, even the allegiance, of current researchers). This disconcerting situation can leave the neophyte with a sense of groundlessness. It also presents a serious methodological trap. It becomes all too easy to cherry-pick from among those ideas that best fit one's argument and ignore the rest. I have sought to avoid this pitfall by reading as widely as I could among the most up-to-date, pertinent research I could find. I have also consulted and corresponded with social psychologists, and several kindly agreed to read those chapters relevant to their own research interests.

I have noted that while psychologists often present their propositions as being in competition with other ideas, many psychological models display a greater degree of complementarity than their champions appear willing to concede. Much current work builds on prior insights rather than in opposition to them.[22] Some researchers, indeed, are actively working to transcend boundaries within the discipline, as they seek a more generalized understanding than that offered by focused studies of particular phenomena. As noted above, the social psychologist Stephen Reicher has

---

[22] For the example of group processes, see J. Szmatka et al., *The Growth of Social Knowledge: Theory, Simulation, and Empirical Research in Group Processes* (Westport, 2002).

called for a historical perspective within the discipline. While the vector of this book runs in the opposite direction to what Reicher has in mind – in that it explores what social psychology can tell us about a particular set of historical circumstances, rather than vice versa – it is very much consonant with his overall approach. It is therefore to be hoped that even if in ten years' time the psychological propositions outlined in what follows are viewed as fossils of bygone models, the methods employed and the historical data assembled here will be of use in the search for a deeper understanding of the issues addressed.

Unlike today's social scientists, ancient historians cannot poll or survey their subjects, bring them into laboratories and conduct experiments on them, or directly observe their behavior to deduce their frames of mind. We rely instead on the scattered and biased testimony of the extant sources, composed mostly by members of the elite and bounded by circumstances of time, geography, gender, and class. This immediately poses a problem, since our interest here is in mass behavior and motivation, and the ancient elite authors rarely reflect the masses' point of view. What little they do say is colored by their social (or religious) prejudices, so that in both pagan and Christian treatises the arena crowd is portrayed as a cruel, uneducated rabble, impressed by the flashy and the frivolous, and incapable of worthwhile pastimes.[23] Such attitudes were wholly typical of the Roman elite's snobbery when confronted by the *plebs* and what it considered their mindless pursuits.[24] That said, it is clear that the sources do not cut their portraits of arena spectators' behavior from whole cloth; rather, they are putting a negative spin on it. Members of the privileged classes attended the games themselves (indeed, they were expected to) and, in their more candid moments, even admitted to enjoying them; some were so enthralled as to participate in the spectacles as performers. Elite descriptions of spectator behavior therefore often stem from autopsy.[25] Nevertheless, we must be alert to the biases of our sources as we advance the analysis.

---

[23] See, e.g., Sen. *Ep.* 7.2–5 = T.20; Salv. *Gub. Dei* 6.10 = T.18, Tert. *Spect.* 21.2–22 = T.29.

[24] See R. MacMullen, *Roman Social Relations, 50 BC – AD 284* (New Haven, 1974), esp. 138–41 (the "Lexicon of Snobbery"). On Christian depictions of the arena crowd, see below, ch. 7, pp. 254–7. Note Polycarp's contempt for the crowd at Smyrna: they were below hearing his defense; see *Pass. Polyc.* 10 (= Musurillo, *Acts of the Christian Martyrs*, 10–11).

[25] Aside from Augustine on Alypius, most commentators on arena crowd behavior (such as Cicero, Pliny, Seneca, Martial, or Tertullian) had clearly seen it with their own eyes. This will emerge clearly from the specific references in the analysis to follow. For elite enjoyment of the games, see, e.g., Cic. *Mur.* 39–40; Tac. *Ann.* 14.21; Dio 75.8.3. Fronto distinguishes between the rabble kept happy with the grain dole, and the whole populace with shows; his comment is explicitly class-based and assumes the attendance of the elite as spectators; see Fronto *Princ. Hist.* 17 = T.8. Some appreciation for the situation with the ancient sources may be gauged by a comparison with negative modern faculty attitudes toward intercollegiate athletics in American colleges and universities; while many

It is worthwhile to make a very obvious point here: the ancients were not aware of social psychology and so do not make expressly social-scientific observations in their writings. This casts the current project as an interpretive one, in that it seeks to draw psychological insights from evidence that is often allusive and necessarily indirect. Matters of genre, literary commonplaces, and authorial intent inevitably obtrude. That said, even if the ancient sources are morally disapproving or ostensibly fictive (a novel or satire, for instance), we can at the very least reckon that their descriptions of spectator behavior reflect the sorts of things arena crowds typically did or were widely thought to do. We must, however, ruthlessly excise from the ancient accounts all editorial glosses, moral judgments, snide asides, sarcastic blasts at the "herd" (*vulgus*), and other such commentary. Our study will then find a firmer foothold in the terrain of observed actions rather than risk sinking into the swamp of subjective opinion.[26] It will also be necessary to read between the lines.

The interpretation of ancient literary evidence is not a zero-sum game. There is more than one way to read pertinent passages in ancient works. Whether an author writes to make a moral, philosophical, rhetorical, satirical, theological, or some other point, there may be embedded in his account valuable observations of psychological relevance. In the face of this fact, the procedure throughout this book is to accept the authors' observations of what the crowd actually *did* while disregarding their editorializing glosses and expressions of snobbishness or moral outrage. Somewhere between reported observations and moral judgmentalism lie those (rare) records of the author's own emotional reactions. Such confessional comments ought not to be dismissed as mere glosses, though there may be a significant moral and formulaic dimension to them. I treat each datum of this sort on a case-by-case basis. By following this procedure I hope to focus the analysis on the crowd's documented actions and verbalizations and avoid getting sidetracked into endless debates about alternative interpretations of particular passages. That does not mean, of course, that such alternative interpretations are disallowed – just that there is little value in entertaining endless permutations.

The scattered and patchy nature of the evidence precludes the possibility of constructing a diachronic analysis that might trace changes in spectator

---

disparage the "sports culture" they see burgeoning around them, they nevertheless attend or watch their school's sporting events, and enjoy doing so. For a recent study, see J. L. Shulman and W. G. Bowen, *The Game of Life: College Sports and Educational Values* (Princeton, 2001), esp. 258–309.

[26] E. Champlin has applied such an approach – with enlightening results – in his study of Nero; see E. Champlin, *Nero* (Cambridge, MA, 2003), esp. 36–52.

demographics, behavior, and attitudes over time or, for that matter, across geographic boundaries within Rome's vast realm. In very many ways arena spectatorship must have been a quite different sort of experience in the Republic as opposed to the High or Late Empire, and different also if you were sitting in the Colosseum in Rome as opposed to some provincial amphitheater, perhaps in ramshackle wooden stands. Circumstances changed over time, socioeconomic inequalities grew wider, codes of conduct in government and administration and public life evolved, and the games became more and more complicated. Our evidence allows us to trace some of these processes, but large gaps remain. While acknowledging these gaps, the best approach is to survey all the available evidence for clues as to the behavior of arena spectators, recognizing all the while that the composite picture we arrive at might not match in all its details any specific *spectaculum* ever staged.[27] This is a problem that dogs all of Roman social history, and we simply have to live with it.

---

[27] As recognized by J. C. Edmondson, "Dynamic Arenas: Gladiatorial Presentations in the City of Rome and the Construction of Roman Society during the Early Empire," in Slater (ed.), *Roman Theater and Society*, 69–112, esp. 75–9.

CHAPTER I

Seeking explanations

The past is a foreign country: they do things differently there.

L. P. Hartley, *The Go-Between* (1953)[1]

Studying ancient Rome should be like visiting some teeming capital in a dangerous and ill-governed foreign country; nothing can be relied on, most of what you see is squalid, sinister or unintelligible, and you are disproportionately grateful when you find something you can recognise as familiar.

T. P. Wiseman, *Catullus and His World* (1985)[2]

Unlike his predecessor Augustus, the emperor Tiberius was no keen sponsor of spectacles. Thirteen years into his reign, he had organized no major shows.[3] So a local magnate at Fidenae saw an opportunity and, supposedly out of a desire for profit, erected a temporary amphitheater and made arrangements for putting on *munera*.[4] Roused by the recent rarity of spectacles, people of all ages, men and women alike, poured into town from the nearby capital. The temporary amphitheater was packed to the point that many were left standing around outside, seeking entrance. The sponsor's entrepreneurial spirit apparently extended to cost-cutting in construction, for as the show progressed the stands collapsed, mangling thousands among the splintered beams. In an irony of no small proportions, violent death

---

[1] L. P. Hartley, *The Go-Between* (London, 1953; reprint, New York, 2002), 17.

[2] T. P. Wiseman, *Catullus and His World: A Reappraisal* (Cambridge, 1985), 4.

[3] See Suet. *Tib.* 47; Sen. *Dial.* 1.4.4. Gladiatorial games were staged by Drusus and Germanicus in AD 15 (Tac. *Ann.* 1.76.5–7; Dio 57.14.3–4), which the emperor did not attend in person. A *venatio* to honor the birthday of Augustus was put on in the same year and for several years afterward (Dio 57.14.3–4). These are the only imperially sponsored shows on record for Tiberius' entire twenty-three-year reign.

[4] Games for profit may have been called *munera assiforana* ("Penny Shows"); see Mosci Sassi, *Linguaggio gladiatorio*, 128. The senatorial decree about gladiatorial games of AD 177 ranks such shows as the least expensive (and thus least impressive) of possible spectacles; see *CIL* 2.6278 = *ILS* 5163, lines 29–30. For a full-scale analysis of the Fidenae incident, see G. Chamberland, "A Gladiatorial Show Produced *In Sordidam Mercedem* (Tac. *Ann.* 4.62)," *Phoenix* 61 (2007), 136–49. Chamberland (esp. 139–47) argues cogently that *munera* were never staged exclusively for financial profit, but that does not rule out desire for profit as an element in this sponsor's motivation.

had come unexpectedly to the crowd which usually watched it from the safe haven of the tiers. In reaction, the entrepreneur was exiled, laws were passed establishing a building code for wooden amphitheaters, and the great houses of Rome were thrown open to tend the wounded.[5] Of particular interest in this disaster story from AD 27 is the diversity of the crowd and its enthusiasm for spectacles. "Those keen for such things (*avidi talium*)," in Tacitus' succinct expression, were willing to walk five miles from Rome and sit in a jerrybuilt (and probably uncomfortable) arena to see men and animals butcher each other.

In AD 52–3 Claudius staged first a vast naval spectacle, and then a gladiatorial show to draw public attention to his draining of the Fucine Lake. Tacitus is explicit (*Ann.* 12.56.1) that the spectacles were intended to augment the size of the crowd assembled to appreciate the engineering achievement of draining the lake; without the spectacles, fewer people would have shown up. Fronto takes it as given "that hand-outs are anticipated less keenly than shows."[6] The size and scale of surviving amphitheaters, among the largest urban structures built by the Romans, offer material confirmation for this enthusiasm. In many cases, they are significantly larger than the estimated populations of the towns that housed them, demonstrating that they served not a community but a region. It would not have been unusual, then, for people to travel some distance to watch.[7] How do we explain such a popular commitment to bloody spectacle? What sense can we make of such a phenomenon?

It is fair to say that historians have tended to offer explanations for the popularity of violent spectacles that are both monocausal in nature and largely "external" in their focus. That is, the tendency is to propose a single overarching model for what was going on, and then to unpack the cultural meaning(s) inherent in particular violent rituals as a way to understand their appeal. Cultural analyses of contact sports, for instance, or "sport entertainment" (such as professional wrestling) take such approaches.[8]

---

[5] See Tac. *Ann.* 4.62–3; Suet. *Tib.* 40. [6] Fronto *Princ. Hist.* 17 = T.8.

[7] See below, ch. 3, p. 97 for discussion of amphitheater capacities. It is true that amphitheaters could serve multiple functions, but their primary purpose was the staging of *spectacula*. The infamous amphitheater riot in Pompeii in AD 59 took place between the Pompeians and their neighboring rivals from Nuceria (Tac. *Ann.* 14.17 = T.26; see ch. 3, pp. 93–6, for analysis) and advertisements for games in neighboring towns are known from outside the Nucerian Gate at Pompeii, which itself lies near the amphitheater there; see Sabbatini Tumolesi, *Gladiatorum Paria*, 91–110 (nos. 63–82).

[8] On sports in general, see J. Horne et al., *Understanding Sport: An Introduction to the Sociological and Cultural Analysis of Sport* (London, 1999); on wrestling, see T. Henricks, "Professional Wrestling as Moral Order," *Sociological Inquiry* 44 (1974), 177–88; S. Mazer, *Professional Wrestling: Sport and Spectacle* (Jackson, 1998), esp. 148–71. Similar approaches are adopted by R. W. Malcolmson, *Popular Recreations in English Society 1700–1850* (Cambridge, 1973).

Ritual public punishments have been variously interpreted as exercises in state propaganda, social control, or moral education that convey distinct political, religious, and symbolic messages to spectators.[9] The attention of work like this has been predominantly on the intentions of the organizers or, to a lesser extent, on the cultural expectations the spectators brought with them to the stadium or the scaffold.[10] In this way, the spectators' psychological stance toward violent spectacle, when it is considered at all, has been very much subordinated to the sociocultural meaning of the spectacle itself.

This is not to say that culturally bounded interpretations are unconvincing or futile (quite the opposite), but that some of their cogency is lost in the face of the striking historical persistence of spectatorship at agonistic, punitive, or religious violent spectacles staged in very different times and places and under a variety of value systems, all embedded within quite divergent religious, social, and political contexts (see below, chapter 2). Yet the ever-present spectator is rarely the concern of study, no doubt in part due to the difficulty in gaining access to the watchers' perspective from surviving sources.[11] A magisterial study of the death penalty in Germany from 1600 to 1987 sets out its agenda as follows: "This book, therefore, tries to give the past a voice, by allowing those who lived through it to talk about their experience: not only the executed, but also and particularly those who prescribed and administered the death penalty: politicians, bureaucrats, judges, lawyers, state prosecutors, judicial officials, executioners."[12]

---

[9] Some prominent studies include: H. Bleackley and J. Lofland, *State Executions Viewed Historically and Sociologically* (Montclair, 1977); M. Foucault, *Discipline and Punish: The Birth of the Prison* (New York, 1977); P. Linebaugh, *The London Hanged: Crime and Civil Society in the Eighteenth Century* (Cambridge, 1992); M. B. Merback, *The Thief, the Cross and the Wheel: Pain and the Spectacle of Punishment in Medieval and Renaissance Europe* (Chicago, 1998), esp. 126–97; J. R. Ruff, *Violence in Early Modern Europe, 1500–1800* (Cambridge, 2001), esp. 73–116; P. C. Spierenburg, *The Spectacle of Suffering: Executions and the Evolution of Repression from a Preindustrial Metropolis to the European Experience* (Cambridge, 1984). See also R. J. Evans, *Rituals of Retribution: Capital Punishment in Germany 1600–1987* (Oxford, 1996), esp. the survey of theoretical approaches at 1–24; J. B. Given, *Inquisition and Medieval Society: Power, Discipline and Resistance in Languedoc* (Ithaca, 1997), 68–90; G. Ruggiero, "Constructing Civic Morality, Deconstructing the Body: Civic Rituals of Punishment in Renaissance Venice," in J. Chiffoleu et al. (eds.), *Riti e rituali nelle società medievali* (Spoleto, 1994), 175–90; R. van Dülmen, *Theatre of Horror: Crime and Punishment in Early Modern Germany* (Cambridge, 1990). See also works cited in introduction, n. 18.

[10] A sermon printed and distributed before the public execution of a thief in Munich in 1771 is unambiguous as to the spectacle's purpose: "See this blood, understand its teachings: Learn to fear and venerate justice" (cited in van Dülmen, *Theatre of Horror*, 125).

[11] Execution accounts become available on a regular basis in Europe from the mid-sixteenth century onwards but from the spectator's perspective only from the eighteenth century onward; see van Dülmen, *Theatre of Horror*, 110.

[12] Evans, *Rituals of Retribution*, 23.

Notably absent are the spectators. This is not a criticism but an observation: the spectators' perspective is not one of this huge book's explicit guiding concerns.[13] Anthropological and sociological analyses have certainly illuminated various and important aspects of public ritual violence, but the favored point of view is overwhelmingly that of the organizers and the victims, rather than of the watchers. The approach is firmly "external": cultural considerations and symbolism dominate the discussion.[14] The attendance of crowds, sometimes running to the tens of thousands, seems hardly to warrant explanation. It is simply assumed that, if pain and death are staged as spectacle, people will come out to watch.

The assumption pervades our ancient evidence too. A striking example is the death of Peregrinus Proteus in the middle of the second century AD. Peregrinus was a dabbler in philosophy and mysticism, who in his younger days had even given Christianity a try while travelling in Syria and Palestine. In AD 165 Peregrinus announced in advance that he would burn himself to death at the Olympic games. Lucian, who was a witness, regarded the whole business as a contemptible display of vainglory. But huge numbers of people (including Lucian himself), already gathered for the games, were determined to watch Peregrinus' self-immolation. As it turned out, the event took place not at Olympia during the festival, but at the nearby town of Harpina the day after the festival ended. The spectators, therefore, had to walk or ride about two miles to see Peregrinus die.[15] Why did they do it?

There is nothing at all obvious or inevitable about the desire to watch. Here was a man who was going to burn himself to death, and not even as part of any organized spectacle of punishment or competition. People

[13] That said, the spectators naturally make sporadic appearances at various junctures throughout Evans' work. Spierenburg (*Spectacle of Suffering*, 81–109) does include a chapter on "the watchers," though virtually nothing is said of what drew them to attend. A study of public executions in England, however, does focus in large part on the spectators and their motives for attending; see V. A. C. Gatrell, *The Hanging Tree: Execution and the English People 1770–1868* (Oxford, 1994), esp. 29–105 and 242–97; see also Ruff, *Violence in Early Modern Europe*, 102–9. Both offer culturally specific explanations for crowd attendance (e.g., expectations of an edifying spiritual experience, desire to witness the manifestation of popular notions of justice, etc.).

[14] Similarly, a study of the role of (non-violent) spectacle in the reign of Louis XIV of France pays attention to the spectators, but adheres to a cultural and symbolic mode of analysis (i.e., spectacle organized and internalized notions of nationhood and the centrality of the monarch to it); see J.-M. Apostolidès, *Le roi-machine: spectacle et politique au temps de Louis XIV* (Paris, 1981), esp. 148–64.

[15] See Lucian, *De mort. Peregr.* esp. 21 (timing of the immolation), 35 (location), 35–6 (the event itself). In actuality, Peregrinus burned during the night, but it had been rumored that he would do so at dawn. Lucian witnessed the event and therefore met many expectant spectators on the road to Harpina on his return journey; see ibid., 38–9. Whether or not Lucian's tale is fact or ficiton is beside the point: the cultural assumptions it reveals about spectatorship at violent spectacle are what matter.

could have ignored him, or not turned up, or gone somewhere else. Various circumstantial explanations can be offered – admiration or contempt for Peregrinus' professed piety, for example – but when set against the historically consistent presence of crowds at violent spectacles, such contextually based explanations appear at best partial. Are people inherently drawn to witness death and pain? This is the conundrum that sits at the heart of this study which, for want of space and the limitations of its author, is restricted to Roman gladiatorial spectacles but carries implications far beyond that context.

THE STORY SO FAR

As noted above, prior studies have inferred the popularity of the Roman arena by theorizing its cultural function.[16] Until the 1970s, the games were seen as a peculiar and titillating aspect of Roman life and certainly not a cultural practice that offered important lessons about Roman civilization.[17] Michael Grant seized the moral high ground and bracketed arena games with the Nazi horrors as among the worst excesses of human cruelty.[18] Roland Auguet built on Juvenal's famous aphorism about bread and circuses (*Sat.* 10.78–81) and explored the meaning of the games and their role in society. They were used by emperors to elevate their own status and to keep the mob occupied and docile; they were mechanisms for interaction between ruler and ruled; they were sustained by the institution of slavery, which conditioned Romans to see people as instruments. The fascination of the games lay in the transformation of the despicable and the lowly into objects of admiration (since the socially outcast gladiators were held in high popular regard). Such analysis moved the games from the periphery to the heart of Roman culture, now audaciously dubbed "a civilization based on games."[19]

---

[16] See Kyle's helpful synopsis of the different models employed to make sense of the Roman games in *Spectacles of Death*, 7–10. Useful review articles include S. Brown, "Explaining the Arena: Did the Romans 'Need' Gladiators," *JRA* 8 (1995), 376–84; and D. G. Kyle, "Rethinking the Roman Arena: Gladiators, Sorrows, and Games," *AHB* 11 (1997), 94–7.

[17] Notwithstanding such excellent older overviews as L. Friedländer, *Darstellungen aus der Sittengeschichte Roms in der Zeit von Augustus bis zum Ausgang der Antonine*, 10th edn., 4 vols. (Leipzig, 1922; reprint, Aalen, 1964), vol. II, 1–162, esp. 50–112 (on the gladiatorial games) and 94–100 (for insightful remarks); E. Daremberg and E. Saglio, *Dictionnaire des antiquités grecques et romaines*, 5 vols. (Paris, 1887–1919), vol. II, 563–99, s.v. "Gladiator."

[18] M. Grant, *Gladiators* (London, 1967), 8.

[19] R. Auguet, *Cruelty and Civilization: The Roman Games* (London, 1972), 184–99 (the quote is the title of this chapter). The usefulness of this book is vitiated by the absence of references, even to ancient works quoted at length in the text.

The transition of *spectacula* from the wings to the limelight was completed in 1983, when Keith Hopkins used the games as a lens through which to interpret various features of Roman culture.[20] The arena now became a manifestation of Rome's status as a warrior state, a reminder to peacetime Romans of their martial heritage and value system. The games represented the power of the state to annihilate its enemies. Brutality and violence were built into the fabric of Roman society and the arena was only one symptom, if a highly visible one, of this wider condition. Like Friedländer and Auguet before him, Hopkins saw the games as a sort of Roman parliament, where the people could address their concerns directly to the emperor. Hopkins also saw the hierarchical nature of Roman society, manifested most harshly in slavery, as central to the phenomenon of the amphitheater.[21]

There followed a flurry of studies in the 1990s probing the deeper meaning of arena violence. A comprehensive survey of the attitudes found in Early Imperial writers concluded that, of the public entertainments available to the Romans, the amphitheater alone was considered edifying and manly, even if its bracing messages were somewhat attenuated by associations with idleness, luxury, and pandering to vulgar tastes.[22] A particularly rich study offered symbological interpretations for the various phases of arena games. The range of exotic animals exhibited and slaughtered in the *venatio* proclaimed the extent of the empire and Rome's power over nature. In a dangerous pre-industrial environment where animals routinely threatened humans as predators or were competitors for resources, watching the destruction of feral beasts, even herbivores, was gratifying. Executions of criminals and enemies symbolized the power of the state to suppress deviance and maintain order, while the favored modes of execution

---

[20] See Hopkins, *Death and Renewal*, 1–30. Hopkins modeled his approach explicitly (ibid., n. 1) on the anthropologist Clifford Geertz's influential essay "Deep Play: Notes on the Balinese Cockfight," *Daedalus* 101 (1972), 1–37 (= C. Geertz, *Myth, Symbol, and Culture* [New York, 1974], 1–37). The technique is to take an apparently banal practice and, through a process of scholarly interrogation, expose the deeper cultural currents running through it.

[21] There have since been expansions on many of these important themes: see, e.g., M. Clavel-Lévêque, *L'empire en jeux: espace symbolique et pratique sociale dans le monde romain* (Paris, 1984), esp. 129–78; M. Clavel-Lévêque, "L'espace des jeux dans le monde romain: hégémonie, symbolique et pratique sociale," *ANRW* 2.16.3 (1986), 2406–563; Edmondson, "Dynamic Arenas"; E. Flaig, *Ritualisierte Politik: Zeichen, Gesten und Herrschaft im Alten Rom* (Göttingen, 2003), 232–60; D. Potter, "Performance, Power and Justice in the High Empire," in Slater (ed.), *Roman Theater and Society*, 129–60. See now also Edwards (*Death*, 46–77) for a perceptive exploration of the games' cultural meaning.

[22] See M. Wistrand, *Entertainment and Violence in Ancient Rome: The Attitudes of Roman Writers of the First Century* AD (Göteborg, 1992), esp. 55–80.

(particularly burning alive and exposure to wild beasts) confronted transgressors with the stark consequences of their choices: stripped of the protection of the social order they had rejected, the condemned were destroyed
by the unfettered forces of chaos with which they had allied themselves in
committing their crimes. A similar analysis of executions staged as mythological motifs or the mass sea battles (*naumachiae*) saw such events as
speaking to the power of the emperor to make real the unreal, to control and deploy natural forces, and to master the fates of thousands.[23]
Gladiatorial bouts demonstrated that, through displays of martial skill and
virtus, men held below contempt by society at large could die bravely or, if
consistently victorious, be reborn into the community. Indeed, the whole
amphitheatrical package was a paean to the Roman concept of *virtus* and,
as such, eagerly embraced by the Romans themselves as well as by those
who wished to declare their Roman-ness to the world. Finally, it is possible
that the slaughter of the games offered a peculiar comfort to the spectators: "the ritualization of the encounter with death had put death in its
place."[24]

Another study emphasized the arena's function as a re-presenter of state
power, a confirmation of the Roman order where enemies were assembled
and slaughtered under the auspices of the goddess Nemesis.[25] A dense
anthropological analysis viewed the games as "liminoid rituals" that sought
to neutralize the destructive and wild forces threatening society by staging
them under controlled conditions. The arena represented a "quest for
security through incorporation of disorder into order," an attempt at the
"incorporation of potential dysfunction to assure proper functioning."
On this view, the games were a sort of cultural vaccination against the
potential for uncontrollable mayhem inherent in violence.[26] Yet another
interpretation saw the games as reinforcers of Roman male concerns such as
honor, competition, and shame, all anchored in the celebration of violence
as the language of empire. The ethic of the games had to do less with death

---

[23] K. M. Coleman, "Fatal Charades: Roman Executions Staged as Mythological Enactments," *JRS* 80 (1990), 44–73; K. M. Coleman, "Launching into History: Aquatic Displays in the Early Empire," *JRS* 83 (1993), 48–74. On the *naumachiae*, see now A. Berlan-Bajard, *Les spectacles aquatiques romains*, CEFR 360 (Rome, 2006).

[24] Wiedemann, *Emperors and Gladiators*, esp. 1–101 (quote at 97). See also Clavel-Lévêque, *L'empire en jeux*, esp. 63–86; S. L. Tuck, "Spectacle and Ideology in the Relief Decorations of the Anfiteatro Campano at Capua," *JRA* 20 (2007), 255–72.

[25] Hornum, *Nemesis*, 43–90, esp. 78–88.

[26] P. Plass, *The Game of Death in Ancient Rome: Arena Sport and Political Suicide* (Madison, 1995), 3–77 (quotes at 8 and 28 respectively).

and more with appearances, with the maintenance of proper comportment in all circumstances, in a word, with style. The spectacles pitched the rational and fixed principle of *virtus* against the irrational and unpredictable workings of *fortuna*. Sudden and unexpected reversals of fortune and sharp contrasts were part and parcel of the games, and the suspense involved in anticipating such reversals was an element of their lure. In the arena, even the lowly and barbarous were expected to maintain the proper appearances. Doing so could make the difference between life and death, for when a fallen fighter appealed for his life, the decision to kill or spare was reached by the sponsor on the basis of how the gladiator had performed in the fight. Ultimately, the games represented an attempt by the emperor to buttress traditional elite values at a time when they were under assault from a growing popular culture.[27]

Mining a similar vein, a poststructural analysis has argued that the arena was an Ideological State Apparatus signifying an ideal world in accordance with elite paradigms. "Were the emperors interpellated by the arena? That is, to what extent was the persona actually the essence of the emperor's subjectivity?" are the sorts of questions asked, while the conclusion – "[t]he ideology of the arena has no outside" – achieves an equal level of obscurity.[28] A more accessible analysis holds that the Imperial games were dynamic replacements for Republican cultural and social values formerly expressed in the defunct popular assemblies (*comitia*) and muster (*dilectus*).[29] A comparative historical approach stresses the games' sacral nature and concludes that they were mass human sacrifices, alike to the more familiar Aztec version practiced in the New World. Naturally, built into all such rituals are potent messages about power and control.[30] Taking a rather different tack, there has even been a quasi-psychiatric analysis

---

[27] J. P. Toner, *Leisure and Ancient Rome* (Cambridge, 1995), 34–52. These ideas are reiterated and tied to others just surveyed (e.g., the role of *virtus*), in J. P. Toner, *Rethinking Roman History* (Cambridge, 2002), esp. 82–128. See also Potter, "Spectacle," esp. 385–6.

[28] E. Gunderson, "The Ideology of the Arena," *CA* 15 (1996), 113–51 (quotes at 132 and 151). See also his "The Flavian Amphitheatre: All the World as Stage," in A. J. Boyle and W. J. Dominik (eds.), *Flavian Rome: Culture, Image, Text* (Leiden, 2003), 637–58.

[29] Edmondson, "Dynamic Arenas." Note Fronto *Princ. Hist.* 17 = T.8 and Juv. 10.78–81 for ancient formulations of these ideas. Pylades, a famed dancer, once quipped to Augustus (Dio 54.17.5): "it is in your interest, Caesar, that the people should devote their spare time to us" (συμφέρει σοι, Καῖσαρ, περὶ ἡμᾶς τὸν δῆμον ἀποδιατρίβεσθαι).

[30] Futrell, *Blood in the Arena*, 169–210. Essential to this view is the overt sacredness of the games, a proposition not without its problems, since religion and religious imagery were so closely integrated into almost everything the Romans did in the public sphere; see M. Le Glay, "Les amphithéâtres: loci religiosi?," in C. Domergue et al. (eds.), *Spectacula I: gladiateurs et amphithéâtres* (Lattes, 1990), 217–25. Note also C. Barton, "The Emotional Economy of Sacrifice and Execution in Ancient Rome," *Historical Reflections/Réflexions Historiques* 29 (2003), 341–60.

proposing that the Roman mind – conceived, it seems, as a monolith – was caught in an emotional vise between desire and despair, a condition for which the games acted as a sort of concentrating lens: "The contradictory and inflammatory desires that infused every aspect of Roman society were, in the arena, focused in a circle of heat."[31]

While many of these analyses offer penetrating insights, none is entirely satisfying in itself as an explanation for the phenomenon of the arena and why people attended in large numbers. Some display distinct weaknesses, and others are a little stretched. The proposition, for instance, that gladiatorial games reminded peacetime Romans of their martial heritage seems less cogent when it is noted that the games proliferated in scale and frequency in the second and first centuries BC, and even more so in the Augustan era – periods when there were plenty of real wars, foreign and civil, to go around. Even under the more settled conditions of the empire, martial values, the emperor's military *virtus*, and far-flung conquests were extolled in the monuments, public statues, and inscriptions of the capital and in the rest of the empire's cities, not to mention on the circulating coinage and in the rhetoric and public ideology of the elite. The soldier-to-civilian ratio in Imperial Rome has been calculated at between 1:125 and 1:25, so that troops were constantly to be seen both in person and in representation on the monuments.[32] Given this, one wonders how much Romans really needed to be reminded of their martial roots through the occasional gladiatorial display. The "liminoid ritual" interpretation of the arena is at odds with other views of the connection between arena violence and wider patterns of behavior in Roman society. Most see the link as causal: a general pattern of violence nurtured the culture of the arena. According to the "liminoid" view, however, the opposite was the case: the games sought to limit and rein in the dangers of general violence. That they failed in doing so is suggested by the evidence (see below, pp. 25–7), but perhaps it is unfair to judge an intention by its results. Despite its Freudian underpinnings (or perhaps because of them), the diagnosis of psychiatric dysfunction for an

---

[31] C. Barton, *The Sorrows of the Ancient Romans: The Gladiator and the Monster* (Princeton, 1993), 3–81 (quote at 80). Barton reconstructs a collective *mentalité*, but it is unclear how it applied to all Romans, of all classes, all across the empire and over several centuries; see the insightful (and critical) review of K. Welch, *Journal of Social History* 27 (1993), 430–3, and Le Goff, "Mentalities."

[32] See the prevalence of military themes in state art, as documented in N. Hannestad, *Roman Art and Imperial Policy* (Aarhus, 1986), and S. Dillon and K. E. Welch (eds.), *Representations of War in Ancient Rome* (Cambridge, 2006). On statues alone, see C. Edwards, "Incorporating the Alien: The Art of Conquest," in C. Edwards and G. Woolf (eds.), *Rome the Cosmopolis* (Cambridge, 2003), 44–70. On soldiers at Rome, both real and represented, see J. C. N. Coulston, "'Armed and Belted Men': The Soldiery in Imperial Rome," in Coulston and Dodge (eds.), *Ancient Rome*, 76–118, and esp. fig. 5.8 (at 81) for the ratios of civilian to soldier in the city.

entire population, let alone one dead 2,000 years, is highly dubious, given the uncertainties that plague the diagnosis of living individuals.[33]

SOME CONTEXTUAL FACTORS

Prior studies, therefore, confront us with a smorgasbord of explanatory possibilities for what the games meant and why the Romans found them so absorbing, not all of them equally appealing or mutually compatible. But they are all culturally specific and tie the games firmly to the particulars of the Roman historical experience and to specific features of their social ecology. That this is to take too narrow a view is a core argument of this book. However, one of the chief values of prior scholarship is that it draws attention to several features of Roman society that seem closely connected to the phenomenon of gladiatorial spectacles, whether as correlates or causes. Before proceeding to the social psychology, these features need to be explored a little more fully, as they constitute prominent elements of the historical context that helped shape the mental dispositions, expectations, and outlook of arena spectators.[34]

First, slavery. Slavery at Rome was as complex as it was ubiquitous.[35] Slaves were everywhere in Roman life, an integral part of the social fabric. Although they were all of a class in a legal sense, slaves actually occupied a variety of status levels, from the elevated to the abject. Estimates of the slave population are hard to arrive at, but most hover around 30 percent in the cities; the situation in the countryside is harder to gauge.[36] When

---

[33] For the notion of neuroses affecting whole populations, see S. Freud, *Civilization and its Discontents* (New York, 1930). It is Barton's expressed wish to produce an emotional map of the Romans – all of them; see Barton, *Sorrows*, 3–8.

[34] The discussion that follows might seem to be undermined by the points made about the documented widespread appeal of violent spectacle below in ch. 2, but that would be a mistake. Every cultural context has features that shape the form and nature of its violent public rituals and also motivate attendance; such features of the Roman context as likely contributed to spectatorship at arena spectacles are the main point under consideration here, and whether or not they find analogs in other contexts does not materially affect the main argument.

[35] The modern bibliography on the topic is vast. For useful overviews, see K. R. Bradley, *Slaves and Masters in the Roman Empire: A Study in Social Control* (Oxford, 1987); K. Bradley, *Slavery and Society at Rome* (Cambridge, 1994); A. Carandini, *Schiavi in Italia: gli strumenti pensanti dei Romani fra tarda Repubblica e medio Impero* (Rome, 1988); M. I. Finley (ed.), *Classical Slavery*, Studies in Slave and Post-Slave Societies (London, 1987); P. Garnsey, *Ideas of Slavery from Aristotle to Augustine* (Cambridge, 1996); K. Hopkins, *Conquerors and Slaves: Sociological Studies in Roman History I* (Cambridge, 1978), esp. 99–132 (with table II.1 at 101); L. Schumacher, *Sklaverei in der Antike: Alltag und Schicksal der Unfreien* (Munich, 2001). Note also the sources assembled in T. Wiedemann (ed.), *Greek and Roman Slavery* (London, 1981).

[36] See, e.g., P. A. Brunt, *Italian Manpower 225 BC – AD 14* (Oxford, 1971), 124–30 and 702–3; W. L. Westermann, *The Slave Systems of Greek and Roman Antiquity* (Philadelphia, 1955), 84–90. A recent

Augustus sought to restrict the numbers of testamentary manumissions in the *lex Fufia Caninia* of 2 BC, classes of slave-owners were classified in a spectrum from those who owned as many as 500 or more down to those with only 1.[37] Households in possession of only one slave stand as paradigms of want in Roman literature, while Cicero appeals to the hideous condition of being entirely slaveless as an indicator of one client's utter destitution.[38] In the countryside, the larger estates of the wealthy were worked by gangs of slaves, often laboring under a steward (*vilicus*), himself frequently a slave. Freeborn small farmers shared living space with their slaves, and shared also the abject poverty of eking out a living from the land.[39] In the towns and cities, slaves were found in practically all contexts: at home, in shops and businesses, at the public fountains, the market, the baths, on the street. They would be encountered in various guises, from the relatively independent *institor* (a slave put in charge of a wing of the owner's business and left alone to run it) or the privileged family accountant (*dispensator*) going about their daily business largely unsupervised, down through the *paedogogus* accompanying the owner's children to school, to the domestic menials sent out to fetch water or shop at the market. It is important to remember that slaves at Rome were not readily distinguishable by their race or outward appearance from the lowly freeborn; slaves in positions of importance in their household apparently looked better off than the urban, freeborn poor.[40] This must have been the case especially for the higher-ranking slaves, who could even move about in public accompanied by a slave retinue of their own. Since slaves could not own property, these underling slaves (termed *vicarii*) were assigned to the favored servant as a designation of status.[41] So in the everyday experience of ancient Romans

assessment reckons the figure of 30 percent as "probably too conservative," see W. Jongman, "Slavery and the Growth of Rome," in Edwards and Woolf (eds.), *Rome the Cosmopolis*, 100–22 (quote at 117). For a survey of problems in estimating Rome's population, see E. Lo Cascio, "La popolazione," in E. Lo Cascio (ed.), *Roma imperiale: una metropoli antica* (Rome, 2000), 17–69.

[37] For the provisions of the *lex Fufia Caninia*, see Gaius *Inst.* 1.42–6. For analysis, see Bradley, *Slavery and Society*, 10–30.

[38] Apul. *Met.* 1.21–3. (one slave); Cic. *Rosc. Am.* 77 and 145 (slavelessness indicative of destitution). Note also W. Fitzgerald, *Slavery and the Roman Literary Imagination*, Roman Literature and Its Contexts (Cambridge, 2000).

[39] Keith Bradley points out (*Slavery and Society*, 90–1) that it is impossible to tell whether Simulus, the impoverished farmer in *Moretum*, a poem ascribed to Virgil, is a slave or a freeborn peasant. Among the poorer classes in towns, slaves would also share the cramped living quarters of their owners; see Apul. *Met.* 1.21–3.

[40] Petron. *Sat.* 57.9; Sen. *Clem.* 1.24.1; *Dig.* 18.1.4–5. On *institores*, see J.-J. Aubert, *Business Managers in Ancient Rome: A Social and Economic Study of Institores 200 BC – AD 250* (Leiden, 1994).

[41] *CIL* 6.5197 = *ILS* 1514; Petron. *Sat.* 30.7–11. In both cases, the high-ranking slave is a *dispensator*, or household accountant, a position that entailed a high degree of trust between slave and owner.

slaves were a fundamental fact of life, and contact with them would have been sustained and, on occasion, intimate.[42]

These circumstances must have had a profound effect on Roman outlooks about human worth in general, and the relative value of individuals in particular. Alongside the world of the freeborn existed a parallel universe inhabited by persons who, as a class, were deemed legally non-existent except as property.[43] Here were people who were subject to every whim of their owners (although some legal restrictions on the treatment of slaves were introduced under the emperors). To be sure, there were kind and decent slave-owners, such as Pliny the Younger, who made the lives of at least some of their slaves more pleasant. But such temperance, drawn in part from lofty philosophical principles of general equality, would apply only to certain classes of owners on the one hand and, on the other, only to slaves who enjoyed frequent contact with the owner – there is little reason to believe that the workforce of Pliny's rural estates or the servants who cleaned his toilets basked in the glow of his warmth or had a decent shot at manumission.[44] The crucial point is that everything hinged on the owner's whim and was quite out of the slave's control. If an owner was a sadist, or a pervert, or a rigid disciplinarian, or wholly apathetic about his servants' welfare, the consequences for the chattel were bound to be unpleasant. Plutarch comments, tellingly: "We see that newly bought slaves do not ask whether their master is superstitious or jealous – but whether he is quick to anger."[45] One of the chief arguments against maltreatment of slaves in the

[42] Quite apart from sexual liaisons between adults, many children in affluent households were raised by slave-minders; see K. R. Bradley, *Discovering the Roman Family: Studies in Roman Social History* (Oxford, 1991), 13–102.

[43] In wills, slaves were passed down as instruments (*instrumenta*) attached to working installations, like farms (*Dig.* 33.7.8 pr) or bathhouses (*Dig.* 33.7.13.1, 33.7.17.2, 33.7.14.1). Ulpian in the *Digest* (50.17.32) expressly states that slaves are legally regarded as nonentities: "as far as the civil law is concerned, slaves count for nothing" (*quod attinet ad ius ciuile, servi pro nullis habentur*).

[44] E.g., Pliny *Ep.* 8.16 and Sen. *Ep.* 47 (mild treatment); Sen. *Clem.* 1.18.1–2 (lofty principles). Columella portrays visits to rural estates by their owners as an occasional event, and stressful for the slaves concerned; he specifically recommends (1.2.1) promising more visits than one intends, to keep the staff on their toes. His strictures find echo in the novel *Daphnis and Chloe* (4.1–18), where an impending inspection by an estate owner causes deep consternation among the slave workforce. Pliny claims (*Ep.* 3.19.7) that he did not use chained slaves on his estates. But chains are only one form of cruelty to which slaves were subjected (see below). Of the 4,116 slaves enumerated in the will of the ex-slave C. Caecilius Isodorus (Pliny *HN* 33.135), how many can have had close enough contact with their master to rate a good chance of gaining their freedom? The same man must have run vast estates: his will counted 3,600 pairs of oxen and 257,000 head of cattle among his belongings. Most of his slave "family" therefore worked the lands, out of sight and mind. As Jongman ("Slavery," 118) comments, "Manumission, after all, was mostly an urban thing."

[45] Plut. *Mor.* 462a: ὁρῶμεν δὲ καὶ δούλους νεωνήτους περὶ τοῦ πριαμένου πυνθανομένους, οὐκ εἰ δεισιδαίμων οὐδ᾽ εἰ φθονερὸς ἀλλ᾽ εἰ θυμώδης.

ancient sources is not the immorality of handling a fellow human being harshly but the deleterious effect such behavior had on the psyche of the owner and the loss of dignity inherent in losing one's temper.[46] In the eyes of prominent Roman jurists, the condition of slavery was likened to death, making slaves the living dead; in an infamous comment, Varro says that some consider slaves "the speaking class of tool" (*instrumenti genus vocale*); and Pliny the Younger comments disapprovingly that some owners regard sick or old slaves as nothing more than a financial liability, an attitude manifested in Cato the Elder's recommendation that old and sick slaves be sold off along with other superfluous burdens on one's estate.[47]

The societal impact of these circumstances has long been appreciated: "The inevitable consequence of slavery is the weakening of pity, of sympathy for pain . . . At equal levels of civilization, a nation which has slaves must be much less compassionate than one which does not."[48] It is therefore reasonable to suppose that pervasive slavery and the attitudes it generated in treating human beings as instruments played a central part in fashioning the culture of the arena. At a very basic level, slavery conditioned the Romans to see certain classes of people as wholly expendable, to be (ab)used and discarded without a thought. As far as the slave performers in the arena were concerned, many spectators would see only the socially dead being converted into the physically dead.[49]

The second main contextual factor is the firm suspicion that widespread violence pervaded Roman society. Put plainly, the sources leave a strong impression that the Roman world was awash with brutality, violence, and degradation of the weak and powerless.[50] Violence, for instance, was part and parcel of the slave's lot. Cicero characterized slavery as coercion and

---

[46] Bradley, *Slavery and Society*, 132–53; W. V. Harris, *Restraining Rage: The Ideology of Anger Control in Classical Antiquity* (Cambridge, MA, 2001), esp. 317–36.

[47] E.g., *Dig.* 1.5.5.2, 35.1.59.2, 50.17.209 (living death); Varro, *Res Rust.* 1.17.1 (speaking tool), cf. Arist. *Pol.* 1.2.4 (= 1253b23–33) for the slave as a "living tool"; Pliny *Ep.* 8.16.3 (financial loss); Cato, *Res Rust.* 2.7 (sell old and sick slaves). The laws were mollified over time, so that grosser abuses were proscribed, at least officially. But the basic circumstances of slavery remained constant; see Harris, *Restraining Rage*, 329–36. On slavery as a form of living death, see O. Patterson, *Slavery and Social Death: A Comparative Study* (Cambridge, MA, 1982).

[48] B. Constant, *Principles of Politics Applicable to All Governments*, trans. D. O'Keeffe (Indianapolis, 2003; originally published 1810), 358.

[49] On the social identity of arena victims, see Kyle, *Spectacles of Death*, 76–127.

[50] The main problem is that levels of casual, criminal, or even state-sanctioned violence cannot be quantified for ancient Rome: the sources for doing so do not exist. One must therefore work from anecdotes and vignettes, cases documented in papyri, and other such scattered data, each of which is bounded by time and space. Such material allows the formation of, at best, impressions and suspicions rather than hard-and-fast, well-documented conclusions. See Coleman, "Contagion of the Throng" and my own thoughts in "Violence in Roman Social Relations," in M. Peachin (ed.), *The Oxford Handbook of Roman Social Relations* (Oxford, forthcoming).

breaking of the will (*Rep.* 3.37), processes he symbolized with the whip, the hook, and the cross (Cic. *Rab. Perd.* 16). The slaves of Plautine comedy strive constantly to avoid beatings, or worse.[51] Galen, from personal experience, tells of a man who was prone to whipping, hitting, kicking, or assaulting his slaves with whatever pieces of wood came to hand. The fellow once became enraged while traveling with Galen and hit two of his slaves over the head with the narrow edge of a sheathed sword, inflicting serious wounds which Galen treated (Galen, *Anim. Pass.* 4 = Kühn 5.18–19). Minucius Basilus, one of Julius Caesar's murderers, was himself murdered by his slaves, "one of whom he was mutilating as a punishment," as Appian casually notes (*B Civ.* 3.98). Violence threatened even the supposedly favored servants who worked in close proximity to their owners. Seneca offers a harrowing picture of the degradations and casual violence meted out to the servers at dinner parties: they were to stand rigid and completely still; a cough, a sneeze, or a hiccup invited a beating with rods; mishaps or murmuring while serving earned an appointment with the lash. Similar unpleasantness is found in Juvenal, as when a mistress tears out the hair of a maidservant for minor infractions.[52] Torturers (*tortores*) were kept on retainer to punish wayward slaves or to preside over "examinations" into crimes or transgressions.[53] Humiliation of slaves was the norm. As Trimalchio plays ball in the baths prior to his infamous *cena*, he urinates, washes his hands, and then dries them in the hair of a nearby slave.[54]

While vulnerability to arbitrary violence was thus one of the cardinal characteristics of the slave's condition, violence extended well outside the slave–owner relationship. The acceptance of violence ran deep in Roman society: "Roman tradition tolerated and even encouraged violence in political and private disputes, and both the law and constitutional precedent

---

[51] Citations collected and discusssed by R. P. Saller, *Patriarchy, Property and Death in the Roman Family* (Cambridge, 1994), 137–8; H. Parker, "Crucially Funny or Tranio on the Couch: The *Servus Callidus* and Jokes about Torture," *TAPA* 119 (1989), 233–46.

[52] Sen. *Ep.* 47.2–3, *Dial.* 5.24–5; Juv. *Sat.* 6.475–93. For further examples and discussion, see J. D'Arms, "Slaves and Roman *Convivia*," in Slater (ed.), *Dining in a Classical Context*, 171–83. On violence and degradation against slaves in general, see Bradley, *Slavery and Society*, 27–30. The anonymously penned *Life of Aesop* (*Vit. Aes.*) is also replete with casual violence (in the form of beatings, slaps, and cuffs) administered to Aesop by his owner; for text, see B. E. Perry, *Aesopica* (Urbana, 1952), 35–208; for translation, see L. W. Daly, *Aesop without Morals: The Famous Fables and a Life of Aesop* (New York, 1961). For analysis of the *Life's* value as a source for social history, see K. Hopkins, "Novel Evidence for Roman Slavery," *Past and Present* 138 (1993), 3–27. See also A. Cutler, "The Violent *Domus*: Cruelty, Gender, and Class in Roman Household Possessions," in E. D'Ambra and G. P. R. Métraux (eds.), *The Art of Citizens, Soldiers and Freedmen in the Roman World*, BAR International Series 1526 (Oxford, 2006), 103–14.

[53] Juv. *Sat.* 6.480; Cic. *Cluent.* 176–7; Petron. *Sat.* 49.6.

[54] See, e.g. Petron. *Sat.* 27.5–6, cf. 28.7, 30.5–11, 34.2, 49, 57.6.

recognized the use of force by private individuals."[55] The head of a Roman household (*paterfamilias*) enjoyed total legal control (termed *patria potestas*) over the bodies and belongings of all who lived under his roof, including the right to inflict corporal punishment and death. Even if historical examples of fatherly severity are all but non-existent, tales of fathers who harshly punished or even killed wayward children appear in the sources as *exempla* of laudable behavior, demonstrating that the private application of violence by right of fatherhood was perfectly acceptable to Roman tastes.[56]

On a less draconian plane, in crowded places, such as public baths, casual hitting of social inferiors who got in your way appears to have been unexceptional.[57] Urban streets and alleyways, especially at night, were the province of muggers and brawlers.[58] When Galen's slave-beating friend later regretted his savage roadside assault on his servants, he asked Galen to flog him in private. "Even remorse took the form of violence," observes Keith Hopkins of this incident.[59] Violence was an integral part of the law, especially as applied to the less-valued members of society, against whom torture and cruel punishments were to be deployed as a matter of course (see below, pp. 28–30). Being a militaristic and imperial culture, the Romans adopted, even celebrated, an ideology of dominance through the application of violence. It has recently been argued that the prevalence of violent iconography found in Roman domestic art and even household objects reflects a deep fascination with violence at the societal level.[60] All of these conditions arguably inured the Roman psyche to accept high levels of violence as a form of entertaining spectacle in a manner that seems, on the surface, alien to the modern consumer of entertainment. As one leading scholar has put it, "Why did the Romans find violence so absorbing? Partly, I suggest, because the Roman world was permeated by violence that had to be absorbed."[61]

[55] A. W. Lintott, *Violence in Republican Rome*, 2nd edn. (Oxford, 1999), esp. 1–51 (quote at 4).

[56] See the *exempla* of Valerius Maximus (5.8) and Seneca (*Clem.* 1.15.1). On the rarity of firmly attested cases, see W. V. Harris, "The Roman Father's Power of Life and Death," in R. S. Bagnall and W. V. Harris (eds.), *Studies in Roman Law in Memory of A. Arthur Schiller* (Leiden, 1986), 81–95. See also Saller, *Patriarchy, Property and Death*, 102–53.

[57] See Pliny *Ep.* 3.14.6–8; Sen. *Dial.* 4.32.2, *Ep.* 107.2.

[58] *Dig.* 9.2.52.1; Juv. *Sat.* 3.235–308; Tac. *Ann.* 13.25.1–2; Sen. *Clem.* 1.8.2; Suet. *Aug.* 45.2. See further T. W. Africa, "Urban Violence in Imperial Rome," *Journal of Interdisciplinary History* 2 (1971), 3–21.

[59] Galen *Anim. Pass.* 4 = Kühn 5.19–20. Quote from Hopkins, "Novel Evidence," 10.

[60] See, e.g., S. Brown, "Death as Decoration: Scenes from the Arena on Roman Domestic Mosaics," in A. Richlin (ed.), *Pornography and Representation in Greece and Rome* (Oxford, 1992), 180–211; Cutler, "Violent Domus."

[61] See Coleman, "'Contagion of the Throng'" (quote at 65). On militarism in Roman culture, see W. V. Harris, *War and Imperialism in Republican Rome, 327–70 BC* (Oxford, 1979), 9–53.

Third, Rome was a society marked by an almost obsessive commitment to hierarchy and status: "Rank must be maintained" declares Cicero as he discusses the finest of status gradations among senators, who perhaps represented two one-thousandths of 1 per cent of the empire's entire population.[62] In sharp contrast to modern Western pretensions of egalitarianism, Roman society was from an early period broken down into legally defined status groups, such as slaves and freeborn, freeborn and freed, citizens and non-citizens (or quasi-citizens). Even the supposedly privileged class of citizens was subdivided into ranks (*ordines*) grounded in birth and wealth, for which specific symbols of status came to be prescribed and policed.[63] As citizenship became increasingly widespread in the course of the second century AD, and then universal for the empire's freeborn population in AD 212, the obsession with rank led to the division of the freeborn into "The More Respectable" (*honestiores*) and "The More Lowly" (*humiliores*) or "The Thinner Ones" (*tenuiores*). These sorts of distinctions were enshrined in the law, where punishments were proportioned according to social status, with the most degrading procedures, including those administered in the arena, reserved for the lowest orders and outcasts, such as prisoners of war, brigands, fugitive slaves, or, later, *humiliores*.[64] The principle underlying the application of socially graded punishment long predated the emergence of the *honestior/humilior* categories, however: "Our ancestors in every case punished slaves more harshly than freemen, the notorious more severely than the respectable," notes a Roman jurist, while a Roman senator praises a correspondent for "preserving the distinctions of class and rank" as he presided over the courts in his province.[65]

---

[62] See Cic. *Planc.* 15 (*servari necesse est gradus*); cf. Epict. 3.14.11–14; Lib. *Or.* 48.31, Pliny *Ep.* 9.5. For the percentage of senators, see MacMullen, *Roman Social Relations*, 88.

[63] For overviews, see G. Alföldy, *The Social History of Rome*, 3rd edn. (Baltimore, 1988), esp. 106–15; G. E. M. de Ste. Croix, *The Class Struggle in the Ancient Greek World* (London, 1981), 327–408; J. Gagé, *Les classes sociales dans l'empire romaine* (Paris, 1964); P. Garnsey and R. P. Saller, *The Roman Empire: Economy, Society, and Culture* (Berkeley, 1987), 107–25. On status symbols, see, e.g., F. Kolb, "Zur Statussymbolik im antiken Rom," *Chiron* 7 (1977), 239–59; M. Reinhold, "Usurpation of Status and Status Symbols in the Roman Empire," *Historia* 20 (1971), 275–302.

[64] *Humiliores* are characterized in the *Digest* (48.19.28.1–5) as those "customarily beaten with clubs" (*fustibus caedi solent*), that is, the sort of people who are punished the way slaves are punished (48.19.10.pr). Elsewhere (*Dig.* 1.15.4) the inhabitants of apartment blocks (*insularii*) are declared subject to summary beating for lighting fires in their quarters. On the logic of such differentiation, see R. A. Bauman, *Crime and Punishment in Ancient Rome* (London, 1996), esp. 141–60; Coleman, "Fatal Charades," 44–9; P. Garnsey, *Social Status and Legal Privilege in the Roman Empire* (Oxford, 1970), 103–52 (differentiated punishments) and 222–3, 260–80 (*honestior/humilior* distinction); R. MacMullen, "Judicial Savagery in the Roman Empire," *Chiron* 16 (1986), 147–66 (= R. MacMullen, *Changes in the Roman Empire: Essays in the Ordinary* [Princeton, 1990], 204–24).

[65] *Dig.* 48.19.28.16: *maiores nostri in omni supplicio severius servos quam liberos, famosos quam integrae famae homines punierunt*; Pliny *Ep.* 9.5: *temperare mihi non possum quominus laudem similis monenti, quod eum modum tenes ut discrimina ordinum dignitatumque custodias.*

It was shocking to elite sensibilities not when a person was tortured and crucified but when a person of inappropriate status was tortured and crucified. Cicero's prosecution of C. Verres (who had been governor of Sicily in 73–71 BC) illustrates these perspectives very clearly. Given the forensic context, it can be assumed that Cicero was expressing sentiments that (he thought) would resonate with jurymen drawn from the upper class, and probably also with the members of the common public who routinely watched prominent trials in the city. He seeks to elicit the indignation of his audience by harping on Verres' having tortured and killed (by crucifixion) Roman citizens in a manner stated as fitting for slaves or public enemies.[66] Similar consideration is extended to a leading citizen of Tyndaris, who was brutalized by Verres in the city's forum (*Verr.* 2.4.86–7), and to other men of prominence in their communities unjustly executed by the cruel governor (*Verr.* 2.5.108–14). But no such indignation attaches to notices of a slave shepherd crucified for carrying a hunting spear (*Verr.* 2.5.7) or a gibbet set up to receive *servi damnati* (*Verr.* 2.5.12). Indeed, Cicero expects uppity slaves and pirate captains to be paraded about in public, lashed, burned, and executed, and finds it rather irritating when they are not (*Verr.* 2.5.14, 2.5.65–7).

And not just Cicero. He insists that the people of Syracuse shared similar expectations.

> In that great gathering at Syracuse, gentlemen of the jury, I saw no man who said they had seen the captive [a pirate captain Verres had captured, but kept at his house], although everyone, as is customary and usually happens, came running, inquired about him, and wanted to see him . . . The seafaring people of Syracuse, who had often heard that leader's name and trembled at it, although they wanted to feast their eyes on his torture and execution and sate their souls, not one of them was given the opportunity to glimpse him.[67]

In these instances, quite aside from the matter of the guilt or innocence of Verres' victims, Cicero calibrates the severity of punishment against the social status of the accused, and he evidently expects the jurors to

---

[66] Cic. *Verr.* 1.5.13 (*cives Romani servilem in modum cruciati et necati*), 2.1.7, 2.1.8, 2.1.9, 2.1.13, 2.3.6, 2.3.59, 2.4.26, 2.5.72–3 (*cives Romani hostilem in modum cruciati et necati*), 2.5.101–22, 2.5.160–72, 2.5.179. For comparanda, see, e.g., Dio 57.19.2, 58.21.3; Gell. *NA* 10.3.17; Suet. *Aug.* 27.4, *Tib.* 60, *Cal.* 32.1, *Claud.* 34; Sen. *Dial.* 5.18–23; Tac. *Ann.* 3.50.2, 11.22.1, 15.56, 16.20.2; and the *Senatus Consultum de Cn. Pisone Patre* (*SCPP*), lines 49–52; see W. Eck et al. *Das Senatus Consultum de Cn. Pisone Patre* (Munich, 1996). In each case, it is not the cruelty of the torments themselves that offends, but that a person of the wrong status had to endure them.

[67] Cic. *Verr.* 2.5.65: *hominem in tanto conventu Syracusis vidi neminem, iudices, qui archipiratam captum sese vidisse diceret, cum omnes, ut mos est, ut solet fieri, concurrerent, quaererent, videre cuperent . . . homines maritimi Syracusis, qui saepe istius ducis nomen audissent, saepe timuissent, cum eius cruciatu atque supplicio pascere oculos animumque exsaturare vellent, potestas aspiciendi nemini facta est.*

do the same – hence his belaboring the point. So in addition to being confronted constantly with slaves, "the talking sort of tool," ever larger swathes of the population came to be classified as fit for degrading and brutal punishment. In this way the power of public distinction (*dignitas*) was maintained. When Cicero comments that "to consign a Roman citizen to chains is a wicked deed, to flog him a crime, to kill him is practically parricide, but what can I say about crucifying him? No word is sufficient to describe such a vile act,"[68] the vileness proceeds entirely from the status of the victim, not the act of crucifixion. Thus was the inflicting of violence closely tied to the implacably hierarchical cast of Roman social thought.

Fourth, pain and death were far more proximate companions to the ancient Roman than they are for most moderns, at least those fortunate enough to live in the developed world. Life expectancy at birth is generally agreed to have been about twenty-five years in ancient Rome (as opposed to roughly seventy-six today), probably even lower among the slave and destitute populations.[69] Infant mortality hovered, appallingly, at about 30 percent. Three famous examples are suggestive. The prominent Republican nobleman, Ti. Sempronius Gracchus and his wife Cornelia had twelve children, of whom only three saw adulthood (Plut. *Gracch.* 3–5). The emperor Antoninus Pius had two natural sons, both of whom perished before he assumed power in AD 138.[70] The second-century senator M. Cornelius Fronto lived to see the deaths of five children and his first grandson, all apparently in infancy (Fronto, *Nep. Am.* 2.1–2, cf. *Ad Ver.* 2.9). In the absence of accurate knowledge about human physiology and the causes of disease, or any awareness of the microbial realm at all, death could come even to adults with a bewildering suddenness: Q. Caecilius Metellus Celer (cos. 60 BC) was seen in the forum fine and healthy one day – and was dead the next (Cic. *Cael.* 59).

It must be appreciated that these melancholy notices concern people at the pinnacle of Roman society, who had available to them the very best the times had to offer in the way of shelter, nutrition, and medical care. How much worse it must have been for the masses teeming in their

---

[68] *Verr.* 2.5.170: *facinus est vincere civem Romanum, scelus verberare, prope parricidium necare: quid dicam in crucem tollere? verbo satis digno tam nefaria res apellari nullo modo potest.*

[69] For recent surveys, see R. P. Duncan-Jones, *Structure and Scale in the Roman Economy* (Cambridge, 1990), 93–105; B. W. Frier, "Roman Demography," in D. S. Potter and D. J. Mattingly (eds.), *Life, Death, and Entertainment in the Roman Empire*, 2nd edn. (Ann Arbor, 2010), 85–109; T. G. Parkin, *Demography and Roman Society* (Baltimore, 1992), esp. 92–111; Saller, *Patriarchy, Property and Death*, 12–25; W. Scheidel (ed.), *Debating Roman Demography, Mnemosyne* Suppl. 211 (Leiden, 2001).

[70] For Antoninus' sons, see *PIR*[2] A 1511 and G 26.

urban slums or huddling in rural hovels.[71] As documented in detail by Alex Scobie's pioneering study of the (un)hygienic conditions in the ancient capital, the corpses of animals and even of humans could be found in the streets, to be picked up by gangs of public slaves for disposal in lime pits, pits excavated on the Esquiline in Rome in the nineteenth century.[72] General nutrition levels were also shockingly low, so that large numbers of people went hungry for much of the time, and this would leave them particularly susceptible to infection and illness.[73] Death rates increased during the later months of summer, when malaria and pulmonary or gastro-intestinal infections flourished in the heat and humidity.[74] Infants and toddlers were constantly at risk, and death in childbirth (from uncontrolled hemorrhaging or infection) was a very real danger facing women. Death, therefore, would have been something with which the Roman adult was intimately familiar. The encounter with it began early and the relationship remained close throughout the subsequent stages of life. This is not to argue that the Romans were indifferent to death through habituation, but rather that it was an accepted part of life, something they were less squeamish about confronting in the flesh, if you will, than are most moderns.[75]

Then there was pain. In the modern world palliatives are a convenience purchasable for a pittance, whereas the Romans had minimal notions of anesthetics. Suffering, from toothaches to surgery, would have to be endured in a manner so vivid as to defy the twenty-first-century ima-gination. Many of the afflictions of old age that are treatable, or at least

---

[71] Pliny the Elder (*HN* 7.180–5) catalogs varieties of sudden natural deaths, while the astrologer Vettius Valens (2.41) reports violent deaths met by some of his clients, including beheading (or throat-cutting), drowning, roasting in a bath, poison, suicide by hanging, and fighting wild beasts. The latter might be taken to suggest death in the arena, but no setting for the fatal struggle is indicated – rustic fields or remote byways are also possibilities.

[72] The Roman jurist Papinian (*Dig.* 43.10.1.2) felt it necessary to prohibit throwing excrement, corpses, or animal skins onto the street. See A. Scobie, "Slums, Sanitation, and Mortality in the Roman World," *Klio* 68 (1986), 399–433, esp. 418–22 on corpses (animal and human) in the street and the attendant dangers of this situation. On the Esquiline dumps, see R. Lanciani, *Ancient Rome in the Light of Recent Discoveries* (Boston, MA, 1889), 64–5. See also V. M. Hope and E. Marshall (eds.), *Death and Disease in the Ancient City* (London, 2000).

[73] P. Garnsey, *Food and Society in Classical Antiquity* (Cambridge, 1999), 34–61.

[74] B. D. Shaw, "Seasons of Death: Aspects of Mortality in Imperial Rome," *JRS* 86 (1997), 100–38; R. Sallares, *Malaria and Rome: A History of Malaria in Ancient Italy* (Oxford, 2002), esp. 201–34; W. Scheidel, *Death on the Nile: Disease and the Demography of Roman Egypt*, Mnemosyne Suppl. 228, (Leiden, 2001), esp. 51–109; W. Scheidel, "Germs for Rome," in Edwards and Woolf (eds.), *Rome the Cosmopolis*, 158–76.

[75] Historians of Early Modern Europe have reasoned along these lines, but to argue for indifference rather than mere familiarity or even heightened fascination; see A. Farge, *Fragile Lives: Violence, Power, and Solidarity in Eighteenth-Century Paris*, trans. C. Shelton (Cambridge, 1993), 185–7; Gatrell, *Hanging Tree*, 76–80. For Rome, see Frier, "Roman Demography," esp. 86–90; Hopkins, *Death and Renewal*, 201–56.

manageable today must have been excruciating in ancient conditions.[76] Pain and suffering, therefore, would have been another immediate and visible feature of the everyday Roman experience. Indeed, it was not unusual for major surgical operations to be performed in public, before an audience (Joh. Chrys. *Hom. de Paralyt.* 4 = *PG* 51.54–6). It is reasonable to suppose that people raised amidst such conditions could gaze on suffering and death in the arena – and the suffering and death of those reckoned worthless, at that – far more readily than would be the case for the average Westerner today. Their threshold of tolerance was a lot higher than ours.[77]

Fifth, specific historical circumstances contributed to the emergence and development of the gladiatorial games at Rome.[78] By the second century BC, the Romans were in possession of a vast empire spanning the Mediterranean basin. Incessant wars generated thousands of prisoners, who staffed the arena displays.[79] Although the pace of expansion slowed under the emperors, occasional efforts at extending the empire's borders or the suppression of internal revolts provided plenty of fodder for the *spectacula*.[80] Likewise, the geographic extent of the empire gave access to large numbers of exotic animals for exhibition on the sand. The agonistic ethos of the Republican oligarchy meant that the games were seized on as a means to outdo rivals, which in turn ensured the elaboration of their production over time. Indeed, the games were but one feature of a wider pattern of ancient euergetism, i.e., the deployment of private wealth for public benefit. In this system, the provision of conveniences (*commoda*) at the expense of the wealthy for the enjoyment of the community played a prominent part.[81] The Republican oligarchy long used such *commoda* as one theater of operations among many in their constant struggle for priority and prominence – and later, under the dynasts of the first century BC, for dominance – while the emperors, having cleared the field of rivals,

---

[76] See, recently, K. Cokayne, *Experiencing Old Age in Ancient Rome* (London, 2003), and T. G. Parkin, *Old Age in the Roman World: A Cultural and Social History* (Baltimore, 2002), esp. 57–89. See also M. Harlow and R. Laurence, *Growing Up and Growing Old in Ancient Rome: A Life Course Approach* (London, 2002).

[77] Cicero (*Rosc. Am.* 92–3), with reference to the widespread murder generated by the Sullan proscriptions in Italy, alludes to the dehumanizing effect that constant exposure to atrocity had even on hardened Roman sensibilities.

[78] The point is well made by Kyle, *Spectacles of Death*, 34–75; see also Ville, *Gladiature*, 57–173.

[79] Hopkins, *Conquerors and Slaves*, 99–106; Jongman, "Slavery."

[80] See, e.g., the fate of the Jewish prisoners taken after the fall of Jersulalem in AD 70: Jos. *BJ* 6.414–19, 7.37–8. The 123 days of spectacles put on by Trajan in AD 107, following his final victory in Dacia the previous year, presumably featured plenty of Dacian prisoners; see Dio 68.15.1.

[81] The seminal study remains P. Veyne, *Le pain et le cirque: sociologie historique d'un pluralisme politique* (Paris, 1976), esp. 539–791.

were simply expected to put on games on the most grandiose scale possible. To have done otherwise would have tarnished the image of the *princeps* as the empire's premier benefactor.[82] The emperors found in the games a useful vehicle for strengthening social and political control, as well as for increasing personal popularity and communicating the paternalistic principles of imperial rule, so sponsoring them was very much in their interest. Foreign conquest also brought the Romans into contact with diverse cultures and societies, some of which may have provided models or inspiration for the particular forms of violence laid on in the arena.[83] In this way, historical contingency played a central role in generating and then shaping the phenomenon of the Roman games, but their advent was not predicated as an inevitable outcome by any one circumstance. Rather, a combination of factors stood behind the emergence of arena spectacles. The historical development of the games would have accustomed the spectators to increasing levels of violence presented in increasingly inventive ways. By the High Imperial period the expectations of the crowd at Rome would have been very high indeed, even if not matched by those of the provincials, who would have been used to more modest displays commensurate with the means of their local sponsors.

The various spheres of experience reviewed above combined to engender, at least as reflected in our primarily elite written sources, a certain callous fatalism about human mortality.[84] Ideas of universal human dignity were all but non-existent and large swathes of the population were seen as morally or inherently worthless. Weak members of society were objects not of compassion but of derision. More than most, Romans lionized strength over weakness, victory over defeat, dominion over obedience. Losers paid a harsh price and got what they deserved, and recalcitrants, rebels, or resisters were to be ruthlessly handled.[85] Such notions permeated Roman society and

---

[82] Mart. *Spect.* 6.4, 24.1–2, 28. Augustus boasts expansively about his gladiatorial games, hunts, and a sea-fight in his *Res Gestae* (22–3), while Suetonius' biographies report each emperor's spectacles and public shows as a matter of course (not all of them necessarily gladiatorial); see Suet. *Iul.* 39, *Aug.* 43–4, *Tib.* 47, *Cal.* 18, *Claud.* 21, *Nero* 11–12, *Vesp.* 19, *Tit.* 7.3, *Dom.* 10.1, 12.1.

[83] The origins of the gladiatorial games are disputed (see above, introduction n. 19) but were almost certainly located outside Rome itself.

[84] "The ethical standards common to the hellenized Mediterranean world, let alone those of the 'barbarian' races, did not place such high value on human existence in itself as ours do now ... The Romans, therefore, laid little weight on the infliction of death or suffering as such, and this attitude was by the same token callous, but removed from sadism"; see Lintott, *Violence*, 35–51 (quotes at 36 and 50 respectively).

[85] See Caesar's comment on the handling of the Catilinarian conspirators (Sall. *Cat.* 51.17), "I do not think his [Silanus'] proposal [that the conspirators be put to death] is cruel, for what can be done to such men that is cruel?" (*verum sententia eius mihi non crudelis – quid enim in talis homines crudele fieri potest?*). See also discussion below, ch. 5, pp. 166–74.

are expressed throughout our sources in such profusion as to defy concise citation. Four examples, drawn from very different planes of Roman life, will suffice to illustrate the breadth and depth of this coldhearted value system.

From the Late Republic onwards, Roman politics became a ruthless game of total winners and abject losers, where moderation and power-sharing were all but impossible. The drive to dominate and not to be forced to bow before a rival was paramount, and the general sanctioning of revenge (*vindicatio, ultio*) as a justifiable pursuit in the private and public spheres added fuel to the fire.[86] Mercy and cooperation were only conceivable within the parameters of an unequal power relationship, where winner-benefactors granted favors to loser-suppliants. Under the emperors, power-sharing was virtually unheard of (except temporarily, usually among siblings or fathers and sons, and nearly always with disastrous results), and the only major attempt to introduce it formally into the administration of the empire, the Diocletianic Tetrarchy, failed on its first test. Thus, for centuries sociopolitical relationships among the elite were governed by the principles of dominance and subjection; how far down the social ladder these attitudes extended remains debatable, but it seems unlikely that the lower orders were largely free from them.

Second, as seen above, the treatment of ever-present slaves was marked by violence and disregard for their welfare. Galen's father advised that slaves ought not to be punished in anger, but only after a period of reflection, coldly and coolly with whips and rods. As a result, owners would not injure their fists administering blows or succumb unhealthily to their passions.[87]

Third, the poor and destitute were omnipresent in Roman society but almost wholly uncared for by the state, and scorned by the elite.[88] Left to

---

[86] On revenge, see Lintott, *Violence*, 22–34, 49–50; Flaig, *Ritualisierte Politik*, 137–54.

[87] Galen *Anim. Pass.* 4 = Kühn 5.17. A similar story was told of Plato (Plut. *Mor.* 10D and 1108A): he once asked his nephew to beat a wayward slave for him, since Plato himself was angry. Plato was concerned not with the welfare of his own knuckles but that his reactions not carry the taint of injustice spurred by emotion.

[88] See Martial's contemptuous jokes about beggars and tramps; *Ep.* 4.53, 11.32, 11.56; or Alciphron's nonchalant description of the poor eating scraps from a market (Alciphr. 3.24; cf. John Chrys. *Hom. in I Cor.* = *PG* 61 passim). A modest exception to elite indifference to the plight of the poor was the alimentary scheme for poor children in Italy run by Nerva and Trajan; see Pliny *Ep.* 1.8.10, 7.18.2–5, *Pan.* 28. The main epigraphic testimony is provided by two tables outlining the scheme for the communities of Ligures Baebiani (*CIL* 9.1455 = *ILS* 6509) and Veleia (*CIL* 11.1147 = *ILS* 6675); see also *CIL* 5.5262 = *ILS* 2927 (Comum) and *ILS* 6106 (Ferentinum). The exact purpose of the scheme remains debated; see, e.g., F. C. Bourne, "The Roman Alimentary Program and Italian Agriculture," *TAPA* 91 (1960), 47–75; R. P. Duncan-Jones, "The Purpose and Organisation of the Alimenta," *PBSR* 32 (1964), 123–46; R. P. Duncan-Jones, *The Economy of the Roman Empire: Quantitative Studies*, 2nd edn. (Cambridge, 1982), esp. 304–10; S. L. Dyson, *Community and Society in Roman*

occupy whatever shacks, hovels, or corners of public buildings they could find, they were abandoned quite literally to rot on the street, as Martial makes harrowingly clear when describing the dying moments of a beggar. The perishing wretch beats off carrion birds by flapping his rags at them, even as dogs gather and squabble over the anticipated feast of his flesh.[89] Poverty is perhaps a perennial feature of society, but rather than doing anything about such manifest misery in their midst, the well-off deluded themselves into thinking the poor were really rather happy folk.[90] The view from the top is nicely summed up by Seneca: "Let the emperor . . . look with pleasure upon one class of his citizenry because they are useful and good – the rest he can leave to make up the numbers." A graffito from Pompeii is rawer still: "I hate poor people."[91]

Set against this backdrop of intimate familiarity with death, pain, and wretched misery, mercy and pity were undervalued as qualities in and of themselves. Seneca's treatise *On Mercy* (*de Clementia*), addressed to Nero, makes for illuminating reading. Quite unlike modern notions of pity and mercy as inherent virtues, Seneca advocates a version of mercy modulated by cold calculation: the merciful prince will have no need of bodyguards, since he is loved by his people.[92] To be fair, Seneca's treatise is addressed to an emperor, so that the manipulative attitude toward clemency he delineates is to be expected. But in the second book, which survives only in part, the philosopher treats "the nature and aspect of mercy" (*Clem.* 1.3.1) in abstract terms. Here we read that mercy is essentially a mechanical act, a considered choice: "all understand that mercy consists in stopping short of what might have been deservedly imposed" (*Clem.* 2.3.2). Mercy is in

---

Italy (Baltimore, 1992), 216–17 and 221–2; P. Garnsey, "Trajan's *Alimenta*: Some Problems," *Historia* 17 (1968), 367–81; G. Woolf, "Food, Poverty and Patronage: The Significance of the Epigraphy of the Roman Alimentary Schemes in Early Imperial Italy," *PBSR* 45 (1990), 197–228.

[89] Mart. *Ep.* 10.5 (the dying beggar). In fact, the very ubiquity (Sen. *Dial.* 12.12.1) and apparent permanence of poverty induced some to embrace a doctrine of inaction: there was simply nothing to be done (Dio Chrys. *Or.* 7.125; Sen. *Dial.* 7.24). Note that John Chrysostom (*Hom. in I Cor.* 34.4–5 = *PG* 61.291–2) includes among "the poor" artisans, construction workers, and farmers.

[90] Sen. *Ep.* 80.6–7; Dio Chrys. *Or.* 7.103–4. Such attitudes die hard. As one contributor to the poverty debates in England in the eighteenth and nineteenth centuries, the Methodist minister Joseph Townsend (1739–1816) commented, "The peasant with a sickle in his hand is happier than the prince upon his throne"; see J. Townsend, *A Dissertation on the Poor Laws* (1786), section 7, cited in W. Richey and D. Robinson (eds.), *William Wordsworth and Samuel Taylor Coleridge: Lyrical Ballads and Related Writings* (Boston, MA, 2002), 177.

[91] Sen. *Clem.* 1.5.7: *princeps alios ex civibus suis, quia utiles bonique sunt, libens videat, alios in numerum reliquat.* Elsewhere Seneca makes it clear that by "the rest" he means the poor (*Dial.* 12.12.1) and he describes people flinging alms contemptuously at the needy while wishing to have no contact with them (*Clem.* 2.6.2). Pompeian graffito: *CIL* 4.9839b.

[92] Sen. *Clem.* 1.13.5, 1.19.3–9. Cicero's contemporary Curio (*Att.* 10.4.8) attributes a similar calculation to Caesar's famed policy of *clementia*.

harmony with strictness (*severitas*), so long as a punisher does not take sick pleasure in the cruelty (*crudelitas*) of a punishment and so transgress into the realm of savagery (*feritas*). Mercy, then, does not dictate that brutality be eschewed entirely, but rather demands calculation in its application.

In contrast, pity (*misericordia*) is not a virtue at all but a perversion of mercy, as cruelty is to severity. Pity is the vice of a feeble nature that succumbs to the sight of other people's misfortunes. It is thus most associated with weak people: old ladies and little women, who are moved by the tears of the most hardened offenders, and who, if they could, would break open their prisons. Pity looks at a condition, not the reason for it; mercy embraces reason.[93] Cicero's opinion is not far removed: "Pity is distress arising out of the wretchedness of another who is suffering undeservedly; for no-one is moved by pity at the punishment of a parricide or a traitor."[94] Such are the views of educated Romans, generally held to stand at the humaner end of the spectrum, as Romans go.[95] Roman sources not uncommonly deride as unworthy of the proper gentleman that he yield to raw emotion, whether kindly or cruel (e.g., Sall. *Cat.* 51.1; Sen. *Dial.* 3–5 *passim*). We have no way of knowing how widely views like this were held among the general population; most *plebs* probably gave such abstract matters little or no thought. We have seen how the people of Syracuse are described by Cicero as thirsting to see a pirate captain paraded, tortured, and killed (Cic. *Verr.* 2.5.65–7); the overall impression one gets from the sources does not suggest that the commoners of the ancient world were awash with *misericordia*.[96]

These cultural and contextual factors must be seen as contributing in important ways to the phenomenon of the Roman games. None is decisive in itself in fully explaining the appeal of the *munera*. There have been

---

[93] I paraphrase Sen. *Clem.* 2.5.1: *est enim vitium pusilli animi ad speciem alienorum malorum succidentis. itaque pessimo cuique familiarissima est: anus et mulierculae, quae lacrimis nocentissimorum moventur, quae, si liceret, carcerem effringerent. misericordia non causam, sed fortunam spectat; clementia rationi accedit.* Seneca concedes in the following sections that not everyone shares this view, and advocates charitable acts, provided they are carried out in a calm and collected manner. Pardon, however, should not be granted to those deserving of punishment (*Clem.* 2.7).

[94] *Tusc.* 4.18: *misericordia est aegritudo ex miseria alterius iniuria laborantis; nemo enim parricidae aut proditoris supplicio misericordia commovetur.*

[95] "Cicero was a humane and cultivated man," according to R. Syme, *The Roman Revolution* (Oxford, 1939), 4.

[96] People are not emotional monoliths, and the *populus* could display *misericordia* on occasion, especially in the face of perceived injustice (e.g., Tac. *Ann.* 14.42–5, 14.60–61.3). This was true even in the arena (see below, ch. 5, pp. 179–82). Their attitude toward those thought deserving of punishment, as Cicero's comments show, was rather more severe (compare, e.g., Tert. *Spect.* 19.2 = T.28; Sen. *Ep.* 7.5 = T.20). For more on classical concepts of pity, see D. Konstan, *Pity Transformed* (London, 2001), esp. 27–74 (on pity in the law and pity versus compassion).

other imperialist or slave-owning or wealthy and unequal societies that never staged gladiatorial-type spectacles. Historically or culturally bounded explanations for Roman *spectacula* are therefore only partial explanations. This is obvious even when they are set against the multicultural background of the ancient Mediterranean basin alone, never mind the deeper perspective of history (for which, see the next chapter). Populations lacking the particular historical experiences or cultural sensibilities of the Romans readily took to arena shows, once they were introduced to them. Provincials in places like Africa or Spain or Gaul or Germany came out in their thousands to witness these most Roman of events. Greeks of the East adapted their circuses, theaters, and stadia to accommodate the violence of Roman *venationes* and *munera* alongside their traditional spectacles of drama and athletics.[97] Why would all these populations be enthralled by an event which was so thoroughly Roman in its symbolism and (by extension) in its appeal?[98] Perhaps, it may be argued, the Romans so thoroughly integrated conquered peoples into their cultural system that to all intents and purposes they *were* Romans and behaved accordingly.[99] Maybe so. But what happened in a suburb of Antioch in 166 BC suggests otherwise. Here, the Seleucid king Antiochus IV, who had spent twelve years at Rome as a hostage, put on a gladiatorial display for his people, the first such spectacle on record in the Greek East. As Livy reports it (41.20.11–13 = T.9), the spectators reacted initially with terror (not revulsion, note) at the novelty of the display, but through repeated exposure and a gradual increase in the level of violence they eventually learned to enjoy the show.[100] This happened,

---

[97] For the popularity of gladiatorial *munera* in the Greek East, see Robert, G*ladiateurs*, esp. 239–66 and, more recently, M. Carter, "The Presentation of Gladiatorial Spectacles in the Greek East: Roman Culture and Greek Identity" (Ph.D. dissertation, McMaster University, 1999); M. Golden, *Greek Sport and Social Status* (Austin, 2008), 68–104; and items cited below, n. 101. On the adaptation of Greek theaters and other arenas for *munera*, see ch. 3, n. 99. For epigraphic evidence of gladiatorial displays and beast hunts in the theater and stadium at Aphrodisias, see C. Roueché, *Performers and Partisans at Aphrodisias in the Roman and Late Roman Period* (London, 1993), 61–80.

[98] The essential Roman-ness of the spectacles is stressed in most of the analyses reviewed above; see esp. K. Welch, "The Roman Arena in Late-Republican Italy: A New Interpretation," *JRA* 7 (1994), 59–80, and Welch, *Roman Amphitheater*, 72–101, esp. 88–91.

[99] What precisely is meant by the so-called Romanization of subject populations, however, is far from clear; see recently, C. Ando, *Imperial Ideology and Provincial Loyalty in the Roman Empire* (Berkeley, 2000); R. MacMullen, *Romanization in the Time of Augustus* (New Haven, 2000); D. Mattingly, *An Imperial Possession: Britain in the Roman Empire* (London, 2006); S. Pilhofer, *Romanisierung in Kilikien? Das Zeugnis der Inschriften* (Munich, 2006); L. Revell, *Roman Imperialism and Local Identities* (Cambridge, 2009); R. E. Roth (ed.) *Roman by Integration: Dimensions of Group Identity in Material Culture and Text*, *JRA* Supplementary Series 66 (Portsmouth, RI, 2007); G. Woolf, *Becoming Roman: The Origins of Provincial Civilization in Gaul* (Cambridge, 1998).

[100] Polybius (30.25–26 = Ath. 5.194c–195f) describes Antiochus' spectacles in more detail and tells us they lasted thirty days. He does not note spectator reactions, however. Diodorus (31.16) mentions

it must be stressed, almost a century before the Seleucid monarchy was washed away and this part of the Mediterranean world fully integrated into the Roman empire. So the Roman games, once people became accustomed to them, appealed to spectators who had been raised well outside the Roman cultural sphere. Later, when gladiatorial combats were introduced into Athens in the first century AD, a visitor to the city noted that "the Athenians ran in crowds to the theater beneath the acropolis to witness human slaughter, and the passion for such sports was stronger there than it is in Corinth today . . . and when the Athenians invited him [Apollonius of Tyana] to attend their assembly, he refused to enter a place so impure and reeking with gore."[101] The philosopher Apollonius' high-minded position stands in stark contrast to the behavior of the Athenian public. There was nothing peculiarly Roman about attraction to violent spectacle, even if the *munera* were indeed peculiarly Roman events.

The point is buttressed by a quick glimpse beyond the Roman context. Many other types of horrendously violent rituals have been very successful in drawing enormous crowds (below, chapter 2). When the Roman games are set against this deeper perspective, limiting the scope of explanation exclusively to historically contingent or culturally bounded factors, for all their insight and worth, looks restrictive. Thinking solely in terms of culture and context is inadequate to explain a widespread pattern of mass attendance at brutal spectacles of degradation, suffering, and death. It seems more than a little stretched to envision that the attention of all such crowds was commanded by quite distinct and unconnected motivations determined by their particular cultural context and historical circumstances. Surely some similarity underlies so consistent a commitment to watching violence laid on as spectacle. I suggest that similarity can be found in the one thing that truly unites spectators at violent spectacles, past, present, and future: our shared human psychology.

---

the festival but omits any mention of gladiators performing at it. For contrasting analyses of this spectacle's nature and cultural-historical significance, see J. C. Edmondson, "The Cultural Politics of Public Spectacle in Rome and the Greek East, 167–166 BCE," in B. Bergmann and C. Kondoleon (eds.), *The Art of Ancient Spectacle* (New Haven, 1999), 77–95, esp. 84–8, and M. Carter, "The Roman Spectacles of Antiochus IV Epiphanes at Daphne, 166 BC," *Nikephoros* 14 (2001), 45–62. See also P. F. Mittag, *Antiochos IV. Epiphanes: Eine Politische Biographie*, Klio Beiträge 11 (Berlin, 2006), 282–95.

[101] Phil. *VA* 4.22 = T.13. For similar sentiments, see Dio Chrys. 31.121 = T.7, who in this passage seems more offended at the location than the nature of the spectacle. For a full discussion, see K. Welch, "Negotiating Roman Spectacle Architecture in the Greek World: Athens and Corinth," in Bergmann and Kondoleon (eds.), *Art of Ancient Spectacle*, 125–45. Mann ("Gladiators in the Greek East," 276–9) shows how gladiatorial games were not foisted on the Greek East by the Romans, but eagerly adopted at the local level. See also M. J. Carter, "Gladiators and Monomachoi: Attitudes to a Roman 'Cultural Performance,'" *International Journal of the History of Sport*, 26 (2009), 298–322.

THE APPLICABILITY OF SOCIAL PSYCHOLOGY

Is there such a thing as a unitary "human nature" shared by all, and is human behavior innate or learned? These fundamental questions have no easy answer. The simplistic dichotomy between "nature and nurture" has been replaced by a more nuanced model in which inherited propensities are interwoven with environmental conditions, but it remains debated how these influences are to be weighted relative to each other.[102] It is well beyond the scope of this book to become embroiled in the multifaceted, politicized, and polemical debate that rages around the core questions of human nature, cognition, culture, and behavior. But if, as some claim, the mental mechanics and behavior of different populations is wholly culture-bound,[103] then any attempt to gain insight into Roman social action using the modern discipline of social psychology, which is dependent on observations made about modern subjects, would be a fruitless endeavor. So the matter of the applicability of modern social psychology to ancient conditions needs to be addressed.

Several propositions are fundamental to the analysis that follows. First, there is no question that the physiology of the human brain is universal. If, as seems reasonable (or even demonstrable in cases of neural injury or malfunction), psychological processes ultimately stem from the physical functioning of the brain (some use the term "pyschobiology"), then we can expect to find similarities in those processes on a species-wide basis. One leading researcher, in fact, argues that we share a universal psychological architecture, "Standard Equipment," as he terms it.[104] A physiologically

---

[102] For recent and detailed expositions of contrasting views (but which all accept the interactive model), see P. Ehrlich, *Human Natures: Genes, Cultures, and the Human Prospect* (Washington, DC, 2000), and R. E. Nisbett, *The Geography of Thought: How Asians and Westerners Think Differently . . . and Why* (New York, 2003) (both of whom advocate the primacy of culture in shaping multiple "human natures"); *contra* S. Pinker, *How the Mind Works* (New York, 1997), and S. Pinker, *The Blank Slate: The Modern Denial of Human Natur*e (New York, 2002). Occupying the middle ground are K. N. Laland and G. R. Brown, *Sense and Nonsense: Evolutionary Perspectives on Human Behaviour* (Oxford, 2002).

[103] As would be claimed by strict cultural determinists, such as Nisbett, *Geography of Thought*, xx: "The social practices promote the world views: the world views dictate the appropriate thought processes; and the thought processes both justify the world views and support the social practices." Cf. M. Hollis and S. Lukes (eds.), *Rationality and Relativism* (Oxford, 1982), 1: "Other minds, other cultures, other languages and other theoretical schemes call for understanding *from within*" (emphasis added).

[104] For some recent summaries of the current state of knowledge on the brain and the likely physiological basis of our thought processes, see J. E. Dowling, *Creating Mind: How the Brain Works* (New York, 1998); C. Koch, *The Quest for Consciousness: A Neurobiological Approach* (Greenwood, 2004); S. Rose (ed.), *From Brains to Consciousness? Essays on the New Sciences of the Mind* (Princeton, 1999); J. E. Swanson, *Brain Architecture: Understanding the Basic Plan* (Oxford, 2003). Voices dissenting

generated psychological architecture, if it exists, does not mean that human actions are genetically determined in the popular sense of there being "a gene for" this or that behavior, but rather that as a species our "psychobiology" generates our cultural systems and sets limits on just how varied they can be.[105] At the same time, the specific facets of the mental constructs and cultural behaviors exhibited by different groups are enormously influenced by the environment confronting them. This suggests that an interdependence between contextual stimulus and psychological propensity shapes behavior.

There are some obvious indications that this is so. Every documented human culture has a rich conceptual world that includes language, music, art, religion, and so on, but not in the same forms. All human cultures also display behavioral propensities for "groupishness" (see chapter 3), ethnocentrism, social differentiation, and the like, but not in the same manner.[106] Such observations tend to support the suggestion that "behavior may vary across cultures, but the design of the mental programs that generate it need not vary."[107] This means that the cultural mediation of psychological processes should not be misunderstood as the cultural generation of those processes. A prevalent view among psychologists and anthropologists can be summed up as follows: "How people think and behave is a product of their genetic predispositions acting under the influence of various environmental factors that include but are not limited to their culture."[108]

Second, the multiplicity of environmental circumstances under which human societies evolved and in relation to which people oriented

from materialism exist but are forced to appeal to vague "mental forces" they insist do not stem from neurophysiology: see J. M. Schwartz and S. Begley, *The Mind and the Brain: Neuroplasticity and the Power of Mental Force* (New York, 2002); C. H. Vanderwolf, *An Odyssey through the Brain, Behavior and the Mind* (Norwell, 2003). On cognition in general, see, e.g., Pinker, *How the Mind Works*, 3–58 (on "Standard Equipment"). For "psychobiology," see R. Edgerton, *Sick Societies: Challenging the Myth of Primitive Harmony* (New York, 1992), 62.

[105] Two examples of crude genetic determinism: M. P. Ghiglieri, *The Dark Side of Man: Tracing the Origins of Male Violence* (New York, 1999); R. J. Herrnstein and C. Murray, *The Bell Curve: Intelligence and Class Structure in American Life* (New York, 1994).

[106] On language, see S. Pinker, *The Language Instinct: The New Science of Language and Mind* (New York, 1994), and S. Pinker, *The Stuff of Thought: Languages as a Window into Human Nature* (New York, 2007). On religious concepts, see S. Atran, *In Gods We Trust: The Evolutionary Landscape of Religion* (Oxford, 2002); P. Boyer, *The Naturalness of Religious Ideas* (Berkeley, 1994), and P. Boyer *Religion Explained: The Evolutionary Origins of Religious Thought* (New York, 2001); D. C. Dennett, *Breaking the Spell: Religion as a Natural Phenomenon* (New York, 2006). On music, see N. L. Wallin et al. (eds.), *The Origins of Music* (Cambridge, MA, 2000).

[107] Pinker, *Blank Slate*, 1–102 (quote at 41). Even Paul Erhlich, who favors a culturally deterministic view of behavior, essentially accepts this point, although in modified form: "There is no reason to believe that the substrata [of our mental life] on which our diverse natures have been built are fundamentally different among different groups" (*Human Natures*, 106).

[108] Edgerton, *Sick Societies*, 62–3.

themselves mentally (ecological, geographic, demographic, historical, social, etc.) guarantees a kaleidoscope of variation in human cultural systems and mental concepts, as traced in detail by ethnography. The hypothesis of psychological "Standard Equipment" would predict that fundamental similarities be identifiable amidst all of this variety. And this is the case. Anthropologists have compiled a long list of human universals, several hundred traits found in all known human societies.[109] Unsurprisingly, the manifestation of universals is not universally similar. If, for example, "male coalitional violence" is a human universal, it may present as family feuds here, tribal raids there, or World War II all over. Furthermore, not all males in a given society will necessarily take part in such violence or even like it, but such individual abstinence does not negate or even undermine the fact of "male coalitional violence" as a human universal.[110] The assessment of universals in specific cultural contexts and their overall significance for anthropology and psychology is ongoing, but their very existence can be read as a powerful indication that there are shared features in human psychological functioning.[111]

The realms of language, religion, and emotion offer good examples of all this. Despite a bewildering variety in documented languages around the world, no tongue has ever been encountered which has successfully resisted all attempts to comprehend it (assuming its full mode of expression is discernible by outsiders).[112] Indeed, all human languages are translatable into

---

[109] D. E. Brown, *Human Universals* (New York, 1991); B. Lloyd and G. Gay (eds.), *Universals of Human Thought: Some African Evidence* (Cambridge, 1981).

[110] This is what social psychologists call the "individual-differences dimension," since social-psychological processes are not manifested mechanically and evenly across a given population. Francis Fukuyama argues that species-typical behaviors can be deemed universal without requiring every single member of the species to display them, or even every group within the species. Rather, such behaviors must represent a statistical median in the species' overall activities; see F. Fukuyama, *Our Posthuman Future: Consequences of the Biotechnology Revolution* (New York, 2002), esp. 129–47.

[111] Note esp. N. Roughley (ed.), *Being Humans: Anthropological Universality and Particularity in Transdisciplinary Perspectives* (Berlin, 2000), esp. the papers by B. Shore ("Human Diversity and Human Nature: The Life and Times of a False Dichotomy," 81–103) and D. E. Brown ("Human Universals and their Implications," 156–74). Brown (ibid., 167) shelters both universals and particulars under the umbrella of human psychology: "Variation is entirely compatible with a panhuman patterning that is the manifestation of a common *design* of the human mind" (emphasis in original).

[112] Necessarily excluded are undeciphered ancient languages such as Linear A, the Harappa script, Etruscan, the stamps on the Phaistos Disk (if these stamps do indeed record a language), or several Near Eastern tongues represented in the cuneiform corpus. These languages resist understanding because their syntactic, morphological, and semantic systems are not fully reconstructable, either because a paucity of examples prevents decipherment (e.g., the Phaistos Disk or Linear A) or because the surviving corpora are too restricted in content to allow an understanding of the wider language (e.g., Etruscan, limited mostly to personal names and official titles in epitaphs). It has recently been forcefully argued, in fact, that the Phaistos Disk is a modern forgery; see J. M. Eisenberg, "The Phaistos Disk: One Hundred Year Old Hoax?" *Minerva* 19 (2008), 9–24.

all other human languages, so that a person who speaks one language can learn that spoken by another, if given the time and inclination to do so. This fact alone points powerfully to a facility for language built into our pscyhological make-up, which transcends cultural boundaries. That even dead languages are also intelligible, despite surviving only via the written word and spoken by no living person, shows that the language facility crosses historical frontiers also. Most linguists today follow a Chomskian model of a "language faculty" hardwired into the human brain.[113] It hardly needs pointing out that the specific language a child acquires using the hardwired language faculty is determined by the environment it grows up in – it is the interweaving of inherited propensity with environment that produces the final behavior, in this case a person speaking their native tongue. It is a telling contrast that attempts to understand communication systems attributed to other species have been markedly less successful. To date, nobody can claim credibly to have deciphered whale songs, dolphin squeaks, bee dances, or even the hoots and screeches of our closest primate cousin, the chimpanzee, even though it seems clear enough that some mode of communication is involved in each case.

Religion too comes in a dazzling variety of forms. Some people worship trees or mountains, others fear witches or malevolent ancestral spirits, some believe in a single universe-creating superdeity, others stand in awe of a pantheon packed with divine multitudes. Nevertheless, an underlying similarity is detectable among the wide variety of supernatural agents that populate these very different belief systems. Such agents are always possessed of senses, emotions, and minds that are strikingly human in nature: they can see things (such as human frailty), hear spoken words (such as prayers), or remember past doings (such as sins). They can also be moved to the very human emotions of pity or anger or jealousy. Whether spirits, ancestral souls, or superdeities, religious supernatural agents always have access to key "strategic information" about our lives, information we would rather not have broadcast about. Furthermore, there are limits on the forms of religious beliefs, no matter how divergent or bizarre their details may appear from without. When confronted with a set of supernatural propositions, a few can be immediately judged as inherently bogus. Consider this list:

---

[113] N. Chomsky, *Language and the Mind* (New York, 1968), and, more recently, N. Chomsky, *On Nature and Language* (Cambridge, 2002). A case has been made along Chomskian lines that a moral instinct is also a human universal; see F. B. M. de Waal, *Good Natured: The Origins of Right and Wrong in Humans and Other Animals* (Cambridge, MA, 1996); M. D. Hauser, *Moral Minds: How Nature Designed our Universal Sense of Right and Wrong* (New York, 2006).

1. There is only one God. He is omniscient but powerless. He cannot do anything or have any effect on what goes on in the world.
2. There is only one God. He knows everything we do and will judge us on our behavior after death.
3. There is only one God. He is omnipotent, but he only exists on Wednesdays.
4. The forest protects us. It gives us game if we sing to it.
5. Dead people's souls wander about and sometimes visit people.
6. Some people can see the future, but they forget it immediately.
7. Some people have invisible organs in their stomachs. That organ flies away at night when they are asleep and does mischief.
8. There are invisible people around who only drink cologne. If someone suddenly goes into a fit and screams for cologne, it is because their body is being controlled by one of these invisible people.
9. The spirits will punish you if you do what they want.
10. Some people suddenly disappear if they are really thirsty.

The truly counterfeit propositions, as opposed to the merely strange, should be instantly recognizable: no religion could hold to such beliefs and command a following for any length of time.[114] This suggests that there are features of all successful religious propositions that reflect the way we think as a species. To put it another way, the human mind sets limits on the variety of religious propositions, while at the same time the diversity of cultural systems ensures great variation among those that endure.

Emotions too appear to be a human universal – all people seem to feel joy, anger, sadness, and so forth – although the cultural and linguistic conventions governing emotional expression diverge significantly, and the scientific understanding of the roots of emotions remains incomplete.[115] Emotions seem partly physiological and partly socially constructed. Everyone can feel, say, disgust (or some form of emotion analogous to our concept

---

[114] The list is adapted from Boyer, *Religion Explained*, 51–3. The bogus items are nos. 1, 3, 6, and 9. Item nos. 2 and 5 should be familiar from mainstream religions. The rest are representative of various systems of belief. On "strategic information," see ibid., esp. 150–5.

[115] J. LeDoux, *The Emotional Brain: The Mysterious Underpinnings of Emotional Life* (New York, 1996); P. Ekman and R. J. Davidson (eds.), *The Nature of Emotion: Fundamental Questions* (Oxford, 1994); M. Lewis and J. M. Haviland (eds.), *Handbook of Emotions*, 2nd edn. (New York, 2000); Pinker, *How the Mind Works*, 363–424; S. Walton, *A Natural History of Human Emotions* (New York, 2005). For a succinct summary of the issues with respect to the scientific basis of anger and pity respectively, see Harris, *Restraining Rage*, 32–49, and Konstan, *Pity Transformed*, 1–21. See also D. Konstan, *The Emotions of the Ancient Greeks: Studies in Aristotle and Classical Literature* (Toronto, 2006), esp. 41–76 (anger) and 201–17 (pity). On the universality of emotions and their (largely neglected) historical importance, see R. MacMullen, *Feelings in History, Ancient and Modern* (Claremont, 2003), esp. 49–78.

"disgust"), but there is considerable cultural variation about what is thought disgusting, most obviously in matters of cuisine.[116] It seems likely that we inherit our emotional propensities, but we express, display, or suppress particular emotions in ways shaped by our cultural environment (although a good case has been made that the facial expression of at least some emotions is universal).[117] This situation includes those instances where either other languages appear to have no way of expressing certain emotions for which English has words or phrases (e.g., "love") or conflate feelings that we conceptualize as naturally distinct (e.g., "fear" and "shame").[118] With regard to the classical world, recent work has examined emotions as they are described in the ancient sources and charted similarities and differences between their conceptualization and expression in the ancient and modern contexts.[119] Similarly, strong cases have been made that the psychological dynamics of battle are at least comparable, if not identical, in the ancient and modern worlds.[120] A practicing psychiatrist working with traumatized Vietnam veterans has identified in Homer's portrayal of Achilles all the symptoms of the psychological (primarily emotional) damage inflicted by prolonged war combat, dubbed today "Post Traumatic Stress Disorder." His analysis points to a universal facet in human psychology that spans time, space, and culture, but which is expressed and understood in culturally specific ways. Behaviors that to Homer's audience were manifestations

---

[116] W. I. Miller, *The Anatomy of Disgust* (Cambridge, MA, 1997). Even within cultural spheres, certain foods will be acceptable in one place and considered revolting in another. Horse, for instance, is commonly consumed in southern Italy but eschewed in the north. See also Walton, *Natural History*, esp. 85–125 on disgust.

[117] Such is the argument of Walton (see previous note), working off C. Darwin, *The Expression of the Emotions in Man and Animals* (Chicago, 1965; originally published 1872), and the works of Paul Ekman, such as P. Ekman (ed.), *Darwin and Facial Expressions: A Century of Research in Review* (New York, 1973), and P. Ekman, *Emotion in the Human Face*, 2nd edn. (Cambridge, 1982).

[118] A. Wierzbicka, *Emotions across Languages and Cultures: Diversity and Universals* (Cambridge, 1999), esp. 273–307.

[119] See MacMullen, *Feelings in History*. See also L. Febvre, "Sensibility and History: How to Reconstitute the Emotional Life of the Past," in P. Burke (ed.), *A New Kind of History: From The Writings of Febvre* (New York, 1973), 12–26; W. M. Reddy, *The Navigation of Feeling: A Framework for the History of Emotions* (Cambridge, 2001). For specific emotions or emotional relationships, see S. M. Braund and G. W. Most (eds.), *Ancient Anger: Perspectives from Homer to Galen* (Cambridge, 2004); D. Cairns, *AIDOS: The Psychology and Ethics of Honour and Shame in Ancient Greek Literature* (Oxford, 1993); Harris, *Restraining Rage*; R. A. Kaster, *Emotion, Restraint, and Community in Ancient Rome* (Oxford, 2005); Konstan, *Pity Transformed*; D. Konstan, *Friendship in the Classical World* (Cambridge, 1997); D. Konstan and K. Rutter (eds.), *Envy, Spite and Jealousy: The Rivalrous Emotions in Ancient Greece* (Edinburgh, 2003); M. Peachin (ed.), *Aspects of Friendship in the Graeco-Roman World*, JRA Supplementary Series 43 (Portsmouth, RI, 2001). For an example of an emotionally focused analysis applied to a different epoch, see C. Z. and P. N. Stearns, *Anger: The Struggle for Emotional Control in America's History* (Chicago, 1986).

[120] See the articles in A. B. Lloyd and C. Gilliver (eds.), *Battle in Antiquity* (London, 1996), and the comments of P. Sabin, "The Face of Roman Battle," *JRS* 90 (2000), 1–17, esp. 3–4.

of an honor-bound and courageous heroic code are today diagnosed as mental dysfunction. But – and here is the crux of the matter – the psychological reaction to combat that underlies the behavior is arguably the same.[121]

In all of the preceding, there is much that remains uncertain and debatable, and gaps persist in basic scientific knowledge about how brain and mind interact. Much will undoubtedly change as research advances. The role of culture is a particularly difficult issue, and this is our third core point. Culture is not only a shaper of human behavior, it is a product of it. Yet the conditions under which culture emerged as a force in our existence, how it came to have such a powerful influence over our actions, what gave rise to certain patterns of behavior – all of these questions have no ready answers, although recent attempts to reconstruct ancient cognition from archaeological remains have been at least plausible, if contentious.[122] So in considering the case for a shared human psychology, it is worth reiterating that culture plays a central, even a constitutive, role in being human. Humans without culture would be unrecognizable as humans.[123] Yet it is also true that without human minds (and brains), there would be no culture. The relationship between mind and culture is best conceived as symbiotic and reciprocal rather than causal and linear. Psychological processes do not float in some ethereal realm disembodied from culture, nor does culture drop independently from the heavens on to human societies. The two – mind and culture – share an intrinsic bond, each forming and influencing the other. Against this backdrop, it seems unconvincing to argue that all human thought and behavior derive solely from the cultural side of our existence. Such a culturally deterministic view is flatly contradicted by observation of the world around us, which is clearly inhabited by a single human species adhering to multiple cultural systems rather than

---

[121] J. Shay, *Achilles in Vietnam: Combat Trauma and the Undoing of Character* (New York, 1994). Note Shay's salutary warning (53–4): "We simply do not know which aspects of emotion are biological universals, like the heartbeat, and which aspects of emotion are culturally constructed." See also his *Odysseus in America: Combat Trauma and the Trials of Homecoming* (New York, 2002).

[122] For "cognitive" analysis of archaeological artifacts, see, e.g., M. Donald, *The Origins of the Modern Mind: Three Stages in the Evolution of Culture and Cognition* (Cambridge, MA, 1991); S. Mithen, *The Prehistory of the Mind: The Cognitive Origins of Art and Science* (London, 1996); T. G. Wynn, *The Evolution of Spatial Competence* (Urbana, 1989). See also the comments of H. A. Orr "Darwinian Storytelling," *New York Review of Books* (Feb. 27, 2003) in his review of Pinker's *Blank Slate*. Orr accepts the fundamental notion of an inherited human psychology (a human nature, if you will) but is concerned by the conjuring up of evolutionary scenarios to explain specific behaviors. Other critics of evolutionary psychology share Orr's discomfort; see D. J. Buller, *Adapting Minds: Evolutionary Psychology and the Persistent Quest for Human Nature* (Cambridge, MA, 2005).

[123] Hence Geertz's famous dictum (*The Interpretation of Cultures* [New York, 1973], 49): "There is no such thing as human nature independent of culture."

by multiple human species, each possessed of a peculiar psychology forged by divergent cultural experience.[124] The analysis in the pages that follow must necessarily include close consideration of cultural context, even as it places emphasis on the mental processes charted by social psychologists. To be absolutely clear: mind and culture should be seen as interlocking cogs in a behavior-generating machine rather than as distinct drives acting independently.

Anthropologists have been in the field for decades recording the mental constructs and *modus vivendi* of people living in hundreds of cultural systems, from small-scale folk communities to technologically advanced urbanized nation-states. This vast ethnography has yet to identify a single cultural nexus that has wholly resisted comprehension by an outside observer trying to understand it (although the logic of specific behaviors or institutions can and does prove elusive). Religious beliefs and rituals, marriage customs, systems of kinship, social groupings, property ownership, leadership and power legitimation, communal eating habits, sports and games – all these variables and more have been documented and categorized by anthropologists in wildly divergent cultures the world over.[125] Specific behaviors may seem at times familiar or strange, expected or surprising, genteel or abhorrent, but patterns of behavior, like languages, are found to be intelligible. If people's psychological functioning varied as widely as their diverse cultural constructs, the behavior of people in alien societies ought to remain virtually impenetrable to an outsider. It does not.

This line of argument can be extended to the discipline of history in general, and to ancient history in particular. It is possible for modern minds to comprehend, analyze, and even empathize with the actions of people in other historical eras. Despite obvious sociohistorical divergences, fictional characters in, say, the epics of Homer or the plays of Euripides, as well as historical personages portrayed in the pages of a Thucydides or a Tacitus, behave in ways we recognize and relate to. They act out of motives, display emotions, and do things we find familiar, or even expect. They can be greedy, ambitious, selfish or altruistic; they can be courageous or cowardly, loyal or false; they seek redress when wronged or rationalize when wronging others; they feel grief in the face of death; they delight in their successes – they are, in short, recognizable human beings. This

---

[124] On this view, different people growing up in different cultures would presumably have different mental architectures; for just such a perspective, see Ehrlich, *Human Natures*; Nisbett, *The Geography of Thought*; Shore, "Human Diversity."

[125] Edgerton, *Sick Societies*, 16–45 (with reference to prior work); see also C. L. Hamlin, *Beyond Relativism: Raymond Boudon, Cognitive Rationality, and Critical Realism* (London, 2002).

is the basis for the celebrated timelessness of great literary works, the reason they are hailed for their deep humanity, psychological insight, and elucidation of the human condition.[126] Even the ordinary and uncelebrated inhabitant of the ancient Mediterranean can appear very immediate to us.[127] Such connectedness stretches across even deeper chronological and cultural divides. A modern Western mind is capable of seeing wisdom and beauty in the ancient teachings of a Confucius or a Buddha, even though the cultural gap between modern Westerners and ancient Asians is far more imposing than that between us and classical antiquity. These circumstances are the bases for studies that seek to employ the power of empathy as a mode of historical analysis.[128] This would not be possible if human psychology (and behavior) were wholly circumscribed by cultural context. The ability to identify with the behavior of people far removed from us chronologically, geographically, and culturally is fundamental to the entire business of history.[129] Without it, the past would not only offer a strange cultural landscape, it would be populated by individuals whose actions and reactions we could not begin to understand, elusive creatures who would forever remain an impenetrable mystery to us. But such is not the case. If, as this chapter's epigraphs assert, the past is a foreign country where everything is unfamiliar, it is nonetheless a foreign country inhabited by fellow human beings behaving in recognizably human ways.[130] There are limits to the bewilderment of culture shock.

[126] See, for instance, the famously touching and tragic scene between Hector, Andromache, and their son Astyanax in Homer's *Iliad* (6.369–502), with commentary by G. S. Kirk, *The Iliad: A Commentary*, 6 vols. (Cambridge, 1984–93), vol. II, 208–25; see further J. Griffin, *Homer on Life and Death* (Oxford, 1980), esp. 103–43. Bernard Knox, in his introduction to Robert Fagles' translation of the *Odyssey* (1990), praises Homer's understanding of human psychology (50–8) and ends with an apt quote from Alexander Pope: "Homer has taken all the inward Passions and Affections of Mankind to furnish his Characters."

[127] See, for instance, emotions expressed on gravestones (Shaw, "Seasons of Death," 109–10) or personal letters and outraged complaints to officials preserved on papyrus; MacMullen, *Roman Social Relations*, 8–12; J. G. Winter, *Life and Letters in the Papyri* (Ann Arbor, 1933).

[128] For an excellent overview, see MacMullen, *Feelings in History*. See also the comments of Hopkins, *Death and Renewal*, xv, and K. Hopkins, *A World Full of Gods: The Strange Triumph of Christianity* (London, 1999), 2.

[129] D. E. Brown, *Hierarchy, History, and Human Nature: The Social Origins of Historical Consciousness* (Tuscon, 1988). For some insightful comments on this issue from an ancient historiographical perspective, see M. Reinhold, "Human Nature as Cause in Ancient Historiography," in J. W. Eadie and J. Ober (eds.), *The Craft of the Ancient Historian: Essays in Honor of Chester G. Starr* (Lanham, 1985), 21–40 (= M. Reinhold, *Studies in Classical History and Society* [Oxford, 2002], 45–53). MacMullen writes of Thucydides (*Feelings in History*, 6): "How can anyone be sure what his personal feelings were? In answer: only through the assumption of our common humanity. It cannot be easily supposed, because it cannot be felt by any of us, that an author could write as this one did, except in the grip of just such emotions as his readers experience, vicariously."

[130] My thanks to Professor Kenneth L. Feder for bringing Hartley's epigram to my attention.

There are thus very good reasons for supposing that psychological processes and the behavioral patterns that partly stem from them transcend time and space. In most cases this supposition is implicit in historical studies, but here it stands as a primary investigative tool. As noted in the introduction, social psychology is the essential instrument for what follows, since it demands integration of cultural considerations into its analysis. Three areas of social psychology are particularly pertinent to the arena crowd: the psychology of groups and crowds in general, and of sports spectators in particular; the psychology of prejudice; and the psychology of attraction to violence as spectacle and entertainment. That the Romans were not immune to these processes is demonstrated even by a cursory glance at the facts. The Roman hierarchical conception of social organization is practically a paean to group processes. The Romans assigned individuals into any number of group categories and treated them accordingly. As we shall see (chapter 3), this group-based social hierarchy was made manifest in the arena's stands. Ancient descriptions of crowd behavior evoke the thrill of participation in watching sport and competition. Prejudice is not only identifiable in the Roman world, it was sanctioned in all sorts of ways, both legally and socially. Finally, the scale and ubiquity of amphitheaters and other venues for gladiatorial shows can hardly leave in doubt the attractiveness of violent spectacle in the Roman world. Even more importantly, as we shall see in the next chapter, the Romans were not alone in succumbing to this attraction.[131]

---

[131] Charles Dickens (Letter to the *Daily News*, 28 Feb. 1846) averred that it was people's "secret nature" to harbor "a dark and dreadful interest in the punishment at issue." A universal brutal streak, if you will.

CHAPTER 2

A catalog of cruelty

No animal could ever be so cruel as a man, so artfully, so artistically cruel.

F. Dostoevsky, *The Brothers Karamazov* (1880)[1]

Vast was the number of Spectators (as always is both there and everywhere else at such unpleasant Sights)

W. Montague, *The Delights of Holland* (1696), on the crowds at Amsterdam executions[2]

Many people in different times and places have been eager to watch people and animals degraded, hurt, and killed as a public spectacle.[3] In this chapter I present just a sample of the vast corpus of comparative evidence, drawn from divergent times and places, for violence staged before spectators. The sheer volume of pertinent data is telling in itself; indeed, there is much that cannot be included without extending the length of this treatment by needless replication of examples. The draw of violent spectacle emerges as not so much the exception but the rule.

PUNISHMENT

The brutal methods of execution employed in the Roman arena are well known. People were burned to death, crucified, exposed to wild beasts, cut down unarmed, or subjected to elaborate execution rituals inspired

---

[1] F. Dostoevsky, *The Brothers Karamazov*, trans. L. Pevear and L. Volokhonsky (New York, 1990; originally published 1880), 238.

[2] W. Montague, *The Delights of Holland* (London, 1696), 179.

[3] As recognized long ago by Friedländer, *Sittengeschichte Roms*, vol. II, 98. See also Kyle, *Spectacles of Death*, 133–40, for a brief collection of ancient comparanda. At the other end of the chronological spectrum, see the astute musings on the modern fascination with horror and violence in S. King, *Danse Macabre* (New York, 1981), and H. Schechter, *Savage Pastimes: A Cultural History of Violent Entertainment* (New York, 2005).

by motifs drawn from classical mythology.[4] Four features stand out. First, spectacular executions in the arena were intentionally degrading and humiliating to the victim. As such, Roman law reserved them for true outsiders (bandits, war captives, slaves, murderers of low social status, etc.). Second, the amphitheater was not the original, or even the primary, place of execution in the Roman world. Public executions had long been held outside the arena, and continued to be so after the emergence and widespread diffusion of arena spectacles (see above, introduction, p. 7). Third, connected to the second, execution methods in the arena were either adapted from earlier modes or invented anew so as to offer the most interesting sight possible for the audience. This is best viewed as a secondary development, the consequence of moving some executions into the context of gladiatorial spectacles or beast hunts. Fourth, arena executions communicated symbolic messages to the crowd about the value of conformity, the power of the emperor, and society's solidarity in the face of threats to the established order. The arena context amplified these messages, insofar as the emperor (or members of the local elite) was personally present and the sociopolitical order was made manifest by the hierarchical seating arrangements.

Historical comparanda are legion for the popularity of rituals of public punishment, sometimes of shocking violence and terrible duration. While surviving documentation necessarily tilts the record in a European direction,[5] large crowds turning out to watch public torture and murder are not restricted to the West or to places colonized by Westerners. In what follows, instances where spectators' attitudes or reactions have been recorded are given special attention, as are occasions when particularly vile punishments were staged in front of large crowds.

In Early Dynastic Mesopotamia (*c.* 3,000–2,350 BC) the execution of prisoners of war appears to have been normative, since the economic infrastructure was insufficiently developed to accommodate and exploit large numbers of slaves efficiently.[6] Evidence is lacking to determine in what circumstances such executions took place, although a relief fragment from the Mesopotamian site of Girsu (modern Tello), now in the Louvre

---

[4] See Barton, "Emotional Economy"; E. Cantarella, *I supplizi capitali in Grecia e a Roma* (Milan, 1991), 153–337 (who adopts an anthropological approach and has little to say about arena executions); Coleman, "Fatal Charades"; Kyle, *Spectacles of Death*, esp. 91–102; C. Vismara, *Il supplizio come spettacolo* (Rome, 1990); Wiedemann, *Emperors and Gladiators*, 68–97.
[5] And is further limited by chronology, as descriptions of execution procedures and spectator reactions only become available in the sixteenth century and after.
[6] F. Gelb, "Prisoners of War in Early Mesopotamia," *JNES* 32 (1973), 70–98.

and dated to *c.* 2,600 BC, shows a bound captive being hit over the head with a mace in the presence of a divinity, suggesting perhaps some sort of ritual involving human sacrifice. (If this conjecture is right, the relief offers an early example of how punitive and religious violence could be combined.) The location – whether on the battlefield or in town – is not clear. Mesopotamian lawcodes stipulate capital punishment or mutilation, particularly partial or total blinding, for many offenses. Given the need to broadcast the effectiveness of the law, we may assume a public context such as the marketplace for most such procedures.[7] The vicious executions and mutilations of the Assyrians are graphically recorded in royal inscriptions and on palace reliefs, but they appear mostly in the context of warfare against recalcitrant cities under siege, and as such are examples of politically motivated terror campaigns aimed at opponents rather than ritual punishments carried out in front of voluntary spectators.[8] There are exceptions. For instance, King Assurnasirpal II (883–859 BC) reports transporting a rebel leader to Nineveh (one of the Assyrian royal cities), flaying him, and draping his skin over the city walls. These circumstances surely imply that the procedure was staged as a spectacle for the edification of Nineveh's populace.[9]

The records of ancient Egypt reveal punitive violence, including blinding, beating with sticks, cutting, amputation, impaling, and, more rarely, burning and frying on a brazier. The places where such rituals were staged are usually not specified, but public spaces appear to have been the norm; we read of executions at the site of a crime, or at the palace gates. The dramatic means of killing alone imply a public dimension: modes of sequestered execution tend to be more mundane and seek less to impress (poisoning, hanging, garroting, suffocating, electrocution, lethal injection, etc.). How frequent public punishments were in Egypt, how many crimes earned them, and the degree, if any, to which the spectacles attracted large crowds are not details recoverable from the laconic tone of the (predominantly)

---

[7] Most lawcodes laconically prescribe death, but sometimes they specify the method as burning, drowning, or impaling; see J. B. Pritchard, *Ancient Near Eastern Texts Relating to the Old Testament*, 3rd edn. (Princeton, 1969), 159–98 (lawcodes of Eshnunna and Hammurabi). In at least one instance, the stipulated penalty was to be "beaten sixty times with an oxtail whip in the assembly"; ibid., 175 (no. 202).

[8] H. W. F. Saggs, "Assyrian Warfare in the Sargonid Period," *Iraq* 25 (1963), 145–54. For examples, see A. K. Grayson, *Assyrian Rulers of the Early First Millennium BC*, 2 vols. (Toronto, 1991–6); E. Bleibtreu, "Grisly Assyrian Record of Torture and Death," *BAR* (Jan./Feb. 1991), 52–61.

[9] Grayson, *Assyrian Rulers*, vol. 1, 199. What is unusual here is the location of the punishment. In most instances, Assyrian atrocities were carried out directly outside the rebel communities, as part of the campaign itself (innumerable examples of which can be gleaned from ibid.).

official evidence for public punishment in Egypt. Presumably, at least some people came to watch.[10]

In a passage in Plato's *Gorgias* Socrates argues that malefactors who make amends by enduring punishment are metaphysically better off than those who escape punishment entirely. His interlocutor, Polus, replies:

> If a man be caught criminally plotting to make himself a despot, and he be straightaway put on the rack and castrated and have his eyes burnt out, and after suffering himself and seeing inflicted on his wife and children a number of grievous torments of every kind, he be finally crucified or burnt in a coat of pitch, will he be happier than if he escapes and makes himself despot, and pass his life as the ruler in his city?[11]

No direct evidence suggests that such vicious measures were regularly applied to real people, and the passage may throw light only on a dark corner of one educated Athenian's imagination. That said, we read that in 514 BC the tyrannicide Aristogeiton was captured alive (his accomplice Harmodios having been killed on the spot) and tortured for a long time ([Aristot.] *Ath. Pol.* 18.4). Herodotus (9.5) reports that Lycidas, who suggested making peace with Xerxes during the Persian Wars, was stoned to death by an angry mob. A mob of Athenian women then moved on to Lycidas' house and, just for good measure, stoned his wife and children to death too. Herodotus also reports (9.120) that the Greeks crucified Artayactes, Persian satrap of the region around Sestus, and forced him to watch his son being stoned to death before his eyes. According to Plutarch (*Per.* 28.1–3), some rebellious Samians were harshly treated by Pericles: they were dragged to the agora, fastened to boards, and exhibited for ten days, then clubbed to death and left unburied. Demosthenes (18.133) refers to an ex-citizen Antiphon being

---

[10] A. Leahy, "Death by Fire in Ancient Egypt," *Journal of the Economic and Social History of the Orient* 27 (1984), 199–206; D. Lorton, "The Treatment of Criminals in Ancient Egypt through the New Kingdom," *Journal of the Economic and Social History of the Orient* 20 (1977), 2–64; J. A. Tyldesley, *Judgement of the Pharaoh: Crime and Punishment in Ancient Egypt* (London, 2000), 60–76 (esp. 65–8 for public locations). Tyldesley (14) doubts that public executions "became the popular spectator events that they were in many societies," but official evidence, which is silent about spectators, does not reflect the totality of the social reality. See the comments of A. G. McDowell in D. B. Redford (ed.), *The Oxford Encyclopedia of Ancient Egypt*, 3 vols. (Oxford, 2001), vol. 1, 315–20, s.v. "Crime and Punishment."

[11] Pl. *Grg.* 473c (Loeb trans.): ἐὰν ἀδικῶν ἄνθρωπος ληφθῇ τυραννίδι ἐπιβουλεύων, καὶ ληφθεὶς στρεβλῶται καὶ ἐκτέμνηται καὶ τοὺς ὀφθαλμοὺς ἐκκάηται, καὶ ἄλλας πολλὰς καὶ μεγάλας καὶ παντοδαπὰς λώβας αὐτός τε λωβηθεὶς καὶ τοὺς αὑτοῦ ἐπιδὼν παῖδάς τε καὶ γυναῖκα τὸ ἔσχατον ἀνασταυρωθῇ ἢ καταπιττωθῇ, οὗτος εὐδαιμονέστερος ἔσται, ἢ ἐὰν διαφυγὼν τύραννος καταστῇ καὶ ἄρχων ἐν τῇ πόλει διαβιῷ; similar lists of dread punishments appear at Ar. *Ran.* 610–25; Pl. *Resp.* 361c; Aesch. *Eum.* 186–90; see also Pl. *Grg.* 525a–c for a theory of justice that emphasizes exemplary punishment. Plutarch (*Them.* 22.2) mentions a spot near the Agora in the Athens of his day where public officers threw out the bodies of the executed.

racked and executed, but he provides no details as to whether the procedure was carried out in public.

All of these examples pertain to times of war or political sedition. It is far less clear that harsh and humiliating punishments were routinely and publicly meted out to common criminals in peacetime. But it may well have been so.[12] Slaves appear to have been tortured under Athenian law, though the details of the practice – even its reality – have been seriously questioned.[13] That public executions took place in ancient Athens, however, emerges from references to the *barathron*, a public execution pit which, in Plato's day, appears to have been located outside the northern wall. There the unburied bodies of the executed were to be seen by passers-by.[14] Classical Athens had a board of public order, the Eleven, that presided over executions, which were carried out by a public slave in service to the board. Corporal punishment was also practiced, predominantly against slaves, as were some punishments of public humiliation, such as fastening in stocks.[15]

Passing beyond Antiquity, our sources for Dark Age punitive practices are not good,[16] but throughout the Middle Ages in continental Europe it is clear that many forms of aggravated execution and public torture were employed, including burning, boiling alive in oil (feet first), decapitation, burial alive, drawing and quartering, branding, flogging, and miscellaneous forms of mutilation. For those guilty of multiple offenses, cumulative punishment could be applied, if stipulated by the court. In this way, lethal and non-lethal punishments were often combined, so that torture preceded execution, or mutilation of the body was carried out *post*

---

[12] Cantarella, *Supplizi*, 19–116, esp. 73–87.

[13] See C. Carey, "A Note on Torture in Athenian Homicide Cases," *Historia* 37 (1988), 241–5; M. Gagarin, "The Torture of Slaves in Athenian Law," *CP* 91 (1996), 1–18; D. Mirhady, "Torture and Rhetoric in Athens," *JHS* 106 (1996), 119–31. See also V. J. Hunter, *Policing Athens: Social Control in the Attic Lawsuits, 420–320 BC* (Princeton, 1994), 70–95 (on slaves and torture). Some of these scholars (notably Gagarin) insist that slave torture was not actually practiced, but was rather a rhetorical topos. Note also Ant. 1.20, 5.30, Dem. 48.16–19, Lys. 7.35 for instances of penal or judicial torture at Athens.

[14] See Hdt. 7.133; Xen. *Hell.* 1.7.20; Plut. *Aristid.* 3, *Them.* 22; Thuc. 2.67. Cantarella, *Supplizi*, 96–105; *RE* 2.2 (1896), 2854, s.v. "*barathron*" (Thalheim). For the visibility of the bodies, see Pl. *Resp.* 439e–40a.

[15] See D. S. Allen, *The World of Prometheus: The Politics of Punishing in Democratic Athens* (Princeton, 2000), 197–242, esp. 200–2 where the discovery of seventeen execution victims in a mass grave at Phalerum is noted; Hunter, *Policing Athens*, 154–84, who comments (184), "The venue chosen for penalties that afflicted the body was calculated to produce large gatherings eager for a spectacle." See also M. Gras, "Cité grecque et lapidation," in *Châtiment dans la cité*, 75–89; V. Hunter, "Crime and Criminals in Plato's Laws," *Museion* 9 (2009), 1–19.

[16] See K. Royer, "The Body in Parts: Reading the Execution Ritual in Late Medieval England," *Historical Reflections/Réflexions Historiques* 29 (2003), 319–39, esp. 325–6 on Anglo-Saxon punishments.

mortem.[17] The Sachsenspiegel, an illuminated German legal code of 1220–35, shows beheading, hanging, hacking, the birching and shearing of a woman tied to a stake, and mutilation. It is not evident from the Sachsenspiegel, however, that these punishments attracted crowds.[18] But there is no reason to think that they did not. In Medieval France, for instance, punishments consistently attracted large crowds of spectators, and the grim human detritus produced by executions was hung from gibbets at the town gates, which extended and further publicized the spectacle.[19] Later engravings suggest that the marketplace was the setting for many such punishments. If so, crowds of spectators would be a natural consequence. In 1488 the town of Mons paid a considerable sum of money to purchase a brigand from a neighboring community, so that he could be quartered in their town. Presumably, the good people of Mons would have spared themselves the expense unless there was considerable public interest in coming out to watch.[20]

Particularly unpleasant was "wheeling," also called "braiding" or "breaking on the wheel" (in France) or "breaking with the wheel" (in Germany). The procedure took many forms and was employed in numerous countries across the European continent and in foreign colonies. The usual method was for the victim to be tied to a scaffold or laid out on the ground with wooden struts to raise the limbs, and a wagon wheel (or a hammer, iron bar, or club) used to break them. Special execution wheels were manufactured, with projecting flanges for added smashing power. Alternatively, victims could be run over repeatedly by heavy wagons. The traditional *dénouement* was for the condemned to have their ruined limbs threaded through the spokes of another wagon wheel – the "braiding" part of the action – which was then hoisted on a pole for display. There the victim, if not dead already, could linger for days. A harrowing eyewitness account from 1607 reports how the victim was transformed "into a sort of huge screaming puppet writhing in rivulets of blood, a puppet with four tentacles, like a sea

---

[17] Evans, *Rituals of Retribution*, 27–35; Foucault, *Discipline and Punish*, 47–51; A. McCall, *The Medieval Underworld* (London, 1979; reprint, Stroud, 2004), 41–81. See also W. Schild, "History of Crime and Punishment," in C. Hinkeldey (ed.), *Criminal Justice through the Ages: From Divine Judgement to Modern German Legislation* (Rothenburg ob der Tauber, 1993), 99–173, esp. 131–64 (survey of methods of execution and mutilation, with many Early Modern woodcuts featuring watching crowds). Also note B. Innes, *The History of Torture* (New York, 1998).

[18] See W. Schild, "History of Criminal Law and Procedure," in Hinkeldey (ed.), *Criminal Justice through the Ages*, 46–98, esp. 65–80 on the Sachsenspiegel.

[19] E. Cohen, "'To Die a Criminal for the Public Good': The Execution Ritual in Late Medieval Paris," in B. S. Bachrach and D. Nicholas (eds.), *Law, Custom and the Social Fabric in Medieval Europe: Essays in Honor of Bryce Lyon* (Kalamazoo, 1990), 285–304.

[20] McCall, *Medieval Underworld*, 72.

monster of raw, slimy and shapeless flesh, mixed with splinters of smashed bones." This mode of execution was employed in France until 1787, and in Germany into the 1840s (it was finally taken off the books in Prussia in 1851).[21] The number of blows to be administered to each limb depended on the heinousness of the crime and could be specified in the sentence; the executioner could also be instructed to work "from the top down" (delivering the killing blow first) or "from the bottom up" (to maximize the suffering). Up to forty blows are stipulated in some instances.

A woodcut (Fig. 1) shows the execution by wheeling of convicted parricide Franz Seuboldt in Nuremberg on September 22, 1589. A sequence of events is enclosed in a single frame. Seuboldt shoots his father at top left and then, in the foreground, is shown being transported to the *Rabenstein* (the ravenstone, the traditional German place of execution) outside town. He sits in a carriage facing two clergymen while an executioner pinches the flesh of his arms with red-hot tongs, which have been heated in a brazier by an attendant wielding bellows. At center right, Seuboldt is shown being broken with the wheel, his limbs raised by wooden blocks to facilitate the smashing of his limbs. In the background can be seen hoisted wheels festooned with the tatters of previous victims, a severed head on a spike, and a gallows with dangling corpses. Around the *Rabenstein* is gathered a crowd of well-dressed gentlemen (two on horseback), as well as women and children, but it is important to recall that all the events portrayed in the woodcut (save the initial murder, of course) would have taken place in public view. Seuboldt's sentence would have been read to him in the town center before large crowds; his transition to the place of execution followed by a crowd, perhaps with schoolboys singing hymns (as was common); and the execution itself carried out before spectators.[22]

When the sources begin to pay attention to the spectators in the eighteenth century, the crowds emerge as substantial to enormous. The beheading of bandit Lips Tullian and four of his accomplices at Dresden in 1715 took place while "more than 20,000 people, 144 carriages, and some 300

---

[21] On the procedure of "wheeling," see G. Abbott, *Execution: The Guillotine, the Pendulum, the Thousand Cuts, the Spanish Donkey, and 66 Other Ways of Putting Someone to Death* (New York, 2006), 39–50; Merback, *The Thief, the Cross and the Wheel*, 126–97 (quote from 1607 at 160–1); van Dülmen, *Theatre of Horror*, 92–6.

[22] See van Dülmen, *Theatre of Horror*, 107–18, who stresses that the public nature of the different phases from sentence to death were key to their very purpose. See also Evans, *Rituals of Retribution*, 65–108 and 238. The latter includes (at 79) a depiction from 1726 of a mass execution by wheeling, hanging, and decapitation before a huge crowd, with the fashionable on horseback and in carriages; for many more such images, see Merback, *The Thief, the Cross and the Wheel, passim*.

Figure 1 Woodcut of the execution of Franz Seuboldt in 1589

horses looked on."[23] When the notorious poacher Matthias Klostermaier was broken with the wheel in Munich in 1771, the event drew so many visitors to town that all the guesthouses of the city were filled, and most of the private houses also. On the day itself, masses assembled at the town hall to watch the reading of the sentence, while others hurried to the place of execution to secure good vantage points. An etching of Klostermaier's demise (Fig. 2) shows an enormous sea of people watching the proceedings. Noteworthy is the presence of carriages, men on horseback, women and children, and a viewing stand in the midst of the crowd, at center right. In the background, latecomers appear to sprint and gallop to the action. Crowds at *ancien régime* executions in France were also routinely vast: the wheeling of the bandit Cartouche in 1721 drew tens of thousands of spectators into the Place de Grève in Paris.[24]

Alexis de Tocqueville quotes the letters of Mme. de Sévigné to her daughter describing the suppression of a peasant revolt in Brittany in 1675. This aristocratic lady, whom de Tocqueville deems no barbarian, describes breakings on the wheel, quarterings, and hangings which she had witnessed. The good lady comments "We are not so broken on the wheel now; one in a week, to keep justice going; it is true that hanging now seems quite a treat."[25] Mme. de Sévigné's habit of watching executions was not idiosyncratic. The opening of Jean Racine's tragedy *Britannicus* in Paris on December 13, 1669 was less well attended than expected, since an execution in a neighboring square attracted away a large portion of the potential audience. They apparently preferred the real thing to a theatrical facsimile.[26] The situation echoes that facing Terence as he presented his new play *Hecyra* in 164 BC: the announcement

[23] Evans, *Rituals of Retribution*, 73–4 (quote at 73).

[24] P. Bastien, *L'exécution publique à Paris au XVIIIe siècle: une histoire des rituels judiciaires* (Seyssel, 2006), 136–7. Crowds of comparable size assembled in England to watch hangings; Gatrell, *Hanging Tree*, 56–8. It is claimed that the execution of St. Pol in Paris in 1475 drew some 200,000 spectators, but this is surely an exaggerated figure; see the *Chronicle of Jean de Troyes*, cited in M. Petitot, *Collection des mémoires relatifs à l'histoire de France*, 130 vols. (Paris, 1819–29), vol. xiv, 25. (My thanks to Professor Paul Friedland for this reference.)

[25] See A. de Tocqueville, *Democracy in America*, trans. H. Reeve, 2 vols. (New York, 1899; originally published 1835), vol. ii, 175. As de Tocqueville comments, what is key to de Sévigné's attitude is the absence of any identification on her part with the victims, who were mere peasants: "Mme. de Sévigné had no clear notion of suffering in anyone who was not a person of quality." It is possible she was being sarcastic, or adopting a fashionable insouciance; see P. Friedland, *Spectacular Justice: Theory and Practice of Executions from the Middle Ages to the French Revolution* (forthcoming; my thanks to Professor Friedland for sharing the relevant pages of his manuscript with me). Even if his reading is correct, the essential point, it seems to me, remains the same: Mme. de Sévigné watched executions as a matter of course.

[26] J. Racine, *Britannicus, Phaedra, Athaliah*, trans. C. H. Sisson (Oxford, 1987), xii.

Figure 2 Execution of the poacher Matthias Klostermaier in 1771

of a gladiatorial show sparked an exodus from the play (Ter. *Hec. prol.* 39–42).

On March 28, 1757 the notorious rake Giacomo Casanova and his debonair companions, three of them women, were in the huge crowd that had assembled at the Place de Grève in Paris to witness the execution of Robert Francois Damiens, who had attempted to assassinate Louis XV only weeks earlier. The vast crowd was comprised of Parisians, countryfolk, and even people who had come from abroad.[27] Eyewitnesses describe people hanging out of chimneys and crowding the rooftops; one couple took a fall and were injured. The rooms around the square were rented to the well-to-do who watched in secluded comfort. Over a period of four hours Damiens' body was literally torn to shreds, piece by piece, until he was left a mere head and torso. Throughout his ordeal, he remained conscious and filled the square with appalling shrieks and wails. Casanova, who considered the spectacle "an offense against our common humanity," reports that he several times closed his eyes and blocked his ears to the atrocity but that his companions were riveted by the spectacle and never once diverted their gaze. They felt no compassion for Damiens, they said, due to the enormity of his crime. Casanova's friend Tiretta even had surreptitious sex with one of the women while the ghastly execution proceeded. Other eyewitnesses describe members of the crowd, especially the ladies, watching with detached disinterest or even chattering and laughing.[28]

As humanizing Enlightenment attitudes took hold, death was prescibed for fewer and fewer crimes and execution rituals were elaborated into protracted and complex displays of state power. If wheeling was retained, it was only for the most serious offenses and all but the most despicable perpetrators were spared its agonies by being strangled before the procedure began. A Prussian regulation of 1749 stipulates that the strangulation is to be carried out "in such a way that the spectators round about will not

---

[27] The English gentleman and MP George Selwyn, whose 1791 obituary noted his "particular penchant for executions . . . that scarcely any great criminal was carried to the gallows, but George was a spectator," traveled to Paris specifically to see Damiens' grisly end. His friends in London wrote to him, lamenting his absence at a well-attended hanging there; see Gatrell, *Hanging Tree*, 253 (attendance), 262 (quote from obituary), and 276 (friends lamenting his absence).

[28] See G. Casanova, *The Memoirs of Jacues Casanova de Seignalt 1725–1798*, trans. A. Machen, 8 vols. (Edinburgh, 1940; originally published 1894), vol. III, 310 and the comments of S.-L. Mercier (*The Picture of Paris*, trans. W. and E. Jackson [London, 1929; originally published 1781–8], 27) on ladies "carried in crowds" to the execution of Damiens: "they were the last to turn their eyes away from the hideous scene," he notes. See also Foucault, *Discipline and Punish*, 3–6; Bastien, *L'exécution publique*, esp. 75–91 and 143–203; P. Friedland, "Beyond Deterrence: Cadavers, Effigies, Animals and the Logic of Executions in Premodern France," *Historical Reflections/Reflexions Historiques* 29 (2003), 295–317; Friedland, *Spectacular Justice*.

notice it"; thereafter, the execution was to proceed as normal. The concern
for the spectators' perceptions is noteworthy. The authorities' motive was
presumably to maintain the deterrent value of the procedure, but there may
also have been an element of fear at the crowd's likely reaction to a faked
execution.[29] Strangulation was also employed in France throughout the
eighteenth century, sometimes as the wheeling proceeded, i.e., the victim
would endure a number of blows and then be strangled.[30]

The cheering mobs who witnessed thousands of aristocrats, dissidents,
and common criminals guillotined during the French Revolution are notorious. Although political partisanship doubtless played a role in drawing
their attendance and shaping their attitudes toward the victims, contemporary testimony insists that many were there for the sport of it all. Despite
the expectation on the part of its employers that *la machine* would inculcate the people with a sense of the law's majesty, the spectators' reaction to
the process of guillotining – the procession from the prison, the exchanges
on the scaffold, the rapid decapitation, the presentation of the severed
head to the crowd – actually fell far short of these expectations. A vengeful and carnival atmosphere marked their attitudes more than did any
expected solemnity. Platforms were erected to allow those equipped with
opera glasses to get a better view. Contemporary engravings often include
depictions of large gatherings of men, women, and children all clearly
animated and cheering around the scaffold (with arms aloft, hats in the
air, etc.).[31] Convicted thief Nicolas Jacques Pelletier earned the dubious
distinction of being the first person beheaded with the guillotine in Paris
on April 24, 1792. The crowd were let down by the (non-)spectacle. They
began shouting for a return to the more brutal methods of the *ancien
régime*. Their dissatisfaction stemmed in part from the very novelty of the
procedure, which departed from familiar rituals. But the guillotine, on its
debut, was disappointing also because it was so efficient. The execution
was over in a flash, death was dealt out impersonally and without much
attention-arresting drama. As the Terror gathered pace, these shortcomings

[29] This is certainly documented in other contexts, where riots could be sparked by the cancellation of
scheduled executions. See below, n. 34.
[30] Prussian regulation: van Dülmen, *Theatre of Horror*, 95. France: Bastien, *L'exécution publique*, 103–6
(who points out examples where the strangulation was done visibly). For a penetrating analysis
of the influence of rationality on modes of execution in the Enlightenment Germany, see Evans,
Rituals of Retribution, 109–49 (with the 1749 regulation at 122–3).
[31] See D. Arasse, *The Guillotine and the Terror* (London, 1989), esp. 87–132; Evans, *Rituals of Retribution*,
140–9; D. Gerould, *Guillotine: Its Legend and Lore* (New York, 1992). Arasse's and Gerould's books
include a sample of engravings, but for a thorough survey, see R. Paulson, *Representations of the
Revolution (1789–1820)* (New Haven, 1983).

were compensated for by prolonging the process, usually with an increase in the number of decapitations staged on a single occasion.[32]

The beheading of Louis XVI on January 21, 1793 was an unusual case, in part because the relative silence of the crowd was exceptional – until the deed was done, that is. Then, as one eyewitness reports,

> The blood flowed and cries of joy from 80,000 armed men struck my ears . . . I saw the schoolboys of the *Quatre-Nations* throw their hats in the air; his blood flowed and some dipped their fingers in it . . . An executioner on the boards of the scaffold sold and distributed little packets of hair and the ribbon that bound them . . . I saw people pass by, arm in arm, laughing, chatting familiarly as if they were at a *fête*.[33]

People are reported dancing around the scaffold.[34] Such was the pull of the guillotine that fully functional miniature versions were manufactured as children's toys and used to decapitate mice and birds.[35]

Things were no better in England, where executions drew enthusiastic and boisterous crowds from the Middle Ages down to 1868, when they were moved behind prison walls.[36] From the early Tudor period down to 1783, for instance, thousands of men, women, and children were hanged at Tyburn outside London at six-week intervals.[37] These hangings ought not to be sanitized as quick and easy. They were usually messy. Terrified victims typically kicked and bucked for five or more minutes on the end of the rope; the executioner often had to pull down on their legs to finish the job. There could be hemorrhaging, or the involuntary expulsion of excreta. The majority of victims were guilty of little more than theft. The crowds of spectators were so consistently large that the owner of a nearby farm

---

[32] See Arasse, *Guillotine*, 27–8 (disappointing inauguration) and 87–132 (subsequent innovations in procedure). Simon Schama reports how hundreds could be decapitated in a single day, at staggering rates: thirty-two heads cut off in twenty-five minutes, or twelve heads in five minutes in Lyons in October 1793; see S. Schama, *Citizens: A Chronicle of the French Revolution* (New York, 1989), esp. 619–847 (growth of the Terror), esp. 782–3 (Lyons beheadings).

[33] Quote in Schama, *Citizens*, 670.

[34] On the reported dancing, see Arasse, *Guillotine*, 191–2. Some spectators danced and reveled as new gallows and scaffolds were erected (to mask their own fear at the sight?); see Spierenburg, *Spectacle of Suffering*, 87–9. In England, disappointed crowds grew troublesome or riotous when scheduled hangings were cancelled; see Abbott, *Execution*, 163–92, esp. 165–6; D. D. Cooper, *The Lesson of the Scaffold: The Public Execution Controversy in Victorian England* (Athens, OH, 1984), 3.

[35] See Gerould, *Guillotine*, 37–9.

[36] See Gatrell, *Hanging Tree*; T. W. Laqueur, "Crowds, Carnival and the State in English Executions, 1604–1868," in A. L. Beier et al. (eds.), *The First Modern Society: Essays in English History in Honour of Lawrence Stone* (Cambridge, 1989), 305–55; Royer, "The Body in Parts."

[37] For detailed studies, see Gatrell, *Hanging Tree*, and Linebaugh, *London Hanged*. The triangular gallows at Tyburn stood roughly where Marble Arch stands in modern London. Hangings were staged at Tyburn eight times a year, or every six and a half weeks; Gatrell, *Hanging Tree*, 56.

built a wooden viewing gallery to cash in, and entrepreneurs rented out carts and ladders to those seeking a better view.[38] As with executions on the continent, the two-mile cavalcade of the condemned from the city to the triangular gallows at Tyburn was attended by mobs of onlookers, sometimes in a merry frame of mind: "No solemn procession" wrote Henry Fielding, "it was just the contrary; it was a low-lived, black-guard merry-making."[39] Snacks were sold as the hangings progressed. Horrifically graphic accounts of the condemned's crimes (usually illustrated), combined with records of their last speeches from the scaffold, were printed and sold briskly on the streets of English towns, as did their counterparts in continental Europe and the colonies.[40]

Samuel Pepys nonchalantly includes notices of witnessing executions at Tyburn and elsewhere among his diary entries. On one occasion, he comments that he sent his wife to book a good spot for him, and even records that the display of one victim's heart and severed head to the crowd occasioned a shout of joy.[41] The novelist Samuel Richardson commented of the Tyburn crowds in 1741 that "the face of everyone spoke a kind of mirth, as if the spectacle they had beheld had afforded Pleasure instead of pain, which I am wholly unable to account for," and over a century later Charles Dickens noted with disgust that execution crowds in central London showed "no sorrow, no salutary terror, no abhorrence, no seriousness, nothing but ribaldry, debauchery, levity, drunkenness, and flaunting vice in fifty other shapes."[42] William Makepeace Thackeray was also amazed

---

[38] Viewing stands were not restricted to Tyburn. In 1747 a viewing stand holding 9,000 spectators collapsed at a beheading at Tower Hill in London, killing twelve; see J. Laurence, *A History of Capital Punishment* (London, 1932; reprint, New York, 1960), 171; for other comparanda, see Cooper, *Lesson of the Scaffold*, 1–26. Note also the viewing stand at center right in Fig. 2.

[39] P. Linebaugh, "The Tyburn Riot against the Surgeons," in D. Hay et al., *Albion's Fatal Tree: Crime and Society in Eighteenth-Century England* (New York, 1975), 65–117 (quote at 68).

[40] Last speeches and moralizing sermons: J. A. Sharpe, "'Last Dying Speeches:' Religion, Ideology and Public Execution in Seventeenth-Century England," *Past and Present* 107 (1985), 144–67; R. Bosco, "Lectures at the Pillory: The Early American Execution Sermon," *American Quarterly* 30 (1978), 156–76. Popular songs and verses about executions and speeches of the condemned also circulated in early modern Germany; see Evans, *Rituals of Retribution*, 150–89. Indeed, the industry in murder- and execution-related broadsheets took on a life of its own in the seventeenth century and continued down to the twentieth in America and England; see, e.g., Gatrell, *Hanging Tree*, 109–96; K. Halttunen, *Murder Most Foul: The Killer and the American Gothic Imagination* (Cambridge, MA, 1998), esp. 7–59; Schechter, *Savage Pastimes*, 27–68.

[41] See, e.g., R. Latham and W. Matthews (eds.), *The Diary of Samuel Pepys: A New and Complete Transcription*, 11 vols. (Berkeley, 1970–83), vol. I, 265 (shout of joy), vol. II, 26–7 and 72–3, vol. III, 67, vol. IV, 60, vol. V, 23, vol. VII, 131 and 205, vol. VIII, 196, vol. IX, 335. Attendance at executions is folded in to Pepys' daily routine, and his execution notices are as laconic as this: "[t]his day two soldiers were hanged in the Strand for their late mutiny at Somerset-house" (ibid., vol. I, 59).

[42] For the quotes, see Laqueur, "Crowds," 330 and n. 61. Public executions were moved from Tyburn to the square outside Newgate prison in central London in 1783.

by the English execution crowd's carnivalesque attitude and regretted his attendance at a hanging as a result.[43] Tyburn-like scenes were reproduced at hangings all around England. Following the hanging, drawing, and quartering of a Catholic priest in Dorchester in July 1642, for instance, the crowd played football with the severed head for six hours.[44] Even if English sensibilities and social norms changed over time, the presence of crowds of spectators at executions, often in cheery form, is strikingly persistent. On the continent, spectators were generally more subdued. People there tended to watch executions with solemnity and regard them as important communal events. Continental executions have been likened to funerals: publicly celebrated, to be sure, but nevertheless serious and weighty ceremonies that affirmed sacred and secular mores.[45] But solemnity did not always prevail. The last public hanging in Vienna in 1869 attracted huge crowds and the whole affair degenerated into a street party, with public drunkenness and fighting. There are records of German executions where tickets were sold and food peddled.[46] But whatever the mood, the main point is that for many centuries, stretching well into the Enlightenment and beyond, Europeans came out in large and sometimes huge numbers to watch people hurt and killed.

The spectacle continued after the death of the condemned. It was regular practice to let the bodies of execution victims hang in public sight until they decomposed (ostensibly as a continued deterrent). Remarkably, spectators could be found who wanted to watch this process too. Well into the nineteenth century, Hounslow Heath in London was the site of up to a hundred gibbeted corpses in various states of putrefaction, such that the stench downwind was often intolerable. These exposed corpses of the executed became destinations for Sunday outings. One gibbeting in England in 1812 drew 100,000 to watch. Children would be brought to gaze upon exposed cadavers as part of their moral education. Alternatively,

[43] W. M. Thackeray, "Going to See a Man Hanged," *Fraser's Magazine* 22 (August 1840), 150–8. The hanging was of Courvoisier, a French valet to Lord William Russell, whom Courvoisier had murdered.

[44] S. D. Amussen, "Punishment, Discipline, and Power: The Social Meaning of Violence in Early Modern England," *Journal of British Studies* 34 (1995), 1–34, esp. 12.

[45] Evans, *Rituals of Retribution*, 99–108. For similar interpretations of executions in other European countries, see E. Cohen, "Symbols of Culpability and the Universal Language of Justice: The Ritual of Public Executions in Late Medieval Europe," *History of European Ideas* 11 (1989), 407–16; Spierenburg, *Spectacle of Suffering*, 91–4. The difference in mood between English and continental executions is observed by Laqueur, "Crowds," 317 and Evans, *Rituals of Retribution*, 106–7. One Victorian commentator caustically dubbed English execution crowds "an avalanche of ordure"; Gatrell, *Hanging Tree*, 58–61 (quote at 60).

[46] Van Dülmen, *Theatre of Horror*, 108.

the body could be "anatomized," that is, dissected for science, often in public. There are descriptions of crowd-pleasing procedures only loosely connected to scientific inquiry, such as hooking the body up to a battery to make it twitch, tanning the hide, or pickling the scalp.[47]

European habits naturally transferred to the colonies. In Spanish colonial America, for instance, executions and corporal punishment were conducted in public squares, the better to cater to the large crowds that were expected (and the crowds were not exclusively European in composition). People are known to have traveled considerable distances to attend. For instance, on November 13, 1630, an "infinite number of persons on foot, on horseback, and in coaches" gathered in Collao in Peru to witness the execution of one Thomas Buesso, who had been convicted of sodomy and bestiality. They also got to see Buesso's African male lover whipped and the offending dog burned.[48] Between 1640 and 1697 a Spanish diarist in Lima noted details of two dozen public executions held in the town's main plaza before huge crowds.[49] Treatment of Amerindian rebels was particularly harsh. Following the suppression of a major Maya revolt in the Yucatan in 1761, the rebel leader Canek underwent public execution in the provincial capital, Merida. The sentence required that Canek's bones be broken with an iron bar, his flesh torn away with pincers, and that he then be suspended in a cage "until he dies naturally." His body was to be burned and the ashes scattered. The entire process lasted five hours. Over the course of the following week, eight more rebels were hanged and over 600 flogged and mutilated, all in front of large crowds.[50] In 1781 Inca rebel Tupac Amaru II was executed in Cuzco's main square. He was forced first to witness the killing of his entire family, and then had his tongue cut out before being tied to horses and torn apart.[51]

[47] In 1752 the British Parliament decreed that the bodies of executed murderers be dissected for science – in public; see Cooper, *Lesson of the Scaffold*, 3. The deterrent effect of the execution was thus prolonged after the actual death of the criminal. See also Evans, *Rituals of Retribution*, 86–98 (exposure of corpses) and 416–17, 656–7, 897–8 (anatomization); Gatrell, *Hanging Tree*, 246–50 (children), 255–8 (anatomization), and 267–70 (gibbeting); Spierenburg, *Spectacle of Suffering*, 90–1. See also Linebaugh, "Tyburn Riot," 69–78.

[48] See M. A. Burkholder and L. L. Johnson, *Colonial Latin America*, 3rd edn. (Oxford, 1998), 228. The arrest, trial, and execution of animal malefactors was standard practice in premodern France; see Friedland, "Beyond Deterrence," 309–13.

[49] See R. R. Miller (ed.), *Chronicle of Colonial Lima: The Diary of Josephe and Francisco Mugaburru, 1640–1697* (Norman, 1975), 26, 83, 85, 109, 126, 131, 136, 210, 267.

[50] See D. E. Dumond, *The Machete and the Cross: Campesino Rebellion in Yucatan* (Lincoln, NB, 1997), 59; R. W. Patch, "Culture, Community, and 'Rebellion' in the Yucatec Maya Uprising of 1761," in S. Schroeder (ed.), *Native Resistance and the Pax Colonial in New Spain* (Lincoln, NE, 1998), 67–83. My thanks to Professor Matthew Restall for these references.

[51] O. Starn et al. (eds.), *The Peru Reader* (Durham, NC, 1995), 157–61.

Public executions consistently attracted spectators in the United States until they were discontinued in the 1930s. On July 27, 1886, for instance, the public hanging of Andrew Green in Denver, Colorado, drew a crowd estimated at 15,000. Many hundreds took up position just to watch the gallows being built. So many people came out to watch that some were a mile distant from the action when Green met his end. The crowd represented a cross-section of Denver society and comprised men, women, and children. Some ladies dressed in their Sunday best, while others enjoyed a picnic. Hucksters sold lemonade and pictures of the condemned man. The *Daily Denver Times* noted that "one would have thought that they were assembled for the purpose of seeing a horse race instead of an execution," and Sam Howe, a local detective who was an eyewitness, commented later that "the hanging was divested of solemnity by the enormous crowd, who seemed to find pleasure in the gruesome spectacle about to be enacted . . . [it] took the situation lightly and was very boisterous." Green's hanging was botched. He writhed on the end of the rope for five minutes. Spectators pushed to secure a position as close as possible to the action; boys and girls surged forward; babies were held aloft for a better view.[52]

The last legal public execution in the United States took place on August 14, 1936, when African-American Rainey Bethea was hanged in Owensboro, Kentucky, for a rape and murder committed a few weeks earlier. An estimated 20,000 people, many in festive humor, descended on the small town from five states by airplane, train, bus, car, horse, and foot. They seized every available vantage point, scaling buildings to occupy the roofs and even hanging off lampposts. Some slept on cots around the gallows throughout the preceding night, and hawkers sold popcorn and hotdogs.[53] Legal public executions aside, another spectacle of public murder attracted large crowds in America until quite recently. In the southern states especially,

---

[52] See W. M. King, *Going to Meet a Man: Denver's Last Legal Public Execution, 27 July 1886* (Niwot, 1990), esp. 115–45 (quotes from the *Times* at 119; from Howe at 132). After the execution, a reformist local newspaper pointedly commented "[The sheriff] had made the people happy. He had given them a spectacle equal in brutality to the exhibitions with which the Roman Emperors were wont to pander to the lowest appetites of their subjects" (ibid., 139).

[53] See P. T. Ryan, *The Last Public Execution in America* (Kentucky, 1992), esp. chs. 24–6. This book is available at www.geocities.com/lastpublichang/ (accessed Jan. 12, 2010). Laqueur ("Crowds," 306) offers a somewhat sensationalized account. The behavior of these American spectators is vividly echoed in descriptions of Old World execution crowds, such as this one from the execution of the bandit Cartouche, November 27, 1721: "All night long, on Thursday 26th, fiacres [four-wheeled cabs] carried passengers to the Place de Grève, until it was jammed with people all waiting for the event. Windows facing the square were lit all night. The cold was biting, but the crowd lit fires right in the square and local merchants sold food and drink. Everyone was laughing, drinking, singing. Most of the spectators had had their places reserved for over a month"; cited in Abbott, *Execution*, 43.

lynchings of African-Americans and white criminals continued into the 1960s.[54] Remarkably, a genre of photography emerged from these events that preserves gruesome images of beaten and often charred or half-charred corpses hanging from trees or lampposts, sometimes in groups. In such photographs, well-dressed crowds of smiling men and women are to be seen, occasionally with their children in tow. Some of the images were made into postcards.[55]

The movement of executions out of the public eye did not diminish the hunger for images of the killings among significant sectors of the modern public.[56] Indeed, as executions became rarer in nineteenth-century Europe and rail transport became available, crowds at public executions in London and elsewhere in England actually *increased* in size.[57] This development was paralleled on the continent. Fearing disorder, the authorities tried to discourage heavy attendance by moving the scaffold further and further outside town. No matter. The spectators simply walked or rode to see the action.[58] Even the total sequestering of executions behind prison walls has not reduced at least a sector of the public's appetite for the details. In 1927, when a photographer from the *Daily News* captured the electrocution of Ruth Snyder with a hidden camera, the image sold an extra 500,000 copies of the tabloid. In the United States even today, crowds routinely gather outside prisons during executions. Some are there to protest the death penalty, but others to celebrate the execution and chant their mockery of the victim, even though there is nothing at all to be seen save bare prison walls and guarded gateways. Illicit photographs leaked from execution chambers, especially electrocutions, circulate widely on the internet, and

[54] See W. F. Brundage, *Lynching in the New South: Georgia and Virginia, 1880–1930* (Urbana, 1993); S. E. Tolnay and E. M. Beck, *A Festival of Violence: An Analysis of Southern Lynchings, 1882–1930* (Urbana, 1995).

[55] J. Allen et al., *Without Sanctuary: Lynching Photography in America* (Santa Fe, 2000). The message on one postcard depicting the horribly burned corpse of Jesse Washington (lynched in Texas on May 16, 1916) reads: "This is the barbecue we had last night. My picture is to the left, with a cross over it. Your son, Joe."

[56] See W. Lesser, *Pictures at an Execution: An Inquiry into the Subject of Murder* (Cambridge, MA, 1993). Lesser's book treats the wider phenomenon of America's obsession with deliberate killing, both legal and illegal.

[57] See also Laqueur, "Crowds"; Linebaugh, *London Hanged*; and Cooper, *Lessons of the Scaffold*, all of whom include striking prints of Victorian hangings with large (and sometimes festive) crowds roiling around the gallows. The woodcuts of William Hogarth (1697–1764) not infrequently depict executions. The quote from William Montague in the epigraph of this chapter refers to large execution crowds in seventeenth-century Amsterdam.

[58] Evans, *Rituals of Retribution*, 41–52 (general process of increase in crowd size), 257–8 (nineteenth-century figures and official measures). Crowds of 20,000 are recorded for hangings outside Newgate prison in England, and the hanging of two highwaymen in 1807 drew 45,000 spectators; see Schechter, *Savage Pastimes*, 99.

sites (such as "World of Death") with video of hostage beheadings from the Middle East and photographs of the aftermath of accidents attract visitors by the tens of thousands. Shaky video on youtube.com of Saddam Hussein's hanging in 2006 has drawn over a million hits, on an informal count.

Although documentation is much scarcer, it is evident that ritual violence conducted as public spectacle is not exclusively a European or Western phenomenon. Among the Iroquois of the north eastern United States, captured warriors and other enemies (such as Jesuit priests) were subjected to protracted rituals of torture, sometimes for days, tied to scaffolds before crowds drawn from the village and its environs. One Jesuit account from 1642 records captives being paraded through several villages and publicly tortured in each.[59] The urban center of the Aztec empire, Tenochtitlan, saw vast rituals of human sacrifice involving progressively larger numbers of victims staged for centuries atop the huge pyramids framing the city's main plaza. The bloody spectacles would therefore be seen from almost any part of the city below. Efforts were made over time to increase the scale of the sacrifices and to vary the methods of killing.[60] The process invites comparison with the quest for novelty notable in other violent spectacles and suggests that more than religious scruple was involved in staging Aztec sacrifices, and that there was a concern also to maintain public interest by avoiding monotony. In addition to sacrifices, Aztec criminals were subjected to vicious public executions (including stoning, clubbing, burning, and crucifixion).[61] Human sacrifice in the New World was not limited to the Mesoamerican region. Until well into the nineteenth century, the

[59] See A. Greer (ed.), *The Jesuit Relations: Natives and Missionaries in Seventeenth-Century North America* (Boston, MA, 2000), esp. 155–85; N. Knowles, "The Torture of Captives by the Indians of Eastern North America," *Proceedings of the American Philosophical Society* 82 (1940), 151–225; D. K. Richter, *The Ordeal of the Longhouse: The Peoples of the Iroquois League in the Era of European Colonization* (Chapel Hill, 1992), esp. 65–70 on torture and adoption rituals among the tribes.
[60] For an overview, see E. M. Brumfiel, "Aztec Hearts and Minds: Religion and the State in the Aztec Empire," in S. E. Alcock et al. (eds.), *Empires* (Cambridge, 2001), 283–310; G. W. Conrad and A. A. Demarest, *Religion and Empire: The Dynamics of Aztec and Inca Expansionism* (Cambridge, 1984), esp. 28–9 and 44–52. For changes in the scale and methods of ritual, see Fr. Diego Durán (died 1588?), *History of the Indies of New Spain*, trans. D. Heyden (Norman, 1994; originally published 1581), 140–3, 169–74, 191–2, 233, 288–90, 322–3, 407, 435–6; note especially 338–40 (80,400 prisoners supposedly sacrificed in one four-day ceremony) and 456–9 (variations in sacrificial techniques, including cardiac excision, partial burning, shooting with arrows, and flaying alive). Such sacrifices often took place before huge crowds; indeed, Durán (231) reports that king Moctezumah I (reigned 1440–69) said, "We shall invite the whole world [to witness a planned mass sacrifice], for an act of such great importance must be known to all, and it is better to make a big display than a little one." It is a sentiment the Roman *munerarius* would fully understand.
[61] See D. Durán, *Book of the Gods and Rites and The Ancient Calendar*, trans. F. Horcasitas and D. Heyden (Norman, 1971; originally published 1574–6), 283–4.

Skidi Pawnee of Nebraska used to sacrifice captive men, women, children, and even infants to the Morning Star. This was done in full view of the village, as victims were tied to a scaffold and tortured before being killed and dismembered. Attempts by one of their leaders, Knife Chief, to stop the practice failed.[62]

By the time of the T'ang Dynasty in ancient China (AD 618–907), five forms of punishment had become enshrined in the law: beating with a light stick, beating with a heavy stick, penal servitude, exile for life, and death. In earlier periods death was inflicted in a variety of ways, including boiling in a large pot, chopping, mashing, sawing in half (lengthwise), or pulling apart by horses. By the T'ang period the preferred methods were strangulation, decapitation, and the infamous "death by a thousand cuts" (*ling chi*). Like wheeling in Medieval Europe, this mode of execution was reserved for those guilty of the most heinous crimes.[63] Drawings from the Ming Dynasty (1368–1644) depict victims tied to stakes being sliced in front of onlookers. Indeed, execution in China was always very much a public affair, as suggested by its designation as *ch'i-shih*, "casting away in the marketplace" and its being staged between one and five in the afternoon, when the marketplace would be busy (public executions in premodern Europe usually also took place on market days, to maximize attendance). Many early modes of execution stipulated the public display of the malefactor's remains, also in the marketplace.[64]

As part of his sojourn among the Zulus in the early nineteenth century, European trader Henry Francis Fynn reports summary public executions under the tyrannnical rule of Shaka. Victims were hit on the head with a knobkerrie (a type of club), their bodies then beaten to a pulp and impaled on a stake through the anus, and left as carrion. Fynn became accustomed to this almost daily procedure, whereas a companion who joined him in Zululand could not bear to watch.[65] The native kingdom of Asante dominated the west African coast in the eighteenth and nineteenth centuries.

---

[62] Edgerton, *Sick Societies*, 142–3.
[63] G. MacCormack, *Traditional Chinese Penal Law* (Edinburgh, 1990), esp. 100–33 on T'ang punishments. See also M. R. Dutton, *Policing and Punishment in China: From Patriarchy to "the People"* (Cambridge, 1992), esp. 109–11 (for earlier punishments). On *ling chi*, see Abbott, *Execution*, 259–61; T. Brooks et al., *Death by a Thousand Cuts* (Cambridge, MA, 2008), esp. 1–4 for an execution carried out at the gate of the vegetable market in Beijing in 1904.
[64] See B. McKnight, *Law and Order in Sung China* (Cambridge, 1992), esp. 446–71 on the death penalty, and 448–51 for the Ming depictions of *ling chi*.
[65] J. Stuart and D. McK. Malcolm (eds.), *The Diary of Henry Francis Fynn* (Pietermaritzburg, 1950), 28–9; N. Isaacs, *Travels and Adventures in Eastern Africa Descriptive of the Zoolus, their Manners, their Customs* (Capetown, 1970; originally published 1836), 62. Note, however, the modern critique of the tradition about Shaka in, e.g., C. Hamilton, *Terrific Majesty: The Power of Shaka Zulu and the*

When European travelers entered its dazzling capital, Kumase, in 1817, they described the great wealth of the place and the warm welcome they received from the king and his court. They also met the royal executioner. He carried about with him an axe encrusted with human blood and fat, and the visitors saw a victim being led away for an appointment with him. The victim was tortured horribly en route, with knives shoved through his cheeks and under his shoulder blades, his ears severed, and the cord used to lead him piercing his nose.[66]

In some parts of the world, public executions continue to be carried out to this day. In Saudi Arabia the condemned are beheaded, normally on Fridays, in one of the main squares in Riyadh, at the rate of about one a week. Women are usually shot, to spare them the indignity of bearing their necks in public. In Iran, China, North Korea, Thailand, and elsewhere executions can be staged before large crowds. In an echo of Medieval European practices, sentencing ceremonies are often staged in China as huge public rallies. In the North Korean city of Hamhung, the place of execution is located beside the town's main bridge, and schoolchildren are brought along in groups to watch (the preferred method is firing squad). Schoolchildren attending for the first time are seated at the very front. Eyewitnesses report crowds in the thousands. As recently as 1988, a public hanging in Pakistan attracted 10,000 spectators.[67]

Each culture has had its own ideas about what public punishment achieves, and no doubt the motivations impelling people to attend have not been monolithic and unitary across so broad a cultural and chronological

---

Limits of Historical Invention (Cambridge, MA, 1998), and D. Wylie, *Savage Delight: White Myths of Shaka* (Pietermaritzburg, 2000).

[66] T. E. Bowdich, *Mission from Cape Coast Castle to Ashantee* (London, 1966; originally published 1819), 31–4.

[67] On the Pakistan hanging, see Linebaugh, *London Hanged*, xvi. The internet provides much information (as well as video and images) about contemporary public executions, although the sources must be vetted carefully. On Saudi Arabia, for instance, see Amnesty International website, s.v. "Saudi Arabia"; available at www.amnesty.org/en (accessed Jan. 12, 2010). On North Korea, see ibid., s.v. "North Korea"; videos of executions have been posted at youtube.com (accessed Jan. 12, 2010). The presence of schoolchildren echoes English practices of the eighteenth and nineteenth centuries, when taking children to the gallows or gibbet was considered an improving and educational experience (one town even declared a school holiday in 1824 to witness a hanging); see Gatrell, *Hanging Tree*, 246–50. On Thailand, see J. Head, "Eyewitness: Thailand's Public Executions," available at http://news.bbc.co.uk/2/hi/asia-pacific/1292812.stm (accessed Jan. 12, 2010). For a particularly nasty public flogging and hanging in Iran in 2005, see "Iran Town Rejoices at Public Hanging," available at http://news.bbc.co.uk/2/hi/middle_east/4355029.stm (accessed Jan. 21, 2010). Indeed, public executions in Iran are often attended by large crowds and televized; see R. Fulford, "Iran's War on its Own," *National Post* (Aug. 11, 2007), available at: www.canada.com/nationalpost/news/issuesideas/story.html?id=02679845–6f28–4db3-ae22–2ae5d7043eda (accessed Jan. 12, 2010).

landscape as that reviewed here. Study of the cultural currents that flowed through such spectacles, and continue to do so, is thus a worthy and very instructive endeavor, and it is not to be doubted that the cultural meaning(s) of spectacles of punishment is closely tied to the facets of each one's historical context. This approach has its limits, however.

MEDIEVAL PUBLIC EXECUTIONS AND THE "GOOD DEATH"

By way of example, let us look a little more closely at the proposal that the ethos of the Christian "good death" infused European executions from the Middle Ages to the early nineteenth century, and that this is what motivated people to come and watch.[68] The "good death" was essentially a public, communal event. Even if people passed away at home, they did so in the presence of friends, neighbors, clergymen, and other onlookers, all of whom were there to witness and celebrate the departure of the deceased's soul to a better place. Death by execution paralleled the "good death," insofar as it was public and presided over by clerics. The latter ensured that the condemned died free from sin and, if they played their prescribed role properly, vocally repentant for past misdeeds. Execution victims could be admired and sanctified for dying under such blessed circumstances (that is, in a state of grace). The condemned also enjoyed the luxury of knowing the precise time of their deaths, so they could thoroughly prepare themselves for the transition to the hereafter. Malefactors habitually wore white on their final march to and on the scaffold, went to their deaths amidst hymns and praying, and interacted with the crowd before being killed. The whole event was thus communal, participatory, and ceremonial, analogous to other public religious rites. Death by public execution was an echo, even a mirror, of the Christian "good death." Therefore, it can be argued, spectators at European executions in this period were drawn to watch out of a solemn spirit of religious celebration.[69]

One window onto popular perceptions of the execution ritual in this era is street ballads, so-called farewell songs, which were performed as street theater before an interested public. Examples from seventeenth- and

---

[68] For expositions of this thesis, see Merback, *The Thief, the Cross and the Wheel,* 126–97; van Dülmen, *Theatre of Horror,* 119–32; Evans, *Rituals of Retribution,* 108–238.

[69] See Friedland, "Beyond Deterrence." He argues (*Spectacular Justice*) that until the eighteenth century, *ancien régime* executions in France were participatory quasi-religious ceremonies that sought to redeem the community from the harm done by the criminal. Spectators are recorded praying and weeping and singing hymns, with the victim sometimes joining in (ibid., 306–7).

eighteenth-century Germany emphasize the condemned's penitence and reconciliation with God. An example from 1683 reads in part:

This day I shall die, / Heaven shall be mine. / This day I'll see God . . . / Soul fly up to Heaven / From the body's cavern / For with Christ to rest. Rest, o soul, in Heav'n, / Rest awhile my limbs / Until the soul returns. / O troubled hearts / Why do you lament over my demise? I've gone to where I should / To where I long since would, / So wipe thy tearful eyes: For I've been sent before/ To where you all must go / Every one of you.

The mutual identification of the condemned and the crowd, partly achieved by the use of the first person direct address but also inherent in the song's theological content, could hardly be clearer. Everyone dies, all good souls go to heaven – the executed just arrive there sooner. Another example, from 1735, ends:

> O dearest Mother, O Mary, Thou must not leave me now, today,
> Command me up to Thee above because I rush along death's way,
> And Mary Magdalena too, stand by me with Thy tears of rue,
> That I may be today with Thee, myself to call right blessed too.

Reconciliation with God and repentance (symbolized by Mary Magdalena) are the core messages – and also core elements in the "good death."[70]

From the perspective of the authorities, however, popular views of the condemned as blessed martyrs rather went against the moral and civic messages that the execution ritual was supposed to communicate to the masses. As eighteenth-century public policy was increasingly shaped by an emerging commitment to rationalism, attempts were made to secularize executions. Clergymen were removed from the public phases of the proceedings, and the nature of the events themselves was altered to emphasize the core lessons the state desired to teach the watching public: deterrence and moral education. Public participation was more and more restricted, public sentencing abandoned, the death march speeded up, white shrouds for the condemned replaced by normal clothes, detachments of soldiers dispatched to maintain order, and the execution ritual stripped down to its bare essentials. Pastors could attend the condemned in their cells, but they were increasingly barred from their side during the procession to the scaffold and at the execution itself. The motive behind these reforms was expressly to reduce the public perception of the execution victim as in any way fortunate or enviable, as one anonymous pamphleteer in Hamburg in

---

[70] Evans, *Rituals of Retribution*, 150–89 (on farewell songs; quotes from "farewell songs" at 153 and 156 respectively).

1784 put it bluntly "the ultimate purpose of public punishment is largely frustrated if the malefactor dies in circumstances that arouse a kind of admiration and respect . . . Terror and repugnance, in accordance with the purposes of criminal justice, are the only emotions which the sight of a malefactor being led to the bloody scaffold should arouse in the spectator's heart." Under these reforms, moral education was furthered by replacing the intimate first-person "farewell songs" with officially sanctioned "moral speeches," composed in the more distant third person and largely devoid of religious imagery. The speeches cataloged the misdeeds and personal failings that had brought the condemned to so terrible an end. All of these measures sought to counter the popular view of the "good death" at executions, and the effort met with resistance: folk songs and other popular media retained elements of the religious view of the execution ritual, which continued to be seen as "almost an act of celebration, with the sanctified soul of the condemned rising up to heaven at the end."[71]

This interpretation of European public executions is sophisticated and nuanced, and carries considerable explanatory weight. Executions emerge as contested cultural space, where official policy butted against popular points of view. Yet there are good grounds for being wary of accepting the "good death" as an all-encompassing explanation of the spectators' *motives* for attendance. A cultural ethos of the "good death" does not require that the throngs at the execution scaffold were filled with admiration or envy for the condemned's fortunate circumstances, or were drawn there to celebrate a quasi-religious ritual. Motives no doubt varied from person to person, but on the collective plane the solemn, religious motive is difficult to reconcile with the boorishly festive mood sometimes noted by observers among execution crowds, which appears to have been the norm in England.[72] Spectators' motives were complicated. The Hamburg pamphleteer of 1784, whose views we have already noted, comments: "The rabble is not motivated by the desire to hear something good and thus be moved and uplifted, but merely by the wish to see something new, and to satisfy its curiosity, even, on many occasions at the cost of human feeling." Similarly, a traveler to Munich in 1781 was appalled

---

[71] Quotes in ibid. at 125 (from the Hamburg pamphleteer) and 188 ("sanctified soul").

[72] Boisterousness is noted even at some German executions, the very paradigm of the "good-death" ritual. An execution in Stuttgart in 1738, for instance, was marked by a festive mood among the crowd, with viewing booths erected for ladies, broadsheets on sale, and street traders plying their wares; see van Dülmen, *Theatre of Horror*, 99. A change in attitude is also charted by Friedland (*Spectacular Justice*) in France where, after the sixteenth century, people's motives to attend became less overtly religious. The detached, callous, or even festive demeanor of delicate ladies particularly appalls the (male) observers.

at the public's interest in execution literature and imagery, much of it extremely graphic:

Instead of reflecting in a mature way on the origins of the horrible crimes that are the occasion for such terrible executions, people read reports on both the crime and its punishment, and even the wretched moral speeches attached to them, with interest ... The physiognomies of the hangmen and executioners are far more repulsive than those of the malefactors; these latter, which should surely arouse the real abhorrence, look like those of martyrs by comparison. The common people gawk at these pictures in a thoughtless way and with complete indifference; children even make jokes about them.[73]

It is tempting to dismiss these views as symptomatic of a condescending elitism, but they carry no less weight as a guide to mass motivation than the equally condescending official sanctions against clergy on the scaffold. The final two sentences of the last quote are particularly telling. Despite noting the "good death" imagery of malefactor-as-martyr, the common people's reaction to it is hardly one of compassion and admiration, but rather titillation and disinterested curiosity. Cultural meaning need not be commensurate with conscious motivation.

More importantly, not every malefactor earned the crowd's sympathy. As reflected in folk songs, the crowd's attitude toward the victim depended in no small measure on the nature of the crime that had brought them to the scaffold in the first place – and only a handful of crimes appear to have generated outright empathy. When a young indigent girl was driven to infanticide by a duplicitous lover, or a cuckolded soldier-husband committed a crime of passion on returning from war, or a bandit was glossed with generous motives and populist virtues – in such instances the crowd might be well-disposed. But for most common murderers who killed in an act of larceny or out of adulterous motives or for other base reasons, as well as multiple murderers, gangs of bandits who terrorized farming communities, suspected witches, old women, "midwives," and loners, when such as these mounted the scaffold, the crowd's attitude was that they were getting what they deserved. A folk song about a robber-gang who carried out a "house invasion" and murdered a family in the process, along with a tenant and a maid, ends with the lines, "They are too wicked for this world! / A hangman's death these men have earned. / And for the ugly bloody deed / Each murderer pays upon the wheel."[74] Likewise in England. When murderers, child-killers, or sexual deviants mounted the gallows, crowd

---

[73] Evans, *Rituals of Retribution*, 124–5 (Hamburg pamphleteer) and 150 (Munich observer).
[74] Ibid., 173–89 (quote at 184).

hostility could be intense. The hanging of the murderous body-snatcher William Burke in 1829 was greeted with loud cheers, and other reviled convicts were routinely yelled, hissed, or shouted at as they faced their final moments.[75] Thus the Christian "good death" only goes so far in explaining the European public's fascination with executions from the Middle Ages onwards. It is bounded by time (it ended by the nineteenth century, even as crowd size at executions increased), by place (it hardly applies to the unruliness that was habitual at Tyburn, and it is wholly inapplicable to spectators in non-Christian contexts), and by circumstance (not all malefactors earned admiration, and even some supposedly "good death" crowds were disorderly, drunken, or riotous).

A wider point emerges here that is applicable to any context-specific explanation for spectatorship at executions: they necessarily carry limited value in understanding the phenomenon across time and space. It would require sustained *ad hoc* reasoning to argue that people's consistent attendance at such rituals in widely divergent sociocultural contexts stems from motivations rooted only in those contexts.[76] Psychological factors must play their part. We shall return later in this book to the most probable psychological processes that help undergird spectator motivations at executions. For now, however, we turn our attention to the second main category of violent spectacle: games, pastimes, and competitions.

COMBAT SPORTS AND BLOODSPORTS

As with watching execution rituals, combats or confrontations staged as spectacle were not unique to Rome. Evidence from ancient Mesopotamia and Egypt makes it clear that combat sports (primarily boxing and wrestling, but also stick-fighting) were known in these societies, and their association with religious festivals suggests a spectacular context for their staging. Royal hunts could also be presented as spectator events. Other Mediterranean societies too, such as the Hittites or Minoans, appear to have featured some version of violent competition staged before spectators.[77]

---

[75] Gatrell, *Hanging Tree*, 68–9 and 100–3. Gatrell suspects that class differences, titillation, and excitement played as much a part in this sort of behavior as did approval at seeing a vile crime punished. But the pitilessness of the spectators on such occasions – which could include toasting the eternal damnation of the executed man's soul with gin – rather points to retributive satisfaction.

[76] Gatrell, *Hanging Tree*, 67–105. He tips his hat in the direction of psychological considerations (ibid., 72–3), but leaves the terrain largely unexplored.

[77] Kyle, *Sport and Spectacle*, 26–53. Note especially the famous "Grandstand Fresco" from Knossos (*c.* 1500 BC) or the "Ramp House Fresco" from Mycenae (*c.* 1450 BC), which show people spectating

The Greeks were enthusiastic for combat sports. Homer's epics contain descriptions of boxing (dubbed "grievous"), wrestling, and armed duels staged as spectacles.[78] Among the most unpleasant of these was the *pankration*, an all-out fight with only two rules: no biting, no gouging (Philostr. *Imag.* 2.6.3). For the Spartans, even these two restrictions were excessive, and many pankratiasts appear to have ignored them anyway. One anecdote tells how a pankratiast dislocated his opponent's ankle to secure victory before dying from his own injuries.[79] Greek boxing was even more punishing. From the fourth century BC onwards, boxers wore thongs of hardened leather over their knuckles that lacerated the opponent's face. (To this the Romans appear to have added pieces of metal and spikes to form the fearsome *caestus*, one of the most vicious sporting accoutrements ever devised.) As with the *pankration*, notices not only of cuts to the face, but eyes and ears lost in the fray make clear the hazards of Greek boxing.[80] Death and severe injury were very real possibilities during these bouts, so that jokes could be made about how the mothers or pets of boxers failed to recognize them.[81] Violent events like these were part of the great panhellenic athletic competitions and were staged before large and enthusiastic crowds. These trends continued into the Hellenistic era, when empire infused the whole with a greater degree of staged excess.[82] Furthermore, the Greeks were also

at staged events; or the Boxer Rhyton from Hagia Triada (*c.* 1550 BC) or the Boxing Boys fresco from Akrotiri on Thera (*c.* 1625 BC), the subject matter of which is self-evident from their modern titles.

[78] Boxing: *Il.* 23.651–700, *Od.* 18.1–107. Wrestling: *Il.* 23.700–39, *Od.* 8.100–3; Armed duel: *Il.* 23.748–825; Kyle, *Sport and Spectacle*, 54–71.

[79] See M. B. Poliakoff, *Combat Sports in the Ancient World: Competition, Violence, and Culture* (New Haven, 1987), esp. 54–63 on the *pankration*; Kyle, *Sport and Spectacle*, 124–6. Note also the remarks of Golden (*Greek Sport*, 72–4) on "violent Greeks." For the posthumous victory, see Philostr. *Imag.* 2.6; Paus. 8.40.1–2. Stephen Miller has remarked that in the *pankration*, "victory went to the survivor"; see S. G. Miller, "The Organization and Functioning of the Olympic Games," in D. J. Phillips and D. Pritchard (eds.), *Sport and Festival in the Ancient Greek World* (Swansea, 2003), 1–40 (quote at 27).

[80] Poliakoff, *Combat Sports*, 68–88 (75–9 on the *caestus*). On the boxing glove, see Kyle, *Sport and Spectacle*, 124–5. An attempt has been made to define the *caestus* down (the spikes reinterpreted as protection for the fingers, for instance); see H. M. Lee, "The Later Greek Boxing Glove and the Roman Caestus: A Centennial Re-evaluation of Jünther's 'Über Antike Turngeräthe,'" *Nikephoros* 10 (1997), 161–78, esp. 170–1. Greek boxing and wrestling were eventually staged as spectacle in Roman baths; see Z. Newby, "Greek Athletics as Roman Spectacle: The Mosaics from Ostia and Rome," *PBSR* 70 (2002), 177–203.

[81] Eight deaths in boxing, wrestling, or *pankration* bouts are documented in the sources; see R. Brophy, "Deaths in the Pan-Hellenic Games: Arrachion and Creugas," *AJP* 99 (1978), 363–90; R. and M. Brophy, "Deaths in the Pan-Hellenic Games: All Combative Sports," *AJP* 106 (1985), 171–98; M. Poliakoff, "Deaths in the Pan-Hellenic Games: Addenda and Corrigenda," *AJP* 107 (1986), 400–2. Failure to recognize: Arist. *Lys.* 614–705; *Anth. Pal.* 11.77.

[82] Coleman, "Ptolemy Philadelphus"; Kyle, *Sport and Spectacle*, 133–5 (Olympic spectators) and 229–50 (Hellenistic developments); A. Kuttner, "Hellenistic Images of Spectacle: From Alexander to Augustus," in Bergmann and Kondoleon (eds.), *Art of Ancient Spectacle*, 97–123.

fond of cock-, quail- and partridge-fighting, an enthusiasm not shared, interestingly, by the Romans.[83]

Looking beyond the Roman era, in the warrior ethos of Medieval Europe training for war involved mock combats between armed men, which developed in the course of the twelfth century into the more structured tournament.[84] This spectacle involved teams of knights on horseback, sometimes numbering in the hundreds, attacking each other with sharp weaponry in a free-for-all termed *mêlée*; it only later incorporated more structured combats and jousts conducted with blunt weapons. Initially, infantry and even archers could be involved in the *mêlée*, which made the larger tournaments closely resemble actual battles.[85] Despite this, the contests were not intentionally lethal – combatants usually fought for honor and ransoms paid for captured opponents – but when the blood was up, matters could get out of hand. In 1241 at Neuss near Cologne, for instance, up to eighty combatants were killed when a tournament degenerated into a real battle. When the English king Edward I was man-handled at a tournament at Chalons in 1273, a struggle broke out that killed dozens of combatants and spectators and became known as the "little battle of Chalons." Aside from these riotous occurrences, there are many notices of deaths and maimings among prominent participants in the course of tourneying that bear witness to the dangers of the pastime.[86] The Church reckoned that tournaments promoted sinful behavior and so officially opposed them, but the popularity of the events ensured that they continued to be staged. Eventually the Church reconsidered its position, not least due to the tournament's usefulness in preparing Crusaders for the rigors of real combat.[87]

The tournament appears to have been a spectator event from quite early in its history. Initially the *mêlée* ranged over an expanse of countryside bounded by palisades and ditches. It would have been possible for an audience to watch from outside the bounds, but only at some remove from the

[83] M. G. Morgan, "Three Non-Roman Blood Sports," *CQ* 25 (1975), 117–22.

[84] See J. M. Carter, *Ludi Medi Aevi: Studies in the History of Medieval Sport* (Manhattan, 1981); J. Fleckenstein (ed.), *Das ritterliche Turnier im Mittelalter* (Göttingen, 1985); J. Fleuri, *Chevaliers et chevalerie au Moyen Âge* (Paris, 1998), 131–52; S. H. Hardy, "The Medieval Tournament: A Functional Sport of the Upper Class," *Journal of Sport History* 1 (1974), 91–105.

[85] The popular image of the tournament, with tilting lists, heraldry, and ornate armor, derives from the events as they were staged in the fourteenth and fifteenth centuries. Combats with sharp weapons were termed *à outrance*, with blunted *à plaisance*. But even the latter were hazardous and could result in injury or death. On the forms of combat featured in the tournament, see J. R. V. Barker, *The Tournament in England, 1100–1400* (Woodbridge, 1986), 137–61.

[86] For these and other details, see M. Keen, *Chivalry* (New Haven, 1984), 83–101.

[87] See Carter, *Ludi Medi Aevi*, 61–73; Keen, *Chivalry*, 94–7.

action. Gradually, however, tournament sites became more localized (outside castles, for instance), and eventually they became permanent arenas with roofed wooden stands. The attendance of women among the spectators at tournaments – attested as early as 1180 outside the castle at Joigny in France – played to chivalric ideals and helped mold the form of subsequent events.[88] The very presence of women, however, proves that the violence of the tournament (even if conducted *à plaisance*, with blunt weapons) had become a spectacle to be watched by an audience, while the gradual provision of permanent stands reflects the tournament's growing popularity. Unfortunately there is little in the Medieval sources about spectator behavior, beyond notices of boisterous participation and the occasional riot.

Bear-, bull-, and badger-baiting, cock-, dog-, and rat-fighting, boxing, wrestling, cudgeling, singlesticking, and fencing remained popular combat entertainments for spectators throughout the Middle Ages right down to modern times (and some of these diversions are still staged in various parts of the world). The object of cudgeling or singlestick bouts was to "break the head," by which was meant the drawing of blood. Samuel Pepys, in his famous seventeenth-century diary, reports a sword-fight he watched in the New Theatre in London on June 1, 1663:

And I with Sir J. Minnes to the Strand May-pole; and there light out of his coach, and walked to the New Theatre, which, since the King's players are gone to the Royal one, is this day begun to be employed by the fencers to play prizes at. And here I come and saw the first prize I ever saw in my life: and it was between one Mathews, who did beat at all weapons, and one Westwicke, who was soundly cut several times both in the head and legs, that he was all over blood: and other deadly blows they did give and take in very good earnest, till Westwicke was in a sad pickle. They fought at eight weapons, three boutes at each weapon. This being upon a private quarrel, they did it in good earnest; and I felt one of the swords, and found it to be very little, if at all blunter on the edge, than the common swords are. Strange to see what a deal of money is flung to them both upon the stage between every boute.[89]

Even if this particular fight appears to have been a duel over some private dispute, it was nevertheless played out before a crowd, and Pepys is quite clear that the New Theatre had been given over to fencing spectacles that were public, bloody, and quasi-professional, insofar as prizes were awarded and money thrown on stage by the crowd. Later the same year, he attended a

---

[88] See Barker, *Tournament*, 100–11.
[89] Latham and Matthews (eds.), *Diary of Samuel Pepys*, vol. IV, 167–8.

cock-fight and noted the great social variety of the crowd, from Members of Parliament to "the poorest 'prentices, bakers, brewers, butchers, draymen, and what not." On May 27, 1667, Pepys went to the "bear-garden," an arena specifically built for bear-baiting, to see two men, a butcher and a waterman, fence for a prize in the pit. The place was so packed with spectators that Pepys had to find a way in through a nearby alehouse. When the waterman was disabled and could fight no longer, a riot broke out between partisans in the crowd, which Pepys stayed to watch, since "they all fell to it to knocking down and cutting many on each side. *It was pleasant to see*, but that I stood in the pit, and feared that in the tumult I might get some hurt. At last the battle broke up, and so I away" (emphasis added).[90]

The popularity of bloody spectacle spurred James Figgs, a heavyweight boxer and expert pugilist in eighteenth-century England, to open the appropriately named "Figgs Amphitheatre" in London in 1719. The Amphitheatre was a huge hit with all classes, drawing rowdy crowds who came to watch the proprietor batter opponents with fists, sticks, and swords. Cock- and bull-fights and brawling Irishwomen were alternative attractions. One onlooker records that, during his visit, the loudest shout went up when Figgs sliced off part of his opponent's calf.[91] The appeal of combat sports continues down to the present, and not just in the familiar forms of boxing or wrestling. In recent years the spectacle of "Mixed Martial Arts" or "Ultimate Fighting" has emerged as immensely popular in North America, indeed so popular that it now has its own professional organization (the UFC, Ultimate Fighting Championship) and is the fastest-growing spectator sport among American males aged 18–34.[92] Ultimate Fighting may be seen as a resurrection of the *pankration*, although with more restrictions (the UFC website lists thirty-one possible fouls; the *pankration* had two). Fighters are put into a boxing ring or an octagonal cage and kick, punch,

[90] Ibid., vol. IV, 427–8 (cock-fight) and vol. VIII, 238–9 (bear-garden). Pepys liked his prize fighting, as he attended the bear-garden again on September 9, 1667 (ibid., vol. VIII, 430) to see a prize fight in which the loser "was so cut in both his wrists that he could not fight any longer." Pepys comments: "The sport very good, and various humours to be seen among the rabble that is there." Note also his comment that a highlight of the play *Catiline's Conspiracy* was the excellent fight sequences; ibid., vol. IX, 395. On stage violence, see ch. 7, p. 234.
[91] See A. Guttmann, *Sports Spectators* (New York, 1986), 53–82, especially 70–1 on Figgs. For an excellent overview of English pastimes in this era – including blood and combat sports – see Malcolmson, *Popular Recreations*, esp. 5–14 and 34–51 (with blood and combat sports at 42–51).
[92] The statistic is quoted by the UFC on its website (www.ufc.com/index.cfm?fa=news.detail&gid=8111; accessed Jan. 12, 2010) and was confirmed in a *60 Minutes* report (aired Dec. 10, 2006). Sport and spectacle are becoming increasingly conflated: a LexisNexis search for "sports w/2 spectacle" yielded 964 results for the period 2005–10.

throw, or wrestle to win the bout. The bouts are very violent and frequently bloody. On television, the camera tends to linger on limbs being twisted or faces cut. Even bloodier is "Ultimate Wrestling" where performers fight it out in a ring of barbed wire, smack each other with hard objects, are flogged with barbed wire, or throw each other on to broken light bulbs. The bouts frequently end with the wrestlers bathed in very real blood from very real injuries. The audience, particularly in the southern United States, laps it all up.

This gruesome catalog has been necessary to underscore the point that the Roman public was not unique in turning out in large numbers to watch people tortured or killed, or both. Indeed what is really quite remarkable is the well-documented persistence of spectators at public rituals of punishment and competition, up to and including the present, in those places where they are still practiced. To be sure, punitive and ludic violent spectacles have varied in form, method, and intent. Some punishments, for instance, have been prolonged and hideous (*ancien régime* punishments in France, wheelings), others relatively quick and not particularly spectacular (hangings, guillotining); some have been overtly religious in intent (mass Aztec sacrifices), others wholly secular (nineteenth-century hangings). Similarly, depending on the competitive event, death and injury are made more or less likely by the rules of engagement, the accoutrements used, and the prevailing values of the historical context.

What unites all these violent spectacles, however, is the readiness of people to watch, which transcends the specifics of each cultural context. Violent spectacles undoubtedly carry cultural meanings particular to each time and place, and spectator motivations for attending are likely to be connected to those meanings. But even if so, such culturally embedded motivations are not likely to have been consciously experienced by the spectators and, in any case, they collapse as explanatory models outside the context to which they are linked. That is, culturally specific explanations for spectator attendance are partial at best. A wider framework of explanation is called for. This book is about the Roman games, so to chart the contours of such a broad explanatory model in detail lies beyond its scope. But we may embark on defining some of its main features by a detailed consideration of how psychological processes played out at the Roman arena. The investigation that follows can tell us much about what the experience of watching the Roman games was like, but its wider historical implications should also be evident from the dismal litany we have just reviewed.

CHAPTER 3

Groups, crowds, and seats

> Every man has a mob self and an individual self, in varying proportions.
>
> D. H. Lawrence, "Pornography and Obscenity" (1929)[1]

That particular pseudo-theory that calls itself crowd psychology thus finds no foothold in the Roman *ludi*. The spectators in the theaters and amphitheaters of the Roman empire were not a "crowd," nor were those in the circus. Anonymity either did not exist at all or was in large measure dissipated; every reaction – at least in the theater and amphitheater – was unequivocally attributable, since it was known which group sat where. Social transparency severely reduced the scope for deviant behavior.[2]

So concludes Egon Flaig in his analysis of Roman political semiotics. Even if it appears a little stretched to claim that tens of thousands of Romans assembled in an arena did not constitute a crowd, the central contention appears nevertheless to be reasonable: the Roman system of assigning seats at spectacles according to social status surely undercut the possibility of what most people imagine as typical crowd behavior – suggestibility, volatility, and a tendency to unruliness generated by a mitigated sense of personal responsibility. The problem is that these assumptions rely on a largely discredited century-old model of crowd dynamics. Flaig bypasses more recent work, founded in group processes, that offers an entirely different model of why crowds behave as they do. This newer model of crowd dynamics better describes what the arena spectators experienced and intersects with the ranked deployment of the crowd in Roman amphitheaters.

---

[1] D. H. Lawrence, "Pornography and Obscenity," in J. T. Boulton (ed.), *The Cambridge Edition of the Works of D. H. Lawrence: Late Essays and Articles* (Cambridge, 2004), 238. The essay was originally published in 1929.
[2] Flaig, *Ritualisierte Politik*, 236 (translated from the German by the author).

GROUP PROCESSES AND THE CROWD

To operate in groups, large and small, is a basic feature of human existence.[3] People, when formed into even temporary groups, quickly develop a cohesion that places an emphasis on conformity. Social psychologists interpret this process in terms of a "social identity," which is distinct from (but not unrelated to) a person's individual sense of self and which orients itself first and foremost to the group.[4] The compass of this orientation is provided by the group's norms, that is, those patterns of behavior or thought that emerge from the membership's interaction and are sanctioned by the group. The cohesion of a group therefore rests in large measure on its norms and its members' conformity to them.[5] An individual normally claims membership in many groups, and so harbors a wide variety of social identities that are appropriate to each group. Social identities are therefore flexible, and people can readily switch between them, depending on circumstances. In this way, group processes are said to be "situationally salient," in that they are elicited by the contexts people find themselves in.

Social categorization is a related basic group process, closely linked to social identity. In their minds, people order their social universe according to group memberships.[6] Social categorization works both for the groups we are a part of or feel close to (ingroups) and also for groups we are not part of or feel removed from (outgroups). In certain circumstances, social categorization can lead people to adopt discriminatory and derogatory attitudes toward outgroup members. Ingroup members tend to strive for a positive social identity, such that fellow ingroupers are viewed favorably and outgroupers are viewed with some degree of suspicion; when conditions require it, this suspicion fosters prejudice and discrimination (for more on

[3] For recent and thorough overviews, with voluminous references to earlier work, see Brown, *Group Processes*; Hogg and Tindale (eds.), *Group Processes*; Szmatka et al., *Growth of Social Knowledge*. P. B. Paulus (ed.), *Basic Group Processes* (New York, 1983), is still informative.

[4] Some argue against a sense of self that is wholly independent of group membership (that is, nobody has a self-conception entirely unconnected to membership of some group, whether family, church, nation, etc.); see D. Abrams and M. A. Hogg, "Collective Identity: Group Membership and Self-Conception," in Hogg and Tindale (eds.), *Group Processes*, 425–60; S. Worchel and D. Coutant, "It Takes Two to Tango: Group Identity to Individual Identity within the Framework of Group Development," in ibid., 461–81.

[5] The cohesiveness of groups also rests on categorization processes, whereby members are evaluated by their relative conformity to a prototypical expectation of what a group member is like. The prototype is characterized by a fuzzy set of attributes that no individual may embody in their entirety (e.g., vague claims about "family resemblance" or the behavior of "people like that").

[6] Why they do so is a matter of dispute: because all people are, in reality, members of several groups? Or is it to simplify and negotiate an immensely complex social environment that might otherwise be bewildering, if everyone were assessed and treated on a strictly individual basis?

prejudice, see chapter 5). It is telling that marginal members of groups are often the most vociferous in their public expression of negativity toward outgroups, precisely because by doing so they broadcast their credentials as ingroupers.[7] Groups are not inherently wanton, violent, or cruel, but they can become so, if aggression or cruelty emerge as group norms and derogation of an outgroup is raised to the level of action. As with any group process, individual members will be affected differently, but the ability of individuals to descend into various degrees of unpleasantness is at least comprehensible in the case of a group whose norms sanction violence – whether direct or indirect – against others. In a nutshell, groups are not essentially nasty, but they can turn so under certain circumstances.[8]

Three influential experiments

Several seminal experiments illustrate these basic processes. The strong grip of group mentality over the human psyche was powerfully demonstrated by the "minimal group" experiments of Henri Tajfel in the 1970s, since replicated in hundreds of studies. Tajfel divided schoolboys into two groups based on some arbitrary criterion (such as their preference for one of two modern painters). Each was given a number, to obscure personal identity, but each knew which of the two groups he himself belonged to. The boys were then asked to assign sums of money to both ingroupers and outgroupers simultaneously using a matrix of paired, linked sums, so that when a chosen sum of money was assigned to an ingrouper, the linked sum automatically went to an outgrouper.[9] Individuals were identified to

---

[7] J. G. Noel et al., "Peripheral Ingroup Membership Status and Public Negativity toward Outgroups," *Journal of Personality and Social Psychology* 68 (1995), 127–37.

[8] Reicher et al. chart a five-step process leading to the ultimate manifestation of intergroup nastiness: genocide. First, ingroup identification generates intragroup cohesion. Second, exclusion blocks targeted groups from access to the ingroup. Third, excluded groups are constructed as threatening the ingroup's cohesion, or even its very existence. Fourth, against this confrontational backdrop, the ingroup is constructed as uniquely virtuous. Fifth, inhumanity perpetrated in defense of the ingroup is glorified as especially virtuous. These processes are not inexorable and they do not play out in a vacuum. Sociopolitical circumstances and active leadership play key roles in shaping group understandings and social actions, and they can be challenged (and usually are) at any stage in their development; see Reicher et al., "Making a Virtue of Evil."

[9] A simple Tajfel reward matrix looks like this (members of Group A see choices 1–9 and 10A; members of Group B see choices 1–9 and 10B):

Choice no.	1	2	3	4	5	6	7	8	9	10A	10B
Group A	16	14	12	10	8	8	6	4	2	24	36
Group B	2	4	6	8	8	10	12	14	16	36	24

each other only by their personal numbers and their group affiliations. Although the boys strove to be fair, their allocations showed a statistically significant favoring of ingroup members over the outgroup.[10]

The truly remarkable feature of the minimal group experiments is that the groups exist solely in the minds of their members: they never meet as groups or partake of any group activities, they have no history of interaction with the other group, and there is no opportunity even for group norms to develop. But, nevertheless, social categorization occurs, social identities emerge, and ingroup members favor each other at the expense of out-groupers. The experimental paradigm further highlights the situationally salient character of ingroup/outgroup membership, that is, social identity and categorization are triggered by circumstance, even if that circumstance is wholly artificial and arbitrary. Membership in some groups may be fixed (one's race, nationality, native language group, etc.), but group member-ship and the effects generated by it are more commonly determined by the situations people find themselves in. The power of these processes to

---

Thus a member of Group A, in chosing no. 1, assigns 16 units to his fellow ingrouper and 2 to the outgrouper. In choosing no. 8, 4 units go to the Group A member and 14 to the Group B member. And so on.

There are four major choice strategies: P, MJP, MIP and MD, as explained in this chart:

Choice strategies	Choice no.	Effect
Parity (P)	5	equality
Maximum Joint Profit (MJP)	10	maximizes overall profit but favors outgroup
Maximum Ingroup Profit (MIP)	10	maximizes ingroup profit but favors outgroup
Maximum Differentiation (MD)	1 (for Group A) *or* 9 (for Group B)	maximizes favoritism but at cost of MIP

The most logical choice is MJP, since everyone comes off the winner. But results are remarkably consistent: allocations usually fall somewhere between P and MIP (nos. 3, 4 or 6, 7 in the above matrix) and the *least* favorite choice is MJP. Thus ingroupers favor each other (though not exclusively) and find it most difficult to betray the ingroup by rewarding the ougroup more generously. The paradigm has been replicated with consistent results for almost four decades, using subjects of different ages, ethnicities, genders, nationalities, religious affiliations, and so on. For the relevant literature, see next two notes.

[10] Original demonstration: H. Tajfel et al., "Social Categorization and Intergroup Behaviour," *European Journal of Social Psychology* 11 (1971), 149–78; H. Tajfel, "The Achievement of Group Differen-tiation," in H. Tajfel (ed.), *Differentiation between Social Groups: Studies in the Social Psychology of Intergroup Relations* (London, 1978), 77–98. Subsequent replication: Brown, *Group Processes*, 281–5; W. P. Robinson (ed.), *Social Groups and Identities: Developing the Legacy of Henri Tajfel* (Boston, MA, 1996). For a lucid guide to the full complexity and interpretive nuance of this experimental paradigm, see R. Y. Bourhis et al., "Intergroup Research with the Tajfel Matrices: Methodological Notes," in M. P. Zanna and J. M. Oleson (eds.), *The Psychology of Prejudice* (Hillsdale, 1994), 208–32.

shape real-world behavior was demonstrated outside the laboratory, when factory workers at an aviation engineering company in England were asked to assign wages to their own unit and also to another unit using a Tajfel reward matrix. Workers consistently preferred the choice with the greatest differential favoring their unit over the other unit, even if a more profitable assignation was available that gave them more money in absolute terms, but at the cost of favoring the other unit.[11]

In 1949, 1953, and 1954 psychologists posing as camp attendants assembled boys at summer camps in Connecticut and at Robbers Cave State Park in Oklahoma. The boys had been deliberately selected to ensure the greatest possible uniformity at the outset: they were all aged between eleven and twelve, were white and middle class, and stemmed from similar backgrounds. After a few days of joint activities, the boys were divided into two groups and sent to separate camps some distance apart at opposite ends of the park. In the first two experiments, friendships that had formed in the initial days were deliberately split between the groups; in the third, the boys did not meet as a single group beforehand and assembled separately at their respective camps.

Separate activities were organized, and soon the boys had cohered into two distinct groups, each with its leaders and norms, as well as group names (such as "Eagles" and "Rattlers"). The two groups were then brought together for competitive activities, such as soft ball or tug-of-war. The winners were given prizes, and the losers received nothing. Intergroup hostility emerged rapidly, to the point that even non-competitive meetings (such as shared dinners or movies) became occasions for aggressive display, such as shouted insults, displays of bravado, and scuffling, especially on the part of the winning group toward the losing group. Erstwhile cross-group friendships were replaced with hostility. Reduction of intergroup conflict was not effected through contact alone but by both groups being forced to cooperate in attaining mutually desired "superordinate" goals (such as helping to start a broken-down truck bringing food to a joint outing). This final stage of cooperation, however, was only reached on the third occasion, since the intense hostility led to the premature abandonment of the first two experiments.[12]

---

[11] R. J. Brown, "Divided We Fall: An Analysis of Relations between Sections of a Factory Workforce," in Tajfel (ed.), *Differentiation between Social Groups*, 395–429. For instance, most workers chose an assignation of £67.30 for themselves where £66.30 went to the other unit, when they could have chosen £69.30 for themselves but with £70.30 going to the other unit. The desire to favor the ingroup trumped even the desire for personal enrichment.

[12] M. Sherif et al. *Intergroup Conflict and Cooperation: The Robbers Cave Experiment* (Norman, 1961); M. Sherif, *Group Conflict and Co-operation: Their Social Psychology* (London, 1966), 71–93.

These experiments demonstrate, once more, the profound grip of group processes on the human psyche. In this instance, mutually incompatible goals led to intense and escalating conflict that could only be reduced by cancelling the experiment or by setting higher goals that required the cooperation of both groups to attain. Ingroup favoritism was elicited by means of a game involving bean counts. Beans were scattered in the grass and the groups asked to pick up and bag as many as possible within a time limit set by the experimenters. The bags were then held up against a strong light, so that beans could be vaguely discerned inside. Each group gave an estimate of how many beans were in their bag and how many in their opponents'. In fact, both groups were shown the very same bag with exactly thirty beans in it. Unsurprisingly, each group overestimated its total bean count while underestimating that of their opponents. The habitually victorious group displayed the greater differential in their estimates.

The Robbers Cave experiment protocol was repeated subsequently in Britain, Lebanon, and Russia.[13] Although the precise behavior of the subjects was not identical in each case (it could hardly be expected to be), most of the basic group processes noted above were observed, but in varying degrees. Ingroup favoritism made an appearance in all cases, though it trailed off rather than intensified in the British context, and aggression and stereotyping were largely absent from one of the Lebanese groups, even if the opposing side amply compensated for that absence. One of the main conclusions reached by the researchers in these cases is that the actions of the subjects were influenced by long-established social norms and traditions outside the experiment's parameters. In other words, cultural context mediated the manifestation of the mental processes. Given that group processes are situationally salient, none of these observations are terribly surprising.

In 1971 twenty-four male volunteers, all college students selected for their stability and overwhelming "normalcy," were divided by the flip of a coin into "guards" and "prisoners" by the psychologist Philip Zimbardo and his team at Stanford University.[14] Early one morning, the prisoners – who had no idea that they had been selected as such – were rounded up by police, booked, fingerprinted, photographed, and transported to a simulated "prison" in a basement on the Stanford campus. The prison had three-man cells, a solitary confinement cell, and an exercise yard. Here the

---

[13] See Smith and Bond, *Social Psychology across Cultures*, 26–8.
[14] By "normalcy" is meant that subjects did not have a history of violence, criminality, drug abuse, etc.

subjects were to be housed for two weeks under a strict prison-like regime. Psychologists had wired the prison for around-the-clock observation.

Some (though not all) of the guards showed very quickly that they revelled in their power and began to treat their charges sadistically. Loud and disruptive counts of prisoners were staged at regular intervals, especially in the dead of night. A "rebellion" by some prisoners was put down using force: prisoners were forced into their cells and sprayed with fire extinguishers. In the wake of the rebellion, harassment of prisoners increased in intensity and inventiveness. At various times, prisoners were made to do push ups, sent to solitary confinement, stripped naked, denied access to food or the toilets, chained together with bags over their heads, or forced to clean toilet bowls with their bare hands. As the stress mounted, some prisoners began to show signs of such emotional strain that they had to be released. With conditions deteriorating rapidly, Zimbardo cancelled the experiment after only six days, fearing that the situation had spiralled out of control.[15]

This experimental model has much to say about issues of authority and obedience, power and powerlessness, and the organization of penal communities. But it also demonstrates the powerful grip of group (or social) identity over the human mind, all the more so since membership had been assigned arbitrarily on the basis of sortition. Both guards and prisoners rapidly cohered as distinct groups with their own normative patterns of behavior. For most of the prisoners, this started out as submissiveness, but their total subjection to the will of the guards reached the point where their group cohesion dissolved entirely and some individuals suffered severe emotional stress. For the guards, group norms of authoritarianism prevailed. Within the concept of the experiment those norms tended to sanction cruelty, so that the formation of the group "guards" acted as a catalyst for the rapid emergence of prejudice (see chapter 5), aggression, and vindictiveness. Even though some guards were "good guys" and treated the prisoners well, none did anything to prevent the degradation and discomfort inflicted by the more enthusiastic members of their group, and none questioned the authoritarian requirements of their role as guards. It is not that the sadistic guards (who had a particularly aggressive leader) were inherently

[15] C. Haney et al., "Interpersonal Dynamics in a Simulated Prison," *International Journal of Criminology and Penology* 1 (1973), 69–97. For more recent reassessments, see P. G. Zimbardo et al. "Reflections on the Stanford Prison Experiment: Genesis, Transformations, Consequences," in T. Blass (ed.), *Obedience to Authority: Current Perspectives on the Milgram Paradigm* (Mahwah, 2000), 193–237; P. G. Zimbardo, *The Lucifer Effect: Understanding How Good People Turn Evil* (New York, 2007). A website is also devoted to the experiment (www.prisonexp.org; accessed Jan. 21, 2010) and a video of it is also available, *Quiet Rage: The Stanford Prison Study*. The German film, *Das Experiment* (2000), offers a fictionalized version of these events.

evil, brutal, or inhumane to begin with. But in certain circumstances, they could become so and, just as strikingly, were given free rein by their more passive colleagues, who stood by and did nothing. Indeed, the experiment's director, Philip Zimbardo, became so immersed in his own role as "prison warden" that he not only sanctioned the harsh treatment of prisoners but even took part in planning some of it. It took strident objections to conditions in the prison from one of his former graduate students to break the illusion and end the experiment. In looking back after thirty years, Zimbardo notes how the Stanford Prison Experiment demonstrates "the power of social situations to overwhelm individual dispositions and even degrade the quality of human nature."[16]

In 2001–2, under the auspices of BBC television, two leading British psychologists repeated the prison experiment protocol as a television series that was broadcast in four, one-hour installments.[17] While the course of events in the BBC prison did not exactly mirror Zimbardo's results, the same group processes were once more manifested, albeit differently than at Stanford. In many ways, they were even more interesting. This time, the prisoners formed a coherent group, but the guards did not. In particular, the guards were reluctant to behave tyrannically. The apparent weakness and vacillation of the guards emboldened the prisoners, who "rebelled" and broke the guards' authority, with the result that everyone, guards and prisoners alike, agreed to form a single commune run on the principle of egalitarianism. But when the commune – in essence, a single group formed from two prior factions – failed to develop rules (norms) that everyone could agree on, a subgroup of four authoritarians plotted to take over the commune and establish a harsh and rigid regime (black berets and sunglasses were to be the order of the day). Surprisingly, their noxious

---

[16] Zimbardo et al., "Reflections," 193–4. His analysis, however, is not uncontested. S. Reicher and S. A. Haslam argue forcefully that the guards did not resort to cruelty out of a mindless submission to circumstances, nor did their cruelty emerge as a "natural" consequence of group membership (as Zimbardo insists). Rather, they note, Zimbardo himself helped construct their harsh attitudes toward the prisoners, and the guards had in their midst strong and aggressive personalities who cowed their fellows. That is, leadership and intragroup dynamics – not helpless and unthinking submission to the context – were key elements in generating the degradation that Zimbardo rightly deplores in the quote above; see Reicher et al., "Making a Virtue of Evil" and items cited in next note.

[17] See S. A. Haslam and S. D. Reicher, *A User's Guide to "The Experiment": Exploring Groups and Power* (London, 2002); S. D. Reicher and S. A. Haslam, "Social Psychology, Science, and Surveillance: Understanding *The Experiment*," *Social Psychology Review* 5 (2002), 7–17; S. D. Reicher and S. A. Haslam, "On the Agency of Individuals and Groups: Lessons from the BBC Prison Study," in T. Postmes and J. Jetten (eds.), *Individuality and the Group: Advances in Social Identity* (London, 2006), 237–57.

scheme found wider support within the failing commune than the experimenters anticipated. The experiment was cancelled, however, before the
authoritarians could make their plan a reality, for fear of the consequences.
The study again highlighted how group processes are not in themselves
pathological or inherently nasty. On the positive side, functioning groups
lent the subjects a sense of validation, worth, cooperation, solidarity, and
agency (among the prisoners initially). On the negative side, when groups
failed, subjects fell into depression and frustration, and were willing to
contemplate authoritarian solutions as the commune foundered. As with
the Stanford scenario, the power of circumstance to guide the directions
taken by group processes is what stands out.[18]

Crowds

Crowds are a particular type of group, defined by their large size and
emotional volatility.[19] They are a problematic category, in part because
analysis of crowds predates the emergence of social psychology as a distinct discipline in the 1920s. The classic appraisals of crowd behavior,
rooted in nineteenth-century ideas, surmise that in crowds the individual
is subsumed into a collective mind. Stripped of personal responsibility and
cognition, crowd members feel a tremendous sense of power, succumb to
their animal instincts, and behave in deviant, often horrible ways. Behavior
spreads through the crowd by "contagion," a process whereby members,
rendered mindless in the crowd, are unable to resist any stimuli that come
their way. This generates the observable suggestibility of the crowd state.
Such were the basic propositions of Gustave Le Bon, in his book *The
Crowd: A Study of the Popular Mind*, which has been continuously in print
since it was first published in French in 1895. Le Bon suggested that in a
crowd "a man descends several rungs in the ladder of civilization. Isolated,
he may be a cultivated individual; in a crowd, he is a barbarian – that is,
a creature acting by instinct."[20] Le Bon's interests lay not with spectators,

---

[18] Note that the Haslam/Reicher analysis places greater emphasis on the role of active agency and the
impact of leadership on the directions taken by the groups than does Zimbardo, who stresses the
power of the situation to "overwhelm" more passive agents.

[19] When does a group become a crowd? This is unclear. Evolutionary biologists suggest that humans
evolved to deal with a circle of family, friends, and acquaintances of 90 and 220 individuals and
note that membership in hunter-gatherer groups typically numbers around 150 (the mean between
90–220); see Ehrlich, *Human Natures*, 157–9, 171–4, 300–4. Perhaps when the membership of a
gathering exceeds a couple of hundred, our "natural" expectations of group-size no longer function
and crowd dynamics supervene.

[20] G. Le Bon, *The Crowd: A Study of the Popular Mind*, 2nd edn. (New York, 1897), 36. The basic
tenets of Le Bon's interpretation continue to find support; see, e.g., E. Canetti, *Crowds and Power*,

but with the sort of active crowds he had witnessed during the Paris Commune of 1871 and, understandably, the main focus of subsequent work has been on the processes by which crowds become violent (as rioters, mass suicides, perpetrators of pogroms or genocide, etc.). Since we are interested in the crowd's rather more passive participation in violence as spectators (though the Roman arena demanded some participation on the part of the spectators), the mental conditions engendered by mere membership in a crowd are more pertinent to our purposes.

There is much to criticize in Le Bon's model. A collective mind is a metaphysical rather than a scientific proposition: its existence cannot be proven or disproven or even tested. It is evident that not all crowds are inevitably barbaric – movements for social justice (e.g., India's independence movement, or American civil rights marches) or resistance to tyranny (e.g., popular demonstrations against Eastern Bloc regimes in 1989) can generate entirely peaceful crowds. So, at best, the Le Bonian model applies only to certain kinds of crowds, and even then only under certain conditions. Le Bon's conservative political orientation made him suspicious of mass popular gatherings. Despite these problems, one of his basic premises – the loss of individual identity in crowd or group contexts – has been recast more recently as "deindividuation."[21] Contrary to Le Bon's notion of a crowd descending into savagery, it has been demonstrated that deindividuation need not in itself lead to aggression or cruelty – it can also generate resistance to such impulses. What really matters are the stimulus cues of a given context that shape the norms of the crowd.[22] Deindividuation is widely accepted as the factor that makes crowd members more suggestible than they would be individually, and its basic premise is rooted in the conviction that individual identity is lost in a crowd.

Not all are convinced by the deindividuation model.[23] A very different approach employs the basic group processes of social identity and social categorization surveyed above as a way to understand crowd dynamics.[24]

---

trans. C. Stewart (London, 1962; reprint New York, 1984); S. Moscovici, *The Age of the Crowd: A Historical Treatise on Mass Psychology* (Cambridge, 1985), 92–105.

[21] See, e.g., E. Diener, "Deindividuation: The Absence of Self-Awareness and Self-Regulation in Group Members," in P. B. Paulus (ed.), *The Psychology of Group Influence*, 2nd edn. (Hillsdale, 1989), 209–42.

[22] For summaries with reference to relevant literature, see Brown, *Group Processes*, 10–19; Reicher, "Psychology of Crowd Dynamics."

[23] The main objection is that, while deindividuation successfully accounts for a Le Bonian submergence of individuality, it does not explain the crowd's sense of power; see Reicher, "Psychology of Crowd Dynamics," 187–9.

[24] See, e.g., S. D. Reicher, "The Determination of Collective Behaviour," in H. Tajfel (ed.), *Social Identity and Intergroup Relations* (Cambridge, 1982), 41–83; and see previous note.

Most explanations of crowd behavior, including Le Bon's, rely on observations made from without. Analysis from inside the crowd reveals a very different picture. Although they are prone to spontaneous action, crowds rarely congregate spontaneously. Rather, they tend to assemble for particular purposes, such as to participate in protest marches, listen to concerts, or watch sporting events. Thus crowds usually have a purpose, which makes their supposed mindlessness *a priori* unlikely. In many crowd situations there is another group (police, rival fans) who constitute an outgroup for the crowd to focus its attention on. Crowd members thus bring to the assembly a social identity against which they categorize both themselves and, where they are present, members of a visible outgroup. Furthermore, a crowd often comprises many subgroups (friends, family members, neighbors, co-workers), who are well known to each other and who can see each other in the crowd. This mutual acquaintance and visibility reinforces and validates actions taken by crowd members. Rioters, for instance, whose actions appear maniacal and bestial from the outside, can speak afterwards of those same actions as generating feelings of purpose, solidarity, and meaning.[25]

The documentation of crowd activity, particularly what crowds actually *do*, can reveal a patterning of action that in turn maps the contours of the crowd's social understanding(s). For instance, surviving accounts by contemporaries of the Peasants' Revolt in England in 1381 express surprise at the purposeful actions of the rampaging mob. The rioting peasants did not target wealthy households and estates at random, but rather focused their rage on those with particular symbolic associations; a similar discernment was displayed in selecting victims for lynching.[26] Agitators and leaders are usually invoked to explain such patterning in mob action, but it occurs also in the absence of any clear leadership. Natalie Davis has shown how the particular types of violence perpetrated by Catholics and Huguenots during religious riots in France in the sixteenth century reflected widespread popular understandings of what manifested the pollution of heresy: for the

---

[25] S. D. Reicher and J. Potter, "Psychological Theory as Intergroup Perspective: A Comparative Analysis of 'Scientific' and 'Lay' Accounts of Crowd Events," *Human Relations* 38 (1985), 167–89; S. D. Reicher, "'The Battle of Westminster:' Developing the Social Identity Model of Crowd Behaviour in Order to Explain the Initiation and Development of Collective Conflict," *European Journal of Social Psychology* 26 (1996), 115–34; S. Reicher et al., "More on Deindividuation, Power Relations between Groups and the Expression of Social Identity: Three Studies on the Effects of Visibility on the In-Group," *British Journal of Social Psychology* 37 (1998), 15–41.
[26] R. B. Dobson, *The Peasants' Revolt of 1381* (New York, 1970), 155–300 (my thanks to Professor Laurel Carrington for this observation and reference). Contemporaries made analogous observations about the Penlez rioters in London in July 1749; see Linebaugh, "Tyburn Riot," 89–102.

Protestants, it lay in the rituals and objects of Catholic idolatry (as they saw it), and so they tended to vandalize crucifixes, churches, statues, holy water, the host, and so forth; for Catholics, heresy was a personal failing of the individual, and so they mostly targeted the Huguenots themselves, whether alive or dead.[27] Both sides took collective action to change the social environment to accord better with their shared (and competing) understandings of that environment. Change was actively sought by rioting on this occasion, but there are times when hoped-for or ideal outcomes are ritually acted out, and this provides satisfaction to those watching: the various violent spectacles surveyed in the previous chapter offer some ready examples, as do modern Hollywood movies that affirm, say, Western or American values. We shall defer for now surveying the actions of Roman arena crowds (see next chapter), but the key point to note here is that what they did and said is likely to reflect things they understood about the world, either as it was or as it should be, and that enacting such understandings played a role in drawing spectators to arena events.

All of this suggests that rather than surrendering their individuality to a collective mind, as Le Bon imagined, crowd members alter their social identities to accord with the larger crowd's norms, which are in turn shaped by shared understandings that underlie the crowd's identity (they are genuinely "shared understandings," because the crowd has assembled for some purpose known to all in advance). Normative behavior becomes defined by crowd actions rather than by individual values. While crowd members are subject to a set of prior expectations for both self-categorization and the categorization of others, the size of the crowd often makes the modes of conformity to its norms unclear, unless the crowd is focused on a strong leader (such as a speaker or an entertainer). In the absence of such a leader, crowd members draw their cues from the people immediately around them who, it will be remembered, are often known to them. This explains how, in some circumstances but not in others, crowd behavior can become volatile and spiral out of control: much depends on the circumstances and context of the crowd's gathering.

[27] N. Z. Davis, "The Rites of Violence: Religious Riot in Sixteenth-Century France," *Past and Present* 59 (1973), 51–91, esp. 75–85. Similar observations are made about food rioters by E. P. Thompson, "The Moral Economy of the English Crowd in the Eighteenth Century," *Past and Present* 50 (1971), 76–136. (My thanks to Professor Stephen Reicher for the Davis and Thompson references.) The approach has also been applied to the pivotal events in Athens in 508/7 BC, where collective action by the *demos* is argued to have saved the city from long-term impotence as an appendage of Spartan dominance; see J. Ober, "The Athenian Revolution of 508/7 BC: Violence, Authority, and the Origins of Democracy," in L. Kurke and C. Dougherty (eds.), *Cultural Poetics in Archaic Greece* (Cambridge, 1993), 215–32 (= J. Ober, *The Athenian Revolution* [Princeton, 1996], 34–52).

A key element in the social-identity model of crowd dynamics is that crowd norms are bounded by a shared understanding of category meanings and the identities that are linked to them. That is to say, crowd members usually know in advance why they are gathering, what the gathering means to their sense of self, what outgroups (if any) will be present, what the prior relationship to those outgroups has been in the past and ought to be at the gathering, and so forth. Such shared understandings will usually connect to (if not derive from) the wider experience of the people who comprise the crowd. In the case of religious riots in sixteenth-century France, for instance, the mobs' conflicting views of what it meant to be Catholic or Calvinist were informed by a lifetime's exposure to church doctrines, purificatory rites, and punitive traditions, and these are what shaped their actions during specific disturbances, which often broke out during holy processions and sacral festivals.[28] It may be that crowds, far from erasing identity, offer unique opportunities for people to express their identities as fully as possible. Work on the role of collective phenomena in giving people powerful feelings of affirmation and validation, cohesion and solidarity, or power and agency is still in the nascent stages.[29] It can reasonably be surmised that the crowd's sense of its own empowerment rests not on deindividuation but rather on the processes that generate feelings of affirmation, cohesion, and belonging. It must be stressed that these psychological processes ought not to be conceptualized as mechanistic and automatic, inevitably generating behavior in a mental domino effect. The specific contextual and cultural mediation of social identities is no less important than the shared psychological processes that underlie them.[30] The crowd, then, is a fine example of how specific contextual factors interlace with shared psychological processes to generate behavior.

From the outside, English football hooligans appear to be a paradigmatic example of the mindless, Le Bonian crowd. The documentation of their activities from within, however, offers a glimpse into the soul of this most

---

[28] Davis, "Rites of Violence," esp. 81–5 and 90–1.
[29] Reicher, "Psychology of Crowd Dynamics," 197. See also S. Reicher and S. A. Haslam, "Beyond Help: A Social Psychology of Collective Solidarity and Social Cohesion," in S. Stürmer and M. Snyder (eds.), *The Psychology of Prosocial Behavior: Group Processes, Intergroup Relations and Helping* (Chichester, 2010), 289–309; the Prayag Magh Mela Research Group, "Living the Magh Mela at Prayag: Collective Identity, Collective Experience, and the Impact of Participation in a Mass Event," *Psychological Studies* 52 (2007), 293–301 (my thanks to Professor Reicher for providing me with pre-publication manuscripts of these papers).
[30] S. D. Reicher, "The Context of Social Psychology: Domination, Resistance, and Change," *Political Psychology* 25 (2004), 40–62.

unruly of crowds.[31] The hooligans are organized as "firms," comprising subgroups of some thirty to forty individuals loyal to well-known leaders, each of whom commands a set of sub-lieutenants. Each football club has its own firms. Members have a strong sense of group identity, or rather, a set of nested identities, which are expressed through tattoos, placards, flags, songs, and chants. Depending on the context, their collective identity revolves around the team (and its firm), city, or nation. As football fans, they gather together for an ostensible purpose, to watch football. But their deeper purposes derive from their nested group identities, namely, to uphold the honor of the team, firm, city, or nation, and to dominate their opponents and denigrate their corresponding identities. Thus the identities expressed on any given occasion are deliberately confrontational: chants of "Fuck the Pope" in Italy or defense of Catholics in England are aimed specifically at offending Catholic and Protestant bystanders respectively.[32] The weekly gatherings and associated violence, so mindless to the outside observer, are reckoned extremely consequential by those engaged in it. As one supporter put it: "We look forward to Saturdays [when football matches are played] all week long. It's the most meaningful thing in our lives. It's a religion, really. That's how important it is to us. Saturday is our day of worship."[33] From this surprising source comes as stark an expression of the affirming value of participation in collective action as one could imagine: beating people up at football matches was, for this subject, tantamount to a religious experience.

THE POMPEII RIOT

The foregoing is not to argue that modern English football thugs represent close analogs for ancient Roman arena spectators or, indeed, for sports spectators in general. For a start, Roman amphitheater crowds did not riot or attack other "fans" as a matter of course.[34] The only arena riot on record

---

[31] G. Armstrong, *Football Hooligans: Knowing the Score* (Oxford, 1998); B. Buford, *Among the Thugs* (New York, 1992). Both books are written by authors who spent many years traveling with hooligans and even took part in their riots. See also D. Brimson, *Eurotrashed: The Rise and Rise of Europe's Football Hooligans* (London, 2003); L. Johnstone, "Riot by Appointment: An Examination of the Nature and Structure of Seven Hard-Core Football Hooligan Groups," in D. Canter and L. Alison (eds.), *The Social Psychology of Crime: Groups, Teams, and Networks* (Aldershot, 2000), 153–88.

[32] Buford, *Thugs*, 43, 95. [33] Ibid., 114.

[34] The same cannot be said of the chariot-racing factions or, bizarrely, supporters of stage performers; see below, ch. 4, n. 64. On the circus factions of the Early and High Empire, see Friedländer, *Sittengeschichte Roms*, vol. II, 32–40; Kyle, *Sport and Spectacle*, 309–10; for the Byzantine period,

is that between the Pompeians and the Nucerians, which took place in Pompeii's amphitheater in AD 59. It is an instructive episode. The spark sprang from an intense local rivalry between Pompeii, a Roman colony since Sullan times, and Nuceria, a colony since the age of Augustus but one that had recently earned enviable imperial recognition – and with it enhanced status – when Nero settled some veterans there only two years earlier (Tac. *Ann.* 13.31.2). Tacitus, in fact, records that an ex-senator, named Livineius Regulus, was convicted of having planned and organized the riot and so suffered banishment as a result, along with unnamed "others" who were his accomplices. Illegal associations (*collegia*) were also banned at Pompeii.[35] Given what we have seen above about the purposefulness of crowds rooted in a shared sense of identity, there is no need to follow the Roman authorities in seeing the riot as deliberately planned and executed, though that possibility cannot be entirely ruled out. It is just as likely that the riot emerged spontaneously from how crowd processes manifested themselves on this occasion.

Aspects of the riot strongly echo facets of crowd dynamics as we have just documented them. The crowd had gathered for a reason, to see a spectacle. The Pompeii riot was essentially over competing social identities anchored in intercity rivalry, which is also one of the driving motives of the English football hooligan. Tacitus charts the crowd's road to violence: what began as taunts between Nucerians and Pompeians became shouted abuse, which grew into stone-throwing, and ended with swords and knives. Similar escalation marked the "Riot of the Statues" in Antioch in AD 387, described by Libanius (*Or.* 19.25–33). It started out as a protest against added taxes and ended in widespread vandalism against the emperor's statues; and journalist

see A. Cameron, *Circus Factions: Blues and Greens at Byzantium* (Oxford, 1976), and J. H. W. G. Liebeschuetz, *Decline and Fall of the Roman City* (Oxford, 2001), 203–20 (at 213–14 Liebeschuetz expressly likens the Byzantine circus factions to English football hooligans) and 249–57 for the riots they were involved in. For discussion of associations of gladiatorial fans, see below (ch. 6, pp. 219–21). Fanaticism could run deep. The funeral of the Red Team driver Felix in the first century AD saw one fan self-immolate on the pyre; see Pliny *HN* 7.168. The emperor Gaius (Caligula) is reported to have had eager circus fans beaten (or killed) with clubs, when they tried to seize free seats at night and/or protest against taxes (Suet. *Cal.* 26.4; see also Dio 59.28.11 and Jos. *AJ* 19.24–6). Note also the riot sparked by the silversmith Demetrius at a public meeting in Ephesus' theater (*Acts* 19:25–7), which may implicate a professional *collegium* of artisans in orchestrating trouble.

[35] Tac. *Ann.* 14.17 = T.26; *CIL* 4.1293, 4.1329, 4.2183. The riot is also famously depicted in a fresco from the House of Anicetus (at 1.3.23); see L. Jacobelli, *Gladiators at Pompeii* (Los Angeles, 2003), 71–3 (fig. 58). For analysis of this event, see D. L. Bomgardner, *The Story of the Roman Amphitheatre* (London, 2000), 50–3; H. Galsterer, "Politik in römischen Städten: Die 'Seditio' des Jahren 59 n. Chr. in Pompeii," in W. Eck et al. (eds.), *Studien zur antiken Sozialgeschichte: Festschrift Friedrich Vittinghoff* (Cologne, 1980), 323–38; W. O. Moeller, "The Riot of AD 59 at Pompeii," *Historia* 19 (1970), 84–95.

Bill Buford traces from personal experience a strikingly similar sequence of events in modern football riots.[36] So far as we can tell, the Pompeii riot was a singular event in the history of the Roman *munera*.[37] The value of the incident, as well as the riot in Antioch, lies in how the sequence of actions of modern turbulent crowds finds echo in the ancient evidence; it is reasonable to infer that the mental processes behind that sequence are also comparable. In both contexts, violence is rooted in competing social identities, and mob action builds to a crescendo rather than commencing at the most intense level. There is no good reason to doubt that the rioters at Pompeii were somehow immune to the well-documented processes of social identity and categorization; and the background against which these mental dynamics played out on this one occasion in AD 59 led to intracrowd rioting.

It has been noted that Tacitus, who was very careful with his word choice, describes the spectacle on that fateful day as a "gladiator-like spectacle" (*gladiatorium spectaculum*), rather than the more common "spectacle of gladiators" (*gladiatorum spectaculum*).[38] He also notes that the senate banned "a similar gathering" (*eius modi coetus*) at Pompeii, rather than *munera* or *spectacula* as such. Given that the senate also disbanded illegal *collegia* at Pompeii, a likely candidate for the "gladiator-like spectacle" is some sort of non-lethal, martial competition between youth associations (*collegia iuvenum*) held in the amphitheater.[39] The presence of large numbers of Nucerians at the event suggests that the youth associations of the two towns had come together to compete against each other.[40] Indeed, in

---

[36] Buford, *Thugs*, 81–93 (Turin) and 282–313 (Cagliari in Sardinia).

[37] A passage in the *Digest* (48.19.28.3) reporting turbulent claques of *iuvenes* who sometimes disrupt unspecified *spectacula* is too vague to be interpreted as referring to regular trouble at amphitheater events.

[38] *Gladiatorum spectaculum*: Tac. *Hist.* 2.67, 2.71, 2.94, 3.32, *Ann.* 3.31.4, 4.62.2, 12.57.2, 13.31.4, 15.32.3. He twice uses the phrase *gladiatorium munus*, where *munus* leaves no doubt that a regular exhibition of gladiators is denoted: *Ann.* 4.63.2 (in express connection with a disastrous show at Fidenae) and *Ann.* 15.34.2 (a *gladiatorium munus* given by Vatinius). *Munus gladiatorium* is widely attested epigraphically to denote regular gladiatorial spectacles; see Fora, *Munera Gladiatoria*, 41 n. 123.

[39] It is known that such youth organizations could have gladiatorial trainers attached to them, perhaps for just this sort of competition; see Apul. *Apol.* 98.7, *AE* 1935.27 = *EAOR* 3.64, *EAOR* 2.36 and 39. On these organizations in general, see P. Ginestet, *Les organisations de la jeunesse dans l'Occident romain*, Collection Latomus 213 (Brussels, 1991). Note also M. Kleijwegt, *Ancient Youth: The Ambiguity of Youth and the Absence of Adolescence in Greco-Roman Society* (Amsterdam, 1991), esp. 109–10 on youth organizations and training.

[40] For the details, see Moeller, "Riot," esp. 90–1, accepted by Galsterer, "Politik," 325–7. Advertisements for games at Pompeii between AD 59 and 69 specify only processions, hunts, and athletes, but no gladiators; see *CIL* 4.1181 = Sabbatini Tumolesi, *Gladiatorum Paria*, 48–9 (no. 19); 4.3883 = Sabbatini Tumolesi, *Gladiatorum Paria*, 40 (no. 12); 4.7818a; 4.7989a = Sabbatini Tumolesi, *Gladiatorum Paria*, 47–8 (no. 18); 4.7993 = Sabbatini Tumolesi, *Gladiatorum Paria*, 40 (no. 13).

this instance, the spectators were not only antagonistic toward each other at the outset, but their attention was focused on representatives of their two towns as they competed against each other, so that preexisting tensions blossomed into violence in the stands. If this interpretation is correct, then the only amphitheater riot on record had nothing to do with regular arena spectacles. By AD 59, Nucerians must have been coming to Pompeii for decades to see spectacles in the amphitheater there. It is telling that trouble only arose when the show was not a gladiatorial *munus* at all, but rather a spectacle that brought to the fore competing social identities latent within the crowd.

So much for rioters and thugs. What of the more typical, passive arena crowd? What can be said of them?

AMPHITHEATERS AND SPECTATOR DEMOGRAPHICS

The way spectators sat in Roman amphitheaters has been well studied and many observations made about its symbolic, political, and sociological ramifications.[41] However, the psychological implications of spectator demographics and seating dispositions have yet to be properly appreciated. The ancient evidence falls into four categories: archaeological, literary, epigraphic, and (to a lesser extent) iconographic. While gladiatorial spectacles, hunts, and executions were staged in the circus, the forum, stadia, or theaters, the amphitheater was a building type designed specifically for viewing such shows.[42] Most surviving examples are in ruinous condition,

This would suggest that gladiatorial bouts were indeed banned by the senate, although two caveats apply. First, the texts have been assigned to this period precisely on the assumption that the absence of gladiators reflects the ban from Rome; see, e.g., J. L. Franklin Jr., "Cn. Alleius Nigidius Maius and the Amphitheatre: *Munera* and a Distinguished Career at Ancient Pompeii," *Historia* 46 (1997), 442–4. But this need not be the case, given the range of events staged as arena spectacles. Second, even if the senatorial ban did cover all gladiatorial bouts at Pompeii in these years, that fact need not necessarily reflect the character of the riotous spectacle of AD 59; the senate may just have been cautious and/or punitive in banning any sort of gladiator-related spectacle in the wake of the riot.

[41] See, e.g., T. Bollinger, *Theatralis Licentia: Die Publikumsdemonstrationen an den öffentlichen Spielen im Rom der früheren Kaiserzeit und ihre Bedeutung im politischen Leben* (Basel, 1969), 1–24; Bomgardner, *Story of the Roman Amphitheatre*, esp. 9–20 (for a case study of seating in the Colosseum); Edmondson, "Dynamic Arenas"; J. C. Edmondson, "Public Spectacles and Roman Social Relations," in *Ludi Romani: Espectáculos en Hispania Romana, Museo Nacional de Arte Romano, Mérida, 29 de julio – 13 octubre, 2002* (Córdoba, 2002), 41–63; E. Rawson, "*Discrimina Ordinum*: The *Lex Julia Theatralis*," *PBSR* 55 (1987), 83–114 (= E. Rawson, *Roman Culture and Society: Collected Papers* [Oxford, 1991], 508–45); P. Rose, "Spectators and Spectator Comfort in Roman Entertainment Buildings: A Study in Functional Design," *PBSR* 73 (2005), 99–130, esp. 100–2; A. Scobie, "Spectator Security and Comfort at Gladiatorial Games," *Nikephoros* 1 (1988), 191–243. See also items in n. 95.

[42] See, e.g., Livy 44.18.8, Pliny *HN* 8.53, *RG* 22.3, Suet. *Claud.* 21.2, Varro, *Sat. Men.* 296, (circus); Livy 2.16.9, Dion. Hal. *Ant. Rom.* 6.30.1, Vitr. *De arch.* 5.1.1 (forum); Dio 78(79).25.3, Eus. *Eccl. Hist.*

but some are sufficiently well preserved to allow the internal arrangements of the *cavea* to be discerned. Capacities can be calculated from the seating area of the auditorium. Using this method, a recent calculation of the seating capacity in the Colosseum in Rome reaches a total of 54,760.[43] This was clearly an untypical case, since it was the largest and most important amphitheater in the empire. A survey of North African monuments reveals an ascending scale of potential seating capacities, ranging from 2,300 at the lower end (a military amphitheater at Tigava Castra in modern Algeria) to 44,000 at the higher end (at Carthage). Average capacities appear related to mode of construction. Where seats rested on simple embankments, an average crowd capacity of 8,740 has been calculated (drawn from fifteen examples); those with filled-in compartments in the *cavea*'s substructures had average capacities of 11,243 (fourteen examples); while three examples with vaulted substructures, modeled on the Colosseum in Rome, could hold an average of 31,933 (Carthage, Thysdrus, Bararus).[44] It is safe to say, therefore, that arena crowds habitually numbered in the thousands, and not uncommonly in the tens of thousands.

In some cases (Pompeii, Nîmes, Arles, El Djem), the seating is well enough preserved for its arrangement to be studied more closely.[45] Rows of

---

4.15.16, HA *Hadr.* 19.3 (stadia); Nic. Dam. *Vit. Caes.* 26A, Dio 44.16.2 (theater). For epigraphic testimony from Italy, see Fora, *Munera Gladiatoria*, 67–9. Tacitus reports (*Hist.* 2.95.1) that gladiatorial displays were held in each district throughout Rome (*tota urbe vicatim*) to celebrate Vitellius' birthday in September AD 69. The venues of such displays are not obvious, but were presumably temporary (and wooden). On the origins of the amphitheater, see Bomgardner, *Story of the Roman Amphitheatre*, 32–60; J.-C. Golvin, *L'amphithéâtre romain: essai sur la théorisation de sa forme et de ses fonctions*, 2 vols. (Paris, 1988), vol. I, 39–63; J.-C. Golvin, "Origine, fonction et forme de l'amphithéâtre romain," in Domergue et al. (eds.), *Spectacula I*, 15–27; Welch, "The Roman Arena in Late-Republican Italy"; Welch, *Roman Amphitheatre*, 30–72.

43 Golvin, *L'amphithéâtre romain*, 380–1 (who postulates three spectators per square meter); see also Bomgardner, *Story of the Roman Amphitheatre*, 234 n. 40 (in agreement with Golvin). On the capacity of the Colosseum, see also ibid., 17–20. See further A. Gabucci (ed.), *The Colosseum* (Los Angeles, 2001); K. Hopkins and M. Beard, *The Colosseum* (London, 2005); Welch, *Roman Amphitheatre*, 128–62. See also the comments of K. M. Coleman, *Martial: Liber Spectaculorum* (Oxford, 2006), lxv–lxxii.

44 Bomgardner, *Story of the Roman Amphitheatre*, 157–83 (survey) and 190–1 (averages). Other major arenas (see ibid., 61–120) include Verona (28,200 or 38,900 depending on whether the *cavea* was topped with a colonnade or wooden seats); Flavian Amphitheater, Puteoli (35,700); Anfiteatro Campano, Capua (47,426); Nîmes (30,500); and Arles (33,400). On average, Bomgardner (ibid., 62) estimates that Imperial amphitheaters held between 40,000 and 60,000 spectators, perhaps reaching 100,000 if standing room was wholly occupied as well; the estimates of Rose ("Spectators," 102–18) are consistent with these figures. Ancient estimates for seating capacities are generally higher. For instance, the Regionary Catalogs cite a capacity of 87,000 for the Colosseum. Coleman (*Liber Spectaculorum*, lxx n. 153) addresses the disparity by noting that ancient people were smaller and probably not as fastidious as moderns in the matter of personal space. Note also the discussion in Futrell, *Blood in the Arena*, 53–76.

45 See Bomgardner, *Story of the Roman Amphitheatre*, 1–31 (Colosseum), 39–58 (Pompeii), 106–20 (Nîmes and Arles) and 146–51 (El Djem); Golvin, *L'amphithéâtre romain*, 341–86, esp. 354–67 for a

seats (*gradus* or *ordines*) were usually divided into three horizontal bands, in increasing distance from the action on the sand: the *ima*, *media*, and *summa cavea*.[46] These concentric bands were often termed *maeniana*.[47] Depending on the luxuriousness of the amphitheater, *maeniana* were separated from one another by a low balustrade (*balteus*) or by a walkway with a raised back wall (*praecinctio*); some *praecinctiones* were raised so that successive *maeniana* were effectively terraced, maximizing the spectators' sight lines on the action below.[48] *Maeniana* were sometimes subdivided into front and rear sections, as was the case at El Djem. The very front row of seats in the amphitheater (and circus) was termed the "podium," which was either subsumed into the first *maenianum* or separated from it by a *balteus*.[49] Stairs gave access to the seats. They ran perpendicular to the *maeniana* and radiated downward toward the arena, thus dividing the tiers vertically into blocks of seats (*cunei*, literally "wedges"). At Pompeii, there are twenty such *cunei* in the *media cavea* (or second *maenianum*) and forty in the *summa*

survey of examples. On the Pompeii amphitheater, see also E. la Rocca, M. and A. de Vos, *Guida archeologica di Pompei* (Verona, 1976), 248–55. Still informative is A. Mau, *Pompeji in Leben und Kunst*, 2nd edn. (Leipzig, 1908), 216–29.

[46] *Cavea* had long been used to designate the viewing area occupied by spectators (Plaut. *Am.* 66). For subdivisions of the *cavea*, see Cic. *Sen.* 48 (*prima cavea*), *Phil.* 1.37 (where the divisions of the *cavea* are inferred in the phrase *a summis, mediis, infimis*) or Suet. *Aug.* 44.2 = T.21 (*media cavea*).

[47] The term *maeniana* was applied to balconies, both public (Pliny *HN* 35.113) and private (Vitr. *De arch.* 5.6.9). As a designation for seating at the amphitheater, see Vitr. *De arch.* 5.1.2 (*maeniana* part of the wooden structures for viewing spectacles in a forum) and *CIL* 6.2059 = 6.32363 = *ILS* 5049 = *EAOR* 6.13 = I.1 (seat assignations in the Colosseum for the Arval Brotherhood, reviewed in detail below). Festus (120L = 135M) records the origin of the term: "Maeniana are named after Maenius the censor, who was the first to extend wooden structures out in front of the columns in the forum to increase the size of the upper viewing areas" (*Maeniana appellata sunt a Maenio censore, qui primus in foro ultra columnas tigna proiecit, quo ampliarentur superiora spectacula*). The passage makes sense, if we imagine wooden balconies extending out from the upper reaches of the basilicas flanking the forum's piazza, a conclusion also reached by Welch, *Roman Amphitheatre*, 32–5. C. Maenius, the most famous member of this family, was censor in 318 BC (*RE* 14.1 [1928], s.v. "Maenius" no. 9 [Münzer]). Golvin (*L'amphithéâtre romain*, 19 n. 41) accepts this early Maenius as the eponymous figure; Rawson ("*Discrimina Ordinum*," 84 n. 10) prefers the later T. Maenius, who was praetor in 186 BC, but never censor. The later date is to be preferred. There is a further complication, however. Festus may confuse an early monument called the *columna Maenia* in the forum with later balconies called *maeniana*; see Coleman, "Entertaining Rome," 249 n. 107; *LTUR*, vol. I, 301–2, s.v. "Columna Maeniana" (Torelli). If so, his explanation for the etymology is misleading. *Maeniana* could be dubbed *primum*, *secundum* and *summum*; the *maenianum secundum*, at the Colosseum at least, may also have been subdivided *I* and *II*, denoting and upper and lower zone, but this depends on how one reads the confusing Arval records assigning seating to the college, especially since this particular passage is badly carved and riddled with errors; see J. Scheid, *Recherches archéologiques à la Magliana: Commentarii Fratrum Arvalium qui Supersunt: les copies épigraphiques des protocoles annuels de la confrérie arvale* (Rome, 1998), 126–9 (no. 48) and commentary.

[48] This could be coupled with a steeper gradient in the upper *maeniana* to facilitate good viewing, as at Thysdrus; see Golvin, *L'amphithéâtre romain*, 344–5. For *praecinctiones* in theaters, see Vitr. *De arch.* 5.3.4, 5.6.2, 5.7.2.

[49] For the podium, see Pliny *HN* 37.45; Juv. *Sat.* 2.147; *AE* 1959.81 (Lyons; Tiberian).

Figure 3 *Cavea* of the amphitheater at Pompeii

cavea (or third *maenianum*), but in other cases the same number of *cunei* is usually found in each of the horizontal sections.[50]

In the front rows (*ima cavea* or first *maenianum*) it is not unusual to find *cuneus*-like divisions. At Pompeii, for instance, six sections are demarcated from each other by short walls (Figs. 3, 4), while at the Colosseum there were originally fourteen *cunei* in the first rank of seats. Two boxes of honor (termed *pulvinaria* or *tribunalia*) were usually situated on the short axes of the podium wall and afforded an optimal view of the proceedings.[51] Usually, the tribunal and the seats on the podium were accessible directly from outside the amphitheater, via special entrances and approach corridors. This was the case even for relatively humble amphitheaters, such as Pompeii's. The crest of the *cavea* could be topped with a colonnade, space for wooden seating, or individual boxes (*tabulationes*), or a combination of such features.

---

[50] Golvin, *L'amphithéâtre romain*, 372–7 (where an average of sixteen *cunei* are known from various examples).

[51] On the *pulvinar*, see C. van den Berg, "The *Pulvinar* in Roman Culture," *TAPA* 138 (2008), 239–73, esp. 258–66. The term applies principally to the viewing box in the circus.

Figure 4 Podium and *cunei* at Pompeii's amphitheater

Given this seating system, a precise seat (*locus* or *linea*) in an arena could be designated quite readily, by *maenianum, cuneus,* and *gradus.*[52] The amphitheater at Verona (possibly of Claudian date) and the Colosseum at Rome both have carved numerals over each entrance, which acted as guides for ticket-holders. Once inside, *cunei* were individually numbered, and the tiers and (sometimes) the individual seats on each tier likewise.[53] The handful of surviving theater and amphitheater tickets (*tesserae*) corroborate these observations by mirroring the designations found on surviving seats. A typical example (from Arles) reads:

[52] Individual places could be marked with paint and/or engraved lines on each row, hence the use of *linea* to denote "seat" or "place"; see Ov. *Ars Am.* 1.141, *Am.* 3.2.19; *CIL* 5.3456 = *EAOR* 2.72 (cited in next note.).

[53] Painted markings have long since faded; J. Kolendo, "La répartition des places aux spectacles et la stratification sociale dans l'Empire Romain: à propos des inscriptions sur les gradins des amphithéâtres et théâtres," *Ktèma* 6 (1981), 301–15, esp. 303. However, the Flavian Amphitheater at Puteoli had carved inscriptions over the entrance to the appropriate stairway: e.g., *AE* 1956.139: *cun(eus)* XXXI ("31st *cuneus*") and, for discussion, A. Maiuri, *Studi e ricerche sull'anfiteatro Flavio Puteolano* (Naples, 1955), 56–60. Note also the second-century example at Lambaesis, *CIL* 8.3293. For numbered tiers and rows, see *CIL* 5.3456 = *EAOR* 2.72 (from Verona), *I (cuneus), loc(us) IIII, lin(ea) I* ("First *cuneus*, section four, place one"). Note also *EAOR* 2.73 and 76 for numbers carved on to seats at Milan. For the complex circulation patterns in the Colosseum, which were regulated by a system of stairways and vaulted ambulatories, see Bomgardner, *Story of the Roman Amphitheatre,* 9–17; Rose, "Spectators."

cav(ea) II, cun(eus) V, grad(us) X, glad(iatorum spectacula) vela

Second *cavea,* fifth *cuneus,* tenth tier; gladiatorial spectacle with awning.

Another, from Pompeii, reads:

cav(ea) II, cun(eus) III, grad(us) VII, Casina Plauti

Second *cavea,* third *cuneus,* seventh tier; Plautus' *Casina.*[54]

That precisely the same system of seat designation was used at both Arles and Pompeii – as well as for very different types of shows – indicates how widespread the system was. Armed with *tesserae* and marked seats, spectators could find their way to their allocated spots quickly and efficiently. It remains unclear to what extent the tickets were paid for or acquired *gratis* through patronage; the unscrupulous selling of tickets cannot be ruled out.[55]

The complexity of the seating in the *cavea* was designed not only for convenience and the efficient movement of people through the building. Social rank was rigidly enforced. Until the early second century BC it seems that people had watched spectacles, of whatever sort, as an undifferentiated mass. In 194 BC senators were separated from the rest and allotted places at the front.[56] Then, in 67 BC, a *lex Roscia* reserved the first fourteen rows at the theater for knights (*equites*).[57] These rows would be immediately behind the senators who, in the theater, would sit in special seats on

---

[54] Both cited in Golvin, *L'amphithéâtre romain,* 353–4. It is noteworthy that these tickets were distributed for specific, named events. *Cavea II* most probably denotes the *media cavea* (or *maenianum secundum*). The holder of such a ticket would therefore be a member of the non-elite.

[55] On the distribution of tickets, see Bollinger, *Theatralis Licentia,* 17–20; Bomgardner, *Story of the Roman Amphitheatre,* 6; M. A. Cavallaro, *Spese e Spettacoli: aspetti economici-strutturali degli spettacoli nella Roma giulio-claudia* (Bonn, 1984), 207–8; Ville, *Gladiature,* 430–2. Martial (*Ep.* 5.24.9 = T.11) describes the popular gladiator Hermes as *divitiae locariorum* ("the riches of the *locarii*"), who would be termed today "ticket touts." Under the Republic, tickets were certainly distributed through patronage (Cic. *Att.* 2.1.5, *Mur.* 72–3), though seats could also be rented out for profit (Plut. *C. Gracch.* 12.3–4). Chamberland ("Gladiatorial Show," 144) suggests that it was habitual for spectators without free seating privileges to be charged entrance fees to arena games; note the inscription (*CIL* 8.6995 = *ILS* 411) that mentions a statue erected "with revenues from seats in the amphitheater on the day of his games" (*ex reditibus locorum amphitheatri [sic] diei muneris*).

[56] Livy 34.44.5, 34.54.3–8; Cic. *Har. Resp.* 24; Val. Max. 2.4.3; J. von Ungern-Sternberg, "Die Einführung speziellen Sitze für die Senatoren bei den Spielen (194 v. Chr.)," *Chiron* 5 (1975), 157–63. The innovation applied to the *ludi Megalenses* and probably extended to theaters and other spectacles shortly thereafter. In surviving amphitheaters, the front rows on the podium are often twice as wide as the other seats, to accommodate the seats of honor (*subsellia*) or double seats (*bisellia*) reserved for senatorial bottoms; see Epict. 1.25.26–7; Golvin, *L'amphithéâtre romain,* 354–7.

[57] Cic. *Phil.* 2.44; Dio 36.42.1; Plut. *Cic.* 13.2–4. Who was eligible to qualify as an *eques* under this law and how further gradations of status within the class of *equites* were maintained is not at all clear; see A. Stein, *Die römische Ritterstand: Ein Beitrag zur Sozial- und Personengeschichte des römischen Reiches* (Munich, 1927), 21–30; Rawson, "*Discrimina Ordinum,*" 102–7.

Figure 5 Dedicatory inscription of the amphitheater at Pompeii

the edge of the orchestra itself and, in amphitheaters, on the podium. Under the Republic, the Vestals enjoyed a favored position at gladiatorial games held in the forum (Cic. *Mur.* 73), and Julius Caesar was awarded the right to sit with the tribunes of the *plebs* in their privileged seats (Dio 44.4.2). Under Caesar, the client king of Judaea Hyrcanus, and his children, gained the right of sitting with the senators during spectacles (Jos. *AJ* 14.210). Socially stratified seating was clearly becoming more refined in the Late Republic. Nevertheless, that Republican magistrates could construct temporary viewing stands for gladiatorial games and hire them out (Plut. *C. Gracch.* 12.3) may suggest a rather loose regulation of non-elite seating under the Republic.

Further evidence of social segregation among Republican spectators at both the theater and gladiatorial spectacles is offered by inscriptions. The dedicatory inscription of the amphitheater at Pompeii (Fig. 5), dating to about 70 BC, states that local magistrates "oversaw the construction of the *spectacula* (i.e., amphitheater) from their own funds and gave the place in perpetuity to the colonists." This refers to the recent settlement in the community of military veterans (*coloni*), who effectively took over the town as its new elite and thereby generated considerable resentment among the now superseded pre-colonial population.[58] In the arena, it has been

---

[58] *CIL* 1².1632 = 10.852 = *ILS* 5627 = *ILLRP* 645. The key phrase is *spectacula . . . de sua | peq(unia) fac(iunda) coer(arunt) et coloneis | locum in perpetuom deder(unt)*. For tensions between colonists and

proposed, this sociopolitical division was made manifest in the seating: the magistrates, decurions, their sons and other honored guests occupied the podium and the *ima cavea*; the new colonists the *media cavea*; and the old Samnite-Oscan inhabitants were relegated to the back.[59] These conditions were peculiar to Pompeii, of course, but they suggest the way localized variations in the ranking of seats may have been manifested in other Republican amphitheaters.

Indications along just such lines are provided by the *lex Ursonensis*, the municipal charter for a Caesarian military settlement *colonia Genetiva Julia* (Urso) in Spain. A section of the charter covers seating arrangements at spectacles.[60] Specific regulations are spelled out about seating at *ludi* (games usually associated with public holidays) and *ludi scaenici* (theatrical performances). In turgid legal language places are set aside for the decurions, magistrates, or visiting officials at *ludi* and heavy fines threatened against illicit occupants and those who aid and abet them. In the case of *ludi scaenici*, a greater number of restrictions apply. Here seating is specified for decurions and magistrates, colonists of the town and its territory (*coloni Genetivi*), non-citizen inhabitants (*incolae*), public guests (*hospites*), and visitors (*adventores*).[61] Fines are to be levied from transgressors and those who aid them. Finally, if a Roman senator, his son, or another official of the Roman people happened to be in town when theatrical shows were being staged, they got to sit in the orchestra.

This inscription raises interesting issues. Presumably, each group was assigned its own section of the auditorium, though the details remain elusive: were assignations by *maenianum*, *cuneus*, or seat bench, or a combination of these elements? More importantly, there is no overt mention of gladiatorial spectacles in the seating prescriptions, unless they are subsumed under the general rubric *ludi*. But until the Late Empire, *ludi* and *munera*

---

locals at Pompeii, see Cic. *Sulla* 60–2 (written in 62 BC); for a modern analysis, see Welch, "Roman Arena," 60–2 and *Roman Amphitheatre*, 76–9.

[59] Bomgardner, *Story of the Roman Amphitheatre*, 42. The suggestion is plausible and attractive, but it does face some uncertainties. The original seating was wooden and was replaced piecemeal with stone tiers during the Augustan and Julio-Claudian periods (ibid., 48–9), a time when (as we shall see) social segregation at spectacles had been legislated in detail. The piecemeal substitution of the seating may imply that the stone seating mirrors the disposition of the original wooden tiers exactly, but this inference is far from secure. Even if the current seating arrangements are exact analogs of conditions in the Republican arena, spectators in the Republic may not necessarily have sat in starkly socially segregated sections, beyond that between the local magistrates and everyone else.

[60] *CIL* 2.5439 = *ILS* 6087, §§125–7. For discussion, see R. Frei-Stolba, "Textschichten in Lex Coloniae Genetivae Iuliae Ursonensis: Zu den Kapiteln 66, 70, 71, 125–127 über die Spielveranstaltungen," *SDHI* 54 (1988), 191–225.

[61] The separate seating for *coloni* and *incolae* at Urso lends some weight to the suggestion just reviewed about the divisions in the amphitheater at Pompeii.

were usually distinguished from each other, as indeed they are elsewhere in this same inscription.[62] Given this, the text cautions against blithely assuming that these seating arrangements for *ludi* applied to gladiatorial games, since those specified for *ludi scaenici* are notably more detailed than are those for mere *ludi*. Which of these two models or, for that matter, whether either applied to crowds at *munera* in Caesarian Urso is not obvious from the charter. Finally, there is uncertainty about the date of the inscription. Since the surviving text is a Flavian copy of a Caesarian original, it has been suspected by some that the seating stipulations are a later, Imperial interpolation, from a time when concern for regulated seating was well established. The case for interpolation, however, is unproven.[63] Assuming that the inscription is authentically Caesarian, its value lies in the clues it provides about the sorts of localized social divisions that may have been commonplace among spectators at theaters on the eve of Augustus' major, empire-wide legislation on the issue (the similarities in seating arrangements attested from architecture and inscriptions from all across the empire demonstrates the empire-wide nature of Augustus' regulations).

The Augustan regime's concern for the maintenance of proprieties and its insistence on respecting rank heralded a new era for the seating arrangements at spectacles. It manifested itself early. A senatorial decree from 39 BC, during the Triumviral era, granted ambassadors from Plarasa and Aphrodisias reserved seats among the senators at contests, gladiatorial games, hunts, and athletic displays held at Rome.[64] However, major

---

[62] *CIL* 2.5439 = *ILS* 6087, §§70–1 (for *munus lu\dosve scaenicos*); cf. Suet. *Nero* 11.1. For more citations, see *TLL* 7.2.1783.61–1784.3, s.v. "ludus" (for the habitual *ludus/munus* distinction) and ibid., 1787.58–77 (for later conflation). The distinction was a fine one, to be sure. In general, *ludi* were games held in honor of the gods, usually in the theater or circus, often sponsored by magistrates on behalf of the state, and funded with public money. Gladiatorial spectacles (*munera*) started out as elements of *ludi funebres*, but were ostensibly private commemorations of dead family members and were always privately financed, at least during the Republic; see Balsdon, *Life and Leisure*, 244–52; F. Bernstein, *Ludi Publici: Untersuchungen zur Entstehung und Entwicklung der öffentlichen Spiele im republikanischen Rom*, Historia Einzelschriften 119 (Stuttgart, 1998); Kyle, *Spectacles of Death*, 41–3; Ville, *Gladiature*, 18–19. The phrase *ludi gladiatorum* appears in Cic. *Sest.* 106 and in the Late Roman schoolbooks; see G. Goetz (ed.), *Corpus Glossariorum Latinorum*, 7 vols. (Leipzig, 1888–1923) vol. III, 642–3 §22 (*colloquium Harleianum*), text cited in ch. 5, n. 54. Note also Clavel-Lévêque, *L'empire en jeux*, 45–86.

[63] See Rawson, "*Discrimina Ordinum*," 88 n. 24 for discussion (she does not favor the interpolation hypothesis). Similar provisions are found in §81 of the Flavian charter from Irni in Spain; see J. González, "The *Lex Irnitana*: A New Copy of the Flavian Municipal Law," *JRS* 76 (1986), 147–243 (§81 at 194–5). But here the text merely confirms the seating provisions of an earlier, now lost statute, on the condition that they comply with imperial decrees from Augustus onwards.

[64] J. M. Reynolds, *Aphrodisias and Rome* (London, 1982), 54–91 (no. 8), lines 75–7 (it is expressly stated in the decree that privilege applies to the city of Rome and within one mile of the city of Rome).

legislation, introduced around 20 BC, set the agenda for future generations. The Julian Law on Theaters (*lex Iulia theatralis*) tightened up the situation in the theaters and then extended the new regulations to amphitheaters.[65] (The situation at the circus, where chariot races were held, is less clear.)[66] Our chief source is a passage in Suetonius' *Life of Augustus* (*Aug.* 44 = T.21). In many ways the passage perfectly encapsulates both the value and the limitations of the ancient literary sources for the topic of crowd demographics and dispositions in the arena. Suetonius tells us that the crowd at spectacles comprised men, women, and children. He specifies ten classes of spectator and implies two others: senators; foreign ambassadors; ex-slaves; soldiers; underage boys; the tutors of underage boys; married commoners (and, by implication, unmarried commoners); citizens with dark clothes (and, by implication, citizens with bright clothes); women, apparently of all classes; and Vestal Virgins. The *praetoris tribunal* seated the imperial family and/or the sponsor of the spectacle, neither of whom qualifies as a class of spectator in the same sense as the rest. It is immediately clear that Suetonius is providing only a partial picture, since there is no mention of slaves or, more tellingly, of knights (*equites*).[67] In all likelihood, Suetonius knew that his readership was perfectly familiar with the imperially mandated seating arrangements at spectacles and so focused on those details he judged particularly interesting.[68] His focus, naturally enough, is on the

Cf. Dio 68.15.2 for Trajan assigning seats among the senators to foreign ambassadors. See below for seats reserved at the Colosseum in Rome for ambassadors from Gades.

[65] A thorough analysis is provided by Rawson, "*Discrimina Ordinum*." Rawson (98–9) dates Augustus' measures either to 22 BC (when he regulated how games would be staged) or 19 BC (when he assumed the *cura morum*, or supervision of morals). The legislation appears to have been called the *lex Iulia theatralis*; see Pliny *HN* 33.32.

[66] Claudius assigned seats to the senators in the circus, but allowed them to sit wherever they wanted to (Suet. *Claud.* 21.3; Dio 60.7.3–4). Nero assigned a section to the *equites* (Suet. *Nero* 11.1), so it appears that social segregation was applied in the circus incrementally and partially, but not along gender lines; see sources cited below, n. 68.

[67] It is not absolutely clear that common slaves (as opposed to *servi publici*) were allowed to attend spectacles. Cicero (*Har. Resp.* 22) refers to bands of disruptive slaves at the theater during the *Megalesia*, but they appear to irrupt from outside. If slaves did watch, they were undoubtedly shunted away to the periphery of the *cavea*. It is likely that only trusted slaves would enjoy the license and freedom of movement to waste time idling at the games.

[68] The same is true of other later sources, who vaguely allude to segregated seating at spectacles as a matter of course: e.g., Tac. *Ann.* 13.54.5; Hor. *Epod.* 4.15; Mart. *Ep.* 5.41; Ov. *Ars Am.* 1.135–70, *Am.* 3.2 (the latter two contrasting the unsegregated seating at the circus with conditions at gladiatorial spectacles), *Tr.* 2.284–5; Juv. 11.201–2. Edmondson ("Public Spectacles," 45–52) separates rules for seating at theaters from those governing seating at gladiatorial displays, but Suetonius (*Aug.* 44.1 = T.21) says that Augustus' rules applied "whenever public spectacles were staged anywhere" (*quotiens quid spectaculi usquam publice ederetur*). The conflation of theatral and gladiatorial events implicit in this wording is borne out by the subsequent details, which includes notice of women being barred from watching gladiators, except from the upper seats.

social hierarchies predominant in the empire's capital. The result is a frustratingly Suetonian blend of specificity and vagueness that makes teasing out the general situation in the *cavea* difficult.

Augustus, says Suetonius, assigned specific places to each of the named groups. Thus, the front row was reserved for senators; when Augustus found out that some foreign ambassadors were ex-slaves, he banned them from the best seats, i.e., the orchestra in theaters or the podium in amphitheaters; soldiers were separated from civilians; married men (*mariti*) from among the commoners received an unspecified number of tiers, while presumably single men (*caelibes*) from the same class got other, less favorable places (directly behind the *mariti*?); young boys got a block (*cuneus*), and their tutors the neighboring block (that the boys have tutors suggests that they stem from the upper echelons of society); dark-clothed *plebs* were debarred from the *media cavea*, so this area was likely the preserve of the light-clothed (toga-wearing) citizens, possibly also that of the boys and tutors just mentioned; women were banished to an upper section (*superior locus*); the Vestals got a reserved place (*locus*); the sponsor, and presumably his family, had their own box (*praetoris tribunal*). Although the governing principle is clear in its general outline – the higher your status, the closer to the front you sat – it is not easy to envisage from Suetonius' vague wording where exactly each group was located in the *cavea*. Where, for instance, were the soldiers seated? How were they differentiated from civilians? By row (*ordo*) or block (*cuneus*)? Were divisions of status among soldiers respected and, if so, how were they manifested? In which *maenianum* were the *cunei* for the boys and their tutors? What, exactly, is meant by the *superior locus* for the women or the *locus* for the Vestals?[69] Confusion is deepened by notices such as that in Martial (*Ep.* 5.8, 5.14) that the *lex Roscia* of 67 BC was reintroduced under Domitian. How did the *lex Roscia* intersect with the Augustan legislation? And how, exactly, had it fallen into abeyance prior to Domitian?[70]

A variety of literary notices attest further gradations of status for various spectator categories.[71] Ex-senators, expelled for whatever reason, could

---

[69] Edmondson, "Public Spectacles," 47 (fig. 2), offers a eye-catching chart of how the seating may have been arranged (he labels it a "hypothetical reconstruction of the ideal seating arrangements envisaged by Augustus' law"; ibid., 46).

[70] A possible explanation is that standards were felt to be slipping somehow and that this induced Domitian to be seen to take appropriate action. To complicate matters further, Pliny (*HN* 33.32) implies that the equestrian right to sit in the fourteen rows came with the *lex Iulia theatralis*. Clearly this is mistaken, since the evidence for the reserved fourteen rows predates Augustus (see above, n. 57).

[71] Many of these notices are extremely allusive and do not specify what sort of event was being watched, or where (forum? circus? amphitheater?). But since the theater and amphitheater were the chief

keep their reserved places in the games, probably in a distinct section (Cic. *Cluent.* 132; Suet. *Aug.* 35.2). It seems likely that colleges of magistrates and priests sat together; at least they appear to have done so by the third century AD. Consulars may have had their own section.[72] Tacitus records seats in the theater (and so likely in the amphitheater also) reserved for "attendants of the tribunes" (*viatores tribunicios*), so that the staff of state officials also enjoyed reserved seating, but where they sat relative to those whom they served is not obvious.[73] He also alludes (*Ann.* 2.83.5) to seating in *cunei* regulated by age (*iuniores* and *seniores*) among the equestrian rows. Cicero (*Phil.* 2.44) provides the detail that special places in the Fourteen Rows were assigned to bankrupt equestrians (*decoctores*). Augustus is said to have readmitted *equites* bankrupted by the civil wars to the privileged rows, which implies that they had in the interim been banished to less desirable tiers (Suet. *Aug.* 40.1). The sources make mention of staff who patrolled the seating, transferring interlopers to their appropriate tiers; the equestrian rows appear to have been the chief objective of these unprincipled sneaks.[74] Some women of the imperial family, at least in the Julio-Claudian period, were given special permission to sit in the front rows or with the Vestals; what the norm was otherwise is not clear, although it seems scarcely conceivable that empresses, princesses, and senatorial women would be abandoned to the wooden seats at the back.[75] It has been suggested that such unsavory proximity to social inferiors, as well as the daunting prospect of climbing dozens or even hundreds of steps – 220 to reach the *tabulationes* at the back of the Colosseum, for instance – may have been specifically intended to dissuade women of quality from attending games at all.[76]

---

venues of segregated seating, it is very unlikely that any form of restricted seating mentioned in our sources did *not* apply in those two locations.

[72] Arnobius *Adv. Nat.* 4.35. A Vespasianic inscription (*CIL* 12.6038 = *ILS* 6964) from Narbonne documents the privileges of a *flamen*, which include (line 5) *[inter decuriones s]enatoresve subsellio primo spectan[di . . .]* ("among the town councillors and senators (the right) of watching (spectacles) from the first row of privileged seats").

[73] Tac. *Ann.* 16.12.1. Even relatively minor officials, such as the *decemviri stilitibus iudicandis*, had special seats assigned to them (Ov. *Fasti* 4.383–4). Many such staffers (*apparitores*) were freedmen, so the logic of the Augustan legislation would bar them from sitting with their officials at the front; see N. Purcell, "The *Apparitores*: A Study in Social Mobility," *PBSR* 51 (1983), 125–73.

[74] Hor. *Epod.* 4.15–16; Juv. *Sat.* 3.153–9; Mart. *Ep.* 3.95.9–10, 5.14, 5.23, 5.35, 6.9. See also Reinhold, "Usurpation of Status."

[75] Tac. *Ann.* 4.16.6 (Livia gets a seat among the Vestals); Dio 59.3.4 (Gaius' sisters sit with the Vestals in the circus, as Livia had before them) and 60.22.2 (Messalina gets a front-row seat); Hdn. 1.8.4 (Commodus' sister Lucilla sits in the imperial box at the theater).

[76] Bomgardner, *Story of the Roman Amphitheatre*, 16–17; Welch, *Roman Amphitheatre*, 159.

Figure 6 Inscriptions on the podium wall of Pompeii's amphitheater

Figure 7 Detail of inscriptions on the podium wall of Pompeii's amphitheater

Soldiers who had won the *corona civica* – a crown awarded for saving the life of a citizen in combat – got exceptionally privileged places in the front rows, somewhere near the senators (Pliny *HN* 16.13). Since military service earned special seats (Hor. *Epod.* 4.15–16; Ovid *Fasti* 4.383), factors such as rank, quality of unit, length of commission, honors and citations earned, and so on, were likely reflected in seat assignations for veterans and serving soldiers. When spectacles were put on to impress visiting dignitaries (Mart. *Spect.* 31), it is hardly likely that those dignitaries were banished from the preferred seating (as Suetonius states they were by Augustus), but it is not clear where they would have been seated. The quality of the represented nation's relationship with Rome appears to have been taken into account. In AD 58, ambassadors from a Germanic tribe, the Frisii, were visiting Rome to petition Nero for land rights along the Rhine. They were taken to a play in the Theater of Pompey and assigned seating in the less prestigious tiers. But they noticed that ambassadors from honored nations were sitting with the senators in the orchestra. The Frisians insisted that their virtue entitled them to sit with such honored guests, and they were duly admitted.[77] Evidence for blocks of seats reserved for professional *collegia* is known from auditoria in both the East and West (see below, pp. 110–11, 116).

All of this literary information is supplemented by surviving inscriptions carved on to arena and theater seats.[78] Inscriptions of Republican date reserving seats for spectators have been tentatively identified at theaters in Corfinium and Aquileia.[79] At Pompeii a series of inscriptions graces the podium wall (Figs. 6, 7). The texts are best interpreted as recording the construction of *cunei* by individual local magistrates and magnates. One reads:

mag(istri) pag(i) Aug(usti) F(elicis) S(uburbani) pro lud(is) ex d(ecurionum) d(ecreto).

The heads of the suburban district Augustus Felix, by decree of the council, instead of games.[80]

---

[77] Tac. *Ann.* 13.54.1–4; cf. Suet. *Claud.* 25.4, who appears to tell the same story, but sets it under Nero's predecessor. As the anecdote about the Frisians shows, however, foreign-born spectators were not necessarily seated by ethnicity, but by status.

[78] Kolendo, "Répartition"; Rawson, "*Discrimina Ordinum*"; and items cited in this chapter, nn. 41, 95, 101–2.

[79] Rawson, "*Discrimina Ordinum*," 110 n. 164.

[80] *CIL* 10.853 = *ILS* 5653e. The district in question has yet to be located. For the other podium inscriptions at Pompeii, see *CIL* 10.854–57 = *ILS* 5653a–d. Most face out toward the arena, but a few face in toward the *cavea*. A typical example is (*ILS* 5653a), *M. Cantrius M. f. Marcellus IIvir pro lud(is), lum(inibus), cuneos III f(aciundos) c(uravit) ex d(ecurionum) d(ecreto)* ("M. Cantrius Marcellus, son of Marcus, *duovir*, instead of games or ornamental lights, oversaw the construction of three *cunei*, by decree of the council"). Cantrius had preferred to fund a construction project to

The crucial words are omitted as self-evident, but the text probably records the construction of a *cuneus* by the *magistri*, since "instead of games" reveals that an outlay of funds was involved. The inscription may also imply that this *cuneus* was reserved to the *magistri*; an inscription from the amphitheater at Carnuntum in Austria notes the *loca pagi Aeleni* ("places for the village of Aelenus").[81] Such block reservation is unequivocally recorded in inscriptions from the podium wall in the Nîmes amphitheater. Here we read:

> *n(autis)* or *n(aviculariis) Atr(icae) et Ovidis loca n(umero) XXV d(ata) d(ecreto) d(ecurionum) N(emausensium).*

To the sailors (or shippers) of the Ardèche and Ouvèze (rivers) were given 25 places by decree of the council of Nîmes.

> *n(autis)* or *n(aviculariis) Rhod(ani) et [A]rar(is) XL d(ata) d(ecreto) d(ecurionum) N(emausensium).*

To the sailors (or shippers) of the Rhône and the Saône (rivers) were given 40 (places) by decree of the council of Nîmes.[82]

In this community, where river commerce was central to the local economy, important players in that commerce occupied seats of high honor in the amphitheater, and the seating was assigned to them in blocks. Indeed, seat inscriptions at Arles, Nîmes, and elsewhere regularly record the standing reservation of blocks of seats, such as the *[lo]ca XX scholast(icorum)*

spending his money giving *lumina ludi* (see *CIL* 14.2121 = *ILS* 5683 for *lumina ludos Junoni Sospiti matri reginae*). *Lumina* were probably decorative lights, it not being unusual for public spaces to be decorated for festivals; see, e.g., Tac. *Ann.* 14.21.3 and S. P. Oakley, *A Commentary on Livy, Books VI–X* (Oxford, 1997), 522. (Alternatively, if the function of the lights was more pragmatic, they may offer evidence of nocturnal games; see Coleman, *Liber Spectaculorum*, 204–5.) The lost town charter of Pompeii (*lex*) apparently gave local magistrates the choice of spending their money either on *ludi* and their accoutrements, or on construction projects; see *CIL* 1².1635 = *CIL* 10.829 = *ILS* 5706 = *ILLRP* 648 for work carried out *ex* | *ea pequnia quod eos e lege* | *in ludos aut in monumento* | *consumere oportuit* ("from those funds which, according to the *lex*, they ought to have spent either on games or in building"). Magistrates at Urso were expected to give *ludi scaenici* in honor of Jupiter, Juno, and Minerva (*CIL* 2.5439 = *ILS* 6087 §§70–1). For more on the podium inscriptions, see Mau, *Pompeji in Leben und Kunst*, 222; La Rocca and de Vos, *Guida archeologica di Pompei*, 252; A. and M. de Vos, *Pompei, Ercolano, Stabia* (Bari, 1982), 152–3.

[81] For this suggestion, see Golvin, *L'amphithéâtre romain*, 348; for the text, see *AE* 1934.264 (Carnuntum). It would make sense for villages within a city's territory to have reserved seats at the arena; outsiders of no significant status would be consigned to the first-come, first-served area.

[82] *CIL* 12.3316–17 = *ILS* 5656 = *EAOR* 5.43–4. The *navicularii* from Arles may also have had reserved seats at the Nîmes amphitheater, although not on the podium; see *CIL* 12.3318e = *EAOR* 45e. The inscriptions are hard to date, but appear to come from the second century AD. A third-century AD inscription from Smyrna (*IK* 24.1.713) records the reservation of front-row seats for the porters from the market.

("the twenty places of the scholars") at Arles or *l(oca) XXV dat[a]* ("25 places given [by local decree]") or just *loca dat[a]* ("places given [by local decree]").[83]

When the groups awarded seating are identified they are specified as representatives of a particular ethnicity, as state or religious functionaries, as citizens of other cities, as workers or businessmen, or as members of particular age groups.[84] In North Africa, spectators appear to have been assigned block seats in the amphitheater according to their membership in the curious and obscure local administrative units called *curiae*; at least this was the case at Lambaesis. Here, in an inscription since lost but transcribed in the 1850s, a fragmentary schematic laid out the seating assignments for named *curiae*. Interestingly, the seats were not assigned to these groups by *cuneus* but by row across several *cunei*, so that the most favored (the *curia Antoniniana*) occupied the front rows of at least five *cunei*, two others (the *curiae Papiria* and *Aurelia*) occupied the second row of at least five *cunei* between them, another (the *curia Saturnia*) the third row of at least two and a half *cunei*, and so on.[85]

Evidence for specific seat assignations is not limited to the provinces. On the seats of the Colosseum in Rome were found a series of very fragmentary inscriptions of High Imperial date that make mention of block seat assignations to various categories of spectator:

[qu]ib(us) in theatr(o) lege pl(ebis)ve [scito sedere | l]icet p(edes) XII

to those who are allowed to sit in the theater by law or by plebiscite, twelve feet

equiti[bus] Rom[anis]

to Roman knights

---

[83] See *EAOR* 5.40–1 (all from Arles and Nîmes). Unspecified seat assignations may have been transferable, vaguely "reserved" for any group the town council wished to honor at any given time, with the details perhaps painted in beside the permanent, inscribed notices. For painted seat inscriptions from the Colosseum, see *CIL* 6.32262 = *EAOR* 6.12.4.

[84] See Kolendo, "Répartition," *passim*, who documents numerous examples. A rough sample assembled from *EAOR*: Ethnicity: 5.78.1 (Arverni, Bituriges Cubi), 5.78.2 (Bituriges Cubi), 5.78.3 (Tricasses), 5.78.8 (Macedones), 5.79.6 (Vellaves), 5.79.7a–c (Aedui or Viromandui or Viducasses). State or religious functionaries: 5.40cii (*pastophororum templi Isidis?*), 5.78.5 (*curatores civium Romanorum*), 5.79.1 (*Augustales*). Citizens of other cities: 5.78.6 (*Glanici*, from Glanum), 5.78.7 (*Antipolitani*, from Antipolis), 5.45d (*Arletanses*, from Arles [at Nîmes]). Workers: see previous note and 5.40ai (*oleariorum diffusorum*), 5.45e and 5.80.15 (*navicularii*), 5.77 (*lorarii* or *loricarii?*). Age groups: 5.81.1b (*iuvenes*). Note also the *loca Augustalium m(unicipii) A(elii) K(arnunti)* ("places of the imperial-cult priests of Municipium Aelium Karnuntum") from Carnuntum in Austria (*AE* 1934.263) or the places of the *iuvenes* at Trier (*CIL* 13.3708 = *EAOR* 5.81.1).

[85] *CIL* 8.3293. For discussion, see Kolendo, "Répartition," 308–9.

[pra]etext[atis | p(edes)] XVIIIS

to underage boys, eighteen and a half feet

[paedagogis p]uero[rum]

to boys' tutors

[hos]pitib[us publicis]

to public guests

client(ibus)

to clients

Gaditanorum

(the seats) of the people of Gades.[86]

Here too we see groups specified by social class, locality, and age group. It is noteworthy how several of the categories echo the wording of Suetonius about Augustus' regulations, notably the underage boys, their tutors, and the public guests (which denotes ambassadors).

The most explicit, detailed, and well-studied seating assignation in an arena is that of the Arval Brothers recorded in their minutes, which were carved on stone at their cult center at Magliana a few miles outside Rome. The Arvals, who saw to the worship of the dea Dia, had a membership of twelve senators, one of whom was always the reigning emperor. However, the brotherhood's activities required a staff of attendants (*calatores* and an *aedituus*) and slaves assigned to it by the state (*servi publici*), so the actual number of people involved in the worship of the dea Dia far exceeded the twelve Arvals. These staffers would be of varying social status (the *calatores*, for instance, were invariably freedmen).[87]

In the year AD 80 the brotherhood received from the office of the *praefectus annonae* their seat assignations in "the amphitheater," i.e., the

---

[86] *CIL* 6.32098a–f, l, m = *ILS* 5654 = *EAOR* 6.14.1–23 = A. Chastagnol, *Le sénat romain sous le règne d'Odoacre: recherches sur l'épigraphie du Colisée au Ve siècle* (Bonn, 1966), 25. The latter notes (26) some fragments found in 1939, one of which (no. 3) reads only . . . *viris* ("for men"); *EAOR* 6.14.8 corrects this latter reading to the measurement *VIIIS* ("eight and a half feet"). Note also Mart. *Spect.* 3 for the diverse ethnicities among those in the arena, many of whom were probably ambassadors; see the comments of Coleman, *Liber Spectaculorum*, 38–41.

[87] On the Arvals, see I. Paladino, *Fratres arvales: storia di un collegio sacerdotale romano* (Rome, 1988); J. Scheid, *Le collège des frères arvales: étude prosopographique du recrutement (69–304)* (Rome, 1990); J. Scheid, *Romulus et ses frères: le collège arvale modèle du culte public dans la Rome des empereurs*, BEFRA 275 (Rome, 1990). For excavations at the site, see H. Broise and J. Scheid, *Recherches archéologiques à la Magliana: le balneum des frères Arvales* (Rome, 1987).

Colosseum, which celebrated its gala opening in this year (see text at I.1).[88] The individual seats are not numbered in the text, but rather space is assigned as a specified width of a tier within numbered *maeniana* and *cunei*. The average width of seats in Roman theaters and amphitheaters was 0.4m, as evidenced by surviving seats where the individual places are marked by permanently carved lines.[89] Since modern metrical equivalents for the Roman system of feet (*pedes*) and fingers (*digiti*) have been worked out,[90] the number of places per tier and section appears to have been as follows:

Location	Roman	Metrical	No. of places
Maenianum 1, *cuneus* 6, 8 rows	*ped.* 42 1/2	12.5205m/0.4	31 1/3
Maenianum 2, *cuneus* 12, 4 rows	*ped.* 22 1/2	6.6285m/0.4	16 1/2
Summum maen. in ligneis, 53rd *tab.*11 rows	*ped.* 63 23/24	18.8415m /0.4	47

It seems that four spectators, more or less, were expected to occupy space in each of the allotted rows and that the Arvals were allotted at least ninety-four places in the Colosseum, perhaps more if the wooden seats were filled to maximum capacity. It has been suggested that the blocks of seats were arrayed in ascending sections, one above the other, in the third quadrant of the arena (at entrance 53, near the Colossus of Nero).[91] Uncertainty over how the *cunei* were numbered at the Colosseum makes testing this suggestion impossible.

Aside from the emperor, there were eleven Arvals, but they cannot have occupied the seats in the first *maenianum* that is mentioned in the text. As senators and state religious functionaries, they would have sat on the podium, which is not mentioned in the inscription and which, in any case, had seven rows of seats and so cannot have been the first *maenianum* of the text (which had at least eight). The seating of the Brethren themselves

---

[88] The text has been long known and subjected to much interpretation since the nineteenth century: see, e.g., C. Hülsen, "Il posto degli arvali nel Colosseo e la capacità dei teatri di Roma antica," *Bull-Com* 22 (1894), 312–24. For recent interpretations, see Bomgardner, *Story of the Roman Amphitheatre*, 18–20; Golvin, *L'amphithéâtre romain*, 350–3; Kolendo, "Répartition," 304–5; Rawson, "*Discrimina Ordinum*," 101; Scheid, *Commentarii*, 127–9.

[89] Golvin, *L'amphithéâtre romain*, 352 (table 43). The incised seat markings in the amphitheater at Arles are particularly clear, see J. Formigé, "L'amphithéâtre d'Arles," *RA* (1965), 1–47, esp. 1–5.

[90] Scheid, *Commentarii*, 129, where 1 *pes* = 0.2946m.

[91] Hülsen, "Il posto degli arvali," 317–18. The suggestion is accepted as plausible by Bollinger (*Theatralis Licentia*, 21–2) but doubted by Golvin (*L'amphithéâtre romain*, 353).

on the podium was felt to be so self-evident that detailed assignation of measured space there was deemed unnecessary. (Indeed, we do not know how permanent seats were assigned within the podium zone.) With the Arvals themselves ensconced on the podium, who occupied the ninety-four assigned places?[92] The first *maenianum*, directly behind the podium, must have included the rows traditionally reserved for *equites*, but it is not clear what *equites* were attached to the Arval Brothers. These rows may have been intended for the grown sons of the Arvals, who were technically classed as *equites* until such a time as they entered the senate; minor sons presumably sat with their peers in a *cuneus* adjacent to their *paedagogi*. That other equestrian dependants of the Brethren were allowed to sit in this section is also a reasonable possibility. Each brother had a footman (*calator*), who was usually of freedman status. As such, the *calatores* would have been barred from the first *maenianum*, but they could have occupied the block of seats allotted in the second *maenianum*, with room for four others. The brothers' wives (and children?), as well as perhaps the slaves attached to the brotherhood, were apparently assigned to the wooden seats (recall Augustus' banishment of all women to a *superior locus*) in the fifty-third box (*tabulatio*).

Finally, there is no mention in the Arval records of the third *maenianum* (*maenianum summum*, or upper *maenianum secundum*) in the Colosseum: the seat assignations jump from the second *maenianum* to the wooden seats at the top of the house. This was because the third *maenianum* was assigned to the ones Suetonius calls "the dark-clothed" (*pullati*), probably in reference to the freeborn but truly impoverished masses who were seated in this section on a first-come, first-served basis. The overall situation with the Arval Brethren's seating in the Colosseum is paralleled in second-century Miletus, where the city councillor M. Aurelius Thelymitres had three rows of seats assigned to him in the theater by decree of the local council. The seats are at the rear of the fourth *cuneus*. The obscurity of this location strongly suggests that the places were intended not for Thelymitres himself but for his dependants; Thelymitres (and his family) would have had more prominent places at the front.[93] In this way, official seat assignations to leading citizens, whether Thelymitres at Miletus or the Arvals at Rome,

---

[92] For various suggestions, see Bollinger, *Theatralis Licentia*, 22–3; Bomgardner, *Story of the Roman Amphitheatre*, 19; Scheid, *Commentarii*, 129. The inclusion of the Arvals brings the total number of places assigned to the Brotherhood to 105 (excluding the emperor, who had his own box).

[93] It has been suggested that Thelymitres' seats were reserved for members of several professional associations of which he was patron; see O. M. van Nijf, *The Civic World of Professional Associations in the Roman East* (Amsterdam, 1997), 223. For the pertinent inscriptions, see W. Günther, "Ehrungen für einen Milesischen Periodoniken," in H. Kalcyk et al. (eds.), *Studien zur alten Geschichte* (Rome,

facilitated the processes of local patronage. The nexus of patronage, indeed, was pretty much how everything got done in ancient Rome, and the ability to attend games was no exception.[94] Going to spectacles in at least some arenas may well have been something of a privilege. If officials as relatively minor as the Arvals had ninety-four places to dispense to their dependants, how many more seats must *pontifices*, augurs, prefects, consuls, ex-consuls, praetors, and other state officers have been entitled to? If each of these had 100 or more reserved seats to dispose of, the unconnected citizen might have had a hard time securing any place in the *cavea* at all. That said, the ancient writers consistently associate gladiatorial spectacles with the entertainments of the common people, which tells us that, despite areas of the *cavea* being reserved for various elite categories, most of those in attendance are likely to have derived from the less privileged classes. Of course, the genuine elite occupied only the very front rows, so the others would have been available for the *plebs* or *populus* or *vulgus*, or however else the upper class chose to designate them.[95] To secure attendance, one's social status may have mattered less than whom one knew.

From the third century onward, seats in amphitheaters were also reserved for individuals, and their names were carved into their places accordingly, usually in the genitive or dative cases to mark the seat as owned or assigned. Over two hundred such names, mostly of senators, are recoverable from seats in the Colosseum and date to between the late third and early sixth centuries AD.[96] Almost a hundred names are known from

---

1986), 313–28. Similarly, the stadium at Aphrodisias has a row of seats reserved for one Claudia Seleucia, probably for the use of her dependants; see Roueché, *Performers and Partisans*, 88–9.

[94] See, e.g., Garnsey and Saller, *Roman Empire*, esp. 148–59; N. Rouland, *Pouvoir politique et dépendance personnelle dans l'antiquité romaine: Genèse et rôle des rapports de clientèle*, Collection Latomus 166 (Brussels, 1979); R. P. Saller, *Personal Patronage under the Early Empire* (Cambridge, 1982); A. Wallace-Hadrill (ed.), *Patronage in Ancient Society* (London, 1989).

[95] Bomgardner (*Story of the Roman Amphitheatre*, 17–20) estimates that the common element in the crowd accounted for only 18 percent of the Colosseum's seating while some 62 percent of seats went to senators, *equites*, and well-to-do citizens. Hopkins and Beard (*Colosseum*, 112) and Rose ("Spectators," 118–19) concur. Yet precise figures for who sat where in the Colosseum are largely guesswork, since sections of the first and second *maeniana* cannot be assigned to known classes of people with any confidence. It should give pause, for instance, that we cannot even identify the well-attested "fourteen rows" reserved for the *equites* at the Colosseum. The plain truth is that we cannot be sure about the exact social status of spectators between the most privileged seats on the *podium* and the wooden benches in the *tabulationes* at the back. Seat inscriptions attest to the role of trade, cult, youth, or neighborhood associations (*collegia*) in securing group seats at spectacles in the mid-regions of the *cavea*, which also points to a predominance of *plebs* in the audience; see Kolendo, "Répartition," 215; Roueché, *Performers and Partisans*, 124–8 (seat inscriptions); Toner, *Leisure*, 34–52 (association of games with vulgar tastes and pursuits).

[96] Chastagnol, *Le sénat, passim* = *EAOR* 6.17.1–178. Note that *EAOR* 6.16.1–74 catalogs High Imperial seat assignations for individuals or members of senatorial families, datable to the late third century and early fourth century AD.

the seats of the amphitheater at Pola in Istria, but others are known from other amphitheaters, nearly always of the fourth and fifth century AD.[97] These are undoubtedly persons of importance. A combination of individual and group reservations is attested in those places where prominent local families, as a whole, had places set aside for them at spectacles.[98]

The evidence reviewed above pertains to the Latin West. In the Greek East purpose-built amphitheaters (like the one at Corinth) are rare, but circuses, theaters, and stadia were used for *munera* and *venationes*, and were sometimes physically adapted to these purposes.[99] Inscriptions even refer to a hybrid building-type, the "amphitheater-stadium."[100] Ranked seating arrangements are also attested for such structures, which highlights the empire-wide nature of the practice.[101] The theater at Hierapolis in Phrygia, for instance, has yielded late second or early third century seat inscriptions that show *cunei* or parts of *cunei* assigned to local administrative units, the tribes (*phylai*).[102] A thoroughgoing analysis of the seating inscriptions at the theater, odeon, and stadium at Aphrodisias has revealed a familiar pattern: seats assigned to or claimed by groups or individuals (the latter, mostly, from the Late Imperial period). The groups are designated by now-familiar categories: profession or job (grain-dealers, tanners, fiscal officers, gardeners, gold-workers, butchers), city of citizenship (Mastaureitans, Milesians?, Antiocheians, Kibyrans), age categories (youths, ephebes), and possibly ethnicity (Jews, Lydians or Lycians?). The names of several groups are no

---

[97] *CIL* 5.86 = *EAOR* 2.75. See Kolendo, "Répartition," 312–14.

[98] Chastagnol, *Le sénat*, 32–3; Kolendo, "Répartition," 313.

[99] Golvin, *L'amphithéâtre romain*, 237–49; Robert, *Gladiateurs*, 34–6; K. Welch, "The Stadium at Aphrodisias," *AJA* 102 (1998), 547–69, esp. 558–69; K. Welch, "Greek Stadia and Roman Spectacles: Asia, Athens and the Tomb of Herodes Atticus," *JRA* 11 (1998), 117–45; Welch, "Negotiating," esp. 133–8 (on the Corinth amphitheater); Welch, *Roman Amphitheatre*, 163–85. Many examples of adaptation are also documented in L. Lavan, "Provincial Capitals of Late Antiquity" (Ph.D. dissertation, University of Nottingham, 2001), 262–78. See also H. W. Pleket, "Mass-Sport and Local Infrastructure in the Greek Cities of Roman Asia Minor," *Stadion* 24 (1998), 151–72.

[100] *IGRR* 4.845, 4.861 (Laodicea; late first century?). At this early date, however, the phrase may mean no more than "stadium in which the seats go all the way around"; see J. H. Humphrey, "'Amphitheatral' Hippo-Stadia," in A. Raban and K. G. Holum (eds.), *Caesarea Maritima: A Retrospective after Two Millennia* (Leiden, 1996), 121–9. Gladiatorial spectacles, executions, and hunts took place in them, but so did more traditional Greek athletic competitions; see Welch, "Greek Stadia."

[101] F. Kolb, "Sitzstufeninschriften aus dem Stadion von Saittai (Lydia)," *EpigAnat* 15 (1990), 107–19; A. Retzleff, and A. M. Mjely, "Seat Inscriptions in the Odeum at Gerasa (Jerash)," *BASOR* 332 (2004), 37–47; D. B. Small, "Social Correlations to the Greek *Cavea* in the Roman Period," in S. Macready and F. H. Thompson (eds.), *Roman Architecture in the Greek World* (London, 1987), 85–93.

[102] F. Kolb, "Zur Geschichte der Stadt Hierapolis in Phrygien: Die Phyleninschriften im Theater," *ZPE* 15 (1974), 225–70. Since theaters in the East were used for staging civic meetings as well as spectacles, the tribal seat assignations may have primarily pertained to the former.

longer decipherable or, where known, are of unclear meaning.[103] From the
Late Imperial period come seat reservations at opposite ends of the theater
for the competing circus factions, the Blues and the Greens. By this time,
these organizations had grown in importance not only as organs of social
and cultural life, but also of municipal administration.[104]

Ancient depictions of arena crowds are rare and not very enlightening. Although the amphitheater spectacles were a popular topic for many
ancient mosaicists, potters and painters, the focus was (understandably)
on the action on the sand rather than the crowd watching.[105] There are
some exceptions, however. A mosaic found in Cologne in 1888 shows an
arena with named gladiators engaged in combat. To one side we see a
group of eight spectators, one of them perhaps a woman (Fig. 8). They
are mostly dressed in tunics and short cloaks, although two appear to be
wearing longer outer garments. The position of the feet of the foremost
pair of spectators shows they are in motion, moving to take up their places
in the seating, which is suggested by a boxed design that looms up behind
and to the left of them.[106] A mosaic of an arena hunt from Thelepte in
Africa shows the crowd as two groups of five rather passive-looking men
enclosed in boxes at the top of the frame. The appearance of the crowd
in such images serves to strengthen the correspondence between looking
at the mosaic and looking at the spectacle itself, since the pavements were
usually commissioned by *munerarii* to commemorate actual shows they
had put on.[107]

An instructive body of arena-related images is found on *appliqué* terracotta rondos from the Rhône valley that were used as pot decorations in the

[103] For example, seats for some *collegia* (*syntechnia*) have lost their genitive modifiers, so the profession
of their membership is unknown. On the seating of professional guilds at spectacles, see van Nijf,
Civic World, 209–40 and 257–9.

[104] The main publication is Rouché, *Performers and Partisans*, 83–128, esp. 83–4 (on estimates of
dating) and 119–28 (for discussion). See above, n. 34 on the factions. See also the comments of
Welch, "Stadium," 561–3.

[105] See R. Lim, "In the 'Temple of Laughter': Visual and Literary Representations of Spectators at
Roman Games," in Bergmann and Kondoleon (eds.), *Art of Ancient Spectacle*, 343–65. Tellingly,
the chapter includes both artistic and literary representations, and it covers the entire gamut of
spectacle: circus races, theatrical displays, and arena events.

[106] K. Parlasca, *Die Römischen Mosaiken in Deutschland* (Berlin, 1959), 82–4 (with Pl. 83,1). The mosaic
was restored in the nineteenth century so that its proper date cannot now be ascertained; see D.
von Boeslager, "Das Gladiatorenmosaik in Köln und seine Restaurierung im 19. Jahrhundert,"
KölnJb 20 (1987), 111–28. The identification of the boxed design as seating is suggested by the
nearby inscription *cav(ea)* (*CIL* 13.12063 = *EAOR* 4.72). Also, the left-most spectator in the fore,
only partially depicted, is bending forward – arranging a cushion?

[107] K. M. D. Dunbabin, *The Mosaics of Roman North Africa* (Oxford, 1978), 65–87 (esp. 69–70
on Thelepte). On the assimilation of arena spectator and mosaic viewer, see Brown, "Death as
Decoration," esp. 187–8.

Figure 8 Mosaic of arena spectators from Cologne

second and third centuries AD. One very well-preserved example, now in Nîmes, shows two named gladiators fighting. A balustrade at the bottom suggests the arena. At the upper end of the image stand four figures, who probably represent the watching public, who shout *stantes missi* ("It's a draw!").[108] Finally, sixth-century consular diptychs (ivory notebook covers

---

[108] See P. Wuilleumier and A. Audin, *Les médallions d'applique gallo-romains de la Vallée du Rhône* (Paris, 1952), 39 (no. 34), where the four figures are interpreted as gods, to whom the *genii* of the gladiators are supplicating. To be sure, the figures are all shown in full and standing, which supports this interpretation. Compare *EAOR* 5, 67–8 (App. 1) where the figures are thought to represent the public with arms outstretched. The proximity of the crowd-related inscription *stantes missi*, located

presented to consuls on entering office) sometimes depict Late Imperial beast spectacles staged in the arena. The crowd, when it appears, is usually shown as a series of six to eight heads peeping over the top of the podium. In some cases, an attempt is made to give a sense of the spectators' serried ranks by setting the occasional head behind the others, as if looking over the shoulders of those in front. These depictions of the spectators may have been patronizingly humorous, in that the common folk are rendered as somewhat gormless and dressed in simple tunics.[109]

The minor poet Calpurnius Siculus imagines a simple countryman coming to Rome to witness a *venatio* staged in the wooden amphitheater erected by Nero in the Campus Martius in AD 57.[110] The passage (Calp. Sic. *Ecl.* 7) is a dialogue between one Lycotas, who stayed home, and Corydon, who made the trip to Rome and is now returning almost three weeks later. Corydon is amazed by what he has seen in Rome (7.13–8). The amphitheater (*spectacula*) itself is a source of wonder: Corydon likens it to a natural valley in scale and form (7.30–4) and describes its luxurious appointments (7.35–6). As a common rustic, Corydon is assigned seating "where the dirty-cloaked mob usually watch, among the women's seats" (7.26–7: *venimus ad sedes, ubi pulla sordida veste / inter femineas spectabat turba cathedras*). He notes the *equites* and tribunes down below, white-clad and glowing in the sun (7.28–9). This would locate his seating in the third *maenianum* where, as we have seen, Suetonius says the *pullati* ("the dark-clothed") were expected to sit. It would have been just below the *summum maenianum* with its *tabulationes* for women, hence the comment about the proximity to the women's seating. Alternatively, if we take Corydon at his word, Nero's temporary arena conflated the lower-class seating with the *tabulationes* for women and slaves. Since seats in the third *maenianum* were not allotted to particular groups, Corydon comments that he chanced to sit beside an old man, a native of Rome who tells him that sights like this are still a marvel to behold, even for one who has lived in the city his whole life (7.39–46).

Needless to say, the show itself amazes Corydon, with beasts of all sorts displayed and pitched against each other (including one combat of [polar]

directly to the right of the four figures, supports this interpretation. On the crowd's participation in arena events, see below, ch. 6, p. 222.

[109] R. Delbrueck, *Die Consulardiptychen und verwandte Denkmäler* (Berlin, 1929), 3–32 (on the diptychs in general) and 75–8 (on the *venatio* scenes). For specific examples, see nos. 9–12 (AD 506), 20–1 (AD 517) and also nos. 37, 57, 59, and 60.

[110] Tac. *Ann.* 13.31.1; Suet. *Nero* 12.1; Pliny *HN* 16.200. See also *LTUR*, vol. 1, 36, s.v. "Amphitheatrum Neronis" (Palombi); G. B. Townend, "Calpurnius Siculus and the Munus Neronis," *JRS* 70 (1980), 166–74.

bears and "sea calves," i.e., seals). He ends his account by wishing he
could have dressed better, so that he could have taken a more forward
seat, and with it, a better view of the godlike Nero (7.79–84). Corydon
therefore implies that he could have disguised himself by his dress to sneak
into the better seats – precisely the situation the authorities sought to
police in the lower *maeniana* and with which the Roman satirists had such
fun. Corydon's experience encapsulates much of what we have seen above
about the seating arrangements in Roman amphitheaters: spectators were
segregated on various criteria into peer groups, which clustered in certain
parts of the *cavea*; there were rules as to who precisely got to sit where;
and the crowd looked at itself as well as the events on the sand, as the
spectators were mutually visible to each other. It is now time to investigate
the workings of crowd dynamics at the Roman arena against this physical
and sociopolitical backdrop.

CHAPTER 4

Crowd dynamics at arena spectacles

> Monday's rioter was Tuesday's voter. Tuesday's voter was Thursday's
> theatregoer. Not necessarily with the same friends and loyalties in
> each context.
>
> N. Horsfall, *The Culture of the Roman Plebs* (2003)[1]

The known facts about crowd demographics and the seating arrangements
in the amphitheater carry important psychological ramifications. The arena
crowd was not an amorphous mass, but was marshaled into distinct subgroups. The fact of strictly segregated seating by social categories in the
cavea meant that spectators sat with people to whom they were connected
in some way. Colleagues in particular professions and crafts sat together
in assigned seats, for instance, as did fellow townsmen, or ex-brothers-in-
arms, and so on. Thus the vast majority of the crowd was seated amongst
groups of peers, many of whom must have known each other already. At
the Flavian Amphitheater at Puteoli, amidst the vaulted substructures that
supported the seating, special chambers were bricked off from the maze
of corridors and entrances. Some of them were chapels (*sacella*) for religious observances, but others, apparently, were hospitality suites reserved
for guilds (*collegia*). One, for instance, is associated with the *scabillarii*,
the cantonet players for theatrical performances.[2] It cannot be ruled out
that these musicians were part of the arena spectacle itself, in which case,
this space was reserved for performers (on the role of music at the games,
see below, chapter 6, pp. 225–6). The same cannot be said, however, of a
schola org[iophantorum] ("chamber of the initiatory priests of Dionysus"),
who are mentioned in an inscription not found *in situ* but can be plausi-
bly associated with another chamber in the substructures.[3] Other vaulted
amphitheaters have not left physical evidence of reception rooms, but such

---

[1] N. Horsfall, *The Culture of the Roman Plebs* (London, 2003), 27.

[2] Maiuri, *Anfiteatro Flavio Puteolano*, 47; Bomgardner, *Story of the Roman Amphitheatre*, 77–80; Welch,
Roman Amphitheatre, 221–5. For the relevant inscription, see *AE* 1956.137.

[3] *AE* 1956.138, with Maiuri, *Anfiteatro Flavio Puteolano*, 46–8 and 53–5.

suites could have been set up easily enough, even temporarily, by means of ropes, wooden screens, or curtains. It is hardly implausible to imagine groups of fellow workers and friends gathering in (rented?) chambers for refreshments before the games or during intervals. This scenario suggests one way groups of people known to each other enjoyed their day at the games; in all likelihood, they would sit in the stands together as well.[4]

Even among the unsegregated masses in the tiers of the third *maenianum*, a strong psychological, as well as social, cohesion was likely in effect. Although apparently undifferentiated in their specific seat allocations, here too people of the same social class were grouped together in a single region of the *cavea*.[5] No doubt many spectators in this section also came to the games in smaller groups, even if not formally categorized and seated as such. Alypius watched from this region of the Colosseum with his friends, and later led others there too (August. *Conf.* 6.13 = T.3) and, it seems, the rustic Corydon did not go to Nero's *venatio* alone: "we came to our seats" (*Ecl.* 7.26: *venimus ad sedes*), he comments, and found himself with an older stranger sitting to his left (*Ecl.* 7.39–40: *senior, lateri qui forte sinistro / iunctus erat*) – the seat on his right, it is inferred, was occupied by someone he knew.

The social psychology of crowd dynamics suggests that the presence and mutual visibility of subgroups in a crowd strengthens the social identities of both the crowd and the subgroups within it, increases sensations of solidarity that stem from those identities, and amplifies the expression of identities that lends crowd members feelings of empowerment. The history of modern English football stadiums and crowd behavior there offers dramatic evidence for these propositions. Traditionally, spectators watched soccer matches in an undifferentiated mass, standing in terraces. As crowd size grew and rivalries intensified, in the 1960s the authorities sought to curb growing hooliganism first by confining rival fans to separate terraces, then by fencing the terraces off from each other, and finally by locking the spectators into the fenced-off "pens" to keep them apart. The effect, however, was the opposite of that desired. Fans – now corralled together in dense packs, bodies pushing and swaying in unison – displayed greater ingroup solidarity and a consequent intensification of outgroup

---

[4] The largest proportion of seat inscriptions from the stadium and theater at Aphrodisias, for instance, refers to groups or associations, both formal (e.g., ephebes, or people from specified cities or members of professions) and informal (e.g., the *philoploi*, "weapons' fans"); See also Roueché, *Performers and Partisans*, 79–80 and 119–28.

[5] Welch (*Roman Amphitheatre*, 159) makes the reasonable suggestion that plebeian spectators had seating regions set aside for them according to tribal or *collegia* membership. If so, the third *maenianum* may also have been partitioned into group-specific zones.

hostility, which took the form of abusive chants during games and off-site violence against rival fans, since on-site violence was now so hard to perpetrate. A new tack was therefore taken in the 1990s, when the "pens" and standing terraces were abandoned in favor of individual, numbered seats with arms that bodily separated individual fans from each other, and which required a paper ticket to occupy. Violence decreased.[6] The point to note is not the fluctuation of rates of violence specifically, but the wider fact that spectator segregation in stadia carries demonstrable consequences for group solidarity (i.e., social identity), for the feelings that underlie it, and for outward behavior – in this case, violent behavior.

SPECTATOR EXPECTATIONS, BEHAVIORS, AND VOCALIZATIONS

We saw in the introduction that the ancient literary evidence as to how the arena crowd behaved is tarnished by the snobbish attitudes of the Roman elite when recounting the behavior of its social inferiors, as well as by the rhetorical commonplaces so readily resorted to by ancient authors. Despite these caveats, the data remain instructive and contain much useful information. Cassiodorus (*Var.* 1.27.5) simply asks "who looks for dignified behavior at spectacles?" (*mores autem graves in spectaculis quis requirat?*), while Tertullian (*Spect.* 21.2–22 = T.29) goes deeper and draws a sharp contrast between the way people behaved in normal life and the way they behaved in the arena, circus, or theater. Conduct reckoned intolerable when displayed by others in a daily context was condoned in the stands. They would shield their daughters from coarse language, but then expose them to it and use it themselves in the *cavea*. They would avert their eyes from the corpse of one who had died naturally, but relish the sight of arena victims ripped and lacerated. They would attempt to break up a fight on the street, but applaud far more violent combats in the arena. They would approve of punishment for murder, but then encourage a gladiator to commit murder. Tertullian frames these remarks in a typically rhetorical manner, as a set of antithetical juxtapositions infused with moral opprobrium. His is a specific and judgmental view of the crowd experience that stresses lack of restraint and baseness of behavior as the salient results of going to the games. The same observations could be made about Seneca's description of a lunchtime visit to the arena (*Ep.* 7.2–5 = T.20), Salvian's

---

[6] See Armstrong, *Football Hooligans*, 105–38; Buford, *Thugs*, 161–74; E. Dunning et al., *The Roots of Football Hooliganism: A Historical and Sociological Study* (London, 1988), 132–83, esp. 164–9; F. Frosdick and P. Marsh, *Football Hooliganism* (Cullompton, 2005), esp. 10–24 and 172–3.

comments about merry spectators enjoying victims fed to beasts (*Gub. Dei* 6.10 = T.18), or Augustine's passage about his friend Alypius' debut at the Colosseum (August. *Conf.* 6.13 = T.3). All of these texts reflect a dominant discourse that emphasizes the themes of intemperance, loss of individual identity, and atavistic vileness.[7] On the surface, then, the ancient portrayal of arena crowds is essentially Le Bonian in character.

But if we dig a little deeper, more can be said. These authors make it quite clear that people behaved differently in the arena, circus, or theater than they did in their everyday environments. Indeed Tertullian and Augustine chart not only changes in behavior, but also shifts in attitude, as their subjects' very thinking is transformed in the crowd. In light of the social identity model of crowd dynamics, these details may be taken to reflect not loss of control or the submergence of individual minds into a collective, but the adaptation of people's social identities and categorizations to the crowd context. The result was a realignment of the spectators' priorities and, just as noteworthy, a vehement expression of crowd-based social identities in ways the ancient authors regard as a descent into vulgarity and barbarism.[8] But the authors' judgments are less significant than their reporting the identity shift and its enthusiastic expression.

Crowd actions and vocalizations echo the social identities brought to the fore by context, identities which are themselves grounded in shared social understandings. Thus, more revealing than moral judgments about crowd behavior are notices about what the spectators actually did and said. The patchwork of surviving evidence, however, makes determining the full scope of social identity content a more difficult, if not an impossible proposition: Roman spectators cannot be polled or interviewed about what they were thinking or feeling as they watched. However, broad suggestions can be made on the basis of the cultural analyses offered by prior studies (see chapter 1, pp. 17–22) combined with direct evidence for what the crowd did and said, much of it drawn from the direct experience of the ancient writers themselves. Like any crowd, arena spectators' social identities would have comprised several elements, drawn from the expectations they brought with them to their seats, shaped by the nature of the events they had come to witness, and influenced by the sharp distinction the physical environment drew between the watchers in the stands and the watched on the sand. It is also likely that the spectators' psychological reactions tracked the different

---

[7] See also the passages assembled and discussed by Wistrand, *Entertainment and Violence*, esp. 14–29.
[8] Such judgments find echo in external observers' reactions to the behavior of modern rioters; see, e.g., Reicher, "'Battle of Westminster.'"

phases of the complex spectacle taking place before them. Thus, their views of the performers and of themselves would be partially fixed, derived as they were from their life experiences and understandings, and partially malleable, as they reacted to changing conditions in the specific spectacle they had come to watch.

We have already charted some of the most relevant features of the Roman social environment that likely shaped the crowd's identities (see chapter 1, pp. 22–38), and many life experiences were common to all parts of the empire over many centuries, such as prevalent slavery, high average mortality, hierarchical social thought, and militarism in state ideology. But some outlooks, such as callous fatalism or the disparagement of pity, were less likely to be so universal and firmly rooted, as they varied over time and space, or even by individual, while the particular elements of spectacles would also vary from case to case. In this way, the social identities of Roman arena crowds should not be conceived as monolithic and homogeneous across time and space, but instead imagined as a dynamic kaleidoscope of attitudes, outlooks, and reactions fashioned from a combination of shared experience and immediate stimuli.

The details of crowd demographics also mattered a great deal. The social identities and understandings of, say, an all-male crowd at an amphitheater attached to a military base are not likely to have been the same as those of the Colosseum crowd at Rome, and both of these would diverge from the identities prevalent among, say, spectators in the Greek East, who brought their own cultural baggage to the shows. Regional and cultural differences like these among arena spectators would have had a powerful formative impact on the content of their social identities, and not just at *munera*.[9] This variety needs to be borne in mind in what follows, where only a composite picture can be constructed from scattered snapshots drawn from divergent contexts.

The hunt probably opened the proceedings at many spectacles. The first thing to note is that not all the beasts sent into the arena were slaughtered, and this was no disappointment to the spectators. Martial was so dumb-founded by a display of lions that had been trained to frolic with hares that he devoted eight poems to the marvel. The poet was no less amazed

---

[9] For instance, twenty-eight amphitheaters are known from the Rhine–Danube frontier, many of them attached to legionary bases (e.g., Vetera, Cologne, Moguntiacum, Vindonissa, Carnuntum etc.); see Futrell, *Blood in the Arena*, 53–76, esp. 58–66 (Britain and the Rhine–Danube frontier). See also P. Le Roux, "L'amphithéâtre et le soldat sous l'empire romain," in Domergue et al. (eds.), *Spectacula*, 203–16. On the Greek East, see Carter, "Gladiators and Monomachoi"; Mann, "Gladiators in the Greek East"; Robert, *Gladiateurs*, esp. 239–66.

by an elephant, who had formerly been pitted against a bull, kneeling before the emperor in apparent submission.[10] The Domitianic poet Statius devotes one of his *Silvae* (2.5) to a tamed lion, whose death was mourned by the people as if it had been a famous gladiator. The behavior of animals, whether they were slaughtered or not, was a matter of general interest, and in itself constituted one lure of the hunt. Pliny (*HN* 8.20 = T.14) comments that the arched flightpaths of shields hurled in the air by a dying elephant specifically delighted the crowd (*voluptati spectantibus erant*), as the sight reminded them of juggling. Symmachus (*Ep.* 4.12.2) reports that the mere running about of leopards amused the crowd at games he staged for his son. This sort of detail highlights the complexity of the spectators' mental orientation to what they were watching and demonstrates that a lot more than raw bloodlust drew people to watch.

While the *venationes* were not necessarily all about blood and death, it cannot be denied that these were amply on display. Competitions between beasts, or between human and beast, shared some of the attractions of the headline event, when gladiators took to the sand. Like the main bouts, outcomes in the hunts were not certain. While the animals were at a distinct disadvantage, there was a very real possibility (as in bull-fighting today) that a huntsman could go down to some fast or unexpected move on the part of a beast.[11] Despite their lesser status as fighters, skill, agility, and dexterity were required of *bestiarii* and *venatores*, and this was appreciated by the crowd. Fronto, for instance, reports that M. Aurelius, as heir-apparent, would free and enfranchise arena huntsmen on the crowd's insistence.[12] As

---

[10] Mart. *Ep.* 1.6, 1.14, 1.22, 1.44, 1.48. 1.51, 1.60, 1.104.12–22 (lions and hares) and *Spect.* 20, 22 (elephant). See also Mart. *Ep.* 1.104.9–10 for a dancing elephant. Roman crowds were amazed by unexpected sights, such as tightrope-walking elephants (Suet. *Galba* 6.1, *Nero* 12.2; cf. Aelian, *NA* 2.11), trickster dogs (Plut. *Mor.* 973E), or sunbathing crocodiles (Strabo 17.814–5).

[11] The Hunting Baths at Leptis Magna show arena hunting scenes in which two of the human performers have come to grief – one is being chewed on by a big cat; see J. B. Ward-Perkins and J. M. C. Toynbee, "The Hunting Baths at Leptis Magna," *Archaeologia* 93 (1949), 165–95, esp. 181. Note also a relief from Apri in Asia Minor showing a shielded huntsman in which one shielded huntsman is being tossed by a bear, another by a bull; see Robert, *Gladiateurs*, 90–1 (no. 27) and plate 24. In a gladiatorial relief from Pompeii (see Jacobelli, *Gladiators at Pompeii*, 95–7 [fig. 77]), a bear is shown chewing a *bestiarius* right out of the gate, while two colleagues raise their arms in alarm or despair.

[12] Fronto *Ad M. Caes.* 1.9.2. The *bestiarius* Carpophorus was celebrated in Flavian Rome and is compared by Martial to Meleager, Hercules, and other legendary hunters; see Mart. *Spect.* 17, 26(?), 32 with Coleman, *Liber Spectaculorum*, ad locc., and Mart. *Ep.* 5.65. An advertisement for games staged at Pompeii promises "Ellios and a hunt" (*Ellios [et] ven(atio) erit*) where Ellios was apparently a famed huntsman; *CIL* 4.1179 = *ILS* 5143 = Sabbatini Tumolesi, *Gladiatorium Paria*, 36–7 [no. 10]). See also Pliny *HN* 8.20 = T.14 for the *magnum miraculum* of an elephant felled by a single javelin to the head, or the implicit admiration of Commodus' hunting prowess at Dio 72(73).10.3, 72(73).18.1–19.1 and Hdn. 1.15.1–6. Note also Dio 72(73).14.1 for a rival hunter, a nobleman named Julius Alexander, who brought down a lion with a javelin thrown from horseback;

with gladiators, the crowd could demand the release of an animal performer it favored, presumably because it had put up a good fight or evaded capture in some impressive manner; they did so by waving their togas or scraps of material, such as napkins or handkerchiefs (Mart. *Ep.* 13.99, 13.100). The hunt offered to the eye exotic, fast-moving, and exciting images. And wagers could be laid. People in other eras have derived pleasure both from merely viewing wild or tamed animals (in circuses and zoos) and from bloodsports involving animals, and the *venatio* combined both attractions. The staging of hunts as stand-alone spectacles tells us that they had their own unique attractions and, probably, their own dedicated fans.[13] Given all this, we may defer further consideration of a major part of the crowd's mental state during the hunt until we turn our attention to sports spectatorship (see below, chapter 6), but we can conclude on the foregoing alone that the spectators' mental orientation to this phase of the spectacle was complex and fluid.

Evidence for what the crowd did or said as the hunts progressed is sparse. Most authors merely report what transpired on the sand, what animals were put on display and in what quantity, or note unusual happenings.[14] That the people expected a good showing, from animal and human performer alike, is well established. M. Caelius Rufus' increasingly frantic pleas to Cicero, as governor of Cilicia, to deliver panthers for a hunt he planned to stage at Rome are well known.[15] A letter of Pliny's (*Ep.* 6.34) illuminates Caelius' concerns. Pliny writes in consolation to a friend, a local magnate in Verona, whose African felines failed to appear on the appointed day. No doubt, the participation of the panthers had been widely advertised in advance, and their absence was a source of terrific and very public embarrassment for the games' sponsor, as can be deduced from the tone of Pliny's letter, which seeks to assure his friend that his efforts at pleasing the people had not gone unappreciated. In Apuleius' *The Golden Ass*, a fictional sponsor of games at Plataea saw his expensive troupe of bears reduced to almost nothing by pestilence, their bodies scavenged by the town's paupers

---

in response, Commodus had Alexander killed. The lesser status of *bestiarii* (and *venatores*) is suggested by their under-representation in arena-related epitaphs, graffiti, and other monuments; see Ville, *Gladiature*, 334–43. Of the 302 documents and monuments assembled by L. Robert, only five certainly commemorate *bestiarii*; Robert, *Gladiateurs*, 87–90 (no. 25), 90–2 (no. 27), 107 (no. 47a), 130 (no. 77), and 234–5 (no. 298). *Bestiarius* appears to have been a term of abuse used in arguments; see Goetz (ed.), *Corpus Glossariorum Latinorum*, vol. III, 643 §24.

[13] Severus deplored a senator who publicly contested at Ostia with a prostitute dressed as a leopard; Dio 75(76).8.2. The chap evidently liked his beast hunts.

[14] Typical would be such notices as, e.g., *RG* 22.3; Dio 53.27.6, 55.10.8, 66.25.1, 68.15.1, 72(73).18.1–2, 72(73).19.1; HA *Ant. Pius* 10.9; Strabo 18.1.44; Suet. *Titus* 7.3.

[15] Cic. *Att.* 6.1.21; Cic. *Fam.* 8.2.2, 8.4.5, 8.6.5, 8.8.10, 8.9.3; cf. HA *Prob.* 19.1–7.

(Apul. *Met.* 4.13–14 = T.1). Centuries later, Symmachus (*Ep.* 6.43, 9.141, 9.151) reports with considerable disgust how crocodiles he had imported at great expense for a spectacle at Rome went on hunger strike and perished. The spectators would voice their disappointment at such no-shows or vent their disapproval at dismal performances featuring emaciated animals or inept hunters. For the sponsor, whose great day this was supposed to be, such an outcome would be nothing less than appalling.

Beyond roaring their approval or disapproval, crowd behavior during the hunts goes largely unreported in the literary sources. A notable exception is the famous incident during Pompey's lavish games in 55 BC, when elephants behaved in such a way as to stir the spectators to sympathy, which caused them to curse Pompey (but note that the slaughter of the elephants was not interrupted).[16] Especially vivid are the eyewitness accounts of Cassius Dio and Herodian concerning Commodus' hunting appearances in the arena.[17] Commodus performed both as a gladiator and a huntsman in the arena. Despite killing or maiming opponents in private pairings, for combats staged in public he fought with wooden weapons. He engaged in hunts with lethal weapons, however. On one occasion the emperor had the arena criss-crossed with catwalks, which he then traversed and used as shooting platforms, killing 100 bears in a single day. When he grew tired, reports Dio, the emperor was given a cup of chilled wine. The arena crowd, people and senators alike, called out in unison the Roman equivalent of "cheers" – "Long life to you!" (Dio 72[73].18.2). Here the crowd imported into the arena context a popular phrase used in another: the tavern or dinner party. In a similar way, the bathing phrase *salvum lotum!* ("Well washed!") was called out as the martyr Saturus was bathed in his own blood while being mauled by a leopard.[18] Such invocations in the arena lent the phrases a macabre humor, but they also suggest that the crowd cast arena violence in the same category as their other, non-violent pastimes from which these phrases were drawn. A deeper irony may be hidden in the case of Commodus: the emperor was wished long life, even as he killed spectacularly.

Mosaic inscriptions are more informative. Among the most famous is the so-called Magerius mosaic, from Smirat in Tunisia (Fig. 9). It is generally agreed, given its content, that this mosaic records a historical *venatio*, put on by a magnate called Magerius, who later commissioned

---

[16] For a full discussion of this incident, below, ch. 7, pp. 249–52.
[17] For claims of autopsy, see Dio 72(73).4.2, 72(73).7.1, 72(73).18.3–4; Hdn. 1.2.5, 2.15.7.
[18] Saturus: *Pass. Perp. et Felic.* 21.2–3 (= Musurillo, *Acts of the Christian Martyrs*, 129–31). For *salvum lotum!*, see Fagan, *Bathing in Public*, 76 n. 4. It may also have carried an allusion to baptism.

Figure 9 The Magerius mosaic, Smirat

the mosaic to be laid on the floor of his house as a private monument to his public generosity. On stylistic grounds, it can be dated to the mid- to late third century AD.[19] The scene presents us with four named huntsmen (*venatores*) from the professional association called the Telegenii. They are spearing four leopards, who are also given names.[20] There is no specific iconographic indication of the arena setting, but that is made evident by the accompanying inscriptions. In two places, Magerius' name appears in the vocative case (*Mageri!*), commemorating the crowd's appreciative shouts. In the middle of the mosaic we get more detailed information. Here a long-haired and well-dressed boy, identified in the text as a herald of the Telegenii, is depicted holding a tray with four bags on it. Each bag bears the symbol for 1,000 (∞).

---

[19] See A. Beschaouch, "La mosaïque de chasse à l'amphithéâtre découverte à Smirat en Tunisie," *CRAI* (1966), 134–57; D. Bomgardner, "The Magerius Mosaic: Putting on a Show in the Amphitheatre," *Current World Archaeology* 3 (2007), 12–21; Dunbabin, *Mosaics of North Africa*, 67–9 (with plates 52 and 53). For the text, see *AE* 1967.549.

[20] There appear to have been several guilds of professional huntsmen operational in the North African provinces, especially Africa Proconsularis and Byzacena, in the third and fourth centuries AD; see A. Beschaouch, "Nouvelles recherches sur les sodalités de l'Afrique romaine," *CRAI* (1977), 486–503; Dunbabin, *Mosaics of North Africa*, 78–84. One of the Telegenii in the Magerius mosaic (the one named Spittara) works from stilts – quite a feat of daring and dexterity.

To the left of the boy is the following inscription, recording the herald's address to the crowd:

per curionem / dictum: "domi/ni mei ut / Telegeni(i) / pro leopardo / meritum ha/beant vestri / favoris, dona/te eis denarios / quingentos.

Spoken through a herald: "My lords, in order that the Telegenii have your favor's reward for each leopard killed, give them 500 *denarii*."

The crowd is addressed as *domini*, "lords." Claudius addressed arena crowds in the same way (Suet. *Claud.* 21.5 = T.22), and Cicero puts both *dominus* and *populus* on the same plane when stating whom the gladiator seeks to please (Cic. *Tusc.* 2.41 = T.5). The pandering is of course unctuous, but the use of the term is also highly significant. Here, in this time and place, the spectators imagined themselves lords for a day, and were addressed as such. This was their place, where they were the "masters."[21] This is why Juvenal (3.36–7) mocks those *arrivistes* who can now afford to give games but must obey the orders of the masses. In the Magerius mosaic, the herald goes on to urge the "lords" to pay the hunting company of the Telegenii a certain amount. But the spectators, of course, would pay the Telegenii nothing whatsoever. Payment would come, rather, from the *munerarius*, Magerius. Yet the crowd is addressed as if they determine how much the huntsmen are to be paid, as if the crowd had control over the event's sponsor, or as if the two – crowd and sponsor – were a single unit. (We shall see below other ways in which the crowd and *editor* were assimilated.) And this is not an isolated incident: the people regularly demanded payment for winners (Juv. 7.243). The symbols on the four moneybags show that Magerius doubled the amount requested and paid 1,000 *denarii* to each of the huntsmen, thereby demonstrating his civic-minded generosity. To the right of the tray-bearer the text continues:

adclamatum est:

"exemplo tuo mu/nus sic discant / futuri! audiant / praeteriti! unde / tale? quando tale? / exemplo quaesto/rum munus edes! / de re tua mu/nus edes! / (i)sta dies!"

---

[21] This is the essential meaning of *dominus*: someone at the head of the household, with rights of control over things; this meaning covers just under eight columns of the entry for *dominus* in *TLL* 5.1911–35 (they are 1913.30–1919.77). It could also be used as a form of address in polite company (Sen. *Ep.* 3.1), but that is too anodyne a usage for this context; this meaning garners just over one column in *TLL* 5.1925.3–1926.26 (although Suet. *Claud.* 21.5 is cited under this rubric). Cf. Cic. *Tusc.* 2.41 for weakened gladiators asking of the *domini* (here designating the crowd?) what their wishes are. The suggestion (Lane Fox, *Classical World*, 637 n. 52) that *domini* in the Magerius mosaic is addressed only to the rich members of the audience appears unlikely, as it suggests that the spectacle had yet to be paid for; see Bomgardner, "Magerius Mosaic," 16–18. On the meaning and usage of *dominus*, see E. Dickey, *Latin Forms of Address: From Plautus to Apuleius* (Oxford, 2002), 77–99.

Magerius do/nat.

"Hoc est habe/re! hoc est posse! / hoc est ia(m)! nox est; / ia(m) munere tuo / saccis missos."

They shouted out:

"By your example let future generations (of sponsors/office-holders?) learn that a *munus* is staged like this! Let past generations (of sponsors/office-holders?) hear about it! Where did such a show come from? When has one like this been staged? As an example for the quaestors, you will put on a spectacle! You will put it on at your own expense! This is your day!"

Magerius gives (the money).

"This is what it is to be rich! This is what it is to have power! – This is it alright! It is night. They have been sent away from your *munus* with their sacks (of money)!"[22]

The sociopolitical meaning of the chants is clear enough: the appreciation of the *editor* and the enhancement of his status within the community by public mass acclamation. What is particularly interesting in terms of content is the focus of the crowd on the sponsor of the games, which is likely due primarily to the mosaic's function as a commemoration of the *editor*'s immense personal outlays in funding spectacles. Yet this very circumstance also gives good reason to believe that some effort was made to recall the actual content of the acclamations on the day, at least those acclamations directed at the sponsor. The inscriptions are therefore likely to relay if not the actual acclamations on Magerius' big day, then at least the sorts of things crowds habitually chanted at sponsors during hunts. What we see happening in the chants is, first, the assimilation of crowd and sponsor in the herald's address, and then the crowd rejoicing in Magerius' capacity to put on games and his generosity in doing so. Magerius is at once acknowledged as the leading man who had enabled this day to come to pass and as the embodiment of the crowd's sense of empowerment. The

---

[22] The translation of this pair of texts is not without difficulty. For instance, does the *ut*-clause of the lefthand inscription express purpose or cause? If the *futuri* of the righthand acclamation is rendered as "future people/generations" or "posterity," then how is *praeteriti* to be translated? "Past (dead) people/generations" or "the past" does not make much sense, hence the suggestion that past and future "sponsors" or "office-holders" are meant. Such benefactors will envy or follow the example of Magerius, as the framing text suggests. Another issue is who the quaestors are: those of the local community, or those in Rome (I tend to favor the former). The final phrase might also be rendered "By your leave they've been sent away with their sacks (of money)." For variant translations (slightly abridged, but with the main sense as above), see Bomgardner, "Magerius Mosaic," 17; Lane Fox, *Classical World*, 637 n. 52; Futrell, *Roman Games*, 49–51; Wiedemann, *Emperors and Gladiators*, 16–17.

spectators are focused as much on themselves and their relationship to the spectacle's organizer as they are on what is happening on the sand below. The spectacle, in fact, is seen to be a vehicle that told the spectators important things about themselves.[23] We can expect their social identities to have been molded accordingly.

From all of this, a variety of attractions can be postulated for the *venationes*. The general appeal of seeing animals would play a basic part in luring people to watch.[24] The pleasures of watching competitive bloodsports involving animals (with the possiblity of betting), pleasures by no means restricted to the Romans, also generated interest. All of this would engender excitement and anticipation. The cultural symbolism of the hunts, in which animal threats or competitors were neutralized under controlled conditions, resonated in an agricultural society like ancient Rome and likely fed into the crowd's social identity for this phase of the *munera*. We may imagine that identity revolving around an "us-versus-them" attitude toward animals deemed to be dangers to humans or rivals for food resources. A shared sense of Roman power over nature also played a role. The spectators would not experience such meanings consciously, of course, but rather as a set of feelings generated by the mental processes of crowd dynamics: satisfaction and relief, wonder and amazement, a general sense of solidarity as humans and Romans categorized over and against the beasts and (largely non-Roman) huntsmen. The latter sensations were strengthened by the intracrowd content of the social identity, which had to do with the spectators' relationship not only to those on the sand, but also to each other and to the games' sponsor. Central to this facet of the experience would be a feeling of shared empowerment and validation, where the *munerarius* had provided an occasion for the crowd, the *domini*, to feel themselves in complete control. The social identities and categorizations of the Roman arena crowd, just for the hunting phase of the spectacles, thus emerge as multifaceted, complex, and dynamic. When hunts were staged as part of a larger conglomerate spectacle, this complexity and dynamism was extended accordingly.

[23] As, indeed, has been recognized in several studies surveyed in chapter 1. The Roman populace employed acclamations in all sorts of public contexts (e.g., triumphs, religious festivals, imperial departures and arrivals, at theaters, circuses, as well as the arena), so that many of these chants were likely traditional and formulaic. The conventions of Roman acclamation are studied in detail by G. S. Aldrete, *Gestures and Acclamations in Ancient Rome* (Baltimore, 1999), esp. 99–164; C. Roueché, "Acclamations in the Later Roman Empire: New Evidence from Aphrodisias," *JRS* 74 (1984), 181–99, esp. 188–90 on the structure of acclamations.

[24] Note, for instance, the books of Pliny's *HN* devoted to animals and their behavior (8–11), as well as Aelian's *De Natura Animalium*. Balsdon, *Life and Leisure*, 302–6; J. M. C. Toynbee, *Animals in Roman Life and Art* (London, 1973; reprint Baltimore, 1986), *passim*.

The execution phase of arena spectacles cannot have been anything other than viscerally brutal. This was sheer murder, the disposal of what was considered human garbage. While Seneca was repelled by what he saw during the lunchtime break (*Ep.* 7.2–5 = T.20), he records various comments the people shouted out as the butchery proceeded: they demanded various types of action (see below, chapter 5, pp. 182–3). Seneca adds a further noteworthy detail, often overlooked: all of this happened when the arena was practically empty.[25] Pure butchery, apparently, was not to everyone's taste (for more on this, see chapter 5, p. 158). Seneca tells the story, of course, to emphasize the theme announced at the start of the passage: that being in a crowd is harmful. Despite his essentially Le Bonian analysis – joining a crowd inevitably entails an insensible descent into barbarism – Seneca's account reveals something of the spectators' mental state. During executions, their ability to direct the course of action on the sand would have strengthened an already formidable sense of empowerment, indeed the ultimate sense of empowerment, over life and death itself. This was one of the clearest manifestations of the crowd as *domini*, lords of the arena. The crowd merely called out its wishes to see them enacted. Corroboration is offered by the Christian martyrologies, which contain numerous notices of the crowd's utterances. As with Seneca's anecdote, it is irrelevant whether the phrases were or were not actually shouted out by a specific crowd on any given day. Rather, the martyrologies report the sorts of actions and expressions their Roman readers would associate (probably from personal experience) with the execution phase of a spectacle.[26]

Polycarp, bishop of Smyrna, was executed in the mid-second century. Polycarp was a well-known figure in the community, so as he entered the amphitheater a huge shout went up. There followed an exchange with the governor, who tried to persuade Polycarp to recant and worship the emperor, to have regard for his age (he was eighty-six at the time), and to declare "Away with the atheists," by which the governor meant Christians. Polycarp instead invoked that very phrase against the spectators while shaking his fist at them. The governor then invited him to try to move the mob with his rhetoric, but he declined – they were not worthy to

[25] See below, ch. 5, n. 86.
[26] For the value of the martyrologies as historical evidence, see G. W. Bowersock, *Martyrdom and Rome* (Cambridge, 1995), 23–39; D. Potter, "Martyrdom as Spectacle," in R. Scodel (ed.), *Theater and Society in the Classical Word* (Ann Arbor, 1993), esp. 56–8. For a recent teasing out of their meaning, see Edwards, *Death*, 207–20. Note also the survey of visual representations of Christian martyrs, J. W. Salomonson, Voluptatem Spectandi Non Perdat Sed Mutet: *Observations sur l'Iconographie du martyre en Afrique Romaine* (Amsterdam, 1979), esp. 42–50, and the recent analysis of martyrdom as an act of communication in A. Carfora, *I cristiani al leone: I martiri cristiani nel contesto mediatico dei giochi gladiatorii. Oi Christianoi 10* (Trapani, 2009).

hear his defense. The governor announced through a herald that Polycarp had confessed to being a Christian, and the whole mob – identified by the martyrologist as pagans and Jews – shouted out that Polycarp was the "schoolmaster of Asia – the father of Christians – the destroyer of our gods – the one who teaches the masses not to sacrifice or do reverence." The stress on the *entire* crowd shouting out these phrases allows us to imagine them chanted in unison. The spectators then demanded that a lion be produced and set on Polycarp. Since the animal shows were over, this was not allowed, so they demanded he be burned alive. The mob then collected wood from various sources, such as workshops and baths, raised a pyre, and saw Polycarp burn.[27] The crowd is here shown not only to make cruel demands in the manner that so horrifed Seneca, but to participate actively in the execution to a remarkable degree: they physically left their seats in the arena, hunted about in the neighborhood for firewood, and then returned to contribute to Polycarp's pyre. In this case, then, the mob were not just participatory witnesses to the enactment of justice (as they saw it), but active agents in its implementation. The spectators had become a lynch mob.[28] The inverse was also possible. At Lugdunum (Lyons) in AD 177, the pagan populace turned on the Christians in their midst. This was a pogrom, where Christians were rooted out, dragged through the streets, beaten and cursed, and hauled before officials for sentencing.[29] Some were killed in the forum, others strangled in prison, and others executed during gladiatorial games staged specially for the occasion. A small group of the condemned perished in the arena under a variety of tortures demanded by the mob (Euseb. *Hist. eccl.* 5.1.38). The same crowd called for the production of the Christian Attalus, who was spared on this occasion because he was a Roman citizen (ibid. 5.1.43–4). After the emperor had reached a decision in his case, Attalus was returned to the arena for burning in a brazen seat. As he burned, he castigated the crowd as cannibals and refused to name his god when the spectators demanded that he do so (ibid. 5.1.52). When Blandina and the boy Ponticus were brought into the arena on the last day of the spectacle, the crowd grew angry at their refusal to honor the pagan

---

[27] *Pass. Polyc.* 9–16 (= Musurillo, *Acts of the Christian Martyrs*, 8–15; quote at *Pass. Polyc.* 12.2 = Musurillo, *Acts of the Christian Martyrs*, 10–11). See also L. L. Thompson, "The Martyrdom of Polycarp: Death in the Roman Games," *Jrel* 82 (2002), 27–52.

[28] Popular justice in the Roman empire was not above summary execution at the hands of a mob; see, e.g., Apul. *Met.* 2.27–9, 7.12–13; Diod. Sic. 37.12; Hor. *Sat.* 1. 2. 41–6. See also Fagan, "Violence in Roman Social Relations."

[29] The whole affair was recorded in a letter Eusebius purports to reproduce; see Euseb. *Hist. eccl.* 5.1–2.8 (= Musurillo, *Acts of the Christian Martyrs*, 62–85); note esp. ibid. 5.1.7, and 5.1.31. For discussion, see Kyle, *Spectacles of Death*, 248–51.

idols and at their habit of insulting their executioners, and this rendered the crowd pitiless, according to the letter cited in Eusebius (ibid. 5.1.53). The crowd's anger extended to the corpses, which were denied burial as a way (the pagans reasoned) of frustrating resurrection. Interestingly, Eusebius notes a variety of attitudes toward the corpses on the part of the pagans, from rage to mockery to a puzzled empathy (ibid. 5.1.59–60). The special circumstances at Lugdunum meant that these arena executions were part of a wider pattern of ongoing mob violence, frequently quite direct, aimed at Christians. Here a lynch mob had become an arena crowd.

In other arena martyrdoms, the spectators retained their more habitual, less active role and limited their participation to vocal expression. They questioned the martyr Carpus (or Pamfilus, in the Latin version) as to why he was smiling at being nailed down to be burned alive and then questioned the very justice of Agathonike's execution.[30] The crowd objected to the nakedness of Perpetua and Felicitas in the arena, but was also enraged by the singing, praying, and contempt of authority expressed by Perpetua, Felicitas, and other Christians in Carthage. They demanded them scourged by gladiators. As noted above (p. 128) the crowd shouted "Well washed!" at Saturus as he suffered at the teeth and claws of a leopard. His unconscious body was then set to one side to have its throat cut, but the crowd insisted that he be brought back into the middle of the arena so they could see the deed done.[31] Apuleius describes how his hero-turned-donkey Lucius was condemned to couple with a murderess in the arena. The crowd roared its appreciation when he appeared in the *pompa*, and was then entertained by innocuous preliminaries – dancers, followed by actors dressed as gods re-enacting the Judgment of Paris on a mountain stage-set. This complete, the crowd demanded the woman and the donkey, but Lucius escaped as the staff were busy getting ready for the show (Apul. *Met.* 10.29–35 = T.2). The inconsistency evident in these crowd interventions – sometimes cruel, sometimes lenient – is enough in itself to reveal the psychological complexity of the spectators' view of what was transpiring before their eyes.

Of the three phases of the *munus*, the midday executions boast the greatest volume of ancient evidence for crowd vocalizations, presumably because this was the phase into which the spectators had the greatest sustained input, and also because the martyrologies provide so much information

---

[30] *Pass. Carp. Pap. et Agathon.* A38–47 and B4.3–6.5 (= Musurillo, *Acts of the Christian Martyrs*, 26–9 and 32–7). See also below, ch. 7, pp. 254–7.
[31] *Pass. Perp. et Felic.* 21.1–10 (= Musurillo, *Acts of the Christian Martyrs*, 128–31).

about crowd behavior. The content of spectator vocalizations is dominated by demands for particular victims to be produced or specific torments to be applied to them. On rare occasions, such as with Agathonike, the crowd voiced disapproval of the proceedings (see below, chapter 5, pp. 179–82). In terms of social identity content, the prevalent elements appear to have been a tremendous sense of empowerment coupled with the conviction that those suffering on the sand were getting what they deserved (a matter investigated more closely in the next chapter). The basic outlook was therefore similar to that which underlay taking enjoyment in the hunts: threats, now in human form, were being neutralized. But the capacity of the crowd to shape the action directly would also lend them a godlike sensation of power over life and death. They could demand that a particular prisoner be brought out, and then insist on the method of killing to be applied to him or her. And as the prisoners perished, they could be mocked or otherwise derided.[32]

We must not conceive of these attitudes as universally held and uniformly expressed by all crowd members, as the varied reactions of onlookers to the treatment of Christian corpses at Lugdunum reminds us. What was taking place on the sand might also cause divisions of opinion within the crowd. One of the freedmen in Petronius (*Sat.* 45.7 = T.12) forecasts how the spectators will argue when a certain Glyco has his domestic accountant (*dispensator*) thrown to the beasts in the forthcoming games. The accountant had committed adultery with the mistress of the house to merit this fate, and the freedman foresees arguments in the stands between jealous husbands and loverboys. The scenario is comedic, but it plays off reality and reveals that the crowd's psychological cohesion was not absolute and did not affect everyone equally. It seems unrealistic to imagine that absolutely everyone in the crowd, for instance, objected to Agathonike's execution or Perpetua's nakedness. In a strong echo of what we have seen for execution crowds in other times and places (see chapter 2, pp. 73–4), the nature of the crime, the identity of the criminal, the validity of the conviction, and the appropriateness of the punishment all played a role in shaping spectator behavior. Kathleen Coleman proposes that the attractions of arena executions were an amalgam of desires and expectations to

---

[32] That crowd mockery of the dying was a common occurrence is not obvious. Most of the primary evidence comes from the martyrologies, and they have an axe to grind with arena spectators. Perhaps, also, the peculiar "crimes" and demeanor of Christian victims – their strange beliefs, apparent know-it-all arrogance in denying the state deities, rumored cannibalism, air of superiority in the face of torments, etc. – invited commentary in a way that would not apply to the execution of, say, a common murderer who displayed the expected terror as s/he perished.

see justice done, the inherent attraction of horrible sights, the thrill of the unexpected when people were exposed to beasts,[33] a morbid fascination with death, and a relief from boredom. The spectators came to the arena with a series of expectations as to what would transpire and how it would play out. Performers and victims had their roles to play, and the crowd anticipated seeing those roles fulfilled. When they were not, disgruntlement could ensue.[34] Appreciation of crowd dynamics, however, allows us to see how this disgruntlement played out psychologically (and we will review another likely psychological factor in chapter 7). By denying the power of the crowd to terrify or cow them, the actions and demeanor of recalcitrant *noxii* (execution victims) challenged a core element of the crowd's social identity, i.e., their role as *domini* whose wishes were made real merely by being uttered. The challenge, naturally, made the spectators angry and vengeful.

Evidence for crowd behavior and expressions during the gladiatorial phase of a spectacle is limited. In Augustine's passage on Alypius (*Conf.* 6.13 = T.3), the crowd issues a unified roar when a gladiator falls. This was presumably standard practice, as it is among modern sports spectators when there is a score or a good chance is missed. When a wound was inflicted, the cry "He's got one!" (*hoc habet!*) went up. If the fighters were hesitant or timid, the crowd would shout "Get stuck in!" (*adhibete!*). Spectators even shouted out tips to the combatants.[35] They would stand and gesticulate as the fights played out, urging on their favorites and stretching out their left hands (which were normally kept inside the toga on formal occasions). As gold coins were counted out to victors, the crowd would count along.[36] As with the other phases of the spectacle, spectators would call for particular gladiators to be brought out.[37] The real moment of truth, however, was when a gladiator was defeated and appealed to the *editor/munerarius* by raising a finger and looking toward the tribunal.[38] While the decision was being made, the crowd shouted its opinion and gesticulated dramatically. The centrality of this moment of decision for arena

---

[33] For instance, an attempt to affix the martyr Saturus to a boar failed when the animal instead gored the gladiator tying Saturus down; *Pass. Perp. et Felic.* 19.5 (= Musurillo, *Acts of the Christian Martyrs*, 126–7).

[34] Coleman, "Fatal Charades," 57–9; Potter, "Matyrdom as Spectacle," 63–71.

[35] For crowd vocalizations and tips, see, e.g., Aug. *Conf.* 6.13 = T.3; Tert. *ad Mart.* 1.2; Fronto *Ad M. Caes.* 1.8.2; Prudent. *C. Symm.* 2.1096–113 = T.16; Don. ad Ter. *Andr.* 1.1.56, Ov. *Ars Am.* 1.165–6. Prudent. *Psychom.* 53, Ter. *Andr.* 83, Virg. *Aen.* 12.296 (*hoc habet!*); Petron. *Sat.* 45.12 (*adhibete!*).

[36] On crowd behavior during bouts, see below, ch. 6, pp. 209–27. See Juv. 7.243 (on gold paid to the winners).

[37] Mart. *Spect.* 23; Suet. *Cal.* 30.2, *Dom.* 4.1.   [38] For sources, see below, ch. 6, n. 78.

games is reflected in its prevalence among mosaic depictions of gladiatorial combat.[39]

A Late Imperial mosaic from Rome, now in Madrid, has two named gladiators fighting in two registers, to be read from bottom to top. In the lower register, the two gladiators (named Habilis and Maternus) approach each other, weapons poised, under the watchful eyes of two officials. In the upper register, Habilis is shown in the act of killing the fallen Maternus, who lies in a pool of blood on the sand. Inscriptions accompany the action. In the lower register we are informed that "Symmachius put the fighters to the sword" (*quibus pugnantibus Symmachius ferrum misit*). This may be something the crowd called out, or it may simply be disembodied narration. Since both gladiators are named, Symmachius can only be the *editor*, an inference confirmed by the texts in the upper register. Here, as in the Magerius mosaic, the name of the *munerarius* appears in the vocative "Symmachius!" with the added acclamation "Happy chap!" (*Symmachi! Homo felix!*). These are crowd acclamations. The simple statement "I kill [him]" (*neco*) appears, and the crowd cries "We see these deeds!" (*Haec videmus!*).[40] Here the *editor* is credited with killing the fallen fighters (cf. Juv. 3.36–7; Petron. *Sat.* 45.11), even though he kills nobody directly. He *does*, however, make the decision on an appeal and, in that sense, he can say "I kill [him]." The crowd then validates his decision, which the spectators had no doubt influenced by expressing their judgments as the *editor* weighed his options – "We see these deeds." At such moments, spectator and sponsor were again psychologically assimilated under the umbrella of the crowd's social identities and in their expression of them; the two parties were in close agreement, jointly determining what happened below. Sponsor and crowd are connected in mutual validation. The crowd praises Symmachius' staging of the games; he stands out as the centerpiece of the great day, and this fact is understandably celebrated in the mosaic Symmachius commissioned to commemorate it. Graffiti acclamations painted on walls at Pompeii honor the Pompeian magnate Cn. Alleius Nigidius Maius, who gave many games at Pompeii over his long local career, which stretched from the 40s AD to the death of the city in AD 79. The graffiti are likely to reflect the sorts of things shouted out by the crowd in the amphitheater on the days of Alleius' games: "Good luck to Alleius Maius,

---

[39] See Brown, "Death as Decoration," esp. 202–7; Ville, *Gladiature*, 410–24.

[40] For the mosaic (of the late third or early fourth centuries AD), see M. E. Blake, "Mosaics of the Late Empire in Rome and Vicinity," *MAAR* 17 (1940), 81–130, esp. 112–13. For the relevant inscriptions, see *CIL* 6.10205 = 6.33979 = *ILS* 5140 = *EAOR* i.114.

prince of the games-givers!"[41] The acclamations recorded in these texts are simple when compared to some of those in the Magerius mosaic (see above), where rather more complex statements appear, despite the packaging of some elements as discrete phrases (*unde tale? quando tale?... ista dies... hoc est habere*, etc.).[42] A whiff of implausibility may hang about the longer and more complicated phrases (*exemplo tuo munus sic discant futuri!... exemplo quaestorum munus edes!*). Yet as long as they were formulaic and rhythmic, complex chants could (and can) be taken up by a lot of people. Romans were accustomed to learning by rhythmic chanting from childhood.[43] In the theater and amphitheater, the crowd could also be instructed: organized cheerleaders and claques were a longstanding feature of spectacles.[44] (In the Late Imperial and Byzantine periods crowd acclamations, now staged in all sorts of contexts but especially in the theater and hippodrome, were organized by professional claques and became essential components in the elevation of emperors. Popular acclamations were even recorded and reported to absent rulers.[45]) Dio, an eyewitness to the events he describes, tells how the senators (and crowd?) at spectacles in which the emperor Commodus appeared in AD 192 were required to chant "You are lord and you are first, of all men most fortunate. You win and win you will; from time everlasting, Amazonian, you win." Dio expressly says the spectators were told what to chant on these occasions and also notes the people habitually chanted rhythmic phrases in praise of Commodus in

---

[41] *CIL* 4.1179b–c, 4.7790 = Sabbatini Tumolesi, *Gladiatorum Paria*, 43 (no. 16), *Cn(aeo) Alleio Maio | principi munerarior[um] | feliciter*. On this magnate, see Franklin, "Cn. Alleius Nigidius Maius and the Amphitheatre"; Sabbatini Tumolesi, *Gladiatorum Paria*, 32–44. Comparable acclamations are sometimes appended to advertisements; see, e.g., ibid., 47–8 (nos. 18–19).

[42] Compare the simple slogan, "Great is Artemis of the Ephesians," rapidly taken up and chanted for two hours during the riot there against Paul; see *Acts* 19:27.

[43] See Aug. *Conf.* 1.13.22; Ov. *Fast.* 3.535–6 (in the theater specifically); Pliny *Pan.* 73.1–2 (spontaneous chants for Trajan). See also Horsfall, *Culture*, 11–19 and 39–42 (on widespread memorization through chanting and theater songs/chants learned in advance).

[44] Claques are attested from the first century BC onward: see, e.g., Cic. *Sest.* 115; Dio 61.20.3, 76(77).2.2, 77(78).10.4; Plaut. *Am.* 65–85; Plut. *Pomp.* 48.7; Tac. *Ann.* 1.16.4, 14.15.8–9, 16.4.4–5.1; Euseb. *Hist. eccl.* 7.30.9. Philo (*Flacc.* 34) records the organization and practice of chants in the gymnasium of first-century AD Alexandria, a practice brought to Rome by Nero (Suet. *Nero* 20.3; cf. Dio 63.10.1, 63.20.5). Dio records, sometimes from personal observation, chants in the Circus in AD 193 (73[74].4.1–3) and 196 (75[76].4.1–6). See further Horsfall, *Culture*, 31–42; Potter, "Performance, Power, and Justice," 142–4; P. J. J. Vanderbroeck, *Popular Leadership and Collective Behavior in the Late Roman Republic (ca. 80–50 BC)* (Amsterdam, 1987), 61–2, 143–4.

[45] J. H. W. G. Liebescheutz, *Antioch: City and Imperial Administration in the Later Roman Empire* (Oxford, 1972), 211–16; Liebescheutz, *Decline and Fall*, 208–10; C. Roueché, *Aphrodisias in Late Antiquity* (London, 1989), 116–32. On the reporting of acclamations to emperors, see *CTh.* 1.16.6, 8.5.32 and various *loci* cited by Roueché, "Acclamations," 181–8.

the theaters and amphitheaters, which they twisted into mockery after his assassination.[46]

Many chants were probably formulaic and familiar from a young age. Given the sparsity of the evidence, it is impossible to say whether portions of the Magerius or Symmachius acclamations were standard material routinely addressed to *munerarii* in their locales, if not further afield. Acclamation formulae likely varied by region, perhaps even by city. Paid claques were used to orchestrate acclamations, in which case they may have been practiced in advance, at least by a section of the crowd. Some political demands or grievances aired to emperors at the games in Rome were of a complex nature, so singing the praises of a local magnate is not likely to have been beyond the capabilities of arena spectators.[47]

Political demands and popular commentary occurred at all sorts of spectacles. At the arena, they do not appear to have been tethered to any particular phase of the events but were just a product of the boisterous crowd who came out to watch. Previous work has stressed the political importance of these demands and comments, since they often took the form of airing grievances at state officials who were present. Because of this, the games have been described as a sort of Roman "parliament," where chants and acclamations mediated relations between rulers and ruled that reflected the symbolic relationship between the giver of the games and his public.[48] The psychological effects of such behavior are no less important than its political and symbolic significance, and with this in mind we turn to the content of the arena crowd's social identities.

SOCIAL IDENTITY CONTENT

From the evidence for the chants and vocalizations and spectator behaviors at the arena, as well as from the hypotheses about the cultural meaning(s) of the games surveyed in chapter 1, it is possible to sketch the contours of

---

[46] Dio 72(73).20.2 (senators) and 73(74).2.3 (people). The senatorial acclamations recorded for Claudius II (HA *Claud.* 4.2–4) are all relatively straightforward: "Claudius Augustus, deliver us from the Palmyrenes" (repeated five times) or "Claudius Augustus, you are brother, father, friend, good senator and truly emperor" (repeated eighty times!).

[47] See Bollinger, *Theatralis Licentia*, 50–71.

[48] For a comprehensive assembly of the evidence and a thoroughgoing political analysis of it, see ibid., 24–73; Cameron, *Circus Factions*, 157–229; A. Lewin, *Assemblee popolari e lotta politica nella città dell'impero romana* (Florence, 1995), esp. 108–12. See also Clavel-Lévêque, *L'empire en jeux*, 153–61; Edmondson, "Dynamic Arenas"; Flaig, *Ritualisierte Politik*, 232–60, esp. 237–42; Hopkins, *Death and Renewal*, 14–20 (16 for the statement "the amphitheatre was their parliament"); Potter, "Performance, Power and Justice." For the relationship between the public and *editor*, see Brown, "Death as Decoration." See also Aldrete, *Gestures and Acclamations*.

Figure 10 Podium wall of amphitheater at Lecce in Apulia, topped with reliefs
of animal hunts

the crowd's social identity content, but only in the broadest strokes; the
caveats outlined above (p. 125) about regional, demographic, and diachronic
variation should always be kept in mind.

The most obvious and overt component of the crowd's social identity
was surely the ingroup–outgroup distinction and its role in promoting
ingroup cohesion among the spectators. The distinction between spectator
and performer was powerfully reinforced by the physical setting, where the
high podium wall separated the two groups (Figs. 3, 4, 10); by the social
and moral degradation of all arena performers relative to the spectators
(see the next chapter); and by the fact that only one side was in any danger
of getting hurt or killed. No matter what the status differentiation was
within the Roman arena crowd, these circumstances applied to all of them
equally and, just as equally, they did not apply to the performers down
on the arena floor. The spectators did not have to work hard at making
social categorizations, since the arena context made them so evident. The
sense of "us-and-them" is thus the most basic and pervasive element of
the arena spectators' psychology. The ingroup–outgroup distinction has

been demonstrated by social psychology as one of the most profoundly influential in human social relations, and it was sustained throughout all phases of the spectacle. Its effect would have been to lend the spectators an overarching sense of psychological cohesion, even if they were socially disparate and sat in segregated subgroups. Indeed, the subdivision of the spectators into peer groups was, if anything, more likely to facilitate the crowd's expression of its ingroup identities rather than to hinder it. The end result of all this would be to inculcate a powerful sense of connectedness and belonging among the spectators.

The symbolism of the arena's seating arrangements, a topic which has already been explored by other scholars, may have further buttressed ingroup cohesion. At spectacles, the Roman social order was made manifest, as each group occupied its proper place in the *cavea* relative to its superiors and inferiors. But no less significantly, that entire social order was visibly and powerfully categorized relative to the threatening and deviant forces paraded across the arena floor.[49] The symbolism of this "community-made-manifest" context, particularly given the presence of well-defined outgroupers occupying a separate physical space below, would have been experienced as feelings of validation in the stands.

Crowds are often at their most cohesive and vocal when they are focused on a leader (a fact recognized by the likes of Hitler).[50] So a further cohering force at the arena was the attention the crowd paid to the *editor*, particularly at crucial moments in the spectacle: at the opening procession (*pompa*), as events were introduced, when certain actions were demanded by the crowd, when defeated gladiators appealed, and when victors were crowned and paid. At these moments, the crowd's identity would be channeled through the games' sponsor, as spectator and *munerarius* were virtually assimilated. It seems from the evidence reviewed above that the *editor* would seek to stress this assimilation by, for instance, addressing the crowd as *domini* (the *editor* would himself be a wealthy *dominus*) or agreeing with, and then enacting, the spectators' judgments about fallen gladiators. The crowd would express its appreciation, and it was precisely for such moments of adulation and oneness with the community that the rich and prominent paid for games out of their own pockets, and why some later

---

[49] That the crowd's wider identity was (at least in part) defined as "the Roman order" vs. the criminal/deviant on the sand is argued by, among others, Coleman, "Fatal Charades," 44–9; Edmondson, "Dynamic Arenas," 83; Gunderson, "Ideology," 133–6; J. Maurin, "Les Barbares aux arènes," *Ktèma* 9 (1984), 102–11; Wiedemann, *Emperors and Gladiators*, 68–91.

[50] See Canetti, *Crowds and Power*. On Hitler, see I. Kershaw, *Hitler, 1889–1936: Hubris* (New York, 1999), 156 and 652 n. 12.

memorialized them in mosaics, reliefs, or other monuments. That said, the unity of sponsor and community was occasional and momentary as the games progressed: the *editor*, it will be recalled, sat apart in his box and also accepted popular acclamations that stressed his social preeminence within the group.

This final detail reminds us, even at the risk of repetition, that we need to be careful in this line of analysis and recognize that the ingroup cohesion charted here was not uniform and untextured. Events on the sand, developments in the wider social or political context, mishaps with the performers or the equipment, or other twists of fortune could cause the spectators to make demands unrelated to the spectacle, to criticize or even curse the *editor*, or to argue among themselves. But at the arena, these occasions appear to have been brief and relatively rare – had they been common, fewer magnates would have risked giving games in the first place. They also appear to have had little impact on the overall spectacle; we do not hear, for instance, of arena games that ground to a halt or were abandoned due to crowd disgruntlement.[51] We may safely imagine that a sustained ingroup cohesion was a prominent element in the crowd's social identity, even if it was occasionally fractured by circumstance.

Ingroup cohesion, and the nature of the spectacle being watched – controlled hunts and the struggles of outgroupers for survival – suggest another element in the spectators' social identity: a sense of privilege and priority generating feelings of empowerment. That arena spectators could directly intervene in the course of executions and enjoyed input into the outcomes of gladiatorial bouts that went to appeal were direct expressions of their power, as they got to experience an almost god-like control over life and death. People like feeling superior to others, and the Roman arena was one place where Romans of all stripes, who expended much energy establishing priority among themselves in other contexts, could feel better about themselves as a group, in comparison to those they had come to see.[52] The presence of the underclasses among the spectators adds another dimension to this psychological scenario. These were the people holding some of the weaker hands Roman society dealt to its members. Even though they did not number among the destitute or rank with the slave population, they lived in cramped apartments amidst discomfort and squalor, enjoyed

---

[51] Contrast this with the disruption or abandonment of executions in more recent times when the spectators (for whatever reason) turned against the event; see above, ch. 2 n. 34 and below, ch. 5, pp. 175–6.

[52] A point well made by Coleman ("Fatal Charades," 57–9) about amphitheater executions, but surely no less applicable to any phase of the conglomerate arena spectacle.

no recognition on the grand stage of imperial grandeur, lived and died in almost complete obscurity, and had to put up with the high-handed condescension of their social superiors. These were the people Seneca advised Nero to leave "to make up the numbers."[53] But at the arena they were the *domini*, and, perhaps more importantly, their right to wield power was publicly acknowledged in a fashion usually denied to them in other contexts.[54] Juvenal mocks the *nouveaux riches* who give games and "when the mob *gives the order* with turned thumbs, kill to popular acclaim."[55] In this formulation, it is the crowd who gives the orders and the *editor* who does the crowd's bidding – the very essence of being a *dominus*. Seneca asks: "Why do the people grow so unjustly angry at gladiators that they think themselves harmed because the men don't go to their deaths willingly? They reckon they've been disparaged, and in their expressions, gestures, and agitation turn from being a spectator to being an adversary."[56] This strange reaction becomes understandable if we conceive of the spectators feeling that their authority was being challenged, and along with it their sense of empowerment, a core element in their social identity. Even worse, outgroupers were the source of the challenge.

The spectators naturally brought with them to their seats a variety of social identities derived from the wider societal context, and at the arena, in addition to a strong ingroup identification within the crowd as a whole, they found some of those identities reinforced by their segregated disposition in the amphitheater's *maeniana* and *cunei*. That fault lines could open up between these localized identities and that of the wider crowd in the *cavea* seems plausible. Yet the very purpose of attending the games played a role in papering over differences: to celebrate qualities held dear by the community as a whole and to see agreed-upon outgroupers pay the penalty they deserved. As sociocultural analyses of the arena have already established, the gladiatorial games reinforced the imperial order

---

[53] Sen. *Clem.* 1.5.7. On the living conditions of Roman commoners, see, e.g., Scobie, "Slums, Sanitation, and Mortality"; Z. Yavetz, "The Living Conditions of the Urban Plebs in Republican Rome," *Latomus* 17 (1958), 500–17 (= R. Seager, *The Crisis of the Roman Republic* [Cambridge, 1969], 162–79).

[54] One is reminded here of the famous phrase of Juvenal's (10.77–81; cf. Fronto *Princ. Hist.* 17) that the people of Rome, formerly masters of kings and granters of *imperium* to magistrates, were now reduced to obsessing about bread and circuses. From the psychological standpoint just reviewed, participation in, say, a Republican electoral assembly and attending the games may have been analogous (but not identical) experiences. Exploring this possibility, however, lies beyond the scope of the current work.

[55] Juv. 3.36–7: *munera nunc edunt, et verso pollice vulgus / cum iubet, occidunt populariter* (emphasis in translation added).

[56] Sen. *Dial.* 3.2.4: *gladiatoribus quare populus irascitur et tam inique, ut iniuriam putet, quod non libenter pereunt? contemni se iudicat et vultu, gestu, ardore a spectatore in adversarium vertitur.* See also above, n. 21.

(especially in the hunts and executions) and (in the gladiator pairings) put into practice essential elements of the Roman male value system: martial skill and endurance, contempt for death and injury, establishing priority in trials of strength, and earning public approval through displays of *virtus*. In gladiatorial bouts the complex social mechanisms by which these values played out under normal conditions were reduced to a particularly raw and basic form and, even more intriguingly, they were seen to operate in those otherwise deemed below social consideration. That the origins of the performers often lay abroad (as captured rebels, bandits, fugitive slaves, professional performers from the provinces, etc.) would only strengthen these intracrowd impressions and feelings.[57] In this way, arena games might be likened to a morality play, where the spectators, through watching outsiders, were told important things about themselves as members of the Roman community. Attendance made them feel valued and connected, their system of beliefs validated and celebrated.[58]

The symbolic and cultural meaning(s) of arena games were thus not experienced as active cognitions but as feelings, impressions, and emotions that addressed themselves to such core human needs as connectedness, validation, belonging, and empowerment. Social identities at the arena were channeled on to the arena floor and subgroup identities within the crowd adapted to these conditions. The self-categorization of small-group members was therefore balanced by a social categorization over against others in the crowd (according to various criteria – recall Corydon's looking down enviously on the privileged seats of the white-clad tribunes and *equites*), but more importantly, by the overarching contrast between the spectators and the unfortunates on the sand below. The issue of prejudice is treated more fully in the following chapter, but its contribution to the crowd's sense of power and superiority should be noted here in passing.

The fluidity of social identities would also mean that individual spectators would switch seamlessly between them as the spectacle progressed. Sharing a section of seats with a group of one's peers, identities might remain confined to the subgroup during intervals, breaks, pauses, or lulls but would morph and adapt in response to specific actions taking place in the spectacle. On occasions, chants or acclamations from the whole

---

[57] On the foreign origins of many gladiators and other arena performers, see Ville, *Gladiature*, 264–7; Wiedemann, *Emperors and Gladiators*, 113–14.

[58] I do not, however, think that the games were a *necessary* means of achieving this – there were other venues and occasions where "Roman-ness" was loudly celebrated as well – and, as such, I question the opinion of those who would locate the games near the center of Roman culture; see below, conclusion.

crowd would generate different psychological responses, perhaps diverting attention briefly to the sponsor's box or to some section of the crowd or to a move made by a performer. The phases of the spectacle would emphasize different aspects of the spectators' suite of identities and cause them to make new categorizations, depending on what was happening and to whom. Unfortunately, we do not have the data to trace these identity shifts in any detail. It can be imagined, however, that moments such as the suspense-filled pause while a decision was reached on life or death would focus the crowd's attention intensely. Spectators would move frequently between their subgroup social identities and the wider crowd's versions of it, as the phases of the spectacle fashioned the psychological environment.

Chanting added to the sense of cohesion. Chants probably came and went, as they were taken up by a part of the crowd or by all of it, as the case may be. In chants, whether organized or spontaneous, a crowd expresses its social identity, particularly when the chants are coincident with the categorization of outgroups: derogatory songs against rival fans, for instance.[59] Chanting reinforces the liberating sense of free expression that courses through a crowd's membership. Unified chants would have greatly increased the crowd's sense of ingroup cohesion, solidarity, and empowerment, especially when they saw their demands not only met but exceeded, as with Magerius' doubling the fee to the hunting company employed in his show.[60] The enclosed, elliptical shape of the arena, particularly when the roof awnings (*vela*) were erected, would have amplified chants emanating from even a part of the crowd and projected it across the auditorium to the spectators sitting opposite.[61] Between acclamations, routine catchphrases elicited by happenings on the sand, crowd demands, or spontaneous reactions to the particulars of a spectacle, we must imagine the arena crowd in a constant state of vocalization, not just cheering and clapping randomly but issuing bursts of organized chanting, aimed at both the performers and the games' sponsor. Bands provided musical cues and rhythmic support for the longer and more complex chants. The din would have been deafening.

The harsh life experiences and attitudes of the spectators (see chapter 1, pp. 22–38) as well as the mostly negative feelings they harbored toward the arena's lowly victims (see chapter 5, pp. 174–82) also played a role

---

[59] Horsfall (*Culture*, 67–8) notes the unifying effect of attending theater and amphitheater events with a large crowd.

[60] Of course chanting, when directed at subgroups within a crowd, can divide the crowd against itself, as we shall see shortly.

[61] See Golvin, *L'amphithéâtre romain*, 342.

in shaping the crowd's social identity. Such were the raw materials from which the arena crowd's norms were fashioned and, it can be suggested, they made them more willing to accept brute violence as entertainment. If in our supposedly egalitarian age with its Universal Declaration of Human Rights, violence has proven to be an enormously popular form of entertainment, how much easier it must have been to accept it in Rome's hierarchical society, where one's worth was a function of birth, group membership, and legally defined status and where raw pity (*misericordia*) was the preserve of women (at least in the opinion of some). The spectators came to the arena without any illusions about what they were about to see, and once arrayed in their segregated seats, group processes and crowd dynamics came into play. A sense of purpose was instilled by the occasion, and the processes of social categorization and the free expression of social identities, all intensified by the presence of mutually visible acquaintances, would generate sensations of liberation and empowerment. From the outside, it would all look so wild and unrestrained. Indeed, the prospect of succumbing to intense emotions constitutes one of the chief objections against going to spectacles aired by elite pagan and Christian writers alike.[62] But arena games were not wild and woolly occasions where people went to lose control. Far from it. The social identity content of arena crowds, as broadly reconstructable from an admittedly patchy body of evidence, instead reveals that they were meaningful and exciting experiences where people went to connect with peers and with the wider community, to have their worldview validated, and to feel what it was like to have power. They did not consciously think of these things as they went along to the arena, of course. The processes of crowd dynamics supplied the means by which it could all be experienced as a suite of dynamic, shifting emotions and sensations felt en masse. And that prospect was quite its own lure.

THEATER AND AMPHITHEATER

It should be clear by now why Flaig's bold assertion, cited at the opening of chapter 3, that crowd psychology is not applicable to Roman arena events is doubly mistaken. First, it assumes the outdated Le Bonian model of crowd dynamics, which posited anonymity (and all that flows from it) as the key to understanding crowd dynamics. The more recent social-identity model

---

[62] See, e.g., Sen. *Ep.* 7.2 = T.20; Tert. *Spect.* 21 = T.29; Joh. Chrys. *Contra Lud. et Theat.* = *PG* 56.263–70 and 64.511–16; [Joh. Chrys.] *De Circ.* = *PG* 59.567–70, *In Abr. et contra theat.* = *PG* 58.541–54; Lact. *Div. Inst.* 6.20. Wiedemann, *Emperors and Gladiators*, 128–64; Wistrand, *Violence and Entertainment, passim.*

sees feelings of purposefulness and belonging as key to understanding crowd behavior. As such, the latter is the diametric opposite of the former. Arena spectators may not have been crowds in the Le Bonian sense, but crowds they most certainly were.

Second, ranked seating and mutual visibility in and of themselves did not guarantee orderly spectators, as Flaig assumes. Spectators at theater events (and possibly the circus, at least in the case of the higher social echelons) were also seated by status, yet they could readily fall to rioting, whereas spectators at the arena appear to have been peaceable, if not quite passive. The details need to be probed a little to resolve the apparent paradox of why spectators at the most violent of Roman spectacles were themselves the least violent of spectator crowds. In the ancient sources, blame for theater tumults uniformly falls on actors and, in particular, a class of entertainers called *pantomimi*, whose act involved a form of dance accompanied by music.[63] We get few clues as to what sparked these fights in the theater but, in those instances where details are provided, the performers and their supporters (*factiones, fautores*) are expressly implicated, even if the contours of the partisans' allegiance remain obscure to us.[64] A fable of Phaedrus about a buffoon and a rustic who compete in making pig noises before a theater audience simply assumes that theatergoers were inherently prone to sharp partisanship; in this case, they prefer the imitation of the buffoon, whom they favor, over that of the rustic, who had concealed a real pig in his clothes! Phaedrus comments on the audience for the rustic's

---

[63] See Luc. *Salt.*; Balsdon, *Life and Leisure*, 274–9 (on pantomimes) and 179–88 (on actors). Dio (61.8.1) explicitly connects disorderly behavior with the theater and circus, but makes no mention of the amphitheater. See also R. C. Beacham, *Spectacle Entertainments of Early Imperial Rome* (New Haven, 1999), 141–6.

[64] Blame: Dio 57.14.10, 57.21.3, 61.8.2–3; Suet. *Tib.* 37.2 (actors); Suet. *Nero* 16.2, 26.2; Tac. *Ann.* 1.54.2, 1.77.2, 4.14.3, 13.25.4, 14.21.4; Lib. *Or.* 41.2–7; Joh. Chrys. *Hom. in Matt.* 37.6 = *PG* 57.425–8, *Hom. de Stat.* 17.2 = *PG* 49.176; Soc. *Hist. eccl.* 7.13 (*pantomimi* and *histriones*). Percennius, a ringleader in the Pannonian mutiny in AD 14, got his start in agitation as a claque for pantomimes (Tac. *Ann.* 1.16.4). Culpable partisans: Suet. *Tib.* 37.2 (*capita factionum*), *Nero* 16.2 (*pantomimorum factiones*), Tac. *Ann.* 1.77.4 (*lascivia fautorum*), 13.25.4 and 13.28.1 (*fautores histrionum*). Claques and pantomimes, however, were not inherently troublesome; see Suet. *Nero* 20.3; Pliny *Ep.* 7.24.7. For fuller treatments, see E. J. Jory, "The Early Pantomime Riots," in A. Moffatt (ed.), *Maistor: Classical, Byzantine, and Renaissance Studies for Robert Browning* (Canberra, 1984), 57–66 (Jory suspects something in the performance aroused spectator passions); W. J. Slater, "Pantomime Riots," *CA* 13 (1994), 120–44 (who sees wider sociopolitical forces at work behind the riots). Note also R. Lim, "The Roman Pantomime Riot of A.D. 509," in J.-M. Carrié and R. Lizzi Testa (eds.), 'Humana Sapit' *Études d'Antiquité Tardive offertes à Lellia Cracco Ruggini* (Turnhout, 2002), 35–42 (where court politics and circus factions are prominently implicated in this riot). Lucian (*Salt.* 83–4) comments on the ability of pantomimes to stir the emotions of their audiences profoundly and mentions rivalries among performers and their supporters: the cocktail of emotion and partisanship could prove explosive on occasion. Libanius claims (*Or.* 64.119) that "Dance . . . does no harm and never will"; the problems stemmed from the partisans.

performance: "There was an even bigger crowd. Their minds were already gripped by partisanship, and you should know that they were there to mock, not to watch."[65] Factions of partisans are also deeply implicated in disturbances at chariot races in the circus.[66] Pliny (*HN* 29.9) notes that actors (*histriones*, a category that includes pantomimes) and chariot racers were followed about by huge retinues in public, which attests a deep bond between fan and performer.

Comparable evidence for popular devotion to individual gladiators or particular types of gladiator exists, but it is sparse when compared to that for stage performers and charioteers. Gladiatorial partisans appear to have been less committed and fanatical (and less numerous?) than those associated with the theater and circus.[67] This relatively low level of arena fan fanaticism may go a long way to explaining why the gladiatorial crowds were so peaceable. But in addition to intense partisanship, a further destabilizing factor in theatrical events was the capacity of actors to interact with the audience (rather than vice versa), as well as the possibility of the shows to be politicized by comments on or allusions to current affairs, whether in word or gesture. This is probably why the authorities often held the performers themselves accountable as active participants in the depradations of their supporters.[68] And these were not isolated incidents. Theaters were felt to be naturally tumultuous and noisy places, to the extent that when a Late Imperial governor was received in Antioch's theater in total silence, he turned white with fright (Lib. *Or.* 33.12). Trouble at the theater was so predictable that a cohort of guards was put on duty during performances in Rome.[69]

---

[65] Phaed. 5.5: *fit turba maior. iam favor mentes tenet / et derisuros, non spectaturos, scias.*

[66] Isidore of Pelusium (*Ep.* 5.185 = *PG* 78.1433–7) expressly identifies circus factions and supporters of pantomimes as a source of civic disturbances; see also Joh. Chrys. *Hom. de Stat.* 15.4 = *PG* 49.159. However, by this date (the early fifth century) the activities of partisan associations appear to have spanned several types of spectacle; see Roueché, *Performers and Partisans*, 44–60.

[67] On circus factions, see above, ch. 3, n. 34. For more on gladiatorial partisans, see below, ch. 6, pp. 219–21.

[68] Tacitus comments that "a rivalrous competition of the actors" (*Ann.* 1.54.2: *discordia et certamine histrionum*) caused disturbances in AD 14. Tiberius judged the performers the source of problems (Tac. *Ann.* 4.14.3), as does Tacitus in an editorial comment (*Ann.* 14.21.4). For politically scurrilous theater performances, sometimes resulting in the banishment of the offending performers, see, e.g., Cic. *Fam.* 12.18.2; Dio 60(61).29.3; Sen. *Dial.* 4.11.3; Suet. *Aug.* 68, *Tib.* 45, *Cal.* 27.4, *Nero* 39.3, *Galba* 13; HA *Verus* 8.4, *Comm.* 3.4, *Maximini* 9.3–5; Tac. *Ann.* 4.14.4. On the two-way interaction between stage performers and the audiences, see Balsdon, *Life and Leisure*, 276; Champlin, *Nero*, 94–6; R. W. Reynolds, "Criticism of Individuals in Roman Popular Comedy," *CQ* 37 (1943), 37–45.

[69] For tumultuous theatergoers and guards at performances, see, e.g., Dio 61.8.3; Lib. *Or.* 19.14; Luc. *Salt.* 5; Tac. *Ann.* 1.16.3, 1.77.1–4, 4.14.3, 6.13.1, 11.13.1, 13.24.1, 13.25.4, 13.28.1, 14.24, 25; Tert. *Nat.* 1.17.

In contrrast to the extensive record of disorder at theaters, the only recorded disturbance at an arena event is the Pompeii riot of AD 59. How do we explain this disparity? Since the seating conditions were the same in both situations, they cannot have been the essential difference. Partisanship was also a feature of both contexts, although much attenuated in the case of gladiators. The really major dissimilarity lay in the divergent nature of the spectacles themselves, so the answer is likely to lie in the crowd's psychological reaction to the different contexts they confronted in the theater and the arena. The point is reinforced by the fact that no disturbances at gladiatorial games are on record, even when they were held in adapted theaters, as they regularly were in the Greek East.[70] It was not the seating or the setting that mattered, as asserted by Flaig, nor even the demographics of the audience (overlap in attendance from event to event must have been substantial, given the reserved seating and the connections needed for the lower orders to secure seats). Rather, the nature of the spectacle and the spectators' mental orientation to it were the key.

In the amphitheater, the crowd was intensely focused on violence being done to and by deviants, criminals, and social outcasts. This focus powerfully reinforced their self-categorization as the ingroup (the spectators) against the outgroup (the victims and performers). The salience of subgroup membership among arena spectators frequently yielded to a more all-embracing self-categorization elicited by what was happening to outgroupers, right there, in front of everyone's eyes. That the spectators, barring some outrage, were not going to suffer any violence strengthened the crowd's self-categorization and sense of connectedness. Their interaction with what was going on, by shouting, making demands, or even directing the action on the sand was overwhelmingly unidirectional (from the stands to the sands), added to the power of the situation, and underlined which party was in charge. Divided into their status groups, the spectators were united, first and foremost, in *not* being one of the unfortunates on the arena floor. Safe in their seats, they were constantly invited to compare themselves and their situation by watching the suffering of outgroupers.

Naturally, there would have been lulls and distractions during which subgroups within the crowd did their own thing; people came and went; perhaps also occasional tensions and localized rivalries would emerge between

---

[70] This observation undermines the assertion that "amphitheater crowds might take fire not only with city rivalries but with their enthusiasms for some star or team of gladiatorial combat, chariot racing, or dramatic dances and plays"; see R. MacMullen, *Enemies of the Roman Order: Treason, Unrest, and Alienation in the Empire* (Cambridge, MA, 1966), 170; this view conflates quite different phenomena. On the use of theaters for gladiatorial shows, see above, ch. 3, n. 99.

groups of spectators as this or that favored fighter made an appearance. The arena crowd, like any other, was not wholly consistent in its behavior, nor should it be imagined as such. It has been cogently argued, using a Foucaultian and anthropological perspective, that the ranked seating rendered arenas socially divisive places.[71] While the psychological analysis offered here may seem to differ sharply from this view, the social-identity model of crowd dynamics can accommodate spasms of divisiveness that interrupted the overall psychological cohesion. What matters, rather, are sustained patterns of categorization as they relate to the situational salience of group membership. In the arena setting, the most consistently salient ingroup was the spectatorship as a whole, categorized against the victim-outgroupers below. If, during the games, groups in the crowd temporarily categorized themselves in opposition to other spectators (over suppport for specific gladiators or styles of armature, for instance), that fact does not lessen the tendency of the context to direct the spectators' attention toward the universally acknowledged outgroups struggling on the sand.

Finally, the very nature of gladiatorial bouts – short in duration, with a frequent rotation of performers – limited the extent to which partisans could direct antipathy against rival supporters in the crowd. Individual bouts cannot have lasted much more than fifteen or twenty minutes, after which new fighters would appear.[72] Even a phenomenally popular gladiator would be in action for only a few minutes, and so the likelihood of his supporters becoming volatile enough to cause trouble was much diminished. The frequent changing of gladiatorial pairs likewise reduced how long the different types of gladiators were exposed to the crowd, and the necessary breaks between fights gave tempers a chance to cool. Individuals or groups of individuals scattered throughout the crowd might cheer vociferously for their champion(s) or favorite style of combatant, but the performers would only be on the sand for a few minutes at a time and, possibly, only a few times a year.[73] In some spectacles, favorites would not

---

[71] E.g., Clavel-Lévêque, *L'empire en jeux*, 153–61; Edmondson, "Dynamic Arenas," 98–111; Potter, "Spectacle."

[72] M. Junkelmann, "*Familia Gladiatoria*: Heroes of the Amphitheatre," in E. Köhne and C. Ewigleben (eds.), *Gladiators and Caesars: The Power of Spectacle in Ancient Rome* (Berkeley, 2000), 31–74, esp. 40. Mark Twain observed students in a German corps (a traditional form of fraternity) duelling with swords in the nineteenth century and noted that their contests lasted up to twenty or thirty minutes, which included brief breaks. These contests were not nearly as intense or as demanding as a gladiatorial pairing, and yet the students were worn out by their exertions; see M. Twain, *A Tramp Abroad*, 2 vols. (Hartford, 1880), vol. 1, 34–40 (ch. 5).

[73] On the frequency of gladiatorial displays, with reference to earlier work, see S. L. Tuck, "Scheduling Spectacle: Factors Contributing to the Dates of Pompeian Munera," *CJ* 104 (2008), 123–43. Tuck concludes that arena games were much more frequent than many prior scholars have imagined (at

appear at all. All of this makes for a very different relationship between spectacle and spectator than that pertaining in the circus and the theater, where fierce partisanships were sustained by the relative uniformity of the spectacle, the block seating of partisans (at least in the Late Empire), and the prolonged exposure of the crowd to their chariot driver or actor heroes.

Theater performances seriously blurred the ingroup/outgroup categorizations between stage and auditorium. Like gladiators, stage performers mostly stemmed from the lower orders and were certainly scorned by the elite and legally stigmatized with "lack of good repute" (*infamia*), but they were not the utter outcasts who made up the ranks of the arena's performers, executioners, and victims. To fight on the sand as a professional gladiator (that is, for money), a citizen was required to abjure his status by taking an oath that cast him among the pariahs; no such requirement was demanded for stage performers.[74] Lucian, in praising the art of pantomime,

least at Pompeii, where the evidence from epigraphic advertisements is fullest). For a contrasting view, see Wiedemann, *Emperors and Gladiators*, 47 and 56. Of course the frequency of *munera* may have little or no bearing on how often a specific fighter was called on to perform.

74 Gladiators swore to submit to be "burned, bound, flogged and killed by the sword"; see Hor. *Sat.* 2.7.58–9; Juv. 11.5–8; Petron. *Sat.* 117.5; Sen. *Ep.* 37.1. In the Republic, amateur actors in Atellan farces were citizens of sufficient standing to be eligible for the military draft (Val. Max. 2.4.4; cf. Macrob. *Sat.* 3.14.6–8). Livy (7.2.12) implies that other actors may also have held citizenship, but belonged to the militarily exempt lowest class. By the early Principate, however, citizen-actors earned the stigma of *infamia* (*Dig.* 3.2.2.5), and bars were put on actors marrying into senatorial families and on senators performing on stage (*Dig.* 23.2.44*pr*; Dio 54.2.5). This did not stop members of the elite from performing, however (Dio 53.32.3, 55.10.11, 62.20.4–5; Tac. *Ann.* 15.65, 16.21.1). The key factor was whether one was paid or not (*Dig.* 3.1.1.6). On stage performers in general, see H. Leppin, *Histrionen: Untersuchungen zur sozialen Stellung von Bühnenkünstler im Westen des Römischen Reiches zur Zeit der Republik und des Principats* (Bonn, 1992), esp. 36–44 (social status), 71–83 (the legalities), and 189–313 (a catalog of all known performers; where status can be determined, the figures are: 24 slaves, 41 freedmen, 5 possible *peregrini*, 11 freeborn, 4 citizens). See also C. Hugoniot et al. (eds.), *Le statut de l'acteur dans l'Antiquité grecque et romaine* (Tours, 2004). On attitudes toward arena performers and executioners, see below, ch. 7, pp. 245–73. H. N. Parker ("The Observed of All Observers: Spectacle, Applause, and Cultural Poetics in the Roman Theater Audience," in Bergmann and Kondoleon [eds.], *Art of Ancient Spectacle*, 163–79) argues (at 164–6) that arena and theater performers were all "outcasts" who were equally degraded by exposing their bodies for the entertainment of others. In this view he has considerable support (cf. also A. Duncan, *Performance and Identity in the Classical World* [Cambridge, 2006], 124–59). While *infamia* may be a consistent legal concept, laws do not encompass the whole of social reality. Prostitutes, gladiators, and other performers were all degraded, yes, but not to the same degree, as Seneca (*Q Nat.* 7.31.3) and Juvenal (8.198–9) imply and the gladiatorial oath suggests; see also *Dig.* 3.1.4.1 for categories of performers judged not to incur *infamia*. Famed actors could enjoy close social connections with prominent people, including members of the imperial household, even as they practiced their trade (e.g., C. Maecenas Bathyllus and C. Julius Pylades under Augustus, or Apelles and Mnester under Caligula and Claudius; Leppin, *Histrionen*, 217–19 [Bathyllus], 284–5 [Pylades], and 261–2 [Mnester]; see also HA *Verus* 8.7, 10–11 with an honorific inscription of AD 199 at *CIL* 14.4254 = *ILS* 5191). The reverse is also true: in AD 15 senators had to be barred by decree of the senate from visiting the houses of pantomimes, and *equites* from taking part in their processions (Tac. *Ann.* 1.77.4). Analogous evidence for close gladiator–patron social interaction is rare; indeed, Cicero (*Cat.* 2.9) includes

says that the performance elicited self-recognition in the spectator so that "each recognizes his own traits, or rather sees in the dancer, as in a mirror, his very self, with his customary feelings and actions."[75] That is to say, psychological lines of distinction between performer and spectator were as clouded in the theater as they were clear in the arena. Unlike most gladiators (who wore helmets) actors could interact vocally with the crowd, and pantomimes could stir their emotions and whip them up into an excited state with music, movement, and gesture.[76] In this situation, rivalries between performers and their supporters in the audience, stoked by actors from the stage and by claques in the seats, combined to divide the audience against itself. Combined with the blurred actor–partisan distinctions, the fanatical following adhering to mimes and actors would have impeded the more inclusive self-categorization that characterized arena crowds, so that localized social identites within the crowd remained more salient at theater events than they did at *munera*.

Unlike gladiatorial bouts, theater events featured only a handful of performers who occupied the stage for several hours.[77] Supporters were therefore exposed to their idols and rivals for sustained periods of time. The possible infusion of political commentary into this already volatile situation added fuel to the fire. The role of theatrical performers in fomenting divisions within their audience reversed the situation in the arena, where

gladiators as among Catiline's close friends (*intimi*) precisely to emphasize the man's depravity; cf. Dio 59.5.2 (on Caligula's gladiator friends). Indeed, Cicero (*Rosc. Am.* 17) uses "gladiator" as a synonym for "scoundrel." Gladiators are attested as bodyguards (e.g., Cic. *Att.* 4.4a.2, 4.8.2; Suet. *Cal.* 55.4; Tac. *Ann.* 13.25.3) or business investments (e.g., Caes. *B Civ.* 1.14.4–5). They are not usually numbered among the intimates of the great and powerful (and dissolute), the way mimes, actors, and other entertainers are. The exception is women of quality who are imagined as sullying themselves with gladiators (e.g., Juv. 6.67–113; HA *Marc.* 19.7), but in general the gladiator was not the sort of person one had over to dinner; see Ville, *Gladiature*, 290–5. The social situation was therefore more complex than the legal sources divulge, and even the legal situation with regard to actors is not wholly consistent; see Edwards, *Politics of Immorality*, 98–136, esp. 123–6 and 131–4.

75 Luc. *Salt.* 81: ἕκαστος τῶν ὁρώντων γνωρίζῃ τὰ αὑτοῦ, μᾶλλον ὥσπερ ἐν κατόπτρῳ τῷ ὀρχηστῇ ἑαυτὸν βλέπῃ καὶ ἃ πάσχειν αὐτὸς καὶ ἃ ποιεῖω εἴωθεν.

76 The gladiator Pacideianus, according to Lucilius (of the second century BC), who is cited in Cicero (*Tusc.* 4.48 = Lucil. 4.155–60K = 4.153–8M = T.10), addressed spectators at a show, presumably in the forum. The notice is exceptional. Pantomimes stirring emotions: Luc. *Salt.* 83.

77 That stage performances lasted hours is clear not only from the length of surviving plays and comments that (apparently private) recitations could stretch over days (Pliny *Ep.* 4.27.1, 8.21.4; cf. ibid. 1.131–3, 6.17.3), but also from other indications. The theatrical show that Caligula attended on the last day of his life lasted from morning at least into the early afternoon, when the emperor left the theater for lunch; Jos. *AJ* 19.84–101; Suet. *Cal.* 57.4, 58.1. Pantomimes may also have had a long duration, if several dances were performed in sequence. Ummidia Quadratilla, for one, would spend hours watching her mimes and pantomimes (who also performed publicly in the theatre); Pliny *Ep.* 7.24.4–87. Crato, the stern interlocutor in Lucian's *The Dance*, implies that watching pantomimes took a lot of time (Luc. *Salt.* 2) and the extent of the mythological cycles performed (ibid. 37–61, 63, 66) also points in the same direction.

the crowd influenced action on the sand, not vice versa, and this further confused the ingroup/outgroup distinctions between performer and spectator.[78] It also blurred the theater spectators' focus outward on to the stage and turned it inward on to themselves. In these psychological circumstances, the division of the spectators into ranks of seats at the theater did not facilitate the expression of a crowd-wide social identity, as it did in the amphitheater, but rather stressed the divisions and disagreements within the audience. At *munera*, the crowd consistently paid attention to outgroups physically removed from it on the sand below; at the theater, the crowd recognized outgroups in its very midst. No wonder there was trouble.[79] It is possible that a psychological environment more akin to that typically found at theatrical events confronted the audience at Pompeii's amphitheater on the day of the riot in AD 59 (reviewed above, chapter 3, pp. 93–6). On this occasion social identities in the crowd coalesced around municipal affiliations, and when the longstanding rivalry between Pompeii and Nuceria was brought to the fore by the nature of the spectacle being staged, the crowd became acutely divided against itself.

A subtheme running through the preceding pages has been how hostile attitudes toward outgroups constituted a core element of the arena spectators' mental state. We now turn to this matter in detail.

---

[78] This is not to say that theater audiences were sedately attentive, they could call out commentary on proceedings (see Luc. *Salt.* 76 for the catcalls of Antiochene audiences). The point is that the communication was markedly more two-way in the theater than in the arena.

[79] The ancients can comment on how theater audiences divided against themselves; Hor. *Epist.* 2.1.180–5; Plut. *Cic.* 13.2–3; Tac. *Ann.* 13.25.4. No comparable statements are found in our sources in connection with arena events. See also Luc. *Salt.* 83, who notes divergent audience reactions to what happened on stage during a performance of the madness of Ajax: when the Ajax character hit Odysseus on the head so hard only the latter's cap saved him from serious harm, the rabble in the audience went wild, while the more discerning spectators at the front applauded in a more restrained fashion. The tensions in the theater are palpable.

CHAPTER 5

Arenas of prejudice

Indeed my proposal is not cruel – for what could be cruel in the case of men such as these?

Caesar, speaking in Sall. Cat. 51.17

Since he has killed, he deserves to suffer.

Sen. Ep. 7.5

Prejudice is a mindset known to bring about not only an emotional distance from the agony of victims of violence but even to give license to revel in it. Prejudice, of course, is not to be invoked as an all-embracing, umbrella explanation for attendance at violent public rituals in all contexts – many psychological factors are likely to have been involved, including excitement (see chapter 6), the attractions of violent spectacle in general (see chapter 7), a morbid fascination with confronting one's mortality, or just plain curiosity. But spectatorship at ritual *punishments* in particular may often be rooted in a conviction that the condemned are getting what they deserve, a stance inherently prejudicial toward the victim, and all the more so if group affiliations are involved, as they were in the Roman arena. Since Roman society was rife with prejudice, and since virulent attitudes toward the arena's victims (and performers) are documentable from the surviving record, the role of prejudice in drawing spectators to arena spectacles warrants closer scrutiny.

As a psychological phenomenon, prejudice is complicated.[1] A classic formulation posits three components: (a) cognitive, or harboring negative

---

[1] The literature on the subject is vast; for lucid overviews, see R. Brown, *Prejudice: Its Social Psychology* (Oxford, 1995); R. Y. Bourhis and J.-P. Leyens (eds.), *Stereotypes, Discrimination, and Intergroup Relations*, 2nd edn. (Hayen, 1999); J. H. Duckitt, *Social Psychology of Prejudice* (New York, 1992); M. Jones, *Social Psychology of Prejudice* (Upper Saddle River, NJ, 2002); T. D. Nelson, *The Psychology of Prejudice*, 2nd edn. (Boston, MA, 2006); T. D. Nelson (ed.), *Handbook of Prejudice, Stereotyping, and Discrimination* (New York, 2009); Zanna and Olson (eds.), *Psychology of Prejudice*. See also Chin (ed.), *Psychology of Prejudice and Discrimination*; J. F. Dovidio et al. (eds.), *On the Nature of Prejudice: Fifty Years after Allport* (Oxford, 2005); J. H. Duckitt, "Prejudice and Intergroup Hostility," in D. O. Sears et al. (eds.), *Oxford Handbook of Political Psychology* (Oxford, 2003), 559–600;

beliefs about others; (b) affective, or harboring negative *feelings* about others; and (c) conative, or harboring negative *intent* toward others. These characteristics are nowadays seen as the separate but interrelated processes of stereotyping (a cognitive process), discrimination (a pattern of behavior), and prejudice proper (an attitude).[2] Aside from being multifaceted, prejudice is also simultaneously social and personal. If an entire society can be organized along prejudicial lines – Nazi Germany or apartheid South Africa come to mind – even in such extreme environments not everyone will share equally in the prejudice. Some may even dissent or actively resist – for every Heinrich Himmler there can be an Oskar Schindler. So in any given prejudiced group there will always be variations among individuals (the so-called "individual-differences dimension") that shape how deep and widespread prejudicial beliefs are, and how they find expression (if at all) at the interpersonal level. A proper psychological understanding of prejudice requires recognition of these interlinked facets. This is why older theories that stressed personality type as the ultimate source of prejudice are now thought unsatisfactory, while more recent notions of prejudice as a product of group processes remain incomplete also. Both are essentially right, but for different planes of the same phenomenon.

A historical survey of how prejudice has been conceptualized in the decades since the 1920s, when social psychology emerged as a discipline, has convincingly demonstrated the salience of historical context in shaping favored theories. Prior to the 1920s prejudice was held to be a natural response to inherently inferior peoples but, in the 1920s and 1930s, as the civil rights movement appeared in the United States, it came to be regarded as an irrational and unjustifiable attitude, a mental aberration. The ascendancy of fascism in Europe in the 1930s and 1940s saw efforts to explain prejudice in psychodynamic terms, such as Freudian projection (transferring what one does not like about oneself on to others), scapegoating (blaming others for one's own problems), or displacement of frustration and hostility (aggressing against those believed to block

---

S. T. Fiske, "Stereotyping, Discrimination and Prejudice at the Seam between the Centuries: Evolution, Culture, Mind and Brain," *European Journal of Social Psychology* 30 (2000), 299–322; R. C. Spears et al. (eds.), *The Social Psychology of Stereotyping and Group Life* (Oxford, 1997). As Jones puts it (*Prejudice*, 74): "Prejudice is such an enigmatic and enduring phenomenon that a multiplicity of approaches is required to fully capture the role that history, culture and society play in it." For a recent use of the social psychology of prejudice to analyze ancient minds, see Holloway, *Coping with Prejudice*.

[2] See G. W. Allport, *The Nature of Prejudice* (Reading, 1954). Duckitt (*Prejudice*, 7–24) prefers a model in which stereotyped beliefs lead to prejudicial attitudes which generate behavior. See also S. T. Fiske, "Stereotyping, Prejudice and Discrimination," in D. T. Gilbert et al. (eds.), *The Handbook of Social Psychology*, 4th edn. (New York, 1998), 357–411; Jones, *Prejudice*, 3–10.

one's goals).[3] Revelation of Nazi horrors engendered a view of prejudice in the 1950s as a pathology, a characteristic of peculiar personality types, especially the "authoritarian" personality. Prejudice now became an individual matter, and this view stands at the root of what is today individual-difference analysis.[4] Such individual-psychological theories of prejudice seemed inadequate in the face of the civil rights crisis in the United States in the 1960s and 1970s, which highlighted how entire societies could be prejudiced. Group theories therefore became dominant. Social categorization is now seen as the engine of stereotypical and prejudicial thinking, so that prejudice, at its roots, is a group process. Set against this perspective, prejudice emerges as an almost inevitable offshoot of group membership.[5]

These bewilderingly diverse approaches to the phenomenon of prejudice may be resolved by adopting an integrative approach, as advocated by one scholar in these terms:

First, certain universal psychological processes build in an inherently human potentiality or propensity for prejudice. Second, social and intergroup dynamics describe the conditions and circumstances of contact and interaction between groups and elaborate this potentiality into normative and socially shared patterns of prejudice. Third, mechanisms of transmission explain how these intergroup dynamics and shared patterns of prejudice are socially transmitted to individual members of these groups. Fourth and finally, individual-differences dimensions determine individual susceptibility to prejudice, and so operate to modulate the impact of these social transmission mechanisms on individuals.[6]

The laudable goal of most modern research on the subject is to understand prejudice the better to reduce its baneful impact on society, but the historian's main interests lie in the psychological roots of prejudice and isolating those social conditions that seem to nurture it. With this in mind, it is apparent that the integrative model of prejudice is only fully applicable to the most recent historical periods for the simple reason that we have

---

[3] On frustration-aggression theory, see below, p. 159.

[4] The standard work in this sphere is T. W. Adorno et al., *The Authoritarian Personality* (New York, 1950). For a recent update on these ideas, see N. Sanford, "The Roots of Prejudice: Emotional Dynamics," in P. Watson (ed.), *Psychology and Rage* (New Brunswick, 2007), 57–75. For a similar approach, but one differently focused, see M. Rokeach, *The Open and Closed Mind* (New York, 1960).

[5] This paragraph summarizes Duckitt, *Prejudice*, 43–65.

[6] Ibid., 62, and restated on 217, 245–6, 249–50. Recently, Alice Eagly has argued for a more integrated understanding of prejudice as emergent from "the interface between individual beliefs and a social structure composed of social roles"; see A. H. Eagly, "Prejudice: Toward a More Inclusive Definition," in A. H. Eagly et al. (eds.), *The Social Psychology of Group Identity and Social Conflict: Theory, Application, and Practice* (Washington, DC, 2004), 45–64 (quote at 45).

neither the data nor the capacity to measure individual variables (such as the prevalence of authoritarian personalities) among dead generations.[7] Thus the first two elements of the model (inherent propensities and social conditions) offer more viable tools to the historian than the second two (mechanics of transmission and individual differences). That said, as we shall see, something may be suggested about the social transmission of prejudice in the Roman context, and if we are in no position to quantify it, there can be no doubt that variations in personal inclination applied in Roman times too, no less so than it did in better-documented ones (see below, conclusion, pp. 275–8). As we have seen, Seneca noted that the arena was practically empty when he witnessed the midday butcheries, and Claudius' preference for staying behind to watch, even after dismissing the people for lunch, is presented as illustrating his singular cruelty.[8] Not everyone, it seems, liked this sort of thing.

There is even more explicit testimony. The *Declamations* of Pseudo-Quintilian note that "there are people who grow upset even at the punishment of condemned criminals, who grow pale at the sight of anyone's blood, and who actually weep over the misfortunes of complete strangers. Then there are the opposite types, who don't even mourn their own relatives."[9] As a child, Caracalla is reported to have burst into tears and turned away from arena executions, and the crowd found this endearing (HA *M. Ant.* 1.5). The people of Rhodes refused to hold gladiatorial fights at all.[10] It is less imperative to quantify how many such sensitive souls there were in ancient Rome than to note their mere existence. By proclivity or circumstance, then, the violence of the arena was not everyone's cup of tea. The focus in the following analysis, of course, is on the broad patterns that elucidate the basic human propensity for prejudice and the social dynamics of its manifestation in the Roman context, especially the arena, but the role of personal preference in modulating the behavior of Romans should be kept firmly in mind at all times.

---

[7] Social psychologists investigate individual-differences factors by means of questionnaires, the answers to which are set against calibrated scales; see Duckitt, *Prejudice*, 161–215; Jones, *Prejudice*, 111–28. From the available evidence, we may justifiably suspect that many Romans shared the traits of the authoritarian personality (a tendency to conformity, respect for tradition and legitimate authority, hostility and aggression toward others, etc.), but we cannot quantify such attitudes.

[8] Sen. *Ep.* 7.4 = T.20 and Suet. *Claud.* 34.2 = T.23.

[9] [Quint.] *Decl.* 9.16: *sunt, quorum mentes etiam nocentium supplicia confundant, qui ad omnium sanguinem pallescant, ignotorum quoque miseriis inlacriment. sunt contra, qui ne suorum quidem misereantur.* In Achilles Tatius' novel (3.15.5) a general and his soldiers, men presumably somewhat habituated to violent sights, could not watch a captive disemboweled by brigands.

[10] Robert, *Gladiateurs*, 248.

THE PHENOMENON OF PREJUDICE

The psychodynamic foundations of the human proclivity for prejudice have been variously explained.[11] For instance, a popular notion in the 1930s and 1940s was frustration-aggression theory, which proposed that frustration over thwarted goals generates aggression and prejudice, both of which are then directed at others believed to be responsible for the thwarting, whether justifiably or not.[12] While this may account for some forms of prejudice (Nazi Germany being both an example and an inspiration for the theory), it collapses as an overarching explanation in the face of the power-infused minimal group experiments, to be reviewed shortly. Instead, the current consensus locates the key to prejudice in the cognitive processes of social categorization and social identity (surveyed in chapter 3).[13] Stereotyping, which is closely related to prejudice, is thought to be an effective means of negotiating a complex social environment by categorizing individuals according to their group memberships. Prejudice is one manifestation of such categorization. According to social identity theory, there will always be a tendency toward a positive identity for the ingroup. Stereotyping and prejudice are conducive to this goal through sharing common assumptions about the members of outgroups. In this way, an individual's categorization of other people depends on what social group the categorizer is currently identifying with. To put it another way, the complexions people perceive in their social surroundings will shift depending on which group memberships are made salient by a given situation.[14] Assumptions about outgroupers are very often negative, in that outgroups are seen not only as different but

[11] Proposals include Freudian projection, ethnocentrism (ingroupers are liked and outgroupers not), universal color bias (people inherently prefer white over black – an observation that is both false and irrelevant for forms of prejudice other than racism), or belief congruence (we like those who agree with us and vice versa). For a lucid overview, see Duckitt, *Prejudice*, 67–91.

[12] The classic formulation is J. Dollard et al., *Frustration and Aggression* (New Haven, 1939). A related idea is "relative deprivation theory," which posits that prejudice can arise from perceptions by one group of disadvantages suffered at the hands of another; see Jones, *Prejudice*, 132–3. A problem with the latter view, however, is that prejudice is often directed by the advantaged against the disadvantaged.

[13] For an overview, see Hogg and Vaughan, *Social Psychology*, 328–39. See also D. Abrams and M. A. Hogg (eds.), *Social Identity Theory: Constructive and Critical Advances* (New York, 1990); S. Reicher, "Rethinking the Paradigm of Prejudice," *South African Journal of Psychology* 37 (2007), 820–34 (who argues for a greater focus on ingroup identity over outgroup stereotyping); H. Tajfel, "The Roots of Prejudice: Cognitive Aspects," in P. Watson (ed.), *Psychology and Rage* (New Brunswick, 2007), 76–95.

[14] This process is most fully elaborated in self-categorization theory, on which see J. C. Turner, *Rediscovering the Social Group: A Self-Categorizaton Theory* (Oxford, 1987); J. C. Turner, "Some Current Issues in Research on Social Identity and Self-Categorization Theories," in N. Ellemers et al. (eds.), *Social Identity: Context, Commitment, Content* (Oxford, 1999), 6–34.

somehow deficient, less worthy, or even less human than the ingroup. In its extreme forms such thinking leads to the complete dehumanization of outgroupers. The problem for social psychologists is that the process of ingroup favoritism predicted by social identity theory is not inevitably twinned with derogation of the outgroup: some outgroups are viewed neutrally, or even positively, as with (most) Americans' attitudes towards their Canadian neighbors.[15] Whether a given outgroup is disregarded, esteemed, or despised depends on factors in the social dynamics of intergroup relations or, in other words, on stimulus cues drawn from context. So the core question becomes "what cues trigger prejudice?"

The centrality of context to prejudice can be appreciated by the simple observation of how greatly intergroup interrelations vary depending on circumstances. In some contexts, prejudice is normative (apartheid in South Africa, religious bigotry in Northern Ireland), but it is not uniformly adhered to (Afrikaaners were notoriously more prejudiced than other groups who shared their context), and it can change over time. For instance, despite some prior stereotyping, Japanese were regarded neutrally by most Americans prior to December 7, 1941, when Pearl Harbor was attacked by the forces of the Japanese empire. Between then and the end of World War II Japanese were habitually seen as sneaky, dishonorable savages and, in American propaganda, openly likened to monkeys. 110,000 Japanese-Americans were rounded up and interned in prison camps without having actually done anything other than being Japanese. Since the end of the war, when a democratized Japan with an American-written constitution has been a key ally in the Far East, American attitudes deintensified considerably and even became positive.[16] Another striking example comes from India. In February 1959 Indian professors polled their students on their attitudes toward their Chinese neighbors. Results were positive: the Chinese were seen as honest, brave, progressive, and cultured. Shortly afterward, a border dispute raised tensions between the two countries. Indian students at the same university were polled again in December of the same year. They now regarded the Chinese as cruel, aggressive, dishonest, and

---

[15] M. B. Brewer, "The Psychology of Prejudice: Ingroup Love or Outgroup Hate?" *Journal of Social Issues* 55 (1999), 429–44; M. B. Brewer, "Ingroup Identification and Intergroup Conflict: When Does Ingroup Love Become Outgroup Hate?" in R. E. Ashmore et al. (eds.), *Social Identity, Intergroup Conflict, and Conflict Reduction* (Oxford, 2001), 17–41.

[16] A. N. Ancheta, *Race, Rights and the Asian American Experience* (New Brunswick, 1998), esp. 61–128. Of course, prejudice was also found on the Japanese side, where Westerners were portrayed as greedy, soft, and dishonorable. It is hardly a coincidence that the two theaters of World War II most openly infused with racial prejudice – the Pacific and the Eastern front in Europe – were characterized by a markedly high level of brutality.

stupid.[17] As a teenager growing up in Ireland, I vividly recall how the inoffensive Argentinians were transformed almost overnight into the demonic "Argies" by the British press in the run-up to the Falklands War of 1982, and how quickly the anti-Argentinian vitriol abated after the conflict ended. In the same period, the British press often succumbed to the crudest anti-Irish sloganeering in the wake of specific IRA atrocities in England (such as the London park bombings in 1982 or the Harrod's car bomb the following year). Prejudice, it seems, can wash over a society in waves.

These examples point to one of the stimulus cues demonstrated by experiment to generate prejudice between groups: competition. Realistic Conflict Theory (RCT) adopts the common-sensical position that competition between groups, in which the success of the winner comes at a tangible cost to the loser, will inevitably lead to prejudicial thinking. The *perception* of conflict is also enough to generate prejudice, provided an outgroup is available for targeting.[18] Further, the minimal group experiments suggest that discrimination and prejudice can arise in the complete absence of conflict altogether. Since group conditions have been whittled down to virtual non-existence in the minimal group paradigm, suspicion of the outgroup in these conditions cannot stem from conflict, real or imagined. Thus another source of prejudice is averred to be "intergroup social competition," a process generated by the raw fact of group membership, which seems to engender a propensity to view outgroupers as threats or competitors. But this is only a propensity. Circumstance determines how intensely it is manifested, and intergroup conflict, whether real or perceived, is one such circumstance.

Another catalyzing circumstance is power differential. Active hostility and prejudice toward outgroups do not normally emerge in the classic minimal group scenario, but when further levels of elaboration are factored in, prejudice clearly emerges. Two factors are basic: first, social cues or circumstances that stress group memberships; and, second, status and power differentials between groups. In such circumstances, particularly where group boundaries are not easily permeable and the status/power

---

[17] A. K. Sinha and O. P. Upadhaya, "Change and Persistence in the Stereotypes of University Students toward Different Ethnic Groups during the Sino-Indian Border Dispute," *Journal of Social Psychology* 52 (1960), 225–31.

[18] For instance, it seems rather unlikely that Jews are actually part of a global conspiracy to rule the world, but many justify their anti-Semitism by appealing to just such an unrealistic scenario. See, e.g., V. M. Esses et al., "Instrumental Relations among Groups: Group Competition, Conflict, and Prejudice," in Dovidio et al. (eds.), *Nature of Prejudice*, 227–43; M. A. Zarate et al., "Cultural Threat and Perceived Realistic Group Conflict as Predictors of Attitudes toward Mexican Immigrants," *Journal of Experimental Social Psychology* 40 (2004), 99–105.

differential is felt by both sides to be stable and legitimate, prejudicial attitudes will emerge as normative among the dominant group.[19] A related observation is that it may be in the interest of the higher status group to foster a *belief* in the subordinate group that they may one day get to join the ranks of the privileged, even if the actual number who do so is miniscule, and even if hostility and prejudice continue to dog those who successfully make the transition.

The Robbers Cave and Stanford Prison Experiments highlight the importance of status, power, and dominance in generating prejudice. In the Robbers Cave Experiments, it will be remembered, the *winning* team expressed the most prejudicial attitudes toward the losers, while the "guards" in the Stanford Prison similarly lorded it over their powerless charges.[20] It was remarkable in both instances how quickly the dominant groups slipped into patterns of prejudicial thinking about their subordinates. Just how fundamental power is in producing prejudice and discriminatory behavior was demonstrated in a minimal group setting that had been suffused with status and power differentials. Canadian university students were divided into three pairs of minimal groups by flipping coins. The students had been told that they would help determine who among them would be awarded an extra class credit (there were no limits on who could get the credit, so there was no competition or realistic conflict). Each pair of groups was told they had a certain degree of influence over how the credit would be distributed: one group was told they had a 100 percent say in the assignation, while their counterparts had 0 percent (that is, a situation of total power was established). Another group was told that their choices carried a 70 percent weight in the assignation, while their counterparts had 30 percent (a situation where a high degree of power differential was at work). The last pair was told they enjoyed equal influence in the assignation (50 percent), and so constituted a control operating under the "standard" minimal group protocol. The results showed that the groups with the same level of power performed as normal minimal groups and slightly favored their respective ingroups. The two dominant groups, however, discriminated more markedly against their subordinates, with the 70 percent group discriminating more than the all-powerful 100 percent

---

[19] When the status differential is felt to be either unstable (under threat somehow) or illegitimate (questioned by members of either party to the relationship), hostility and prejudicial attitudes will often intensify in the dominant group. Where group boundaries are permeable, members of oppressed groups have the option of escape, so neither the status differential nor its attendant prejudice can long endure.

[20] In the BBC-sponsored version of this experimental protocol, the prisoners were initially dominant; see above, ch. 3, pp. 87–8.

group. This was presumably because the 70 percent group did not feel as confident in its power as did the 100 percent group, while the 100 percent group, secure in its omnipotence, could display some *noblesse oblige* toward its utterly powerless underlings. The 30 percent group discriminated less than the parity group, but still somewhat, and the 0 percent not at all. These results suggest that exercising discrimination requires real power and that the degree of discrimination is proportional to the degree of real power wielded. The powerless, by definition, have no power to wield, and so they cannot discriminate. Indeed, it may be in their interests to placate the powerful, in the hope of future benefits. These results were replicated several times and shown to apply even across significant group boundaries, such as gender (that is, dominant groups of women discriminated no less than dominant groups of men).[21]

Once more, the minimal group paradigm generated stark results. Here, we are not just dealing with ingroup favoritism but choices that actively and needlessly denied outgroupers a coveted reward – there was no good reason why everyone could not have received the extra credit, particularly since the groups carried no meaning in the real world. Prejudice and discrimination, it seems, emerged directly from group memberships imbued with power and status differentials. Furthermore, it has been posited that in situations where a social identity is made particularly salient over a personal identity – say, in a crowd – stereotypical thinking about outgroups also becomes more salient.[22] The importance of group membership in generating prejudice, stereotypes, and discrimination appears to be absolutely fundamental.

The most obvious reason why power and dominance lead to prejudicial thinking is that prejudiced beliefs rationalize and justify unequal relationships.[23] As a rule, people think about outgroups in attributional rather than in circumstantial terms, that is, they tend to see conditions

---

[21] I. Sadchev and R. Y. Bourhis, "Social Categorization and Power Differentials in Group Relations," *European Journal of Social Psychology* 15 (1985), 415–34; I. Sadchev and R. Y. Bourhis, "Status Differentials and Intergroup Behaviour," *European Journal of Social Psychology* 17 (1987), 277–93; R. Y. Bourhis, "Power, Gender, and Intergroup Discrimination: Some Minimal Group Experiments," in Zanna and Oleson (eds.), *Psychology of Prejudice*, 171–208. (Naturally, all the participating students got the extra credit.) See also T. K. Vescio et al., "The Stereotypic Behaviors of the Powerful and their Effect on the Relatively Powerless," in T. D. Nelson (ed.), *Handbook of Prejudice, Stereotyping, and Discrimination* (New York, 2009), 247–65.

[22] S. A. Haslam et al., "Social Identity Salience and the Emergence of Stereotype Consensus," *Personality and Social Psychology Bulletin* 25 (1999), 809–18.

[23] J. Sidanius and F. Pratto, *Social Dominance: An Intergroup Theory of Social Hierarchy and Oppression* (Cambridge, 1999). Stereotypes can also induce subordinate groups into thinking that the unequal system is fair and just; see J. T. Jost and M. R. Banaji, "The Role of Stereotyping in System-Justification and the Production of False Consciousness," *British Journal of Social Psychology* 33 (1994), 1–27.

facing outgroups as stemming from attributes inherent in the nature of outgroupers rather than from a less visible set of social or historical circumstances. For ingroupers, this tendency is inverted: successes are interpreted through an attributional lens, and failures assigned to circumstance: unemployed ingroupers face a tight job market (circumstance), while unemployed outgroupers are just plain lazy, like the rest of their ilk (attribute).[24] When applied by the dominant to the oppressed, such attributional thinking is termed "victim-blaming." A situation that allows a longstanding and stable inequality to persist between groups will reinforce the dominant group's belief in the self-evidently inferior attributes of its subordinates.

These processes draw on the effects of the wider societal context – what social psychologists call "macrosocial conditions" or "macrocontext" – on intergroup relations. For instance, an enduring and stable status or power differential will often limit intergroup contact to situations where group memberships (and any status differentials attendant on them) are consistently brought to the fore, which further buttresses stereotypical and prejudicial thinking by providing, from the perspective of the dominant group, yet more evidence for group X's inherent inferiority and unworthinesss. Master–servant or employer–worker roles are prime examples of this type of intergroup contact. The situational salience of basic group processes therefore plays a key role in elaborating prejudice. Other macrosocial conditions are considered by social psychologists to be important in shaping prejudice and discrimination. The greater the number of fields where distinctions are highlighted in intergroup situations – dress, religion, language and accent, political orientation, etc. – the greater the degree of prejudice, since there will be few intergroup situations where group membership is not highlighted. Differential treatment by third-party agencies (the law, or social institutions) is another significant factor in maintaining prejudice, especially when one group is consistently favored over another. Group size also seems to be relevant. It is noteworthy that majorities usually discriminate against minorities, although this is not a hard and fast rule (think of apartheid South Africa). There are thus several features of a social order's structure that can work to reinforce prejudicial thinking in a variety of situations.[25]

---

[24] M. Hewstone, "The 'Ultimate Attribution Error'? A Review of the Literature on Intergroup Causal Attribution," *European Journal of Social Psychology* 20 (1990), 311–35; T. F. Pettigrew, "The Ultimate Attribution Error: Extending Allport's Cognitive Analysis of Prejudice," *Personality and Social Psychology Bulletin* 5 (1979), 461–76.
[25] Duckitt, *Prejudice*, 93–125; Jones, *Prejudice*, 129–50. Another good example is intractable conflict, where negative stereotypes promulgated on both sides are entrenched by virtue of the roles fixed by

The perpetuation of society-wide prejudices rests on the social transmission of such attitudes to individuals. Various media, not all of which are applicable to the ancient world, are reckoned to play their part in this process. Socialization of children is an obvious starting point. A society infused with prejudice can pass its attitudes on to its children through direct tuition by parents, peer emulation, children observing and imitating peer or adult behaviors, and the educational system. (Today, of course, there are also the mass media.) There is much empirical research on child socialization that supports these contentions. However, people do not retain their childhood habits of thought unaltered throughout their lives. Other factors beyond childhood socialization must also play a part. Conformity pressure is one such factor, which inclines individuals to behave and believe as others around them do.[26] The most disturbing demonstration of conformity pressure was Stanley Milgram's infamous obedience experiments in the early 1960s. Here individual subjects were instructed by authoritative "scientists" (men in white coats) to ask questions of an unseen partner and "punish" any wrong answers with an electric shock. The voltage increased with each wrong answer. A startling number of subjects took the punitive (but counterfeit) voltage to harmful, even lethal levels following the instructions of the "scientists," despite screams and other signs of distress emanating from the interrogee's booth.[27] Obeying direct commands, however, is only one form of conformity: peer pressure (social sanction for deviating from group norms, rewards for compliance) and continuous conformity, which may eventually become internalized, all appear to perpetuate prejudiced beliefs after childhood socialization. (As always, individual differences play a crucial role in mediating the degree of conformity from person to person.) Sustained experience of macrosocially conditioned contact with subordinate groups reinforces prejudicial thinking, particularly through perceptual and attribution errors. All of these media of social transmission are under ongoing investigation by social psychologists, and the means by which they interact constantly reviewed.[28] Nevertheless, the processes outlined here seem central to the perpetuation of prejudices in a society.

the conflict; see Bar-Tal and Teichman, *Stereotypes and Prejudice in Conflict*. Racial stereotyping and discrimination in the United States offer another obvious example; see, e.g., Chin (ed.), *Psychology of Prejudice and Discrimination*, vol. 1: *Racism in America*.

[26] See S. Guimond, "Group Socialization and Prejudice: The Social Transmission of Intergroup Attitudes and Beliefs," *European Journal of Social Psychology* 30 (2000), 335–54; Haslam et al., "Social Identity Salience."

[27] See S. Milgram, *Obedience to Authority: An Experimental Overview* (New York, 1974).

[28] See, e.g., Duckitt, *Prejudice*, 127–59 and the papers collected in Dovidio et al. (eds.), *Nature of Prejudice*.

In sum, the phenomenon of prejudice exists on several planes, not all of which are accessible to historical inquiry. Social-psychological research suggests that, first, prejudice is a universal human propensity that appears to stem from basic mental processes. Second, like any mental proclivity, prejudice does not operate in an automatic fashion but requires environmental stimuli to be elicited and elaborated into action. Third, group processes, especially when combined with power and status differentials, appear to be among the most basic requisites for this elaboration, where prejudice is invariably directed toward outgroups. Fourth, wider social conditions are identifiable which facilitate and nurture the expression of prejudice, including stable and legitimate status differentials, structured intergroup contacts that emphasize the salience of group membership, and differential treatment by third parties. Finally, through socialization, conformity, and experience of the wider social context, prejudiced attitudes can be passed on to individuals and perpetuated in a society.

Much of this can be demonstrated to apply to the Roman context in general, and to the arena in particular.

THE ROMAN MACROCONTEXT

However prejudice manifests at the individual level, it is especially potent when given free rein in a group context. When an entire society succumbs to prejudicial thinking, the result can be systematic discrimination against outgroups, even their wholesale dehumanization and attempted eradication.[29] The spectrum of people categorized by the Romans as outgroups was extensive. Stereotypes and prejudices marked relations between such categories as Roman and non-Roman, free and unfree, town and country, rival cities and villages, and even districts within individual cities. Prejudicial thinking also colored the lenses of the official *ordines* of citizens as they regarded each other, at least looking from the top down.[30] In sharp contrast to the modern concern with personal rights, Roman social thought emphasized group membership over individual worth. From the second century AD onwards, physiognomics promoted the belief that outward appearance reflected inner character; and since different peoples had

---

[29] There are those who insist that prejudice and stereotyping are first and foremost group and societal phenomena; see Bar-Tal and Teichman, *Stereotypes and Prejudice*, 4–8.

[30] MacMullen, *Enemies of the Roman Order*, esp. 163–241 and 255–68; MacMullen, *Roman Social Relations*, esp. 67–73 and 135–7 on urban–district rivalries. See also, e.g., J. P. V. D. Balsdon, *Romans and Aliens* (London, 1979); Y. A. Dauge, *Le barbare: recherches sur la conception romaine de la barbarie et de la civilisation*, Collection Latomus 176 (Brussels, 1981); S. Faller (ed.), *Studien zu antiken Identitäten* (Würzburg, 2001).

their own peculiar appearance, their characters were also deemed to be set. There can therefore be no doubt that the wider context of ancient Roman society – that is, the macrosocial conditions at Rome – not only harbored but actively endorsed stereotyping, prejudice, and discrimination. A full analysis of Roman prejudice and its variegated manifestations cannot be undertaken here, but a few illustrative examples are worth reviewing.[31]

Slaves represented an outgroup of gargantuan proportions, and freeborn attitudes toward them were openly prejudicial. Although the evidence mostly pertains to the elite, there is no *prima facie* reason to think that harsh attitudes toward slaves did not permeate all levels of the freeborn community. The Greeks had developed the philosophical doctrine of natural slavery, which postulated that some people were inherently suited for servitude, particularly the peoples of Asia.[32] The Romans viewed Syrians, Jews, and Asiatic Greeks in this light. A slave stereotype was a corollary of such attitudes, and it typically posited a person fit for hard labor, lacking deliberative powers, lazy, cunning, shirking, and obsequious.[33] Even if the slave-owning *plebs* did not read such philosophy, and even if slavery was considered by some jurists to be an unnatural construct (*Dig.* 1.5.4.1), the notion of a slave character was likely to have been widely assumed among the freeborn of all classes. It is readily invoked in rhetorical contexts to smear ex-slaves with their supposedly servile attributes.[34] The social position of slaves was widely equated with that of beasts of burden or other mute animals.[35] The habit of thought revealed by attitudes like this is a textbook example of the attribution error in prejudicial thinking, which justifies a persistently unequal relationship between groups by appealing to supposedly inherent attributes of the oppressed.

[31] See B. Isaac, *The Invention of Racism in Classical Antiquity* (Princeton, 2004), esp. 149–63 on physiognomics.

[32] The basic text is Arist. *Pol.* 1.2.2–23 (= 1253b15–1255b40), though the idea appears elsewhere in the Aristotelian corpus. For discussion, see Isaac, *Invention of Racism*, 170–94. Greek attitudes to slaves (and foreigners) were complex and could vary by case; see the discussion of J. M. Dillon, *Salt and Olives: Morality and Custom in Ancient Greece* (Edinburgh, 2004), 127–54.

[33] For insightful discussions, see Bradley, *Slavery and Society*, 133–45 (natural slavery and other philosophical views), and Bradley, *Slaves and Masters*, 26–30 (the slave stereotype).

[34] Note, e.g., Cic. *Rosc. Am.* 140 and 142; Suet. *Dom.* 11.1 (freedmen referred to as *servi nequissimi*, "worthless slaves"). The surviving portion of Petronius' *Satyricon* is a scathing portrait of a freedman's base vulgarity in the form of Trimalchio, who stems from Asian slave stock (Petron. *Sat.* 75). See also S. M. Treggiari, *Roman Freedmen during the Late Republic* (Oxford, 1969), 215–27 on social relations between freedmen and patrons.

[35] In Greek, slaves were called *andrapeda*, "man-footed creatures." For a full analysis, see K. Bradley, "Animalizing the Slave: The Truth of Fiction," *JRS* 90 (2000), 110–25 (*andrapedon* at 110). The pattern of thought extended to foreigners; see Isaac, *Invention of Racism*, 194–215.

Stereotypical and largely negative attitudes extended also to barbarians, foreigners, and other outsiders (such as bandits, pastoralists, or nomads), both within and without the empire. These attitudes were not necessarily hostile. It was taken as self-evident that different peoples (*nationes, gentes, ethne*) had their peculiar characteristics, which were expressed as stereotypes.[36] Some foreign groups were regarded neutrally, a handful even admired. What seems clear, however, is that Roman attitudes toward foreigners were not founded in analogs of modern racial categories.[37] (In other words, while the patterns of thought in ancient and modern bigots might be similar, the particular forms they took diverge according to context.) Prejudicial and stereotypical beliefs about all manner of outgroups, both within and without the empire, are traceable into Late Antiquity.[38]

That slaves were integrated into practically every plane of daily life and were found in virtually every conceivable context means that Romans were accustomed to social situations that laid stress on group memberships imbued with power differentials. And this applied not only to the interactions between slave and freeborn. The slave population was itself ranked into a hierarchy based on a variety of considerations (possession of desirable skills, tasks performed, proximity to the owner, level of trust earned, urban or rural setting for their labors, etc.). Slaves of the emperor ranked higher than those of everyone else; those of senators ranked over those of

---

[36] Such attitudes can turn up in the most unexpected places, such as Vitruvius' *On Architecture* (6.1.3–12), where there is a discussion of the geographic influence on national character.

[37] Juv. *Sat.* 3 is the *locus classicus* of anti-foreigner prejudice. Roman-era works with an ethnographic component – such as Strabo's *Geography*, Caesar's *Gallic War* or Tacitus' *Germania* – often adhere to negative stereotypes of the outsider but also single out particular traits (or sometimes whole tribes or peoples) for positive assessment. The benchmark for investigating ancient stereotyping and "proto-racism" is now Isaac's magisterial treatment in his *Invention of Racism*. For some older work that remains valuable, see Balsdon, *Romans and Aliens*, 18–71; Dauge, *Barbare*; J. Gaudemet, "L'étranger dans le monde romain," *StClas* 7 (1967), 37–47; D. Noy, *Foreigners at Rome: Citizens and Strangers* (London, 2000), esp. 31–52; A. N. Sherwin-White, *Racial Prejudice in Imperial Rome* (Cambridge, 1967); L. A. Thompson, *Romans and Blacks* (London, 1989), esp. 86–8 and 157–64; I. Weiler and H. Grassl (eds.), *Soziale Randgruppen und Aussenseiter im Altertum: Referate vom Symposion "Soziale Randgruppen und Antike Sozialpolitik" in Graz (21. bis 23. September 1987)* (Graz, 1988); T. Wiedemann, "Between Men and Beasts: Barbarians in Ammianus Marcellinus," in I. Moxon et al. (eds.), *Past Perspectives: Studies in Greek and Roman Historical Writing* (Cambridge, 1985), 189–229. On bandits, pastoralists, and nomads, see B. D. Shaw, "'Eaters of Flesh and Drinkers of Milk': The Ancient Mediterranean Ideology of the Pastoral Nomad," *AncSoc* 13–14 (1982–3), 5–31; B. D. Shaw, "Bandits in the Roman Empire," *Past and Present* 102 (1984), 3–52. For a case study for the ethnic portrayals in Cicero's speeches, see A. Vasaly, *Representations: Images of the World in Ciceronian Oratory* (Berkeley, 1993), 191–243.

[38] J. Vogt, *Kulturwelt und Barbaren: Zum Menschheitsbild der spätantiken Gesellschaft* (Wiesbaden, 1967). See also the ancient sources assembled and discussed in R. M. Mathisen, *People, Personal Expression, and Social Relations in Late Antiquity*, 2 vols. (Ann Arbor, 2003), vol. I, 42–70 (slaves and the lower orders) and 113–40 (various outsiders).

equites; and so on down the line.[39] Similarly, slaves who performed skilled tasks necessitating regular interaction with their owners (such as butlers, secretaries, accountants, or estate stewards) ranked higher than menial laborers who rarely saw the owner, if at all (such as farmhands, cleaners, or water-carriers). As a class, town-based slaves (*urbani*) were considered superior to their rural counterparts (*rustici*). Snobbery and prejudice were not likely to have been lacking in the interactions between these status groups in the slave hierarchy, and there is no convincing evidence that a unifying class consciousness existed among the ethnically diverse and divergently employed slave population. The existence of *vicarii* – slaves loaned by owners to serve more exalted slaves, and paraded in retinues to declare status in public – is enough in itself to support the inference. But of detailed evidence we get, at best, merely hints.[40]

Snobbery and exclusivity marred relations within the freeborn population as well. The common mob was looked down on by the elite, especially if they were unemployed or had to sell their labor to make a living.[41] Contact between status groups was often highly structured. Many social situations were heavily ritualized, and care was taken to maintain the proper status distinctions in public as thoroughly as possible. Indeed, concern for status was the one constant that permeated Roman social relations.[42] The

[39] On the imperial slaves, see P. R. C. Weaver, *Familia Caesaris: A Social Study of the Emperor's Freedmen and Slaves* (Cambridge, 1972). Weaver also charts differentiations in status within this vast *familia*.

[40] For a survey of slave tasks, see Bradley, *Slavery and Society*, 57–80, esp. 65–73 where the slave hierarchy, naturally enough, can only be reconstructed from the perspective of slave-owners; see also R. P. Saller, "The Hierarchical Household in Roman Society: A Study of Domestic Slavery," in M. L. Bush (ed.), *Serfdom and Slavery: Studies in Legal Bondage* (New York, 1996), 112–29; S. M. Treggiari, "Domestic Staff at Rome in the Julio-Claudian Period, 27 B.C. to A.D. 68," *Histoire Sociale/Social History* 6 (1973), 241–55; Weaver, *Familia Caesaris*, esp. 199–294 (with *vicarii* discussed at 200–6). Intraslave snobbery is difficult to document, since no literature survives from slaves themselves, though attempts have been made to fill the vacuum; see, e.g., Hopkins, "Novel Evidence"; F. Kudlien, *Sklaven-Mentalität im Spiegel antiker Wahrsagerei* (Stuttgart, 1991), with the comments of W. Scheidel, "Slavery and the Shackled Mind: On Fortune-telling and Slave Mentality in the Graeco-Roman World," *AHB* 7.3 (1993), 107–14. For glimpses of slave snobbery see, e.g., Cic. *Parad. Stoic.* 5.36 (slaves of major houses think themselves superior); *Vit. Aes.* G13 (Aesop, about to be sold, rues the prospect of obeying another slave's orders, rather than his true master's), cf. ibid. G14–19; Petron. *Sat.* 30.6–11 (a slave accountant, a *dispensator*, is about to beat a slave assigned to him, a *vicarius*, for having lost his cloak at the baths) and 47.11–13 (a cook is threatened with demotion to the *decuria* of *viatores*); Apul. *Met.* 1.15–16, Mart. *Ep.* 7.86, Petron. *Sat.* 30.5–6, Sen. *Ep.* 19.11 (freeborn guests at the behest of slave secretaries and doorkeepers). Slaves as a group were ranked only slightly above beasts of burden, which extended the hierarchy across species; see Bradley, "Animalizing." At one point in Apuleius' *The Golden Ass* Lucius, transformed into an ass, finds particular humiliation in being beaten by the very slave who had served him when he had human form (Apul. *Met.* 3.27).

[41] See, e.g., Luc. *Somn.* 1.8. For a collection of relevant *loci*, see F. Meijer and O. van Nijf, *Trade, Transport, and Society in the Ancient World: A Sourcebook* (London, 1992), 3–20.

[42] The powerful concern for status, and the way in which status was tied to legal privilege, is vividly illustrated by the case of Petronia Iusta, attested from wax tablets found in Herculaneum. She went

morning visit, the *salutatio* ("greeting"), by clients to their patrons; the street procession of the influential and their train of dependants as they moved about in public; the reclining arrangements, food served, and plate used at the evening dinner party; the quantity and quality of gifts given out at cash hand-outs or public banquets staged as communal benefactions; and, as we have seen, the seating arrangements at the theater and arena – in all of these situations and more the Roman macrocontext regulated status-group interaction in such a way as to make group membership and attendant status differentials salient for all participants. Even in the supposedly equalizing context of the public baths, great effort was expended to ensure that the relative status of the bathers was clear to everyone.[43] In the domestic sphere, the appearance of apsidal reception halls and ceremonial dining areas in Late Imperial rich mansions and villas reflects an elevated level of pomp and circumstance in the interaction of the privileged with everyone else.[44]

As if this were not enough, we have already seen how the law discriminated actively between the status groups in Roman society. People were ranked into classes and treated differentially in accordance with that ranking.[45] The vilest punishments, such as crucifixion or exposure to wild beasts in the arena, were reserved for the humblest members of society (*humiliores* or *tenuiores*), while less humiliating penalties, such as exile or fines, were specified for the privileged (*honestiores*). If modern liberal democracies try to legislate certain forms of prejudice into non-existence and consider everyone equal before the law, ancient Roman social and cultural prejudices were built right into the law itself.

to court to prove that she was the freeborn daughter of a freedwoman and not a freedwoman herself, since the determination of her status carried implications for her marital and property rights; see J. F. Gardner, "Proofs of Status in the Roman World," *BICS* 33 (1986), 1–14; A. Lintott, "Freedmen and Slaves in the Light of Legal Documents from First-Century A.D. Campania," *CQ* 52 (2002), 555–65, esp. 560–4; E. Metzger, "The Case of Petronia Iusta," *Revue internationale des droits de l'antiquité* 47 (2000), 151–65.

[43] The details can be traced in the general social histories of Rome; see ch. 1, n. 63. For public baths, see, e.g., G. G. Fagan, *Bathing in Public in the Roman World* (Ann Arbor, 1999), 206–19, and F. Yegül, *Bathing in the Roman World* (Cambridge, 2010), esp. 5–39. For dinner parties, see the articles collected in *Roman Dining, AJP Special Issue*, *AJP* 124.3 (2003); K. M. D. Dunbabin, *The Roman Banquet: Images of Conviviality* (Cambridge, 2003); O. Murray (ed.), *Sympotica: A Symposium on the Symposium* (Oxford, 1990); W. J. Slater (ed.), *Dining in a Classical Context* (Ann Arbor, 1991). For public banquets, see J. F. Donahue, "Toward a Typology of Roman Public Feasting," *AJP* 124 (2003), 423–41; Dunbabin, *Roman Banquet*, 72–102; S. Mrozek, *Les distributions d'argent et de nourriture dans les villes italiennes du Haut-Empire romain*, Collection Latomus 198 (Brussels, 1987).

[44] S. P. Ellis, "The End of the Roman House," *AJA* 92 (1988), 565–76; F. Guidobaldi, "L'edilizia abitativo unifamiliare nella Roma tardoantica," in A. Giardina (ed.), *Società romana e impero tardoantico*, 4 vols. (Rome, 1986), vol. II, 165–237.

[45] See above, chapter 1, pp. 28–30.

Access to various social institutions was also legally restricted. At the upper end, the *ordines* ("ranks") of senators, knights, and decurions were defined by birth and high property qualifications; at the lower stood the rigid official boundaries between the slave and free, citizen and non-citizen (at least until AD 212), with status symbols legally regulated for each. Professional and private associations (*collegia, factiones,* or *synedria*) were formed among the lower orders for some ostensible reason – to ensure proper burial of members, or as artisan associations, for instance. The legal designation for such associations was "associations of the indigent" (*collegia tenuiorum; Dig.* 47.22.3.2), which demonstrates their particular connection with the lower classes.[46] The existence of these clubs represented an attempt to achieve some form of exclusivity within that undifferentiated stratum of society the elite dubbed "the herd" (*vulgus*). The *collegium* was an institution with restricted access that marked off members from everyone else, that offered the prospect of attaining status and importance through tenure of club offices (president, vice-president, secretary, etc.), and that also offered the possibility of advantageous interaction with patrons drawn from the more elevated social echelons. Interestingly, slaves and freedmen could be admitted into private *collegia*, if the members and patrons were amenable.[47] It seems highly unlikely, however, that slaves were eligible for club offices or enjoyed all the privileges of the freeborn and freed members.

The socially determined scales of punishment in Roman law and the internal workings of *collegia* are excellent examples of third-party agencies that reinforced and legitimized status-group distinctions by consistently favoring certain groups over others. In psychological terms, it is safe to say that power-and-status differentiated groups predominated in the Roman macrocontext, which would tend to guarantee the perpetuation of stereotypes as a pervasive element in the Roman mental universe. Despite the wishful thinking of some, there is little convincing evidence that the lower classes did not buy into this prejudicial value system, let alone resist it.[48]

---

[46] Famous examples are the epigraphically attested funerary clubs at Lanuvium of AD 136 (*CIL* 14.2112 = *ILS* 7212) and that of Aesculapius and Hygia in Rome of AD 153 (*CIL* 6.10234 = *ILS* 7213).

[47] J. S. Kloppenborg, "Collegia and *Thiasoi*: Issues in Function, Taxonomy and Membership," in J. S. Kloppenborg and S. G. Wilson (eds.), *Voluntary Associations in the Graeco-Roman World* (London, 1996), 16–30; van Nijf, *Civic World*, esp. 3–69. Slaves were less welcome in the professional associations, it seems. This is true at least for the builders' *collegia* at Rome and Ostia, for which no slave members are attested; see J. DeLaine, "Building the Eternal City: The Construction Industry of Ancient Rome," in Coulston and Dodge (eds.), *Ancient Rome*, 119–41, esp. 121.

[48] See, e.g., de Ste. Croix, *Class Struggle*, esp. 31–111 (who argues the Marxist line of class consciousness and struggle in ancient societies). System-justification Theory takes the view that pervasive stereotypes can cause the disadvantaged to accept a system that keeps them in a subordinate position; see Jost and Banaji, "The Role of Stereotyping."

The social transmission of prejudice across generations, as we saw above, is a key feature of its perpetuation in any given society. The process of social-ization among the Romans is not a matter easily investigated, but some avenues of inquiry lie open for exploration. Since the family was "the fun-damental unit of social reproduction" in ancient Rome, it seems likely that prejudicial attitudes would find fertile soil within Roman households.[49] Interaction with slaves offers a ready starting point. Encounters with slaves would have been a near-universal experience for the freeborn, from infancy onwards and at all levels of society (and the reverse was true for the slaves, of course, especially those born into the condition). Among the upper classes, children were regularly raised by slaves in the house, whether nurses (*nutrices* or *nutritores*) or, later, tutors and other child-minders (*paedagogi*). To be sure, bonds of affection could develop between child-minder and charge, but it must have become clear to the child early on that one party to the relationship was in every meaningful sense disadvantaged.[50]

The same lessons would be learned on a daily basis by observing the interactions of adults. Surviving Roman schoolbooks of the third century AD and later, called *hermeneumata*, are mostly lists of words in Latin and Greek to be learned by rote. A common element in such books, however, are *colloquia*, vignettes of daily life that required the children to practice common vocabulary (some have rubrics like, "Daily Conversation," *de sermone cotidiano*, or "Daily Tales," *de fabulis cotidianis*). The "hero" of these *colloquia* is often the child, but adults occasionally take the lead role. In these *colloquia* the teacher is usually addressed as *magister*, a type of educator whose pupils were typically between seven and eleven years old.[51] Slaves lurk in the text as near-invisible entities at whom orders

[49] R. P. Saller and B. D. Shaw, "Tombstones and Family Relations in the Principate: Civilians, Soldiers, and Slaves," *JRS* 74 (1984), 124–56 (quote at 145).
[50] On the pervasiveness of slavery in even lower-class Roman family life, see P. R. C. Weaver, "Recon-structing Lower-Class Roman Families," in S. Dixon (ed.), *Childhood, Class and Kin in the Roman World* (London, 2001), 101–14; B. Rawson, "Family Life among the Lower Classes at Rome in the First Two Centuries of the Empire," *CP* 61 (1966), 71–83. On slave child-rearers, see Bradley, *Discovering the Roman Family*, 13–102.
[51] For the texts of the *colloquia*, see Goetz, *Corpus Glossariorum*, vol. III, 637–59; for the appearance of the term *magister*, see ibid., vol. III, 637 §3 (*colloquium Leidense*), vol. III, 646 §2 (*colloquia Monacensia*), vol. III, 654 §2 (*colloquium Montepessulanum*). In addition to the *magister*, a *praeceptor* (instructor) and *subdoctor* (assistant teacher) appear in these passages. For another *colloquium* and an explication of the genre as a whole, see A. C. Dionisotti, "From Ausonius' Schooldays? A Schoolbook and its Relatives," *JRS* 72 (1982), 83–125. On Roman schools and teachers, see H.-I. Marrou, *Histoire de l'éducation dans l'antiquité*, 6th edn. (Paris, 1965). Dionisotti ("From Ausonius' Schooldays?," 110) suggests that *grammatici* might be assumed in a section of his *colloquium*, in which case the children could conceivably be a little older (roughly between eleven and fifteen); a *grammaticus* is expressly mentioned in Goetz, *Corpus Glossariorum*, vol. III, 638 §1 (*colloquium*

are barked in the unsparing imperative mood.[52] The schoolbooks present pupils with phrases useful in various contexts, such as greetings, questions, or conversations. At one point we read:

And [will] you beat me? I am afraid. Your status is high... Do you revile me, bad head? May you be crucified. You behave badly and don't know that it doesn't benefit you. Why? Because I am a freeborn man but you are a useless slave. Be quiet. So you want to learn: I am not like you. You aren't, impostor? I want to find out whether he is a slave or a freedman. I [shall] not give you an explanation. Why? Because you aren't worthy. Let's go to your master. Maybe. For I [am] a freeman known to everyone and the master of a house. [That] is apparent from your face. Let's go.[53]

The concern for establishing status that pervades this entire passage – which imparts phrases useful in an argument – is remarkable. To be effective teaching tools, these phrases must have echoed daily encounters, and so would have taught young Roman children to treat certain categories of people brusquely. Prejudicial attitudes started early. We cannot trace in any detail how attitudes toward foreigners, criminals, and other outsiders were passed on, but imitation and emulation of parents and peers likely played a major part. The Roman social hierarchy placed a premium on group-based conformity and compliance, reinforced by continuous encounters with subordinates in structured and ritualized situations. The legal, political, and social institutions of the Roman state confirmed all this by dividing people into dozens of categories, assessing them on the basis of their group memberships, and treating them accordingly.

Harleianum). Marrou (*Histoire*, 389–99), however, associates the *hermeneumata* firmly with primary schools, catering to seven- to eleven-year-olds; see also Quint. 1.1.15–18. Note that one schoolroom scene (Goetz, *Corpus Glossariorum*, vol. III, 646 §2) is populated by little boys (*pusilli*) and bigger boys (*maiores*), all learning together.

[52] The orders start as soon as the child wakes up – "Dress me... Give me my sandals and slippers and trousers... Bring me water for my hands..." – and continue throughout the schoolbook's "day." Sometimes the slave is addressed directly, never by name but only as "boy" (*puer*). The same imperative tone is evident in the *colloquium* published by Dionisotti (text at "From Ausonius' Schooldays?," 97–105).

[53] Goetz, *Corpus Glossariorum*, vol. III, 642 §§17–18 (*colloquium Harleianum*): *et c<a>edis me? Timeo. Magna tua dignitas... maledicis me, malum caput? crucifigaris. male facis et nescis quod non expedit tibi. qua re? quoniam ego ingenuus homo sum, tu autem nequam servus. silentium habe. vis ergo discere. non sum tibi par. non, inpostor? volo discere utrum servus aut libertus. non do tibi rationem, qua re? quoniam non es dignus. eamus ad dominum tuum. fortasse. ego enim ingenuus omnibus notus et pater familias. apparet a facie tua. eamus nos.* (Text and translation by E. Dickey; my thanks to Professor Dickey for sharing with me parts of her forthcoming edition of the *colloquia*.) The reading is difficult, but it seems clear that these are disembodied phrases, not part of a connected dialogue; see Goetz, *Corpus Glossariorum*, vol. III, 640 §1. The concern for status is echoed in §§9–10 of Dionisotti's text ("From Ausonius' Schooldays?," 97–8), "I dress myself, as is fitting, being the son of the house and a freeborn person" (*vestio me, ut decet, filium familias, hominem ingenuum*).

Thus freeborn Roman arena spectators, who comprised the vast majority of the amphitheater crowd, would have been reared from infancy in the habit of viewing the world through the lens of group memberships that prioritized status and power differentials. And let us not forget that children attended the games. Augustus reserved a section of seating at spectacles for underage boys and an adjacent one for their minders, a situation confirmed by one of the *colloquia*: "If all [goes] well, the day after tomorrow there [will] be a circus, and afterwards gladiatorial games. So let's watch something newly (*sic*) and thus go to the baths with him, when the games let out."[54] Roman youngsters, long schooled in the ways of superiority and dominance, were thus exposed early to violence on the sand, one of their value system's most impressive manifestations. The arena was a place where the ongoing socialization of prejudicial attitudes among young Romans was both articulated and advanced.

THE ARENA AND PREJUDICE

If the Romans indulged their social prejudices wholeheartedly in their wider society, they did so in an intense, microcosmic form at the arena. The power differential between spectator and victim in the amphitheater was represented physically by the podium wall, usually between six and twelve feet high (Figs. 4 and 10).[55] But a more important gulf separated the two groups. Prejudice most obviously pervaded the execution phase of the spectacle. Those condemned to exposure to wild beasts, burning, crucifixion, or straight butchery were self-evidently enemies of the Roman order. They were non-citizen outlaws, people of the lowest status, brigands, common murderers, criminals, fugitive slaves, rebels, captured enemy warriors forced to fight in massed pitched battles, or members of proscribed antisocial cults – the ultimate outgroupers.[56] The law stated that those condemned to execution lost both their citizenship and freedom.[57] Tacitus

---

[54] See Suet. *Aug.* 44 = T.21. Imperial princes habitually attended spectacles, and we may reasonably expect the children of the elite (especially boys?) to have done so too; see, e.g., Dio 55.9.4; Suet. *Aug.* 55.2; HA *M. Ant.* 1.5. For the schoolbook entry, see Goetz, *Corpus Glossariorum*, vol. III, 642–3 §22 (*colloquium Harleianum*): *si omnia bene, tertium diem circus est, et postea ludi gladiatorum. noviter ergo spectemus et sic cum illo lavemur quando dimittunt spectacula* (text and translation by E. Dickey). See also Tac. *Dial.* 29.3 for children habituated to arena games "pratically in the womb" (*paene in utero*).

[55] Surviving podium walls stand anywhere between 2.00m (6.6ft) to 3.6m (11.8ft); Golvin, *L'amphithéâtre*, 71–223 *passim* (for multiple surviving examples). For example, the podium at Pompeii's amphitheater (Figs. 4 and 6) is 2.18m (7.1ft) high, that at Lecce (Fig. 10) is 2.05m (6.7ft), while the Colosseum's is 3.6m (11.8ft) high.

[56] On the identity of *noxii*, see Coleman, "Fatal Charades," 54–7; Kyle, *Spectacles of Death*, 91–5; Ville, *Gladiature*, 234–40.

[57] *Dig.* 48.19.29 (Callistratus on the *Lex Julia et Papia* of *c.* 18 BC). Such convicts were dubbed *servi poenae*, "slaves of the punishment"; cf. Pliny *Ep.* 10.31.2.

(*Ann.* 1.76.5) comments on the worthlessness of arena victims when he condemns Drusus, the son of Tiberius, for watching arena games and the shedding of blood, "however vile" (*quamquam vili sanguine nimis gaudens*). The bishop of Thmouis in Egypt, Phyleas, writing to his flock, describes the torments he and his fellow Christians were put through at Alexandria during the Great Persecution. At one point the governor told his torturers "not to have the least particle of regard for us, but to be so disposed and act as if we were no longer of any account" (Euseb. *Hist. eccl.* 8.10.7). Worthlessness knew no age limit: not even minors were spared the sword, the scaffold, or the jaws of the beasts (Lib. *Or.* 19.37; Euseb. *Hist. eccl.* 5.1.53–4). And the arena spectators were focused on them and their fate completely.[58]

Legitimacy in victim-selection has been shown to be an important shaper of crowd attitudes toward the condemned. Provided the crowd were convinced that wrong-doers deserved their fates, they were more than willing to watch them tormented and killed. Before Peregrinus self-immolated near Olympia in AD 165 (on which, see above, chapter 1, pp. 16–17), Lucian himself claims to have delivered a denunciation of Peregrinus and his followers as charlatans and fools (*De mort. Peregr.* 7–30). The bystanders, convinced by Lucian's oration, began calling for the immediate burning not only of Peregrinus but also of his disciples: "Let them be burnt right now! They deserve the flames!" (31). The notion of just deserts was key to the crowd's reaction, and it did not take much convincing to have them baying for death. On the other side of the coin, a suspicion of illegitimacy in the proceedings could cause execution spectators in later ages to reject the punishment to the point of boycotting the execution or even trying to free the condemned (sometimes successfully).[59] The authorities of sixteenth-century Seville commuted a seventeen-year-old murder convict's sentence to toil in the galleys, fearing crowd disturbances at this planned execution. The reason? Doubts about the conviction.[60] In 1788, Jean Louschart was scheduled to be broken on the wheel for parricide. But there was a general feeling that the conviction was unsound and that Louschart had been guilty of manslaughter rather than murder. Before the execution could proceed,

[58] When the martyr Pionius closed his eyes after being nailed up for burning in the arena, the crowd noticed and thought he was dead; they were clearly watching very closely. See *Pass. Pion.* 21.7 (= Musurillo, *Acts of the Christian Martyrs*, 164–5).

[59] See below, p. 179 for Roman examples. By way of comparison, see the cases discussed by Spierenburg, *Spectacle of Suffering*, 107–8, and the comments of Gatrell, *Hanging Tree*, 99–103 and 280–321. Spectators had to be convinced that the penalty was legitimate. So hangings for mere theft became increasingly unpopular in Early Modern Europe. The execution of rebels, with whom the spectators might sympathize, were volatile occasions; see Spierenburg, *Spectacle of Suffering*, 100–9. Botched executions could also cause the crowd to reject the procedure entirely; see Gatrell, *Hanging Tree*, 50–1; Linebaugh, "Tyburn Riot," esp. 102–3.

[60] Spierenburg, *Spectacle of Suffering*, 93.

the crowd rushed the scaffold, freed Louschart, and smashed and burned the apparatus of execution.[61]

In ancient Rome the legitimacy of arena punishments was established in a variety of ways. The accusation, trial, and conviction of the condemned prior to execution usually took place in full public gaze before crowds of observers in the open setting of the forum or the basilica, as is made clear, for instance, from regular inclusion of public-hearing scenes in the *Acts of the Christian Martyrs*. Spectators at Roman trials could intervene, comment on what was taking place, or otherwise interfere in the process.[62] Cicero (*Verr.* 2.5.106) records the indignation of the *populus* at unjust charges being read out in court in the marketplace of Syracuse. Novels provide an illuminating ground-level view of Roman society, and so offer valuable information from a unique perspective.[63] Apuleius' novel *The Golden Ass* includes the story of how a poisoned woman ran to the governor's house and accused her poisoner before falling dead at the governor's feet – all before large crowds. The governor had the perpetrator's slaves tortured for information, and finally "although it was less than she deserved, but because no other fitting torture could be devised, he condemned her to the beasts, at least."[64] We must imagine the trial and condemnation taking

---

[61] Abbott, *Execution*, 52–4.

[62] Trials at Rome were habitually staged in the open forum, witnessed by a circle (*corona*) of spectators; see L. Bablitz, *Actors and Audience in the Roman Courtroom* (London, 2007), 121–40; F. Millar, *The Crowd in Rome in the Late Republic* (Ann Arbor, 1998), 41–5. For explicit mention of (often participant) spectators at martyrs' trials see, e.g., *Pass. Carp. Pap. et Agathon.* A30 and B3.2, B.6 (= Musurillo, *Acts of the Christian Martyrs*, 26–7 and 30–1); *Pass. Apoll.* 11 (= Musurillo, *Acts of the Christian Martyrs*, 92–3); *Pass. Perp. et Felic.* 6.1 (= Musurillo, *Acts of the Christian Martyrs*, 112–13); *Pass. Pion.* 3.6, 5.1, 7.1, 10–11.1, 15.1, 15.4, 17–18.8 (= Musurillo, *Acts of the Christian Martyrs*, 138–9, 142–3, 144–5, 148–51, 156–7, 158–61); *Acta Cypr.* 3.1. 5.1 (= Musurillo, *Acts of the Christian Martyrs*, 172–3); *Pass. Mar. et Iacob.* 9.2 (= Musurillo, *Acts of the Christian Martyrs*, 206–7); *Pass. Mont. et Luc.* 18.1, 20.4–5 (= Musurillo, *Acts of the Christian Martyrs*, 230–1, 232–3). The proceedings against Christians at Lugdunum in AD 177 were very public; Euseb. *Hist. eccl.* 5.1.7, 10, 15, 17, 29–31, 35, 47, 50. Spectators are implicit in notices that locate hearings before a tribunal (e.g., *Pass. Agap. Iren. et Chion.* 3.1 = Musurillo, *Acts of the Christian Martyrs*, 282–3) or in the forum (e.g., *Acta Maxim.* 1.1 = Musurillo, *Acts of the Christian Martyrs*, 244–5). Note also [Quint.] *Decl.* 9.8 = T.17 and 9.11 for mention of the great throng standing around during the speaker's (fictional) trial. The so-called *Acta Alexandrinorum*, or *Acts of the Pagan Martyrs*, are a collection of courtroom scenes in which crowds of spectators repeatedly appear; for text see H. Musurillo, *The Acts of the Pagan Martyrs* (Acta Alexandrinorum) (Oxford, 1954); for analysis, see A. Harker, *Loyalty and Dissidence in Roman Egypt: The Case of the* Acta Alexandrinorum (Cambridge, 2008), 141–73. See also Bowersock, *Martyrdom and Rome*, 41–57; L. Grig, *Making Martyrs in Late Antiquity* (London, 2004); Potter, "Martyrdom as Spectacle," esp. 63–71.

[63] On Apuleius alone see, e.g., Bradley, "Animalizing"; F. Millar, "The World of the *Golden Ass*," *JRS* 71 (1981), 63–75; W. Riess, *Apuleius und die Räuber: Ein Beitrag zur historischen Kriminalitätsforschung* (Stuttgart, 2001), esp. 348–76. Note also Hopkins, "Novel Evidence."

[64] Apul. *Met.* 10.28 = T.2. Recent work has stressed the importance of visibility in Roman public life; see, e.g., Beacham, *Spectacle Entertainments*; D. Fredrick (ed.), *The Roman Gaze: Vision, Power and the Body* (Baltimore, 2002); Flaig, *Ritualisierte Politik*; Millar, *The Crowd in Rome*.

place before crowds too, as had the earlier mock-trial of Apuleius' hero in the forum and theater at Hypata (*Met.* 3.2–11). On that occasion, the crowd crammed every available space to witness the proceedings – they filled the whole of the *cavea*, the entrances and the roof, they hung out of the columns and statues and peered through windows and over the cornices. The only unusual thing about this situation was not the crowd's size or its craving to watch, but its laughter, since the entire trial was a sham (*Met.* 3.2). *Leucippe and Clitiphon*, the novel by Achilles Tatius of Alexandria, also includes a lengthy murder trial, which takes place before spectators; when the alleged murder is proven never to have taken place, the observers crowd around the incorrectly convicted hero to prevent his unjust imprisonment (Ach. Tat. 7.7–16).

In the schoolbooks too, the child takes part in or watches court cases in the forum. Two cases are described:

The defendant brought into court is a bandit. He is questioned as he deserves: he is tortured, beaten by the interrogator, his chest pummelled, he's strung up, stretched, lashed with rods, thrashed thoroughly – he goes through the whole series of torments, and still he denies his guilt. He must be punished: the sentence is death, and he's led away to the sword.[65]

Another case follows, in which a rich man with eloquent friends pleads his way to acquittal so effectively that the *colloquium* does not even bother to note the charge against him. The torture of the bandit took place in the court, a not unusual circumstance, it seems. The martyr Perpetua's father was beaten with rods in court, merely for attempting to dissuade her from persisting in her confession of Christianity; the man was beaten for trying to further the presiding governor's cause, but in an impertinent manner. Indeed, the Christian martyrologies contain frequent scenes of torture and violence ordered by the presiding official during public hearings.[66] At the mock trial of Lucius, the hero of Apuleius' *The Golden Ass*, the magistrate

---

[65] Goetz, *Corpus Glossariorum*, vol. III, 648 §4, and vol. III, 656 §10 (speakers as participants in a case); Dionisotti, "From Ausonius' Schooldays?," 104–5 §§74–7 (speaker watches). Quote at ibid., 105 §7): *reus sistitur latro, interrogatur secundum merita; torquetur, quaestionarius pulsat, ei pectus vexatur, suspenditur, crescit, flagellatur fustibus, vapulat, pertransit ordinem tormentorum, et adhuc negat. puniendus est: perit poena, ducitur ad gladium.*

[66] *Pass. Perp. et Felic.* 6.5 (= Musurillo, *Acts of the Christian Martyrs*, 114–15). See also, e.g., *Pass. Carp., Pap. et Agathon.* A23, A35 (Gk. recension) and B2.4 B3.5 (Latin recension) (= Musurillo, *Acts of the Christian Martyrs*, 24–5, 26–7 and 30–1, 32–3); *Pass. Pion.* 20.1–2 (= Musurillo, *Acts of the Christian Martyrs*, 162–3); *Vers. Ruf.* (= Musurillo, *Acts of the Christian Martyrs*, 324–7); Euseb. *Hist. eccl.* 5.1.14, 18–27 (note that the last phase of torture is explicitly located in dungeons to contrast it with the prior, public phases) and 10.8.8. Note also Ach. Tat. 7.12.2 where preparations are made in the courtroom to torture a convicted murderer for more information pertaining to another case.

orders the defendant tortured with fire, wheel, and the lash (Apul. *Met.* 3.8–9). Similar courtroom torture is reported by John Chrysostom, who personally witnessed the tribunals held in the wake of a riot in Antioch in AD 387. Although the city was largely empty due to fear of official reprisals, Chrysostom found the courthouse full of spectators, many of them relatives of the defendants, who were being brutally scourged for information, filling the air with their wails and shrieks.[67] For the Later Empire, this sort of thing was standard practice in courtroom proceedings.[68]

The public nature of Roman legal proceedings validated the arena crowd's psychological prejudices against the condemned when they finally appeared on the sand. Even if the same people had not themselves witnessed the forensic preliminaries, everyone could rest assured that proper procedure had been followed and that only the deserving had been selected for exhibition. In the case of prisoners of war or captured rebels, their status as enemies was self-evident. Tertullian identifies one motive for attendance at the games as "approval of punishment for murder" and characterizes the arena spectator's attitude toward execution victims in these terms: "It's a good thing when the guilty are punished. Who will deny this, unless themselves guilty?" (*Spect.* 19.2 = T.28). Tertullian embraces this very same attitude and shifts it to the cosmic plane when he looks forward to the greatest spectacle of them all: Judgment Day. On that happy day Christians in heaven can look forward to watching the persecutors, the philosophers and sages, the poets and actors, the charioteers and athletes writhe and liquefy in hellfire – "What shall be my wonder, my laughter, my joy and exultation?!," he writes.[69] Seneca echoes this sentiment when it comes to the condemned in the arena: "Since he has killed, he deserves to suffer," and he elsewhere comments on "the sad sight of entirely just punishments" which affects us. The sight may be sad, but the punishment is deemed justified.[70] Lucian, similarly, reckons that the charlatan Alexander of Abonoteichus

---

[67] Joh. Chrys. *Hom. de Stat.* 13.2–3 = *PG* 49.138–41; Lib. *Or.* 19.37. For a full analysis of this incident, see R. Browning, "The Riot of AD 387 in Antioch: The Role of the Theatrical Claques in the Later Empire," *JRS* 42 (1952), 13–20.

[68] Amm. Marc. 15.7.3–5, 28.2.16; Lib. *Or.* 4.37, 27 *passim*, 28.13–14, 45.29, 54.51; P. Garnsey, "Why Penalties Become Harsher: The Roman Case," *Natural Law Forum* 13 (1968), 141–62; MacMullen, "Judicial Savagery."

[69] Tert. *Spect.* 30.3: *quid admirer? quid rideam? ubi gaudeam, ubi exultem!*

[70] Sen. *Ep.* 7.5 (= T.20; "since he has killed") and Sen. *Dial.* 4.2.4 ("sad sight": *movet mentem . . . iustissimorum suppliciorum tristis aspectus*). Cf. Sen. *Controv.* 7.1.9: "But if someone is now standing in this crowd [in court] they are saying: 'Ought anyone spare this man, who killed his brother, and proves that he killed him?'" (*si quis nunc stat in turba, hoc dicit: huic quisquam parcat, qui fratrem suum occidit et occidisse se probat?*). Even the Christian Lactantius (*Div. inst.* 6.20.10), when warning against the pleasures of watching people killed, feels obliged to add "no matter how justly condemned" (*quamvis ob merita damnatum*) they may be.

should really be torn apart by foxes or apes in front of a vast amphitheater crowd (*Alex.* 2). Similar attitudes are found in other sources.[71]

The importance of a sense of legitimacy attaching to arena victims is highlighted by those occasions where people, even of low birth, were reckoned to have been put into the arena unjustly. Such instances are consistently presented in our sources as shocking travesties.[72] In one version of the martyrdom of Agathonike, the young mother is inspired by the spirit of god as she watches Carpus die, steps forward, and volunteers herself for death. The crowd plead with her to consider her young son, but the proconsul does nothing to prevent her throwing herself on the pyre. "It is a terrible sentence," shout the spectators, "these are unjust decrees."[73] The requirement of legitimacy held even in the case of slaves. When the death of 400 household servants belonging to the urban prefect Pedanius Secundus had been decreed by the senate in the wake of Secundus' murder by one of their number in AD 61, popular sentiment was against the unjust decision, and a mob attempted, unsuccessfully, to prevent the executions. The senate house was threatened with arson, and the route the doomed slaves took to their deaths had to be lined with troops to maintain order (Tac. *Ann.* 14.42–5). But such instances were rare (cf. Pliny *Ep.* 8.14.12–26). Conversely, Cicero (*Verr.* 2.5.134) regards with indignation the prospect of a guilty man watching a punishment rather than being its victim.

The legitimacy of a punishment was also partially established by its serving the public good, ridding society of those detected through due process as transgressors or threats. When there was a suspicion that some other motive stood behind punishment, the public's attitude changed. Tacitus reports how Nero, having blamed the Christian sect for the great fire at Rome in AD 64, presided over their demise:

[71] See, e.g., MacMullen, "Judicial Savagery," esp. n. 13.

[72] See, e.g., Dio 59.10.3, 72(73).20.3; Pliny *Pan.* 33.3 = T.15; Suet. *Cal.* 27–35, *Claud.* 34.2 = T.23, *Dom.* 10.1 = T.25. Whether historically accurate or not, the anecdotes indicate what was thought inappropriate; crowd reactions are not specifically recorded. Commodus' breach of the spectator/performer barrier by moving between the arena and his seats is reckoned by Dio as so disconcerting and egregious that he apologizes even for writing about it; see Dio 72(73).17–21 (apology at 72[73].18.3–4).

[73] *Pass. Carp. Pap. et Agathon.*, A42–7 (quote at 45) (= Musurillo, *Acts of the Christian Martyrs*, 26–9). In the Latin version (Recension B), Agathonike goes through a trial before being martyred; *Pass. Carp. Pap. et Agathon.*, B6 = (Musurillo, *Acts of the Christian Martyrs*, 34–7). This would explain the crowd's strange complaint about the unjust decrees in the earlier, Greek version (Recension A), since no trial is mentioned there and Agathonike simply emerges from the crowd to throw herself onto the pyre. Such voluntary martyrdoms fell out of favor when the church fathers condemned suicide in the third and fourth centuries. This required that a trial scene be inserted in Recension B and made implicit in the crowd's odd comment in Recension A; see the remarks of Bowersock, *Martyrdom and Rome*, 38–9 and 59–74. See also the observers' objections to the condemnation to the beasts of the Christian convert Thecla in *The Acts of Paul and Thecla* 27 (at §32 the crowd in the arena at Antioch continues the argument over Thecla's conviction); see J. K. Elliott (ed.), *The Apocryphal New Testament* (Oxford, 1993), 370–89.

Mockery was added as they died, as they were covered in wild beasts' skins and died torn apart by dogs, or fixed to crosses or, when daylight faded, burned to serve as torches at night. Nero provided his own gardens for the spectacle and put on a show in the circus, where he mixed with the commoners in a charioteer's outfit or stood in his vehicle. As a result, despite deserving the most innovative punishments for their guilt, a pity arose for them, since it was felt they were being killed not for the public good but to sate the savagery of one man.[74]

In Tacitus' mind at least, it is not sympathy for the victims of brutal and degrading treatment that moves popular opinion – the punishment is expressly stated to have been legitimate – but the sadistic selfishness of the motives suspected to stand behind its application. The Romans, like other execution crowds, could tolerate almost any form of savagery inflicted on the guilty, so long as it was seen as legitimate and carried out for the public good. As Caesar asked in the debate over the fate of the Catilinarian conspirators: "For what could be cruel in the case of men like these?" (Sall. *Cat.* 51.17).

Legitimacy was further reinforced in the arena itself. Heralds and/or placards broadcast what enormities the condemned had committed to earn their place on the sand. When a spectator rashly insulted the class of gladiator favored by Domitian, he was thrown to dogs in the arena with a placard declaring, "A favorer of the Thracians who spoke impiously" (Suet. *Dom.* 10.1 = T.25). The Christian Attalus was paraded around the arena at Lyons behind a placard declaring, "This is Attalus, the Christian" (Euseb. *Hist. eccl.* 5.1.43–4). In the story of Androcles and the lion, placards communicate the strange tale to the spectators (Gell. *NA* 5.14; for discussion, see below, chapter 7, pp. 257–60). Informers (*delatores*), a category of offender especially despised by the aristocracy, were ritually humiliated by being paraded in the amphitheater with placards declaring their crimes.[75] Claudius in the arena and Hadrian at the circus communicated with crowds through placards (Suet. *Claud.* 21.5; Dio 69.16.3). A herald announced three times to the arena crowd that Polycarp, bishop of Smyrna, had confessed to being a Christian. When the female martyr Agathonike was brought into the arena in Smyrna, the proconsul (who was

---

[74] Tac. *Ann.* 15.44.4–5: *et pereuntibus addita ludibria, ut ferarum tergis contecti laniatu canum interirent aut crucibus adfixi [aut flammandi atque], ubi defecisset dies, in usu[m] nocturni luminis urerentur. hortos suos ei spectaculo Nero obtulerat, et circense ludicrum edebat, habitu aurigae permixtus plebi vel curriculo insistens. unde quamquam adversus sontes et novissima exempla meritos miseratio oriebatur, tamquam non utilitate publica, sed in saevitiam unius absumerentur.*

[75] K. M. Coleman, "'Informers' on Parade," in Bergmann and Kondoleon (eds.), *Art of Ancient Spectacle*, 231–45. A relief from Miletus depicts bound prisoners and their guard, with a placard carried by the former; see ibid., 237 (fig. 4).

presiding over the show) asked her in the presence of the crowd to sacrifice to the gods. When she refused, she was burned alive. It seems that the spectators did not relish the prospect of killing a beautiful young mother who had recently given birth, and by publicly highlighting her criminal recalcitrance, the proconsul was trying to re-establish the legitimacy of the proceedings.[76] It was thus habitual for spectators to be informed about what the condemned had done to deserve their fates, or to mock their criminal presumption: "Jesus of Nazareth, King of the Jews" is perhaps the most famous such written notification.[77] Knowledge of the convicts' crime(s) would fan the crowd's prejudices against the condemned, all of whom stemmed from marginalized groups to begin with. As Martial writes of one Laureolus:

Just as Prometheus, chained on Scythian crag, fed the tireless bird on his prolific breast, so Laureolus, hanging on no false cross, gave up his defenceless entrails to a Scottish bear. His mangled limbs were still alive, though the parts were dripping with blood, and in his whole body there was actually no body. Then what heinous crime merited such severe punishment? Either in his guilt he had stabbed his master in the throat, or in his madness had robbed a temple of its hoard of gold, or stealthily set you alight with brutal torches, Rome. The miscreant had surpassed crimes recounted in tales of old; in this case, what had been legend really was punishment.[78]

Note that Martial is unsure what exactly Laureolus had done to deserve so brutal a fate, but the point is that he *is* certain it was something atrocious: murder or sacrilege or arson – whatever! Acceptance that something awful stood behind the horrible punishment was sufficient to take pleasure in the gory death.

The contours of the spectators' attitude toward execution victims are discernible in a famous incident related by Cicero and Pliny the Elder.

---

[76] *Pass. Polyc.* 12 (= Musurillo, *Acts of the Christian Martyrs* 10–11); *Pass. Carp. Pap. et Agathon.* A42–7, B6 (= Musurillo, *Acts of the Christian Martyrs* 34–5). See Thompson, "Martyrdom of Polycarp."

[77] Of course Jesus' placard was not displayed in the arena, but it served a not dissimilar function. For heralds in the arena, see Dio 60.13.5 and the Magerius mosaic (above, ch. 4, pp. 128–32). See also, e.g., Gell. *NA* 5.14.29; Mart. *Spect.* 4, 7, 9; Pliny *Pan.* 34–35; Petron. *Sat.* 45.7; Strabo 6.2.6; Sen. *Ep.* 7.5; Suet. *Cal.* 30.2 (for another placard proclaiming a crime, although not in the setting of the arena, see ibid. 32.2), *Claud.* 21.5. Placards were also used to communicate quite complicated information to spectators at Roman triumphs and are depicted in triumphal scenes in ancient art; see Plut. *Pomp.* 45.1–3; Suet. *Iul.* 37; M. Beard, *The Roman Triumph* (Cambridge, MA, 2007), 45 (fig. 9) and 126–7 (fig. 21). The practices echo the use of broadsheets and moral speeches to communicate the atrocities of the condemned to early modern execution spectators; see above chapter 2, n. 40; Cooper, *Lesson*, 1–26.

[78] Mart. *Spect.* 9; trans. K. Coleman, *Liber Spectaculorum*, 82; note Coleman's insightful comments ad loc.

In the games to celebrate the opening of his theater (or, more properly, the temple of Venus that crowned it), Pompey exhibited a large group of elephants who were hunted by javelinmen. But the demeanor of the beasts, with their cries and gestures of entreaty, earned the sympathy of the crowd, who began to curse Pompey. The reason for the crowd's change of heart is noted by Cicero, an eyewitness, as "a sort of belief that the huge beast had something in common with the human race." The assumption here is that, under normal circumstances, the crowd would regard arena victims (whether beasts or criminals) as having nothing in common with humanity.[79] A tamed lion, a favorite of the crowd, was mourned by senators and crowd alike after its death precisely because it had exhibited the human qualities of discipline, skill, and courage. This caused the crowd to conceive of the lion as similar to a favorite gladiator – a revealing equivalence.[80] In the case of Perpetua and Felicitas, the crowd objected to their execution on the basis of their youth and Felicitas' recent childbirth. Comparable reactions are recorded to the self-immolation of the Christian martyr Agathonike or when men refused to consummate (or watch) the forced prostitution of Irene at Thessalonika. In these instances, the appearance or demeanor of the victims lay stress on their humanity and so undermined the crowd's habitually hostile attitude; the response of the authorities was to cover up Perpetua and Felicitas in unbelted tunics, thus obscuring their femininity (although they did not stop Agathonike's death). A similar motive likely stood behind the shaving of the martyr Crispina's head before she was exhibited on the sand.[81]

But for most of those condemned to execution (*noxii*), the hostility of the crowd appears to have been intense. When the Cynic philosopher Demonax tried to dissuade the Athenians from introducing Roman-style games into the Theater of Dionysus, he urged them first to pull down the Altar of Pity (Luc. *Demon.* 57). Seneca records the vitriol yelled down from the seats during the midday executions:

[79] Cic. *Fam.* 7.1.3 (*opinio eiusmodi esse quamdam illi belluae cum genere humano societatem*). The point is well made by Coleman, "Contagion," 75: "This anecdote, much quoted and embroidered in Antiquity, surely encapsulates a fundamental truth about violent spectacle at Rome: it was allowable and indeed proper so long as it exploited non-persons, be they animals, or slaves, or prisoners of war, or condemned criminals." See chapter 7, pp. 249–52 for a more detailed examination of this incident.

[80] Stat. *Silv.* 2.5. The identification of human-like qualities in animals that confounded spectator expectations also underlay the non-lethal display of animals in the arena; see above, ch. 4, pp. 125–6.

[81] *Pass. Carp. Pap. et Agathon.* 42–7 (= Musurillo, *Acts of the Christian Martyrs* 26–9); *Pass. Perp. et Felic.* 20.2–3 (= Musurillo, *Acts of the Christian Martyrs* 128–9); *Pass. Agap. Iren. et Chion.* 6.2 (= Musurillo, *Acts of the Christian Martyrs*, 290–1); *Pass. Crisp.* 3.1 (= Musurillo, *Acts of the Christian Martyrs* 306–7).

"Kill him! Lash him! Burn him! Why does he meet the sword so timidly? Why does he kill so lamely? Why won't he die more willingly? Drive him to his wounds with the lash; let's have each accept their blows with naked and exposed chests!" There's an intermission: "Let's have throats cut, so there's *something* happening."[82]

Christian sources are especially detailed in recording the harsh expression of the crowd's prejudices against the martyrs, as they order extra punishments inflicted on them or brutally mock their torment. We have seen how the mob at Carthage shouted "Well washed!" at the martyr Saturus, bathed in his own blood.[83] The phrase (*salvum lotum*) is habitually found in association with the more congenial atmosphere of the public baths, which makes its invocation in the arena especially vicious. Toward the end of this same spectacle, the mob demanded the butchery of the whole group of martyrs in the middle of the arena, so that they could see the swords penetrate the martyrs' flesh.[84] Similarly, Salvian insists that crowds took great pleasure at the sight of living human beings reduced to animal feed (Salv. *Gub. Dei* 6.10 = T.18). In a protracted description of the martyrdoms in Lugdunum (Lyons) in AD 177, Eusebius includes many details of the crowd's cruelty toward the victims (Euseb. *Hist. eccl.* 5.1). The mob was present at the trials and shouted down attempts by the Christians to defend themselves and sometimes assaulted them. In the arena, they called out for high-profile victims by name or issued commands to the torturers in the amphitheater.[85]

Two points need to be stressed. First, given variations in personal inclination, it seems unlikely that the whole crowd participated in the vocal vilification of execution victims. The shouters and jeerers perhaps represented only a particularly hard-hearted section of the crowd. The arena appears to have been sparsely attended during the more brutal midday executions.[86] So while shouting for blood and torments and jeering at suffering may

---

[82] Sen. *Ep.* 7.5 = T.20.

[83] *Pass. Perp. et Felic.* 21.2–3 (= Musurillo, *Acts of the Christian Martyrs*, 129–31).

[84] *Pass. Perpet. et Felic.* 21.7 (= Musurillo, *Acts of the Christian Martyrs*, 128–9).

[85] Polycarp was also called for by name by the arena crowd at Smyrna and, on his appearance, there supposedly ensued an extensive exchange between martyr and mob; see *Pass. Polyc.* 3, 9–13 (= Musurillo, *Acts of the Christian Martyrs*, 5, 9–13).

[86] Sen. *Ep.* 7.4 = T.20. That *dum vacat harena* denotes the entire facility rather than the performing area is suggested by notices that spectators were usually dismissed for lunch at midday; see Suet. *Claud.* 34.2; cf. Dio 60.13.4. The same criticism may be implicit in Tacitus' comment (at *Ann.* 1.76.5) that Drusus, son of Tiberius, liked to watch the shedding of all sorts of blood in the arena, no matter how vile. That is, Drusus stayed to watch the midday executions – and, notes Tacitus, the *populus* disapproved of his doing so. On *(h)arena* as denoting the whole building, see Fronto *Princ. Hist.* 17 (*scaenae aut circi aut harenae*) and relevant citations, mostly late, in *TLL* 6.3.2350.30–2351.23, s.v. "(h)arena."

indeed have expressed the crowd's prejudices, such behavior was not likely typical for everyone present.[87] Second, as we shall see below, prejudice extended to all the performers in the *munera*, not just the unfortunate execution victims. Gladiators were also held in broad contempt, even as they were popularly admired (a paradox addressed below, chapter 6).

It would be a mistake, however, to conclude from such evidence that because the jeerers may have been relatively few in number, prejudices against the arena's victims were restricted only to a vocal minority of fanatics. Seneca may have seen some midday butchery enjoyed by only a portion of the crowd, but *damnatio ad bestias* and "fatal charades" were expensive to stage and were therefore hardly reserved only for a handful of die-hard gore fans. Indeed, as expressions of the emperor's power, "fatal charades" aimed to reach as many spectators as possible. There is no hint in a source like Martial's *Book of Spectacles* or the *Acts of the Christian Martyrs* that seeing arena victims ripped by carnivores or women raped by bulls appealed only to a minority of the crowd, let alone that such spectacles were intended only for the enjoyment of a small segment of the spectatorship.[88] Variations in attendance rates depended on such factors as when and where games were being held, who was putting them on, and who was performing, and this variety likely accounts for the conflicting pictures painted by the sources. While the crowd as a whole shared the prejudices they brought to their seats, only some of them were impelled to revel outright in the cruelty. The larger point is driven home by noting how the deaths of the martyrs united in prejudice both Jews and pagans, two groups not otherwise noted for their harmonious relations. On several occasions in the martyrologies, the presence and shared expression of anti-Christian prejudice by these constituencies is expressly noted.[89] While this may in part be ascribed to the overtly anti-Semitic tone of some of these works, it nevertheless reflects the psychological unity that sating shared prejudices can foster.[90]

On a broader perspective, the desire to see the guilty punished was certainly not the preserve of the arena's midday denizens. It was a

---

[87] Clearly, a substantial quorum was interested in watching the executions, as is made clear by some advertisements for games that include specific mention of execution victims (*noxii*), *CIL* 4.9968 ("slaves ordered to be bled with the sword"), 4.9983a ("there'll be crucifixions, a hunt, and the awning"), 9.3437 = *ILS* 5063 ("he gave gladiatorial games for three days and (exhibited) four execution victims"), and so on. See further, Sabbatini Tumolesi, *Gladiatorum Paria*, 143–5.

[88] Coleman, "Fatal Charades," esp. 62–3; Tuck, "Spectacle and Ideology," esp. 264–71.

[89] E.g., *Pass. Polyc.* 12.2 and 13.1 (= Musurillo, *Acts of the Christian Martyrs*, 10–11 and 12–13); *Pass. Pion.* 3.6 and 4.8–23 (= Musurillo, *Acts of the Christian Martyrs*, 138–9 and 139–43).

[90] As noted by Bowersock (*Martyrdom and Rome*, 42–3), "[Martyrdom spectacles] served to unite non-Christian citizens in the expression of prejudice, most conspicuously in the combined hostility of Jews and polytheists towards the Christians."

communal thing. We noted above (chapter 1, p. 29) how Cicero vividly evokes the vengeful mood in Syracuse in the wake of the capture of a pirate ship, but the incident also has much to say about harsh popular attitudes toward criminals. The ship was brought to port, the old and ugly crew members executed, the handsome or talented ones distributed as slaves among the staff of the corrupt governor Verres (whom Cicero was prosecuting), but the captain was nowhere to be seen, apparently having bribed his way to freedom. The invisibility of the pirate captain Cicero judges truly extraordinary, since captured enemy leaders were habitually paraded "before the eyes of all" (*ante oculos omnium*). Yet nobody at Syracuse set eyes on the elusive pirate captain, which outraged the locals.[91] When other pirate captains had been captured in the past, people poured in from all over the region to watch "the happiest of spectacles" (*hoc iucundissimum spectaculum*), namely, "to see those whom one has frequently feared led off in chains to execution."[92] Centuries later, the Latin Panegyricist of Constantine could declare German prisoners thrown to beasts as "a deed lovelier than his triumph" done "for the pleasure of us all."[93] Even given the evident rhetorical exaggeration, the communal expectation (and keen anticipation) of brutal retribution meted out to enemies and outlaws is striking, as is the centrality of spectatorship to the whole exercise. Both requirements were amply met at the arena, and these comments (like those cited above, p. 183) indicate what types of outlook the crowd as a whole brought to bear on the *noxii* to be executed there. Here were demonstrated enemies, threats to the safety and welfare of all, captured and punished. Satisfaction derived from fears assuaged and prejudices sated.

Echoes of these attitudes can be identified in mosaics depicting execution victims facing their grisly ends. The expendability of the condemned is made manifest by their pusillanimous gestures and carefully depicted facial expressions, all of which suggest timidity, fear, and cowardice in the face of death. The vileness of the execution victims was only highlighted by their

---

[91] For text see above, ch. 1, n. 67.
[92] Cic. *Verr.* 2.5.66: *hoc iucundissimum spectaculum omnibus vinctorum captorumque hostium praebebat... nihil est victoria dulcius, nullum est autem testimonium victoriae certius quam, quos saepe metueris, eos te vinctos ad supplicium duci videre.*
[93] *Pan.* 12.23.3 [AD 313]: *Nam quid hoc triumpho pulchrius, quo caedibus hostium utitur etiam ad nostrum omnium voluptatem, et pompam munerum de reliquiis barbaricae cladis exaggerat? Tantam captivorum multitudinem bestiis obicit, ut ingrati et perfidi non minus doloris ex ludibrio sui quam ex ipsa morte patiantur.* ("For what is lovelier than his triumph, in which he uses the slaughter of enemies for the pleasure of us all and enhances the games' opening procession with the remnants of the barbarian defeat? He throws so vast a number of captives to the beasts that the ingrates and oath-breakers suffers no less pain from their humiliation than from their very deaths.") It was standard practice to throw barbarian captives to the beasts in this era: *Pan.* 6.12.3, 8.17.1.

being exhibited as a precursor to the bravery and endurance of the trained gladiators.[94] To the Roman eye, such images would have resonated with the prejudices that had allowed them to watch the brutal executions in the first place: the inherent worthlessness of the condemned was on obvious display, right to the very last. For the *munerarius* to decorate the public spaces of his house with such scenes attests to the perceived rightness of arena justice and suggests an attempt was being made to extend the experience of watching indefinitely. In the *Acts of the Christian Martyrs*, it is precisely the martyrs' behaving in a brave and admirable fashion that drives the spectators into paroxysms of anger and vitriol.[95] They were clearly guilty, legitimately selected for punishment, belonged to inferior groups, and yet they failed to play their prescribed roles as cowering *noxii* deserving of their fate. In doing so, they called into question the legitimacy of the crowd's prejudicial attitudes: the condemned were not supposed to display *virtus* (and, as we saw in chapter 4, such behavior also challenged core elements of the crowd's social identity).

Without the ability to poll Roman spectators, it is hard to determine with any precision what specific facets of prejudicial thinking were active in the arena crowd. In all likelihood, there was probably a complex of outlooks. Given that brigands, rebels, or prisoners of war were natural enemies of the Roman order, Realistic Conflict Theory may well apply. Certainly the retributive mindset charted by Cicero – a desire to see feared pirates paraded, tortured, and killed, or great satisfaction at fearsome leaders humiliated and executed – is consistent with that model. The demographics of execution victims, who stemmed from already marginalized groups, makes plausible also the application of the social-competition model, which is founded on the basic group processes of social categorization and social identity. Not only were the condemned of the arena guilty of specific crimes, they generally belonged to outgroups already viewed with suspicion, fear, and anxiety. There was a distance between arena victims and the watching crowd.[96] Those on the sand were marked as the social (or political) other,

---

[94] For full discussion, see Brown, "Death as Decoration."

[95] See Euseb. *Hist. eccl.* 5.1.39 and 53–4; *Pass. Polyc.* 3 (= Musurillo, *Acts of the Christian Martyrs*, 4–5). Indeed, the language of the martyrologies often employs athletic imagery to present its protagonists as going forth bravely to meet an adversary: see, e.g., Euseb. *Hist. eccl.* 5.1.43, *Pass. Perp. et Felic.* 19.2 (= Musurillo, *Acts of the Christian Martyrs*, 126–7), *Acta Maxim.* 3.2 (= Musurillo, *Acts of the Christian Martyrs*, 248–9), *Pass. Iren.* 5.2 2 (= Musurillo, *Acts of the Christian Martyrs*, 298–9).

[96] Shelby Brown ("Death as Decoration") cleverly traces this distance between the viewer and the viewed from the forty or so arena mosaics still extant. For instance, in discussing the Magerius mosaic (ibid. 198–200; see Fig. 9) she notes how all the huntsmen and animals look at each other or the ground; the two deities (Diana and Dionysus) gaze at Magerius; and only Magerius and

and this would mitigate any tendencies toward sympathizing with their sufferings. As if that were not enough, the wider social context combined with the particular circumstances of the arena to infuse a tremendous and very obvious power differential between spectator and victim that reinforced prejudicial attitudes prevalent in the crowd, while the crowd dynamics reviewed in the previous chapters facilitated the gratifying and empowering expression of those attitudes.

While our focus in this chapter has been on the execution phase of proceedings, prejudice extended also into the hunts and gladiatorial combats (explored in more detail below, chapter 7). And yet for all its salience in the arena setting, prejudice was by no means the only relevant aspect of the crowd's mental state at the games. Prejudice does not in itself explain the presence of the crowd at the arena, since Romans, as we have seen, indulged their prejudices in all sorts of contexts, of which the arena was but one. Other factors were clearly at play. One such may have been a "morbid fascination with risk and violence."[97] If so, that fascination is not unique to the Roman context, any more than is popular interest in violent spectacle. Plain curiosity may also have been involved. The large crowd that walked several miles from Olympia to witness the self-immolation of Peregrinus at Harpina was hardly motivated by prejudice. They were just curious to see something unusual (Luc. *De mort. Peregr.* 35–9): a man of senatorial status burning himself to death in public to sate his delusions was not an everyday occurrence. However, the categories "curiosity" and "morbid fascination," are too vague to be meaningfully explored in the Roman context.[98] Since so many of the seats at spectacles were reserved or otherwise pre-assigned (see above, chapter 3, pp. 96–120), the viewing public was arguably drawn from a rather limited pool of people, who had for the most part seen it all before. In such a context, the drawing power of pure curiosity may well have been mitigated[99] (which explains

---

the herald look out at the viewer of the mosaic. The viewer is thus drawn into collusion with the games' sponsor, who acts as the agent of the depicted deities, and a sharp demarcation is drawn between "us" (the viewers) and "them" (the viewed). And this, argues Brown, likely reproduces the viewer-viewed dynamics of arena spectacles themselves.

[97] Coleman, "Entertaining Rome," 216.

[98] On curiosity at executions, e.g., Gatrell, *Hanging Tree*, 250–8; note especially the rich vein of source material (letters, diaries, newspaper reports, novels, etc., etc.) available for his investigation. See also the studies collected in J. A. Crook et al. (eds.), *Morbid Curiosity and the Mass Media* (New York, 1984). Our efforts are hampered by a lack of such spectator-centered material from the Roman world.

[99] Cicero (*Fam.* 7.1.3) expresses tedium at seeing the same old sights in the animal hunts Pompey staged in 55 BC (though he may be taking a swipe at Pompey's show by feigning boredom). Cf. M. Aur. *Med.* 6.46.

the observable elaboration of arena spectacle over time), although it is perfectly reasonable to propose common-sensical motivations such as curiosity or ghoulishness as further factors behind crowd attendance, even if they cannot be definitively demonstrated from the ancient evidence.

The mental dynamics of crowd processes and prejudice at the arena, while certainly major contributors to the arena spectators' experience of the games, did not in themselves generate the raw desire to watch. Insofar as these dynamics would be encountered in a wide variety of contexts in the Roman world, they may be considered part of the psychological background, the foundations for the superstructure of the arena spectators' mental edifice. More particular pulls must have been the excitement and anticipation of watching intense and potentially lethal competitions and, even more basically, the attraction of violence as an entertaining diversion. These central issues are the focus of the following two chapters.

CHAPTER 6

Gladiators and sports spectatorship

> We, in games, are not fascinated by death, its nearness and its avoidance. We are fascinated by victory and we replace the avoidance of death by the avoidance of defeat.
>
> E. Hemingway, *Death in the Afternoon* (1932)[1]

> The first thing that comes into my head is the cheering everytime somebody gets hit into the boards and a fight breaks out; everyone stands up and cheers that kind of thing, and when they see blood. A lot of fans came to see that and they got bored if there wasn't some kind of violence going on.
>
> Collegiate-level ice hockey player (2004)[2]

If arena executions can hardly be classed as sport, the same does not apply to the morning hunts or to the fights of trained, professional fighters that were the headline event. The classification of gladiatorial combats – and, by extension, the hunts – as forms of sport has generated controversy. While they certainly bear some resemblance to combat sports or bloodsports, for some analysts gladiatorial combats do not meet basic criteria for what constitutes sport and ought to be excluded from consideration as such. As one leading authority puts it, sport is

activity in which a person physically competes against another in a contest with established regulations and procedures, with the immediate object of succeeding in that contest under criteria for determining victory that are different from those that mark success in everyday life . . . A gladiator fighting to kill or disable his opponent and save himself in any manner possible is not participating in a sport but in a form of warfare for spectators.[3]

---

[1] E. Hemingway, *Death in the Afternoon* (New York, 1932), 22.
[2] Quoted in N. T. Pappas et al., "Athlete Aggression on the Rink and off the Ice: Athlete Violence and Aggression in Hockey and Interpersonal Relationships," *Men and Masculinities* 6 (2004), 291–312 (quote at 302). Quotation brought to my attention in R. Collins, *Violence: A Micro-sociological Theory* (Princeton, 2008), 301.
[3] See M. B. Poliakoff, *Combat Sports in The Ancient World: Competition, Violence, and Culture* (New Haven, 1987), 7. A similar conclusion is reached by G. Horsmann, "Sklavendienst, Strafvollzug oder

Others are willing to admit gladiatorial combats into the category of sport, but Donald Kyle has effectively sidelined this entire dispute by arguing that the categories "sport" and "spectacle" were not strictly distinguished in ancient usage. Since the banishment of gladiatorial games from the domain of sport stems in no small part from a modern desire to separate supposedly pure Greek sport from debased Roman spectacle, Kyle's stressing the similarities rather than the differences between the two categories draws them closer together: just as Greek sport could be a form of spectacle, so could Roman spectacle be a form of sport.[4]

Indeed, it is difficult to see how gladiatorial bouts can be removed entirely from the realm of sport, however it is defined. In the first place, modern definitions of sport have been developed to describe contemporary phenomena far removed from ancient contexts: what we consider sport and what the ancients understood as such do not necessarily coincide. The ancients had no specialized word for "sport" in the modern sense and employed vaguer designations, such as "contest" (*agon, athlos, certamen*) or "game/pastime" (*diatribe, ludus*). These words applied in a variety of contexts, from gymnastics to war to politics.[5] For their part, ancient writers can mention gladiators and athletes in the same breath, suggesting at least a perceived affinity between their respective spheres of activity.[6] Indeed,

Sport? Überlegungen zum Charakter der römischen Gladiatur," in H. Bellen and H. Heinen (eds.), *Fünfzig Jahre Forschungen zur antiken Sklaverei an der Mainzer Akademie, 1950–2000: Miscellanea zum Jubiläum*, Forschungen zur antiken Sklaverei 35 (Stuttgart, 2001), 225–41 (who also emphasizes the unfree status of gladiators). See also J.-P. Thuillier, *Le sport dans la Rome antique* (Paris, 1996), esp. 8 and 12–13 (who recognizes the sport-like nature of gladiatorial combats, but nevertheless excludes them from his analysis). Gladiators are also passed over in silence by H. A. Harris, *Sport in Greece and Rome* (Ithaca, 1972).

[4] For acceptance of gladiatorial games as sport, even if with some unique characteristics, see, e.g., N. B. Crowther, *Sport in the Ancient World* (Westport, 2007), 119–23; Golden, *Greek Sport*, 68–104, esp. 89–104; Grant, *Gladiators*, 8; A. Guttmann, "Roman Sports Violence," in J. H. Goldstein (ed.), *Sports Violence* (New York, 1983), 7–19, esp. 9; A. Guttmann, *Sports: The First Five Millennia* (Amherst, 2004), 26–38; M. Junkelmann, *Gladiatoren: Das Spiel mit dem Tod* (Mainz, 2008), 12–18; Kyle, *Spectacles of Death*, 8; Kyle, *Sport and Spectacle*, esp. 251–339; Lane Fox, *Classical World*, 444–5; S. Müller, *Das Volk der Athleten: Untersuchungen zur Ideologie und Kritik des Sports in der griechisch-römischen Antike* (Trier, 1995), 227–9; J. Pearson, *Arena: The Story of the Colosseum* (New York, 1973), 107–12; D. S. Potter, "Gladiators and Blood Sport," in M. M. Winkler (ed.), *Gladiator: Film and History* (Oxford, 2004), 73–87; D. Sansone, *Greek Athletics and the Genesis of Sport* (Berkeley, 1988), 61–2 and 116–17; Wistrand, *Entertainment and Violence*, 14–15. Paul Plass' book *The Game of Death in Ancient Rome* is subtitled *Arena Sport and Political Suicide*, while Fik Meijer's study *The Gladiators* bears the subtitle *History's Most Deadly Sport*. For the sensible comments of Kyle on sport and spectacle, see *Sport and Spectacle*, 18–22.

[5] Kyle, *Sport and Spectacle*, 9–11.

[6] See, e.g., Cic. *Fam.* 7.1.3; Dio 71(72).29.3; Quint. 10.1.4 and other citations below, n. 83; *RG* 22; Robert, *Gladiateurs*, 16–23 (technical language of athletics applied to gladiatorial combats in Greek East); Golden, *Greek Sport*, esp. 74–9 and 84–7. See also Carter, "Gladiators and Monomachoi," 309–10, and Mann, "Gladiators in the Greek East," for Greek athletic and gladiatorial terminology.

gladiatorial shows might include athletic competitions as added attractions (or vice versa).[7] An inscription from Pompeii reports that thirty pairs of athletes were exhibited as an integral part of a gladiatorial *munus*; that the athletic pairings parallel the gladiatorial bouts may imply that boxing, or wrestling or some such combat sport was involved.[8] Second, gladiatorial combats meet most of the criteria for sport, even those set out in the definition (cited above) that seeks to exclude them: they were physical competitions "with established regulations and procedures," and the criteria

---

[7] Gladiators or animal hunts never appeared at the regularly scheduled Greek athletic festivals, but the Romans appear to have staged mixed athletic/gladiatorial spectacles. Livy (39.22.1–2) reports that M. Fulvius Nobilior staged a spectacle that included actors, athletes, and a hunt in 186 BC; Plutarch (*Luc.* 23.1) says that Lucullus staged festivals, processions, and athletic and gladiatorial shows in Asia Minor, but it is left ambiguous whether the gladiators and athletes appeared together; the same can be said of Caesar's mixed games reported by Suetonius (*Iul.* 39.1). Dio (72[73].19.2) reports Commodus fighting in public with wooden weapons and being pitted against a gymnast or a gladiator armed with a wand. See *CIL* 4.9970 = Sabbatini Tumolesi, *Gladiatorum Paria*, 104–5 (no. 75) for a *munus* at Puteoli with gladiators, a hunt, athletes, and the awning. Another text from Pompeii (*CIL* 10.1074d = *ILS* 5053 = Sabbatini Tumolesi, *Gladiatorum Paria*, 18–21 [no. 1]) commemorates two sets of games staged in honor of attaining the duumvirate (a sort of joint municipal mayorship) and notes, on the first occasion, that "in the forum (he laid on) a parade, bulls, bull-fighters, fast runners (avoiding the bulls?), three pairs of bridge-fighters, a company of boxers, and Greek boxers" (*in foro pompam, / tauros, taurocentas, successores, pontarios / paria III, pugiles catervarios et pyctas*). *Taurocentae* appear to have been bull-wrestlers; a relief (from Smyrna?) now in the Ashmolean Museum in Oxford shows horsemen tackling bulls; see Junkelmann, "*Familia Gladiatoria*," 71–2 (with fig. 78). *Pontarii* were gladiators who fought for control of a platform (*pulpitum*) or bridge (*pons*); see Mosci Sassi, *Linguaggio gladiatorio*, 155–6, s.v. "pontarius" and Sabbatini Tumolesi, *Gladiatorum Paria*, 19 (esp. n. 11). They may be depicted in a relief from Trieste and a graffito from Perge, and M. Junkelmann re-enacted this form of contest as part of his experimental testing of gladiatorial fighting styles; see Augenti, *Spettacoli del Colosseo*, 98–9 (no. 55); Junkelmann, *Gladiatoren*, 155 (with Abb. 262–5); M. Langner, *Antike Graffitizeichnungen: Motive, Gestaltung und Bedeutung*, Palilia Band 11 (Wiesbaden, 2001), no. 767. Although not strictly part of a gladiatorial *munus*, these sorts of displays bracket together athletes and particular types of gladiators (*pontarii*) and also suggest what sorts of combat events arena athletes staged. A famous mosaic from Gafsa (ancient Capsa) in Tunisia shows athletic competitions with wrestlers, boxers, and runners; see, in general, Z. Newby, *Greek Athletics in the Roman World: Victory and Virtue* (Oxford, 2005), and esp. pl. 4 (for the Gafsa mosaic). See also Newby, "Greek Athletics as Roman Spectacle." It has been argued that the experience of spectatorship at athletic events diverged considerably from that at gladiatorial spectacles, which would have made watching mixed athletic–gladiatorial shows all the more dynamic; Müller, *Das Volk der Athleten*, 224–95. Note also the comments of J. König, *Athletics and Literature in the Roman Empire* (Cambridge, 2005), 214–17.

[8] *CIL* 10.1074d = *ILS* 5053 = Sabbatini Tumolesi, *Gladiatorum Paria*, 18–21 [no. 1]: "(He displayed) in the amphitheater, on his own, thirty pairs of athletes and five pairs of gladiators and, with his colleague, (he displayed) thirty-five pairs of gladiators, a hunt, bulls, bull-fighters, boars, bears, and the other varieties of hunt" (*solus in spectaculis athletas / par(ia) XXX, glad(iatorum) par(ia) V, et gladiator(um) par(ia) XXXV et / venation(em), tauros, taurocentas, apros, ursos / cetera venatione varia cum collega*). The parallel between thirty pairs of athletes and five pairs of gladiators on the one hand, and thirty-five pairs of gladiators on the other shows that the athletic element here was no sideshow but a core element of this *munus*. Note also Lucullus, who exhibited a combination of athletes and gladiators in Asia Minor in 70 BC (Plut. *Luc.* 23.1). See above, ch. 3, n. 40, for advertisements for spectacles involving athletes that do not mention gladiators.

for victory did differ "from those that mark success in everyday life." Death was not the expected, or even the likely outcome of contests in which a variety of moves or maneuvers could disarm or so disadvantage an opponent that he was forced to concede by appealing to the *editor*/*munerarius* (see below, and chapter 7). Third, categorizing events as sport (or not) by measuring the degree of coercion applied to their participants is a dubious procedure. How can we be certain what motivates any athlete? Can we be sure none feel coerced by coaches, peers, family, life circumstances, or even the state? Roman chariot racers (*agitatores*) were often slaves, acting under compulsion. Does this mean chariot racing was not a sport? In any case, we know that at least some gladiators were volunteers, so not all of them were coerced.[9] Finally, the characterization of the gladiator as "fighting to kill or disable his opponent and save himself in any manner possible" is seriously misleading. Gladiators did not thrash about in a terrified attempt to save their own skins. They were trained professionals competing in combats structured by rules and regulations and conducted in the presence of umpires. There are clearly defined features of sports that make them appealing to watch, such as the display of skill and endurance, rules governing play, uncertainty of outcome, and the possibility (in most instances) of betting on results. Gladiatorial bouts appear to have had all of these characteristics.[10]

That said, it hardly needs emphasizing that modern sports and gladiatorial events are not, in and of themselves, directly comparable. We need to view the ancient phenomenon against the backdrop of its historical context. The world of modern professional sports is a corporate, commercial enterprise. Teams, stadia, leagues, tournaments, special events, all the spin-off products of the sports industry – these things exist to make money. Furthermore, spectators and fans can watch in person amidst large crowds,

---

[9] For volunteer gladiators see, e.g., Dio 48.43.3, 56.25.7, 59.10.2, 65.15.2; Petron. *Sat.* 45.4 = T.12; Suet. *Aug.* 43.3, *Tib.* 35.2, *Nero* 12.1; Tac. *Hist.* 2.62.2. See also C. A. Barton, The "Scandal of the Arena," *Representations* 27 (1989), 9–10; Hopkins, *Death and Renewal*, 20–1; Ville, *Gladiature*, 246–63. Naturally, there is no way to determine the relative percentages of willing and unwilling gladiators, but repeated imperial bans on elite participation suggests that upper-class volunteers were at least perceived as a persistent problem by the authorities. Guttmann ("Roman Sports Violence," 9) notes the complete absence of any mention of coercion in gladiatorial epitaphs, even for trained slaves; instead they stress themes such as fate, skill, or glory. See also below n. 16. Kyle (*Sport and Spectacle*, 198–9) stresses the powerful social forces that compelled many Greek athletes to compete so intensely.

[10] The ancient evidence for betting on gladiatorial bouts is admittedly thin (the most explicit being Ov. *Ars. Am.* 1.163 70), but it is hardly implausible to suggest it was a regular feature of arena spectacles: see also Hopkins, *Death and Renewal*, 26.

or alone and remotely, on television. While some sports certainly entail risk, even life-threatening danger, there are few modern sports in which death, maiming, or severe injury are regarded as part and parcel of the regular run of play (Mixed Martial Arts, aka "Ultimate Fighting," comes close to being an exception). The rules of most modern full-contact and combat sports – such as ice hockey, rugby, American football, boxing – seek to limit the violence inherent in the action. Violent transgressors are removed from play, not rewarded with victory.[11] None of this applied to gladiatorial combats, which were not staged for commercial reasons (even if a lot of money could be made in the support industries), which could only be watched in person, and in which killing or crippling an opponent were accepted as valid ways to secure victory. The rules for gladiatorial combat do not appear to have set limits on the degree of violence the fighters could do to each other in the regular run of play.[12]

As with the appeal of public executions across time and space, therefore, the central issue here is not whether gladiatorial combats were, as events, comparable in form to this or that sporting spectacle from a different cultural context. Rather, the core question is whether the psychological experience of the spectator at gladiatorial fights was comparable to that of the modern sports fan, especially the fan of combat or full-contact events.[13] Did gladiatorial fights attract and entertain the spectator in a fashion similar to the way modern sports spectaculars do? There is good reason to think that they did.

Caligula once ordered five *retiarii* to be pitted against five *secutores* simultaneously (gladiatorial pairs usually engaged one-on-one).[14] When the *retiarii* yielded without a fight, their appeal was denied, and they faced death. The emperor was appalled when one *retiarius* suddenly snatched up his trident and slew all five victorious *secutores*; Caligula issued a proclamation decrying this act of "vicious murder" (*crudelissima caedes*) and excoriated those who had tolerated witnessing it (Suet. *Cal.* 30.3). It is noteworthy indeed that Caligula – an emperor not known for his delicate sensibilities when it came to violence (cf. ibid. 27–8) – did not expect

---

[11] Norbert Elias and Eric Dunning have famously argued that the relative tameness of modern sport is evidence for a "civilizing process," i.e., a rise in manners and polite society ongoing since the eighteenth century; see N. Elias, *The Civilizing Process: The History of Manners* (New York, 1978). On its application to sport, see N. Elias and E. Dunning, *Quest for Excitement: Sport and Leisure in the Civilizing Process* (Oxford, 1986).

[12] For works adopting a counterview, see below n. 104.

[13] See I. Weiler, *Der Sport bei den Völkern der Alten Welt*, 2nd edn. (Darmstadt, 1988), 235–6.

[14] For the habit of staging of stand-alone pairings, see Sen. *Controv.* 4 *praef.* 1 = T.19.

the arena crowd to revel in sheer, formless murder and was offended by this breaking of the rules. In contrast, his successor Claudius gave orders that any gladiator who fell in any show, even by accident, should be killed (Suet. *Claud.* 34.1 = T.23). The story is reported as an example of Claudius' excessive cruelty, since it contravened codes of gladiatorial etiquette, if not the actual rules of engagement. These notices reflect a deep concern for the established rules and procedures of arena combat. Even if we can no longer reconstruct the contents of the gladiatorial rule-book, the presence of umpires in images of gladiatorial bouts, which sometimes show them intervening in the action, can leave no doubt that such rules existed and were enforced on the sand.[15] In this respect, watching a gladiatorial bout shared other key features of watching combat sports: the object of the spectators' focus was a structured and monitored competitive activity that required years of training to prepare for and was staged before crowds familiar with both its rules and professional choreography. The arena audience did not turn out to watch disorganized, frenzied flailing by desperate men struggling to stay alive. They expected quality exhibitions of artistry and daring.[16] The Romans do not stand alone in history in finding such bloody contests appealing (see chapter 2). It seems reasonable to surmise, then, that people's drive to watch athletic competitions, especially violent ones, was another psychological process at play in the arena.

It may be objected at this point, however, that unlike the Roman games, death is not a habitual outcome in most combat events.[17] This may be so,

---

[15] The umpire was termed *summa rudis* ("Supreme Stick"); an assistant umpire, the *secunda rudis*, is also attested: see *EAOR* 1.48–53, 2.36, 3.63–4, 5.12, 59; Ville, *Gladiature*, 367–72. In ancient images, the umpire usually wears a striped tunic and wields his eponymous stick, which was probably used to intervene from a safe distance when rules were broken; see, e.g., Augenti, *Spettacoli del Colosseo*, 104–7 (nos. 60–1) and 122–3 (no. 74). Note especially the scene from Zliten where an umpire physically holds back the arm of a victorious gladiator while the decision on his fallen opponent is being reached (both umpire and gladiator look "out of frame," probably toward the sponsor's box); see ibid., 98–9 (no. 56), and Aurigemma, *Mosaici di Zliten*, 155 (fig. 90). It is not clear that umpires were drawn from among ex-gladiators; Robert (*Gladiateurs*, 263) thought this made sense, while Ville (*Gladiature*, 325–6 and 370–1) saw the suggestion stemming from a confusion between freed gladiators (termed *rudiarii*) and umpires (*summae/secundae rudes*) and presented evidence for enslaved umpires. On the *lex pugnandi*, see below, p. 215.

[16] That gladiatorial epitaphs express pride in achievement corroborates this interpretation; see the evidence collected by K. M. Coleman, "Bonds of Danger: Communal Life in the Gladiatorial Barracks of Ancient Rome," Fifteenth Todd Memorial Lecture (Sydney, 2005), 13–15. (My thanks to Professor Coleman for kindly sending me a copy of this lecture.) Some epitaphs are cited below, and in the Appendix at I.5–9. For a focused and thoughtful study of the latter class of evidence, see V. Hope, "Fighting for Identity: The Funerary Commemoration of Italian Gladiators," in A. Cooley (ed.), *The Epigraphic Landscape of Roman Italy*, *BICS* supplement 73 (London, 2000), 93–113.

[17] Note that Edward I of England (r. 1272–1307) issued a statute that sought to limit the actual violence of tournaments, but it had little demonstrable impact; see Keen, *Chivalry*, 86.

but in fact the same is true for gladiatorial matches, even if death was a fair and accepted result. A variety of non-lethal outcomes were possible, and gladiators who fought well but lost due to injury or to an opponent's superior skills could appeal and be spared (see below on possible outcomes). Seneca comments that bouts could be fixed by collusion between the combatants; indeed, he reports this as a proverbial occurrence (*vetus proverbium*).[18] Martial praises the famed gladiator Hermes, "taught to win but not to harm."[19] One *munerarius* from Tergeste in Italy erected a tomb for a pair of gladiators who had both perished fighting each other during his games. Such mutual destruction was clearly a highly unusual outcome and, as an unexpected oddity, generated popularity (*favor*) for the sponsor.[20] We also read of games held *sine missione* ("without a sending [away]/release"), which is usually taken to mean that all combatants either won or perished. In fact, the precise meaning of the phrase is unclear and, in any case, this form of spectacle was itself a rarity and banned by Augustus.[21] So while the nature of gladiatorial combat certainly made participation very risky and

---

[18] Sen. *Ep.* 22.1. One of Petronius' freedmen makes the comment (*Sat.* 45.12 = T.12) that the sole worthy performer in an otherwise pathetic gladiatorial exhibition fought "by the book" (*qui et ipse ad dictata pugnavit*), which reveals the existence of set moves for such bouts.

[19] Mart. *Ep.* 5.24.7 = T.11: *Hermes vincere nec ferire doctus.* Some gladiators' epitaphs boast that the fighters had "harmed no one"; see, e.g., Robert, *Gladiateurs*, 84–5 (no. 20) and other examples cited in M. J. Carter, "Gladiatorial Combat: The Rules of Engagement," *CJ* 102 (2007), 97–113, esp. 106–8.

[20] *CIL* 5.563 = *ILS* 5123 = *EAOR* 2.19: "Constantius, *munerarius*, to his gladiators on account of the popularity of the show; he provided a funerary monument for Decoratus, who killed the *retiarius* Caeruleus and then fell, himself killed; the trainer's rod killed them both, the funeral pyre covers them both. Decoratus, the *secutor*, veteran of nine fights, bequeathed primarily grief to his wife Valeria." (*Constantius munerarius gladia/toribus suis propter favorem muneris munus sepulcrum dedit / Decorato retiarium, qui peremit / Caeruleum et peremptus deci/dit; ambos extincxit rudis, utro/sque protegit rogus. Decoratus secutor, pugnarum VIIII, / Valer{i}ae uxsori dolore(m) primum reliquit.*) What it was about the result the crowd appreciated – its rarity, the drama of the contest, the total commitment shown by the combatants, or all of the above – we can only speculate about. For comparable scenarios playing out on the sand, see Mart. *Spect.* 31; Suet. *Claud.* 34.2; R. Merkelbach and J. Stauber, *Steinepigramme aus dem griechischen Osten*, 3 vols. (Stuttgart, 1998), 03/02/54.

[21] See Livy, 41.20; Suet. *Aug.* 45.3; Sen. *Ep.* 92.26. The ban appears to have been ignored in third-century Gaul; see *CIL* 13.3162 = *EAOR* 5.58. On the meaning of the term, see Robert, *Gladiateurs*, 258–61, and Ville, *Gladiature*, 403–5 (the standard view). Potter ("Entertainers in the Roman Empire," in Potter and Mattingly (eds.), *Life, Death and Entertainment*, 331) interprets the phrase *sine missione* to mean "ends only in a clear victory," which precluded the possibility of a draw. If so, as Potter puts it ("Entertainers," 331), "There was no such thing as a mandatory fight to the death between gladiators." See also Carter, "Rules of Engagement," 102–3, and Potter's comments in his review of Wiedemann, *Emperors and Gladiators* in *JRS* 84 (1994), 229–31. It is a clever and attractive proposition. However, draws appear to have been a real rarity, and *missio* means "a sending (away)" or "release," where the "release" saw a loser spared and freed from his obligation to the games' sponsor to fight. Without the option of "release," how could a clear victor be determined, except by severe injury or death? See K. M. Coleman, "*Missio* at Halicarnassus," *HSCP* 100 (2000), 487–500, esp. 490–1 (*stans missus* a rarity). The logic of *missio* assumes that death is the "natural" way victory is

the delivery of wounding or fatal blows was accepted to a degree that is unusual by the standards of other combat sports, there was no guarantee of death as an outcome, nor can we say that it was expected or longed for by the spectators, who appear to have appreciated just as much the art of winning without bloodshed.[22] The data are insufficient, unfortunately, to calculate average fatality rates among gladiators.[23]

At the very least, gladiatorial combats were sport-like phenomena. The fights watched by arena crowds had about them the air of sport, even if some details diverge from modern expectations of what happens at sporting events, notably death and injury as accepted results or the spectators' occasional role in directly determining outcomes. But these details, like the coercion applied to some performers, ought not blind us to the sporting appeal of arena events. As such, the spectators' experience of the gladiatorial phase of *munera* – and, arguably, the hunts – can be analyzed psychologically in terms of watching sports.

SPORTS AND SPECTATORS

Sport is a complex cultural phenomenon in its own right. It can be analyzed at the macrolevel (i.e., as a societal or anthropological phenomenon) or at the microlevel (i.e., as a personal, psychological experience). Much work has been done on the nature and social function of sport, its meaning and place in society, or as a historical phenomenon.[24] The psychology and motivations of athletes and team performance has also been the subject of intensive investigation.[25] Crowds of spectators, particularly of the violent

---

determined in gladiatorial bouts, a process short-circuited by the act of "release." This again would suggest that *sine missione* reverts to allowing this "nature" to take its course. Note that Suetonius (Suet. *Aug.* 45.3) reports the Augustan ban in the context of regulations that favored performers, which would make sense for gladiators if games "without release" were especially lethal.

[22] This is not to say that the violence went unappreciated by the crowd: recently published reliefs from Hierapolis from Phrygia are noticeably brutal in their details; see T. Ritti and S. Yilmaz, *Gladiatori e venationes a Hierapolis di Frigia*, Atti della Accademia Nazionale dei Lincei, serie 9, volume 10, fascicolo 4 (Rome, 1998), and comments of Coleman, "Bonds of Danger," 2–3.

[23] For what it is worth, Ville studied the results of 100 fights in the Early Empire and found that, of the 200 combatants, 19 perished (but how was unclear – in the fight, later of wounds, or following a failed appeal). The death rate may have increased in the third century; see Ville, *Gladiature*, 318–23; and Hopkins and Beard, *Colosseum*, 86–94; Junkelmann, "*Familia Gladiatoria*," 69–70; Kyle, *Spectacles of Death*, 86–7; Wiedemann, *Emperors and Gladiators*, 119–22. Note also the skeletal evidence from the gladiator cemetery at Ephesus, which included evidence of recovery from serious wounds, discussed below, ch. 7, pp. 269–70.

[24] For overviews of the different sociological approaches to sport, see R. Giulianotti, *Sport: A Critical Sociology* (Cambridge, 2005); J. Sugden and A. Tomlinson (eds.), *Power Games: A Critical Sociology of Sport* (London, 2002).

[25] See, for instance, J. Kremer and A. P. Moran, *Pure Sport: Practical Sport Psychology* (London, 2008); D. Lavallee et al., *Sport Psychology: Contemporary Themes* (Basingstoke, 2004); R. Lidor and

bent, have also been scrutinized.[26] Out of all of this work, however, what interests us here are the very basic questions of what draws spectators to watch sport, why spectators get so emotionally involved in what they are watching, and, finally, how spectator psychology can elucidate the mental state of Romans watching gladiatorial combats.

As we have seen, sporting contests contain some inherent attractions. They are competitive events bounded by rules familiar to the player and spectator alike; skill and artistry are required to secure victory; uncertain outcomes make the run of play unpredictable and offer the opportunity for betting on results. All of these features alone will draw people to watch. But the psychological motivation and disposition of the spectator is a more complicated matter. Unless they become violent and riotous, sport spectators have attracted relatively scant scholarly attention. As a result, the motivations of the "ordinary" spectator, as opposed to the hooligan, remain relatively obscure, even if various (notably vague) theories have been advanced.[27] It has been proposed, for instance, sports draw like-minded spectators to socialize with each other; to enjoy the skill of the competing athletes; to heighten personal self-esteem by associating with winners (a process termed BIRGing, or "Basking In Reflected Glory"); to profit financially from betting; to take pleasure in the victory of favorites or the defeat of rivals (an emotion termed "eustress," an antonym for "distress"); to escape from boredom or, conversely, to find relaxation from overstimulation; or just for raw entertainment. In most cases, these proposals stress either the *process* or the *outcomes* of sport as the pleasure-conferring elements.

K. P. Henschen (eds.), *The Psychology of Team Sports* (Morgantown, 2003); A. P. Moran, *Sport and Exercise Psychology: A Critical Introduction* (London, 2004); J. L. van Raalte and B. W. Brewer (eds.), *Exploring Sport and Exercise Psychology*, 2nd edn. (Washington, DC, 2002); R. S. Weinberg and D. Gould, *Foundations of Sport and Exercise Psychology*, 3rd edn. (Champaign, 2003). The *Journal of Sport and Exercise Psychology* is currently in its third decade.

26 See, e.g., V. Burstyn, *The Rites of Men: Manhood, Politics, and the Culture of Sport* (Toronto, 2000); Guttmann, *Sports Spectators*; A. Guttmann, "The Appeal of Violent Sports," in J. Goldstein (ed.), *Why We Watch: The Attractions of Violent Entertainment* (Oxford, 1998), 7–26; L. Mann, "Sports Crowds and the Collective Behavior Perspective," in J. H. Goldstein (ed.), *Sports, Games, and Play: Social and Psychological Viewpoints*, 2nd edn. (Hillsdale, 1989), 299–331; D. L. Wann et al., *Sport Fans: The Psychology and Social Impact of Spectators* (London, 2001). On spectator violence, see above, ch. 3, n. 31. See also E. Dunning et al., "Spectator Violence at Football Matches: Towards a Socio-logical Explanation," in Elias and Dunning, *Quest for Excitement*, 245–66; J. H. Kerr, *Understanding Soccer Hooliganism* (Buckingham, 1994); P. Murphy, *Football on Trial: Spectator Violence and Devel-opment in the Football World* (London, 1990); Wann et al., *Sport Fans*, 93–152.

27 An excellent overview is provided by L. R. Sloan, "The Motives of Sports Fans," in Goldstein (ed.), *Sports, Games, and Play*, 175–240. See also Guttmann, *Sports Spectators*, 175–85; G. W. Russell, *The Social Psychology of Sport* (New York, 1993), 237–40 (highly speculative); Wann et al., *Sport Fans*, 23–90.

Such theories apply first and foremost to the modern era, awash as it is in pertinent information. In the absence of detailed data about arena spectators, most are untestable for Roman conditions. For example, "personal investment theory" sees people drawn to watch sports on the basis of several personal calculations, such as perceived options (cost of tickets, parking conditions, availability of free time), a sense of self (e.g., identifying with a team or player), and various personal incentives (group affiliation with fellow fans, possible promotional give-aways at the game, etc.).[28] To establish criteria like these for attendance, detailed demographic knowledge and questionnaires are required, and neither is available for the Roman historian. Another view holds sporting events to have a particular lure for the marginalized in society, since frustrations engendered by the wider social context are vented at sporting events with impunity. Again, demographic data are lacking to test this proposal for Roman conditions, especially on an empire-wide basis. But it does seem to be the case that most of the seats in venues for spectacles were pre-assigned according to the criteria laid out in detail in chapter 3. This being so, many, if not most, of those at the games were likely to be people of some social standing, or at least somehow attached to them. A recent calculation of seating assignments and crowd capacity at the Colosseum in Rome concludes that less than 20 percent of the crowd derived from the underclasses. If this proportion is right, a frustration motive on the part of marginalized groups is unlikely to have been a prime factor in drawing people to the Roman arena.[29]

Since our evidence is so patchy and diversely sourced, this model for spectator demographics at the Colosseum is far from secure, and, in any case, the Colosseum was a special case among amphitheaters. Rome, after all, was likely to have a higher share of elite inhabitants than any other city in the empire. Their proportional representation at the games would therefore be correspondingly higher and so unrepresentative of spectator demographics elsewhere (in, say, a place like Nemausus or even at major centers like Carthage or Antioch). Even at the Colosseum itself, it is a difficult business to tie the physical remains to the literary and epigraphic testimony about who exactly sat where. Too many gaps persist to be certain that less than a fifth of the crowd constituted "the mob." Even in the case

---

[28] Wann et al., *Sports Fans*, 53–66.

[29] See Bomgardner, *Story of the Roman Amphitheatre*, 17–20, who comments (20), "First and foremost the Colosseum was a monument dedicated to the social contract of Roman society: the symbiotic relationship between the emperor and the senatorial and equestrian classes, on the one hand, and the relatively well-to-do Roman citizens, on the other." For more thoughts on this matter, see above, ch. 3, n. 95.

of the seats assigned to the Arval Brothers, we cannot know for certain the social status of the ninety-four dependants who occupied them: those seated in the first *maenianum* probably hailed from the elite, while those stationed in the *tabulationes* at the back may have stemmed from the less-elevated classes. And even if we did know for certain that large portions of the crowd at the Colosseum derived from the lower orders, limitations in our demographic knowledge would prevent us from investigating to what degree, if any, resentment at social marginalization motivated attendance. Since arena victims and performers themselves came from marginalized groups and were the targets of intense prejudice from the crowd, it remains an intriguing, if untestable, possibility that seeing them suffer and struggle somehow lessened the feelings of inadequacy that may have afflicted Roman society's less valued members as they watched from the tiers. The best we can say is that self-esteem issues *may* have played a role in some of the spectators' motivations.

Common also as explanations for the draw of sport, especially of a violent bent, are theses of purgation, or "catharsis." The basic proposition is traceable to Aristotle's *Poetics*, where the great philosopher suggested that people enjoy watching tragedy because they are purged of emotions (primarily fear and pity) and so brought back to a healthy emotional equilibrium.[30] Rather like Paul Plass' theory of arena games as "liminoid ritual," the arena can be interpreted as a means of defusing violent urges by experiencing them vicariously. The idea, however, has not been verified by researchers. Simply put, catharsis lacks empirical support. It has been repeatedly shown that people who watch violent spectacles (e.g., American football, boxing, hockey, or horror movies) leave in a more aggressive frame of mind than when they went in, and are certainly more aggressive in outlook than spectators who had watched non-violent events (e.g., gymnastics or swimming). If anything, watching aggression and violence heightens, rather than purges, aggressive impulses. This reaction holds true even for different events within the same sport – a violent ice hockey game as compared to a relatively fight-free one, for instance.[31]

---

[30] Arist. *Poet.* 6.2 (= 1449b28); cf. Arist. *Pol.* 8.7.3–6 (= 1341b27–42a17). See also E. S. Belfiore, *Tragic Pleasures: Aristotle on Plot and Emotion* (Princeton, 1992), 255–360; D. Wiles, "Aristotle's *Poetics* and Ancient Dramatic Theory," in M. McDonald and J. M. Walton (eds.), *The Cambridge Companion to Greek and Roman Theatre* (Cambridge, 2007), 92–107, esp. 98–100.

[31] R. L. Arms et al., "Effects of Observing Athletic Contests on Hostility of Spectators Viewing Aggressive Sports," *Social Psychology Quarterly* 42 (1979), 275–9; J. H. Goldstein and R. L. Arms, "Effects of Observing Athletic Contests on Hostility," *Sociometry* 34 (1971), 83–90; Guttmann, *Sports Spectators*, 147–58; G. W. Russell, "Psychological Issues in Sports Aggression," in Goldstein (ed.),

A useful social-psychological concept about the enticement to watch sport is "representational sport."[32] In this analysis, the crowd considers its team or favored athlete a representative of itself, and so invests enormous emotional stock in their performance. The representation is perforce group-based, in that the crowd (or subgroups within it) feel that the players represent them, their values, or their aspirations *as a group*. How the group identification is established varies. It can relate to location (a city rooting for its baseball team, or the intense local rivalries between the London-based teams in English soccer), or of nationality (World Cup or Davis Cup fans supporting the national team), or of ethnicity (supporters of black or white boxers). A clear indication of how deeply such representational feelings can run is provided by "The Soccer War" of 1969 between El Salvador and Honduras. While tensions between these neighboring nations mounted for other reasons, armed conflict was finally sparked by the result of a World Cup qualifying match. In such cases, then, the representative role of the players, whether individuals or teams, maps on to the self-categorization of the spectators as a group.

Can we apply the "representational-sport" model to the arena?[33] It might at first seem so. Gladiators have long been analyzed as manifesting Roman *virtus* ("manliness, courage, virtue"), in that they displayed martial skill, discipline, endurance, bravery, and a contempt for suffering and death. That members of the lowest social class could behave so nobly made the point all the more starkly. As Cicero comments, "when condemned men fought with swords, there could be no sturdier training for the eye against pain and death" (Cic. *Tusc.* 2.41 = T.5). Pliny asserts that Trajan's spectacles presented "nothing flaccid or dissolute to soften and weaken men's spirits, but something to rouse them to accept lovely wounds and hold death in contempt, since even in the bodies of slaves and criminals was seen a love of glory and a lust to win."[34] Elsewhere, Pliny describes the gladiators

Sports Violence, 157–81, esp. 164–8; Russell, *Social Psychology of Sport*, 211–35; Wann et al., *Sport Fans*, 115–16, with references to the relevant empirical studies.

[32] First proposed by P. Weiss, *Sport: A Philosophical Inquiry* (Carbondale, 1969) and reprised many times since; see, e.g., Guttmann, *Sports Spectators*, 175–85.

[33] The basic phenomenon finds echo in the annals of antiquity. Tacitus, for instance, tells the story (*Hist.* 2.68) of a wrestling match between a Roman legionary and a Gallic auxiliary that degenerated into a riot resulting in the annihilation of two cohorts; the legionary spectators objected to the mockery heaped by the Gaul on his defeated Roman opponent and attacked the Gallic spectators. Impulses stimulated by representative sentiments likely stood behind the legionaries' actions.

[34] Pliny *Pan.* 33.1 = T.15. For an overview of such notions, see Wistrand, *Entertainment and Violence*, 12–29. Wistrand (55–9) notes that the arena was the only form of popular entertainment rated positively in the writings of the nine first-century AD authors he surveys. See also Ville, *Gladiature*, 334–44.

displayed by Trajan as men whose courage matched their massive physical strength (Pliny *Pan.* 34.3). Martial's poems contain many references to arena events, including an entire book of epigrams possibly inspired by the opening of the Colosseum in AD 80 (*Liber Spectaculorum*, or "The Book of Spectacles"), yet nowhere in it do we find expressions of contempt for gladiators (executed criminals are a different matter). Rather, Martial admires the professional fighters and often identifies them by name, as he does also with some prominent huntsmen (*venatores* or *bestiarii*).[35] Seneca encapsulates the worldview underlying this respect for gladiators when he pronounces "*virtus* is keen for risk and contemplates what it's aiming for, not what it may suffer, since even what it will suffer is part of its glory."[36] By using this sort of evidence in a "representational" analysis, it could be argued that arena spectators viewed gladiators as manifesting those qualities they most admired in themselves, and so they got emotionally involved in the contests.

Horace expresses dismay that people get all worked up over which of two gladiators was the best (Hor. *Sat.* 2.6.44). But the poet's derision of such emotions proves their existence. The question is, did these emotions rest on the arena crowd's feeling that their better angels were "represented" by the brave and skillful gladiators competing on the sand? As attractive as this idea may be, it is unlikely to have applied to the arena in any systematic way. For the "representational" model to apply, Roman spectators would have to identify *as a group* with the slaves, criminals, convicts, and other outcasts who performed in the arena.[37] To put it another way, to feel "represented" the spectator must feel tied to the athlete by a perception of a shared group membership. In the modern context, race, nationality, or regional affiliation meet this essential criterion, but it seems highly unlikely to have held true in the Roman arena, especially when set against a wider social context that emphasized group membership as the determinant of individual

---

[35] Famous and admired gladiators are named frequently in Roman literature; see, e.g., Hor. *Ep.* 1.18.19, *Sat.* 2.7.96; Lucil. 4.151–4K = 4.149–52M (= Nonius, s.v. "spurcum"); Mart. *Ep.* 5.24, *Spect.* 15, 22, 28; Plut. *Galba* 8.5, 9.2; see also Wistrand, *Entertainment and Violence*, 20–2. The encomiastic tone of Martial's *Liber Spectaculorum*, aimed especially at the emperor/sponsor of the games, no doubt contributed to the poet's positive presentation of these gladiators; see Coleman's edition and commentary, *Liber Spectaculorum*, lxxix–lxxxi.

[36] Sen. *Dial.* 1.4.4: *avida est periculi virtus et quo tendat, non quid passura sit cogitat, quoniam etiam quod passura est gloriae pars est.* Compare the related comments of Cicero that pain yields to *virtus* (*Tusc.* 2.31) and that contempt of pain and death are the two greatest duties (*munera*; a nice play on words) of fortitude (ibid. 2.43).

[37] On the gladiators' and other arena performers' degraded status, see, e.g., Kyle, *Spectacles of Death*, 79–90; Wiedemann, *Emperors and Gladiators*, 1–54; Ville, *Gladiature*, 339–44; Wistrand, *Entertainment and Violence*, 15–29. See also above, ch. 4, n. 74.

worth. At the arena, sharp social distinctions divided the spectator decisively from the degraded performer. Displays of skill or the manifestation of admired group traits are not proven bases for a representational analysis in modern sports. Rather, these are factors that affect the affective dispositions of the spectators with regard to particular performers (an issue we will return to in more detail in the next chapter). If we could be sure that, for instance, some ethnic or regional characteristic of gladiators connected them to sections of the crowd that viewed themselves as sharing that ethnicity or characteristic, we would be on a firmer footing. But no such evidence exists (the ethnic markers in gladiatorial epitaphs say nothing about how the spectators viewed themselves vis-à-vis the combatants). A telling exception is the riotous spectacle at Pompeii in AD 59 (see above, chapter 3, pp. 93–6), where a gladiator-like competition between Pompeian and Nucerian youths included the element of representation, since the crowd would naturally regard their town's youths as representing their community, and, in any case, intense fractiousness had long marked Pompeii's relations with its neighbor. But that spectacle was atypical, as was the (very modern-sounding) riot it spawned. If this is the exception that proves the rule, it indicates that a representational bond between spectator and performer were not regular features of watching arena spectacle.

The core contention of the representational model is to assert the alignment of spectator with actor, and there are bases for such alignment other than a sense of shared group membership. We shall see in the next chapter how violent spectacles achieve this alignment psychologically by manipulating the audience's attitudes to perpetrators of violence (what psychologists call the "affective dispositions" of the audience); the approach has been applied also to sports spectatorship, but we shall defer detailed consideration of it until the following chapter.[38] In sports, there is also the spectators' well-known excitement and emotional involvement in what transpires on the field of play.[39] This emotional factor warrants further consideration.

EXCITEMENT: THE EMOTIONAL FACTOR

It is a truism that sports spectators are usually in an excited state. We may regard their emotional involvement in the event as a form of excitement, since that is the dominant state of mind while the contest is underway

---

[38] See, e.g., D. Zillmann et al., "Enjoyment from Sports Spectatorship," in Goldstein (ed.), *Sports, Games, and Play*, 241–78.
[39] See Sloan, "Motives of Sports Fans," 178–9.

and the outcome still uncertain. In one sense crowds of sports spectators can be read as little different from those at any collective event for which likeminded people have gathered, such as at concerts, or political rallies or protests, community fêtes, large religious festivals, and so forth. The content and parameters of the social identities and categorizations involved differ in each case, but the psychological mechanics are the same. For sports spectatorship to be meaningful, there has to be some bond between the spectators and the competing athletes, or else the contest carries little interest. This is the essence of the representational or affective dispositional models of sport spectatorship mentioned above. Indeed, spectators who are neutral in respect to the competing parties may arbitrarily "pick a side" in order to make the event more engaging; they seek to experience the excitement of watching sports vicariously, as it were, by manufacturing a temporary bond with participants. So the mere mental processes of social identity and categorization in crowds, and all that they entail – feelings of agency and empowerment, affirmation and validation, connectedness and solidarity, purposefulness and meaning, etc. (see above, chapter 4) – are in themselves capable of generating a form of collective excitement, even euphoria, that Émile Durkheim dubbed "collective effervescence."[40] This offers at least a partial explanation for why attending sports events is an enticing experience. Sports fans are together with others who share their enthusiasm for the activity being watched; more particularly, they will generally be supporters of one of the competing teams or athletes, and so identify with them in one way or another; there is suspense while the outcome is undecided; the success of their side in overcoming the sport's obstacles to secure victory will therefore be intensely gratifying ("we" did it!), and will be celebrated by those who share an identification both with fellow fans and with the competing team or athlete. "Spectators attend for the collective effervescence, the flow of dramatic emotions building up tension into group energy and solidarity."[41] It is not hard to see why all this is an alluring prospect.

All that said, it is also the case that spectators can derive much pleasure from watching sports more or less alone or in small groups at home, at some remove from the crowd at the live event. It could be argued

---

[40] E. Durkheim, *The Elementary Forms of Religious Life* (Oxford, 2001; originally published 1912), 154–68 and 280–5. Buford (*Thugs*, 194) talks of the "high energy and jubilant authority of suddenly being in a crowd" of soccer hooligans setting out on a rampage; elsewhere he describes it in terms of heat, intoxication, and excitement. Such sensations constitute "collective effervescence" and they are not only elicited by the company of thugs; see the Prayag Mela Research Group, "Living the Magh Mela at Prayag."

[41] Collins, *Violence*, 283–5 (quote at 285).

that their social identity within an imagined community of supporters is sufficient to account for this fact, but it seems just as likely that some other elemental form of excitement is at work.[42] Psychologically, excitement is a phenomenon that is linked to the physiological condition of arousal.[43] The symptoms of arousal are familiar: heart-pounding, stomach-churning, dry-mouthed sweatiness. Interestingly, precisely the same symptoms of arousal have been recorded in people who claim to be both excited (a pleasant state) and anxious (an unpleasant state). What differentiates anxiety from excitement is how people *interpret* the circumstances causing the arousal, of which there are very many. Taking life-endangering risks (mountain-climbing, racing cars), playing sports, sexual activity, playing the stock-market, vandalism – there is no shortage of ways whereby people generate excitement for themselves. But when the arousal-generating stimulus is interpreted negatively, it causes anxiety. The same person can, within a fraction of a second, move from one interpretation of an experience to the other (say, on a rollercoaster ride) and either seek to retreat from the situation (arousal-avoidance) or press on to maximize the excitement (arousal-seeking).[44]

The interpretive strategy whereby people feel safe from the potentially negative consequences of taking risks is termed the "protective frame." This is what allows people to approach "the dangerous edge" between safety and trauma, and to enjoy the excitement of doing so. The protective frame is a psychological construct and is not necessarily realistic or trustworthy: the five people (thus far) who have perished since 1829 going over Niagara Falls in various vessels no doubt did so within a protective frame, but one that proved somewhat misleading. When the frame is absent or collapses,

---

[42] A personal anecdote: the 2008 Men's Wimbledon Championship final between Roger Federer and Rafael Nadal had me in a state of heart-pounding excitement, jumping about, and shouting at the screen. I was quite alone.

[43] The basis for this analysis (see the following footnotes for references) is less experimental than is the case with group processes, crowd dynamics, or prejudice. Rather, it deals with mental "states" – emotional or attitudinal – that everyone is familiar with through direct personal experience of them. It is possible to construct experimental protocols to test the mental states of sports spectators, but the logistics of implementation are very difficult; see further, Sloan, "Motives of Sports Fans," 202–12.

[44] For this and what follows, see M. J. Apter, *The Dangerous Edge: The Psychology of Excitement* (New York, 1992). The model is part of Apter's much wider "theory of reversals," on which see M. J. Apter, *The Experience of Motivation: The Theory of Psychological Reversals* (London, 1982); M. J. Apter, (ed.), *Motivational Styles in Everyday Life: A Guide to Reversal Theory* (Washington, DC, 2001). The basic contention of "reversal theory" is that much of human psychology (particularly in the realm of motivation) is not marked by stability or median continuity, but rather by opposed mental states, such as anxiety or excitement, altruism or selfishness, etc. Thus, the same action can be approached in opposite ways, sometimes on the same occasion. For some prior theories, see below, n. 49.

excitement turns to anxiety or terror and causes most people to retreat from the dangerous edge. This transition can take place in a split second, with the (sickening) realization that all is not going as one expected it would.

The protective frame comes in various forms, which can be divided into three main categories. The *confidence frame* applies to those who actually engage in risky endeavors, such as extreme sports, and it allows them to take what, to outside observers, may seem insane risks and feel confident in their mastery of the skills necessary to remain safe. The *safety-zone frame* applies to those who feel that they are far removed from any real trauma, but get aroused nonetheless (by playing recreational sports, for instance). Sports and games establish artificial rules that allow people to take "risks" and skirt "danger" within the confines of the safety zone, since the real world consequences of, say, touching an inflated ball with your hand are zero, but in the self-contained world of soccer they can be very serious. (This is the psychological essence of Hemingway's observation cited in the epigraph of this chapter, as it applies to bull-fighting.) Finally, there is the *detachment frame*. This makes people feel removed from risky action and allows them to enjoy risk-taking vicariously.

The detachment frame is what applies to the sports spectator. It has three subcategories: self-substitution (imagining oneself as the actor or character one is watching); make-believe (fantasizing about arousing but unreal circumstances, such as winning the lottery); and retrospection (remembering an arousing experience). In all three instances, the protective frame is one of detachment from the action, even as emotional involvement is high and leads to the desired arousal/excitement. Again, only the self-substitution version of the detachment frame applies to the sports spectator or, indeed, to any spectator. Self-substitution is key to all sorts of entertainment, whether plays, operas, movies, books, or TV news. The ability of people to feel as if they are the competing athletes they are watching, or the characters portrayed on stage or in a book is central to the success of these media.[45] Without self-substitution, people's detachment would be too complete for them to retain any interest in what is transpiring before their eyes. Deeply implicated in the process of self-subsitution are parapathic emotions.[46] These are emotions which are usually unpleasant when experienced directly, but when experienced within a protective frame they are pleasurable. So when we watch things happening to other people, we

---

[45] The affective dispositional model essentially agrees with this assessment, but differs on how "identification" plays out mentally; see below, ch. 7, pp. 241–5.

[46] On this concept, see Apter, *Experience of Motivation*, 107–35.

can feel "anger" or "terror" without actually becoming angry or terrified. Feelings like this impel us to root for (or against) a player or a team or a character in a book, and, while they can be intensely felt, they rarely persist for long and are always pleasurable, even if the real version of the emotion is not, such as "sadness" at the end of a tragic movie, or "fear" during a thriller. Parapathic emotions experienced within a detachment frame draw no distinction between fact and fiction. We can be moved and aroused as readily by the ending of a good fictional book as by a news report of some real but far-off natural disaster. As long as the detachment frame is in place, parapathic emotions can be enjoyed. This is why bad news predominates on the airwaves: good news simply does not stir the parapathic emotions of the audience. Hollywood and television producers, authors, actors, and entertainers of all stripes exploit our parapathic emotions to their profit.

What sorts of situations elicit these responses? A large number of arousing stimuli are to be found in the environment and they can be encountered passively or actively. Passive stimuli are those that act on our senses, even if we are supine. Examples might include sun-bathing, swimming, or enjoying natural beauty while hiking. However, some environments (e.g., a circus, amusement park, or night club) are specifically designed to be maximally stimulating, with flashing lights, bright, changing colors, loud music or sounds, varieties of sights, and fast-moving objects. The sports arena is one such environment. Active stimuli are those things that people do to achieve arousal/excitement: exploration (any journey into the unknown, whether physical, emotional, or intellectual); confronting frustration to achieve a goal (most rules in sports are designed to put frustrating obstacles in the way of players' success); overcoming human limitations (driving fast, hang-gliding, skiing, amusement park rides); or negativism (consciously contravening social norms, rules, orthodoxies, or taboos). Within these various types of stimuli, people seem especially aroused by "cognitive synergies," those stimuli that juxtapose opposites or confound expectations. Good examples include the "twist" in a thriller, when a formerly good guy turns out to be a villain (or vice versa); confounding perspectives (as in the art of Maurits Escher); or even the use of a striking metaphor in a poem. In all instances, it is the jarring nature of the combinations, the sudden reversal or proximity of opposites, that leaves us aroused and excited.[47]

---

[47] See A. S. Coulson, "Cognitive Synergy," in Apter (ed.), *Motivational Styles in Everyday Life*, 229–48. It goes without saying that not all stimuli are exciting/arousing to the same degree.

In all this, differences in personality, perception, or the particulars of circumstance can determine whether individuals are arousal-seekers, or arousal-avoiders in any given situation. Most people move between the two states frequently and seamlessly. So, as with all social-psychological processes, there will be divergences between how individuals react to any given situation. Dio (72[73].20.2) reports how the populace of Rome avoided the arena on one occasion in September AD 192 when the emperor Commodus was scheduled to perform. One reason Dio gives for the people's absence was that "many" were ashamed at seeing an emperor degrade himself in the amphitheater. Perhaps. But this admirable sense of shame had not stopped the populace from reveling in Nero's public performances or, for that matter, in Commodus' frequent arena appearances earlier in his reign. Indeed Herodian reports (1.15.1) that spectators flocked from Rome, Italy, and nearby provinces precisely to see Commodus perform. The other reason Dio gives is more telling. At this late stage of his reign (and life), Commodus' identification with Hercules had attained an alarming intimacy, and it was rumored that he was going to shoot arrows at spectators in imitation of Hercules and the Stymphalian Birds.[48] Rather than feeling shame at the emperor's by now familiar arena performances, it seems far more likely that for "many" this rumor destroyed the protective detachment frame within which they normally enjoyed arena violence, and the arousal-avoiders, their prospects for enjoyment destroyed by the fear of being shot by Hercules-Commodus, stayed away. But the Colosseum was not entirely empty on that day in 192. Others *did* go along regardless – these were arousal-seekers, and we can only imagine how they constructed their protective frames to approach the dangerous edge: "I am very unlikely to be hit in a crowd of so many thousands" or "the rumor is bogus," perhaps. They would have found the thrill quite arousing.

Various versions of excitement- or stress-seeking theories have been around for several decades.[49] Very recently, neurophysiology has raised dramatic possibilities for what may stand behind this and many other psychological phenomena. In the 1980s and 1990s a team at the University of Parma was studying the brain patterns of macaque monkeys by recording the firing of specific neurons and neuron-clusters as the monkeys performed various tasks. One day, the neuron activity of the monkeys had been recorded as they reached for food. With the machinery left on, a researcher,

---

[48] Herodian (1.15.7–9) tells the same story, but leaves out the fear motive for the people staying away.
[49] See, e.g., Elias and Dunning, *Quest for Excitement*; M. J. Ellis, *Why People Play* (Englewood Cliffs, 1972); S. Z. Klausner (ed.), *Why Man Takes Chances* (Garden City, 1968); M. Zuckerman, *Sensation Seeking: Beyond the Optimal Level of Arousal* (Hillsdale: 1979).

within sight of the monkeys, reached for a bowl of fruit to have a snack, and the monkeys' neurons fired up *as if they themselves were reaching for food*. That is, when the monkeys saw that the lab assistant was about to eat, their brains reacted as if they themselves were doing the same. The potential importance of the discovery of "mirror neurons" for understanding the roots of human (and primate) imitative behavior, learning, some disabilities (such as autism), and even the basis of culture itself is obvious. But the research is still in its infancy, and much more needs to be done in figuring out how the mirror neuron system works. In particular, its explanatory limitations, as well as its strengths, need to be probed.[50] For our purposes, the discovery of mirror neurons points to a potentially neurophysiological basis for the psychological processes we have been examining in this section. When watching sports, spectators' brains may actually make them *feel* as if they themselves are participating in the action, so that they feel the same emotions (or parapathic versions of them) that the players are feeling.[51] The pronounced emotional involvement of spectators watching a violent (or any) sport, or for that matter, any form of entertainment, might therefore have a neurobiological basis, but it is far too early to assert this as demonstrated fact.

The psychology of excitement, particularly of parapathic emotions experienced within a protective frame of detachment (and, possibly, the operation of mirror neurons), offers one of the best avenues for understanding what it is about watching sport that people find exciting. The approach has the added benefit of encompassing both the process and the outcome of sporting competitions: the uncertainty of the outcome and the run of play generate arousal and excitement as the contest progresses, and a positive result will (and does) generate euphoric excitement. Sports and games are universally appealing to humans and can be shown to have been so across historical time and space. No doubt, particular cultural currents run through games and sports that draw people in, but those currents

---

[50] See further, G. Rizzolatti and L. Craighero, "The Mirror-Neuron System," *Annual Review of Neuroscience* 27 (2004), 169–92; G. Rizzolatti and C. Sinigaglia, *Mirrors in the Brain: How Our Minds Share Actions and Emotions*, trans. F. Anderson (Oxford, 2008); G. Rizzalotti and M. Fabbri-Destro, "The Mirror Neuron System," in G. G. Bernston and J. T. Cacioppo (eds.), *Handbook of Neuroscience for the Behavioral Sciences*, 2 vols. (Hoboken, 2009), vol. 1, 337–57. Note also C. D. Frith and D. M. Wolpert (eds.), *The Neuroscience of Social Interaction: Decoding, Imitating, and Influencing the Actions of Others* (Oxford, 2003), esp. 109–218 (on mirror neurons, by various authors). For evidence of emotion-sharing in ancient art appreciation, see Philostr. *Imag.* 2.18.3 and 30.3, 3.

[51] This idea had been proposed long ago from a physiological analysis of sports fans' reactions, quite without knowledge of mirror neurons; see Sloan, "Motives of Sports Fans," 179.

will be specific to historical contexts and cannot be used to explain the documented universality of the lure of sports, particularly violent ones. But every person (at least occasionally) gets aroused and excited, and since watching sports and games generates these very reactions, herein lies their most basic appeal. In a nutshell, it is fun to watch.

GLADIATORIAL SHOWS AS SPORTS SPECTACULARS

Armed with an undersanding of how people are excited by watching sport, we can revisit gladiatorial combats and analyze them as psychological stimuli analogous to sports spectaculars. (I recognize that doing so underplays their religious significance, but the entire issue of how "religious" or not *munera* were is poorly evidenced and hotly debated.) Our focus here is on the gladiatorial phase of the events, since they (and, arguably, the hunts) constituted the games' most obviously sporting elements. It is notable that the fights were also the most important and expensive element of a *munus*, the headline event that earned top-billing. This is made clear by surviving advertisements for games, where the gladiators take pride of place and the hunts and executions, if any, are noted as added attractions, ranked alongside promises of the awning, distributions of prizes, lesser performers, and so forth.[52] Hunts or executions, as we saw in the introduction, could be staged as stand-alone events, but when gladiators were included the whole show was dubbed *gladiatorum munus* or by some other gladiator-emphasizing formulation.[53] The gladiators were what people came to see.

Before a gladiatorial spectacle was staged, programs (*libelli gladiatorum* or *munerarii*) circulated among potential spectators.[54] These programs probably stand behind advertisements (*edicta muneris*) announcing forthcoming spectacles that were painted on walls about town. Many such *edicta* have survived from Pompeii, and the information in them is revealing.[55] Most are rather vague, such as this example:

---

[52] For a full discussion of gladiatorial advertisements at Pompeii, see Sabbatini Tumolesi, *Gladiatorum Paria*, and examples discussed below.

[53] *TLL* 6.2004.64–2007.36, s.v. "gladiator," and ibid. 8.1665.78–1666.12, s.v. "munus (gladiatorum munus)"; on *ludus*, see above ch. 3, n. 62.

[54] Cic. *Phil.* 2.97, *ad Fam.* 2.8.1; HA *Claud.* 5.5; Ovid *Ars Am.* 1.167; Pliny *Ep.* 3.18.4; Tac. *Dial.* 9.3. *Libelli* were not exclusive to gladiatorial games and were issued in advance of other entertainments as well (for instance, the example cited from Pliny refers to a literary recitation).

[55] Sabbatini Tumolesi, *Gladiatorum Paria*, passim.

Celer wrote (this notice), Twenty pairs of gladiators sponsored by D. Lucretius Satrius Valens, lifetime priest of Nero Caesar, son of Augustus, and ten pairs of gladiators sponsored by D. Lucretius Valens, his son, will fight at Pompeii on April 8–12. There will also be a suitable hunt, and the awning. *Aemilius Celer wrote (this notice), alone at night.*[56]

While the number of gladiators (sixty in all) is announced, no further information is given about them. The same goes for the hunt, which is baldly proclaimed. The *editor* had contracted a professional sign-painter to advertise the event. Unlike such anticipatory advertisements, most epigraphic testimony about the content of spectacles comes to us in the form of *post factum* recognition by the community of a sponsor's generosity, on inscribed statue bases, for instance. They too are usually cursory and note only the most salient features of the spectacle. It is not unreasonable to suppose that the details provided in such texts were to be found also in the program that preceded the spectacle. So when we read that a benefactor "produced as an embellishment for Beneventum a four-day show that featured four wild animals, sixteen bears, four convicts, and the rest herbivores"[57] or "he generously staged a happy day (of games) . . . with a general hunt comprising tens of beasts, four toothed wild animals, and four pairs fighting with swords, and other very fine looking gear"[58] we can imagine that this information was available to the spectators in advance.

The walls of Pompeii have yielded a model of a *libellus gladiatorum* in all its precision.[59] The text, being a graffito, is very fragmentary, but enough exists to discern its format and contents. A heading across the top announces two spectacles and identifies the *editores* by name. Dates for the *munera* are provided, May 2 and 11–15, respectively (the year is uncertain, but it surely comes from the later phases of the city's existence).[60] Below this

[56] *CIL* 4.3884 = *ILS* 5145 = Sabbatini Tumolesi, *Gladiatorum Paria*, 27–8 (no. 5) = Fora, *Munera Gladiatoria*, 123 (no. 28) = I.2.

[57] See above, introduction, n. 14, for text.

[58] *CIL* 10.3704 = *ILS* 5054 (Naples; late second – mid-third century AD), *diem felicissim(um) . . . venatione pass(iva), denis bestiis et IIII feris dent(atis) et IIII paribus / ferro dimicantib(us) ceteroq(ue) honestissim(o) apparatu largiter exhibui[t].*

[59] *CIL* 4.2508 = Sabbatini Tumolesi, *Gladiatorum Paria*, 71–4 (no. 32) = Fora, *Munera Gladiatoria*, 128 (no. 57) = I.3. For prior discussions, see Hopkins, *Death and Renewal*, 25–6; Sabbatini Tumolesi, *Gladiatorum Paria*, 69–74. See *CIL* 11.7444 = *EAOR* 2.53 for a more fragmentary comparandum from Ferentinum.

[60] Sabbatini Tumolesi (*Gladiatorum Paria*, 71 and 114) suggests a date of AD 54–62 for this text, based on the presence of "Neroniani" among the combatants. Given the possibility of a ban on gladiators at Pompeii following the riot of AD 59, we may narrow the date further, to AD 54–9; see Fora, *Munera Gladiatoria*, 128 (no. 57).

introductory material, arrayed in columns, are lists of the upcoming bouts, which look like this (I quote only some of the most complete pairings):

Thracian vs. Murmillo
(won)   Pugnax, of the Neronian School, 3 fights
(died)   Murranus, of the Neronian School, 3 fights

Hoplomachus vs. Thracian
(won)   Cycnus, of the Julian School, 9 fights
(spared)   Atticus, of the Julian School, 14 fights

Essedarii
(spared)   Publius Ostorius, 51 fights
(won)   Scylax, of the Julian School, 26 fights

Thracian vs. Murmillo
(died)   Lucius Fabius, 9 fights
(won)   Astus, of the Julian School, 14 fights

The pairings and the order of their appearance are designated in advance, providing the spectator with a detailed program of events.[61] In each case, the bout is identified first and foremost by the style of gladiators involved (Thracian, *murmillo*, *essedarius*, etc.; see below for more on gladiatorial armatures). Next, the name of the fighter is given, usually as a single moniker. The favored forms are evocative epithets or nouns, or ironic names.[62] In most cases, the fighter's training school is indicated next, in this case either the Julian or Neronian *ludus*, established in Campania by Julius Caesar and Nero respectively.[63] The inclusion of the training school spoke to two facts of interest to the fan: first, the quality of the gladiators themselves (one can expect that imperially owned *ludi* would turn out a top-class product) and, second, the generosity of the *editor* in contracting from the best available sources (Julian or Neronian gladiators are unlikely to have come cheap).[64] Then comes each gladiator's fight record to date, expressed as a simple digit ("nine [fights]").[65] Finally, someone else came

---

[61] Note also [Quint.] *Decl.* 9.8 for mention of "the designated pairing" (*destinatum par*) entering the arena.

[62] On gladiator names, see below, ch. 7, p. 237.

[63] See Sabbatini Tumolesi, *Gladiatorum Paria*, 147–9, who considers the Julian and Neronian *ludi* to be one and the same place. If so, the distinct "credentialing" for each fighter here seems redundant.

[64] Sabbatini Tumolesi (*Gladiatorum Paria*, 69–70) suggests that the *munerarius*, one M. M(a)esonius, may have been himself the owner of a gladiatorial troupe. On the procedure for contracting gladiators, see M. Carter, "Gladiatorial Ranking and the *SC de Pretiis Gladiatorum Minuendis*" (*CIL* 11 6278 = *ILS* 5163)," *Phoenix* 57 (2003), 83–114, esp. 103–8.

[65] It is unclear whether these numbers represent fights or victories; Sabbatini Tumolesi (*Gladiatorum Paria*, 47) favors fights, while Futrell (*Roman Games*, 85–6) prefers victories. The high figure

along after the show and penciled in the results, noted above in parentheses: "won," "spared," or "died."

The legible entries for five of the performers deviate from this format. These men have regular freeborn Roman names, such as Lucius Fabius or Publius Ostorius, and they have no training-school affiliation. These onomastic features leave no doubt that here were volunteer gladiators, members of the freeborn community who willingly subjected themselves to the rigors of the arena by contracting themselves out to a trainer or directly to the *editor*. Similar status distinctions can be traced in the albums of gladiatorial training schools.[66] Such volunteers (termed *auctorati*, "contract fighters") have proven a problematic category for scholars to interpret. Why would anyone take such risks? The ancient sources offer moral or economic reasons for such behavior; modern scholars have been no more certain.[67] But, really, they are not that baffling a phenomenon at all. These are Roman excitement-seekers, the same sort of people who are daredevils or test pilots or mountain-climbers today.[68] They saw the arena as a place to approach the "dangerous edge" directly and thrillingly, and they likely did so within a confidence frame, in that they placed great faith in their combat skills. This may offer a partial explanation for their particular appeal to the spectators.[69]

(fifty-one) ascribed to P. Ostorius, however, favors a fight total (or appearances), especially since he lost on this occasion to a less experienced opponent. This may also have been advantageous for betting, since it conveyed the experience level of each combatant, without revealing his degree of success. In many inscriptions, such as epitaphs, there are two figures separated by a backward facing "C" (for *coronatus*, "crowned [winner]"); it is likely that the first figure is the number of appearances, the second the number of victories; see also inscriptions cited below in next note and n. 74.

[66] See *CIL* 9.466, 26–7 = *ILS* 5083a = *EAOR* 3.68 = I.4 and *CIL* 9.465 = *ILS* 5083 = *EAOR* 3.67 (the *familia* of the *lanista* C. Salvius Capito) for apparently unrelated examples from Venusia. Note also that M. Antonius Exochus, the Thracian gladiator under Trajan and Hadrian, fought first a slave and then a freeborn opponent eight days apart in the same spectacle honoring Trajan's triumph over Parthia; see *CIL* 6.10194 = *ILS* 5088 = *EAOR* 1.92 = I.5.

[67] For discussion with ample reference to the ancient data, see, e.g., Hopkins, *Death and Renewal*, 23–5; Kyle, *Spectacles of Death*, 87–90; B. Levick, "The *Senatus Consultum* from Larinum," *JRS* 73 (1983), 97–115, esp. 101–2; F. Meijer, *The Gladiators: History's Most Deadly Sport* (New York, 2005), 42–50; Slater, "Pantomime Riots," 131–2; Ville, *Gladiature*, 246–62; Wiedemann, *Emperors and Gladiators*, 106–9. A famous case is the senator Gracchus, "better born . . . than all the spectators on the podium" (*generosior . . . omnibus ad podium spectantibus*) who fought as a *retiarius* in the Colosseum – and fled disgracefully; Juv. 2.143–8 and 8.199–210. Juvenal posits financial pressures as the reason men of quality signed up; see Juv. 11.1–23.

[68] The *murmillo* Triumphus, looking back on the glory days of Augustus' reign from the spectacle-starved desert of Tiberian Rome, declared: "what a lovely age has passed!" (*quam bella, inquit, aetas periit!*); Sen. *Dial.* 1.4.4. Balsdon (*Life and Leisure*, 290) got it right decades ago: "In any society there are men to whom danger appeals." This is not to discount entirely financial desperation or moral depravity as elements in the motivation of some, but there were surely less perilous ways to alleviate debt or indulge the baser impulses.

[69] Petron. *Sat.* 45.4 = T.12 suggests that freedmen, at least, were valued as high-quality performers (*familia non lanisticia, sed plurimi liberti*). Ville (*Gladiature*, 251–2) has his doubts. See also *CIL*

Unlike coerced combatants bought by or condemned to the *ludi*, volunteer gladiators were likely to be willing, even eager fighters, and one assumes they were quite good. Risk-takers derive pleasure from facing danger and trauma and beating it by skill and courage. These are ideal traits for a gladiator. That said, of the five freeborn performers listed in the Pompeian *libellus* for whom a result is legible, none were victorious: two died, three were spared.[70] The deaths tell us that these were no dummy or exhibition bouts (termed *paegniaria*), but the real thing. That the *essedarius* (chariot-fighter) Publius Ostorius had fifty-one fights under his belt reflects at least this man's devotion to his favored pastime. It just seems that, on a day in mid-May in Pompeii's arena, five Roman thrill-seekers discovered their limits in the form of imperially trained, professional opponents. "Everyone takes his pleasure where he finds it," reads the epitaph of a noble gladiator.[71]

The *libelli gladiatorum*, then, provided the spectator with a great deal of information about forthcoming games. This may have aided the customer in betting strategies, since the *libellus* was a type of "form" book that allowed fans to select winners based on relevant information.[72] That fans engaged closely with the information in these *libelli* is demonstrated by gladiatorial graffiti, crude etchings of fighters scratched into walls and often found with accompanying text that directly echoes the contents of the *libelli*.[73] Gladiators were known to aficionados by name and repute: "Sigh of the girls! The Thracian (gladiator) Celadus, three fights, three victories."[74]

4.9978 = Sabbatini Tumolesi, *Gladiatorum Paria*, 100–1 (no. 72) for an announcement of games highlighting *lib(eri)* or *lib(erti)* ("freeborn" or "freed") on the first day. Note the story in Suetonius (*Vitell.* 12.1) telling how Vitellius sold his favorite freedman, Asiaticus, to a travelling *lanista* but, on seeing him reserved for the end of a show (which may imply special billing for a socially prominent fighter), he spirited him away and saved him.

[70] And see above, n. 67, for Juvenal on Gracchus, the cringing senatorial *retiarius*.

[71] Quoted in Auguet, *Cruelty and Civilization*, 157. I have been unable to track down the original citation.

[72] See above, n. 10, on betting at gladiatorial bouts.

[73] See below pp. 223–4. Compare also other gladiatorial bouts and career "stats," mostly cited in epitaphs; e.g., *CIL* 4.538 = *ILS* 5138, *CIL* 6.10203 = 33978 = *EAOR* 1.102, *CIL* 6.33980 = *ILS* 5139 = *EAOR* 1.110, *CIL* 6.33988 = *EAOR* 1.109, *CIL* 6.33989 = *EAOR* 1.104, *CIL* 6.33990 = *EAOR* 1.103, *CIL* 9.1671 = *ILS* 5134, *CIL* 12.2747 = *ILS* 5133, *CIL* 12.5696.42 = *ILS* 5137, *CIL* 15.6244 = *ILS* 5135, *CIL* 15.6247 = *ILS* 5136; *EAOR* 1.101, 107, 2.57.

[74] *CIL* 4.4342 = *ILS* 5142a: *suspirium puellarum!* | *T(h)r(aex)* | *Celadus Oct. III ⊃ III*. Interestingly, a record of games from Pompeii (*CIL* 4.9986 = Sabbatini Tumolesi, *Gladiatorum Paria*, 63–7 [no. 29]) notes a Celatus of the Julian school who fought six times. So this Celadus may have been well known in the region. See also below n. 89, and Martial (*Mart. Ep.* 5.24 = T.11) on the gladiator Hermes, renowned at Rome. Senea the Elder refers to a famed Thracian gladiator when he writes (*Controv.* 3 *praef.* 16), "If I were a Thracian, I'd be Fusius" (*si Thraex essem, Fusius essem*). See also Hor. *Sat.* 2.6.44; Petron. *Sat.* 52.3.

What all this means for our purposes is that anticipatory excitement would mount in advance of a spectacle, but not in some vague, generalized way. Devotees of arena games would be alerted as to what stars, what familiar favorites, and what newcomers would be appearing. They would be told what style of gladiator they could expect to see, in what order, and in what style each named individual would be fighting,[75] what records each fighter had built to date, and whether new talent would be pitched against a peer or a skilled veteran. They could assess the quality of the performers' training, whether they were slaves who came from particular schools or were self-contracted, freeborn (or freed) volunteers. All of this would have generated a terrific sense of anticipation in the community, sparking speculations among fans as to who would overcome whom, and how (see below n. 87). Excitement, therefore, preceded the event itself. The day before the spectacle, the public could view the gladiators who were to perform as they dined; the same was done for huntsmen and, it seems, even for some of the prisoners slated for execution, as well as animals.[76] This would also have allowed final adjustments to betting strategies, and ratcheted up expectations still further. Anticipation of the fighters' appearance thus ran high in advance of the games and as they progressed (cf. Sen. *Controv.* 4 *praef.* 1 = T.19).

On the day itself, the spectators would gather at the amphitheater (or theater or stadium, or wherever the games were being held). The amphitheater especially was a place of powerfully arousing stimuli, a public space specifically demarcated to allow relatively free rein to excitement and its expression. The noise of the crowd as it congregated, accompanied by music and chanting, would set the tone, elevate the spectators' anticipatory arousal, and pave the way for what was to come. The gladiators themselves entered the arena in a parade (the *pompa*), their armor and

---

[75] This information about armatures was important, not only for obvious reasons, but also because some gladiators could fight in more than one style; see Mart. *Ep.* 5.24; *InscIt* 10.5.305 = *EAOR* 2.41 (*Smara|gido, mu|rmilloni, oplomaca|rio* ["to Smaragdus, *murmillo, hoplomachus*"]) or ibid. 2.42 (*Antigono | myrmilloni | qui et | provocatori* ["to Antigonos, a *murmillo* who was also a *provocator*"]). See also *ILGN* 436 = *EAOR* 5.14 (*murmillo* and *contraretiarius*), *CIL* 13.1997 = *ILS* 5097 = *EAOR* 5.62 (*dimachaerus* and *essedarius*). Most gladiators, however, fought in a single style, as suggested by their self-identification on epitaphs, and from the membership of gladiatorial *collegia* or *familiae* (see, e.g., above. n. 66, *CIL* 6.631 = *ILS* 5084 = *EAOR* 1.45, and *CIL* 9.465–6 = *ILS* 5083 = *EAOR* 3.67–8) all of which associate individual fighters with one style of combat.

[76] For the gladiatorial banquet (*cena libera*), see Plut. *Mor.* 1099B; Symmach. *Ep.* 2.46; *Pass. Perp. et Felic.* 17.1 (= Musurillo, *Acts of the Christian Martyrs*, 124–55); M. Z. Brettler and M. Poliakoff, "Rabbi Simeon ben Lakish at the Gladiator's Banquet: Rabbinic Observations on the Roman Arena," *HTR* 83 (1990), 93–8; Ville, *Gladiature*, 366; Wiedemann, *Emperors and Gladiators*, 116–17. A famous mosaic from El Djem shows huntsmen at table, with their bulls asleep in front of them; see Dunbabin, *Mosaics of Roman North Africa*, 78–81.

weapons carried before them, led by the *editor*.[77] It is not hard to imagine the huge cheer that greeted their appearance, the appreciative chants of the crowd for the person offering the spectacle or, perhaps, for one or more favorites among the performers.

We do not know what rules governed gladiatorial combat, but that they existed is certain.[78] Ancient images of arena events regularly depict unarmored umpires enforcing regulations with rods; in the Zliten mosaic, one even physically restrains the killing hand of a victor while an appeal is decided. The arena crowd would know these rules intimately, another feature they shared with modern sports spectators who, obviously, know how the game they are watching is supposed to be played. But not only that. The informed spectator knows how the game is supposed to be played *well* and what sort of tricks are possible in the quest for victory.[79] This collusion on rules – and how to bend them – between spectator and competitor adds to the general excitement of sporting events, as a crowd will often react to the calls of referees and umpires no less than to the moves of the players. Arena spectators knew what made for a good gladiatorial bout, what a good combination of moves was, what skills were being displayed, and in what degree. Indeed, Tertullian comments that even for a trained professional fighter advice shouted out by the crowd can be put to good use (Tert. *Ad. Mart.* 1.2), a detail that suggests a high degree of familiarity with gladiatorial moves among the spectators.

Evidence for connoisseurship of gladiatorial artistry is revealed in various ways in the ancient sources.[80] Gladiatorial epitaphs express a certain pride

[77] On the *pompa*, see Tert. *Spect.* 7.2–3; [Quint.] *Decl.* 9.6 = T.17; *Pan.* 12.23.3. It is recorded in inscriptions: see, e.g., above n. 7 and *CIL* 4.3883 = Sabbatini Tumolesi, *Gladiatorum Paria*, 40 (no. 13), *CIL* 4.7993 = Sabbatini Tumolesi, *Gladiatorum Paria*, 40 (no. 12), *AE* 1947.53 = 1976.144 (Herculaneum); see also Ville, *Gladiature*, 399–401. A gladiatorial *pompa* is depicted in a famous relief from a tomb in Pompeii, found outside the Stabian Gate in 1843 and now in the National Museum in Naples. It shows the *pompa* in progress and features the sponsor (accompanied by lictors), musicians blaring horns, religious artifacts, men (the gladiators?) carrying equipment, and horses; see Augenti, *Spettacoli del Colosseo*, 82–3 (no. 45); Jacobelli, *Gladiators at Pompeii*, 95–7 (fig. 77; cf. fig. 18); Junkelmann, *Gladiatoren*, 130–1; Wiedemann, *Emperors and Gladiators*, 93–4.

[78] [Quint.] *Decl. Maj.* 9.9 = T.17, Mart. *Spect.* 31 and Coleman, *Liber Spectaculorum*, ad loc. (the gladiatorial *lex pugnandi*, "law of combat"); Quint. *Inst.* 8.5.12, 20, Mart. *Spect.* 31.4–5 (fight continues *ad digitum*, until the finger is raised in surrender); see also Carter, "The Rules of Engagement," esp. 102–6; Ville, *Gladiature*, 403–6. S. Tuck ("*De Arte Gladiatoria*: Recovering Gladiatorial Tactics from Artistic Sources," paper delivered at the AIA Annual Meeting 2005) offers a creative reconstruction of gladiatorial combat moves, drawn from comparison with German Renaissance "Fight Manuals" (*Fechtbücher*), while Junkelmann (*Gladiatoren*, 129–69) uses an experimental-archaeological approach to investigate how the combats likely unfolded.

[79] An analogous close familiarity with theatrical gesture on the part of audiences has been demonstrated; see Aldrete, *Gestures and Acclamations*, 51–67.

[80] Similar appreciation applied to other spectacle entertainments as well; see Potter, "Entertainers," 321–2, and Potter, "Spectacle," 392–400.

in achievement and skill, when they chart the fight records of the deceased. The Thracian M. Antonius Exochus, for instance, rather than record one of his bouts as a straight win declares instead how he caused an opponent to be spared (*missum fecit*). The implication of the wording is that Exochus' skill forced his rival to appeal, and this is what the victor wished to emphasize.[81] In epitaphs of gladiators killed during shows, the emphasis is on how they were deceived or tricked by fate, or just unlucky; being outfought by a superior opponent is nowhere acknowledged. In one instance, the commemorators complain that the deceased was "deceived by a bandit," which casts the victor as a scoundrel.[82] Such epitaphs attest maneuvers and move combinations in gladiatorial combats that the audience was surely familiar with from repeated exposure to them. Further evidence comes from elite writers, who regularly use gladiatorial and athletic metaphors and analogies to evoke the cut-and-thrust of rhetorical debate (note the close association of the athletic and gladiatorial realms), the philosopher facing the adversities of life, or the inner struggles of the mind.[83] Cicero (*De Orat.* 2.84) refers to the "skillful use of arms in sport" as having value for the gladiator – even somebody as un-martial as Cicero could recognize an artful fighter when he saw one. Cicero reveals a telling attitude when he writes in a letter to his friend Atticus (*Att.* 4.8.2), "You might write to me about your gladiators [Atticus had contracted some for a show], but only if they acquit themselves well. If not, I'm not interested." Cicero only wants to hear about a quality performance, something which he

---

[81] *CIL* 6.10194 = *ILS* 5088 = *EAOR* 1.92 = I.5. See below, n. 105. See also above, n. 19.

[82] See, e.g., *ILS* 5111: "deceived by fate, not by a man" (*fato deceptus, non ab homine*); *CIL* 3.8830 = *ILS* 5112: "deceived by a bandit" (*deceptus a latrone*; the reading is complicated as the stone reads *latrone.bos*); *CIL* 5.3466 = *ILS* 5121 = *EAOR* 2.47 = I.9, "I recommend that each of you look after his own fate; don't put your trust in Nemesis, that's how I was deceived" (*Planetam suum procurare vos moneo; in Nemese ne fidem habeatis: sic sum deceptus*); *CIL* 5.3468 = *ILS* 5122 = *EAOR* 2.52: "veteran of ten fights, deceived in the eleventh" (*pugnar(um) X, hic XI deceptus*). On these revealing documents, see Hope, "Fighting for Identity." Even when a gladiator admits to defeat, he is loathe to concede it was due to superior skill: "I was not beaten by skill, but a young man overpowered an old body" (οὐχὶ τέχνῃ λειφθείς, | ἀλλὰ νέος γεραρὸν σῶ|μα κατειργάσατο); epitaph of Polynices from Alabanda in Caria, Merkelbach and Stauber, *Steinepigramme*, 23/03.

[83] See, e.g., Cic. *De Orat.* 2.84, 2.325 and possibly 2.316; Cic. *Orat.* 243; Quint. *Inst.* 2.12.2, 2.17.33, 5.13.54, 8.3.34, 9.1.20(?), 10.5.20; Sen. *Controv.* 3 praef. 13 and 16, 7.1.10, 9 praef. 4 (my thanks to Dr. Jon Hall for the Quintilian references). See also O. Grodde, *Sport bei Quintilian* (Hildesheim, 1997), esp. 14–57 (on gladiators and athletes). Polemo likens the gladiator waiting to fight to the sophist waiting to speak; see Philostr. *VS* 541. Devotion to the inner life of the mind is also rhetorically framed in terms of training for war, athletics, or the arena; see Fronto, *Nep. Am.* 2.2; Gell. *NA* 13.28; Sen. *Dial.* 9.3.1, *Ep.* 37.1–3, 78.16, 96.5, 117.25. Seneca's treatise *De Providentia* (= *Dialogus* 1) extensively draws on the arena imagery as it charts the philosopher's course through life; see Edwards, *Death*, 75–7. Prudentius in the *Psychomachia* uses the metaphor of battle and single combat to frame the struggle for the soul. Apuleius (e.g., *Met.* 2.15–17) uses the metaphors of war and gladiatorial games for sex, as does the novelist Achilles Tatius (e.g., 2.5.2).

assumes is readily recognizable. (Unfortunately, we do not have Atticus'
reply.) Caesar trained his African legions to fight not in the normal way
"but as a *lanista* trains his recruits," and he even specifies particular moves
he imparted to them, which shows that gladiatorial moves were easily
identifiable.[84] Juvenal mocks one Catullus, who would praise the "fights
and blows of the Cilician gladiator" (4.121), which points in the same
direction. Petronius likens the gesticulations of Trimalchio's dinner-table
scissor ("cleaver" or "carver," which was also a type of gladiator) to the
blade strokes of gladiators.[85] Some gladiators are praised for not harming
anyone over their whole career, and Nero once gave *munera* in his wooden
arena in the Campus Martius in which nobody was killed, not even *noxii*.[86]
The only reason people would come to watch harmless gladiators or a
bloodless spectacle was to appreciate a display of martial skill as an end in
itself. There are snobbish disparagements about plebeians discussing the
relative merits of individual performers. Epictetus frets over what might
happen if one is forced to talk to a commoner: "What are you going to
do, if he talks about gladiators, or horses, or athletes, or, still worse, about
people: 'So-and-so is bad, so-and-so is good; this was well done, this ill.'"[87]
That is, "sports talk" – which presupposes at least some familiarity with the
sport, its rules, and the skills needed to compete – was the ancient arena
fan's province no less than among modern sports fans.

---

[84] Caes. *B Afr.* 71. Note also Ammianus' comment (16.12.49) that the Romans at the battle of Strasbourg
(AD 357) "protected themselves like murmillos" (*seque in modum mirmillonis operiens*), which again
assumes knowledge of gladiatorial techniques.

[85] Petron. *Sat.* 36.6. Dinner carvers varied their strokes according to the meat being carved; see Juv.
5.120–4. For the gladiator *scissor*, see *CIL* 9.466, 26–7 = *ILS* 5083a = *EAOR* 3.68 = I.4 (album of
a gladiatorial *familia* from Venusia). A possible *scissor* is shown in the relief of the heavily armored
gladiator Myron, of unknown provenance and now in the Louvre, whose left arm is covered in a
device that ends in a crescent-shaped blade, clearly a very specialized piece of equipment. Robert
(*Gladiateurs*, 235–6 [no. 299]), comparing this scene with a relief from Tomis that shows the same
piece of equipment discarded on the sand, reasonably suggests that it was designed to slice through
a *retiarius'* net (the adversary in the Tomis relief is a *retiarius*). But it has recently been argued – on
the basis of a relief from Satala in Lydia, two reliefs and accompanying inscriptions from Hierapolis
in Phrygia, and a comment in Artemidorus (2.32) – that such gladiators were termed *arbelai* (after
a semi-circular cobbler's knife), at least in the Greek East; and the Hierapolis reliefs show them
fighting each other, not *retiarii*; see M. Carter, "Artemidorus and the Arbelas Gladiator," *ZPE* 134
(2001), 109–15; Ritti and Yilmaz, *Gladiatori e venationes*, 469–79 (nos. 6 and 7). But there is no
reason to expect that the armaments, the terminology, or the formats of gladiatorial bouts were
perfectly consistent across the empire, so that gladiators of this type could surely be dubbed both
scissores and *arbelai* and appear in diverse pairings.

[86] See above, n. 19, for winning without wounding. Nero's bloodless *munus*: Suet. *Nero* 12.1.

[87] Epict. 3.16.3–4: τί γὰρ ποιήσεις, ἂν περὶ μονομάχων λαλῇ, ἂν περὶ ἵππων, ἂν περὶ ἀθλητῶν,
ἂν τὸ ἔτι τούτων χεῖρον περὶ ἀνθρώπων· "ὁ δεῖνα κακός, ὁ δεῖνα ἀγαθός· τοῦτο καλῶς
ἐγένετο, τοῦτο κακῶς." See also Amm. Marc. 14.6.25; Hor. *Sat.* 2.6.44; Mart. *Ep.* 5.24; Tac. *Dial.*
29.3–4.

The crowd's ability to detect collusion between fighters is a particularly strong indication of their intimate familiarity with, and appreciation of what constituted good gladiatorial moves. Spectators readily recognized when a gladiator was fighting "by the book" (*ad dictata*) or not really trying at all.[88] Pseudo-Quintilian describes how a veteran gladiator handles a novice making his debut on the sand. He turns the fury and aggression of an inexperienced opponent back on his attacker, and dodges the frantic attacks of the newcomer with swift moves of his body (*Decl.* 9.9 = T.17; discussed in more detail below, chapter 7). Strikingly direct evidence is provided by a graffito from Pompeii which identifies one "Albanus, a left-hander, freeborn" and depicts him in a sketch. Left-handedness would have been an advantage in gladiatorial confrontations, allowing easier access to a right-handed opponent's less-protected side; the notation of Albanus' freeborn status may refer to his aggressive style of fighting (see above, pp. 212–13), which was clearly appreciated. The graffito implies much about the crowd's detailed knowledge of the different gladiatorial panoplies and the advantages and disadvantages each entailed, as well as their recognition of specific combat moves and how they could best be performed.[89] Martial says of the gladiator Hermes that he was "taught to win but not to harm" (Mart. *Ep.* 5.24.7 = T.11). The key word here is "taught" (*doctus*), which makes it plain that Hermes was specifically trained in this way and so implies that winning without causing injury was a desirable skill in a gladiator. (Seneca *Dial.* 3.11.1) makes the observation that "skill (*ars*) protects gladiators, anger strips them naked," which again demonstrates knowledge of the conditions and artistry of gladiatorial fights. The effective fighter kept his cool, but emotion reduced his concentration and so left him vulnerable. Much the same could be said of modern boxers. That said, it goes too far to suggest, as some have done, that gladiatorial combat was mostly non-lethal.[90] It was an incredibly dangerous activity to engage in – which is why thrill-seekers sought it out – and the possibility of death or crippling injury was very real indeed. Dio (71[72].29.3) reports that M. Aurelius was so averse to seeing bloodshed that he used to equip gladiators with blunted weapons and watch them perform "like athletes" (i.e., without risk

---

[88] See Sen. *Ep.* 22.1 (collusion); and Petron. *Sat.* 45.12 = T.12 with Suet. *Iul.* 26.3 ("by the book").

[89] See K. M. Coleman, "A Left-Handed Gladiator at Pompeii," *ZPE* 114 (1996), 194–6; Jacobelli, *Gladiators at Pompeii*, 49 (fig. 41); Langner, *Graffitizeichnungen*, no. 1024. An epitaph from Rome (*CIL* 6.10180 = *ILS* 5105 = *EAOR* 1.75) commemorates the gladiator Lycus who fought as *mur(millo) scaev(a pugna)*, "a murmillo with left-handed fighting style"; see also *EAOR* 1.99, *CIL* 11.7444 = *EAOR* 2.53. Commodus was left-handed; see Dio 73(72).19.2; cf. Sen. *Controv.* 3 *praef.* 10.

[90] See M. J. Carter, "Gladiatorial Combat with 'Sharp' Weapons (τοῖς ὀξέσι σιδήροις)," *ZPE* 155 (2006), 161–75; Potter, "Gladiators and Blood Sport," esp. 75–80.

of death). This tells us two important things: first, that it was uncommon for gladiators to engage in bloodless contests, at least in Imperial shows (if not, why Dio's notice?); and, second, that a spectator could watch and enjoy gladiators purely for their combat skills.

Spectator partisanship, we know, applied to chariot races and theatrical events, and it is attested also for gladiators, but in mitigated form. Fans appear to have been devoted either to particular performers (as shown by the sorts of graffiti reviewed above, which attest to the "sports hero" status of some named gladiators), or to a style of armature. Many different gladiatorial armatures are known from written or visual sources: *eques* ("Cavalryman," with a medium-sized round shield, rimmed and feathered helmet, short sword, and tunic), *Thraex* ("Thracian," elaborate helmet, small shield, greaves and curved short sword), *murmillo* ("Fish-man," helmet, large shield, greaves, short sword), *retiarius* ("Net-man," scantily clad with only one arm and shoulder protected, and carrying a trident and dagger), *secutor* or *contraretiarius* ("Pursuer" or "Anti-net-man," armored opponent of the *retiarius*, with smooth helmet, large shield, and short sword), *hoplomachus* ("Equipped Fighter," helmet, spear, buckler, dagger), *essedarius* ("Chariot-fighter," not necessarily mounted, oval shield, helmet, sword), and so on. Variations within the types were possible, by equipping them with long swords, for instance, when they were dubbed *spatharius* ("armed with a *spatha*," the long cavalry sword of the Roman army). There are also some bizarre types, such as the *scissor* ("Cleaver") who wore a vicious device on his left arm that featured a half-crescent blade; or the *andabata* (of uncertain derivation), who appears to have fought blind, perhaps in a completely enclosed helmet.[91]

Out of all these possibilities, however, only two "factions" among arena fans are attested: the *parmularii* ("small-shielders," who supported Thracians) and *scutarii* ("rectangular-shielders," who favored *murmillones*).[92]

---

[91] See Junkelmann, *Gladiatoren*, 43–128, for detailed discussion and modern reconstructions of various armatures. Junkelmann documents some eighteen different named kinds of fighter, but a great variety of armatures are documented in images and not all of them can be given names from surviving sources; see also Junkelmann, "*Familia Gladiatoria*," 31–74, esp. 35–64; Mosci Sassi, *Linguaggio gladiatorio, passim* (where fifteen armatures are documented); Ville, *Gladiature, passim* but esp. 306–11. On the *scissor*, see above, n. 85.

[92] See, e.g, M. Aurel. *Med.* 1.5; Quint. *Inst.* 2.11.2; *CIL* 6.9719 = *ILS* 7492; *Bull. Ép.* 1971.423 and 1972.294 (where Robert argues that such associations were organized like any other *collegia*, with patrons, purses, and regulated membership). See further Roueché, *Performers and Partisans*, 79–80 and 110 (ad 46.H.9) for "Thrax" cut into a seat at Aphrodisias' theater and the advice "Don't quarrel"; Robert, *Gladiateurs*, 24–7 (and nos. 200–2); Ville, *Gladiature*, 443–5. See also *TLL* 10.1.412.9–20, s.v. "parmularius." The very brevity of this latter entry attests to the relative rarity of references to gladiatorial partisanship; cf. *TLL* 6.137.41–79, s.v. "factio" for circus or theater factions.

Caligula, for instance, not only favored Thracians, he was actively hostile toward *murmillones*, while Domitian was so partial to *murmillones* that he considered criticism of them an insult to his imperial majesty.[93] That spectators backed types of armature, as well as individual fighters, makes a lot of sense. The fights were conceived with specific pros and cons in mind, and the combatants armed accordingly: the largely unprotected *retiarius'* long reach with trident and entangling net was pitched against the more armored *secutor's* short sword and large shield. The latter's task was to get in close to bring his short weapon to bear, the former's to keep his opponent at bay with the trident and try to ensnare him with the net. The careful balance in most armatures between protecting extremities and exposing the torso encouraged acts of derring-do and made for a more exciting engagement. Each armature would therefore engender a distinct style of fighting, an inference corroborated by the existence of specialist trainers (*doctores*) for particular types of gladiators (*doctor murmillonum*, for instance) in gladiator schools (*ludi*).[94] The backing of different armatures by members of the crowd was thus an expression of preference for particular styles of fighting and combinations of moves, and this further corroborates a connoisseurship of technique in a knowledgeable audience.[95] Since all gladiators but the *retiarius* wore a face-covering helmet, the ready identification of individuals on sight was difficult. This may be part of the reason the detailed program was announced in advance, with the roster of bouts clearly laid out in the order they would be staged; no doubt heralds and placards supplemented the program immediately before each fight. Under such circumstances, it would be natural for the fan to plump for a specific type of fighter to help maintain interest in the proceedings, at least while named favorites were off-stage.

It is noteworthy that the ancient evidence for the persistence and pervasiveness of *parmularii* and *scutarii* is far slimmer than it is for the circus or

---

[93] Suet. *Cal.* 54.1, *Titus* 8.2 = T.15 (favoring Thracians); Suet. *Cal.* 55.2 (dislike of *murmillones*); Suet. *Nero* 30.2, *Dom.* 10.1, cf. Pliny *Pan.* 33.3–4 = T.24 (favoring *murmillones*).

[94] See, e.g., *IGRR* 1.207 = *EAOR* 1.54 (*epistates* of *essedarii*); *CIL* 6.4333 = *ILS* 5116 = *EAOR* 1.60 (*doctor secutorum*); *CIL* 5.1907 = *EAOR* 2.37, *CIL* 6.10175 = *ILS* 5103 = *EAOR* 1.55 and *CIL* 6.10174 = *EAOR* 1.56 (*doctor myrmillonum*); *CIL* 6.10181 = *ILS* 5099 = *EAOR* 1.58 and *CIL* 6.37842 = *ILS* 9341 = *EAOR* 1.57 (*doctor oplomachorum*); *CIL* 5.4502 = *ILS* 5108a = *EAOR* 2.38 (*doctor provokatorum*); *CIL* 6.10192 = *ILS* 5091 = *EAOR* 1.61 (*doctor Thraecum*); *CIL* 6.37844 = *ILS* 9342 = *EAOR* 1.62 (*doctor velitum*). Some inscriptions record gladiators in a certain class who were also *doctores*, which suggests that when they retired from the arena, they joined the *ludus* as trainers of that class; see, e.g., *CIL* 6.10183 = *ILS* 5110 = *EAOR* 1.59 (*provactor spatharius* and *doctor*), *CIL* 12.3332 = *ILS* 5087 = *EAOR* 5.13 (*Thraex* and *doctor*).

[95] Artemidorus (2.15, 32) provides evidence for the different moves associated with different gladiators.

theater factions. It just does not appear that arena events elicited quite the same sustained intensity of partisanship as was found at those other venues. Why, for instance, did only two styles of gladiator attract supporters, so far as we know? Perhaps it stemmed from so mundane a reason as frequency of appearance. *Murmillones* and Thracians are among the most common type of gladiator attested in the sources, and they also dominate the *libellus* from Pompeii reviewed above. Many of the more exotic gladiators were probably a rarity; there would be no point in being an ardent "Cleaver" supporter if such a specialist only appeared occasionally. Despite the Thracian and *murmillo* support groups, it is clear that partisanship adhered more closely to individual, named combatants; graffiti devoted to gladiators do not mention *parmularii* or *scutarii*, but they nearly always name a particular fighter.[96] This fact alone would mitigate the virulence of partisanship in the arena crowd, since support would be atomized across a fan base distributed throughout the *cavea* in a way that was not true for the circus (where there were only four colors – briefly augmented to six under Domitian – which were on constant display, and fans of which tended to sit together) or for the theater (where famed actors were regulars on the stage). In addition, there was the fluidity of the gladiatorial spectacle itself, where bouts cannot have lasted much longer than fifteen to twenty minutes each.[97] This means that fighters and armatures rotated regularly, as new pairs fought it out, even if Thracians and *murmillones* made frequent re-appearances.

Before the gladiatorial phase of a *munus* got underway, the crowd had already been treated to animal hunts, executions, burlesque mock-fights and (on occasion) athletic displays. Excitement would have therefore been high already. Now the gladiators, the headline event, appeared in the arena, armored, oiled, and looking good (Cic. *De Orat.* 2.316). They warmed up in their pairings, sparring with *arma lusoria* (mock weapons), in what was called the *prolusio* (Cic. *De Orat.* 2.325). Like the *libellus* and the *pompa* that preceded it, the *prolusio* must have raised anticipation to a yet higher pitch, as the crowd's heroes were on display, fitted out, and ready for action. Driving music added to the atmosphere, as noted by Pseudo-Quintilian: (*Decl.* 9.6 = T.17), "the trumpets began to sound their fatal blare." Before

---

[96] Some texts even mention the "admirers" (*amatores*) of particular individuals, which evokes the fan clubs of modern sports stars: e.g., *CIL* 5.5933 = *ILS* 5115 = *EAOR* 2.50 = I.7 and *CIL* 5.3466 = *ILS* 5121 = *EAOR* 2.47 = I.9. For gladiators known to the crowd by name, see, e.g., Mart. *Spect.* 23, *Ep.* 5.24 = T.11; Petron. *Sat.* 52.3; Suet. *Claud.* 21.5 = T.22. For gladiators depicted or named in graffiti, see Langner, *Graffitizeichnungen*, 45–9 and 51–4.

[97] See above, ch. 4, p. 151.

the first pair engaged, the weapons were brought out, presented to the *editor*, and tested for sharpness.[98]

When the combats got underway, excitement would be at its greatest pitch. The crowd surged at the vicissitudes of the fight, shouted out tips, and called out at various junctures.[99] There were four possible ways for a bout to end.[100] A combatant might win. He might be killed outright (noted as *periit* or with a *theta nigra* in programs and inscriptions), or he might be disabled, outmaneuverd, or otherwise forced by his opponent to concede. At this point, he raised his index finger in appeal to the *editor* for a decision.[101] The *editor*, to curry favor with the masses, would abide by the majority decision of the crowd, who would shout out *missus!* ("discharge!") or *iugula!* ("cut his throat!") while flapping their togas or waving napkins or handkerchiefs (for release), or making an appropriate motion with their thumbs (for death).[102] The *editor*, responding to the crowd, would either order the defeated gladiator sent away (*missus*) or killed (*iugulatus*). The gladiator whose appeal was rejected was expected to accept the death blow magnanimously and stretch out his neck for the *coup de grâce*.[103] While the patchy ancient evidence will not allow us to calculate averages for gladiatorial results, gravestones and other sources suggest that being spared was not an uncommon result (see I.3, for instance, where only a few combatants are marked as *periit*).[104] It was also possible for gladiators to fight each other to a standstill, when both were too exhausted or otherwise unable to continue, and neither could gain a decisive advantage over the other. Both would then be "sent (away) standing" (*stantes missi*), which

---

[98] Dio 68.3.2 (at a show Nerva offers gladiatorial weapons for inspection to conspirators he knows are plotting against him); Suetonius (*Titus* 9.2) tells the same story of Titus.

[99] On crowd vocalizations and tips, see above, ch. 4, n. 35. Standing up and/or gesticulating as blows landed appears to have been normal spectator behavior; see Prudent. *C. Symm.* 2.1096 = T. 16; [Quint.] *Decl.* 9.9 = T.17; Suet. *Claud.* 21.5 = T.22, cf. Dio 60.13.5 (on Claudius at spectacles).

[100] I omit here the rare format called *munera sine missione*, on which, see above n. 21.

[101] Thus gladiatorial fights went "to the finger" (*ad digitum*); see Quint. *Inst.* 8.5.12, 20; Mart. *Spect.* 31.4–5 with Coleman, *Liber Spectaculorum*, 223–6; Mosci Sassi, *Linguaggio gladiatorio*, 70–2.

[102] The calls are recorded in a relief (now lost) from Beneventum showing a gladiator fighting a large phallus with the expressions *missus missus* and *iugula iugula* inscribed alongside; see *CIL* 9.1671 = *EAOR* 3.72. The precise form of the thumb turning (Juv. 3.36–7; Prudent. *C. Symm.* 2.1099 = T.16) remains unclear: thumbs up or down, or turned inward toward the neck in a jabbing action? See A. Corbeill, *Nature Embodied: Gesture in Ancient Rome* (Princeton, 2004), 41–66 (who argues cogently for an upright position of the thumb in this gesture), and Mosci Sassi, *Linguaggio gladiatorio*, 57–8. For the use of togas or handkerchiefs to signal release, see Mart. *Ep.* 12.28.8.

[103] For the sort of behavior that was expected of the doomed gladiator, see Cic. *Tusc.* 2.41 = T.5; Sen. *Dial.* 9.11.1–6, *Ep.* 30.8.

[104] M. Carter and D. Potter have followed evidence like this to argue for the relative non-lethality of gladiatorial bouts; see, e.g., Carter, "Rules of Engagement" and "'Sharp' Weapons"; Potter, "Entertainers," 335–41; and above, n. 90.

meant neither defeat nor victory had been achieved and the bout was a draw.[105]

It is not hard to imagine how tremendously exciting all this must have been to watch. Seneca the Elder (*Controv.* 4 *praef.* 1 = T.19) notes that sponsors usually rolled out new pairs of gladiators on successive days of his games, "to keep the anticipation of the people going… [and] both to delight the crowd and keep them coming back." Popular excitement was therefore ratcheted up in advance of the spectacle and deliberately manipulated as it progressed. In watching the fights, spectators could indulge their partisanship for individual combatants whose careers they were tracking or for a particular style of fighter (or both). To help in both processes, they could scrutinize the *libellus* for the track records of the performers slated to appear. Degree of experience and prior success rate were helpful markers, but no more determinative than they are in modern sports. Therein lay part of the pleasure and excitement. On the day, it was impossible to say what was going to happen.

Graffiti from Pompeii offer striking corroboration for these possibilities by recording the debut of the newcomer M. Attilius (a freeborn or freed contract-gladiator, as his name reveals). In his opening match, Attilius, fighting as a *murmillo*, was pitched against a Thracian named Hilarus ("Merry"). We know Attilius was making his debut, since there is no track record after his name, and he is expressly labelled a "beginner" (*t(iro)*). On paper, the fight looked like a mismatch. Hilarus was a formidable opponent, a product of the Neronian training school and a veteran of fourteen fights, who had been crowned victor in twelve of those contests. Yet Attilius won. That Hilarus was spared reveals the match to have been a good one, in which both parties fought well. Attilius' next appearance is depicted nearby on the same wall. Now with one match and one victory under his belt, he went up against another daunting adversary. L. Raecius Felix, as his name reveals, was also a contract gladiator, but he already had twelve fights behind him and was unbeaten. But again Attilius won and

---

[105] On *stantes missi*, see ch. 3, n. 108, and Wuilleumier and Audin, *Médallions*, 78–9 (no. 111c). All four outcomes are amply attested from gladiatorial epitaphs, which can include the career statistics of the deceased; see, e.g., the epitaph of M. Antonius Exochus, from Alexandria, who fought as a Thracian in the games given to mark Trajan's posthumous triumph over Parthia in AD 117 (*CIL* 6.10194 = *ILS* 5088 = *EAOR* 1.92 = I.5), "on the second day, as a beginner, he secured a draw (*stans missus*) with Araxis, imperial slave; at Rome, on the ninth day of the same show he caused to be spared Fimbria, freeborn, with nine fights' worth of experience, (*missum fecit*)"; or Flamma, the *secutor* (*CIL* 10.7297 = *ILS* 5113 = *EAOR* 3.70 = I.6), "He lived 30 years. He fought 34 times, won 21 times, drew 9 times, and was spared 4 times." See also Coleman, "*Missio*."

his defeated opponent was spared – another good pairing.[106] These graffiti show that Attilius was a formidable fighter, who defeated two veterans in his opening two fights.[107] The excitement of informed spectators as they witnessed the dramatic arrival of this new talent in the arenas of Campania is not hard to imagine. The bouts can be viewed against the background of cognitive synergy, where reversal of expectations or close juxtaposition of opposites generates a state of excitement. Indeed, the entire arena spectacle has been analyzed as one giant exercise in jarring contrasts and unexpected reversals (see above, chapter 1, p. 20), but these elements were at their most intense during the gladiatorial combats.[108]

All manner of incident and drama can be reconstructed from gladiatorial epitaphs. We noted above (p. 195) the games given by Constantius at Tergeste, where a *secutor* killed a *retiarius* and then himself perished of his wounds. It was an extraordinary outcome that caused the *munerarius* to pay for their shared tomb and its accompanying inscription. In the text Constantius specifically notes that the remarkable events of his spectacle earned him the *favor* ("applause, goodwill, affection") of the people. The unusual or out-of-the-ordinary was always appreciated. Seneca the Elder, quoting Fulvius Sparsus, supplies a possible scenario to explain what had happened here: "Even among gladiators the worst situation for a winner is to fight a dying man. Fear no opponent more than the one who cannot live, but can

---

[106] The graffiti were etched on to the plaster surfaces of a tomb outside the Porta Nocera at Pompeii; see *CIL* 4.10236–8 = Sabbatini Tumolesi, *Gladiatorum Paria*, 98–100 (no. 71), and Tav. XII; note also Jacobelli, *Gladiators at Pompeii*, 51 (fig. 43), and Langner, *Graffitizeichnungen*, nos. 1007–8 and 1038. The pertinent texts read (*CIL* 4.10238 and 4.10236 respectively): *M. Attilius t(iro) v(icit); Hilarus Ner(onianus) XIV ⊃ XII m(issus)* ("M. Attilius, beginner, won; Hilarus, of the Neronian school, fourteen fights, twelve crowns, spared") and *M. Attilius I ⊃ I v(icit); L. Raecius Felix XII ⊃ XII m(issus)* ("M. Attilius, one fight, one crown, won; L. Raecius Felix, twelve fights, twelve crowns, spared"). Hilarus' fight record, which clearly impressed the graffitist, is also etched over a nearby image (*CIL* 4.10237). The armatures can be deduced from the accompanying figured drawings. We cannot tell if Attilius' fights were part of one spectacle in which he fought twice, or if they took place in different spectacles perhaps weeks or months apart, so that the dedicated graffitist was "tracking" Attilius' early appearances as they unfolded over time. For comparable, though less instructive graffiti from other regions of the West, see *EAOR* 2.57, 6.18–25 and Langner, *Graffitizeichnungen*, nos. 769–916 and 1003–57.
[107] Surviving evidence suggest that newcomers were rarely pitted against veterans. Did the excitement-seeker Attilius specifically seek out bouts with veterans?
[108] Other graffiti etched on the peristyle walls of a house in Pompeii records dramatic fights. *CIL* 4.1421 = Langner, *Graffitizeichnungen*, no. 1003: *Asteropaeus Ner(onianus) CVII v(icit); Oc<ean>eanus l(ibertus) VI m(issus)* ("Asteropaeus, of the Neronian school, 107 fights [or possibly "crowned seven times"], won; Oceanus, freedman [or freeborn], six fights, spared"); *CIL* 4.1422 = Langner, *Graffitizeichnungen*, no. 1040: *Priscus N(eronianus) VI v(icit); Herennius l(ibertus) XIIX p(eriit)* ("Priscus, of the Neronian school, six fights, won; Herennius, freedman [or freeborn], eighteen fights, died.") The latter encounter echoes the evidence about Attilius, in that an experienced veteran met his end at the hands of a relative newcomer.

still kill."[109] A gladiator's epitaph from Ephesus notes "I slaughtered the one who killed me."[110] Another epitaph implies a similar result in the case of Vitalis ("Lively"), an unbeaten *retiarius* of Batavian birth: "He courageously fought it out to the end on an equal footing with his opponent; he was fast in his fights." That the inscription is on Vitalis' grave, that he is specifically noted as unbeaten (*invictus*) and having fought his opponent *pariter* ("equally, on an even footing") suggests that Vitalis too perished of his wounds without losing (the fate of his opponent is not recorded).[111] The mournful epitaph of a gladiator who died in his eighth fight at the age of twenty-two warns "I recommend that each of you look after his own fate; don't put your trust in Nemesis, that's how I was deceived!"[112] Similar is this admonition, issued by Urbicus the *secutor* from beyond the grave; "I recommend that he who beats a man should kill him."[113] This bitter comment would suggest that, in the course of his thirteen-bout career, Urbicus had fought a *retiarius* who was spared. The same pairing was later repeated, and this time the defeated *retiarius* killed Urbicus.

Information like this reflects the high drama that attended quality gladiatorial bouts. One can imagine, for instance, that spectators were well aware in advance that the *secutor* Urbicus would be having a rematch with a *retiarius* he had previously defeated. There would be gossip and speculation in advance of the bout. Tracking careers and speculating about past outcomes and future bouts was all part of being a knowledgeable arena spectator, but given that there were four potential outcomes, nobody would know for sure how any one encounter might turn out. That programs stress the training pedigree of professionals, as well as their past performances, offers a glimpse into a hierarchy of gladiatorial reputations, from the stars of the imperial capital, to the locally renowned fighters who performed in major provincial cities, down to those squaring off in more modest settings.[114]

As the bouts progressed, the band played on, since the action was accompanied by musical bands, some of which appear in images of arena

---

[109] Sen. *Controv.* 9.6.1: *inter gladiatores quoque victoris condicio pessima est cum moriente pugnantis. nullum magis adversarium timeas quam qui vivere non potest, occidere potest.*
[110] Merkelbach and Stauber, *Steinepigramme*, 03/02/04: τὸν κτείν[ο]ντ᾽ ἐφόνευσ[α].
[111] *CIL* 11.1070 = *ILS* 5118 = *EAOR* 2.46 = I.8.   [112] *CIL* 5.3466 = *ILS* 5121 = *EAOR* 2.47 = I.9.
[113] *CIL* 5.5933 = *ILS* 5115 = *EAOR* 2.50 = I.7. For discussion of these, and other, fascinating texts, see Hope, "Fighting for Identity."
[114] Carter ("Gladiatorial Ranking," esp. 87–98) demonstrates how gladiators were ranked in the *palus*-system, whereby the combatants were classified by armature and then ranked as "*primus palus*" ("first stake"), *secundus palus* ("second stake"), etc., apparently in reference to the training post used in gladiatorial schools. Factors other than skill (such as number of victories and popularity) probably also played a role in the ranking system.

events.[115] The instruments in common use were trumpets, both of the curved military type (*cornu*) and the straight version (*tuba*), water organs, flutes and pipes, and probably some sort of percussion. A tomb relief in the National Museum in Naples depicts the *pompa* that preceded the gladiatorial games and shows trumpeters accompanying the participants, the famous arena mosaic from Zliten in Libya shows a band comprising a brass section and a water organ (*hydraulis*), while gladiatorial graffiti on a tomb outside the Nucerian gate at Pompeii shows trumpeters blasting away as two gladiators engage.[116] One scholar has argued that gladiatorial fights were choreographed to music, with trumpet blasts used to highlight the blows and other incidents of the duel, all against the constant backdrop of the organ's drone.[117] These musical accents probably played a role in guiding or stimulating the crowd's acclamations, claques, and the chanting of slogans.[118] The musicians would have added to these expressions from the crowd, perhaps accentuating thrusts, parries, feints or standard sequences of moves with a tune, announcing with a trumpet blast when a blow had landed (encouraging a loud cheer in response?), filling the tense moments during a fallen gladiator's appeal with suspense-heightening notes, or even playing a jingle at the granting of an appeal or a dirge on denial.

---

[115] See, e.g., Ovid *Fasti* 6.657–60; Juv. 3.34; Petron. *Sat.* 36.6; [Quint.] *Decl. Maj.* 9.6 = T.17; Ville, *Gladiature*, 372–5. For arena images, see next note.

[116] On the *hydraulis*, see Vitr. *De arch.* 10.8.3–6 and Heron *Pneum.* 1.42. Juvenal (3.34–5) notes bands of trumpeters and horn-blowers (*cornicines*) who toured provincial games. For the Zliten mosaic, see Aurigemma, *Mosaici di Zliten*, 149 (with figs. 87–9). For the Pompeii scenes, see Jacobelli, *Gladiators at Pompeii*, 94–5 (fig. 77; *pompa*) and 51 (fig. 23; graffiti), and, for the latter, see also Langner, *Graffitizeichnungen*, no. 1007, and Sabbatini Tumolesi, *Gladiatorum Paria*, Tav. XII.1. See also the *hydraulis* and *cornu* depicted in a gladiatorial mosaic from Nennig in Germany; Parlasca, *Römischen Mosaiken*, 35–8 (esp. Taf. 37.2).

[117] See C. J. Simpson, "Musicians and the Arena: Dancers and the Hippodrome," *Latomus* 59 (2000), 633–9. See especially Petron. *Sat.* 36.6 and the flute-player's epitaph (*CIL* 10.4915 = *ILS* 5150), which reads, in part: "In the strains of a flutist I modulated an alternating melody / and by my summons I called to arms the swordsmen of Mars, spurring them with my intonation" (*Tibicinis cantu modulans alterna vocando | Martios ancentu [sic] stimulans gladiantes in arma vocavi*). Note also the epitaph of the gladiator Absolas from Laodicea, which reads in part (line 3) "I hear no more the call of the brass-forged trumpet" (χαλκελάτων δὲ βοὴν σαλπίνγων οὐκέτ'[ἀκούω]), a comment echoed on the tombstone of the *retiarius* Melanippos from Alexandria Troas (lines 4–7) that "I no longer hear the sound of the brass-forged trumpet, nor rouse the din of the uneven flutes as I compete" (οὐκέτι χαλκε[λ]|άτου φωνὴν σάλπιγγος ἀκο[ύω]| [οὐ]δ̓ἀνίσω αὐλῶν κέλαδον ἀ|[εθ]λῶν ἀνεγείρω); see, respectively, Merkelbach and Stauber, *Steinepigramme*, 02/14/09 and 07/05/01 (= Robert, *Gladiateurs*, 234–5 [no. 298]). Apuleius (*Met.* 10.31) describes a "warlike Dorian tune" played on the flute (*tibicen Dorium canebat bellicosum*) during a non-violent re-enactment of the Judgment of Paris that opens a gladiatorial spectacle; note that the martial strains of the melody were readily identifiable.

[118] See D. Potter, "Performance, Power, and Justice in the High Empire," in Slater (ed.), *Roman Theater and Society*, 29–59; see also above, ch. 4, pp. 123–40.

Music, chanting, and crowd vocalizations would have accentuated the emotional arousal of the crowd and helped guide its interpretation of events. That is to say, music probably played a role in the Roman arena similar to that in many sporting spectacles today, including North American football, baseball, basketball and ice hockey, as well as Spanish bull-fights. In these modern contexts, the music (whether canned or live) heightens the crowd's excitement by underlining dramatic moments in the action. The audience, in fact, is usually familiar with the specific musical motifs that highlight particular incidents, so that the music is another means to interpret events that have often transpired very quickly and some distance away (the modern sports event crowd has the added benefit of instant replays on large television screens). While no arena tunes have come down to us from Roman times, it is not hard to imagine music punctuating and heralding the different phases of the spectacle and highlighting especially dramatic moments. Music raised the emotional pitch of arena events, and so affected the level of arousal in the crowd, since music addresses itself first and foremost to the emotions. The very presence of musicians at the games thus constitutes a compelling piece of indirect evidence for the excited and aroused state of the Roman arena crowd, even if their scores no longer sound in our ears.

ARENA SPORT

The foregoing strongly suggests that gladiatorial bouts entertained Roman spectators in a manner very similar to the way that modern sports do. Gladiators were professionally trained experts (or they were talented volunteers) who competed in structured fights governed by rules, which were enforced on the sand by umpires. Individuals were trained in a particular armature which entailed a certain style of fighting, and the pitting of different styles against each other was carefully thought out to maximize entertainment value. Anticipation of the games generated excitement before anyone had taken to the sand. Arena aficionados scrutinized the advertised pairings, discussed past records, and speculated about upcoming matches. Many of the fighters were known to the spectators by name (and/or reputation); some also favored *murmillones* or Thracians as a class of combatant. The arena (or wherever the games were being staged) was a stimulating space where the usual rules of decorum did not apply. It was noisy, roiling, colorful. Trumpets blared. The giver of the games and the performers appeared in procession, no doubt greeted by huge cheers of appreciation and anticipation.

Various diversions preceded the headline bouts themselves: animal displays, hunts, executions, athletes, mock bouts. The spectators' anticipatory excitement mounted. When the weapons had been inspected, the combatants came out in the order listed in the program (*libellus*). The fights were surrounded by drama, but not equally for everyone. Some would look forward to seeing their favorites or heroes in the scheduled pairings, but they would be on the sand only for a few minutes at a time. Others would root for particular types of fighter. Variety was a key feature of arena spectacle, so sights were constantly changing. Parapathic emotions (particularly of self-substitution) deeply involved the spectators in the action. The fact that death and injury were folded into the rules (even if they were not inevitable in every case) raised the stakes and sharpened the tension as the crowd followed the fights. The excitement of self-substitution would have been heightened by the high risks involved in the combat. The crowd was knowledgeable about what was going on and appreciated the skill and artistry of a good fight. It is significant that many ancient notices of crowd vocalizations at the arena record applause, praise, and appeals for freedom and/or rewards for a good performance.[119] This alone demonstrates that arena spectators were not a mindless baying mob, but a keen audience that knew the rules, knew what a good fight looked like, and appreciated the proper execution of difficult moves. They expected quality and knew what to look for as the bouts progressed. They were quite willing to demand extra rewards for quality performances.

The possibility of betting and the uncertainty of outcomes lent the engagements a diverting fascination. For those immersed in gladiatorial statistics, or closely following a participating fighter's (or fighters') career trajectory, the bouts would be totally absorbing. Music helped accentuate moments in the fight, chants focused the crowd's attention on the action, the intensity of the combat, the lethal risks involved, the unified cheers or groans as events transpired, the crowd shouting out tips or requests or calls as wounds were incurred, and the opposing chants at the moment of appeal, some for death, some for sparing – all of this made for a highly arousing psychological experience that has many parallels in the world of watching modern sports, particularly of the more aggressive variety. Spectatorship at gladiatorial bouts, I suggest, was not far removed from that at a boxing spectacle, an ice hockey or rugby match, an American football game, or an Ultimate Fighting tournament. Again, this is not to

---

[119] See, e.g., Gell. *NA* 5.14; Dio 72(71).29.3–4; Pollio ap. Cic. *Fam.* 10.32.2; Suet. *Calig.* 35.3, *Claud.* 21.5 = T.22.

say that these spectacles are in themselves related to the Roman arena, but rather that watching them elicited comparable psychological responses to those operative in the *cavea* of the arena all those centuries ago. Seneca sums it up neatly: "we get worked up at the struggles of others."[120]

All that said, there was little of sporting interest in the executions that preceded the pairings of gladiators, but these appear to have been no less absorbing, at least for some members of the audience. This leads us to consider a basic psychological impulse underlying the entire discussion so far, one that encompasses the whole range of events staged during Roman *munera*: why do people like to watch violence as entertainment?

[120] Sen. *Dial.* 4.2.5: *effervescimus ad aliena certamina.*

CHAPTER 7

The attractions of violent spectacle

In the flabby American spirit there is a buried sadist who finds the bullfight contemptible – what he really desires are gladiators.

N. Mailer, *The Presidential Papers* (1963)[1]

You can't have violence without a sense of humour.

British soccer hooligan, quoted in Buford,
Among the Thugs (1992)[2]

Consider a hypothetical scenario. As I write (February 2010), there are 225 inmates on death row in Pennsylvania, USA, where I live.[3] The cost of killing them, when all appeals have been exhausted, lies in the order of millions of dollars each.[4] Nationwide, the death-row inmate waits on average ten or more years for his date with death, and in Pennsylvania it is just under twelve years. Some death-penalty advocates reckon such delays to be an unacceptable deferment of justice.[5] Now imagine that some future

---

[1] N. Mailer, *The Presidential Papers* (New York, 1963), 11.   [2] Buford, *Thugs*, 116.

[3] Across the United States (as of July 2009), 3,279 inmates were housed on death row by thirty-five states, the US Military, and the US Government. (Unless otherwise indicated, these and subsequently cited facts about the death penalty have been gleaned from the Death Penalty Information Center in Washington, DC; see www.deathpenaltyinfo.org [accessed Feb. 21, 2010], especially their year-end report for 2009, available at www.deathpenaltyinfo.org/reports.)

[4] On average it costs over two million dollars more to kill someone than to imprison them for thirty to forty years. No comprehensive study has been carried out on how much the death penalty costs Pennsylvania, but figures are available for, e.g., Maryland ($37 million spent per executed prisoner [five since 1976]); New Jersey ($253 million spent 1983–2006 with no executions); Florida (estimated $24 million spent per executed prisoner [sixty-nine since 1976]); California (estimated $250 million per executed prisoner [thirteen since 1976]). These figures reflect the amount of money spent on the death penalty by each state *in toto* averaged against the number of inmates actually killed.

[5] The Pennsylvania average (11.7 years) is documented by the Bureau of Justice Statistics and reported to me by e-mail (dated Nov. 17, 2007) from the Death Penalty Information Center. For irritation at delays between sentencing and execution, see, e.g., the comments of then Deputy Attorney General William Parr that "The fundamental unfairness in our death penalty system is not a lack of procedures to raise meritorious claims. Rather, it is the abuse of the writ of habeas corpus to delay, and ultimately to avoid, just punishment" (*New York Times*, Letters to Editor, Sept. 26, 1990). For a more academic presentation of an analogous argument, see J. M. Shepherd, "Murders of Passion, Execution Delays, and the Deterrence of Capital Punishment," *Journal of Legal Studies* 33 (2004), 283–322, or several

governor of Pennsylvania decides that, in the interests of saving taxpayers' money and of ensuring that justice is done speedily, death-row inmates are to be trained to fight to the death with edged weapons. He arranges a *Spectacle of Justice*, to be staged in a major sports arena – Penn State's Beaver Stadium, with a capacity of close to 110,000, would be ideal. As an incentive to fight, winners will have their death sentences commuted to life imprisonment, while the losers will either perish in the combat, and so suffer their legal sentences, or, if injured or outmaneuverd in the bout, will be allowed to appeal to the spectators for their lives. The governor proudly declares the latter provision a sign of his deep commitment to democratic ideals, as well as his trust in the wisdom and judgment of the good people of the Commonwealth of Pennsylvania. To be sure, there would be vociferous opposition to such a spectacle from various quarters, but is there any real doubt that enough people would be found to fill the 110,000 seats in Beaver Stadium? That, indeed, spectators would pour in from all over the country, even from around the world, to see such a thing? That television companies would vie for broadcast rights? The scenario probably appalls many reading it, but we all know intuitively that it would appeal to others.[6]

Underlying this intuition is the abundant evidence all around us for the attraction of violence as spectacle and entertainment. To take an extreme example, the global box-office success of films featuring "superviolence" or "torture porn" (e.g., the *Saw* franchise) demonstrates that the draw of intensely gruesome sights, at least on film, is a very real phenomenon.[7] If indeed some basic penchant for violent sights and images could be located in the human psyche, then a fundamental explanation for the Roman games would quickly emerge.[8] This possibility suffers from two main difficulties in formal demonstration, at least on the current state of knowledge. First, it has

---

other articles traceable through the pro-death penalty Criminal Justice Legal Foundation (website: www.cjlf.org/deathpenalty/DPinformation.htm; accessed Feb. 22, 2010).

[6] Some people I have presented the scenario to – decent, civilized people – admit with a disconcerting candor that they themselves would go along, out of sheer curiosity, if nothing else. One or two have said, heck yeah, they'd attend: these are dead men walking, right? Why not dead men fighting?

[7] The global success of such movies further suggests that their appeal is not limited to any particular cultural system; see D. Zillmann, "The Psychology of the Appeal of the Portrayal of Violence," in Goldstein (ed.), *Why We Watch*, 179–21, esp. 180. Tom Wolfe coined the term "pornoviolence" (*Esquire*, July 1967) to describe the rising fad for violence (represented at that time by *The Dirty Dozen*, *Gunsmoke*, or the James Bond movies). Pornoviolence is portrayed from the perpetrator's perspective, and so de-emphasizes the suffering of the vicitm.

[8] Sam Peckinpah – director of such violent extravaganzas as *The Dirty Dozen* (1967), *The Wild Bunch* (1969), or *Cross of Iron* (1977) – is on record saying that movie violence is "a terrible, ugly thing. And yet there's a certain response that you get from it, an excitement because we're all violent people"; quoted in D. Weddle, *If they Move, Kill 'Em: The Life and Times of Sam Peckinpah* (New York, 1994), 334.

been insufficiently investigated by psychologists. While the broad question of human aggression has generated a vast bibliography, the prevalence of violence in modern entertainment has been examined overwhelmingly for its effects on the spectator and its (disputed) capacity to generate aggressive behavior.[9] Only a handful of social psychologists have looked at the more fundamental question of why people are drawn to watch violence in the first place, and most work in that subfield deals specifically with audiences of modern films or television (their findings are reviewed below).[10]

Second, any suggestion that indulgence of aggressive tendencies, such as watching people and/or animals getting hurt as a spectacle, may derive from an inherent psychological trait is likely to meet with fierce resistance from various quarters. While the source of human aggression is an enormous and highly politicized controversy, which stands well outside the purview of this book, we have reviewed sufficient comparative data (above, chapter 2) to demonstrate that, at the very least, substantial numbers of people in different times and places have been more than willing to witness unimaginable harm done to human beings (and animals) in the context of public spectacle. Even if not all of these spectacles were intended as entertaining diversions, we have also seen sufficient evidence that they could be treated as such by the spectators. If we are to appreciate what was likely a fundamental reason the Romans packed their arenas, we must explore what sort of explanations have been offered for why people find violence attractive.

THE ATTRACTION(S) OF VIOLENT SPECTACLE

There is a great variety of ways violence can be staged and witnessed as spectacle. As we saw above (Introduction p. 5), violent spectacles can be classed as punitive, ludic, or religious, or some combination of these

---

[9] For some recent studies of violence in modern entertainment, see T. Grimes et al., *Media Violence and Aggression: Science and Ideology* (Thousand Oaks, 2008); D. Haugen (ed.), *Is Media Violence a Problem?* (Detroit, 2007); W. J. Potter, *On Media Violence* (Thousand Oaks, 1999), esp. 11–24 (for attraction to violent spectacle); W. J. Potter, *The 11 Myths of Media Violence* (Thousand Oaks, 2003); G. G. Sparks and C. W. Sparks, "The Effects of Media Violence," in J. Bryant and D. Zillmann (eds.), *Media Effects: Advances in Theory and Research*, 2nd edn. (Mahwah, 2002), 269–85. See also M. Barker and J. Petley (eds.), *Ill Effects: The Media/Violence Debate*, 2nd edn. (London, 2001); J. L. Freedman, *Media Violence and its Effect on Aggression: Assessing the Scientific Evidence* (Toronto, 2002); J. D. Torr (ed.), *Is Media Violence a Problem?* (San Diego, 2002); D. Trend, *The Myth of Media Violence: A Critical Introduction* (Oxford, 2007). Note also the series of US Federal Trade Commission Reports (2000 and 2002), *Marketing Violent Entertainment to Children.*
[10] See, e.g., G. G. and C. W. Sparks, "Violence, Mayhem, and Horror," in D. Zillmann and P. Vorderer (eds.), *Media Entertainment: The Psychology of Its Appeal* (Mahwah, 2000), 73–91; Zillmann, "Psychology of the Appeal." See also Trend, *Myth of Media Violence,* 117–21, and several papers in J. B. Weaver and R. Tamborini (eds.), *Horror Films: Current Research on Audience Preferences and Reactions* (Mahwah, 1996).

categories. The violence itself can be real or represented; it can be lethal, injurious, or even playful; it can be an inherent and intentional element of the spectacle or an accidental consequence of how events play out; and it can be watched live, in large crowds or small groups, or remotely via television or on a computer, usually alone or in small groups. It hardly needs to be stressed that psychological analyses of why people like to watch violent entertainment pertain overwhelmingly to modern mass media – violent films or television – and therefore to simulated acts of violence. (Some work has been done, to a lesser degree, on live sports violence.)[11] So a natural and very basic point would be to question whether findings derived from modern studies are applicable to the Roman arena. "After all," a critic might point out, "the violence of modern movies is a faked representation, and doesn't the audience *know* it's unreal? This surely is a world apart from watching actual murder done before your very eyes, as the Romans did." The point is a reasonable one on the face of it. It is indeed the case that most explicit violent entertainment today is watched through the lens of our telecommunication age, which removes it from the direct experience of the viewer. Media violence is often highly stylized (accompanied by dramatic music or depicted in slow motion, for instance) and thereby proclaims its unreality to the viewer. On the surface, then, the ancient and modern experiences appear worlds apart and fundamentally incomparable. Can a single psychological mechanism really stand behind such different types of experience?

The short answer is "yes." Before seeing why this is so, two observations help refine our approach. First, the modern appetite for violent sights is not restricted to the fakery of the movies. The immense popularity of that brand of "reality TV" that documents actual car chases, accidents, injuries, and death, or the video compilations of hockey-fights or football hits excised from their sporting contexts, trumpet their reality as a point of attraction. The news is dominated by stories of death and destruction. Lurid tales of murder are especially popular and can seize public attention for weeks, months, or even years. At the extreme end of the scale, the video series *Faces of Death* offers the viewer what claims to be footage of actual executions, the slaughter of animals in abattoirs, or the aftermath of fatal car accidents. At the time of writing, there are six volumes in the series. There is a dispute as to how many of the images are genuine and how many are staged recreations.[12] The more important point is that the chief

---

[11] See above, chapter 6, pp. 196–202.

[12] *Faces of Death V* (1995) and *VI* (1996) are recycled highlights from the first four volumes (released 1978–90). The producers have cashed in on the "controversy" over the disputed reality of the series by making the "mockumentary" *Faces of Death: Fact or Fiction?* (1999).

selling point of the series is the alleged reality of its images.[13] To date, the series has reportedly grossed $35 million worldwide. More recently, videos posted on Islamist websites showing the decapitation of captives with large kitchen knives have scored hundreds of thousands, if not millions of hits.[14] There was no doubt about the stark reality of these images. There is, then, a documentable taste, even in the telecommunication age, for witnessing real-world violence.

The flipside of this coin is that filmmakers spend huge sums of money on special effects to make the brutal consequences of contrived film violence as realistic-looking as possible.[15] And this requirement is not peculiar to the video age. Medieval and Renaissance drama often demanded a high degree of explicit violence – including dismemberment, mutilation, infanticide, and cannibalism – and it was staged as realistically as the technology of the age allowed.[16] Between 1897 and 1962, the infamous Grand Guignol theater in Paris drew thousands of patrons with the promise of staged depravity, carnage, and deviance. Much care was taken to make the results of the violence look as convincing as possible, and censors frequently intervened to shut the more offensive productions down. So popular was the genre, a Grand Guignol theater opened in London in the early 1920s.[17] In a live environment, such as modern American professional wrestling spectacles, the line between stagecraft and realism is blurred to the point where it does not matter to the cheering crowd whether the fights are

---

[13] The compilation, *Worst of Faces of Death* (1987) carries the tagline, "a journey into the depths of depravity to some of the most bizarre and grisly death experiences ever recorded." The matter is complicated by the producers' evidently playing on the expected audience's familiarity with faked gore and death from films, which would not have applied in the Roman context. That said, the touting of the images' "reality" is simply expected to draw viewers, as it seems to do.

[14] In the weeks following the decapitation of Nick Berg on May 7, 2004, websites featuring video of the atrocity became the single most popular search on the internet in the USA, according to a May 21, 2004 AFP report. I personally know several perfectly decent people who watched (one with the sound turned off).

[15] The observation applies to the gory *results* of violence rather than to the mechanics of the staged violent situations, which are often preposterously unrealistic, such as the bloody demise of hordes of shuffling zombies, a barful of people erupting into an all-out brawl, or a lone hero mowing down dozens of attackers; see Collins, *Violence*, 10–19. The focus here is on conveying the "reality" of the blood and gore rather than how the blood and gore are generated.

[16] See M. Charney, "The Persuasiveness of Violence in Elizabethan Plays," *Renaissance Drama* 2 (1969), 59–70; J. S. Gatton, "'There Must Be Blood': Mutilation and Martyrdom on the Medieval Stage," in J. Redmond (ed.), *Violence in Drama* (Cambridge, 1991), 79–91. See also Schechter, *Savage Pastimes*, 69–98.

[17] J. M. Callahan, "The Ultimate in Theatre Violence," in Redmond (ed.), *Violence in Drama*, 165–75; M. Gordon (ed.), *The Grand Guignol: Theatre of Fear and Terror*, rev. edn. (New York, 1997), esp. 45–50; R. J. Hand, *Grand-Guignol: The French Theatre of Horror* (Exeter, 2002), esp. 33–66. On the London theater, see R. J. Hand and M. Wilson, *London's Grand Guignol and the Theatre of Horror* (Exeter, 2007).

fixed or the blood fake (although in many instances, it is not). Clearly, film special effects or staged live events do not have to be strictly realistic to be effective. Their primary purpose is to evince a visceral reaction from the audience – the group groan at a bone-crunching ejection from the ring or the spontaneous gasp at a spectacular on-screen killing. Such sights play more to the psychological expectations of the spectators than to their sense of what is strictly real. But underlying those expectations is a basic requirement that the realism be sufficiently convincing.[18] For modern consumers of violent images, then, the realms of the staged and the real overlap significantly.

Our second preliminary observation is that the same is arguable for the Romans. Arena violence, despite its reality, was in no small measure packaged for its audience and, in its own way, was as stylized and staged to meet their expectations as modern movie violence or professional wrestling is to meet ours. The games took place in buildings that evolved specifically to cater to them. The spectacle was preceded by a procession (*pompa*) of the games' sponsor, the performers, their gear, and pertinent religious icons.[19] Programs (*gladiatorum libelli*) circulated in advance of the event. Depending on the sponsor's means, the spectacle could feature exotic and unusual animals imported from all corners of the empire, some of them perhaps never before seen by the crowd. More exotic still was the staging of some executions and punishments as mythological re-enactments (e.g., an "Orpheus" savaged by a bear, an "Attis" castrated) which blurred the boundaries between the real and unreal.[20] Great care was taken to erect impressive staging, in the form of artificial hills and landscapes, elaborate frameworks, or trapdoors that suddenly yawned in the sand to discharge fresh animals or combatants.[21] The gladiators themselves looked like no

---

[18] I would suggest that this is why the manner of portraying violence on screen tends toward the more graphic over time: audience expectations are calibrated against the most recent limit reached. In this way the "pornoviolence" of, say, *The Dirty Dozen*, while horrifyingly realistic on its release in 1967, today looks almost parodic when set beside the likes of *Saving Private Ryan* (1998) in its own war-film genre, let alone examples of "torture porn" such as *Saw* (2004), *Hostel* (2006), or *Captivity* (2007). These latter films go out of their way to show violence in as unflinching a manner as possible.

[19] On the *pompa*, see above, ch. 6, n. 77.

[20] See Coleman, "Fatal Charades." Such elaborate executions appear to have been staged in the provinces also; see Tert. *Apol.* 15.4–5, who probaby saw such "charades" in Carthage; cf. *Pass. Perp. et Felic.* 18.4–6 (= Musurillo, *Acts of the Christian Martyrs*, 126–7). The arena's blurring of fact and fiction is one of the major themes of Martial's *Liber Spectaculorum* (e.g., 1, 5).

[21] On stage sets (*apparatus, automata* or *pegmata*), see, e.g., Strabo 6.2.6; Suet. *Iul.* 39.3–4, *Claud.* 21.6 and 34.2 = T.23, *Nero* 12.1–2, *Dom.* 4.1–2; Juv. 4.121–2; Varro *Rust.* 3.5.3. An inscription mentions a spectacle put on with "splendid staging" (*adpa[ratu m]agnifico*) as a particular point of pride: *CIL* 9.2237 = *ILS* 5060 = *EAOR* 3.28 (Telesia; late first/early second century AD). Sets are sometimes

known warriors, fitted out in panoplies specifically designed for arena events, which alone lent the duels an air of make-believe.[22] As we saw in the previous chapter, the violence of the gladiatorial pairings was no mindless butchery for butchery's sake, but a carefully crafted contest of skill and endurance bounded by rules enforced by umpires.[23] Gladiators were inculcated with some suggestive values, such as to reckon an uneven match ignominious, to think that fighting without risk was to fight without glory, or to recognize that pleasing their masters and the people constituted their prime objectives.[24] This reveals that the requirement to put on a good show was enshrined in what might be termed a "gladiator ethos," which was likely to have been internalized and was taken very seriously by at least some of the fighters, as their epitaphs show. Taken as a whole, then, gladiatorial spectacles had about them a powerful aura of stagecraft and artificiality, no matter how real their violence. They were performances, designed to be watched, and they presented themselves as such.

This fact is driven home by inscriptions where *ludi scaenici* (theatrical games), *ludi circenses* (chariot races), and *munera* (gladiatorial spectacles) are often categorized together – staged as alternative spectacles by the same benefactor, for instance – indicating that to Roman minds such events were all of a kind.[25] The dedication of Pompey's theater in 55 BC featured a

depicted in iconography, as in a relief from Trieste showing a *retiarius* perched on a platform as a *secutor* mounts a ramp to gain access to him (these are apparently the "bridge fighters" [*pontarii*] named in some inscriptions; see ch. 6, n. 7); or the relief from Sofia showing *venationes* and *noxii* exposed to beasts amid various stage sets; see Augenti, *Spettacoli del Colosseo*, 44–6 (nos. 16 and 17; *venationes*), 98–9 (no. 55; *pontarii*). The phenomenon is best illustrated by the *naumachiae*, staged sea-fights which, it seems, could be performed in the Colosseum before the subterranean tunnels were installed (and the tunnels themselves were to serve the stagecraft demanded by the arena); see Coleman, "Launching into History," 58–60.

22 On gladiatorial equipment, see above, ch. 6, n. 91. The argument has been made that gladiators were armed to evince Rome's barbarian enemies, which may well be true for such fighters as the "Thracian" (*Thraex*), the "Samnite" (*Samnis*), or the "Gaul" (*Gallus*), but hardly applies to all the armatures: no barbarian tribe went into battle with a net and trident (as did the *retiarius*); see Maurin, "Barbares." Of course, exotic gladiatorial armatures may have denoted no more than the vague category "foreigner" and were hardly based on detailed ethnographic knowledge.

23 See above ch. 6, nn. 15 and 78. Even a savage like Caligula expected the rules to be respected, otherwise it was just "vicious murder" (*crudelissima caedes*); see Suet. *Cal.* 30.3.

24 At least, according to Seneca *Dial.* 1.3.4: "A gladiator reckons it ignoble to be matched with an inferior opponent and knows that he who is beaten without risk is beaten without glory" (*ignominiam iudicat gladiator cum inferiore componi et scit eum sine gloria vinci qui sine periculo vincitur*). On pleasing people and owner, see Cic. *Tusc.* 2.41= T.5.

25 Gladiatorial games and *ludi scaenici* put on by same benefactor: *CIL* 9.2350/1 = *ILS* 5059 = *EAOR* 3.26/7 (Allifae; second half of first century AD); *AE* 1961.109 = *EAOR* 3.40 (Corfinium; late second century AD). See also *CIL* 11.5265 = *ILS* 705 = *EAOR* 2.20.19–20 and 33–4 (rescript of Constantine from Hispellum; AD 337) which mentions *ludos schenicos et gladiatorum munus* and *spectaculum tam scenicorum ludorum quam gladiatorii muneris*. The phrase *ludi gladiatorum* (in the sense of "gladiatorial games" as opposed to "gladiator schools") makes an appearance in the schoolbooks: see above, ch. 3, n. 62.

spectacle of Greek and Oscan plays, athletes, chariot races, and a beast hunt (the latter two staged in the circus, but still part of the same dedicatory celebration).[26] Philo records an event staged in the theater at Alexandria which opened with a morning show of Jews scourged, stretched, bound to wheels, and beaten before being led off for crucifixion. This was followed by dancers, mimes, flute-players and all the usual elements of *ludi scaenici* (Philo *In Flacc.* 84–5). Gladiator names offer a further indication of theatricality. The earliest attested are in Lucilius, where the blandly named Aeserninus ("The Man from Aesernia") fights the uninspiringly monikered Pacideianus (etymology uncertain, but possibly evoking peaceability). But as their popularity grew, gladiators' names became evocative, sexy, or ironically humorous. Thus we get Advolans ("Attacking"), Astus ("Cunning"), Ferox ("Fierce"), Iaculator ("[Net?] Thrower"), Mucro ("Blade"), Pardus ("Panther"), Pugnax ("Aggressive"), Scorpio ("Stinger"), Tigris ("Tiger"), and Velox ("Speedy"); or Cupido, Eros (both "Lust") and Pulcher ("Pretty Boy"); or Clemens ("Gentle"), Columbus ("Dove"), Cycnus ("The Swan," which might refer to grace of movement), Murranus ("Perfume Boy," presumably because he was pampered), Palumbus ("Pigeon"), and Serenus ("Cheerful/Calm Boy").[27] That is to say, gladiators took stage names.

The gulf that apparently separates the Roman arena spectator from the consumer of modern violent entertainment is thus not quite so wide as it might first appear. Yet there is no consensus as to why people find violent sights attractive. Social psychologists have made a series of propositions, but so far no one theory has emerged to combine them into a unified conceptual model. Perhaps part of the difficulty is the variegated nature of violence itself and the variety of ways people can derive enjoyment from it. As a leading researcher in the field, Dolf Zillmann, notes: "there is no single quality of violence, nor a single circumstance in the exposure to its depiction, that could adequately explain the apparent attraction of the portrayals [of violence] . . . Rather, there seem to exist a multitude of conditions that are poorly interrelated and, hence, difficult to integrate into a universal theory."[28] As a result, the best that can be done here is to outline briefly some of the main lines of inquiry.

---

[26] Cic. *Fam.* 7.1.2–3; Dio 39.38.1–5 = T. 6.

[27] For Aeserninus and Pacideianus, see Lucil. 4.151–4K = 4.149–52M (= Nonius, s.v. "spurcum") and 4.155–60K = 4.153–8M = Cic. *Tusc.* 4.48 = T.10; Cic. *Q. Fr.* 3.4.2; see also, on gladiator names, Junkelmann, *Gladiatoren*, 267–8; Mosci Sassi, *Linguaggio gladiatorio*, 183–96; Ville, *Gladiature*, 306–10. Also popular were names derived from mythology, especially from the Trojan Cycle (Achilles, Ajax, Astyanax, Diomedes, Hector, etc.).

[28] Zillmann, "Psychology of the Appeal," 209.

One broad way of thinking about the draw of violent spectacle that was once prominent but is no longer held in high esteem is catharsis, i.e., "purification" or "purgation" (on which see above, chapter 6, p. 199). The proposition was readily extended from an analysis of tragedy and drama to the watching of aggression, on the argument that viewing violence purges spectators of their own aggressive impulses.[29] Quite aside from the lack of a convincing demonstration that some all-pervasive fear and terror motivate people to watch mayhem (the purgation of which then generates pleasure), empirical testing has rendered the catharsis hypothesis untenable.[30] Another unconvincing explanation is that violence and destruction carry inherent aesthetic appeal.[31] Even if that were so – and it is far from proven – the observation merely asserts the appeal of violence more than it offers an explantion for it. And, as with catharsis, empirical data do not support the claim. It has been found that spectators derive no pleasure from decontextualized images of pure violence – they are generally disgusted by them.[32]

Some explanations are not applicable to or testable for conditions at the Roman arena. For instance, horror films are particularly popular among adolescents to such an exent that they have been dubbed "teenpics."[33] It has been argued that the horror movie is tantamount to a modern *rite de passage* where young males and females act out gender roles sanctioned by society. Thus, during the horror film, the male viewer displays constancy and mastery over the threats on the screen, while the female betrays helplessness and terror. The pleasure derives not from the violence *per se*, but

[29] L. Berkowitz, *Aggression: Its Causes, Consequences, and Control* (Philadelphia, 1993), 339–44; Sparks and Sparks, "Violence, Mayhem, and Horror," 82; Zillmann, "Psychology of the Appeal," 183.

[30] C. McCauley, "When Screen Violence is not Attractive," in Goldstein (ed.), *Why We Watch*, 144–62, esp. 147–9; Sparks and Sparks, "Violence, Mayhem, and Horror," 82; Zillmann, "Psychology of the Appeal," 182–7. The related notion of desensitization – confronting fears to overcome them, for instance – is no more rigorous in conception and no more supported by empirical data than are theories of purgation; see J. Bryant and D. Miron, "Entertainment as Media Effect," in Bryant and Zillmann (eds.), *Media Effects*, 549–82, esp. 559; Sparks and Sparks, "Violence, Mayhem, and Horror," 82–4.

[31] T. Heller, *Delights of Terror: An Aesthetics of the Tale of Terror* (Urbana, 1987) (on horror literature); J. Hoberman, "'A Test for the Individual Viewer': Bonnie and Clyde's Violent Reception," in Goldstein (ed.), *Why We Watch*, 116–43; Sparks and Sparks, "Violence, Mayhem, and Horror," 75–6.

[32] It may be the case that certain *kinds* of violent or destructive images have a majestic appeal, such as explosions or scenes of large-scale destruction. Soldiers in the field have indeed reported finding such sights compellingly alluring; see J. G. Gray, *The Warriors: Reflections on Men in Battle* (New York, 1967; originally published 1959), esp. 28–39. Other types of violent imagery – animals slaughtered in an abattoir or radical facial surgery conducted on children – are perhaps less inherently appealing; see McCauley, "Screen Violence."

[33] B. S. Sapolsky and F. Molitor, "Content Trends in Contemporary Horror Films," in Weaver and Tamborini (eds.), *Horror Films*, 33–48, esp. 33–5.

from successfully performing these expected roles.[34] While convincingly demonstrated for the horror film, the observation is not applicable to the Roman arena, where the genders were separated, at least for gladiatorial spectacles (the situation at the circus is less clear)[35] and the proportion of adolescent spectators at *munera* cannot be determined with any specificity. That said, the findings alert us to the role of social setting in rendering reception of violent images enjoyable. Another problematic set of explanations are those that rely on individual personality or character traits as the key to understanding why people attend violent entertainments. Thus notions that sensation seekers or cravers of the novel are drawn to such things – while certainly plausible, and conceivably applicable to a portion of the arena crowd – just cannot be systematically investigated for Roman conditions.[36]

The spectrum of other explanations is so broad as to defy easy subclassification;[37] it also cannot be discussed in any great detail here. The complexity of the subject also needs to be borne in mind in order to avoid

---

[34] D. Zillmann et al., "Effects of an Opposite-gender Companion's Affect to Horror on Distress, Delight, and Attraction," *Journal of Personality and Social Psychology* 51 (1986), 586–94; D. Zillmann and R. Gibson, "Evolution of the Horror Genre," in Weaver and Tamborini (eds.), *Horror Films*, 15–31; D. Zillmann and J. B. Weaver, "Gender-Socialization Theory of Reactions to Horror," in ibid., 81–101. The results were quite stark. Males paired with emotionally unresponsive females reported not enjoying the movie or their partners' company as much as males paired with suitably terrified females. Females paired with cowering males reported the same negative reactions.

[35] See Ov. *Ars Am.* 1.135–70, *Am.* 3.2, *Tr.* 2.284–5. In the first passage cited, Ovid likens the loose seating arrangements at the circus to those at *munera* staged in the forum – a strange comment, given that Augustus' *lex Iulia theatralis* was already in effect (as is clear from *Ars Am.* 1.89–134 with ibid. 1.137–40; on this law, see above, ch. 3, pp. 104–6). Perhaps the regulations with respect to gender separation at *munera* were not applied as rigidly to spectacles staged in the traditional Republican venue of the Roman Forum; see the comments of A. S. Hollis in his edition of the *Ars Amatoria Book I* (Oxford, 1977), 63. Note that Ovid does not advocate comforting the lady spectator in the manner of modern adolescents at scary movies (as asserted, for instance, by Zillmann, "Psychology of the Appeal," 198), but rather he recommends looking out for her physical comfort, cheering on her favored charioteer, sneaking a peak at her ankles, etc. Despite the separation of the genders at *munera*, a connection between the arena and eroticism is certainly traceable; see, e.g., Juv. 6.102–12; Dio 60.28.2; HA *M. Aurelius*, 19.1–9; Barton, *Sorrows*, 65–6, 72–3, and 79–81; C. Ewigleben, "'What These Women Love Is the Sword': The Performers and their Audience," in Köhne and Ewigleben (eds.), *Gladiators and Caesars*, 125–39, esp. 132–3; Hopkins, *Death and Renewal*, 21–2; Meijer, *Gladiators*, 68–76.

[36] See, e.g., Sparks and Sparks, "Violence, Mayhem, and Horror," 77–8; M. Zuckerman, "Sensation Seeking and the Taste for Vicarious Horror," in Weaver and Tamborini (eds.), *Horror Films*, 147–60.

[37] Note that Sparks and Sparks ("Violence, Mayhem, and Horror") divide modern theories into three groups: the inherent attraction of violence (e.g., novelty, sensation seeking); violence as a secondary element attendant on other attractions (e.g., preference for an actor or director); or delayed gratification (e.g., catharsis, enacting gender roles). Zillmann ("Psychology of the Appeal") and Goldstein ("Why We Watch," in Goldstein (ed.), *Why We Watch*, 212–26) apply entirely different categories.

the trap of reductionism, since the individual-differences dimension in social psychology, as always, applies (that is, individuals will be attracted to watch for different reasons), and it is quite possible that different forms of violent spectacle may carry their own, specific attractions. So what follows is a partial list of the more prominent ideas.[38]

- Response tendencies to danger imbued over millennia of human evolution (aka the "fight-or-flight" response) were once very useful in the so-called environment of evolutionary adaptedness (EEA) in which humans originally evolved, and these responses continue to exert influence over the emotions today. As a result, images of violent threats are naturally attention grabbing and fascinating to the human mind. (The hypothesis neatly explains why people find such sights interesting, but not why enjoyment is derived from watching them; on its own logic, violent or threatening sights ought to be distressing and fearful).

- Consciousness of our own mortality imbues us with a curiosity about death and different ways of dying (although, again, the emotional response should be one of anxiety and distress, not enjoyment and pleasure).

- "Excitation transfer" is rooted in the physiological responses to fear, terror, or increased aggression induced by horrific or violent sights (a form of "arousal"). These feelings endure after the fact and are sharpened by relief at a satisfying outcome (e.g., the "bad guy" gets his due). The greater the arousal, the greater the relief afterwards. Anticipation of the arousal itself and of the subsequent euphoric state draws people to watch.

- It is enjoyable to watch others violate accepted social norms with impunity, since this is so rare in real life.

- Boys and men are in general more drawn to violent entertainment than are girls and women (precisely why this should be so is hotly debated). More specifically, watching violent sights appeals to males in groups. Male social identity may therefore have a role to play in drawing people to watch (see above on gendered roles at horror films).

- Historical context influences the attractiveness of violence. Frequent exposure to real violence is likely to generate greater demand for violence as entertainment. War play and increased demand for war toys have

---

[38] The list is distilled from Goldstein, "Why We Watch"; Guttman, *Sports Spectators*, esp. 175–85; McCauley, "Screen Violence," 146–53; Sparks and Sparks, "Violence, Mayhem, and Horror"; Zillmann, "Psychology of the Appeal." The tentative nature of these proposals needs to be appreciated, as Goldstein (ibid. 223) observes baldly: "What we don't know about the attractions of violent entertainment could fill a book." That observation stands today, over a decade after Goldstein made it.

been shown to correlate against the backdrop of an ongoing actual war.[39]

Research along these lines posits at best a series of interrelated psychological processes, attitudes, and outlooks at work in the attraction to violent sights; it remains to be seen if the complex can be fashioned into a universal theory. As it stands, these processes have social, contextual, and emotional components. Although some of the propositions are not mutually exclusive – if violence and destruction carry an inherent aesthetic appeal, this may be particularly alluring to certain types of personality – others clearly are: an inherent aesthetic appeal of violence does not sit well with the acting out of gender roles, which requires a negative reaction to the violence to play out. The various elements of attraction to violent sights may combine in ways that remain opaque in the current state of research. For our purposes, none of these ideas have been sufficiently well developed or are sufficiently transferable to the Roman context to be of much utility in understanding the Roman arena crowd's attraction to violent spectacle. Despite the prevailing confusion in the atomized theorizing in attraction-to-violence studies, one well-worked-out theory warrants scrutiny.

AFFECTIVE DISPOSITIONS

Disposition theory was originally developed for audience engagement with drama and comedy, but it has since been applied successfully to a variety of other genres, including violent entertainment.[40] The basic notion – well documented by extensive survey and experiment – is that deriving enjoyment from watching human agents is contingent on the spectator having a certain orientation toward those agents. This orientation is termed "affective disposition," and it has the power to determine how a spectator feels about the agents, their actions, or experiences (including violent

---

[39] See J. H. Goldstein, "Immortal Kombat: War Toys and Violent Video Games," in Goldstein (ed.), *Why We Watch*, 53–68, esp. 56–9 (on war toys in wartime).

[40] For what follows, see, e.g., D. Zillmann, and J. R. Cantor, "A Disposition Theory of Humour and Mirth," in A. J. Chapman and H. C. Foot (eds.), *Humour and Laughter: Theory and Applications* (London, 1976), 93–115; D. Zillmann, "The Experimental Exploration of Gratifications from Media Entertainment," in K. E. Rosengren, et al. (eds.), *Media Gratifications Research: Current Perspectives* (Beverly Hills, 1985), 225–39; D. Zillmann, "Mechanisms of Emotional Involvement with Drama," *Poetics* 23 (1994), 33–51; D. Zillmann, "Psychology of the Appeal," esp. 199–209. Zillmann (now professor emeritus at the University of Alabama) is a leader in the field and one of the few psychologists to investigate systematically the question of why people like to watch violence (among other things). The works cited here contain ample reference to earlier studies.

actions or experiences).[41] Thus, when good things happen to a liked agent, spectators respond with pleasure (termed "euphoria"), when bad things, with distress ("dysphoria"). The inverse is also true: if an agent is disliked, spectators react euphorically when bad things happen to that agent and dysphorically when good things happen to him or her.[42]

Two features of affective dispositions must be noted. First, spectators are aware of their role as witnesses. They do not identify wholly with the agents they are watching, but rather feel connected to them in what are termed "parasocial relations," which impel spectators to react to agents as if they were real friends (or foes). This is evident from the fact that spectators will not watch nonchalantly as an agent is threatened by an unseen menace (e.g., a killer lurking in the shadows, or a hero creeping up on a villain). In such circumstances, they will cringe when a liked agent is at risk and keenly anticipate the nastiness threatening a disliked agent. Second, a process of "moral monitoring" is constantly at work, in that spectators form their attitudes about agents (their "dispositional alignments") on the basis of moral assessments and anticipate outcomes in terms of deserts: some characters become liked by doing things judged good and are then felt to "deserve" their rewards, whereas other characters are disliked because they do bad things and are judged not to deserve positive outcomes. The reverse also applies: liked agents do not deserve adverse outcomes, but disliked agents deserve any ugliness that befalls them. These relationships are proportional: the more intensely liked an agent is, the greater the dysphoria sparked by undeserved misfortune and the greater the euphoria at success; the more intensely disliked an agent is, the greater the dysphoria at undeserved good fortune and the greater the euphoria at well-earned unpleasantness.[43]

In drama, film, or books, affective dispositions are elicited through narrative structure and character development. In violent narratives, negative dispositional alignments (that is, dislike of a character) allow viewers to enjoy violence when they consider it just and righteous. This attitude is

---

[41] Affective dispositions are to be distinguished from prejudice, in that they are ephemeral, personal, and elicited by the events being watched, whereas prejudices are more deeply seated, prevalent, and persistent. As will become clear below, affective dispositions can also be positive or negative, whereas prejudices are virtually always negative.

[42] In the context of dramatic representations, a neutral affective disposition is also possible, and it usually drains all pleasure from the experience of watching. Hence the common complaint of the unsatisfied viewer: "I just *didn't care* about any of the characters."

[43] In addition to items in n. 40, see D. Zillmann, "The Logic of Suspense and Mystery," in J. Bryant and D. Zillmann (eds.), *Responding to the Screen: Reception and Reaction Processes* (Hillsdale, 1991), 281–303; D. Zillmann, "Basal Morality in Drama Appreciation," in I. Bondebjerg (ed.), *Moving Images, Culture, and the Mind* (Luton, 2000), 53–63.

usually brought about by dwelling on the horrific and unjustified violence of a villain prior to the hero meting out often no less horrific but justified violence to that villain and his minions. As Zillmann puts it, "displays of monstrous gratuitous slaughter and the distress they evoke are a *necessary prelude* to the portrayal of righteous maiming and killing that is to spark euphoric reactions."[44] It is not the violent actions themselves that elicit enjoyment or disgust, but rather who is doing what to whom, and for what reason. The attitude of the viewer toward both the perpetrator and the victim converts these considerations into moral assessments of the violence as either monstrous or magnificent. The moral components of the viewer's alignment render anticipated outcomes intensely satisfying – or not, if expected outcomes fail to materialize or are reversed. To quote Zillmann again, "Negative affective dispositions, then, set us free to thoroughly enjoy punitive violence."[45] This response is termed "counterempathy," the flip-side of the empathic sentiments that spectators feel for liked characters.

A seven-stage model for the working of positive and negative emotional responses to viewing violence runs as follows: (1) spectators perceive and assess agent actions; (2) they then form moral judgments about those actions; (3) positive or negative affective dispositions toward the agents emerge from these judgments; (4) dispositional alignments impel spectators to anticipate appropriately negative or positive outcomes for the agent; (5) they perceive and assess the outcomes as they materialize; (6) their responses are correspondingly euphoric or dysphoric; and (7) their moral judgment of the outcomes as appropriate (or not) instills satisfaction (or not).[46] The relationship between these elements is neither stable nor strictly linear. As we just noted, spectator responses adjust proportionally to the degree of like or dislike felt for an agent. Furthermore, dispositions can affect moral assessments as well as emerge from them, in that dubious actions by liked characters tend to be forgiven, whereas kindnesses on the part of hated characters are deemed suspect and intensify dislike. Moral judgments about outcomes can also revise, even reverse, previously held

---

[44] Zillmann, "Psychology of the Appeal," 208 (emphasis added).   [45] Ibid., 202.

[46] Ibid. p. 202–6, esp. fig. 9.1 (at 204); Bryant and Miron, "Entertainment," 567–70. An example of these processes in response to a violent narrative might be: (1) character brutally murders innocent person; (2) spectator judges action as unconscionable; (3) spectator hates murderer as a result; (4) spectator eagerly anticipates murderer suffering deserved punishment; (5) murderer is himself hideously killed by hero-character; (6) spectator displays euphoric response to this punitive killing; (7) spectator judges outcome appropriate and finds narrative satisfying. Purveyors of suspense- and thrill-infused narratives intuit the affective dispositions of their audience and manipulate them, for instance by introducing "twists" that call into question or even reverse affective dispositions and their related moral judgments.

dispositions. If, for example, hotly anticipated punitive violence is judged too severe, empathy and liking for a hated victim can emerge along with corresponding dislike for a formerly liked agent.[47] But so long as punitive violence is judged righteous and deserved, then there is virtually no limit to the awfulness people can witness being inflicted on transgressors.[48] Related factors are habituation and thrill maximization. Anticipation of satisfying outcomes generates excitement, which is a partly physiological response dubbed "arousal" (on which, see above, ch. 6, p. 204).[49] It has long been recognized that arousal from excitement diminishes with repeated exposure, requiring the subject to seek greater thrills to re-experience the initial "rush."[50] In other words, as audiences habituate to violent stimuli, violence and destruction will tend to escalate in graphicness and scope over time, as indeed is traceable across most modern media over the decades.[51]

So much for the role of affective dispositions in audience appreciation of fictional and dramatic narratives of violence. What has this got to do with real violence done to real people? In this connection two findings are particularly striking.[52] First, affective dispositions do not distinguish between the fictive and the factual.[53] The same mechanisms of disposition-formation as those charted for fiction have been shown to be at work when people watch news reports: they can empathize with victims they are positively disposed toward, and feel satisfied by the sufferings and setbacks of those they dislike. Second, since people in the news will generally be already known to the viewer, narrative structure and character development

---

[47] Zillmann, "Basal Morality," 59–60.

[48] D. Zillmann and J. B. Weaver, "Viewer's Moral Sanction of Retribution in the Appreciation of Dramatic Representations," *Journal of Experimental Social Psychology* 11 (1975), 572–82. The degree of retributive violence judged appropriate is linked to prevailing cultural norms. Furthermore, escalation in villainous violence tends to justify enhanced levels of retributive hero violence.

[49] See also D. Zillmann, "Television Viewing and Physiological Arousal," in Bryant and Zillmann (eds.), *Responding to the Screen*, 103–33.

[50] Zillmann, "Psychology of the Appeal," 206–9 (with citation of prior literature).

[51] G. Gerbner, *Violence and Terror in the Mass Media* (Paris, 1988). Screen violence has only increased since Gerbner's report, although a debate rages about the significance of this fact; see Sapolsky and Molitor, "Content Trends." Note the comments of James Boswell (1740–95), lawyer and friend of Dr. Johnson and David Hume: "Still, however, I persisted in attending [executions], and by degrees my sensibility abated; so that I can now see one with great composure" (quoted in Gatrell, *Hanging Tree*, 292).

[52] See D. Zillmann et al., "News as Nonfiction Theater: How Dispositions toward the Public Cast of Characters Affect Reactions," *Journal of Broadcasting and Electronic Media* 42 (1998), 153–69; Zill-mann, "Basal Morality," 57–9; D. Zillmann and S. Knobloch, "Emotional Reactions to Narratives about the Fortunes of Personae in the News Theater," *Poetics* 29 (2001), 189–206.

[53] Indeed, the fictional and factual realms are closely linked in disposition-formation, since watchers of fiction draw on reality in forming their moral judgments about whom to like and dislike, or be neutral about. In this way, reality informs the reception of fiction.

are not necessary for dispositions to take shape. Rather, viewers' affective dispositional alignments are "predeveloped" from a general knowledge of the wider context. When prior information about a subject is limited or non-existent, news reports assist in the formation of dispositions by framing stories in a certain way, and audiences respond accordingly. Thus a story about a murder victim that begins "Young community volunteer John Doe was found murdered . . . " is likely to meet with empathic responses for the victim and outrage at the crime, while the introduction "Convicted child rapist John Doe was found murdered . . . " will spark a rather different reaction. Nevertheless, it remains a curious phenomenon that people seem drawn to bad or tragic news rather than to good news.[54] Disposition theory can partly explain this fact, but other factors might be at work as well, such as "parapathic emotions" (see above chapter 6, pp. 205–6); "social comparison," whereby tragic news engenders a satisfaction in the viewer that they are safe and not under threat; or moral rationalizations that allow viewers to think the victims somehow deserved what happened to them, that they were "asking for it" (for instance, by not taking proper precautions).[55]

As noted in the introduction (pp. 2–3), Keith Hopkins suggested some time ago that part of the appeal of "murderous games" to Roman audiences was likely to be found in the processes of crowd dynamics but also "in the psychological mechanisms by which some spectators identify more readily with the victory of the aggressor than with the sufferings of the vanquished."[56] Disposition theory is just such a mechanism, in that it allows people to take satisfaction (or even revel) in lethal violence meted out to certain parties deemed deserving of it. As such, it holds great promise for understanding a core element in the Roman arena crowd's state of mind.

AFFECTIVE DISPOSITIONS AT THE ARENA

If the attitude of Roman spectators toward arena performers can only be surmised from scattered scraps of evidence, the character of the arena

---

[54] Zillmann and Knobloch, "Emotional Reactions," 190–1.

[55] Ibid., 202–4. Arasse (*Guillotine and the Terror*, 91) notes of the crowd at guillotinings in Revolutionary France: "The spectator of the Terror shuddered at the *terribilitas* of what he saw, yet enjoyed the knowledge that it could do him no harm." Good (if extreme) examples of moral rationalizations for tragic news were offered by some conservative American religious leaders – always quick to moralize – when they declared that the September 11, 2001 attacks were divine retribution for various features of American society the leaders disapproved of; or that the December 2004 tsunami in the Indian Ocean "punished" the lands it ravaged for supporting Islamic terrorism; or that Hurricane Katrina in August 2005 was a "punishment" on New Orleans for a planned gay pride parade.

[56] Hopkins, *Death and Renewal*, 27.

context prompts two general, prefatory suggestions. First, given the broad prejudice toward the social outcasts on the sand, and given the announcement of event details in advance, it is reasonable to assume that spectator dispositional alignments were largely predeveloped and tended to the negative. This is not to say that they were uniformly and consistently so, but rather that they would naturally incline in these directions. This leads to the second suggestion, namely, that the crowd's attitudes likely changed and shifted with the phases of the spectacle. Even a cursory review of arena personnel is enough to make this probable, since that category included animals, professional huntsmen, helpless execution victims, forced mass combatants, trained and professional gladiators, volunteer fighters, and possibly also athletes and mock-fighters (*paegniarii*).[57] It is highly unlikely, on the face of it, that the crowd adopted a uniform emotional orientation toward all of these performers and victims. It is much more plausible that their attitudes and alignments would alter in response to developments on the sand – and that would make for a dynamic and exciting psychological experience.

Much of the direct ancient testimony for spectator attitudes has already been reviewed in connection with crowd vocalizations and social identity (see chapter 4, pp. 123–47). There is no need to review it all again here, but some particularly illustrative examples may serve to show how the evidence can be interpreted to explore the sentiments of the crowd toward the performers during different stages of the spectacle. Particularly instructive are those occasions when the spectators' attitudes are recorded as having turned. These incidents are readily explained in terms of shifts in dispositional alignments, and although they may have been rare – to be fair, we cannot gauge their actual frequency, although reports about them are few and far between – their exceptionalism indicates what was normal in spectator outlooks.

Animal shows

We cannot expect arena spectators to have emotionally aligned themselves with the animals displayed during hunts as fully as they would with human performers, so the contours of their affective dispositons during the *venationes* remain more indistinct than for the other phases of the event. If, as

---

[57] On the variety of performers, see Kyle, *Spectacles of Death*, 76–127; Ville, *Gladiature*, 345–79. See now also S. Brunet, "Dwarf Athletes in the Roman Empire," *AHB* 17 (2003), 17–32; S. Brunet, "Female and Dwarf Gladiators," *Museion* 4 (2004), 145–70. *Paegniarii* appear to have fought with play-weapons or no weapons at all; see Suet. *Cal.* 26.5; Mosci Sassi, *Linguaggio gladiatorio*, 146–7.

has been argued, the hunting spectacles symbolized human, and specifically Roman, control over forces of nature deemed dangerous in the agrarian context of antiquity, then the outlooks of the crowd toward arena animals would have been generally negative: carnivores menaced people and live-stock alike, while undomesticated herbivores threatened crops.[58] So the controlled slaughter of both, whether by "natural" means in the animal-on-animal spectacles or at the hands of trained human hunstmen, would have been satisfying to watch. That said, crowd attitudes appear to have been more complicated than this. The animal shows included appearances by tamed beasts, which were very popular with the spectators. This fact alone points not to a fixed negative outlook on animal performers, but to a kaleidoscope of shifting attitudes and emotional reactions to them.

In the tame shows, the spectators were intrigued by the reversal of their expectations, the gentle behavior of the supposedly savage beasts confound-ing widespread beliefs about the feral (and so threatening) animal realm.[59] As we saw in chapter 6 (p. 206) such surprising sights generate arousal and excitement as examples of "cognitive synergy," whereby expectations are not met, or opposites are set in close proximity, and are thus enthralling and fas-cinating. The poet Martial, for instance, when confronted by a spectacle of lions allowing hares to gambol in and out of their open mouths unscathed, reasons that they must do so because hares are too puny a form of prey for the mighty lion – dogs are the natural enemies of the hare. Another, more sycophantic reason he offers is that Caesar's authority (and, by implication, his innate beneficence) extends to the lions: "this clemency is not brought about by practice / The lions know whom they serve."[60] The point to

---

[58] Note, for instance, Luxorius *Ep.* 60 (trans. M. Rosenblum) which reads, in part, "The fertile land loses nothing, the plants grow in greater abundance / while all the wild beasts fear their fates here [in the arena]" (*fecundus nil perdit ager, plus germina crescunt / dum metuunt omnes hic sua fata ferae*). This notice applies to a private amphitheater associated with a seaside villa. See Wiedemann, *Emperors and Gladiators*, 55–67. Wiedemann makes much of such evidence as this poem from Vandal-era North Africa preserved in the Latin Anthology (*Anth. Lat.* 186 and 187 SB): "Human power can correct the frenzy of wild beasts; / See! The great beast fears the puny person . . . In dying, what had been a terror beforehand becomes a game" (*vis humana potes rabiem mutare ferinam / ecce hominem parvum belua magna timet. . . / fit moriens ludus, qui fuit ante pavor*; lines cited in Wiedemann, *Emperors and Gladiators*, 98 n. 25). See also Tuck, "Spectacle and Ideology."

[59] On Roman attitudes toward the animal kingdom, see M. Beagon, *Roman Nature: The Thought of Pliny the Elder* (Oxford, 1992), esp. 153–6; Toynbee, *Animals*, 15–31 (animals in general) and 61–9 (lions, an arena favorite).

[60] See above, ch. 4, n. 10 for the relevant references (quote at Mart. *Ep.* 1.104.21–2: *haec clementia non paratur arte / sed norunt cui serviant leones*). On the encomiastic tone of Martial's arena-related epigrams, see Coleman, *Liber Spectaculorum*, esp. lxxii–lxxv. The rhetorical devices at work in Martial's presentation – praise of the emperor, or juxtaposing strength and weakness – do not diminish its value as evidence for audience attitudes. Indeed the contrasts he stresses between lions and hares are just the sort of thing cognitive synergies are made of.

note is the mental process of the poet, as he worked through his emotional reaction to what he saw (amazement) to reach certain conclusions, poetic and panegyric as they may be. In a similar manner, Statius eulogizes a tame lion killed in the arena and anthropomorphizes the beast by comparing it to a dying and valiant soldier staggering on toward his enemy; he notes that the lion's death was mourned like that of a famous gladiator (Stat. *Silv.* 2.5). These attitudes were not restricted to the poetic imagination. Let us not forget that, just as they did with gladiators and hunters, spectators appealed for the release (*missio*) of animals they judged to have successfully evaded capture or death for a long time.[61] All of this suggests that the spectators could form positive dispositions toward some of the animal performers for some of the time (if not actively positive dispositions, then at least neutral dispositions that inclined them to clemency).[62] Since most of the *venatio* was devoted to the grim work of slaughter, this outlook is likely to have been as rare as it was fleeting, a reaction occasionally elicited by peculiar circumstances.

   Humans were put into the mix in animal spectacles in two quite distinct roles: as huntsmen and handlers (*bestiarii, venatores, magistri*) or as helpless victims exposed to the beasts (*damnati ad bestias*). In the former capacity, people were cast as beastmasters; in the latter, they were prey. It is reasonable to assume that the crowd would tend to back the human hunters over their quarry. Despite the fact that *bestiarii*, like all arena performers, were of low social repute and appear to have been held in even lower esteem than gladiators, we saw above (chapter 4) how the crowd appreciated hunting prowess to the point that the emperor Commodus sought to pander to the masses by himself appearing in the arena as a huntsman.[63] That he often did so in the guise of Hercules, protector of the common people against the threats of the wild, may be read as indirect evidence for a generally negative disposition of the crowd toward Commodus' animal victims, an emotion Commodus was seeking to manipulate for the benefit of his image. In psychological terms, negative attitudes in the crowd toward the animals would help dispose the spectators positively toward Commodus, who cast himself as the righteous neutralizer of the feared threats. Presumably, similar outlooks extended to arena huntsmen in general. They may not have been

---

[61] Mart. *Ep.* 13.99 (a gazelle) and 13.100 (an onager). Gazelles are particularly fast and agile, and the onager had evaded "the hunt of the Erythraean tusk."

[62] We do not have the evidence to deduce on what basis such positive dispositions were formed, but anthropomorphization is as reasonable a possibility as any; see below, pp. 249–52 on Pompey's elephants.

[63] See above, ch. 4, pp. 126–7.

heroes of the arena in the fashion of gladiators, but they were at least its stalwarts.[64]

This reconstruction of spectator dispositional alignments during beast spectacles is corroborated by the story of Pompey's elephants. This incident has been alluded to on several occasions in the preceding chapters, but it now warrants closer scrutiny.[65] To dedicate the completion of his permanent stone theater in Rome, the first in the city's history, in the autumn of 55 BC Pompey staged magnificent games that combined theatrics, athletics, and animal bloodsport. Cicero, who was there in person and writes about the games to an absent friend, notes that on the last day of the five-day hunt elephants appeared and "on that day a great wonder arose in the common mob, but no pleasure. Indeed a certain pity resulted, a sort of belief that the huge beast had something in common with the human race."[66]

Cicero does not provide details about what gave rise to the "certain pity" and "sort of belief" in the crowd, but he does say that it caused them to derive no pleasure from the spectacle, despite their amazement at it. We can now see that what he likely noted in the circus was a shift in the crowd's affective disposition toward the elephants. What prompted the shift? Pliny's account, written about a century after the event, fills in the details and was evidently compiled from the testimony of earlier writers (Pliny includes the comment *ut qui tradunt*, "as some report"). Twenty elephants (or, "as some report," seventeen) were pitted against Gaetulian javelinmen in the circus. One wounded elephant put up a great fight and, with its feet pierced, crawled on its knees toward its attackers, grabbed their shields with its trunk and hurled them in the air. The spectators delighted in the arcs described by the shields as they fell to earth. There followed the wondrous sight of an elephant taken down with a single javelin to the eye. But then the elephants stampeded as a group and threatened to break

---

[64] See above, ch. 4, n. 12, for evidence of huntsmen freed on the crowd's insistence.

[65] The main sources are Cic. *Fam.* 7.1.3; Dio 39.38.2–3 = T.6; and Pliny *HN* 8.20–1 = T.14. Two other accounts of these games – Plut. *Pomp.* 52.4 and Sen. *Dial.* 10.13.6–7 – make no mention of the mishap with the elephants. For thoroughgoing analyses, see A. Bell, *Spectacular Power in the Greek and Roman City* (Oxford, 2004), 151–98, on elephants in general and 157–72 on Pompey's elephants in particular; J.-A. Shelton, "Elephants, Pompey, and the Reports of Popular Displeasure in 55 BC," in S. N. Byrne and E. P. Cueva (eds.), *Veritatis Amicitiaeque Causa: Essays in Honor of Anna Lydia Motto and John R. Clark* (Wauconda, 1999), 231–71. Shelton suggests (267–8) that organized claques may have had a hand in orchestrating the crowd's expressions of displeasure, but they are not a necessary ingredient. As we have seen (ch. 3, pp. 90–1), apparently organized behavior can emerge spontaneously in a crowd context.

[66] Cic. *Fam.* 7.1.3: *extremus elephantorum dies fuit; in quo admiratio magna vulgi atque turbae, delectatio nulla exstitit. Quin etiam misericordia quaedam consecuta est atque opinio eiusmodi, esse quamdam illi belluae cum genere humano societatem.* Note that Cicero was writing to his friend M. Marius to console him for having missed Pompey's games, so he is likely to have downplayed their positives.

out of the iron barriers confining them, which understandably worried the spectators. At the end of the spectacle, the elephants lamented and wailed in such a way that the crowd interpreted their actions as appeals for mercy, which generated empathy for them (Pliny says the crowd wept) and anger at Pompey to the point that they cursed the benefactor, a curse, notes Pliny darkly, that was realized soon enough (in that Pompey went on to lose his war against Caesar and suffer ignominious death while seeking refuge in Ptolemaic Egypt).

At first, the crowd was unconcerned by the elephants' suffering and took delight in a hard-fighting pachyderm, shields arcing through the air, and displays of javelineering skill. Things changed when the elephants stampeded. Now the spectators were concerned, but for their own safety, not the elephants'. This was certainly bad news for Pompey, since one of the cardinal clauses in the unspoken contract between *editor* and spectators was that, despite watching great violence done to others, they themselves would suffer no harm. (Threats of harm to the spectators, in fact, would undermine one of the main pillars of their social identity at the arena: masters of the proceedings.) Despite this, when the elephants lamented pitiably, the crowd's attitudes shifted again, this time in favor of the elephants and against Pompey. I suggest that the really important dispositional shift occurred with the stampede, which undermined the spectators' alignment with Pompey out of fear for themselves, since it was the *editor*'s job to assure the crowd's safety at the games he sponsored.[67] This shift in turn colored the spectators' moral assessment of the elephants' dying moments. Note that at the end, the crowd expressed anger at Pompey rather than at the Gaetulian javelinmen doing the killing and, more to the point, their anger swamps their pity, since they curse Pompey rather than petition for the release of the elephants. This would suggest that the dispositional shift was less in favor of the elephants (although there was some of that going on) and more against Pompey.[68]

---

[67] See Scobie, "Spectator Security."

[68] The closing comment about the crowd's curses against Pompey later being realized is a detail found only in Pliny's account and suggests that Pliny (or his source) was more concerned to stress the results of this spectacular failure for Pompey than he was about accurately recording either the elephants' behavior or the crowd's reaction to it. Indeed, Dio (39.39.1) reports that Pompey's spectacles (as a whole) pleased the people, but his military arrangements with Crassus displeased them; see Plut. *Pomp.* 52.4–53.1 for a similar comment; and Shelton, "Elephants, Pompey," 258–61, who posits Stoic or Epicurean philosophical considerations underpinning the crowd's reactions. All this *may* cast doubt over the historicity of the detail about the crowd being angry at Pompey but, again, this is not a key point: what matters is that the motif of the mob cursing an *editor* if they grew displeased was plausible enough to be used by Pliny; Pliny the Younger's consolatory letter to his friend at

Dio provides yet another perspective, also drawn from previous writers ("so as to give rise to the report"). As they were being killed, the elephants stopped fighting and walked about with their trunks raised, issuing piteous cries that sounded like laments. Thinking that the raised trunks showed that the animals were appealing to heaven, a rumor spread that the elephants were protesting the breaking of oaths that had been made to them when they showed reluctance to board the ships transporting them from Africa. The drivers had pledged that the elephants would suffer no harm. The content of this report is certainly consistent with Cicero's less precise comment on the crowd's pity, as well as with what we surmised above about tame animals, in that the dying elephants are thoroughly anthropomorphized. They are now portrayed as understanding human speech and the concept of justice, comprehending pledges to the point of protesting oath-breaking, and appealing to the gods for recompense. If these perceptions of the elephants' behavior were contemporary and not just embellishments added to the tale in transmission,[69] it provides a different psychological reason for the change in the crowd's attitude: the elephants had been done an injustice. Negative dispositional alignments toward the victims of retributive violence, recall, become untenable if the spectators regard the violence as excessive or unjustified. In this scenario, the violence done to the elephants was no longer justified, and so the spectators regarded their fates with pity instead of pleasure.

We have dwelt at length on this episode, since it is rich in information about spectator behaviors and outlooks that is normally lacking in elite authors' observations of arena crowd reactions. A corollary of Cicero's comment that the crowd's changed outlook on the elephants was rooted in an inchoate belief that the beasts had "something in common with the human race," is that ordinarily spectators would not feel that way about arena animals and, arguably, all or most arena victims or performers.[70] Such a sweeping dehumanization, ultimately rooted in widespread prejudices against social outcasts and outgroupers, may well have characterized the crowd's default attitude toward all those on the sand. At the same time,

---

Verona (*Ep.* 6.34) about a failed spectacle there goes out of its way to make the man feel appreciated, which implies that the crowd was displeased on the day when panthers failed to appear and made its displeasure abundantly clear.

[69] Pliny (*HN* 8.3) reports that elephants "are believed" to understand religious matters to the point of not boarding ships until their handler (*rector*) swears they will return. If such lore was widely disseminated in the first century BC, the crowd may well have conceived of the elephants' actions in the terms set out by Dio. On the religiosity of elephants as perceived by the ancients, see Coleman, *Liber Spectaculorum*, 157–8.

[70] See above, ch. 5, n. 79.

we must beware the pitfall of being overly simplistic or monolithic in our conceptions of the crowd's mental state. Whether or not the specific inferences made above about the basis for the crowd's shifting attitudinal alignments are accurate, Pliny's account is sufficient to establish that crowd reactions could shift several times even during a single event, which was itself part of a multifaceted spectacle. Dio's version provides a different basis for the spectator's change of outlook, but the basic point remains the same: here we have excellent evidence for the complexity and mutability of spectator affective dispositions as spectacles progressed. The crowd may generally have been ill-disposed toward arena performers, but that could change depending on what was going on at any given time. That all this applies to an incident involving animals makes the likelihood of affective dispositional variation during the human-centered phases of the spectacle all the greater.

Executions

There can be little doubt that execution victims were the targets of powerful prejudices in the arena (see chapter 5), and so of negative affective dispositions among the spectators. Predeveloped negative attitudes toward them derived from several sources. It would be generally assumed that the likes of captured rebels, prisoners of war, pirates, bandits, and others of that ilk were bad seeds who deserved what they were getting. When it came to individual criminals, such as murderers or arsonists, details of their crimes would have diffused from the public trials that preceded the spectacle. Just to be sure, heralds or placards on the day of execution would further "frame" the imminent spectacle by reminding the crowd of the heinous deeds that had brought the victims to their current pass. Martial, as we saw, made a suite of assumptions about the possible crimes committed by one Laureolus, whom he saw crucified and then torn to shreds by a beast in the Colosseum, although he was not particularly concerned about the accuracy of any of the charges.[71]

So in general, more so even than for the beast hunts, negative attitudes rooted in widely held prejudices and reinforced by the known specifics of criminal infractions would have been the order of the day among the spectators during executions. It is a clear sign of this fact that, whereas the crowd could call for the release of gladiators, huntsmen, and even

---

[71] Mart. *Spect.* 9. See also multiple examples of all these strategies for informing the crowd cited in ch. 5, pp. 175–81.

animal performers, there is only one recorded instance of them doing so for an execution victim, and that appears in a fable. The fate of the condemned was sealed. The harsh sentiments of the crowd are recorded in the Christian martyrologies (see chapter 5), and in the shouts and catcalls of the audience at the midday spectacle that so horrified Seneca (Sen. *Ep.* 7.5 = T.20). It is worth noting here that the crowd's attention was focused on the victims rather than on their executioners. This is consistent with what is known about the workings of affective dispositions. A negative dispositional alignment is sated by the righteous suffering of the hated party and is not necessarily twinned with a positive disposition toward the agent inflicting suffering. While it is all well and good when a movie villain is killed personally by the hero, the audience will still cheer if the villain is eaten by a monster or mangled by a machine, and the cheering will not be *for* the monster or the machine but *against* the villain. Likewise in studies of people's reactions to news reports, people negatively disposed toward real-life personalities take pleasure in their suffering at the hands of, say, a disease or some other impersonal force.[72] The arena crowd's focus on the victims of the execution represents an expression of such negative attitudinal alignments. This is obvious in cases of exposure to beasts (what spectator would really get behind the beasts?), but it applied also when victims were killed by arena personnel.[73] Roman executioners, like their counterparts in the Early Modern period, were not exactly the sorts of people the crowd could readily get behind. They were liminal figures, dealers in death and associated with pain, suffering, dirt, and dishonor. Indeed, the Latin word denoting "executioner" (*carnifex*) was used in slang to mean "villain" or "scoundrel." They did not display courage or *virtus* the way gladiators did by facing armed and trained opponents, but worked on helpless victims.[74] These considerations coupled with the direct evidence,

[72] Zillmann and Knobloch, "Emotional Reactions," 198–202.

[73] The martyrologies mention such officials as *carnifices, gladiatores, milites, ministri, stratiotai,* or *venatores*; see, e.g., *Pass. Carp. Pap. et Agathon.* A40, B4.4 (= Musurillo, *Acts of the Christian Martyrs,* 26–7, 32–3), *Pass. Perp. et Felic.* 18.9, 19.5, 21.1, 21.4, 21.9 (= Musurillo, *Acts of the Christian Martyrs,* 126–7, 128–31); *Pass. Pion.* 21.2 (= Musurillo, *Acts of the Christian Martyrs,* 162–3); *Pass. Mar. et Iacob.* 12.1 (= Musurillo, *Acts of the Christian Martyrs,* 210–11). See also Apul. *Met.* 10.34 (a soldier goes to get an execution victim).

[74] On attitudes to Early Modern executioners, see (for Germany) Evans, *Rituals,* 56–64, and K. Stuart, *Defiled Trades and Social Outcasts: Honor and Ritual Pollution in Early Modern Germany* (Cambridge, 1999), 69–93 and 149–85; and (for France), Friedland, "Beyond Deterrence," 299–303. On Roman executioners, see G. Clark, "Desires of the Hangman: Augustine on Legitimized Violence," in H. A. Drake (ed.), *Violence in Late Antiquity* (Burlington, 2006), 137–46. For the meanings of *carnifex,* see *OLD* s.v. and *TLL* 3.478.1–479.7, s.v., esp. 478.59–83 for *loci* attesting to their low status.

then, suggests that during executions the spectators were dispositionally aligned more against execution victims than with their killers.

Even during this phase, when prejudicial attitudes and negative dispositions were surely at their height, shifts in spectator sentiments were possible. Fructuosus, bishop of Tarragona, was accompanied to the amphitheater by a sympathetic crowd, though the reactions of the spectators inside the arena to his immolation are not recorded.[75] Petronius (*Sat.* 45.7–8 = T.12) has the freedman Echion note over Trimalchio's dinner that the damnation to the beasts of an adulterous household accountant (*dispensator*) would generate strife in the stands at an upcoming show, as jealous husbands debated the merits of the case with loverboys. Although a satire, there is no reason to doubt that Petronius' picture connects to known social realities. His scenario is not inherently implausible, even if the identity of the debating parties is humorously incongruous. As noted above (chapter 5, pp. XXX), doubts about the soundness of a conviction or the justice of a penalty are known to turn execution crowds against the procedure. Roman arena or execution crowds could feel the same way. They objected to Agathonike's sudden martyrdom at Pergamum.[76] We have already noted how the brutality of the punishments Nero meted out to suspected Christian arsonists in AD 64 engendered not pleasure or appreciation in the spectators, but pity for the victims, "since it was felt they were being killed not for the public good but to sate the savagery of one man."[77] Here doubts about the legitimacy and motivation of the punishment caused a shift in dispositional alignments, and so rendered the scene of suffering unenjoyable.

In a different way, the behavior of some Christians in the arena worked to undermine the spectators' enjoyment of their punishment and generated, in part, the paroxysms of crowd anger and vitriol documented in the martyrologies. The final sufferings of the martyrs Perpetua, Felicitas, and their companions are a case in point. The group entered the arena with serene and joyful expressions on their faces. They did not avert their eyes from the gaze of the spectators, but stared right back. This defiance was probably rather annoying, but not as annoying as what happened next.[78]

---

[75] *Pass. Fruct. et al.* 3.1 (= Musurillo, *Acts of the Christian Martyrs*, 178–9).

[76] *Pass. Carp. Pap. et Agathon.* A42–7 and B6 (= Musurillo, *Acts of the Christian Martyrs*, 26–9 and 34–7). As noted earlier (ch. 5, n. 73), Agathonike probably did not undergo a trial proper, but the spectators nevertheless took no pleasure in her sudden and unjustified (from their perspective) death.

[77] Tac. *Ann.* 15.44.4–5; see above, ch. 5, pp. 179–80.

[78] Pliny the Elder notes (*HN* 11.144) that gladiators who stared down a threat without blinking were reckoned unbeatable. On the defiance inherent in Perpetua's counter-gaze, see B. D. Shaw, "The Passion of Perpetua," *Past and Present* 115 (1987), 3–45, esp. 4.

The three male members of the party – Revocatus, Saturninus, and Saturus – began to threaten the mob (we are not told with what, but presumably eternal damnation). They also gesticulated in the direction of Hilarianus, the proconsul who had sentenced them to die in the arena, in such a way that it was clear they were invoking God's condemnation on him. The crowd grew very angry at this and demanded the group be scourged by a line of huntsmen. The Christians welcomed the scourging. Revocatus and Saturninus were then placed on a platform and savaged by a leopard and a bear (they apparently died, since they are not mentioned again in the text). An attempt to fix Saturus to a boar failed when the animal attacked the attendant instead, so that Saturus was only dragged about. He was then tied up on a bridge as bait for a bear, but the animal refused to come out of its cell, so Saturus was withdrawn. The crowd's reaction to all this is not recorded.

When Perpetua and Felicitas were brought out stripped naked but wrapped in netting, the crowd objected to their nakedness and to Felicitas' evident post-partum condition (she had given birth in prison). Brought back dressed, they were exposed to a mad cow. Felicitas was crushed to the ground, Perpetua tossed about. Picking herself up, Perpetua complained that her hair had been mussed and declared that she did not want to appear to be mourning her hour of triumph. She went over and helped Felicitas to her feet, and both were sent out of the arena, "since the heartlessness of the crowd had been defeated," as the text puts it. Something new would be required to finish them off. Saturus was now returned to the middle and a leopard loosed on him. As he was bathed in his own blood, the crowd yelled "Well washed!" at him. He passed out and was tossed to the side with the others, all of whom were to have their throats cut. The crowd, however, insisted that this be done in the middle, so they could see the metal entering the flesh. The martyrs voluntarily mounted a platform to die (Saturus, now conscious, was the first to go). Perpetua cried out in pain when the sword thrust of a nervous newcomer gladiator cut to the bone, but gamely guided the weapon to her own throat in the end.[79]

A comparable interplay between the martyrs' defiance and the crowd's anger and demands for intensified torments can be traced in the case

---

[79] *Pass. Perp. et Felic.* 18–21 (= Musurillo, *Acts of the Christian Martyrs*, 124–31); quote at 20.7 (= ibid. 128–9): *et populi duritia devicta*. Shaw interprets the surviving texts ("Passion of Perpetua," esp. 31–45) as exemplifying an appropriation of Perpetua's simple and honest prison diary by the male-dominated church hierarchy, and so would cast doubt on some of these details of her execution as attempts to reframe her as a typical Roman matron (concerned about her hair, etc.). In contrast, Bowersock (*Martyrdom and Rome*, 36) is convinced that the document was composed by an eyewitness.

of the martyrs of Lyons. Condemned at trial, Sanctus, Maturus, Attalus, and Blandina were brought into the arena and subjected to a standard repertoire of rough treatment: whips, exposure to beasts, and anything else the crowd demanded. (Maturus appears to have perished at this juncture, as he is not mentioned again.) Placed in an iron roasting seat, Sanctus would only repeat his confession of faith. Blandina was hung up and exposed to beasts, but none would touch her, so she was taken down. The spectators loudly demanded Attalus, and he was brought out and paraded around the arena behind a placard declaring he was a Christian. The crowd worked itself into a considerable rage against him, but when the governor heard he was a citizen, he was sent back to prison to await the emperor's decision. Despite the imperial response ordering the decapitation of citizen Christians, Attalus was brought back into the arena (apparently some time later), this time partnered with a Phrygian named Alexander, and subjected to a variety of torments. Alexander did not cry out during his ordeal, while Attalus chose instead to berate the crowd as cannibals for looking at him in the roasting seat. When they asked him to name his god, he refused to reply. Blandina was then returned to the arena, this time with a young boy named Ponticus. Attempts to make them swear by idols under torture failed, so the crowd grew angry and demanded new tortures: scourges, exposure to beasts, and grilling alive. Ponticus died, but Blandina survived to be put into a net, exposed to a bull, and tossed to death.[80]

The *Passion of Perpetua and Felicitas* has been judged a "public blood bath" that is "a difficult document to read on many levels"; the same could be said of most of the other martyrologies, and this makes it easy to dismiss spectator behavior as reflecting nothing more than simple barbarity or unvarnished sadism.[81] But they are actually much more interesting texts than that, as they suggest the psychological currents running through the experience of watching execution spectacles in the arena, and how people could take enjoyment from it. The harsh spectator reactions were sparked by the Christians welcoming their deaths or appearing indifferent to what was being done to them. We suggested above (chapter 4, pp. 133–7) that this behavior challenged the spectators' social identity as "lords" of the arena and that this was part of what frustrated and angered them. Disposition theory adds another dimension to spectator reactions. In order for negative dispositions to be sated, villains have to suffer. If they are smiling or

---

[80] Euseb. *Hist. eccl.* 5.1.17, 37–43, 50–6 (= Musurillo, *Acts of the Christian Martyrs*, 66–7, 72–5, 78–81).
[81] Shaw, "Passion of Perpetua," 10 (quote). See also Auguet, *Cruelty and Civilization*, 194–5; Grant, *Gladiators*, 113–15.

laughing or talking back to the spectators, they do not give much of an impression of suffering, and so the crowd's enjoyment of the proceedings is undermined. The logical antidote for such obstructionist behavior on the part of the condemned would be to demand more and worse torments to ensure suffering – and this is precisely the dynamic we see playing out in the martyrologies. Rather than resort to explanations that are little more than moral condemnations – understandable though such condemnations might be – we are better off appreciating the psychological bases for why the Romans derived pleasure from watching brutal violence done to others, and to recognize that these bases have been (and are) shared by people in different historical contexts.

The crowd, despite its anger and frustration at Christian behavior, nevertheless retained certain standards: it objected to Perpetua's youthful beauty and Felicitas' recent motherhood. To refine the point further, the spectators objected to these qualities of the victims being made evident by their nudity, since the executions continued once the women were brought back suitably clothed. The reason for the crowd's objection is opaque, but concern over their nakedness is not convincing. Nudity, or near nakedness, was part of the humiliation of *noxii*, and images of arena executions routinely show naked victims, sometimes female; indeed, we have just seen how Blandina was covered with netting during her final ordeal in Lyons, and so was presumably otherwise naked, and there the crowd offered no objection.[82] It has been suggested that religious scruple or concern over a crude affront to motherhood were involved in moving the spectators at Perpetua's and Felicitas' martyrdom to object as they did.[83] But the crowd may have objected on this occasion because the youth of Perpetua and the recent motherhood of Felicitas broke through the fog of dehumanization that ordinarily hung about execution victims, and so undermined their status as outgroupers and, along with it, the negative dispositions of the spectators toward them. Enjoyment in the spectacle was threatened. Covering them up readmitted the possibility of taking enjoyment from their fates. Of course, we cannot be certain about the root of the crowd's objection, but its mere manifestation is another example of sudden shifts in attitudes among arena spectators to what they were watching.

A classic fable offers another vivid example. The story of Androcles (or Androclus) and the lion is told by the Antonine writers Aelian (*NA* 7.48)

---

[82] Images:, e.g., Shaw, "Passion of Perpetua," 8; Vismara, *Supplizio*, 42–60. Blandina: Euseb. *Hist. eccl.* 5.1.56 (= Musurillo, *Acts of the Christian Martyrs*, 78–81).

[83] J. E. Salisbury, *Perpetua's Passion: The Death and Memory of a Young Roman Woman* (London, 1997), 142–3; Shaw, "Passion of Perpetua," 8–9.

and Aulus Gellius (*NA* 5.14). The latter's version is the more famous and is expressly stated (*NA* 5.14.1–6) to have derived from a now-lost book on Egyptian wonders by Apion, the son of Posidonius and resident of Alexandria, who lived and wrote in the Julio-Claudian era. Even more remarkably, Gellius reports that Apion claims to have witnessed the events described personally, possibly during his visit to Rome as part of the Greek delegation to Gaius Caligula in AD 39–40, which is described in detail from the Jewish side in Philo's *Legatio ad Gaium*.[84] In all likelihood, however, the story is pure fiction. It finds echo in other ancient tales about friendly lions (Pliny *HN* 8.56–8, Sen. *Ben.* 2.19.1), and in some carved gems from Egypt.[85] Nevertheless, fictional material can transmit much sociocultural information, whether about general expectations of what was typical or illuminating specifics added as "color" to lend a story or anecdote an air of authenticity.[86] There is no reason to doubt, then, the validity of arena-related details reported in this story, many of which can be corroborated from other sources in any case.

Apion, according to Gellius, starts his tale in the Circus Maximus, where he had gone to see a *venatio*. "Many savage wild animals were there, exceedingly large beasts, and all of them strange in appearance and uncommon in their ferocity."[87] Especially remarkable was a vast lion, which drew all the eyes in the crowd. Among those condemned to fight the beasts was one Androclus, the slave of an ex-consul. Yet this huge lion approached Androclus slowly, wagged its tail, and began licking his hands and feet. Androclus, who had turned away from the fearsome animal in terror, looked at the lion, and the two seemed to recognize each other. The people, astonished, broke into shouts. Gaius Caligula, who was presiding over the spectacle, called Androclus over to explain himself. The slave related a strange and marvelous story. The cruelty of his master, the proconsul of Africa, had forced Androclus to flee into the desert. There he had hidden

---

[84] See Jos. *AJ* 18.257–60; cf. Philo *Leg.* 349–72. Note that Philo makes no mention of Apion.

[85] Fable: G. Anderson, "Aulus Gellius as Storyteller," in L. Holford-Strevens (ed.), *The Worlds of Aulus Gellius* (Oxford, 2004), 105–17, esp. 112–13; K. Ranke, "Androklus und der Löwe," in K. Ranke (ed.), *Enzyklopädie des Märchens: Handwörterbuch zur historischen und vergleichenden Erzählforschung*, 12 vols. (Berlin, 1977–present), vol. 1, 501–8 (my thanks to Joe Howley for these references). Gems: C. Bonner, "Eros and the Wounded Lion," *AJA* 49 (1945), 441–4. The relationship of the various accounts to one another – did Aelian rely on Gellius for his account, or did both rely on Apion independently? – remains a matter of considerable uncertainty. That the story was a fable makes it possible that none of the surviving accounts relied on any of the others.

[86] See, e.g., ch. 1, n. 52, and ch. 5, n. 63. See also R. P. Saller, "Anecdotes as Historical Evidence for the Principate," *Greece and Rome* 27 (1980), 69–83.

[87] Gell. *NA* 5.14.7: *multae ibi saevientes ferae, magnitudines bestiarum excellentes omniumque invisitata aut forma erat aut ferocia.*

in a remote cave, only to discover that it was a lion's lair. On entering, the lion approached the terrified Androclus meekly and extended its paw. Androclus saw a large splinter embedded there, extracted it, and treated the wound. Lion and man then shared the cave for three years. When his hair had grown too long and became itchy, Androclus left the cave, was captured, and sent back to his master in Rome, who condemned him to the beasts. The lion was evidently captured too, and now the two had been reunited in the *venatio*. Caligula had the tale relayed to the spectators via placards and, "with everyone demanding it" (*cunctis petentibus*), both lion and man were released (*dimissum*). Apion, via Gellius, adds a postscript: the lion was given to Androclus "by vote of the people" (*suffragiis populi*) and the two were frequently seen about town, where passers-by showered them with money and flowers and were wont to declare: "This is the lion that was host to a man, this the man that was doctor to a lion."

Several points are worth noting. The stated characteristics of the beasts in the spectacle evidently represent a sort of wish list that illustrates spectator expectations and can be corroborated from other sources.[88] Size, exoticness, and ferocity were all key desirables. Androclus is not in that class of execution victim bound and exposed to beasts, but rather he was expected to fight the animals, apparently barehanded.[89] The astonishment of the crowd was not evinced by the sight of the ferocious lion failing to attack and kill Anroclus, but rather by its being gentle with him. This is clear from the lack of similar astonishment recorded in cases where animals simply refused to attack, such as those of Saturus or Blandina just reviewed. The amazement, then, must have come from the lion's unforeseen tenderness, which elicited the same sort of spectator response as exhibitions of tame animals in the arena. As we saw above, the key here was the reversal of spectator expectations of what constituted the "normal" behavior of feral beasts, and may be read as further corroboration of the crowd's usually negative disposition toward both the animals and their victims: animals should attack, vicitms should die. The use of placards to convey information to the crowd is confirmed by other sources, as is the interaction of emperor and people at the games.[90] The idea that the people voted to give

---

[88] See above, ch. 4, pp. 125–32.

[89] Gell. *NA* 5.14.10: "Among many others consigned to fight beasts was brought in a slave [Androclus]" (*introductus erat intra compluris ceteros ad pugnam bestiarum datos servus*). See also Ville, *Gladiature*, 235–40. The briefer notice in Seneca (*Ben.* 2.19.1) goes further and identifies the human character as a *bestiarius*, who was protected from the other beasts by a lion, whose handler (*magister*) the huntsman had formerly been. In this detail, Seneca's story more closely echoes Aelian's version (see below) than Gellius'.

[90] See above, ch. 5, pp. 180–1. On emperor and people at the games, see ch. 1, p. 18.

the lion to Androclus is a neat evocation of the games as a replacement for popular participation in governance.[91] Nothing in Gellius' portrayal of arena protocol or of the crowd's behavior is outlandish or implausible, despite the main content of the fable being both.

Finally, when Gellius' version is put alongside Aelian's more prosaic account, the sort of detail Gellius (or Apion) added to "beef up" the fable comes into high relief, as do some interesting divergences in the arena scene. Most of the omissions or divergences are irrelevant to our current purposes,[92] but some are illuminating. Androcles (as the hero is named in the Greek version) and the lion are released into the arena alone, so the fearsome and exotic menagerie of Gellius' version is absent. When man and lion are reconciled, the crowd's reaction is not astonishment and curiosity, but suspicion and vindictiveness: Androcles is judged a sorcerer (by whom is not specified, but "all present" is as good a guess as any) and a leopard is sent in to finish him off. The lion protects Androcles by ripping the leopard to shreds. Only at this juncture is the crowd dumbfounded. Thus, Greco-Roman writers like Gellius and Aelian, not to mention their readers, who doubtless had first-hand experience of arena conditions, found either of these two reactions – astonishment or vindictiveness – plausible for spectators at the games when their expectations were confounded. This alone attests to the variegated dispositions and emotional unpredictability of the crowd. The *editor* of Aelian's games, although they take place at Rome, is not the emperor but just "the one giving the games." In Aelian, the details of Androcles' story spread through the crowd, and there is no mention of placards. And Aelian's tale ends not with Androcles and the lion shopping in Rome, but with a restatement of the passage's main theme: memory is a feature of animal behavior. The fable of Androcles and the lion thus provides useful information about spectator outlooks during the execution phase of arena spectacles.

Gladiatorial combats

The bases for spectator dispositional alignments for or against gladiators is more opaque. We have already noted the favoritism of some spectators for

---

[91] See, e.g., Juv. 10.77–81; Fronto *Princ. Hist.* 17 = T.8; Gunderson, "Ideology"; Hopkins, *Death and Renewal*, 14–20.

[92] E.g., Aelian's story is framed as an example of animal memory; the story is told in chronological order, rather than beginning with the *venatio*; Androcles is a senator's slave, not a proconsul's; Androcles cooks his food in the lion's cave, rather than drying it out (as Androclus does in the Apion-Gellius version); etc.

particular types of gladiator: the *parmularii*, who supported "Thracians," and the *scutarii*, who backed *murmillones*, but we have also seen that these categories of enthusiast are poorly attested, and that the intensity of their support was attenuated in comparison to the fanatical partisanship elicited by circus factions, actors, or pantomimes.[93] It seems, rather, that spectators usually got behind fighters as individuals, as stand-alone "heroes of the arena."[94] But how so? Why one gladiator, and not another? Affective dispositions were undoubtedly at work here also, but it remains unclear on what basis. There is no evidence, for instance, that gladiators adopted "good guy" or "bad guy" personae in the manner of modern professional wrestlers, who frame their bouts in such a way as to assist in disposition formation among spectators.

Presumably, success bred popularity and garnered a following. It is arguable, then, that a form of narrative structure surrounded the contests and was put in place by arena programs and advertisements, which informed spectators about the identities and track records of the scheduled fighters in advance. The inclusion of this same information as "career stats" in gladiatorial epitaphs underscores the importance of consistent performance to the gladiators' sense of their own worth.[95] The spectators shared this sense, since they judged appeals on the basis of performance. So it is not hard to imagine dramatic narratives emerging from this focus on ongoing reputations, as suggested above for the newcomer Attilius (chapter 6, pp. 223–4). Trimalchio proudly boasts, "I have the fights of Hermeros and Petraites on goblets," possibly in reference to a widely celebrated rivalry.[96] Such a milieu allows for repeat bouts and "grudge" matches, as the fame of ongoing rivalries spread.

Nevertheless, the true heroes can have been few and far between, and we cannot accurately judge from the scattered data how often spectators would

---

[93] See above, ch. 6, pp. 219–21. The non-record of arena riots is enough to demonstrate that gladiator fandom lacked the sort of intensity of the theater or circus. See above, ch. 4, pp. 147–54, for some suggestions as to why this was so.

[94] See, e.g., Barton, *Sorrows*, 11–81; Edwards, *Death*, 68–75; Hopkins, *Death and Renewal*, 20–7; Junkelmann, "*Familia Gladiatoria*"; Ville, *Gladiature*, 334–9.

[95] Carter, "Rules of Engagement," 106–12; Hope, "Fighting for Identity."

[96] Petron. *Sat.* 52.3: *nam Hermerotis pugnas et Petraitis in poculis habeo.* See the comments of H. T. Rowell, "The Gladiator Petraites and the Date of the Satyricon," *TAPA* 89 (1958), 12–24 (who suggests on the basis of comparanda that the two celebrated gladiators did not necessarily meet in combat, a proposition the wording allows: "the fights of Hermeros *and* Petraites" rather than "the fights of Hermeros *against* Petraites"); see also M. S. Smith, *Petronius: Cena Trimalchionis* (Oxford, 1975), 139–40. It is possible that depictions of gladiatorial pairings in mosaics, reliefs, or terracotta media refer to ongoing rivalries, especially when the combatants are named (see, e.g., the Madrid mosaic, above, ch. 4, p. 138).

get to see their favorites in action. So what about the less exalted contestants? Why did people get behind them? The symbolic role of gladiators as living exemplars of cherished Roman virtues – courage, endurance, discipline and martial skill, lust for glory, and the desire to win – may have played a part in aligning members of the crowd behind certain individuals (although not within a representational model), even when the real stars were not on show. The educational character of watching gladiator fights has been discussed above,[97] but it seems possible that this view is more of an upper-class intellectual rationalization of arena brutality than a widely felt popular sentiment. And even the symbolism of the gladiator's working through pain and the risk of death to strive for victory was no more likely to be cognitively acknowledged by the Roman arena spectator than is the military symbolism of modern sporting contests by the average sports fan. Neither take their seats for a cultural education.

So the basis for affective disposition formation remains moot in cases, surely not uncommon, where spectators backed gladiators who were little known, or even altogether unknown to them (as would be the case with a newcomer, for instance). A different perspective on the complicity of audiences and the perpetrators of violence offers useful avenues of approach to this question. A microsociology of violence has been proposed by the sociologist Randall Collins and it runs as follows.[98] In social interactions of any sort, human beings are keenly attuned to the emotional cues given off by other people. The natural tendency is for people to seek solidarity with others in a given situation, by synchronizing with their emotional cues and thereby enhancing the situation's "emotional energy."[99] By attuning to the emotional and physical cues of their fellows, a process called "entrainment," people feel comfortable in the presence of others. In contrast, violent encounters (of whatever type) are inherently uncomfortable and marked by an emotional field of tension and fear, since people in confrontations seek to impose themselves as dominant over the situation which, by its very nature, requires them to ignore the emotional cues of others, or worse, to

---

[97] See, esp., Wiedemann, *Emperors and Gladiators*, 1–54; Wistrand, *Entertainment and Violence*, 15–29; and above, ch. 6, pp. 200–1.

[98] For what follows, see Collins, *Violence*, esp. 1–82. There are deeper theoretical layers to Collins' arguments, but I focus here on those core propositions that are most relevant to the present study.

[99] "Emotional energy" (EE) is not some vague New-Agey concept but a description of the interactional dynamics of a situation. As Collins (*Violence*, 19) explains it, "EE varies with the degree that the people present [in the situation] become entrained in each other's emotions and bodily rhythms, and caught up in a common focus of attention . . . In these successful interaction rituals, individuals come away with feelings of strength, confidence, and enthusiasm for whatever the group was doing: these feelings are what I call emotional energy."

seek to turn those cues against them, as when a mugger exploits the evident fear of his victim by intensifying his aggression. As a result, people generally try to avoid violent conflicts. This is clear from the fact that most people are not violent and live their lives peaceably. Even those deemed very violent – such as serial killers, muggers, or paid assassins – are not violent all or even most of the time, but only in short bursts. Violent encounters are therefore usually brief, confined to a single punch, slash, or shot, and are more often a matter of bluster and bravado than the infliction of real violence, since the parties to a violent encounter try first and foremost to extricate themselves from it.[100]

When real violence does occur, people are largely incompetent at it, flailing about ineffectually in a one-on-one fight, for instance, or firing wildly (or not at all) in military combat. This incompetence is generated by the tension/fear inherent in the conflict situation itself. Violence, then, can be defined simply as "a set of pathways around confrontational tension and fear,"[101] in that it can occur only when these emotional barriers have been overcome. The two primary pathways around tension/fear are, first, attacking the weak and, second, setting limits on the violent encounter by, for instance, staging fights with rules.[102] Although the violence of a staged fight still can be extreme, even lethal (think of Ultimate Fighting or duels), tension/fear is reduced in such encounters on two levels. First, the combatants are in solidarity ("mutually entrained") by agreeing on the rules. The most comprehensive manifestation of rule-agreement is to undertake training in fighting clubs (such as martial arts, boxing, or fencing schools) and to pay careful attention to the etiquette of the staged confrontation (i.e., the rules in duels, or the many formal procedures in martial arts). Confrontational tension/fear is absorbed by directing focus on to the rituals surrounding the fight – when to start and when to stop, what types of blows or moves are permitted and which are not, and so on. It is an added bonus that fighters so trained conceive of themselves as an elite, and are often widely perceived by outsiders as a caste apart from the ordinary mortal, who typically comprises the staged fighters' audience.[103]

---

[100] The macrosociological elements of violence (social conditions, violence-promoting ideologies or institutions, gender) have their role to play in all this too, but Collins' focus is on the interactional dynamics of violence as a process that plays out in real time, which constitutes the "microsociological" perspective.

[101] Collins, *Violence*, 8.

[102] Under "staged fights" Collins groups a wide variety of confrontations, from duels, to boxing matches, to schoolyard fights, to spontaneous brawls that attract even a small group of watchers (but in which "unfair" moves are widely recognized). Naturally, fights staged as organized spectacles also fall under this category.

[103] Collins, *Violence*, 207–11 (on fighting clubs).

The presence of an audience, in fact, constitutes the second main way confrontational tension/fear is reduced in staged fights, since spectators offer emotional support and encouragement to the fighters. Indeed, spectators can often determine the contours of the contest, enforce rules, curtail cheaters, and even intervene to stop a fight if the rules are flouted.[104] Data show that the degree of audience attention to and support of a fight correlates with its duration and intensity: the more enthusiastic the spectators, the longer and harder the fighters will contend; if no audience assembles or spectators are apathetic, the fight can be curbed or even aborted altogether as the fighters descend into shows of bluster and shouting insults while trying to exit the situation and save face. The audience that shows up to a pre-arranged fight is a self-selected group, and so most likely to be very enthusiastic and supportive. The fights they witness will tend to be correspondingly long and intense.[105] Crowds at large-scale fighting spectacles will be of this type, and while such spectacles fall under the category of "staged fights" rather than "sports" in this analysis, there is one feature of sports crowds that requires mention here. Large crowds at mass sports events are emotionally synchronized (or "entrained"), both with each other and with the athletes they are watching. They feel a powerful sense of solidarity with each other, focused as they are on their heroes' struggle to overcome obstacles and achieve victory. From the sociological perspective, this is what lends these occasions their emotional power to draw huge crowds.

The microsociology of violent confrontations offers a different and illuminating point of view on the complicity of performer and spectator in violent spectacles, particularly staged fights. Fighter and audience are attuned to each other, and the one feeds the other. The more keenly the spectators focus on the fighters and the more they voice their support and encouragement, the more the confrontational tension/fear inherent in the fight is reduced. This may result in an increase in fighting competence (or at least, it ought to inhibit incompetence), but it is very likely to intensify and prolong the bout. These circumstances excite the spectators still further and make them keener in their expressions of support, which in turn influences the course of the fight. The emotional field strengthens itself in a feedback loop.

---

[104] Collins contends (*Violence*, 206–7) that breaking the agreed-upon rules of a staged fight allows confrontational tension/fear to creep back in and, with it, incompetent violence. An audience will not linger to watch incompetents brawl.

[105] Collins, *Violence*, 193–241, esp. 198–207 and 229–37 (on spectators and fights).

This line of analysis prompts several suggestions about spectator involvement in gladiatorial bouts. Before proceeding, a caveat. To be fully and properly applied to a pairing, we would need to chart the course of a fight in detail, as a process taking place in real time. How did gladiators approach each other? How did they set up? Where did the umpires stand and with what signal did they start the fight? What moves were typical and what rules bounded those moves? At what point did the fight stop? Did the rules change over time or vary across the empire?[106] For the most part, we cannot answer these questions or, to put it more accurately, we can only offer partial answers.[107] The following details are ascertainable from the evidence: there were two umpires; there was a signal to start (*signum pugnae*), accompanied by trumpet blasts; there may have been an opportunity for the fighters to taunt each other; weaker fighters who fled were forced to fight with whip, torch, and hot irons (the media mentioned in the fearsome gladiatorial oath); and the fight ended in the ways we surveyed above.[108] The fullest account of a gladiatorial bout comes from an exercise composed by a professional teacher of rhetoric (or one of his students) and ascribed, wrongly, to Quintilian.[109] In this instance, the speaker

---

[106] See, by way of comparison, Collins' treatment of duels, ibid., 212–20. See also K. McAleer, *Dueling: The Cult of Honor in Fin-de-Siècle Germany* (Princeton, 1994), esp. 43–84.

[107] Such is the dearth of evidence that Georges Ville (*Gladiature*, 408–9) could fill a mere $1\frac{1}{2}$ of 472 printed pages on the topic "the fight up to the request for *missio*" (their contents are summarized in what follows). See also Carter, "Rules of Engagement"; Junkelmann, *Gladiatoren*, 129–69; and Tuck, "*De Arte Gladiatoria*", for imaginative attempts to reconstruct the course of gladiatorial bouts.

[108] Two umpires: above, ch. 6, n. 15. *Signum pugnae*: Sen. *Ep.* 117.25. Taunting: Festus, 285M = 358L (though note that this is a *retiarius* talking, and he was unique in not wearing a helmet); Lucil. 4.155–60K = 4.153–8M = Cic. *Tusc.* 4.48 = T.10. Fleeing: *CIL* 4.2351, 4.5214, Petron. *Sat.* 45.11–12 = T.12, and on the oath, see above, ch. 4, n. 74. Outcomes: above, ch. 6, pp. 222–3. Note also the Zliten scene of the umpire restraining a victorious gladiator; see above, ch. 6, n. 15. We do get some hints as to other matters. Cic. (*De Orat.* 2.325) notes that the gladiators called Samnites, during the *prolusio* (warm up), would brandish spears they would not be using in the fight itself – pure showmanship.

[109] These are termed *controversiae* and challenged the aspiring orator with some fictional situation he had to write a speech about; see Seneca the Elder's eponymous collecton of *controversiae*; on the genre, see, e.g., W. L. Clarke, *Rhetoric at Rome: A Historical Survey*, rev. edn. by D. H. Berry (London, 1996), esp. 85–99. In this case, labelled *Declamatio Maior IX*, the exercise lays out a situation as follows: a poor man and rich man are enemies, but their sons are friends. The rich man's son is captured by pirates and sold as a gladiator, but since the rich father is slow in paying the ransom, the poor son sets off to find his friend. He finds him about to enter the arena and fight. The poor son approaches the *editor* of the games to take the rich son's place on the condition that the rich son is to support the poor father, if he needs it. The poor son is then killed in the fight. The rich son returns home and starts supporting the poor father, at which point his own (rich) father disowns him, and so disinherits him and cuts him off from support. The rich son brings suit to contest his father's decision, and the exercise is the speech for this case. The relevant passage is [Quint.] *Decl.* 9.5–9 = T.17. For text of and commentary on this work, see G. Krapinger, *[Quintilian] Der Gladiator (Größere Deklamation, 9)* (Cassino, 2007).

enters the arena in the procession (*pompa*) to find the spectators assembled and ready. The *editor* (dubbed here *dominus*, thereafter *munerarius*) takes his seat. The speaker imagines that, since his status as a rich freeman is unknown to anyone present, the mismatch of his fight would earn him pity with *some* of the crowd (*apud quosdam*).[110] Instruments of death and suffering are everywhere being prepared – swords sharpened, metal plates heated, scourges and whips readied. Trumpets blast, stretchers are brought in and then . . . the account gets vague. "Everywhere were wounds, groans, gore; the totality of my peril lay before my eyes" ([Quint.] *Decl.* 9.6 = T.17). The speaker goes off on a digression about his immense fear, laments his lost social status, and resigns himself to await his turn with the "bloody butcher" (*cruentum illum confectorem*). His death is assured, since "even the bravest among us, it seemed, was killed" (ibid., 9.7). These lines may suggest that a spectacle *sine missione* was underway, since the speaker appears to know about the handiwork of his opponent before his turn on the sand comes around; alternatively, he could be expressing such a lack of confidence in his own fighting abilities that he sees no way he can win against any experienced opponent.

At this crucial juncture the speaker's friend, a poor man's son, shows up, presents himself to the games' sponsor, and substitutes himself for the speaker on the sand, who now becomes a spectator. There is much by way of rhetorical flourish as the speaker holds forth on the selfless act of his friend and much drama as he attempts to talk his poor friend down. Of course he fails, and the speaker gives his armor to his friend, who joins the already announced pairing (*destinatum par*). At this point, the poor man begs his friend to support his poor father, the rich man kisses him through his helmet (which tells us that he is not a *retiarius*), the attendants (*ministri*) scatter, and "Mars was allowed." This may be the official formula indicating that a fight could begin. There follows an instructive passage, as the speaker watches (from where?) his friend fight a veteran gladiator.

How anxious I was looking on! How terrified was my heart! How I matched his body's movements! How many times did I duck the hostile blade, as if I were its target! How many times did I raise myself up to his thrusts! Wretched imagination! The cruel nature of fear! Justifiably, my friend, did you prefer to fight. It's a real crime that that courageous fervor had not joined the army and served in military combat, where real courage is not curtailed[111] by any rules of fighting. With what force did he charge in, angry as if his adversary were still mine! But his every attack

---

[110] Judging from the harsh attitudes of Cicero (see below, n. 129) toward weak gladiators, this hope appears misplaced.

[111] The reading here is uncertain.

was deftly parried by the guile of the veteran gladiator, all his thrusts turned back on himself. Still, he'd have had no difficulty securing release, especially under the terms of his contract, but he did not want to live as a gladiator. Therefore, now offering his bared body to his opponent's blows so that he might pay the entire ransom for me at one go, he died still standing (*stans periit*).[112]

The peculiarly close connection between this particular gladiator and this specific spectator would seem to caution against generalizing too much from the passage. But it is one of the fullest ancient accounts we possess of spectator behavior during a gladiatorial bout, and the context of the work offers good reason to be optimistic about its value as historical evidence. In composing an oratorical exercise pertaining to a wholly fictional and contrived situation, the writer would necessarily need to appeal to the general experiences and expectations of his audience in order to render his words vivid and effective. We can assume that, as members of the educated elite, author and audience alike were personally familiar with the experience of watching gladiatorial fights. It would therefore be very much in the author's interest to impress his listeners with his ability to capture, even if in stylized rhetorical language, what that experience was like by accurately evoking the spectator's emotional involvement. For this reason, it is reasonable to interpret the passage as capturing something of the "typical" in spectator behavior.

While the mass of spectators is absent from the account, the speaker represents that mass in the tension and excitement of his own watching, here expressed as a series of exclamations in the opening lines. The speaker's focus is on the successive moves of the fight, as keen anticipation of possible outcomes shapes his mental and physical reactions. Will this thrust hit home, that blow land? He twists and ducks and dives in time with the fighters' movements. The speaker is, of course, linked closely to one of the combatants, but we can read in this an exaggerated expression of what rooting for a favorite fighter was like. Imitative movements mirrored those of the favored fighter. The comment that he raised himself up "to his thrusts" (*ad conatus*) is noteworthy but ambiguous.[113] Does it mean that

---

[112] [Quint.] Decl. 9.9 = T.17.
[113] It finds echo in Prudentius (*C. Symm.* 2.1096 = T. 16) that the Vestal Virgin at the arena "jumps to her feet at the wounds" (*consurgit ad ictus*). See also sources cited above, ch. 6, n. 99. Note [Caes.] *B Afr.* 71.1 for the sorts of movements with which a *lanista* trains a tiro gladiator: how to approach and retreat, or to turn to face an opponent in a compact one. The lithe movements of gladiators may be alluded to in a newly published epigram from Caria, in which a deceased fighter laments how his opponent Achilles "killed me, Droseron, with newfangled dances of Fate" (ἔκτανέ με Δρόσερον καινοῖς ὀρχήμασι μοίρης); Achilles, apparently, had previously been a stage performer, perhaps a pantomime, so the comment may also be a sneer at his first choice of a career;

the speaker jumped up in support when his friend made a thrust, or that he stood erect, in imitation of his friend, to avoid the opponent's blows? The latter interpretation is perhaps to be favored, since we know that a crouch was the habitual combat stance of the gladiator, as it is depicted in many images of gladiators (and one of a legionary) prepared to fight. The crouch reduced the target area presented to an opponent and, for those carrying larger shields, afforded protection to most of the body; it also tensed the leg muscles in readiness to move forward.[114] By quickly standing upright, perhaps coupled with a move to the side, a thrust could be adroitly evaded from such a stance. The contrast drawn in the passage between gladiatorial fighting and regular military combat is curious, since some Roman armies are known to have been trained in the gladiatorial style.[115] But the basis for the contrast here lies not in matters of technique but in the latitude afforded by each context for displays of courage (*virtus*), which is said to be curtailed by the "law of fighting" (*lex pugnandi*). Given that a convincing display of *virtus* is precisely what would keep a gladiator alive if he lost and appealed, the contrast is little more than a rhetorical flourish and not much ought to be read into it. That the veteran gladiator uses cunning (*astus*) not only to parry the fierce assaults of his novice opponent but to turn them against him is particularly noteworthy, as this is a skill advocated in many forms of contemporary staged fighting, such as wrestling, boxing, or martial arts. The speaker's friend is apparently fighting well, since he is angry (*iratus*) and aggressive: Lucilius has the star gladiator Pacideianus declare his hatred for and anger toward an opponent, which were apparently seen as advantageous qualities in a combatant.[116] This is why he muses that his friend could easily have secured *missio*, especially under the terms of his volunteer contract (*auctoramentum*) with the games' sponsor. The stipulations of his contract are nowhere given, but it seems clear that he was expected to fight in more than this one encounter, since "he did not want to live as a gladiator" (*sed noluit gladiator vivere*).[117]

---

see C. P. Jones, "Gladiator Epigrams from Beroea and Stratonikeia (Caria)," *ZPE* 163 (2007), 45–8; G. Staab, "Zu den neuen Gladiatorenmonumenten aus Stratonikeia in Karien," *ZPE* 161 (2007), 35–44.

[114] See numerous examples in Augenti, *Spettacoli del Colosseo*, esp. 76 (no. 39), 85 (no. 47), 86–7 (no. 48), 90 (no. 50), 104 (no. 60); Junkelmann, "*Familia Gladiatoria*," and Junkelmann, *Gladiatoren*, esp. 129–69, where the bent forward knee captures the combat crouch. For the legionary relief (from Mainz, Germany), see A. Goldsworthy, *The Complete Roman Army* (London, 2003), 175.

[115] See above, n. 113; Wiedemann, *Emperors and Gladiators*, 7 and 39.

[116] Lucil. 4.155–60K = 4.153–8M = Cic. *Tusc.* 4.48 = T.10. In contrast, note Sen. *Dial.* 3.11.1, where anger renders a gladiator unprotected.

[117] See also the speaker's later comments at 9.22 about his friend chosing death over the ignominy of life in the *ludus*. For an example of a one-fight contract, see Luc. *Tox.* 57–60.

The final comment, that he died standing, is both a play on the term for a drawn match (*stantes missi*) and an indication that there was a hierarchy of honor in how one perished on the sand. At the lowest end was having one's throat cut with the rest of the ensemble following a poor showing all around, next came voluntary offering of the neck after a failed appeal, and, best of all, dying upright in the course of combat.[118]

The find in 1993 of a gladiators' graveyard in Ephesus has brought to light sixty-eight individuals aged twenty to thirty, all but one of them male. All the male skeletons showed signs of being well-fed, and in general did not exhibit multiple perimortal injuries, in contrast to, say, Medieval battle victims. This would seem to reflect the rule-bound nature of the combats, whereby certain types of blow were allowed, others proscribed. These were not all-in free-for-alls. Twenty-one individuals had suffered a total of twenty-six head injuries; eleven of the victims had survived the trauma ("antemortem trauma"), and five of those had suffered multiple head injuries, apparently on different occasions. Seven of the sixteen ante-mortem head injuries were caused by blunt force, possibly the result of the gladiator's own helmet being driven on to his head by a blow. The high proportion of healed cut or puncture head injuries caused by sharp weapons (9/16) is suprising, given that most gladiators fought in helmets. Furthermore, most of the antemortem injuries (11/16) were to the frontal zone of the skull, which reflects the face-to-face nature of the fights and perhaps suggests that a head wound inflicted early in a bout would cause the combat to end, the injured party then being spared to heal. Peri-mortem (lethal) injuries, in contrast, were mostly to the parietal regions of the skull (8/10) – likely killing blows administered by the victor or the hammer-wielding arena attendant in the garb of Dis Pater, who finished off hopeless cases. Three of the individuals had suffered penetrating trident blows to the head, one of them lethal. This physical evidence thus goes a long way to confirming and supplementing written accounts of gladiator

---

[118] Throat cut: Petron *Sat.* 45.12 = T.12, Suet. *Iul.* 26.3, *Claud.* 21.6, Tac. *Ann.* 12.56.5. Voluntary offering of neck: Cic. *Tusc.* 2.41 = T.5, *Mil.* 31, *Sest.* 80, Plut. *Cic.* 48.5, Sen. *Dial.* 9.11.5, *Ep.* 30.8. Dying upright: Sen. *Ep.* 37.2. Dying on one's feet obviated the ignominy of taking a fall, appealing, and awaiting the uncertain judgment of the spectators and sponsor. The man killed outright died, in this sense, unbowed, as Seneca (*Ep.* 37.2) suggests in an analogy drawn from the arena: "You must die upright and unbeaten" (*recto tibi invictoque moriendum est*). All four outcomes – victory, death, release, or draw – are recorded in gladiatorial epitaphs; see Hope, "Fighting for Identity." Draws seem to have been rare. Martial (*Spect.* 31 and Coleman, *Liber Spectaculorum*, ad loc.) notes a remarkable incident where two gladiators fought to a standstill while the crowd clamored for release (apparently *stantes missi*, though that is not expressly stated); the emperor awarded both men victory and their freedom – the sponsor again exceeding the demands of the crowd. See further, Robert, *Gladiateurs*, 258–61; Ville, *Gladiature*, 408–25.

bouts, sketchy though they are, but the high proportion of head wounds, both lethal and non-lethal, requires explanation, especially since three were caused by tridents, and so were likely inflicted by *retiarii* on their normally helmeted opponents.[119]

Instructive though all this evidence is, it is still not detailed enough to be used in a "fight-as-process" microsociological analysis. The precise movements of the bout remain, at best, shadowy.[120] We are left to fall back on some general observations. Staged fights, recall, reduce tension/fear by being rule bound and consequently directing the combatants' focus on to fight rituals and etiquette, and by taking place in the presence of an audience. Gladiatorial fights had rules that were enforced by umpires in the arena. That the fights were surrounded by ritual – from the *signum pugnae* to the appeal by finger – and also by etiquette is also clear, even if the details remain obscure. The addition of a self-selected and eager audience to these circumstances means that confrontational tension/fear in this kind of staged fight was reduced on both levels simultaneously. The tendency would therefore be that, despite the extreme danger inherent in the contest, when two experienced, skilled, or willing gladiators came to blows in front of "their public," the fight would be both protracted and intense.[121] That is what the crowd had come to see. That is what they expected.[122]

Collins argues that staged fights, going all the way back to the *Iliad*, pit socially equal "heroes" against each other before an audience of peers or social inferiors.[123] At the arena the precise opposite held true: despised

---

[119] F. Kanz and K. Grossschmidt, "Head Injuries of Roman Gladiators," *Forensic Science International* 160 (2006), 207–16. In the case of antemortem puncture wounds to the frontal regions, it is possible that a javelin, or strong trident- or sword-thrust penetrated the helmet. The perimortem parietal wounds may be the result of killing blows after a failed appeal. The five antemortem cut wounds are harder to explain, unless they were not incurred in formal bouts and were perhaps unconnected to the gladiatorial lifestyle entirely (people can cut their heads in lots of ways, after all).

[120] Even Edwards' (*Death*, 55–9) valiant attempt to model a structure for gladiatorial bouts is necessarily painted in the broadest of brush strokes.

[121] It is important to stress that this constitutes a *general tendency* and not a description of all gladiatorial pairings fought all over the empire for centuries, since any number of variables could derail the ideal confrontation, and much depended on the means of the *editor* and the sort of show being put on. The inclusion of untrained and terrified POWs or convicts, for instance, would have produced a different sort of fight profile to that of professionally trained gladiators; see, e.g., Phil. *VA* 4.22 = T.13 for an exhibition of criminals fighting each other (a form of execution) in Athens. Collins' own data (*Violence*, 203–4, tables 6.1, 6.2) show that a cheering audience does not inevitably help stimulate a serious fight; even a slight reduction in cheering, let alone neutral spectators, can have a limiting effect on the course of a contest.

[122] Petron. *Sat.* 45.11–12 = T.12. Suetonius (*Iul.* 26.3) notes that whenever gladiators fought "when the spectators were hostile" (*infestis spectatoribus*), Caesar would save them for himself. The crowd was not reserved in voicing its disapproval of a poor show, and the implication here is that the disappointing performers were all killed, as Petronius states.

[123] Collins, *Violence*, 193–8.

outcasts fought before an audience of social superiors. That said, gladiators could lay claim to the sort of elite status that accrues to those who join and train in fighting clubs. While little can be said about what went on inside the gladiatorial school (*ludus*) due to lack of evidence, few would contest that residence in a *ludus* represents one of the most extreme examples of fighting club memberships in world history.[124] Thus, despite being drawn from the dregs of Roman society to join one of its most despised outgroups, the gladiator was also an admirable figure who could prompt a kind of hero-worship. This paradox – what Georges Ville dubbed "the ambivalence of the gladiator" – has been noted by many commentators, ancient and modern alike, and has usually been explained in terms of the debased gladiator symbolizing cardinal Roman values (courage, discipline, endurance, contempt for death, etc.) as he strove for the glory of victory.[125] While not denying this possibility, the current analysis points in a rather different direction. The gladiator was indeed a social nothing, an outgrouper whose life or death was, in the grand scheme of things, neither here nor there. But when he was in the arena he acquired a temporary status by virtue of his combat skill and membership in an elite group of trained fighters. The true contrast, then, was less between the hero-celebrity who prompted admiration and the hired killer who prompted horror (although this sensibility may well have prevailed among the elite class represented by our surviving authors), and more between the expendable outcast and the elite fighter. When he was on the sand fighting before his public, the gladiator was the hero-combatant; everywhere else, he was a nothing.

This suggestion offers a basis for understanding, in general terms at least, how dispositional alignments worked during the gladiatorial phase of a *munus*. The spectators had come to see a good show put on by trained professionals, and on this basis they got behind gladiators as they fought it out. The audience favored the aggressive and the fearless. As we have already seen (above, chapter 6, pp. 215–19), arena spectators were knowledgeable and knew what a good fight looked like; they recognized deft moves and

---

[124] It is sobering to realize that one of the fullest literary sources for life in the *ludus* is the oratorical exercise just reviewed – [Quint.] *Decl.* 9 – which alludes several times to life in the *ludus*: 9.5 = T.17 (terrible, yet fattening food and an education in criminality), 9.21 (life in the *ludus* is worse than being a criminal in prison), and 9.22 (a cell to live in, training, diet, coaches, and criminal deeds). See, further, Carter, "Gladiatorial Ranking," esp. 89–95; Coleman, "Bonds of Danger"; Ville, *Gladiature*, 301–3 (note again the brevity of the latter, due to lack of evidence).

[125] See above, ch. 6, pp. 200–1, and above, n. 94. Ambivalence: Ville, *Gladiature*, 344 ("the gladiator was at once hero and assassin: the former an admired celebrity, but the latter a source of horror, and it's for this reason that the gladiator fascinates"). See also the comments of Edwards, *Death*, 49–51.

smart maneuvers; they could tell the difference between a humdrum fight-by-the-book and something special; and it seems they could detect collusion between the fighters. As long as the gladiators met audience expectations, they enjoyed a brand of admiration as an elite caste of fighting specialists. Consistent performance earned fame and built a devoted fan-base. But the key point is this: the crowd's admiration and the status that flowed from it were ephemeral, strictly contingent on performance, and did not apply outside the arena. Gladiators were esteemed solely as effective fighters. And so fighters who fled their opponents, or showed reluctance to engage, or put on a bad display, or lost their bout in some derisory fashion abandoned their claim to elite-fighter status and reverted, on the spot, to expendable nothings. These are the mental dynamics behind the appeal for *missio*.

The entire situation is neatly summed up by Tertullian when he comments:

Take the very sponsors and administrators of spectacles: the charioteers, actors, athletes, and arena performers, those great lovers, to whom men surrender their souls, and women their bodies as well, on whose account they commit the sins they censure. They glorify these people for the same skill they degrade and diminish them; indeed, they condemn them openly to ignominy and loss of citizen rights, shut them out of the council chamber, the speaker's platform, the senate, equestrian status, all honors whatsoever, and some distinctions. What towering perversity! They love whom they punish, they devalue whom they admire; the art they glorify, the artist they stigmatize. What brand of judgment is it that a man be hidden out of sight for that which brings him to the fore? What a confession it is of evil conditions! Their authors, at the height of their popularity, are in disgrace.[126]

We must set aside the moralizing elements of Tertullian's Christian, anti-spectacle perspective to focus on the key observation of the passage: "The art they glorify, the artist they stigmatize."[127] This gets to the heart of the apparent paradox of the gladiator's status as an admired fighter and a despised outcast. Approval was conditional on the display of skill (*ars*), and the gladiator was reduced to nothing more than a breathing medium of that skill (*artifex*); beyond that, he was entitled to no consideration. Like any slave in the Roman world, the gladiator's personhood had been absorbed by his function.[128]

---

[126] Text. *Spect.* 22.2–4 = T.29.
[127] Note that Tertullian's assessment applies not only to gladiators but also to the other types of entertainer listed at the start of the passage.
[128] As such, the gladiator existed solely as a tool to be used for the benefit of others. The gladiator's owner was whoever owned his training school, which rented him out to *munerarii* to serve as an instrument of that person's desire for popularity and social recognition. For an example of the latter process, see Franklin, "Cn. Alleius Nigidius Maius."

The mutual emotional "entrainment" of the spectators with the fighters carried consequences for the experience of watching. The more aggressively the gladiators fought, the more the audience would encourage them, which itself would tend to prolong the fight and increase the level of aggression on display. If the combatants flagged, the crowd would shout encouragement ("Get stuck in!") to get it going again. Gladiators knew that they had to put on a display of fighting skill and bravado to meet the crowd's expectations; doing so was literally a matter of life and death and, if their epitaphs are any indication, also of pride and status among their peers.[129] Such considerations may well have impelled gladiators to fight hard and seriously, and the more they did so, the more the crowd would urge them on.[130] Gladiator and spectator were thus partners in the arena's dance of violence, and each played a key role in its lethal choreography.

[129] See Cicero's comment (*Mil.* 92 = T.4; echoed in Sen. *Dial.* 9.11.4 and ibid. 3.1.2.4–5) that gladiators who beg for their lives are hated, those who fight courageously and spiritedly earn the spectators' mercy. Epitaphs: Hope, "Fighting for Identity."

[130] Although made in the context of war, a comment by Caesar (*B. Gall.* 7.80) is enlightening. He observes how a cavalry engagement on the plain before Alesia was watched by both Gauls and Romans, which had the effect of spurring the combatants on: "Because the engagement played out before the eyes of all, it was impossible to hide a good deed or a disgraceful one, and both sides were stirred to courage by a lust for glory and fear of disgrace" (*Quod in conspectu omnium res gerebatur neque recte ac turpiter factum celari poterat, utrosque et laudis cupiditas et timor ignominiae ad virtutem excitabant.*)

Conclusion: the lure of the arena

> There is no spectacle without disturbance to the spirit . . . For even if
> a man enjoys spectacles modestly and uprightly, as befits his status or
> age or even his natural disposition, his soul is not unstirred and he is
> not without a silent rousing of the spirit.
>
> Tertullian *On Spectacles* 15.3, 5[1]

In his study of hangings and English society between 1770 and 1868,
Victor Gatrell posits a variety of motives for popular attendance: titillation,
excitement, ghoulish curiosity, confronting fear of death, and emotions
stirred by the nature of the crime or the identity of the criminal. What
often appeared to elite commentators as the crowd's vulgar boorishness,
fickle callousness, or even outright joy in the face of death – puns and
jokes following the drop, hats thrown in the air, cheering, bawdiness and
drunkenness, abrupt shifts of mood – may actually reflect a deep-seated
unease among the spectators. And this suggests that not everyone was there
for the same reason. The historian of more modern eras has the advantage
of working with an abundance of evidence composed by contemporaries
who observed the execution crowd, many of them snobbishly dismissive
and condescending, to be sure, but not a few shrewd and incisive. On
this basis, the hanging crowd's behavior has been read in two ways: as a
festive, carnival experience that fundamentally subverted the point of public
punishment by trivializing it; or as a serious-minded affirmation of a legal
procedure, whereby consent was manifested in spectator attendance.[2] That

---

[1] Latin text: *omne enim spectaculum sine concussione spiritus non est . . . nam et si qui modeste et probe
spectaculis fruitur pro dignitatis vel aetatis vel etiam naturae suae condicione, non tamen immobilis animi
est et sine tacita spiritus passione.*

[2] Gatrell, *Hanging Tree*, 67–105 and 225–321; note also Laqueur, "Crowds, Carnival and the State."
One particularly astute contemporary commentator was Edward Gibbon Wakefield (1796–1862),
himself a former inmate in Newgate prison (outside of which hangings were staged between 1783 and
1868). Wakefield suspected that the crowd behaved erratically as it tried to suppress its deep-seated
terror at the spectacle of enforced death: "More or less, all the world tremble at the thought of dying,
and, therefore, behave as if they were born to live forever" (cited in Gatrell, *Hanging Tree*, 75–6). On
contemporary festivals and pastimes, see Malcolmson, *Popular Recreations.*

is to say, not every hanging crowd manifested the same tone, nor was the emotional state of spectators at any given hanging necessarily consistent.

In the foregoing chapters, an attempt has been made to trace some contours of the Roman arena crowd's psychological landscape, on the basis of universal mental processes demonstrated by observation and experiment. From this we may generate a mental map, if you will, of what was going on in the stands and thereby gain an impression of what brought people to fill them in the first place. Our map necessarily displays serious gaps, given the patchwork of ancient evidence and our inability to question or observe arena-goers directly. Luckily many of our elite sources provide eyewitness accounts of arena crowd behavior and, once the limitations of this class of evidence are realized, it can be deployed to great benefit. In light of Gatrell's observations about the better-documented English hanging crowds, it is unreasonable to expect that the psychological state of Roman arena spectators was uniform and consistent, or unvarying across the vast territory of the Roman empire over its long duration. The spectacles themselves were complicated events that employed a wide range of human and animal performers, featured elaborate stage sets, and moved through a sequence of phases. All of this means that spectator tastes and expectations, as well as their reactions to what they were seeing, were likely to shift and adjust over time, by region, or even during a single spectacle. Spectators were not emotional automatons, reacting in lockstep unison to what confronted them. There would naturally be divergences in how they made sense of the show, what meanings they derived from them, and so what sorts of emotions they experienced while watching.[3] These sorts of divergences are accounted for in social psychology by the "individual-differences dimension," which allows for variaton in psychological reactions and social behaviors.

Divergence in individual tastes can be securely documented for the best-documented Romans: emperors and the elite. At one end of the scale stood the likes of M. Aurelius, who found the games tedious and repetitive (M. Aur. *Med.* 6.46) or Tiberius, who eschewed them as soon as he came to power (Suet. *Tib.* 47). Julius Caesar appears to have had little interest in shows. Although he staged and attended them (Suet. *Iul.* 31.1, 39), he did

---

[3] See, e.g., Catharine Edwards' enlightening discussion (*Death*, 214–16) of Augustine's insistence that pagans and Christians watched arena martyrdoms in entirely different ways: the pagans saw the victims' torture (*cruciatus*), the Christians, their courage (*virtus*). One wonders to what extent such a formulation represents intellectual wishful thinking on Augustine's part – and he is almost certainly being prescriptive, as he tells the Christian community how to interpret martyrs and martyrologies – or to what extent it was based on real, observed behavior. Either way, it illustrates at least a recognition that different spectators could see different things in what they were watching.

paperwork as they progressed, much to the crowd's irritation. Augustus, therefore, made a point of paying attention at spectacles, either to avoid popular opprobrium or because he was genuinely interested, as he himself proclaimed. Nevertheless, the first emperor did make himself scarce for several hours or even for whole days during protracted games, offering his excuses and appointing proxies to preside over them in his stead (Suet. *Aug.* 45.1). Aside from the pressing concerns of state he necessarily confronted, Augustus' behavior implies at least some ambiguity in his attitude toward arena spectacle. Cicero's stance also comes across as ambivalent. In private, he shares aspects of Marcus Aurelius' negative assessment of the games as repetitive, while nevertheless appreciating the sheer scale and magnificence of what could be presented (Cic. *Fam.* 7.1.3), but in his published work he usually refers to spectacles approvingly, and even claims to have enjoyed them.[4] Cicero's and Augustus' public positions on the games demonstrate what an important a part of civic life they had become and make implicit a degree of eagerness for them among the Roman elite: attendance (and expressions of appreciation) were all but obligatory for the upper classes, at least in Rome. That said, neither man can be classed as an enthusiast.

The same cannot be said for Caligula or Claudius. After the dearth of spectacles during Tiberius' reign, Caligula staged many shows, at which he displayed his characteristic cruelty (Suet. *Cal.* 18, 27). But even he was not as devoted as his uncle Claudius, who used to go down to the arena at dawn and even stay in his seat during the midday executions; apparently, this was bad form for an emperor. So cruel was Claudius, in fact, that he gave orders to cut the throats of all gladiators who fell, even by accident, and he used to scrutinize the death throes of *retiarii*, to study their facial expressions as they perished (Suet. *Claud.* 34.1–2 = T.23). Claudius was not alone. Drusus, the son of Tiberius, was such a fan of arena combat (as well as being personally prone to violence) that he was nicknamed "Castor" after a contemporary gladiator. Nero's paternal grandfather, L. Domitius Ahenobarbus, staged a *munus* so savage that Augustus first warned him off in private and, when that did not work, corrected him by public edict.[5]

There are traceable among the elite, then, degrees of enthusiasm for gladiatorial games and, by implication, a variety of motives for attending them. There are indications that a similar spectrum of attitudes extended

---

[4] E.g., Cic. *Mil.* 92 = T.4, *Mur.* 39–40, *Tusc.* 2.41 = T.5, 4.48. Facing his executioner, Cicero extended his neck in the fashion of a doomed gladiator (Plut. *Cic.* 48.5), so he at least took away something from the shows.

[5] Dio 57.14. 9, Tac. *Ann.* 4.3.2, Hor. *Ep.* 1.18.19 (Drusus/Castor); Suet. *Nero* 4 (Domitius).

downwards into the lower echelons of the social order. Tacitus, in describing the amphitheater collapse at Fidenae, notes that "those keen for such things" (*avidi talium*) made the five-mile trek from Rome to Fidenae to watch the spectacle there (Tac. *Ann.* 4.62.3). By implication, there were those not keen for such things who just stayed home. The sort of people who were drawn to Fidenae were presumably of the same cast as those who enjoyed the notoriously nasty spectacle put on by Nero's grandfather, who would hardly have incurred the vast expense of staging it had he not expected to earn the popular favor that was the *editor*'s expected return on his investment. Seneca notes in disgust (*Ep.* 7.4 = T.20) that "very many people" (*plerique*) prefer the straight butchery of the midday shows to the regular gladiatorial matches. (We can name at least one of these people: Claudius.) But then there were Nero's *munera* during which nobody was killed, "not even *noxii*," reports a perplexed Suetonius (Suet. *Nero* 12.1). A non-lethal gladiatorial show is a typical Neronian inversion of traditional norms, but the inference just drawn about his grandfather's brutal games applies here too – Nero apparently expected people to come to watch, but presumably people of somewhat different inclinations to those enamoured of extreme brutality (and there is no indication that this show was a failure with the masses). And so a variety of motives for attendance at the arena is directly attestable for the elite and implicit for the lower orders. Some craved the games, others were disinterested in them but felt obliged to attend; some went for the maximum savagery, others for reasons unconnected to watching brutality. And some just stayed away.

The latter point can be corroborated by a simple observation. In a city of some one million inhabitants only a tiny proportion – 50–80,000, or between 5 and 8 percent – could attend games staged in the Colosseum on any given day, especially since large sections of the *cavea* were reserved for favored groups already. (Theaters and other venues sat fewer still.) Elsewhere, amphitheaters like those at Pompeii or El Djem may have been sufficiently large to serve the town and the neighboring regions, but even in these cases not everyone would go, whether by choice or circumstance. This is not to downplay the popularity of spectacles – the large venues still filled, and sponsors staged spectacles to increase their own popularity – but rather the observation drives home the simple point that *munera* were not to everyone's taste. This means that those people who did watch constituted a self-selected group. Apart from those upper-class persons who went along out of a sense of obligation, most spectators were voluntarily present, and thus eager and excited to watch. In consequence, the centrality of arena events to the Roman sense of self has probably been overstated in some quarters,[6] given that not everyone could (or wanted) to go, not to mention the variations in crowd demographics, or differences in the shape of shared values, social understandings, historical experience, and cultural meaning across the expanse of time and space occupied by the Roman empire. That a homogeneous concept of Roman-ness was shared by all the regional cultures of the empire for so many centuries is most unlikely, so we must imagine a corresponding variation in local orientations toward the games over time. Future work may elucidate some of these divergent understandings by close analysis of differences in staging or representing games in different parts of the empire, perhaps recoverable through close attention to arena iconography and epigraphy.

Naturally, our interest in this book has focused on those people who went to the games, not those who stayed away. Individual proclivities aside, the focus of social psychology is on general patterns of behavior rather than on individual actions, and in this realm several interlocking processes were at work at the arena. To understand what brought people to the games, we have posited the importance of crowd dynamics, the satiation of prejudice, excitement at sporting events, and the attraction of violence as entertainment. These should not be seen as the *only* pertinent mental processes operating in the *cavea*, and the vaguer suite of emotions charted by Gatrell for English hanging crowds – titillation or morbid curiosity, for instance – were arguably present as well.[7] But the four major, well-documented psychological phenomena studied in the preceding chapters contain greater explanatory promise than speculating about indistinct sentiments, such as fear of death or simple curiosity (the latter in any case inapplicable to the true devotee of arena games).

Recent work has shown that crowd membership, far from generating anonymous, mindless behavior and licensing deviance, can be among the most powerful emotional experiences available to people. Crowd dynamics, rooted in the basic group processes of social identity and social categorization, generate a suite of emotions that find particularly strong manifestation

---

[6] See, e.g, Brown, "Death as Decoration," 184: "The games were not merely an entertainment but virtually a requirement of Imperial Roman social and political life"; or Carter, "Gladiators and Monomachoi," 305: "The *munus* as cultural performance may have played an important role in the creation and maintenance of a Roman sense of identity." See also Brown, "Explaining the Arena"; Müller, *Das Volk der Athleten*, 294; Toner, *Leisure*, 34–52, esp. 39; Wiedemann, *Emperors and Gladiators*, esp. 1–54.

[7] See, e.g., Edwards, *Death*, 60: "The fascination these spectacles exercised over their audiences stems to a significant degree from the desire to see how gladiators will behave in the face of death." This comment envisions a lure somewhere between morbid curiosity and confronting fear of death.

and vivid expression in the crowd context. Since crowds usually comprise large numbers of likeminded people who have assembled in subgroups of mutual friends and acquaintances for a pre-determined reason, deeply consequential sensations of connectedness, validation, purposefulness, agency, and empowerment come to the fore and bind the crowd together in its social identity. The liberating expression of this shared identity in the crowd, Durkheim's "effervescence," generates excitement and sensations of belonging and solidarity. The crowd might, indeed, be one of the few places where people can freely express who they really feel themselves to be, where an "imagined community" can share an expression of how they see the world, both as it is and how they think it ought to be.[8]

The operation of these processes made attendance attractive (for those to whom it appealed, of course). Likeminded spectators had assembled to witness threatening natural or social forces neutralized and to see gladiators manifest, in a particularly raw and direct manner, values widely celebrated in Roman culture and ones that, perhaps, resonated more with some members of the crowd than with others: courage, strength, the disciplined deployment of learned martial skill, contempt for pain and death, and a willingness to struggle and endure for the sake of victory. In the stands, the crowd was subdivided into peer groups that made the social order of Rome manifest in the serried tiers. The presence of an *editor*, a leading member of the community or the emperor himself, acted as a lens to focus the crowd's sense of its identity. Here was the "imagined community," the ingroup made real and visible, assembled to watch the life-and-death struggles of outgroupers on the sand. As other scholars have stressed, the arena was in some sense the world made ideal, at least to Roman male (and elite?) eyes.[9] It was a place where social distinctions were manifest, recognized, and respected, all the way from rulers to slaves; where Roman values played out ideally – the strong, courageous, and skillful prevailed and were rewarded, and the weak got what they deserved; and where human beings mastered the capricious and threatening forces of nature and punished social and political threats. The capacity of the spectators to intervene at various junctures and shape the course of events on the arena floor sharpened the feelings of agency already elicited by mere membership in the crowd. At the arena, they were lords for a day and enjoyed a god-like power of life and death over others. The situational salience of social identity meant that

---

[8] See, e.g., B. Anderson, *Imagined Communities*, rev. edn. (London, 1991), and Reicher, *The Crowd*, ch. 1 (my thanks to Professor Reicher for sharing with me the pre-publication text of this chapter).
[9] See the various studies reviewed in chapter 1, where these points are made cogently and lucidly in works by Bomgardner, Coleman, Edmondson, Hopkins, Toner, and Wiedemann.

feelings and emotions fluctuated in response to specific occurrences in the spectacle, and that made spectating all the more dramatic and energizing. Crowd dynamics, aided unwittingly by the segregated seating arrangements that divided the spectators into subgroups, thus generated a set of powerful sensations, the experience of which can be posited, in itself, as one of the chief lures of the arena.

Of course, the arena was not the only place where groups of Romans experienced crowd dynamics, but the particular set of social identities and categorizations elicited by the spectacle would be unique to that context, as perhaps were some of the feelings and expressions drawn out by it. Among the peculiarly strong currents running through arena events was prejudice. Indulgence of prejudice has been shown to license people to take pleasure in the sufferings of its targets. In psychological terms, prejudice is a multifaceted phenomenon comprising attitudes, cognitions, emotions, and actions. Prejudice appears linked to ingroup/outgroup social identities and categorizations in group and crowd processes, to the personality traits of individuals, to media of cultural transmission, and to wider societal conditions. While the interaction of these elements is still under investigation by social psychologists, it is safe to say that the Roman arena was a place suffused with prejudice from top to bottom. All performers on the sand were *infames* ("of ill-repute") and were therefore unworthy, as a group, of consideration. In the case of the gladiator and, to a lesser extent, the beast hunter, prejudice was temporarily mitigated by the contingent admiration these performers enjoyed by virtue of their skill at arms and risk-taking courage. As with the expression of social identity, to which it was linked at the arena, satisfaction at the satiation of prejudicial attitudes was more likely to wash over the crowd in waves rather than find steady and uniform expression as the spectacle proceeded. The midday executions, in particular, can be surmised as a primary phase for indulging prejudice, since this was when demonstrated villains, the dregs of the social order and guilty of despicable crimes, were getting their just deserts. The legitimacy of their brutal punishment was established by general considerations of who they were, the public nature of criminal interrogations and trials, and by heralds and placards at the arena reminding the crowd of the condemned's enormities immediately prior to the executions. Satisfied that they were confronting "the worst of the worst," arena spectators were free to vent their spleen and derive enjoyment from the ghastly torments inflicted on these unfortunates.

Whereas the execution of prisoners was a spectacle with only one possible result and did not offer much by way of suspense, the beast hunts and gladiatorial combats were something different. Uncertain outcomes, rules of engagement, skill in weapons handling, and the possibility of betting put them into a different category from the purely punitive spectacles of the lunch hour. While history provides many comparanda (e.g., animal-baiting in designated pits and arenas, tournaments staged before audiences, or cudgeling), the status of these contests as sports remains disputed. What seems clearer, though, is that arena bouts shared enough features with other combat sports or bloodsports to offer comparable lures to spectators. As just noted, part of the excitement at live, mass sporting events stems from crowd dynamics and the ensuing "effervescence" generated by them. But the attraction of watching sporting contests lies also in the excitement derived from the spectators' emotional involvement in the action, even if they watch alone and on television. The process of seeking arousal by watching violent clashes within a frame of mental detachment, which entails cognitive synergies (sudden and unexpected reversals or confounding expectations) and elicits parapathic emotions (negative when real, but always pleasurable when experienced from a detached perspective), was probably part of what was going on in the *cavea* during the fights. Arena spectators were knowledgeable about gladiatorial techniques, anticipated seeing named favorites, were prepared to support those favorites and/or particular styles of fighter, and arrived at their seats informed as to which gladiators would be appearing, in what order, what their records were, and in what style they would be fighting. These circumstances, combined with elite condescensions about *plebs* blathering on about their fighting favorites, indicates that a sport-like air hung over the matches. Thrilling and dramatic engagements can be reconstructed from gladiatorial graffiti and other sources, and the very fact that common Romans went to the trouble of scribbling gladiator graffiti at all is testimony to the popular enthusiasm that swirled about the stars of the sand and motivated the tracking of performance from fight to fight. In all of this, much more than raw bloodlust was at work, since appreciation of gladiatorial artistry was not in itself an indulgence of sadism.

And yet there can be little doubt that Roman arena spectacles represent one of the most colossally cruel exhibitions ever put on before an audience. For a typical *munus*, the crowd filing through the arena's arches harbored few illusions about what they were about to witness. What brings people to witness such things? How can enjoyment be derived from watching brutality? While prior scholars have sought to understand the arena solely within the confines of Roman culture and history, a central argument of this book has been that any answers so offered can only ever be partial. For it is depressingly evident that many populations at some remove from the Romans turned out in significant numbers to witness appalling brutalities inflicted on people and animals alike. Indeed this case can be made, to a degree, from within the ancient Mediterranean context itself. Peoples and cultures who had not experienced the specifics of the Romans' own particular historical and cultural evolution, when exposed to the horrors of the arena, took to them enthusiastically (e.g., Dio Chrys. 31.121 = T.7). As we have stressed on several occasions already, the Romans were not alone in finding the sight of people and animals tormented and killed alluring.

The psychological understanding of this perplexing phenomenon remains incomplete. Vague generalizations (such as morbid curiosity), sweeping claims (satiation of fear of death), or disproven hypotheses (catharsis) still do the rounds in the research literature. Perhaps the great variety of ways in which violence can be manifested means that no one explanation fits all. More work needs to be done, as researchers concentrate more on why people watch, and less on what happens to them as a result of watching. Nevertheless, the most systematic attempt to date to explain the attraction of violent spectacle focuses not on the acts of violence themselves, nor even on whether they are real or faked, but on the viewer's emotional orientation towards the perpetrator and victim. "Affective dispositions" shape the alignment of watchers for or against agents and determine how they judge the violent deeds they witness. Good things will be hoped for a liked agent ("positive dispositional alignment"), with whom the viewer will have empathy; but bad things will be wished for a disliked agent ("negative dispositional alignment"), who will elicit a counterempathic response. Counterempathy means that, so long as it is judged justified and righteous, there is virtually no limit to the degree of hideousness spectators will enjoy watching meted out to those against whom they harbor negative affective dispositions. Brutal outcomes for hated agents are intensely satisfying.

The dispositional model can be applied readily to the hunts and executions of the arena, where the crowd would naturally tend to align with human huntsmen over animals, and perhaps stronger animals over weaker ones.[10] Cases where the crowd's alignments suddenly shifted in

---

[10] Although not invariably; see Martial on the lions and hares (above, ch. 4, n. 10) or *Spect.* 33 where sympathy is shown for a doe fleeing hounds, though only because the animal appeared to throw itself on Caesar's mercy.

response to some occurrence in the spectacle reflect the workings of affective dispositions and attest to the fluidity and volatility inherent in spectator dynamics. As documented in the martyrologies, the crowd's default attitude was one of relentless dislike, so that the counterempathic response of taking pleasure in violence inflicted on the condemned was the norm. When it comes to the gladiators, the workings of dispositional alignments become more opaque. The bases for spectator support appear to have been quality of performance, and despite the powerful prejudice against all arena performers, much evidence shows that gladiators could be admired, even idolized. How to account for this ambivalent attitude within the parameters of disposition theory proves challenging, especially since we cannot observe or question the Romans in their seats. An illuminating and complementary perspective is provided by applying the microsociological analysis of violent encounters. This model holds that all violent confrontations are marked by an emotional field of tension and fear and that violence can only occur when these obstacles have been overcome (as people naturally tend to avoid tension and fear). One way to achieve the latter is to stage fights with rules that circumscribe the violence in some way (but not necessarily its intensity, or even lethality) and then to provide an audience that will encourage the fighters.

Gladiatorial matches meet these criteria, and the largely self-selected nature of the spectators would guarantee an eager and excited audience. Furthermore, since participants in staged fights are often objects of admiration to their "public," we arrive at a psychological explanation for how gladiators could be both despised and admired at once. The admiration was ephemeral and strictly contingent on their continued high performance in matches. If they disappointed the crowd by a poor showing, admiration evaporated on the spot and they reverted to the despicable *infames* who could be killed without a second thought. There is the further implication that encouragement of the self-selected and enthusiastic crowd would tend to intensify and prolong the combats, the thrills of which fed the enthusiasm even more, which then flowed back into encouraging the fights. Audience and gladiator emerge as mutual facilitators of arena violence, bound together in an emotional field that worked to reduce the tension/fear inherent in the combats themselves. As the emotional atmosphere intensified, excitement reached fever pitch. There can have been few psychological experiences quite like it. Spectator affective dispositions during the fights would therefore be volatile and fluid, attached less to the perceived content of the gladiators' character as

inherently heroic or villainous – to a degree, they were both simultaneously – and more to the nature of their performance. This is why a poor
performance would generate in the spectators a vitriolic counterempathic
response, leading to feelings not just of disappointment at a bad show but
of anger and even resentment toward the performers.[11] Between them, disposition theory and the microsociology of violence offer an illuminating
framework for understanding what the crowd was experiencing as they
watched.

It is important to appreciate that arena spectators experienced all of
these sensations and feelings at once, not in a linear sequence with each
demarcated from the other. To be sure, phases of the spectacle or specific
incidents on the sand would have made one or more of the mental processes
temporarily more salient than the others – prejudice and counterempathic
emotions coming to the fore during executions, for instance. But it is not
that crowd dynamics switched off when prejudicial attitudes were being
fully indulged, but rather that the prejudicial attitudes became part and
parcel of the crowd's social identity and categorizations, and thus also a
part of how the crowd dynamics manifested at that moment. It is not
that negative affective dispositions replaced or swamped prejudice during
executions, but that the prejudice contributed to the formation of the
dispositions in the first place. Indeed, it was precisely this dynamism and
vividness that made the arena's psychological environment so powerful.
Admittedly, these can only be suggestions. But they are plausible and
reasonable suggestions that give a sense of what the experience of watching
the games was actually like, in real time.

In concluding his study of ancient anger, W. V. Harris hopes "to read
no more universal pontifications about anger founded on questionnaires
administered to well-fed middle-class American or British twenty-year-
olds."[12] On the one hand, Harris highlights a prominent pitfall in applying
modern psychological research to past eras, since it is often based on just
the sort of questionnaires he denigrates. On the other hand, the social-
psychological processes explored in this book (crowd dynamics, prejudice,
sports excitement, and attraction to violent entertainments) are not mirages
conjured by modern questionnaires to undergraduates but very real phenomena observable in everyday life, readily recognizable to (and experienced by) most of us, and abundantly documentable from Roman sources.

---

[11] Sen. *Dial.* 3.2.4; see above, ch. 4, p. 144, for text and translation. This *Dialogus* of Seneca is entitled
De Ira ("On Anger").
[12] Harris, *Restraining Rage*, 409.

To trace their functioning at the arena is therefore instructive, even if the underlying assumption that mental mechanics transcend time and space is apt to make historians of any era come over all nervous and fidgety. So it is worth stating once more that commonality of psychological process (the Romans were no less human than we are) does not entail commonality of behavior. How behavior generated by shared psychological processes plays out on the ground is mediated by culture, since humans are cultural beings who derive meaning from the cultural systems they construct. The pertinent features of the wider Roman social context addressed at various junctures in the book – ubiquitous slavery, hierarchical groupishness dominant in social thought, intimate familiarity with pain and death, and so forth – must not be seen as mere buttresses to the social-psychological analysis, but as inherent features of it. In some ways, the arena offered the distilled essence of many of these prominent features of Roman culture, and that circumstance would have contributed still further to its psychological lure.

A new interpretive framework for the phenomenon of the games has been proposed in this book. It is a framework that emphasizes the lived motivations and impulses of the arena crowd over the implicit symbolism and subconscious attractions of what they were watching. The immediate lure of the arena lay in the psychologically generated experiences of excitement, belonging, validation, and agency; enjoyment at prejudices sated (especially during hunts and executions); emotional involvement in competitive sports and appreciation of skill and dexterity in professional performers; and, for at least some of those present, the *frisson* of watching violence meted out to those judged deserving of it. The centrality of cultural context to social psychology means that acknowledgment of these sensations does not entail replacing or overriding the culturally specific analyses of prior studies, or denying the significance of the anthropological, religious, political, or symbological role of *munera* in Roman culture. Rather, the psychology supplements and complements such approaches. Indeed, the particular contribution of social psychology is to elucidate the mental mechanisms by which the sublimated and culturally embedded meanings of arena games were translated into the spectators' lived experience as a suite of sensations and feelings. By focusing on the latter, we gain a sense of what the arena had to offer, less in terms of what transpired on the sand and more in terms of what was felt in the stands. The Roman games ought not to be viewed as a singular phenomenon, as so often has been the case in the past, but rather as one calibration on a spectrum of ritual violence, which can be demonstrated to exert a strong pull on spectators' attentions across the ages. Indeed, stressing the uniqueness of the arena provides a comforting distance between us and the Romans in their arena seats. An emphasis on the historically contingent and culturally specific aspects of Roman gladiatorial spectacles allows us to turn away, secure in our confidence that we are nothing like that.[13] Appreciation of the psychological dynamics that coursed through those far-away spectators leads to the rather more unsettling realization that the lure of the brutalities staged in the Roman arena may well lie closer to home than many of us might like to think.

---

[13] See, e.g., Edwards, *Death*, 77: "It is hard for the modern reader not to be alienated by the idea that the sight of a man struggling against the pain of a fatal wound can constitute a source of edification and indeed visual joy"; Kanz and Grossschmidt, "Head Injuries," 216: "The brutality of this ancient spectacle still remains incomprehensible to today's socialized humans"; E. Köhne, "Bread and Circuses: The Politics of Entertainment," in Köhne and Ewigleben (eds.), *Gladiators and Caesars*, 8–30, esp. 12: "Roman civilization and culture is never so utterly remote from our understanding as in the matter of these life-and-death games"; Salisbury, *Perpetua's Passion*, 124–34, esp. 124: "We may gather to watch sports events and be temporarily transformed by the crowd enthusiasm . . . But we do not go to such displays to watch people die." Note also Coleman's assessment ("Launching into History," 49) that the Romans exhibited a different *mentalité* "which is largely alien to our modern outlook: a passion for novel and elaborate ways of mounting spectacle" (the annually increasing scale of death and destruction in summer blockbuster movies rather suggests otherwise).

Appendix: *select literary and epigraphic* testimonia *for arena crowd behavior and related issues*

Entries are listed alphabetically by author's name. Literary (entries marked with "T") and epigraphic (entries marked with "I") *testimonia* are listed separately. The texts are drawn from Teubner editions, where available. All translations are the author's, unless otherwise indicated. Very useful also is the collection of sources at the Spectatores website (www-gewi.uni-graz.at/spectatores), on which see W. Petermandl, "Zuschauer der Geschichte: Ein Internet-Archiv zum Publikum im Altertum," *Nikephoros* 19 (2006), 45–56.

SECTION A: LITERARY TEXTS

T.1 Apuleius, *The Golden Ass* 4.13–14

[13] Ibi famam celebrem super quodam Demochare munus edituro gladiatorium deprehendimus. Nam vir et genere primarius et opibus plurimus et liberalitate praecipuus digno fortunae suae splendore publicas voluptates instruebat. Quis tantus ingenii, quis facundiae, qui singulas species apparatus multiiugi verbis idoneis posset explicare? Gladiatores isti famosae manus, venatores illi probatae pernicitatis, alibi noxii perdita securitate suis epulis bestiarum saginas instruentes; confixilis machinae sublicae turres structae tabularum nexibus ad instar circumforaneae domus, floridae picturae, decora futurae venationis receptacula. Qui praeterea numerus, quae facies ferarum! Nam praecipuo studio foris etiam advexerat generosa illa damnatorum capitum funera. Sed praeter ceteram speciosi muneris supellectilem totis utcumque patrimonii viribus immanis ursae comparabat numerum copiosum. Nam praeter domesticis venationibus captas, praeter largis emptionibus partas, amicorum etiam donationibus variis certatim oblatas tutela sumptuosa sollicite nutriebat.

[14] Nec ille tam clarus tamque splendidus publicae voluptatis apparatus Invidiae noxios effugit oculos. Nam diutina captivitate fatigatae simul et aestiva flagrantia maceratae, pigra etiam sessione languidae, repentina correptae pestilentia paene ad nullum redivere numerum. Passim per plateas

287

plurimas cerneres iacere semivivorum corporum ferina naufragia. Tunc vulgus ignobile, quos inculta pauperies sine dilectu ciborum tenuato ventri cogit sordentia supplementa et dapes gratuitas conquirere, passim iacentes epulas accurrunt.

[13] [*Speaker is a bandit*] "There [Plataea] we caught wind of a widespread rumor about a certain Demochares, who was about to put on a gladiatorial show. A man of high birth, very great wealth, and outstanding liberality, he was providing public entertainments with a splendor worthy of his fortune. Who has enough talent, enough eloquence as to describe with appropriate words the individual elements of the show's complex equipment? The gladiators were of renowned valor, the huntsmen of proven agility, and condemned criminals too, their safety lost, providing fattening food for the beasts in a banquet of themselves. There was a wooden pile construction, towers erected with fastenings of boards fashioned like an itinerant house, pretty pictures, and fine cages for the hunt to come. And besides, how many and how impressive the wild beasts! For with outstanding effort he had brought even from abroad those generous tombs for the condemned. But aside from the rest of the paraphernalia for a splendid show, using the entire wealth of his inheritance he assembled an ample troop of huge bears. Besides bears captured in hunts conducted by his own servants or those acquired in costly purchases, there were those provided by his friends, as they vied with each other with varied gifts. These animals he carefully fed and maintained at great expense.

[14] But such brilliant and splendid gear for a public show did not escape the malignant eyes of Envy. For the bears, worn out by their protracted captivity, weakened by the intense summer heat, and made limp from idly sitting about, were attacked by a sudden illness and their numbers were reduced to almost nothing. You could see the wreckage of the animals, their half-alive bodies, lying about in most of the town's streets. Then the common mob, driven by raw poverty without choice in their foodstuffs to seek out vile supplements and free meals for their emaciated bellies, ran to the banquets lying around all over the place."

T.2 Apuleius, *The Golden Ass* 10.18, 23, 28–9, 34–5

[18] Thiasus – hoc enim nomine meus nuncupabatur dominus – oriundus patria Corintho, quod caput est totius Achaiae provinciae, ut eius prosapia atque dignitas postulabat, gradatim permensis honoribus quinquennali magistratui fuerat destinatus, et ut splendori capessendorum responderet fascium, munus gladiatorum triduani spectaculi pollicitus

latius munificentiam suam porrigebat. Denique gloriae publicae studio tunc Thessaliam etiam accesserat nobilissimas feras et famosos inde gladiatores comparaturus, iamque ex arbitrio dispositis coemptisque omnibus domuitionem parabat . . .

[23] Nec gravate magister meus voluptates ex eius arbitrio largiebatur, partim mercedes amplissimas acceptando, partim novum spectaculum domino praeparando. Incunctanter ei denique libidinis nostrae totam detegit scaenam. At ille liberto magnifice munerato destinat me spectaculo publico. Et quoniam neque egregia illa uxor mea propter dignitatem neque prorsus ulla alis inveniri potuerat grandi praemio, quae mecum incoram publicans pudicitiam populi caveam frequentaret. Eius poenae talem cognoveram fabulam . . .

[28] . . . atque illam, minus quidem quam merebatur, sed quod dignus cruciatus alius excogitari non poterat, certe bestiis obiciendam pronuntiavit.

[29] Talis mulieris publicitus matrimonium confarreaturus ingentique angore oppido suspensus exspectabam diem muneris, saepius quidem mortem mihimet volens consciscere, priusquam scelerosae mulieris contagio macularer vel infamia publici spectaculi depudescerem . . . Dies ecce muneri destinatus aderat. Ad consaeptum caveae prosequente populo pompatico favore deducor. Ad dum ludicris scaenicorum choreis primitiae spectaculi dedicantur . . .

[34] Ecce quidam miles per mediam plateam dirigit cursum petiturus iam populo postulante illam de publico carcere mulierem, quam dixi propter multiforme scelus bestis esse damnatam meisque praeclaris nuptiis destinatam. Et iam torus genialis scilicet noster futurus accuratissime disternebatur lectus Indica testudine perlucidus, plumea congerie tumidus, veste serica floridus. At ego praeter pudorem obeundi publice concubitus, praeter contagium scelestae pollutaeque feminae, metu iam mortis maxime cruciabar, sic ipse mecum reputans, quod in amplexu Venerio scilicet nobis cohaerentibus, quaecumque ad exitium mulieris bestia fuisset immissa, non adeo vel prudentia sollers vel artificio docta vel absistentia frugi posset provenire, ut adiacentem lateri meo laceraret mulierem, mihi vero quasi indemnato et innoxio parceret.

[35] Ergo igitur non de pudore iam, sed de salute ipsa sollicitus, dum magister meus lectulos probe coaptando districtus inseruit, et tota familia partim ministerio venationis occupata partim voluptario spectaculo adtonita meis cogitationibus liberum tribuebatur arbitrium, nec magnoque quisquam custodiendum tam mansuetum putabat asinum, paulatim furtivum pedem

proferens portam quae proxima est potitus, iam cursu memet celerrimo
proripio, Cenchreas pervado, quod oppidum audit quidem nobilissimae
coloniae Corinthiensium, alluitur autem Aegaeo et Saronico mari.

[18] Thiasus – for my master was announced [in public] under this name –
came from Corinth, the capital of the entire province of Achaea. As his
lineage and position demanded, he had advanced through the grades of
local office and had been elected to the five-yearly magistracy, and to
respond to the distinction of gaining the fasces, he had promised a three-day
gladiatorial spectacle and was offering his munificence quite expansively.
In his enthusiasm for public glory he had even gone to Thessaly to collect
there the most celebrated wild beasts and famed gladiators. Now after he
arranged and bought everything according to plan, he was readying to
come home . . . [*the journey back is described; Lucius' fame as a gifted ass
spreads in Corinth; a local woman of standing falls in love with him and he
sleeps with her; the unusual coupling is reported to Thiasus, who decides to
include it in his forthcoming spectacle*] . . .

[23] My trainer was not reluctant to bestow these pleasures on her whenever
she wished, partly because he was getting a very large fee, and partly
because he was readying a new spectacle for his master. He didn't hesitate
to expose the entire drama of our lust to him. The master rewarded his
freedman lavishly and slated me to appear in his public spectacle. And
since that outstanding wife of mine could not appear on account of her
social position, and nor could any other woman be found even for a high
price, a worthless nobody was acquired, one sentenced to the beasts on the
governor's order, who would prostitute her virtue with me and throng the
stands with people. I learned the following tale of her conviction . . . [*the
story of the multiple-murdering woman is told, as is her denunciation to the
governor at his house*] . . .

[28] . . . Although it was less than she deserved, but because no other fitting
torture could be devised, he [the governor] condemned her to the beasts
at least.

[29] Such was the woman I was to celebrate a public wedding with, and I
waited for the day of the show with great anxiety and extreme suspense. Very
often I wanted to take my own life before being besmirched by that wicked
woman's pollution or shamed by the disgrace of a public spectacle . . . And
so the appointed day of the show arrived. I was led to the adjacent precinct
of the venue, with the people following along in an enthusiastic procession.
The opening phases of the spectacle were given over to theatrical stage
dancers . . . [*a lengthy description of an intricate dance show follows, and of a*

re-enactment of the Judgment of Paris staged on a wooden mountain complete
with bushes and trees, an artificial river, and grazing goats] . . .

[34] As the people were now demanding her, a soldier made straight across
the performance area to fetch from the public jail the woman who, as I've
said, had been condemned to the beasts on account of her diverse crimes
and was slated for a splendid marriage to me. Now a couch – clearly meant
to be our conjugal bed – was being meticulously laid out, shining with
Indian tortoise-shell, fat with a feathered mattress, bright with silken covers.
But I, besides the shame of sleeping with this woman in public, besides the
infection of this wicked and polluted woman, was racked especially by a fear
of death and thought to myself that, when indeed we were joined together
in Venus' embrace, whatever beast was let into the arena to make an end
of the woman could not possibly be so skilled in intelligence, learned in its
trade, or honest in its moderation as to tear the woman lying beside me but
spare me, on the grounds that had I not been convicted and was innocent.

[35] And so worried not only for my self-respect but also for my very life,
while my trainer was focusing on fitting the couch together properly, and
the entire slave workforce was occupied, some with readying the hunt,
others astonished at the sensual spectacle, free rein was accorded to my
designs. Nobody thought particularly that so tame an ass had to be guarded,
so gradually by furtive steps I reached the nearest gate, and hurled myself
with the fastest sprint and reached Cenchreae, which one hears is a town
in the most renowned territory of Corinth and is lapped by the waters of
the Aegean and Saronic seas.

T.3 Augustine, *Confessiones* 6.13

Romam praecesserat [sc. Alypius] ut ius disceret, et ibi gladiatorii spectaculi hiatu incredibili et incredibiliter abreptus est. cum enim aversaretur et
detestaretur talia, quidam eius amici et condiscipuli, cum forte de prandio
redeuntibus pervium esset, recusantem vehementer et resistentem familiari
violentia duxerunt in amphitheatrum crudelium et funestorum ludorum
diebus, haec dicentem: "si corpus meum in locum illum trahitis, numquid
et animum et oculos meos in illa spectacula potestis intendere? adero itaque
absens, ac sic et vos et illa superabo." quibus auditis illi nihilo setius eum
adduxerunt secum, id ipsum forte explorare cupientes, utrum posset effi-
cere. quo ubi ventum est et sedibus quibus potuerunt locati sunt, fervebant
omnia immanissimis voluptatibus. ille clausis foribus oculorum interdixit
animo ne in tanta mala procederet. atque utinam et aures opturasset! nam
quodam pugnae casu, cum clamor ingens totius populi vehementer eum

pulsasset, curiositate victus et quasi paratus, quidquid illud esset, etiam
visum contemnere et vincere, aperuit oculos, et percussus est graviore vul-
nere in anima quam ille in corpore quem cernere concupivit, ceciditque
miserabilius quam ille quo cadente factus est clamor: qui per eius aures
intravit et reseravit eius lumina, ut esset, qua feriretur et deiceretur audax
adhuc potius quam fortis animus, et eo infirmior, quo de se praesumpserat,
qui debuit de te. ut enim vidit illum sanguinem, immanitatem simul
ebibit et non se avertit sed fixit aspectum et hauriebat furias et nesciebat,
et delectabatur scelere certaminis et cruenta voluptate inebriabatur. et non
erat iam ille, qui venerat, sed unus de turba, ad quam venerat, et verus
eorum socius, a quibus adductus erat. quid plura? spectavit, clamavit, exar-
sit abstulit inde secum insaniam qua stimularetur redire non tantum cum
illis a quibus prius abstractus est, sed etiam prae illis et alios trahens.

He [Alypius] had gone to Rome to study the law and there he was carried
away to an extraordinary extent by an incredible yearning for gladiatorial
games. For although he avoided and detested such spectacles, certain friends
and fellow students of his brought him with lighthearted force (since he
was objecting fiercely and resisting) to the amphitheatre on days of cruel
funeral games. He said, "Even if you drag my body to that place, can you
direct my mind and eyes to the spectacle? I will be present while absent,
and so defeat both you and the show." When they heard this, they dragged
him in with them nevertheless, perhaps wanting to find out whether he
could do it. When they arrived there and had gotten what seats they could,
the whole place seethed with its monstrous pleasures. Alypius closed the
doors of his eyes and forbade his soul to engage in such evils. If only he
had shut his ears too! But at a certain fall in the fight, when a huge roar
from the entire crowd struck him powerfully, he was overcome by curiosity
and, telling himself he was ready to condemn the sight, whatever it might
be, and to rise above it, he opened his eyes. And so he was struck with a
more serious wound in his soul than was he, whom he wanted to see, in
his body, and he fell more pitiably than he whose fall had generated the
roar. That roar entered through his ears and unlocked the sight by which
his soul, daring rather than brave up to this point, was flogged and cast
down. And he was all the weaker for having presumed about himself when
he ought to have relied on you. For when he saw the blood, he drank in the
savagery and did not turn away but fixed his gaze on it. Unaware of what
he was doing, he devoured the mayhem and was delighted by the wicked
contest and drunk on its cruel pleasure. He was no longer the man who
had come to the show, but one of the crowd he had come to, and a true
partner of those who had brought him along. Why say more? He looked,

he shouted, he was fired up, and he carried away with him the madness that would goad him to return, not only with his original companions but even as their leader dragging others along.

T.4 Cicero, *Pro Milone* 92

Etenim si in gladiatoriis pugnis et infimi generus hominum condicione atque fortuna timidos atque supplices et ut vivere liceat obsecrantis etiam odisse solemus, fortis atque animosos et se acriter ipsos morti offerentis servare cupimus, eorumque nos magis miseret, qui nostram misericordiam non requirunt, quam qui illam efflagitant, quanto hoc magis fortissimis civibus facere debemus?

For if in gladiatorial bouts, where the fate of the lowest class of mankind is concerned, we usually loathe the cowardly suppliants who beg to be allowed to live, while we want to spare the brave and vigorous ones who enthusiastically expose themselves to death, and feel more pity for those who do not seek our pity than those who importune us for it, then how much the more ought we do this in the case of our bravest citizens?

T.5 Cicero, *Disputationes Tusculanae* 2.41

Gladiatores, aut perditi homines aut barbari, quas plagas perferunt! quo modo illi, qui bene instituti sunt, accipere plagam malunt quam turpiter vitare!... quis cum decubuisset, ferrum recipere iussus collum contraxit?... crudele gladiatorum spectaculum et inhumanum non nullis videri solet, et haud scio an ita sit, ut nunc fit: cum vero sontes ferro depugnabant, auribus fortasse multae, oculis quidem nulla poterat esse fortior contra dolorem et mortem disciplina.

Gladiators, whether ruined men or barbarians, what wounds they endure! See how the well trained prefer to accept a wound rather than disgracefully avoid it!... Who, when he has fallen, stretches out his neck when ordered to accept the sword?... A gladiatorial spectacle usually appears cruel and inhuman to some and I am inclined to agree, as they are now staged. But when condemned men fought with swords, there could be no sturdier training for the eye against pain and death, though perhaps there were many for the ear.

T.6 Dio 39.38.1–5

Κἀν ταῖς αὐταῖς ἡμέραις ὁ Πομπήιος τὸ θέατρον, ᾧ καὶ νῦν λαμ-πρυνόμεθα, καθιέρωσε, καὶ ἔν τε ἐκείνῳ θέαν καὶ μουσικῆς καὶ ἀγῶνος γυμνικοῦ κἀν τῷ ἱπποδρόμῳ καὶ ἵππων ἅμιλλαν καὶ θηρίων πολλῶν καὶ παντοδαπῶν σφαγὰς ἐποίησεν. [2] λέοντές τε γὰρ πεντακόσιοι ἐν πέντε ἡμέραις ἀναλώθησαν, καὶ ἐλεφαντες ὀκτωκαίδεκα πρὸς ὁπλίτας ἐμαχέσαντο. καὶ αὐτῶν οἱ μὲν παραχρῆμα ἀπέθανον, οἱ δὲ οὐ πολλῷ ὕστερον. ἠλεήθησαν γάρ τινες ὑπὸ τοῦ δήμου παρὰ τὴν τοῦ Πομπηίου γνώμην, ἐπειδὴ τραυματισθέντες τῆς μάχης ἐπαύσαντο, [3] καὶ περιι- ιόντες τάς τε προβοσκίδας ἐς τὸν οὐρανὸν ἀνέτεινον καὶ ὠλοφύροντο οὕτως ὥστε καὶ λόγον παρασχεῖν ὅτι οὐκ ἄλλως ἐκ συντυχίας αὐτὸ ἐποίησαν, ἀλλὰ τούς τε ὅρκους οἷς πιστεύσαντες ἐκ τῆς Λιβύης ἐπεπερ- αίωντο ἐπιβοώμενοι καὶ τὸ δαιμόνιον πρὸς τιμωρίαν σφῶν ἐπικαλού- μενοι. [4] λέγεται γὰρ ὅτι οὐ πρότερον τῶν νεῶν ἐπέβησαν πρὶν πίστιν παρὰ τῶν ἀγόντων σφᾶς ἔνορκον λαβεῖν, ἦ μὴν μηδὲν κακὸν πείσεσθαι. καὶ τοῦτο μὲν εἴτ’ ὄντως οὕτως εἴτε καὶ ἄλλως πως ἔχει, οὐκ οἶδα· [5] ἤδη γάρ τινες καὶ ἐκεῖωο εἶπον, ὅτι πρὸς τῷ τῆς φωνῆς τῆς πατριώτιδος αὐτοὺς ἐπαΐειν καὶ τῶν ἐν τῷ οὐρανῷ γιγνομένων συνιᾶσιν, ὥστε καὶ ἐν ταῖς νουμηνίαις, πρὶν ἐς ὄψιν τοῖς ἀνθρώποις τὴν σελήνην ἐλθεῖν, πρός τε ὕδωρ ἀείνων ἀφικνεῖσθαι κἀνταῦθα καθαρμόν τινά σφων ποιεῖσθαι.

(Loeb trans.): During these same days Pompey dedicated the theatre in which we take pride even at the present time. In it he provided an entertainment consisting of music and gymnastic contests, and in the circus a horse-race and the slaughter of many wild animals. [2] Indeed, five hundred lions were used up in five days, and eighteen elephants fought against men in heavy armour. Some of these beasts were killed at the time, and others a little later. For some of them, contrary to Pompey's wish, were pitied by the people when, after being wounded and ceasing to fight, [3] they walked about with their trunks raised toward heaven, lamenting so bitterly as to give rise to the report that they did so not by mere chance, but were crying out against the oaths in which they had trusted when they crossed from Africa, and were calling upon heaven to avenge them. [4] For it is said that they would not set foot upon the ships before they received a pledge under oath from their drivers that they would suffer no harm. Whether this is really so or not, I do not know; [5] for some in time past have further declared that in addition to understanding the language of their native country they also comprehend what is going on in the sky, so that at the time of the new moon, before that luminary comes within the gaze of men, they reach running water and there perform a kind of purification of themselves.

T.7 Dio Chrysostom 31.121

νῦν δὲ οὐθέν ἐστιν ἐφ’ ὅτῳ τῶν ἐκεῖ γιγνομένων οὐκ ἂν αἰσχυνθείη τις. οἷον εὐθὺς τὰ περὶ τοὺς μονομάχους οὕτω σφόδρα ἐζηλώκασι

Κορινθίους, μᾶλλον δ'ὑπερβεβλήκασι τῇ κακοδαιμονίᾳ κἀκείνους καὶ τοὺς ἄλλους ἅπαντας, ὥστε οἱ Κορίνθιοι μὲν ἔξω τῆς πόλεως θεωροῦσιν ἐν χαράδρᾳ τινί, πλῆθος μὲν δυναμένῳ δέξασθαι τόπῳ, ῥυπαρῷ δὲ ἄλλως καὶ ὅπου μηδεὶς ἂν μηδὲ θάψειε μηδένα τῶν ἐλευθέρων, Ἀθηναῖοι δὲ ἐν τῷ θεάτρῳ θεῶνται τὴν καλὴν ταύτην θέαν ὑπ'αὐτὴν τὴν ἀκρόπολιν, οὗ τὸν Διόνυσον ἐπὶ τὴν ὀρχήστραν τιθέασιν· ὥστε πολλάκις ἐν αὐτοῖς τινα σφάττεσθαι τοῖς θρόνοις, οὗ τὸν ἱεροφάντην καὶ τοὺς ἄλλους ἱερεῖς ἀνάγκη καθίζειν.

(Loeb trans.): But as matters now stand, there is no practice current in Athens that would not cause any man to feel ashamed. For instance, in regard to the gladiatorial shows the Athenians have so zealously emulated the Corinthians, or rather, have so surpassed both them and all others in their mad infatuation, that whereas the Corinthians watch these combats outside the city in a ravine, a place that is able to hold a crowd but is otherwise dirty and such that no one would even bury there any freeborn citizen, the Athenians look on this fine spectacle in their theater under the very walls of the Acropolis, in the place where they bring their Dionysus into the orchestra and stand him up, so that the very seats in which the hierophant and other priests must sit are sometimes spattered with blood.

T.8 Fronto, *Principia Historiae* 17

[Traianus erat] ut qui sciret populum Romanum duabus praecipue rebus, annona et spectaculis, teneri; imperium non minus ludicris quam seriis probari; maiore damno seria, graviore invidia ludicra neglegi; minus acribus stimulis congiaria quam spectacula expeti; congiariis frumentariam modo plebem singillatim placari ac nominatim, spectaculis universum <populum conciliari>.

[Trajan was a man] who knew that the Roman people are kept in line by two things above all else – the grain dole and spectacles; that power meets with approval no less from amusements as from serious undertakings; that serious business is neglected with greater loss, amusements with greater ill will; that hand-outs are anticipated less keenly than shows; and that the grain dole pleases only the plebs individually and by name, whereas spectacles win over the entire people.

T.9 Livy, *Ab Urbe Condita* 41.20.11–13

Gladiatorum munus, Romanae consuetudinis, primo maiore cum terrore hominum, insuetorum ad tale spectaculum, quam uoluptate dedit; [12]

deinde saepius dando et modo volneribus tenus, modo sine missione, etiam [et] familiare oculis gratumque id spectaculum fecit, et armorum studium plerisque iuvenum accendit. [13] itaque qui primo ab Roma magnis pretiis paratos gladiatores accersere solitus erat, iam suo . . . <*vacat*>

He [*sc* Antiochus] gave a gladiatorial show after the Roman fashion, at first to the greater terror than pleasure of people who were unused to such sights. [12] Then by successive iterations, initially limiting the action to wounds and then not sparing the defeated, he made the sight familiar and pleasing, and stirred a zeal for arms in most of the young men. [3] In this way he who had at first usually imported his trained gladiators from Rome at great expense, now with his own . . . <*text breaks off*>

T.10 Lucilius 4.155–60K = 4.153–8M = Cic. *Tusc.* 4.48

(*Part of a discussion about philosophical concepts of distress and disorder*)

An vero vir fortis, nisi stomachari coepit, non potest fortis esse? Gladiatorium id quidem. Quamquam in eis ipsis videmus saepe constantiam:

Conlocuntur, congrediuntur, quaerunt aliquid, postulant, ut magis placati quam irati esse videantur. Sed in illo genere sit sane Pacideianus aliquis hoc animo, ut narrat Lucilius:

> "Occidam illum equidem et vincam, si id quaeritis," inquit,
> "Verum illud credo fore: in os prius accipiam ipse
> Quam gladium in stomacho spurci ac pulmonibus sisto.
> Odi hominem, iratus pugno, nec longius quicquam
> Nobis, quam dextrae gladium dum accommodet alter;
> Usque adeo studio atque odio illius ecferor ira."

Or is it that a truly brave man cannot be brave unless he becomes enraged? It seems so with gladiators. Although in these very same men we often see equanimity:

They converse, meet, ask something, make demands so that they seem more calm than angry. But there may be in that class of person someone quite like Pacideianus, with a spirit such as Lucilius tells us about:

> "I will kill him, oh yes I will, and win, if you ask it," he says,
> "But I think it will be like this: I will get one in the face
> Before I plant my sword in that swine's belly or chest.
> I hate the fellow, I fight angry, nor do we wait any longer
> Than for each of us to fit the sword into our right hands;
> I am transported by my anger to such a passionate hatred for him."

T.11 Martial, *Epigrams* 5.24

Hermes Martia saeculi voluptas,
Hermes omnibus eruditus armis,
Hermes et gladiator et magister,
Hermes turbo sui tremorque ludi
5   Hermes, quem timet Helius, sed unum,
Hermes, cui cadit Advolans, sed uni,
Hermes vincere nec ferire doctus,
Hermes suppositicius sibi ipse,
Hermes divitiae locariorum,
10   Hermes cura laborque ludiarum,
Hermes belligera superbus hasta,
Hermes aequoreo minax tridente,
Hermes casside languida timendus,
Hermes gloria Martis universi,
15   Hermes omnia solus et ter unus.

Hermes the martial delight of the age,
Hermes skilled in all arms,
Hermes, both gladiator and trainer,
Hermes, whirlwind and tremor of his school,
Hermes, whom Helius fears, him alone,
Hermes, before whom Advolans falls, before him alone,
Hermes, trained to win but not to harm,
Hermes, himself his own substitute,
Hermes, the riches of the ticket touts,
Hermes, the love and labor of gladiators' women,
Hermes, proud with warlike spear,
Hermes, threatening with marine trident,
Hermes, fearful with drooping helmet,
Hermes, the glory of Mars universal,
Hermes, all things at once and three times unique.

T.12 Petronius, *Satyricon* 45.4–13

Tu si aliubi fueris, dices hic porcos coctos ambulare. Et ecce habituri sumus munus excellente in triduo die festa; familia non lanisticia, sed plurimi liberti. [5] Et Titus noster magnum animum habet, et est caldicerebrius. Aut hoc aut illud, erit quid utique. Nam illi domesticus sum, non est mixcix. [6] Ferrum optimum daturus est, sine fuga, carnarium in medio, ut amphitheater videat. Et habet unde. Relictum est illi sestertium tricenties: decessit illius pater †male† ut quadringenta impendat, non sentiet patrimonium illius, et sempiterno nominabitur. [7] Iam nannos aliquot habet et mulierem essedariam et dispensatorem Glyconis, qui deprehensus est cum dominam suam delectaretur. Videbis populi rixam inter zelotypos et amasiunculos. [8] Glyco autem, sestertiarius homo, dispensatorem ad bestias dedit. Hoc est se ipsum traducere. Quid servus peccavit, qui coactus est facere? Magis illa matella digna fuit quam taurus iactaret. Sed qui asinum non potest, stratum caedit. [9] Quid autem Glyco putabat Hermogenis filicem unquam bonum exitum facturam? Ille miluo volanti poterat ungues resecare; colubra restem non parit. Glyco, Glyco dedit suas; itaque quamdiu vixerit, habebit stigmam, nec illam nisi Orcus delebit. [10] Sed sibi quisque peccat. Sed subolfacio quia nobis epulum daturus est Mammea, binos denarios mihi et meis. Quod si hoc fecerit, eripiat Norbano totum favorem. [11] Scias oportet plenis velis hunc vinciturum. Et revera, quid ille nobis boni fecit? Dedit gladiatores sestertiarios iam decrepitos, quos si sufflasses, cecidissent; iam meliores bestiarios vidi. Occidit de lucerna equites; putares eos gallos gallinaceos: alter burdubasta, alter loripes, tertiarius mortuus pro mortuo, qui habe\<ba\>t nervia praecisa. [12] Unus alicuius flaturae fuit Thraex, qui et ipse ad dictata pugnavit. Ad summam, omnes postea secti sunt; adeo de magna turba 'Adhibete' acceperant: plane fugae merae. 'Munus tamen,' inquit, 'tibi dedi': et ego tibi plodo. [13] Computa, et tibi plus do quam accepi. Manus manum lavat.

[*Freedman Echion speaking*] "If you lived somewhere else, you'd say roast pork walks the streets. In any case, we're about to have an excellent show on the holiday, three days away. No gladiator troop from the training school, but most of them freedmen. [5] Our Titus is ambitious – he's a real hothead too. One way or another, there'll be something worthwhile. I'm a close friend of his, and he's not a man for half measures. [6] He'll give us the best fighting, with no running away, a butcher's shop in the middle, so the amphitheater can see it. And he has the means. Thirty million sesterces was left to him: his father died, sadly, so that he spends 400,000 without his estate feeling the pinch. His name will be forever remembered. [7] He has some dwarves, a female *essedaria*, and Glyco's head accountant, who was caught pleasuring the mistress of the house. You'll see the people arguing, jealous husbands against loverboys. [8] But Glyco, that cheapskate, has given his accountant to the beasts. That's the same as giving himself over to them. What transgression did a slave commit, who was forced to do it? That piss-pot wife of his is more deserving to be thrown by the bull. But he who can't lash the donkey, lashes the saddle blanket. [9] Why did Glyco think that worthless daughter of Hermogenes would turn out well? He could cut the claws off a flying kite; a snake doesn't father rope. Glyco, O Glyco, he's paid the penalty himself. As long as he lives, he'll carry a stigma that only death can erase. [10] But we all sin against ourselves. But I catch a whiff that Mammea will put on a banquet for us, two *denarii* for me and mine. If he does that, he may strip Norbanus of his popularity entirely. [11] I'm sure you know he'll have plain sailing to victory. In fact, what good has Norbanus ever done us? He gave a show of two-bit gladiators, already decrepit, who'd have fallen over if you blew on 'em. I've seen better beast-men. He killed pint-sized knights – you'd have thought them farmyard cocks. One was thin as a rake, another bandy-legged, and the reserve was a corpse substituting for a corpse – hamstrung in advance. [12] Only one showed any fighting spirit, a Thracian, but even he fought by the book. In short, they all had their throats cut afterwards, for they'd had shouts of 'Get to it!' from the large crowd. It was a total shambles. 'But I gave you a show,' he says. And I applaud you. Do the math, and I'm giving you more than I got from you. One hand washes the other.

T.13 Philostratus, *Vita Apolloni* 4.22

οἱ Ἀθηναῖοι ξυνιόντες ἐς θέατρον τὸ ὑπὸ τῇ ἀκροπόλει προσεῖχον σφαγαῖς ἀνθρώπων, καὶ ἐσπουδάζετο ταῦτα ἐκεῖ μᾶλλον ἢ ἐν Κορίνθῳ νῦν, χρημάτων τε μεγάλων ἐωνημένοι ἤγοντο μοιχοὶ καὶ πόρνοι καὶ τοιχωρύχοι καὶ βαλαντιοτόμοι καὶ ἀνδραποδισταὶ καὶ τὰ τοιαῦτα ἔθνη, οἱ δ᾽ ὥπλιζον αὐτοὺς καὶ ἐκέλευον ξυμπίπτειν. ἐλάβετο δὲ καὶ τούτων ὁ Ἀπολλώνιος, καὶ καλούντων αὐτὸν ἐς ἐκκλησίαν Ἀθηναίων οὐκ ἂν ἔφη παρελθεῖν ἐς χωρίον ἀκάθαρτον καὶ λύθρου μεστόν. ἔλεγε δὲ ταῦτα ἐν ἐπιστολῇ. καὶ θαυμάζειν ἔλεγεν "ὅπως ἡ θεὸς οὐ καὶ τὴν ἀκρόπολιν ἤδη ἐκλείπει τοιοῦτον αἷμα ὑμῶν ἐκχεόντων αὐτῇ . . . ".

(Loeb trans.) The Athenians ran in crowds to the theater beneath the acropolis to witness human slaughter, and the passion for such sports was stronger there than it is in Corinth today; for they would buy for large sums adulterers and fornicators and burglars and cut-purses and kidnappers and suchlike rabble, and then they took and armed them and set them to fight with one another. Apollonius then attacked these practices, and when the Athenians invited him to attend their assembly, he refused to enter a place so impure and reeking with gore. And this he said in an epistle to them, that he was surprised "the the goddess had not already fled the Acropolis when you shed such blood under her eyes . . . ".

T.14 Pliny, *Historiae Naturales* 8.20–1

Pompei quoque altero consulatu, dedicatione templi Veneris Victricis, vig-
inti pugnavere in circo aut, ut quidam tradunt, XVII, Gaetulis ex adverso iac-
ulantibus, mirabili unius dimicatione, qui pedibus confossis repsit genibus
in catervas, abrepta scuta iaciens in sublime, quae decidentia voluptati spectantibus erant in orbem circumacta, velut arte, non furore belvae, iaceren-
tur. magnum et in altero miraculum fuit uno ictu occiso; pilum autem sub
oculo adactum in vitalia capitis venerat. [21] universi eruptionem tempta-
vere, non sine vexatione populi, circumdatis claustris ferreis. qua de causa
Caesar dictator postea simile spectaculum editurus euripis harenam cir-
cumdedit, quos Nero princeps sustulit equiti loca addens. sed Pompeiani
amissa fugae spe misericordiam vulgi inenarrabili habitu quaerentes sup-
plicavere quadam sese lamentatione conplorantes, tanto populi dolore, ut
oblitus imperatoris ac munificentiae honori suo exquisitae flens universus
consurgeret dirasque Pompeio, quas ille mox luit, inprecaretur.

In the second consulship of Pompey, at the dedication of the temple of
Venus Victrix, 20 [elephants] fought in the circus or, as some report, 17
against Gaetulian javelinmen. As one animal was putting up a remarkable
fight, its feet pierced through, it crawled on its knees against the mob of
its attackers, snatched their shields away and threw them high into the air;
as they fell back to earth the shields charted a curve, to the delight of the
spectators, almost as if they had been thrown by skill [i.e., juggling] and not
by the fury of a wild beast. Another marvel in a different instance was when
one elephant was killed with a single wound; the javelin penetrated below
the eye and reached the vitals of the head. [21] Despite an enclosure of iron
fencing, the entire elephant troop attempted a break-out, which disturbed
the people. For this reason, Caesar the Dictator, when he was about to stage
a similar spectacle later, threw a water channel around the arena, which
Nero demolished in adding seats for the Equestrian class. But Pompey's
elephants, having lost hope of getting away, sought the sympathy of the mob
with their indescribable posture as they begged and wailed for themselves in
a sort of lamentation. So great was the grief of the people that, forgetting the
general and the meticulous generosity he had staged for their honor, they
all wept and stood up, invoking curses on Pompey, which he soon paid for.

T.15 Pliny, *Panegyricus* 33.1–4

. . . Visum est spectaculum inde non enerve nec fluxum, nec quod animos
virorum molliret et frangeret, sed quod ad pulchra vulnera contemptumque

mortis accenderet, cum in servorum etiam noxiorumque corporibus amor laudis et cupido victoriae cerneretur. [2] quam deinde in edendo liberalitatem, quam iustitiam exhibuit omni adfectione aut intactus aut maior!... [3] iam quam libera spectantium studia, quam securus favor! Nemini impietas ut solebat obiecta, quod odisset gladiatorem; nemo e spectatore spectaculum factus miseras voluptates unco et ignibus expiavit. [4] demens ille verique honoris ignarus, qui crimina maiestatis in harena colligebat, ac se despici et contemni, nisi etiam gladiatores eius veneraremur, sibi male dici in illis, suam divinitatem suum numen violari interpretabatur, cumque se idem quod deos idem gladiatores quod se putabat.

... We saw a spectacle – nothing flaccid or dissolute to soften and weaken men's spirits, but something to rouse them to accept lovely wounds and hold death in contempt, since even in the bodies of slaves and criminals was seen a love of glory and lust to win. [2] What generosity in putting on the show! What fairness he displayed, untouched by all emotion, or above it!... [3] How free was the enthusiasm of the spectators, how secure their support! No one was charged with disloyalty, as used to be the case, for hating a gladiator; none of the spectators was made into a spectacle, appeasing wretched pleasures with hook and flame. [4] He [Domitian] was a lunatic, ignorant of his own position, who collected charges of treason at the arena and thought himself despised and disparaged unless we also revered his gladiators, who interpreted insults against them as insults against himself and reckoned his divine spirit maligned; he thought himself equal to the gods, and his gladiators equal to himself.

T.16 Prudentius, *Contra Symmachum* 2.1091–113

(Discussing and disparaging the Vestal Virgins)

> inde ad consessum caveae pudor almus et expers
> sanguinis it pietas hominum visura cruentos
> congressus mortesque et vulnera vendita pastu
> spectatura sacris oculis. sedet illa verendis
> 1095 vittarum insignis phaleris fruiturque lanistis.
> o tenerum mitemque animum! Consurgit ad ictus
> et quotiens victor ferrum iugulo inserit, illa
> delicias ait esse suas, pectusque iacentis
> virgo modesta iubet converso pollice rumpi,
> 1100 ne latet pars ulla animae vitalibus imis,
> altius inpresso dum palpitat ense secutor.
> hoc illud meritum est, quod continuare feruntur

excubias Latii pro maiestate Palati,
quod redimunt vitam populi procerumque salutem,
1105 perfundunt quia colla comis bene vel bene cingunt
tempora taeniolis et licia crinibus addunt,
et quia subter humum lustrales testibus umbris
in flammam iugulant pecudes et murmura miscent?
an quoniam podii meliore in parte sedentes
1110 spectant aeratam faciem quam crebra tridenti
inpacto quatiant hastilia, saucius et quam
vulneribus patulis partem perfundat harenae
cum fugit, et quanto vestigia sanguine signet?

Thence to the gathering in the stands goes that nourishing chastity
And piety free from blood, to see bloody combats and deaths of men
To watch with sacred eyes wounds sold for sustenance.
She sits there standing out in the venerable trappings of her veils
And enjoys those of the trainer.
Oh gentle, mild spirit! She jumps to her feet at the wounds
And whenever a winner shoves his sword into a throat,
She declares him her darling; the modest virgin
Orders the chest of a fallen fighter pierced with a turn of her thumb,
So that no vestige of life lies hidden in his deepest vitals,
While the *secutor* trembles at the sword pushed deeper.
Is this their value, that they are said to keep continuous watch
For the greatness of Latium's Palatine?
That they secure the life of its people and well-being of its nobles,
Since they spread their hair over their necks nicely or nicely
Wreathe their brows with little ribbons and add threads to their hair,
And since they cut the throats of lustral cattle at a fire underground
And with ghosts as their witnesses mutter and murmur prayers?
Or is it since, sitting in the better section of the podium,
They watch how often the spearshaft rattles the bronze face
When the trident has struck,
And how the wounded fighter from gaping gashes spatters his part
      of the arena
When he flees, and with how much blood he leaves his marks?

T.17 [Quintilian] *Declamationes* 9.5–9

[5] . . . Audite, audite, iudices, novam captivi querelam: iam miser aput piratas non eram. Alebat devotum corpus gravior omni fame sagina, et inter dedita noxae mancipia contemptissimus tiro gladiator, ut novissime perderem calamitatis meae innocentiam, discebam cotidie scelus. Haec tamen omnia sustinui, tuli; adeo difficile est etiam sua causa mori.

[6] Et iam dies aderat, iamque ad spectaculum supplicii nostri populus convenerat, iam ostentata per harenam periturorum corpora mortis suae pompam duxerant. Sedebat sanguine nostro favorabilis dominus, cum me, cuius, ut interiecto mari, non fortunam quisquam nosse, non natales, non patrem poterat, una tamen res faceret apud quosdam miserabilem, quod videbar inique comparatus; certa enim harenae destinabar victima, nemo munerario vilius steterat. Fremebant ubique omnia apparatu mortis: hic ferrem acuebat, ille accendebat ingibus laminas, hinc virgae, inde flagella adferebantur. Homines piratas putares. Sonabant clangore ferali tubae, inlatisque Libitinae toris ducebatur funus ante mortem. Ubique vulnera, gemitus, cruor; totum in oculis periculum. Si quid est in me abdicatione dignum, iudices, unum crimen agnosco, quod in haec amicum meum misi. Est quidem felicibus difficilis miseriarum vera aestimatio, figurare tamen potestis qui tunc animus mihi, quae cogitatio fuerit.

[7] Namque et natura redit in extremis tristis praeteritae voluptatis recordatio, et mihi, cum generis conscientia, cum fortunae conspicuus aliquando fulgor, cum liberales artes, cum omnia quondam honestiora munerario meo, domus, familia, amici ceteraque numquam videnda in ultima mortis expectatione succurrerent tenenti servilia arma et ignominiosa morte perituro, tum, si ulla miseris fides est, quid horum omnium ignari agerent propinqui, nihil peius de fortuna mea suspicantes, quam quod scripseram. Illud tamen gravissimum, quod patrem, qui tamdiu non veniret, captum putabam. Ergo tota cogitatione intentus in mortem expectabam cruentum illum confectorem. Quis enim dubitet quid futurum fuerit, si ego pugnassem? Ille quoque occisus est, qui inter nos, ut apparet, fortior fuit. His cogitationibus attonito et in mortem iam paene demerso inopinata subito amici mei species offulsit. Obstupui totumque corpus percurrit frigidus pavor, neque aliter, quam si vana obiceretur oculis imago, mente captus steti. Ubi primum lux rediit laxatumque est iter voci, "quid tu," inquam "quo casu pervenisti huc, miser? Numquid et te vendidere piratae?" At ille complexus cervices meas, effusis in pectus meum lacrimis solutus, intercepto prope iam spiritu, <mi>sero iam trepidante me, primam vocem et diu solam edidit: "Satis vixi." Ut vero causas itineris reddidit et venisse se ad redimendum indicavit, "Et unde" inquam "tibi pecunia, nisi redistis in gratiam, et te pater meus misit?"

[8] Audite gentes, audite populi! Non solita iudicium nostrum corona circumstet, sed, si patitur natura rerum, totus ad cognitionem talis exempli orbis circumfluat. Tacete, priora saecula, in quibus tamen a primordio generis humani paucissima amicitiae paria admirabiliora fecerat longa

temporibus nostris fides †intercepta†. Quicquid historiae tradiderunt, carmina finxerunt, fabulae adiecerunt, sub hac conparatione taceant. Quis crederet, si dubitari posset, inter duos amicos, quorum alterum immunem malorum omnium fortuna fecerat, alterum piratis ac lanistae tradiderat, meliorem condicionem fuisse captivi? "si dives essem," inquit "pecuniam pro te attulissem. Quod unum pauperibus praesidium est, manus habeo. Has piratis daturus fui, has pro te in pugnam vicarias dabo."

Ignosce, pater, quod nimia contentione adfectus paene tibi orbitatis vulnus inpresserim. Testor deos non per me stetisse, quod vivo. Neque enim ita me efferarat ludus, aut in tantum duraverat animum caedis longa meditatio, ut eum amicum vellem occidi, qui pro me mori poterat. Vindicabam mihi fortunam meam et adhuc necessitatis gladiator depugnare etiam volebam, neque ullis precibus poteram evinci, quamquam se non superfuturum alioquin minabatur idque unum adfirmabat interesse, utrum vicarium mallem habere mortis an comitem. Non vici. Quid igitur actum sit, quaeritis? Duxit me ad munerarium, iudices. Quas ego illius preces, quam pertinaces lacrimas, quam miserabilem obtestationem vidi! Nemo umquam sic rogavit missionem. Transferuntur in illum detracta corpori meo arma, et male aptatis insignibus destinatum par producitur.

[9] Quid me admonetis supremarum amici mei precum, quibus haec alimenta caro empta inopi patris senectuti petit[a]? Adiutorium hoc ad causam putatis? Me pudet, quod rogatus sum. "Per hanc" inquit "mihi lucem ultimam, per notissimam amoris nostri fidem, non sinas mendicare parentem meum. Sustineas, adiuves, praestes affectum. Si mereor, tu sis illi vicarius meus." Nec plura dicendi tempus fuit, iamque suprema per galeam dederam oscula, digressisque in diversum ministris permissus Mars erat. O quam sollicitus spectavi! Quam attonita mente! Quam simili corporis motu! Quotiens ad infestum mucronem, quasi ipse peterer, me summisi, quotiens ad conatus erectus sum! O misera cogitatio, o crudelis natura metus! Merito tu, amice, pugnare maluisti. Facinus indignum illum animum, illum ardorem non contigisse castris, non bellicis certaminibus, ubi vera virtus nulla pugnandi lege †praemium scribitur†. Qua vi proelium invaserat iratus etiamnum tamquam adversario meo! At omnis impetus excipiebatur callide, veterani gladiatoris astu; omnes conatus contra se erant. Nec difficilem tamen sub illo praesertim auctoramento habuisset missionem, sed noluit gladiator vivere. Igitur iam nudum corpus vulneribus offerens, ut totam pro me mercedem semel solveret, stans periit. Cui licuit in patria, in domo, inter propinquos securo consenescere aevo, cui tranquillam sine reprehensione agere vitam, iacet confectus vulneribus, et primo iuventae flore fraudatus periit miser fato meo. At ego, qui debebar illi fortunae,

quem mors sibi destinaverat, emissus ludo nocentior quam venditus, etiam viatico illius infelicis revertor. Placeamus licet nobis fortuna nostra, pater, pauperi solvendo non sumus.

[5] Listen, gentlemen of the jury, listen to a novel complaint from a captive: by now I was not suffering among the pirates. Fattening food, more grievous than any starvation, fed my accursed body. Among slaves handed over for punishment, the novice gladiator is the most scorned and, in order finally to lose my innocence in this catastrophe, I began learning villainy on a daily basis. All of this I nevertheless suffered and bore: so difficult it is to die, even when it's your purpose in life.

[6] Now the day arrived, and already the people had gathered to watch our punishment, already the bodies of those destined to perish had been displayed throughout the arena and had led the formal procession of their own deaths. The sponsor, popular because of our blood, was sitting down, although one factor made me (whose fate, family or father nobody could know, since a sea intervened) an object of pity: that I appeared unevenly matched. For I was marked as a certain victim of the arena; nobody stood in lower esteem with the sponsor. The whole place hummed with all the machinery of death: one sharpened a sword, another heated iron plates in the fire; here rods were brought out, there whips. You would think these men pirates. The trumpets began to sound their fatal blare, the stretchers of doom were brought in, and my funeral procession got underway before my death. Everywhere were wounds, groans, gore; the totality of my peril lay before my eyes. If I am worthy of disowning at all, gentlemen, I admit one crime: that into all of this I sent my friend. A true reckoning of my miseries is indeed difficult for you fortunate people, yet you can imagine of what mind I was then, what my thinking was.

[7] Yes, it is natural in extreme sadness for the memory of past delight to return, and when this occurred to me as I grasped a slave's weapons and was about to die a ignominious death – knowledge of my lineage, the illustrious splendor of my former fortune, my liberal education, all those other features of my life, more respectable than those of my sponsor (my home, family, friends, and all the other things never to be seen again in my last expectation of death) – then, if any trust can be put in a wretch, I thought what my relatives would do, who were ignorant of all this, suspecting nothing worse about my fate than what I had written. But my most weighty concern was that I thought my father, who had not arrived in so long a time, had been captured. And so I focused all my thoughts on death and awaited that bloody butcher. For who would doubt what

would have happened, if I had fought? For even the bravest among us, it seemed, was killed. While I was dumbstruck by these thoughts and almost already plunged into death, suddenly the unexpected sight of my friend burst upon me like a bright light. I was astounded and the cold chill of fear ran through by entire body. I stood, my mind paralyzed, no differently than as if a spectral shade hove into view. When first light returned to my mind and I regained the power of speech, I said "What brings you here, my poor friend, and under what circumstances? Surely pirates didn't sell you too?" But he embraced my neck, cried out his tears onto my chest, and with his breathing almost cut short, as I, a wretch, trembled, he issued his first and only statement for a long time: "I've lived enough." When he told me the reasons for his journey and indicated he'd come to ransom me, I said "So where did you get the money, unless you have regained my father's favor and he sent you?"

[8] Listen nations, listen peoples! Let no common crowd of spectators stand around our court, but if the nature of things allows it, let the whole world gather about to recognize such a fine example. Be silent, ages past, in which even from the beginning of the human race long-lasting loyalty, which no longer exists in our time, had made a handful of pairs of friends more admirable than we were. Whatever histories have passed down, poems have invented, or stories have exaggerated, let them fall silent in the face of this comparison. Who would believe, if it could be doubted, that between two friends, of whom fortune had made one immune to every evil but handed the other over to pirates and the gladiator trainer, the captive would be in the better position? "If I were rich," he said, "I would have brought money for your ransom. I have that which is the pauper's only assistance: my hands. I was going to give them to the pirates; I will give them as a replacement for you in the fight."

Forgive me, father, because moved by excessive tension I almost inflicted on you the wound of losing your child. I call on the gods to testify that it is not my fault that I live. For the gladiatorial training school had not made me such a savage, nor had my prolonged practicing for butchery hardened my heart to such a point that I wanted him to be killed, he a friend who was able to die in my place. I was taking up my own fate and, as a gladiator of necessity up to this point, I even wanted to fight it out to the end. I could not be dissuaded by any of his entreaties, although he was threatening not to survive in any case and asserted that one thing mattered: did I prefer to have a substitute in death, or a companion? I did not prevail. So what happened next, you ask? He brought me to the sponsor, gentlemen. What pleas, what stubborn tears, what pitiable entreaties I saw! No one ever asked for release from the arena like this. My armaments were taken off my body and passed over to him. With his trappings barely attached, the designated pairing was led forth.

[9] Why do you remind me of my friend's final pleas, by which he sought this support, bought so dearly, for the destitute old age of his father? Do you think this helps my case? I am ashamed that I was asked. He said, "By the light of this, my final day, by the well-known trust of our affection for each other, do not let my father become a beggar. Please support him, help him, extend your affection to him. If I earn the right, please be my substitute for him." There was no time to say more, and I had already given him my final kisses through his helmet. The attendants scattered in different directions, and Mars was allowed. How anxious I was looking on! How terrified was my heart! How I matched his body's movements! How many times did I duck the hostile blade, as if I were its target! How many times did I raise myself up to his thrusts! Wretched imagination! The cruel nature of fear! Justifiably, my friend, did you prefer to fight. It's a real crime that that courageous fervor had not joined the army and served in military combat, where real courage is not curtailed by any rules of fighting. With what force did he charge in, angry as if his adversary were still mine! But his every attack was deftly parried by the guile of the veteran gladiator, all his thrusts turned back on himself. Still, he'd have had no difficulty securing release, especially under the terms of his contract, but he did not want to live as a gladiator. Therefore, now offering his bared body to his opponent's blows so that he might pay the entire ransom for me at one go, he died still standing. He, who might have grown old safely in his country, in his home, and among his relatives, who might have lived a quiet life free from reproach, lay there dead, finished off by his wounds, cheated of the first flowers of youth, my poor friend died my death. But I, who ought to have suffered that fate, whom death had earmarked for itself, was sent out of the gladiatorial training school, more guilty than when I'd been sold into it. I even came back using my unlucky friend's travel allowance. We may take pleasure in our wealth, father, but we are in no position to pay back this poor man.

T.18 Salvian, *De Gubernatore Dei* 6.10

Primum, quod nihil ferme vel criminum vel flagitiorum est quod in spectaculis non sit: ubi summum deliciarum genus est mori homines aut, quod est morte gravius acerbiusque, lacerari, expleri ferarum aluos humanis carnibus, comedi homines cum circumstantium laetitia conspicientium voluptate, hoc est non minus paene hominum aspectibus quam bestiarum dentibus devorari.

In the first place, there is practically no crime or disgrace that is not a feature of the spectacles. Here the highest grade of pleasure is that people be killed or, what is worse and more brutal than death, that they be torn to shreds and the bellies of wild animals filled with human flesh, that people be eaten amidst the joy and delight of the onlookers standing about; that is, to have men devoured hardly any less by the eyes of people as by the teeth of beasts.

T.19 Seneca, *Controversiae 4 praefatio* 1

Quod munerarii solent facere, qui ad expectationem populi detinendam nova paria per omnes dies dispensat, ut sit quot populum et delectet et revocet, hoc ego facio . . .

I am doing what *munerarii* usually do when, in order to keep the anticipation of the people going, they spread new pairs across all the days of a spectacle, so that there is something both to delight the crowd and keep them coming back . . .

T.20 Seneca, *Epistulae* 7.2–5

[7.2] Inimica est multorum conversatio; nemo aliquod nobis vitium aut commendat aut inprimit aut nescientibus adlinit. utique quo maior est populus, cui miscemur, hoc periculi plus est. Nihil vero tam damnosum bonis moribus quam in aliquo spectaculo desidere. tunc enim per voluptatem facilius vitia subrepunt. [7.3] quid me existimas dicere? avarior redeo, ambitiosior, luxuriosior, immo vero crudelior et inhumanior, quia inter homines fui. Casu in meridianum spectaculum incidi lusus expectans et sales et aliquid laxamenti, quo hominum oculi ab humano cruore adquiescant; contra est. quicquid ante pugnatum est, misericordia fuit. nunc omissis nugis mera homocidia sunt. nihil habent quo tegantur, ad ictum totis corporibus expositi numquam frustra manum mittunt. [7.4] hoc plerique ordinariis paribus et postulaticiis praeferunt. quidni praeferant? non galea, non scuto repellitur ferrum. quo munimenta? quo artes? omnia ista mortis morae sunt. mane leonibus et ursis homines, meridie spectatoribus suis obiciuntur. interfectores interfecturis iubent obici et victorem in aliam detinent caedem. exitus pugnantium mors est; ferro et igne res geritur. haec fiunt, dum vacat harena. [7.5] "sed latrocinium fecit aliquis, occidit hominem." quid ergo? Quia occidit ille, meruit ut hoc pateretur; tu quid meruisti miser, ut hoc spectes? "Occide, verbera, ure! quare tam timide incurrit in ferrum? quare parum audacter occidit? quare parum libenter moritur? plagis agatur in vulnera, mutuos ictus nudis et obviis pectoribus excipiant." intermissum est spectaculum: "interim iugulentur homines, ne nihil agatur."

[7.2] Associating with a crowd is harmful; there is nobody who does not recommend some vice to us, or force it on us, or smear us with it when we're not paying attention. To be sure, the larger the crowd, the greater the danger. Nothing is more damaging to good character than to languish at some spectacle. For then vice more easily creeps in under the guise of pleasure. [7.3] What do you think I'm talking about? I come home greedier, more ambitious, more wanton, even more cruel and inhumane, since I have been among humans. I happened upon a midday spectacle expecting playful humor, some respite that relieved the eye of human carnage. Quite the opposite. Whatever fighting came before was compassion itself. All trifles now set aside, it's pure murder. They have nothing to protect themselves and their entire bodies are exposed to blows, a strike is never in vain. [7.4] Very many people prefer this to the ordinary pairings and request bouts. And why shouldn't they? No helmet, no shield deflects the steel. Where's the protection? Where's the skill? Those things just delay death. In the morning men are thrown to lions and bears, in the afternoon they are thrown to the spectators. They order the killers thrown to those who will kill them, and they keep the winner around for further butchery. Death is the exit for these fighters; fire and sword gets the job done. This goes on while the arena is empty. [7.5] "But he's a bandit, or a killer." So what? Since he has killed, he deserves to suffer; but what did you do, wretch, to deserve to watch? "Kill him! Lash him! Burn him! Why does he meet the sword so timidly? Why does he kill so lamely? Why won't he die more willingly? Drive him to his wounds with the lash; let's have each accept their blows with naked and exposed chests!" There's an intermission: "Let's have throats cut, so there's *something* happening."

T.21 Suetonius, *Augustus* 44

Spectandi confusissimum ac solutissimum morem correxit ordinavitque motus iniuria senatoris, quem Puteolis per celeberrimos ludos consessu frequenti nemo receperat. facto igitur decreto patrum ut, quotiens quid spectaculi usquam publice ederetur, primus subselliorum ordo vacaret senatoribus, Romae legatos liberarum sociarumque gentium vetuit in orchestra sedere, cum quosdam etiam libertini generis mitti deprendisset. [2] militem secrevit a populo. maritis e plebe proprios ordines assignavit, praetextatis cuneum suum, et proximum paedagogis, sanxitque ne quis pullatorum media cavea sederet. feminis ne gladiatores quidem, quos promiscue spectari sollemne olim erat, nisi ex superiore loco spectare concessit. [3] solis virginibus Vestalibus locum in theatro separatim et contra praetoris tribunal dedit. athletarum vero spectaculo muliebre secus omne adeo summovit, ut pontificalibus ludis pugilum par postulatum distulerit in insequentis diei matutinum tempus edixeritque mulieres ante horam quintam venire in theatrum non placere.

He [Augutus] corrected and regulated the utterly disordered and indiscriminate manner of watching spectacles after being upset by an insult to a senator, to whom nobody gave a seat in a crowded gathering at some very well-attended games at Puteoli. So the senate issued a decree that, whenever public spectacles were staged anywhere, the first tier of seats (*subsellia*) be reserved for senators and, at Rome, he forbade ambassadors from free and allied nations to sit in the orchestra, since he was informed that some of them were appointed even from the class of ex-slaves. [2] He separated soldiers from civilians. He assigned to married men from among the plebs their own tiers, to underage boys their own *cuneus*, and the neighboring one to their tutors. He further decreed that none of those wearing dark clothes sit in the middle banks of seats (*media cavea*). He did not allow women to watch even gladiators, unless it was from the upper section; formerly it was usual for women and men to watch them mixed up together. [3] Only to the Vestal Virgins did he give a separate spot in the theater, opposite the praetor's box. He removed women so entirely from displays of athletes that when a boxing match had been requested at his pontifical games, he deferred it until the early morning of the next day and issued an edict that women were not allowed to come to the theater before the fifth hour.

T.22 Suetonius, *Claudius* 21.5

nec ullo spectaculi genere communior aut remissor erat, adeo ut oblatos victoribus aureos prolata sinistra pariter cum vulgo voce digitisque numeraret ac saepe hortando rogandoque ad hilaritatem homines provocaret, dominos identitem appellans, immixtis interdum frigidis et arcessitis iocis:

qualis est ut cum Palumbum postulantibus daturum se promisit, si captus esset. illud plane quantumvis salubriter et in tempore: cum essedario, pro quo quattuor fili deprecabantur, magno omnium favore indulsisset rudem, tabulum ilico misit admonens populum, quanto opere liberos suscipere deberet, quos videret et gladiatori praesidio gratiaeque esse.

At no other type of spectacle [than the gladiatorial] was he more affable or cheerful, to the extent that he stretched out his left hand as the mob did and counted aloud on his fingers the gold coin given to the winners, and by his frequent encouragement and requests [of the performers] he provoked the crowd to hilarity, calling them "Masters" and occasionally throwing in flat and strained jokes; one such was when the crowd demanded Palumbus ["Pigeon"] he promised he would get him for them, if he could catch him. Another quip, however, was both salutary and timely: when he had conferred the wooden sword on an *essedarius*, on whose behalf four sons were making entreaties, and the people expressed their approval in loud applause, he immediately sent out a placard advising the people that they should be keen to have children, whom they saw offered protection and service even to a gladiator.

T.23 Suetonius, *Claudius* 34.1–2

quocumque gladiatorio muneri, vel suo vel alieno, etiam forte prolapsos iugulari iubebat, maxime retiarios, ut exspirantium facies videret. [2] cum par quoddam mutuis ictibus concidisset, cultellos sibi parvulos ex utroque ferro in usum fieri sine mora iussit. bestiariis meridianisque adeo delectabatur, ut et prima luce ad spectaculum descenderet et meridie dimisso ad prandium populo persederet praeterque destinatos etiam levi subitaque de causa quosdam committeret, de fabrorum quoque ac ministrorum at id genus numero, si automatum vel pegma vel quid tale aliud parum cessisset. induxit et unum ex nomenculatoribus suis, sic ut erat togatus.

Whenever there was a gladiatorial spectacle, whether his own or someone else's, he ordered that even performers who fell accidentally have their throats cut, especially the *retiarii*, so he could see their faces as they died. [2] When a pair of gladiators inflicted wounds on each other and fell together, he immediately ordered little knives made for himself from both their swords and put them to use. He so delighted in the beast hunts and midday shows that he would go down to the arena at dawn and, having dismissed the people for lunch at noon, he would stay in his seat. Aside from those already on the program, he would for trivial and sudden reasons, match some of his workmen and assistants and people of that sort, if a machine or a stageset or something of the kind had failed. He even sent in one of his pages, just as he was, in a toga.

T.24 Suetonius, *Titus* 8.2

quin et studium armaturae Thraecum prae se ferens saepe cum populo et voce et gestu ut fautor cavillatus est, verum maiestate salva nec minus aequitate.

In addition he openly preferred the Thracian-armed gladiator and often joked with the people by word and gesture as a supporter does, but he maintained his majesty no less than his sense of fairness.

T.25 Suetonius, *Domitianus* 10.1

patrem familias, quod Thraecem murmilloni parem, munerario imparem dixerat, detractum spectaculis in harenam canibus obiecit cum hoc titulo: "impie locutus parmularius."

A man who was head of his household, because he had said that a Thracian gladiator was a match for a *murmillo* but not for the giver of the games, he had dragged from the seats and thrown to dogs on the sand, with this placard: "A Thracian supporter who spoke disloyally."

T.26 Tacitus, *Annales* 14.17

sub idem tempus levi initio atrox caedes orta inter colonos Nucerinos Pompeianosque gladiatorio spectaculo quod Livineius Regulus, quem motum senatu rettuli, edebat. quippe oppidana lascivia in vicem incessentes probra, dein saxa, postremo ferrum sumpsere, validiore Pompeianorum plebe, apud quos spectaculum edebatur. ergo deportati sunt in urbem multi e Nucerinis trunco per vulnera corpore, ac plerique liberorum aut parentum mortis deflebant. cuius rei iudicium princeps senatui, senatus consulibus permisit. et rursus re ad patres relata, prohibiti publice in decem annos eius modi coetu Pompeiani collegiaque quae contra leges instituerant dissoluta; Livineius et qui alii seditionem conciverant exilio multati sunt.

About the same time, a minor incident led to serious slaughter between the colonists of Nuceria and Pompeii at a gladiator-like spectacle which Livineius Regulus, who had been expelled from the senate, put on. During an exchange of insults, typical of the petulance of country towns, they resorted to abuse, then to stones, and finally to steel; the greater strength lay with the populace of Pompeii, where the show was being exhibited. As a result, many of the Nucerians were carried maimed and wounded to the capital, while a very large number mourned the deaths of children or of parents. The trial of the affair was delegated by the emperor to the senate; by the senate to the consuls. On the case being again laid before the members, the Pompeians as a community were debarred from holding any similar assembly for ten years, and the associations which they had formed illegally dissolved. Livineius and the other fomenters of the outbreak were punished with exile.

T.27 Tertullian, *De Spectaculis* 15.5

Nam et si qui modeste et probe spectaculis fruitur pro dignitatis vel aetatis vel etiam naturae suae condicione, non tamen immobilis animi est et sine tacita spiritus passione.

For even if a man enjoys spectacles modestly and uprightly, as befits his status or age or even his natural disposition, his soul is not unstirred and he is not without a silent rousing of the spirit.

T.28 Tertullian, *De Spectaculis* 19.2

bonum est cum puniuntur nocentes. qui hoc nisi tamen nocens negabit?

It's a good thing when the guilty are punished. Who will deny this, unless themselves guilty?

T.29 Tertullian, *De Spectaculis* 21.2–22

[21.2] sic ergo evenit, ut, qui in publico vix necessitate vesicae tunicam levet, idem in circo aliter non exuat, nisi totum pudorem in faciem omnium intentet, ut et qui filiae virginis ab omni spurco verbo aures tuetur, ipse eam in theatrum ad illas voces gesticulationesque deducat, [3] et qui in

plateis litem manu agentem aut compescit aut detestatur, idem in stadio
gravioribus pugnis suffragium ferat, et qui ad cadaver hominis communi
lege defuncti exhorret, idem in amphitheatro derosa et dissipata et in
suo sanguine squalentia corpora patientissimis oculis desuper incumbat,
[4] immo qui propter homicidae poenam probandam ad spectaculum
veniat, idem gladiatorem ad homicidium flagellis et virgis compellat invi-
tum, et qui insigniori cuique homicidae leonem poscit, idem gladiatori
atroci petat rudem et pilleum praemium conferat, illum vero confectum
etiam oris spectaculo repetat, libentius recognoscens de proximo quem
voluit occidere de longinquo, tanto durior, si non voluit . . . [22.1] quid
mirum? inaequata ista hominum miscentium et commutantium statum
boni et mali per inconstantiam sensus et iudicii varietatem. [2] etenim
ipsi auctores et administratores spectaculorum quadrigarios scaenicos xys-
ticos arenarios illos amantissimos, quibus viri animas, feminae autem illis
etiam corpora sua substernunt, propter quos se in ea committunt quae
reprehendunt, ex eadem arte, qua magnifaciunt, deponunt et deminu-
unt, immo manifeste damnant ignominia et capitis minutione, arcentes
curia rostris senatu equite ceterisque honoribus omnibus simul et orna-
mentis quibusdam. [3] quanta perversitas! amant quos multant, depretiant
quos probant, artem magnificant, artificem notant. [4] quale iudicium
est, ut ob ea quis offuscetur, per quae promeretur? immo quanta con-
fessio est malae rei! cuius auctores, cum acceptissimi sint, sine nota non
sunt.

[21.2] So it happens that the man who will hardly lift his tunic in public on
his bladder's necessity, will take it off in the circus in such a way as to expose
himself fully in the face of all; or he who shields his virginal daughter's
ears from any foul language, will himself bring her to the theater, to those
very utterances and gestures; or he who subdues a disagreement in the
streets as it comes to blows, or expresses his detestation of it, will in the
stadium approve of far more serious fights; or he who abhors the corpse of
a man who died according to the shared law of humankind, will in the
amphitheater stare down from above with the most tolerant eyes on chewed
and ripped apart bodies, caked with their own blood; and even he who
goes to the spectacle on account of his approval of punishment for murder,
will drive the reluctant gladiator to murder with whips and rods; or he
who demands a lion for some infamous murderer will petition for the
wooden sword and cap of freedom for a brutal gladiator; indeed he will
demand back the body of the dead one to gaze on his face, and more gladly

inspect from close quarters the man he wished killed from afar; and if he didn't wish it, all the more pitiless is he . . . [22.1] Why wonder? That is the unevenness of humankind, as it mingles and interchanges the conditions of good and evil through inconstant sentiment and variable judgment. [2] Take the very sponsors and administrators of spectacles: the charioteers, actors, athletes, and arena performers, those great lovers, to whom men surrender their souls, and women their bodies as well, on whose account they commit the sins they censure. They glorify these people for the same skill for which they degrade and diminish them; indeed, they condemn them openly to ignominy and loss of citizen rights, shut them out of the council chamber, the speaker's platform, the senate, equestrian status, all honors whatsoever, and some distinctions. [3] What towering perversity! They love whom they punish, they devalue whom they admire; the art they glorify, the artist they stigmatize. [4] What brand of judgment is it that a man be hidden out of sight for that which brings him to the fore? What a confession it is of an evil condition! Their authors, at the height of their popularity are in disgrace.

SECTION B: INSCRIPTIONS

I.1   *CIL* 6.2059 = 6.32363 = *ILS* 5049 = Henzen, *Acta Fratrum Arvalium,* 106–7 = Pasoli, *Acta Fratrum Arvalium,* 25–6 = Scheid, *Commentarii Fratrum Arvalium qui Supersunt,* 126 (#48) = *EAOR* 6.13 Rome, AD 80/1.
Colosseum seats assigned to the Arval Brethren. The stone was recut and corrected (badly), which renders the surviving text confused and confusing.

Loca adsignata in amphiteatro | L. Aelio Plautio Lamia, Q. Pactumeio Fr<o>nto co(n)s(ulibus) | acceptum ab Laberio Maximo, procuratore praef(ecto) annonae, | L. Ven{n}uleio Apron<i>ano mag(istro), curatore Thyrso l(iberto). | Fratribus arvalibus: maeniano (primo), cun(eo) (duodecimo), gradib(us) marm(oreis) (octo): gradu (primo) p(edes) (quinque quadrantem semunciam sicilium), | grad(u) (octavo) p(edes) (quinque quadrantem semunciam, sicilum). F(iunt) ped(es) (quadraginta duo semis). {Gradu (primo) uno ped(es) viginti duo semis}. Et m<a>eniano {summo}| (secundo), cun(eo) (sexto), grad(ibus) marm(oreis) (quattuor): gradu (primo) {uno}p(edes) viginti duo semis. Et maeninano | summo in ligneis, tab(ulatione) (quinquagesima tertia), gradibus (undecim): gradu (primo) ped(es) (quinque) (trientem semunciam), grad(u) | (undecimo) ped(es) (quinque deuncem sicilicum). F(iunt) ped(es) (sexaginta tres deunx semuncia). | Summa ped(es) (centum undetriginta deunx semuncia).

Space assigned in the amphitheater. When L. Aelius Plautius Lamia and Q. Pactumeius Fronto were consuls, received from Laberius Maximus, procurator, prefet of the grain supply, when L. Venuleius Apronianus was president of the brotherhood with his freedman Thyrsus as curator. To the Arval Brethren (the following seats are assigned): in the first *maenianum*, twelfth *cuneus*, eight marble tiers: on the first tier five feet, one quarter, one twenty-fourth, one forty-eighth; on the eighth tier five feet, one quarter, one twenty-fourth, one forty-eighth. That makes forty-two feet and one half. And in the second *maenianum* sixth *cuneus*, four marble tiers: on the first tier <five feet, one half, one twelfth, one twenty-fourth. That makes> twenty-two feet and one half. And in the uppermost *maenianum*, in the wooden seats, in the fifty-third *tabulatio*, eleven tiers of seats: on the first tier, five feet, one third, one twenty-fourth; on the eleventh tier five feet, one half, one forty-eighth. That makes sixty-three feet, eleven-twelfths, one twenty-fourth. Total: one hundred and twenty nine feet, eleven twelfths, one twenty-fourth.

NOTES: The original inscription was copied from a document sent to the brethren from the office of the *praefectus annonae*, and it appears to have been recopied in antiquity so that confusion has crept into line 30, where wording – *gradu (primo) uno ped(es viginto duo semis)* and *maeniano summo* – has been mistakenly carved into this spot from the line directly underneath. The likeliest solution, proposed by Hülsen at *CIL* 6.32363 and adopted here, is that the detailed arrangements in the second *maenianum* have been omitted by mistake. The nature of the missing information can be worked out by comparison with the stated arrangements for the first *maenianum* and by reference to the surviving total for the second *maenianum* (22 1/2 *pedes*). The translation reflects this emendation. The system of fractions used in the text seems immensely complex for the purposes of so simple a task as seat assignation and has been simplified considerably by Hülsen ("Il posto degli arvali," 314–17). The inscription uses a unit of one twelfth (*uncia*). The Roman foot (*pes*) was based on a unit of one sixteenth, since 1 *pes* = 16 *digitus*. By converting the twelfths into sixteenths, we can reduce the measurements to simpler *pedes* and *digitus*. Thus the measurements can be simplified as follows:

First *maenianum*, twelfth *cuneus*:
pedes 5 + 3/12 (= 12/48) + 1/24 (= 2/48) + 1/48 = *pedes* 5 15/48 =
ped. 5 *dig.* 5
This multiplied by the 8 tiers =
ped. 40 *dig.* 40 = *ped.* 42 and 1/2 (*dig.* 8), corresponding to the printed sum for this section.
Second *maenianum*, sixth *cuneus* (calculated from analogy with first *maenianum* and total):
pedes 5 + 6/12 (= 24/48) + 1/12 (= 4/48) + 2/48 = *pedes* 5 30/48 =
ped. 5 *dig.* 10
This multiplied by the 4 tiers =
ped. 20 *dig.* 40 = *ped.* 22. and 1/2 (*dig.* 8), corresponding to the printed sum for this section.
Summum maenianum in ligneis, fifty-third *tabulatio*:
First *gradus*:
pedes 5 + 4/12 (= 16/48) + 1/24 (= 2/48) = *pedes* 5 18/48 =
ped. 5 *dig.* 6
Eleventh *gradus*:
pedes 5 + 1/2 (= 24/48) + 5/12 (= 20/48) + 1/48 = *pedes* 5 45/48 =
ped. 5 *dig.* 15

The upper seats in this section were therefore marginally wider than the lower ones (forced by the curvature of the building?). In all likelihood, the shift from narrower to wider was effected incrementally over the eleven rows. Hülsen ("Il posto degli arvali," 316) postulates seven tiers of wider seats (*ped.* 5 *dig.* 15) and four of narrower (*ped.* 5 *dig.* 3/8 (= 9/4 + 18/4 + 27/4)) and, by means of a speculative and complex calculation, brings his total into line with that stated in the text, which should therefore be accepted. That total is

ped. 63 + 11/12 (= 22/24) + 1/24 = *ped.* 63 23/24.

Thus the total space allotted to the Arvals in each *maenianum* is as follows:

first *maen.*:	*ped.* 42 1/2
second *maen.*:	*ped.* 22 1/2
summum maen. in ligneis:	*ped.* 63 23/24
Total	*ped.* 128 23/24

This overall total is out by one *pes* from that stated in the text (129 + 11/12 + 1/24 = 129 23/24). The most likely solution (Hülsen, "Il posto degli arvali," 317) is that the incompetent copyist has miscarved cxxvIIII for cxxvIII on the stone.

I.2 *CIL* 4.3884 = *ILS* 5145 = Sabbatini Tumolesi, *Gladiatorum Paria*, 27–8 (no. 5) = Fora, *Munera Gladiatoria*, 123 (no. 28). Advertisement for games, Pompeii.

Scr(ipsit) | *Celer. D(ecimi) Lucreti* | *Satri Valenti, flaminis Neronis Caesaris Augusti fili* | *perpetui, gladiatorum paria* xx *et D(ecimi) Lucreti{o}Valentis fili* | *glad(iatorum) paria* X *pug(nabunt) Pompeis* vi, v, iv, ii *pr(idie)* | *idus Apr(iles), venatio legitima* | *et vela erunt.* | *Scr(ipsit)* | *Aemilius* | *Celer sing(ulus)* | *ad luna(m).*

Celer wrote (this notice): Twenty pairs of gladiators sponsored by D. Lucretius Satrius Valens, lifetime priest of Nero Caesar, son of Augustus, and ten pairs of gladiators sponsored by D. Lucretius Valens, his son, will fight at Pompeii on April 8–12. There will also be a suitable hunt and the awning. *Aemilius Celer wrote (this notice), alone at night.*

I.3 *CIL* 4.2508 = Sabbatini Tumolesi, *Gladiatorum Paria*, 71–4 (no. 32) = Fora, *Munera Gladiatoria*, 128 (no. 57). Gladiatorial program painted on a wall, with results added later.

Pri[mum] | *munus M(arci) [M]eso[nii–]* | *[–]*vi *nonas Maias*

(First column)
Tr(aeces)   M(urmillones)
    [–]nator Ner(onianus) (pugnarum) ii *[–]*
    Tigris Iul(ianus) (pugnarum) I*[–]*
    [–]ci[-]s Ner(onianus) (pugnarum) iii *m(issus?)*
    Speculator (pugnarum) lxix
    v(icit?) Essed(arius) R(etiarius) (?)
    Crysantus [–] (pugnarum) ii
    M. Artorius [–]
(Second column)
O(plomachi)   M(urmillones)
    m(issus?) [–]p[–]eacius Iul(ianus)[–]
    M[–] Iul(ianus) (pugnarum) lv *[–]*
    v(icit?) [–] iu[s–]
    [–]ur[–]
[–] [T]r(aex?)

[–]b[–] Ner(onianus) [–]
[–]

Munus [–] v, iv, iii prid[ie] idus, idi[bus] Mais

(First column)

Di[machaeri?]	*O[plomachi?]*
m(issus)	*I[–]ciens Ner(onianus) (pugnarum) xx[–]*
v(icit)	*Nobilior Iul(ianus) (pugnarum)* ii
T(raex)	*M(urmillo)*
m(issus)	*L. Semproniu[s–]*
v(icit)	*Platanus Iu[l(ianus)–]*
T(raex)	*M(urmillo)*
v(icit)	*Pugnax Ner(onianus) (pugnarum)* iii
p(eriit)	*Murranus Ner(onianus) (pugnarum)* iii
O(plomachus)	*T(raex)*
v(icit)	*Cycnus Iul(ianus) (pugnarum)* viiii
m(issus)	*Atticus Iul(ianus) (pugnarum)* xiv
T(raex)	*M(urmillo)*
v(icit)	*Herma Iul(ianus) (pugnarum)* iv
m(issus)	*Q. Petilius [–]*
Ess(edarii)	
m(issus)	*P. Ostorius (pugnarum)* li
v(icit)	*Scylax Iul(ianus) (pugnarum)* xxvi
T(raex)	*M(urmillo)*
v(icit)	*Nodu[–] Iul(ianus) (pugnarum)* vii
m(issus)	*L. Petronius (pugnarum)* xiv
T(raex)	*M(urmillo)*
p(eriit)	*L. Fabius (pugnarum)* viiii
v(icit)	*Astus Iul(ianus) (pugnarum)* xiv

(Second column): Dimaechari – Oplomachi
Laudand[–] io[–](pugnarum) xi *?*
[–]ng[–](pugnarum) xiv *?*
(Second column): Traeces – Murmillones
No[–] m(issus?)
Ri[–] [–]ecius[–]

First show of M. Mesonius(?), 2 May
(First column)
Thracians vs. Murmillones
       [–]nator, of the Neronian School, 2 fights [–]

Tigris, of the Julian School, ? fights [–]
[–]ci[-]s, of the Neronian School, 3 fights, spared
Speculator, 69 fights,
won? Essedarius vs. Retiarius
Crysantus [–] 2 fights
M. Artorius [–]
(Second column)
Oplomachi vs. Murmillones
spared? [–]p[-]eacius, of the Julian School, [–]
M[–], of the Julian School, 55 fights, [–]
won? [–] iu[s–]
[–]ur[–]
[–] [Th]r(acian) ?
[–]b[–], of the Neronian School, [–]
[–]

Show [of –], May 11–14 and 15
(First column)
Dimachaeri? vs. Oplomachi?
spared   I[–]ciens, of the Neronian School, 2? fights
won   Nobilior, of the Julian School, 2 fights
Thracian vs. Murmillo
spared   L. Semproniu[s–]
won   Platanus, of the Julian School, [–]
Thracian vs. Murmillo
won   Pugnax, of the Neronian School, 3 fights
died   Murranus, of the Neronian School, 3 fights
Oplomachus vs. Thracian
won   Cycnus, of the Julian School, 9 fights
spared   Atticus, of the Julian School, 14 fights
Thracian vs. Murmillo
won   Herma, of the Julian School, 4 fights
spared   Q. Petillius [–]
Essedarii
spared   P. Ostorius, 51 fights
won   Scylax, of the Julian School, 26 fights
Thracian vs. Murmillo
won   Nodu[–], of the Julian School, 7 fights
spared   L. Petronius, 14 fights

Thracian vs. Murmillo
>died   L. Fabius, 9 fights
>won   Astus, of the Julian School, 14 fights

(Second column, under "Dimachaeri vs. oplomachi")
Laudand[–] io[–] 11 fights ?
[–]ng[–], 14 fights ?
(Second column, under "Thracians vs. Murmillones")
No[–] spared
Ri[–] [–ecius] [–]

I.4   *CIL* 9.466, 26–7 = *ILS* 5083a = *EAOR* 3.68.
Members of a *familia gladiatoria* from Venusia;
first half of the first century AD.

[–]
Oceanus Avil(ianus) t(iro)
Sag(ittarius):
Dorus Pis(inianus) v(ictoriarum) VI, *c(oronarum)* IIII.
Veles:
Mycter Ofil(ianus) v(ictoriarum) II.
Opl(omachus):
Phaeder Avil(ianus), t(iro)
Thr(aeces):
Donatus Ner(onianus) v(ictoriarum) XII, *c(oronarum)* VII;
Hilario Arr(ianus) v(ictoriarum) VII, *c(oronarum)* V;
Aquila Pis(inianus) v(ictoriarum) XII, *(coronarum)* VI;
Quartio Munil(ianus) v(ictoriae) I;
C(aius) Perpernius, t(iro).
Mur(millones):
Amicus Munil(ianus) v(ictoriae) I;
Q(uintus) Fabius v(ictoriarum) V, *c(oronarum)* III;
Eleuther Munil(ianus) v(ictoriae) I;
C(aius) Memmius v(ictoriarum) III, *c(oronarum)* II;
Anteros Munil(ianus) v(ictoriarum) II;
Atlans Don(atianus) v(ictoriarum) IIII, *c(oronae)* I.
Esse(darius):
Inclutus Arr(ianus) v(ictoriarum) V, *c(oronarum)* II.
Sam(nes):
Strabo Don(atianus) v(ictoriarum) III, *c(oronarum)* III.
Ret(iarius):

C(aius) Clodius v(ictoriarum) 11.
Scisso(r):
M(arcus) Caecilius, t(iro).
Gallu(s):
Q(uintus) Granius, t(iro).
———

Oceanus, of the Avili, beginner.
Archer:
Dorus, of the Pisini, 6 victories, 4 crowns.
Swifty:
Mycter, of the Ofilii, 2 victories.
Hoplomachus:
Phaeder, of the Avilii, beginner.
Thracians:
Donatus, of the Neronian training school, 12 victories, 7 crowns;
Hilario, of the Arrii, 7 victories, 5 crowns;
Aquila, of the Pisinii, 12 victories, 6 crowns;
Quartio, of the Munilii, 1 victory;
Gaius Perpernius, beginner.
Murmillones:
Amicus, of the Munilii, 1 victory;
Quitnus Fabius, 5 victories, 3 crowns;
Eleuther, of the Munilii, 1 victory;
Gaius Memmius, 3 victories, 2 crowns;
Anteros, of the Munilii, 2 victories;
Atlans, of the Donati, 4 victories, 1 crown.
Chariot-fighter:
Inclutus, of the Arrii, 5 victories, 2 crowns.
Samnite:
Strabo, of the Donati, 3 victories, 3 crowns.
Net-man:
Gaius Clodius, 2 victories.
Cleaver:
Marcus Caecilius, beginner.
Gaul:
Quintus Granius, beginner.

NOTES: the names (in the adjectival form Avilianus, Pisinianus, etc.) either refer to the training school of the slave gladiators (see *CIL* 9.2237 = *ILS* 5060 = *EAOR* 3.28 for a *familia [glad(iatoria) Arr]ianorum*) or to some sort of patron. The matter remains a little obscure.

I.5 *CIL* 6.10194 = *ILS* 5088 = *EAOR* 1.92.
Epitaph of M. Antonius Exochus, Thracian.

M. Antonius Exochus. | Thraex. | M. Antonius | Exochus nat(ione) | Alexandrinus: | Rom(ae) ob triump(hum) | Divi Traiani, die II, | tir(o) cum Araxe Cae(saris) | st(ans) miss(us); | Rom(ae) mun(eris) eiusd(em) | die VIIII Fimbriam | lib(erum), (pugnarum) VIIII, miss(um) fe(cit); Rom(ae) mun(eris) eiusd(em) . . .

M. Antonius Exochus. Thracian. M. Antonius Exochus, by birth an Alexandrian, (in the games given) at Rome on account of the triumph of the Deified Trajan, on the second day, as a beginner, he secured a draw with Araxis, imperial slave; at Rome, on the ninth day of the same games he caused to be spared Fimbria, freeborn, with nine fights' worth of experience; at Rome (on the X day) of the same show . . .

I.6 *CIL* 10.7297 = *ILS* 5113 = *EAOR* 3.70.
Epitaph of Flamma, *secutor*.

Flamma sec(utor), vix(it) an(nis) XXX; | pugna<vi>t XXXIIII, vicit XXI, | stans VIIII, mis(sus) IIII, nat(ione) Syrus; hui<c> Delicatus coarmio merenti fecit.

Flamma, *secutor*. He lived 30 years. He fought 34 times, won 21 times, drew 9 times, and was spared 4 times. Syrian by birth. Delicatus made (this tomb) for a worthy comrade-at-arms.

I.7 *CIL* 5.5933 = *ILS* 5115 = *EAOR* 2.50.
Epitaph of Urbicus, *secutor*.

D(is) M(anibus) | Urbico, secutori, | primo palo, nation(e) Flo|rentin(o), qui pugnavit XIII, | vixsit ann(is) XXII, Olympias, | filia quem reliquit me(n)si(bus) V, | et Fortune(n)sis filiae | et Lauricia uxor, | marito bene merenti, | cum quo vixsit ann(is) VII. | Et moneo ut quis quem vic[e]|rit, occidat. | Colent Manes amatores ipsi|us.

To the souls of the departed. For Urbicus, *secutor* of the first rank, by birth Florentine, who fought 13 times. He lived 22 years. Olympias, his daughter, whom he left at 5 months old, and Fortunensis, his daughter's slave, and Lauricia his wife (built this tomb) for a deserving husband, with whom she lived for 7 years. I recommend that he who beats a man should kill him. His admirers will nurture his shade.

I.8   *CIL* 11.1070 = *ILS* 5118 = *EAOR* 2.46.
Epitaph of Vitalus, *retiarius.*

[D(is] M(anibus] | Vitalis, invic|ti retiari, nati|one Bataus; | hic sua virtu|te, pariter cum | adversario de[pu|gnav]it; alacer fu[it] | [p]ugnis. Hi[me?]n convi|[cto]r eius . . .

To the souls of the departed. (Tomb of) Vitalis, unbeaten *retiarius*, Batavian by birth. He courageously fought it out to the end on an equal footing with his opponent. He was fast in his fights. Himen (?), his fellow winner, . . .

I.9   *CIL* 5.3466 = *ILS* 5121 = *EAOR* 2.47.
Epitaph of Glaucus, gladiator.

D(is) M(anibus) | Glauco n(atione) Muti|nensis, pugnar(rum) vii (theta nigrum = obiit) viii (pugna). vixit | ann(is) xxiii, d(iebus) v; | Aurelia marito | b(ene) m(erenti) et amatores | huius. Planetam | suum | procurare | vos moneo; in | Nemese ne fidem | habeatis: | sic sum deceptus! Ave! Vale!

To the souls of the departed. For Glaucus, born at Mutina, veteran of seven fights, killed in the eighth. He lived 23 years, five days. Aurelia, along with his admirers, (made this tomb) for a most deserving husband. I recommend that each of you look after his own fate; don't put your trust in Nemesis, that's how I was deceived! Hello. Goodbye.

Bibliography

Abbott, G., *Execution: The Guillotine, the Pendulum, the Thousand Cuts, the Spanish Donkey, and 66 Other Ways of Putting Someone to Death*. New York, 2006.

Abrams, D. and M. A. Hogg, "Collective Identity: Group Membership and Self-Conception," in Hogg and Tindale (eds.), *Group Processes*, 425–60.

Abrams, D. and M. A. Hogg (eds.), *Social Identity Theory: Constructive and Critical Advances*. New York, 1990.

Adamopoulos, J. and R. Bontempo, "Diachronic Universals in Interpersonal Structures: Evidence from Literary Sources," *Journal of Cross-Cultural Psychology* 17 (1986), 169–89.

Adorno, T. W., E. Frenkel-Brunswick, D. Levinson, and R. Sanford, *The Authoritarian Personality*. New York, 1950.

Africa, T. W., "Urban Violence in Imperial Rome," *Journal of Interdisciplinary History* 2 (1971), 3–21.

Aldrete, G. S., *Gestures and Acclamations in Ancient Rome*. Baltimore, 1999.

Alföldy, G., *The Social History of Rome*, 3rd edn. Baltimore, 1988.

Allen, D. S., *The World of Prometheus: The Politics of Punishing in Democratic Athens*. Princeton, 2000.

Allen, J., H. Als, J. Lewis, and L. F. Litwack, *Without Sanctuary: Lynching Photography in America*. Santa Fe, 2000.

Allport, G. W., *The Nature of Prejudice*. Reading, 1954.

Amussen, S. D., "Punishment, Discipline, and Power: The Social Meaning of Violence in Early Modern England," *Journal of British Studies* 34 (1995), 1–34.

Ancheta, A. N., *Race, Rights and the Asian American Experience*. New Brunswick, 1998.

Anderson, B., *Imagined Communities*, rev. edn. London, 1991.

Anderson, G., "Aulus Gellius as Storyteller," in L. Holford-Strevens (ed.), *The Worlds of Aulus Gellius* (Oxford, 2004), 105–17.

Anderson, J. K., *Hunting in the Ancient World*. Berkeley, 1985.

Ando, C., *Imperial Ideology and Provincial Loyalty in the Roman Empire*. Berkeley, 2000.

Anglo, S., *The Great Tournament Roll of Westminster*, 2 vols. Oxford, 1968.

Apostolidès, J.-M., *Le roi-machine: spectacle et politique au temps de Louis XIV*. Paris, 1981.

Apter, M. J., *The Experience of Motivation: The Theory of Psychological Reversals.* London, 1982.

The Dangerous Edge: The Psychology of Excitement. New York, 1992.

Apter M. J. (ed.), *Motivational Styles in Everyday Life: A Guide to Reversal Theory.* Washington, DC, 2001.

Arasse, D., *The Guillotine and the Terror.* London, 1989.

Arms, R. L., G. W. Russell, and M. L. Sandilands, "Effects of Observing Athletic Contests on Hostility of Spectators Viewing Aggressive Sports," *Social Psychology Quarterly* 42 (1979), 275–9.

Armstrong, G., *Football Hooligans: Knowing the Score.* Oxford, 1998.

Atran, S., *In Gods We Trust: The Evolutionary Landscape of Religion.* Oxford, 2002.

Aubert, J.-J., *Business Managers in Ancient Rome: A Social and Economic Study of Institores 200 BC – AD 250.* Leiden, 1994.

Augenti, D., *Spettacoli del Colosseo nelle cronache degli antichi.* Rome, 2001.

Auguet, R., *Cruelty and Civilization: The Roman Games.* London, 1972; reprint London, 1994.

Aurigemma, S., *I mosaici di Zliten*, Africa italiana 2. Rome, 1926.

Aymard, J., *Les chasses romaines des origines à la fin du siècle des Antonins.* Paris, 1951.

Bablitz, L., *Actors and Audience in the Roman Courtroom.* London, 2007.

Balsdon, J. P. V. D., *Life and Leisure in Ancient Rome.* London, 1969.

Romans and Aliens. London, 1979.

Bar-Tal, D. and Y. Teichman, *Stereotypes and Prejudice in Conflict: Representations of Arabs in Israeli Jewish Society.* Cambridge, 2005.

Barker, J. R. V., *The Tournament in England, 1100–1400.* Woodbridge, 1986.

Barker, M. and J. Petley (eds.), *Ill Effects: The Media/Violence Debate*, 2nd edn. London, 2001.

Barrett, L., R. Dunbar, and J. Lycett, *Human Evolutionary Psychology.* Princeton, 2002.

Barringer, J. M., *The Hunt in Ancient Greece.* Baltimore, 2001.

Barton, C. A., "The Scandal of the Arena," *Representations* 27 (1989), 1–36.

The Sorrows of the Ancient Romans: The Gladiator and the Monster. Princeton, 1993.

"The Emotional Economy of Sacrifice and Execution in Ancient Rome," *Historical Reflections/Reflexions Historiques* 29 (2003), 341–60.

Bastien, P., *L'exécution publique à Paris au XVIIIe siècle: une histoire des rituels judiciaires.* Seyssel, 2006.

Bauman, R. A., *Crime and Punishment in Ancient Rome.* London, 1996.

Beacham, R. C., *Spectacle Entertainments of Early Imperial Rome.* New Haven, 1999.

Beagon, M., *Roman Nature: The Thought of Pliny the Elder.* Oxford, 1992.

Beard, M., "The Triumph of the Absurd: Roman Street Theatre," in Edwards and Woolf (eds.), *Rome the Cosmopolis*, 21–43.

The Roman Triumph. Cambridge, MA, 2007.

Belfiore, E. S., *Tragic Pleasures: Aristotle on Plot and Emotion.* Princeton, 1992.

Bell, A., *Spectacular Power in the Greek and Roman City*. Oxford, 2004.

Bergmann, B. and C. Kondoleon (eds.), *The Art of Ancient Spectacle*. New Haven, 1999.

Berkowitz, L., *Aggression: Its Causes, Consequences, and Control*. Philadelphia, 1993.

Berlan-Bajard, A., *Les spectacles aquatiques romains*, CEFR 360. Rome, 2006.

Bernstein, F., *Ludi Publici: Untersuchungen zur Entstehung und Entwicklung der öffentlichen Spiele im republikanischen Rom*, Historia Einzelschriften 119. Stuttgart, 1998.

Beschaouch, A., "La mosaïque de chasse à l'amphithéâtre découverte à Smirat en Tunisie," *CRAI* (1966), 134–57.

"Nouvelles recherches sur les sodalités de l'Afrique romaine," *CRAI* (1977), 486–503.

Black, J., *The Aesthetics of Murder: A Study in Romantic Literature and Contemporary Culture*. Baltimore, 1991.

Blake, M. E., "Mosaics of the Late Empire in Rome and Vicinity," *MAAR* 17 (1940), 81–130.

Bleackley, H. and J. Lofland, *State Executions Viewed Historically and Sociologically*. Montclair, 1977.

Bleibtreu, E., "Grisly Assyrian Record of Torture and Death," *BAR* (Jan./Feb. 1991), 52–61.

Bogeng, A. E. (ed.), *Geschichte des Sports aller Volker und Zeiten*, 2 vols. Leipzig, 1926.

Bok, S., *Mayhem: Violence as Public Entertainment*. New York, 1998.

Bollinger, T., *Theatralis Licentia: Die Publikumsdemonstrationen an den öffentlichen Spielen im Rom der früheren Kaiserzeit und ihre Bedeutung im politischen Leben*. Basel, 1969.

Bomgardner, D. L., *The Story of the Roman Amphitheatre*. London, 2000.

"The Magerius Mosaic: Putting on a Show in the Amphitheatre," *Current World Archaeology* 3 (2007), 12–21.

Bond, M. H. (ed.), *The Cross-Cultural Challenge to Social Psychology*. Newbury Park, 1988.

Bonner, C., "Eros and the Wounded Lion," *AJA* 49 (1945), 441–4.

Bonte, E. P. and M. Musgrove, "Influences of War as Evidenced in Children's Play," *Child Development* 14 (1943), 179–200.

Bosco, R., "Lectures at the Pillory: The Early American Execution Sermon," *American Quarterly* 30 (1978), 156–76.

Bourhis, R. Y., "Power, Gender, and Intergroup Discrimination: Some Minimal Group Experiments," in Zanna and Olson (eds.), *Psychology of Prejudice*, 171–208.

Bourhis, R. Y. and J.-P. Leyens (eds.), *Stereotypes, Discrimination, and Intergroup Relations*, 2nd edn. Hayen, 1999.

Bourhis, R. Y., I. Sadchev, and A. Gagnon, "Intergroup Research with the Tajfel Matrices: Methodological Notes," in Zanna and Olson (eds.), *Psychology of Prejudice*, 208–32.

Bourne, F. C., "The Roman Alimentary Program and Italian Agriculture," *TAPA* 91 (1960), 47–75.

Bowdich, T. E., *Mission from Cape Coast Castle to Ashantee*. London, 1966; originally published 1819.

Bowersock, G. W., *Martyrdom and Rome*. Cambridge, 1995.

Boyer, P., *The Naturalness of Religious Ideas*. Berkeley, 1994.

    Religion Explained: The Evolutionary Origins of Religious Thought. New York, 2001.

Bradley, K., *Slavery and Society at Rome*. Cambridge, 1994.

Bradley, K. R., *Slaves and Masters in the Roman Empire: A Study in Social Control*. Oxford, 1987.

    Discovering the Roman Family: Studies in Roman Social History. Oxford, 1991.

    "Animalizing the Slave: The Truth of Fiction," *JRS* 90 (2000), 110–25.

Braund, S. M. and G. W. Most (eds.), *Ancient Anger: Perspectives from Homer to Galen*. Cambridge, 2004.

Brettler, M. Z. and M. Poliakoff, "Rabbi Simeon ben Lakish at the Gladiator's Banquet: Rabbinic Observations on the Roman Arena," *HTR* 83 (1990), 93–8.

Brewer, M. B., "The Psychology of Prejudice: Ingroup Love or Outgroup Hate?," *Journal of Social Issues* 55 (1999), 429–44.

    "Ingroup Identification and Intergroup Conflict: When Does Ingroup Love Become Outgroup Hate?," in R. E. Ashmore, L. Jussim, and D. Wilder (eds.), *Social Identity, Intergroup Conflict, and Conflict Reduction* (Oxford, 2001), 17–41.

Brimson, D., *Eurotrashed: The Rise and Rise of Europe's Football Hooligans*. London, 2003.

Broise, H. and J. Scheid, *Recherches archéologiques à la Magliana: le balneum des frères Arvales*. Rome, 1987.

Brooks, T., J. Bourgon, and G. Blue, *Death by a Thousand Cuts*. Cambridge, MA, 2008.

Brophy, R., "Deaths in the Pan-Hellenic Games: Arrachion and Creugas," *AJP* 99 (1978), 363–90.

Brophy, R. and M., "Deaths in the Pan-Hellenic Games II: All Combative Sports," *AJP* 106 (1985), 171–98.

Brown, D. E., *Hierarchy, History, and Human Nature: The Social Origins of Historical Consciousness*. Tucson, 1988.

    Human Universals. New York, 1991.

    "Human Universals and their Implications," in Roughley (ed.), *Being Humans*, 156–74.

Brown, P., *Augustine of Hippo: A Biography*, 2nd edn. Berkeley, 2000.

Brown, R., *Prejudice: Its Social Psychology*. Oxford, 1995.

    Group Processes: Dynamics Within and Between Groups, 2nd edn. Oxford, 2000.

Brown, R. J., "Divided We Fall: An Analysis of Relations between Sections of a Factory Workforce," in Tajfel (ed.), *Differentiation between Social Groups*, 395–429.

Brown, S., "Death as Decoration: Scenes from the Arena on Roman Domestic Mosaics," in A. Richlin (ed.), *Pornography and Representation in Greece and Rome* (Oxford, 1992), 180–211.

"Explaining the Arena: Did the Romans 'Need' Gladiators?," *JRA* 8 (1995), 376–84.

Browning, R., "The Riot of AD 387 in Antioch: The Role of the Theatrical Claques in the Later Empire," *JRS* 42 (1952), 13–20.

Brumfiel, E. M., "Aztec Hearts and Minds: Religion and the State in the Aztec Empire," in S. E. Alcock, T. N. D'Altroy, K. D. Morrison, and C. M. Sinopoli (eds.), *Empires* (Cambridge, 2001), 283–310.

Brundage, W. Fitzhugh, *Lynching in the New South: Georgia and Virginia, 1880–1930*. Urbana, 1993.

Brunet, S., "Dwarf Athletes in the Roman Empire," *AHB* 17 (2003), 17–32.

"Female and Dwarf Gladiators," *Mouseion* 4 (2004), 145–70.

Brunt, P. A., *Italian Manpower 225 BC – AD 14*. Oxford, 1971.

Bryant, J. and D. Miron, "Entertainment as Media Effect," in Bryant and Zillmann (eds.), *Media Effects*, 549–82.

Bryant, J. and D. Zillmann (eds.), *Responding to the Screen: Reception and Reaction Processes*. Hillsdale, 1991.

Media Effects: Advances in Theory and Research, 2nd edn. Mahwah, 2002.

Buford, B., *Among the Thugs*. New York, 1992.

Buller, D. J., *Adapting Minds: Evolutionary Psychology and the Persistent Quest for Human Nature*. Cambridge, MA, 2005.

Burkholder, M. A., and L. L. Johnson, *Colonial Latin America*, 3rd edn. Oxford, 1998.

Burstyn, V., *The Rites of Men: Manhood, Politics, and the Culture of Sport*. Toronto, 2000.

Cairns, D., *AIDOS: The Psychology and Ethics of Honour and Shame in Ancient Greek Literature*. Oxford, 1993.

Callahan, J. M., "The Ultimate in Theatre Violence," in Redmond (ed.), *Violence in Drama*, 165–75.

Cameron, A., *Circus Factions: Blues and Greens at Byzantium*. Oxford, 1976.

Canetti, E., *Crowds and Power*, trans. C. Stewart. London, 1962; reprint. New York, 1984.

Cantarella, E., *I supplizi capitali in Grecia e a Roma*. Milan, 1991.

Carandini, A., *Schiavi in Italia: gli strumenti pensanti dei Romani fra tarda Repubblica e medio Impero*. Rome, 1988.

Carey, C., "A Note on Torture in Athenian Homicide Cases," *Historia* 37 (1988), 241–5.

Carfora, A., *I cristiani al leone: I martiri cristiani nel contesto mediatico dei giochi gladiatorii. Oi Christianoi 10* (Trapani, 2009).

Carter, J. M., Ludi Medi Aevi: *Studies in the History of Medieval Sport*. Manhattan, 1981.

Carter, M., "The Presentation of Gladiatorial Spectacles in the Greek East: Roman Culture and Greek Identity," Ph.D. dissertation, McMaster University (1999).

"Artemidorus and the Arbelas Gladiator," *ZPE* 134 (2001), 109–15.

"The Roman Spectacles of Antiochus IV Epiphanes at Daphne, 166 BC," *Nikephoros* 14 (2001), 45–62.

"Gladiatorial Ranking and the *SC de Pretiis Gladiatorum Minuendis* (*CIL* II 6278 = *ILS* 5163)," *Phoenix* 57 (2003), 83–114.

Carter, M. J., "Gladiatorial Combat with 'Sharp' Weapons (τοῖς ὀζέσι σιδήροις)," *ZPE* 155 (2006), 161–75.

"Gladiatorial Combat: The Rules of Engagement," *CJ* 102 (2007), 97–113.

"Gladiators and Monomachoi: Attitudes to a Roman 'Cultural Performance,'" *International Journal of the History of Sport*, 26 (2009), 298–322.

Casanova, G., *The Memoirs of Jacues Casanova de Seignalt 1725–1798*, trans. A. Machen, 8 vols. Edinburgh, 1940; originally published 1894.

Cavallaro, M. A., *Spese e Spettacoli: aspetti economici-strutturali degli spettacoli nella Roma giulio-claudia*. Bonn, 1984.

Chamberland, G., "A Gladiatorial Show Produced *In Sordidam Mercedem* (Tac. *Ann.* 4.62)," *Phoenix* 61 (2007), 136–49.

Champlin, E., *Nero*. Cambridge, MA, 2003.

Charney, M., "The Persuasiveness of Violence in Elizabethan Plays," *Renaissance Drama* 2 (1969), 59–70.

Chastagnol, A., *Le sénat romain sous le règne d'Odoacre: recherches sur l'épigraphie du Colisée au Ve siècle*. Bonn, 1966.

Chesnais, J.-C., "The History of Violence: Homicide and Suicide through the Ages," *International Social Science Journal* 43 (1992), 217–34.

Chin, J. L. (ed.), *The Psychology of Prejudice and Discrimination*, 4 vols. Westport, 2004.

Chomsky, N., *Language and the Mind*. New York, 1968.

On Nature and Language. Cambridge, 2002.

Clark, G., "Desires of the Hangman: Augustine on Legitimized Violence," in H. A. Drake (ed.), *Violence in Late Antiquity* (Burlington, 2006), 137–46.

Clarke, W. L., *Rhetoric at Rome: A Historical Survey*, rev. edn. by D. H. Berry. London, 1996.

Clavel-Lévêque, M., *L'empire en jeux: espace symbolique et pratique sociale dans le monde romain*. Paris, 1984.

'L'espace des jeux dans le monde romain: hégémonie, symbolique et pratique sociale," *ANRW* 2.16.3 (1986), 2406–563.

Cohen, E., "Symbols of Culpability and the Universal Language of Justice: The Ritual of Public Executions in Late Medieval Europe," *History of European Ideas* 11 (1989), 407–16.

"'To Die a Criminal for the Public Good': The Execution Ritual in Late Medieval Paris," in B. S. Bachrach and D. Nicholas (eds.), *Law, Custom and the Social Fabric in Medieval Europe: Essays in Honor of Bryce Lyon* (Kalamazoo, 1990), 285–304.

Cokayne, K., *Experiencing Old Age in Ancient Rome*. London, 2003.

Cole, M., *Cultural Psychology: The Once and Future Discipline*. Cambridge, MA, 1996.

Coleman, K. M., "Fatal Charades: Roman Executions Staged as Mythological Enactments," *JRS* 80 (1990), 44–73.

"Launching into History: Aquatic Displays in the Early Empire," *JRS* 83 (1993), 48–74.

"A Left-Handed Gladiator at Pompeii," *ZPE* 114 (1996), 194–6.

"Ptolemy Philadelphus and the Roman Amphitheater," in Slater (ed.), *Roman Theater and Society*, 49–68.

"'The Contagion of the Throng': Absorbing Violence in the Roman World," *European Review* 5 (1997), 401–17 = *Hermathena* 164 (1998), 65–88.

"'Informers' on Parade," in Bergmann and Kondoleon (eds.), *Art of Ancient Spectacle*, 231–45.

"Entertaining Rome," in Coulston and Dodge (eds.), *Ancient Rome*, 210–58.

"*Missio* at Halicarnassus," *HSCP* 100 (2000), 487–500.

"Bonds of Danger: Communal Life in the Gladiatorial Barracks of Ancient Rome," Fifteenth Todd Memorial Lecture. Sydney, 2005.

Martial: Liber Spectaculorum. Oxford, 2006.

Collins, R., *Violence: A Micro-sociological Theory*. Princeton, 2008.

Conrad, G. W. and A. A. Demarest, *Religion and Empire: The Dynamics of Aztec and Inca Expansionism*. Cambridge, 1984.

Constant, B., *Principles of Politics Applicable to All Governments,* trans. D. O'Keeffe. Indianapolis, 2003; originally published 1810.

Cooper, D. D., *The Lesson of the Scaffold: The Public Execution Controversy in Victorian England*. Athens, OH, 1974.

Corbeill, A., *Nature Embodied: Gesture in Ancient Rome*. Princeton, 2004.

Coulson, A. S., "Cognitive Synergy," in Apter (ed.), *Motivational Styles in Everyday Life*, 229–48.

Coulston, J. and H. Dodge (eds.), *Ancient Rome: Archaeology of the Eternal City*. Oxford, 2000.

Coulston, J. C. N., "'Armed and Belted Men': The Soldiery in Imperial Rome," in Coulston and Dodge (eds.), *Ancient Rome*, 76–118.

Cripps-Day, F. H., *The History of the Tournament in England and France*. London, 1918.

Crook, J. A., J. B. Haskins, and P. G. Ashdown (eds.), *Morbid Curiosity and the Mass Media*. New York, 1984.

Crowther, N. B., *Sport in the Ancient World*. Westport, 2007.

Cutler, A., "The Violent Domus: Cruelty, Gender, and Class in Roman Household Possessions," in E. D'Ambra and G. P. R. Métraux (eds.), *The Art of Citizens, Soldiers and Freedmen in the Roman World*, BAR International Series 1526 (Oxford, 2006), 103–14.

Daly, L. W., *Aesop without Morals: The Famous Fables and a Life of Aesop*. New York, 1961.

Daremberg, E. and E. Saglio, *Dictionnaire des antiquités grecques et romaines*, 5 vols. Paris, 1887–1919.

D'Arms, J., "Slaves and Roman *Convivia*," in Slater (ed.), *Dining in a Classical Context*, 171–83.

Darwin, C., *The Expression of the Emotions in Man and Animals*. Chicago, 1965; originally published in 1872.

Dauge, Y. A., *Le barbare: recherches sur la conception romaine de la barbarie et de la civilisation*, Collection Latomus 176. Brussels, 1981.

Davis, N. Z., "The Rites of Violence: Religious Riot in Sixteenth-Century France," *Past and Present* 59 (1973), 51–91.

de Ste. Croix, G. E. M., *The Class Struggle in the Ancient Greek World*. London, 1981.

de Tocqueville, A., *Democracy in America*, trans. H. Reeve, 2 vols. New York, 1899; originally published in 1835.

de Vos, A. and M., *Pompei, Ercolano, Stabia*. Bari, 1982.

de Waal, F. B. M., *Good Natured: The Origins of Right and Wrong in Humans and Other Animals*. Cambridge, MA, 1996.

DeLaine, J., "Building the Eternal City: The Construction Industry in Ancient Rome," in Coulston and Dodge (eds.), *Ancient Rome*, 119–41.

Delbrueck, R., *Die Consulardiptychen und verwandte Denkmäler*. Berlin, 1929.

Dennett, D. C., *Breaking the Spell: Religion as a Natural Phenomenon*. New York, 2006.

Dickey, E., *Latin Forms of Address: From Plautus to Apuleius*. Oxford, 2002.

Diener, E., "Deindividuation: The Absence of Self-Awareness and Self-Regulation in Group Members," in P. B. Paulus (ed.), *The Psychology of Group Influence*, 2nd edn. (Hillsdale, 1989), 209–42.

Dillon, J. M., *Salt and Olives: Morality and Custom in Ancient Greece*. Edinburgh, 2004.

Dillon, S. and K. E. Welch (eds.), *Representations of War in Ancient Rome*. Cambridge, 2006.

Dionisotti, A. C., "From Ausonius' Schooldays? A Schoolbook and its Relatives," *JRS* 72 (1982), 83–125.

Dobson, R. B., *The Peasants' Revolt of 1381*. New York, 1970.

Dollard, J., L. Doob, N. E. Miller, O. Mower, and R. Sears, *Frustration and Aggression*. New Haven, 1939.

Domergue, C., C. Landes, and J.-M. Pailler (eds.), *Spectacula I: gladiateurs et amphithéâtres*. Lattes, 1990.

Donahue, J. F., "Toward a Typology of Roman Public Feasting," *AJP* 124 (2003), 423–41.

Donald, M., *The Origins of the Modern Mind: Three Stages in the Evolution of Culture and Cognition*. Cambridge, MA, 1991.

Dostoevsky, F., *The Brothers Karamazov*, trans. L. Pevear and L. Volokhonsky. New York, 1990; originally published 1880.

Dovidio, J. F., P. Glick, and L. A. Rudmanet (eds.), *On the Nature of Prejudice: Fifty Years after Allport*. Oxford, 2005.

Du châtiment dans la cité: supplices corporels et peine de mort dans le monde antique, CEFR 79. Paris, 1984.

Dowling, J. E., *Creating Mind: How the Brain Works*. New York, 1998.

Duckitt, J. H., *The Social Psychology of Prejudice*. New York, 1992.
"Prejudice and Intergroup Hostility," in D. O. Sears, L. Huddy, and R. Jervis (eds.), *Oxford Handbook of Political Psychology* (Oxford, 2003), 559–600.

Dumond, D. E., *The Machete and the Cross: Campesino Rebellion in Yucatan*. Lincoln, NE, 1997.

Dunbabin, K. M. D., *The Mosaics of Roman North Africa*. Oxford, 1978.
The Roman Banquet: Images of Conviviality. Cambridge, 2003.

Duncan, A., *Performance and Identity in the Classical World*. Cambridge, 2006.

Duncan-Jones, R. P., "The Purpose and Organisation of the Alimenta," *PBSR* 32 (1964), 123–46.
The Economy of the Roman Empire: Quantitative Studies, 2nd edn. Cambridge, 1982.
Structure and Scale in the Roman Economy. Cambridge, 1990.

Dunning, E., P. Murphy, and J. Williams, "Spectator Violence at Football Matches: Towards a Sociological Explanation," in Elias and Dunning, *Quest for Excitement*, 245–66.
The Roots of Football Hooliganism: A Historical and Sociological Study. London, 1988.

Durán, D., *Book of the Gods and Rites and The Ancient Calendar*, trans. F. Horcasitas and D. Heyden. Norman, 1971; originally published 1574–6.
History of the Indies of New Spain, trans. D. Heyden. Norman, 1994; originally published 1581.

Durkheim, E., *The Elementary Forms of Religious Life*. Oxford, 2001; originally published 1912.

Dutton, M. R., *Policing and Punishment in China: From Patriarchy to "the People."* Cambridge, 1992.

Dyson, S. L., *Community and Society in Roman Italy*. Baltimore, 1992.

Eagly, A. H., "Prejudice: Toward a More Inclusive Definition," in A. H. Eagly, R. M. Baron, and V. L. Hamilton (eds.), *The Social Psychology of Group Identity and Social Conflict: Theory, Application, and Practice* (Washington, DC, 2004), 45–64.

Eck, W., A. Caballos, and F. Fernández, *Das Senatus Consultum de Cn. Pisone Patre*. Munich, 1996.

Edgerton, R. B., "The Study of Deviance – Marginal Man or Everyman?," in G. D. Spindler (ed.), *The Making of Psychological Anthropology* (Berkeley, 1978), 444–76.
Sick Societies: Challenging the Myth of Primitive Harmony. New York, 1992.

Edmondson, J. C., "Dynamic Arenas: Gladiatorial Presentations in the City of Rome and the Construction of Roman Society during the Early Empire,' in Slater (ed.), *Roman Theatre and Society*, 69–112.
"The Cultural Politics of Public Spectacle in Rome and the Greek East, 167–166 BCE," in Bergmann and Kondoleon (eds.), *Art of Ancient Spectacle*, 77–95.
"Public Spectacles and Roman Social Relations," in *Ludi Romani: Espectáculos en Hispania Romana, Museo Nacional de Arte Romano, Mérida, 29 de julio – 13 octubre, 2002* (Córdoba, 2002), 41–63.

Edwards, C., *The Politics of Immorality in Ancient Rome*. Cambridge, 1993.
  "Incorporating the Alien: The Art of Conquest," in Edwards and Woolf (eds.),
    Rome the Cosmopolis, 44–70.
  Death in Ancient Rome. New Haven, 2007.
Edwards, C. and G. Woolf (eds.), *Rome the Cosmopolis*. Cambridge, 2003.
Ehrlich, P., *Human Natures: Genes, Cultures, and the Human Prospect*. Washington,
    DC, 2000.
Eisenberg, J. M., "The Phaistos Disk: One Hundred Year Old Hoax?," *Minerva*
    19 (2008), 9–24.
Ekman, P. (ed.), *Darwin and Facial Expressions: A Century of Research in Review*.
    New York, 1973.
  Emotion in the Human Face, 2nd edn. Cambridge, 1982.
Ekman, P., and R. J. Davidson (eds.), *The Nature of Emotion: Fundamental Ques-
    tions*. Oxford, 1994.
Elias, N., *The Civilizing Process: The History of Manners*. New York, 1978.
Elias, N. and E. Dunning, *Quest for Excitement: Sport and Leisure in the Civilizing
    Process*. Oxford, 1986.
Elliott, J. K. (ed.), *The Apocryphal New Testament* (Oxford, 1993), 370–89.
Ellis, M. J., *Why People Play*. Englewood Cliffs, 1972.
Ellis, S. P., "The End of the Roman House," *AJA* 92 (1988), 565–76.
Esses, V. M., L. M. Jackson, J. F. Dovidio, and G. Hodson, "Instrumental Relations
    among Groups: Group Competition, Conflict, and Prejudice," in Dovidio
    et al. (eds.), *Nature of Prejudice*, 227–43.
Evans, R. J., *Rituals of Retribution: Capital Punishment in Germany 1600–1987*.
    Oxford, 1996.
Ewigleben, C., "'What These Women Love Is the Sword': The Performers and
    their Audience," in Köhne and Ewigleben (eds.), *Gladiators and Caesars*,
    125–39.
Fagan, G. G., *Bathing in Public in the Roman World*. Ann Arbor, 1999.
  "Violence in Roman Social Relations," in M. Peachin (ed.), *The Oxford Hand-
    book of Roman Social Relations* (Oxford, forthcoming).
Faller, S. (ed.), *Studien zu antiken Identitäten*. Würzburg, 2001.
Farge, A., *Fragile Lives: Violence, Power, and Solidarity in Eighteenth-Century Paris*,
    trans. C. Shelton. Cambridge, 1993.
Febvre, L., "Sensibility and History: How to Reconstitute the Emotional Life of
    the Past," in P. Burke (ed.), *A New Kind of History: From The Writings of
    Febvre* (New York, 1973), 12–26.
Finley, M. I. (ed.), *Classical Slavery*. Studies in Slave and Post-Slave Societies.
    London, 1987.
Fiske, S. T., "Stereotyping, Prejudice, and Discrimination," in D. T. Gilbert,
    S. T. Fiske, and G. Linzey (eds.), *The Handbook of Social Psychology*, 4th edn.
    (New York, 1998), 357–411.
  "Stereotyping, Discrimination and Prejudice at the Seam between the Centuries:
    Evolution, Culture, Mind and Brain," *European Journal of Social Psychology*
    30 (2000), 299–322.

Fitzgerald, W., *Slavery and the Roman Literary Imagination*. Roman Literature and Its Contexts. Cambridge, 2000.

Flaig, E., *Ritualisierte Politik: Zeichen, Gesten und Herrschaft im Alten Rom*. Göttingen, 2003.

Fleckenstein, J. (ed.), *Das ritterliche Turnier im Mittelalter*. Göttingen, 1985.

Fleuri, J., *Chevaliers et chevalerie au Moyen Âge*. Paris, 1998.

Fora, M., *I Munera Gladiatoria in Italia: Considerazioni sulla loro documentazione epigrafica*. Naples, 1996.

Formigé, J., "L'amphithéâtre d'Arles," *RA* (1965), 1–47.

Foucault, M., *Discipline and Punish: The Birth of the Prison*. New York, 1977.

Franklin, J. L. Jr., "Cn. Alleius Nigidius Maius and the Amphitheatre: *Munera* and a Distinguished Career at Ancient Pompeii," *Historia* 46 (1997), 435–7.

Fredrick, D. (ed.), *The Roman Gaze: Vision, Power and the Body*. Baltimore, 2002.

Freedman, J. L., *Media Violence and its Effect on Aggression: Assessing the Scientific Evidence*. Toronto, 2002.

Frei-Stolba, R., "Textschichten in Lex Coloniae Genetivae Iuliae Ursonensis: Zu den Kapiteln 66, 70, 71, 125–127 über die Spielveranstaltungen," *SDHI* 54 (1988), 191–225.

French, K., *Screen Violence*. London, 1996.

Freud, S., *Civilization and its Discontents*. New York, 1930.

Friedland, P., "Beyond Deterrence: Cadavers, Effigies, Animals and the Logic of Executions in Premodern France," *Historical Reflections/Reflexions Historiques* 29 (2003), 295–317.

  Spectacular Justice: Theory and Practice of Executions from the Middle Ages to the French Revolution (forthcoming).

Friedländer, L., *Darstellungen aus der Sittengeschichte Roms in der Zeit von Augustus bis zum Ausgang der Antonine*, 10th edn., 4 vols. Leipzig, 1922; reprint Aalen, 1964.

Frier, B., "Roman Demography," in Potter and Mattingly (eds.), *Life, Death, and Entertainment*, 85–109.

Frith, C. D. and D. M. Wolpert (eds.), *The Neuroscience of Social Interaction: Decoding, Imitating, and Influencing the Actions of Others*. Oxford, 2003.

Frosdick, F. and P. Marsh, *Football Hooliganism*. Cullompton, 2005.

Fukuyama, F., *Our Posthuman Future: Consequences of the Biotechnology Revolution*. New York, 2002.

Fulford, R., "Iran's War on its Own," *National Post* (Aug. 11, 2007). Available online at: www.canada.com/nationalpost/news/issuesideas/story.html?id=02679845–6f28–4db3-ae22–2ae5d7043eda (accessed Jan. 12, 2010).

Futrell, A., *Blood in the Arena: The Spectacle of Roman Power*. Austin, 1997.

  The Roman Games: A Sourcebook. Historical Sources in Translation. Oxford, 2006.

Gabucci, A. (ed.), *The Colosseum*. Los Angeles, 2001.

Gagarin, M., "The Torture of Slaves in Athenian Law," *CP* 91 (1996), 1–18.

Gagé, J., *Les classes sociales dans l'empire romaine*. Paris, 1964.

Galsterer, H., "Politik in römischen Städten: Die 'Seditio' des Jahren 59 n. Chr. in Pompeii," in W. Eck, H. Galsterer, and H. Wolff (eds.), *Studien zur antiken Socialgeschichte: Festschrift Friedrich Vittinghoff* (Cologne, 1980), 323–38.

Gardner, J. F., "Proofs of Status in the Roman World," *BICS* 33 (1986), 1–14.

Garnsey, P., "Trajan's *Alimenta*: Some Problems," *Historia* 17 (1968), 367–81.

"Why Penalties Become Harsher: The Roman Case," *Natural Law Forum* 13 (1968), 141–62.

Social Status and Legal Privilege in the Roman Empire. Oxford, 1970.

Ideas of Slavery from Aristotle to Augustine. Cambridge, 1996.

Food and Society in Classical Antiquity. Cambridge, 1999.

Garnsey, P. and R. P. Saller, *The Roman Empire: Economy, Society, and Culture*. Berkeley, 1987.

Gatrell, V. A. C., *The Hanging Tree: Execution and the English People 1770–1868*. Oxford, 1994.

Gatton, J. S., "'There Must Be Blood': Mutilation and Martryrdom on the Medieval Stage," in Redmond (ed.), *Violence in Drama*, 79–91.

Gaudemet, J., "L'étranger dans le monde romain," *StClas* 7 (1967), 37–47.

Geertz, C., "Deep Play: Notes on the Balinese Cockfight," *Daedalus* 101 (1972), 1–37 (= Geertz, *Myth, Symbol, and Culture*, 1–37).

The Interpretation of Cultures. New York, 1973.

Myth, Symbol, and Culture. New York, 1974.

Gelb, F., "Prisoners of War in Early Mesopotamia," *JNES* 32 (1973), 70–98.

Gerbner, G., *Violence and Terror in the Mass Media*. Paris, 1988.

Gergen, K. J., "Social Psychology as History," *Journal of Personality and Social Psychology* 26 (1973), 309–20.

Gerould, D., *Guillotine: Its Legend and Lore*. New York, 1992.

Ghiglieri, M. P., *The Dark Side of Man: Tracing the Origins of Male Violence*. New York, 1999.

Giebel, M., *Tiere in der Antike: Von Fabelwesen, Opfertieren, und treuen Begleitern*. Darmstadt, 2003.

Ginestet, P., *Les organisations de la jeunesse dans l'Occident romain*, Collection Latomus 213. Brussels, 1991.

Giulianotti, R., *Sport: A Critical Sociology*. Cambridge, 2005.

Given, J. B., *Inquisition and Medieval Society: Power, Discipline and Resistance in Languedoc*. Ithaca, 1997.

Goetz, G. (ed.), *Corpus Glossariorum Latinorum*, 7 vols. Leipzig, 1888–1923; reprint Amsterdam, 1965.

Golden, M., *Greek Sport and Social Status*. Austin, 2008.

Goldstein, J. H., "Immortal Kombat: War Toys and Violent Video Games," in Goldstein (ed.), *Why We Watch*, 53–68.

Goldstein, J. H. (ed.), *Sports Violence*. New York, 1983.

Sports, Games, and Play: Social and Psychological Viewpoints, 2nd edn. Hillsdale, 1989.

Why We Watch: The Attractions of Violent Entertainment. Oxford, 1998.

Goldstein, J. H. and R. L. Arms, "Effects of Observing Athletic Contests on Hostility," *Sociometry* 34 (1971), 83–90.

Goldsworthy, A., *The Complete Roman Army*. London, 2003.

Golvin, J.-C., *L'amphithéâtre romain: essai sur la théorisation de sa forme et de ses fonctions*, 2 vols. Paris, 1988.

"Origine, function et forme de l'amphithéâtre romain," in Domergue et al. (eds.), *Speculata I,* 15–27.

Golvin, J.-C. and C. Landes, *Amphithéâtres et Gladiateurs*. Paris, 1990.

González, J., "The *Lex Irnitana*: A New Copy of the Flavian Municipal Law," *JRS* 76 (1986), 147–243.

Gordon, M. (ed.), *The Grand Guignol: Theatre of Fear and Terror*, rev. edn. New York, 1997.

Grant, M., *The Gladiators*. Harmondsworth, 1970.

Gras, M., "Cité grecque et lapidation," in *Du châtiment dans la cité*, 75–89.

Gray, J. G., *The Warriors: Reflections on Men in Battle*. New York, 1967; originally published in 1959.

Grayson, A. K., *Assyrian Rulers of the Early First Millennium* BC, 2 vols. Toronto, 1991–6.

Greer, A. (ed.), *The Jesuit Relations: Natives and Missionaries in Seventeenth-Century North America*, Boston, MA, 2000.

Griffin, J., *Homer on Life and Death*. Oxford, 1980.

Grig, L., *Making Martyrs in Late Antiquity*. London, 2004.

Grimes, T., J. A. Anderson, and L. Bergen, *Media Violence and Aggression: Science and Ideology*. Thousand Oaks, 2008.

Grodde, O., *Sport bei Quintilian*. Hildesheim, 1997.

Grodzynski, D., "Tortures mortelles et catégories sociales: Les Summa Supplicia dans la droit romain au IIIe et IVe siècle," in *Du châtiment dans la cité*, 361–403.

Guidobaldi, F., "L'edilizia abitativo unifamiliare nella Roma tardoantica," in A. Giardina (ed.), *Società romana e impero tardoantico*, 4 vols. (Rome, 1986), vol. II, 165–237.

Guimond, S., "Group Socialization and Prejudice: The Social Transmission of Intergroup Attitudes and Beliefs," *European Journal of Social Psychology* 30 (2000), 335–54.

Gunderson, E., "The Ideology of the Arena," *CA* 15 (1996), 113–51.

"The Flavian Amphitheatre: All the World as Stage," in A. J. Boyle and W. J. Dominik (eds.), *Flavian Rome: Culture, Image, Text* (Leiden, 2003), 637–58.

Günther, W., "Ehrungen für einen Milesischen Periodoniken," in H. Kalcyk, B. Gulath, and A. Graeber (eds.), *Studien zur alten Geschichte* (Rome, 1986), 313–28.

Guttmann, A., "Roman Sports Violence," in Goldstein (ed.), *Sports Violence*, 7–19.

Sports Spectators. New York, 1986.

"The Appeal of Violent Sports," in Goldstein (ed.), *Why We Watch*, 7–26.

Sports: The First Five Millennia. Amherst, 2004.

Halttunen, K., *Murder Most Foul: The Killer and the American Gothic Imagination*. Cambridge, MA, 1998.

Hamilton, C., *Terrific Majesty: The Power of Shaka Zulu and the Limits of Historical Invention*. Cambridge, MA, 1998.

Hamlin, C. L., *Beyond Relativism: Raymond Boudon, Cognitive Rationality, and Critical Realism*. London, 2002.

Hand, R. J., *Grand-Guignol: The French Theatre of Horror*. Exeter, 2002.

Hand, R. J. and M. Wilson, *London's Grand Guignol and the Theatre of Horror*. Exeter, 2007.

Haney, C., C. Banks, and P. Zimbardo, "Interpersonal Dynamics in a Simulated Prison," *International Journal of Criminology and Penology* 1 (1973), 69–97.

Hannestad, N., *Roman Art and Imperial Policy*. Aarhus, 1986.

Hardy, S. H., "The Medieval Tournament: A Functional Sport of the Upper Class," *Journal of Sport History* 1 (1974), 91–105.

Harker, A., *Loyalty and Dissidence in Roman Egypt: The Case of the* Acta Alexandrinorum. Cambridge, 2008.

Harlow, M., and R. Laurence, *Growing Up and Growing Old in Ancient Rome: A Life Course Approach*. London, 2002.

Harris, H. A., *Sport in Greece and Rome*. Ithaca, 1972.

Harris, W. V., *War and Imperialism in Republican Rome, 327–70 BC*. Oxford, 1979.
   "The Roman Father's Power of Life and Death," in R. S. Bagnall and W. V. Harris (eds.), *Studies in Roman Law in Memory of A. Arthur Schiller* (Leiden, 1986), 81–95.
   Restraining Rage: The Ideology of Anger Control in Classical Antiquity. Cambridge, MA, 2001.

Hartley, L. P., *The Go-Between*. London, 1953; reprint New York, 2002.

Haslam, S. A. and S. D. Reicher, *A User's Guide to "The Experiment": Exploring Groups and Power*. London, 2002.

Haslam, S. A., P. J. Oakes, K. J. Reynolds, and J. C. Turner, "Social Identity Salience and the Emergence of Stereotype Consensus," *Personality and Social Psychology Bulletin* 25 (1999), 809–18.

Haugen, D. (ed.), *Is Media Violence a Problem?* Detroit, 2007.

Hauser, M. D., *Moral Minds: How Nature Designed our Universal Sense of Right and Wrong*. New York, 2006.

Heller, T., *Delights of Terror: An Aesthetics of the Tale of Terror*. Urbana, 1987.

Hemingway, E., *Death in the Afternoon*. New York, 1932.

Henricks, T., "Professional Wrestling as Moral Order," *Sociological Inquiry* 44 (1974), 177–88.

Henzen, G., *Acta Fratrum Arvalium quae Supersunt*. Berlin, 1874.

Herrnstein, R. J. and C. Murray, *The Bell Curve: Intelligence and Class Structure in American Life*. New York, 1994.

Hewstone, M., "The 'Ultimate Attribution Error'? A Review of the Literature on Intergroup Causal Attribution," *European Journal of Social Psychology* 20 (1990), 311–35.

Hinard, F., "Spectacle des exécutions et espace urbain," in *L'urbs: Espace urbain et histoire* (Paris, 1984), 111–25.

Hinkeldey, C. (ed.), *Criminal Justice through the Ages: From Divine Judgement to Modern German Legislation*. Rothenburg ob der Tauber, 1993.

Hoberman, J., "'A Test for the Individual Viewer': Bonnie and Clyde's Violent Reception," in Goldstein (ed.), *Why We Watch*, 116–43.

Hofstede, G., *Cultures and Organization: Software of the Mind*. New York, 1991.

Culture's Consequences: Comparing Values, Behaviours, Institutions and Organizations across Nations, 2nd edn. Thousand Oaks, 2001.

Hogg, M. A. and R. S. Tindale (eds.), *Group Processes: Blackwell Handbook of Social Psychology*. Oxford, 2001.

Hogg, M. A. and G. M. Vaughan, *Social Psychology*, 2nd edn. London, 2001.

Hollis, M., and S. Lukes (eds.), *Rationality and Relativism*. Oxford, 1982.

Holloway, P. A., *Coping with Prejudice: 1 Peter in Social Psychological Perspective*. Tübingen, 2009.

Hönle, A. and A. Henze, *Römische Amphitheater und Stadien: Gladiatorenkämpfe und Circusspiele*. Zurich, 1981.

Hope, V., "Fighting for Identity: The Funerary Commemoration of Italian Gladiators," in A. Cooley (ed.), *The Epigraphic Landscape of Roman Italy, BICS* supplement 73 (London, 2000), 93–113.

Hope, V. M. and E. Marshall (eds.), *Death and Disease in the Ancient City*. London, 2000.

Hopkins, K., *Conquerors and Slaves: Sociological Studies in Roman History I*. Cambridge, 1978.

Death and Renewal: Sociological Studies in Roman History II. Cambridge, 1983.

"Novel Evidence for Roman Slavery," *Past and Present* 138 (1993), 3–27.

A World Full of Gods: The Strange Triumph of Christianity. London, 1999.

Hopkins, K. and M. Beard, *The Colosseum*. London, 2005.

Horne, J., A. Tomlinson and G. Whannel (eds.), *Understanding Sport: An Introduction to the Sociological and Cultural Analysis of Sport*. London, 1999.

Hornum, M. B., *Nemesis, the Roman State, and the Games*. Leiden, 1993.

Horsfall, N., *The Culture of the Roman Plebs*. London, 2003.

Horsmann, G., "Sklavendienst, Strafvollzug oder Sport? Überlegungen zum Charakter der römischen Gladiatur," in H. Bellen and H. Heinen (eds.), *Fünfzig Jahre Forschungen zur antiken Sklaverei an der Mainzer Akademie, 1950–2000: Miscellanea zum Jubiläum*, Forschungen zur antiken Sklaverei 35 (Stuttgart, 2001), 225–41.

Hugoniot, C., F. Hurlet, and S. Milanezi (eds.), *Le statut de l'acteur dans l'Antiquité grecque et romaine*. Tours, 2004.

Hülsen, C., "Il posto degli arvali nel Colosseo e la capacità dei teatri di Roma antica," *BullCom* 22 (1894), 312–24.

Humphrey, J. H., "'Amphitheatral' Hippo-Stadia," in A. Raban and K. G. Holum (eds.), *Caesarea Maritima: A Retrospective after Two Millenia* (Leiden, 1996), 121–9.

Hunter, V., "Crime and Criminals in Plato's Laws," *Museion* 9 (2009), 1–19.

Hunter, V. J., *Policing Athens: Social Control in the Attic Lawsuits, 420–320 BC*. Princeton, 1994.

Innes, B., *The History of Torture*. New York, 1998.

Isaac, B., *The Invention of Racism in Classical Antiquity*. Princeton, 2004.

Isaacs, N., *Travels and Adventures in Eastern Africa Descriptive of the Zoolus, their Manners, their Customs*. Capetown, 1970; originally published 1836.

Jacobelli, L., *Gladiators at Pompeii*. Los Angeles, 2003.

Johnstone, L., "Riot by Appointment: An Examination of the Nature and Structure of Seven Hard-Core Football Hooligan Groups," in D. Canter and L. Alison (eds.), *The Social Psychology of Crime: Groups, Teams, and Networks* (Aldershot, 2000), 153–88.

Jones, C. P., "Gladiator Epigrams from Beroea and Stratonikeia (Caria)," *ZPE* 163 (2007), 45–8.

Jones, M., *Social Psychology of Prejudice*. Upper Saddle River, 2002.

Jongman, W., "Slavery and the Growth of Rome," in Edwards and Woolf (eds.), *Rome the Cosmopolis*, 100–22.

Jory, E. J., "The Early Pantomime Riots," in A. Moffatt (ed.), *Maistor: Classical, Byzantine, and Renaissance Studies for Robert Browning* (Canberra, 1984), 57–66.

Jost, J. T. and M. R. Banaji, "The Role of Stereotyping in System-Justification and the Production of False Consciousness," *British Journal of Social Psychology* 33 (1994), 1–27.

Junkelmann, M., "*Familia Gladiatoria*: Heroes of the Amphitheatre," in Köhne and Ewigleben (eds.), *Gladiators and Caesars*, 31–74.

Gladiatoren: Das Spiel mit dem Tod. Mainz, 2008.

Kanz, F. and K. Grossschmidt, "Head Injuries of Roman Gladiators," *Forensic Science International* 160 (2006), 207–16.

Kaster, R. A., *Emotion, Restraint, and Community in Ancient Rome*. Oxford, 2005.

Keane, C. C., "Theatre, Spectacle, and the Satirist in Juvenal," *Phoenix* 57 (2003), 257–75.

Keen, M., *Chivalry*. New Haven, 1984.

Kenrick, D. and V. Sheets, "Homicide Fantasies," *Ethology and Sociobiology* 14 (1994), 231–46.

Kerr, J. H., *Understanding Soccer Hooliganism*. Buckingham, 1994.

Kershaw, I., *Hitler, 1889–1936: Hubris*. New York, 1999.

King, S., *Danse Macabre*. New York, 1981.

King, W. M., *Going to Meet a Man: Denver's Last Legal Public Execution, 27 July 1886*. Niwot, 1990.

Kirk, G. S., *The Iliad: A Commentary*, 6 vols. Cambridge, 1984–1993.

Klausner, S. Z. (ed.), *Why Man Takes Chances*. Garden City, 1968.

Kleijwegt, M., *Ancient Youth: The Ambiguity of Youth and the Absence of Adolescence in Greco-Roman Society*. Amsterdam, 1991.

Kloeren, M., *Sport und Rekord: kultursoziologische Untersuchungen zum England des sechzehnten bis achtzehnten Jahrhunderts*. Leipzig, 1935; reprint New York, 1966.

Kloppenborg, J. S., "Collegia and *Thiasoi*: Issues in Function, Taxonomy and Membership," in J. S. Kloppenborg and S. G. Wilson (eds.), *Voluntary Associations in the Graeco-Roman World* (London, 1996), 16–30.

Knowles, N., "The Torture of Captives by the Indians of Eastern North America," *Proceedings of the American Philosophical Society* 82 (1940), 151–225.

Koch, C., *The Quest for Consciousness: A Neurobiological Approach.* Greenwood, 2004.

Köhne, E. and C. Ewigleben (eds.), *Gladiators and Caesars: The Power of Spectacle in Ancient Rome.* Berkeley, 2000.

Kolb, F., "Zur Geschichte der Stadt Hierapolis in Phrygien: Die Phyleninschriften im Theater," *ZPE* 15 (1974), 225–70.

"Zur Statussymbolik im antiken Rom," *Chiron* 7 (1977), 239–59.

"Sitzstufeninschriften aus dem Stadion von Saittai (Lydia)," *EpigAnat* 15 (1990), 107–19.

Kolendo, J., "La répartition des places aux spectacles et la stratification sociale dans l'Empire Romain: à propos des inscriptions sur les gradins des amphithéâtres et théâtres," *Ktèma* 6 (1981), 301–15.

König, J., *Athletics and Literature in the Roman Empire.* Cambridge, 2005.

Konstan, D., *Friendship in the Classical World.* Cambridge, 1997.

Pity Transformed. London, 2001.

The Emotions of the Ancient Greeks: Studies in Aristotle and Classical Literature. Toronto, 2006.

Konstan, D. and K. Rutter (eds.), *Envy, Spite and Jealousy: The Rivalrous Emotions in Ancient Greece.* Edinburgh, 2003.

Krapinger, G., *[Quintilian] Der Gladiator (Größere Deklamation, 9).* Cassino, 2007.

Kremer, J. and A. P. Moran, *Pure Sport: Practical Sport Psychology.* London, 2008.

Kudlien, F., *Sklaven-Mentalität im Spiegel antiker Wahrsagerei.* Stuttgart, 1991.

Kuttner, A., "Hellenistic Images of Spectacle: From Alexander to Augustus," in Bergmann and Kondoleon (eds.), *Art of Ancient Spectacle,* 97–123.

Kyle, D. G., "Rethinking the Roman Arena: Gladiators, Sorrows, and Games," *AHB* 11 (1997), 94–7.

Spectacles of Death in Ancient Rome. London, 1998.

Sport and Spectacle in the Ancient World. Oxford, 2007.

La Rocca, E., and M. and A. de Vos, *Guida archeologica di Pompei.* Verona, 1976.

Laland, K. N., and G. R. Brown, *Sense and Nonsense: Evolutionary Perspectives on Human Behaviour.* Oxford, 2002.

Lanciani, R., *Ancient Rome in the Light of Recent Discoveries.* Boston, MA, 1889.

Lane Fox, R. L., *The Classical World: An Epic History from Homer to Hadrian.* New York, 2006.

Langner, M., *Antike Graffitizeichnungen: Motive, Gestaltung und Bedeutung,* Palilia Band 11. Wiesbaden, 2001.

Laqueur, T. W., "Crowds, Carnival and the State in English Executions, 1604–1868," in A. L. Beier, D. Cannadine, and J. M. Rosenheim (eds.), *The First Modern Society: Essays in English History in Honour of Lawrence Stone* (Cambridge, 1989), 305–55.

Lavallee, D., J. Kremer, and A. P. Moran, *Sport Psychology: Contemporary Themes.* Basingstoke, 2004.

Latham, R. and W. Matthews (eds.), *The Diary of Samuel Pepys: A New and Complete Transcription*, 11 vols. Berkeley, 1970–83.

Laurence, J., *A History of Capital Punishment*. London, 1932; reprint New York, 1960.

Lavan, L., "Provincial Capitals of Late Antiquity," PhD dissertation, University of Nottingham (2001).

Lawrence, D. H., "Pornography and Obscenity," in J. T. Boulton (ed.), *The Cambridge Edition of the Works of D. H. Lawrence: Late Essays and Articles* (Cambridge, 2004; essay originally published in 1929), 233–53.

Le Bon, G., *The Crowd: A Study of the Popular Mind*, 2nd edn. New York, 1897.

Le Glay, M., "Les amphithéâtres: loci religiosi?," in Domergue et al. (eds.), *Spectacula*, 217–25.

Le Goff, J., "Mentalities: A History of Ambiguities," in J. Le Goff and P. Nora (eds.), *Constructing the Past: Essays in Historical Methodology* (Cambridge, 1985), 166–80.

Le Roux, P., "L'amphithéâtre et le soldat sous l'empire romain," in Domergue et al. (eds.), *Spectacula*, 203–16.

Leahy, A., "Death by Fire in Ancient Egypt," *Journal of the Economic and Social History of the Orient* 27 (1984), 199–206.

LeDoux, J., *The Emotional Brain: The Mysterious Underpinnings of Emotional Life*. New York, 1996.

Lee, H. M., "The Later Greek Boxing Glove and the Roman Caestus: A Centennial Re-evaluation of Jünther's 'Über Antike Turngeräthe,'" *Nikephoros* 10 (1997), 161–78.

Leppin, H., *Historionen: Untersuchungen zur sozialen Stellung von Bühnenkünstler im Westen des Römischen Reiches zur Zeit der Republik und des Principats*. Bonn, 1992.

Lesser, W., *Pictures at an Execution: An Inquiry into the Subject of Murder*. Cambridge, MA, 1993.

Levick, B., "The *Senatus Consultum* from Larinum," *JRS* 73 (1983), 97–115.

Lewin, A., *Assemblee popolari e lotta politica nella città dell'impero romana*. Florence, 1995.

Lewis, M. and J. M. Haviland (eds.), *Handbook of Emotions*, 2nd edn. New York, 2000.

Lewontin, R. C., S. Rose, and L. J. Kamin, *Not in Our Genes: Biology, Ideology and Human Nature*. New York, 1984.

Lidor, R. and K. P. Henschen (eds.), *The Psychology of Team Sports*. Morgantown, 2003.

Liebeschuetz, J. H. W. G., *Antioch: City and Imperial Administration in the Later Roman Empire*. Oxford, 1972.
  Decline and Fall of the Roman City. Oxford, 2001.

Lim, R., "In the 'Temple of Laughter': Visual and Literary Representations of Spectators at Roman Games," in Bergmann and Kondoleon (eds.), *Art of Ancient Spectacle*, 343–65.

"The Roman Pantomime Riot of A.D. 509," in J.-M. Carrié and R. Lizzi Testa (eds.), 'Humana Sapit' *Études d'Antiquité Tardive offertes à Lellia Cracco Ruggini* (Turnhout, 2002), 35–42.

Linebaugh, P., "The Tyburn Riot against the Surgeons," in D. Hay, P. Linebaugh, J. G. Rule, E. P. Thompson, and C. Winslow, *Albion's Fatal Tree: Crime and Society in Eighteenth-Century England* (New York, 1975), 65–117.

The London Hanged: Crime and Civil Society in the Eighteenth Century. Cambridge, 1992.

Lintott, A. W., *Violence in Republican Rome*, 2nd edn. Oxford, 1999.

"Freedmen and Slaves in the Light of Legal Documents from First-Century A.D. Campania," *CQ* 52 (2002), 555–65.

Lloyd, A. B. and C. Gilliver (eds.), *Battle in Antiquity.* London, 1996.

Lloyd, B. and G. Gay (eds.), *Universals of Human Thought: Some African Evidence.* Cambridge, 1981.

Lo Cascio, E., "La popolazione," in E. Lo Cascio (ed.), *Roma imperiale: una metropoli antica* (Rome, 2000), 17–69.

Lorton, D., "The Treatment of Criminals in Ancient Egypt through the New Kingdom," *Journal of the Economic and Social History of the Orient* 20 (1977), 2–64.

McAleer, K., *Dueling: The Cult of Honor in Fin-de-Siècle Germany.* Princeton, 1994.

McCall, A., *The Medieval Underworld.* London, 1979; reprint, Stroud, 2004.

McCauley, C., "When Screen Violence is not Attractive," in Goldstein (ed.), *Why We Watch*, 144–62.

MacCormack, G., *Traditional Chinese Penal Law.* Edinburgh, 1990.

MacKinnon, M., "Supplying Exotic Animals for the Roman Amphitheatre Games: New Reconstructions Combining Archaeological, Ancient Textual, Historical, and Ethnographic Data," *Museion* 6 (2006), 137–61.

McKnight, B., *Law and Order in Sung China.* Cambridge, 1992.

MacMullen, R., *Enemies of the Roman Order: Treason, Unrest, and Alienation in the Empire.* Cambridge, MA, 1966.

Roman Social Relations, 50 BC – AD 284. New Haven, 1974.

"Judicial Savagery in the Roman Empire," *Chiron* 16 (1986), 147–66 (=MacMullen, *Changes in the Roman Empire*, 204–17).

Changes in the Roman Empire: Essays in the Ordinary. Princeton, 1990.

Romanization in the Time of Augustus. New Haven, 2000.

Feelings in History, Ancient and Modern. Claremont, 2003.

Mailer, N., *The Presidential Papers.* New York, 1963.

Maiuri, A., *Studi e ricerche sull'anfiteatro Flavio Puteolano.* Naples, 1955.

Malcolmson, R. W., *Popular Recreations in English Society 1700–1850.* Cambridge, 1973.

Mann, C., "Gladiators in the Greek East: A Case Study in Romanization," *International Journal of the History of Sport* 26 (2009), 272–97.

Mann, L., "Sports Crowds and the Collective Behavior Perspective," in J. H. Goldstein (ed.), *Sports, Games, and Play: Social and Psychological Viewpoints*, 2nd edn. (Hillsdale, 1989), 299–331.

Marrou, H.-I., *Histoire de l'éducation dans l'antiquité*, 6th edn. Paris, 1965.

Mathisen, R. M., *People, Personal Expression, and Social Relations in Late Antiquity*, 2 vols. Ann Arbor, 2003.

Mattingly, D., *An Imperial Possession: Britain in the Roman Empire*. London, 2006.

Mau, A., *Pompeji in Leben und Kunst*, 2nd edn. Leipzig, 1908.

Maurin, J., "Les Barbares aux arènes," *Ktèma* 9 (1984), 102–11.

Mazer, S., *Professional Wrestling: Sport and Spectacle*. Jackson, 1998.

Meijer, F., *The Gladiators: History's Most Deadly Sport*. New York, 2005.

Meijer, F. and O. van Nijf, *Trade, Transport, and Society in the Ancient World: A Sourcebook*. London, 1992.

Merback, M. B., *The Thief, the Cross and the Wheel: Pain and the Spectacle of Punishment in Medieval and Renaissance Europe*. Chicago, 1998.

Mercier, S.-L., *The Picture of Paris*, trans. W. and E. Jackson. London, 1929; originally published 1781–8.

Merkelbach, R. and J. Stauber, *Steinepigramme aus dem griechischen Osten*, 3 vols. Stuttgart, 1998.

Metzger, E., "The Case of Petronia Iusta," *Revue internationale des droits de l'antiquité* 47 (2000), 151–65.

Milgram, S., *Obedience to Authority: An Experimental Overview*. New York, 1974.

Millar, F., "The World of the *Golden Ass*," *JRS* 71 (1981), 63–75.

    The Crowd in Rome in the Late Republic. Ann Arbor, 1998.

Miller, R. R. (ed.), *Chronicle of Colonial Lima: The Diary of Josephe and Francisco Mugaburru, 1640–1697*. Norman, 1975.

Miller, S. G., "The Organization and Functioning of the Olympic Games," in D. J. Phillips and D. Pritchard (eds.), *Sport and Festival in the Ancient Greek World* (Swansea, 2003), 1–40.

Miller, W. I., *The Anatomy of Disgust*. Cambridge, MA, 1997.

Mirhady, D., "Torture and Rhetoric in Athens," *JHS* 106 (1996), 119–31.

Mithen, S., *The Prehistory of the Mind: The Cognitive Origins of Art and Science*. London, 1996.

Mittag, P. F., *Antiochos IV. Epiphanes: Eine Politische Biographie, Klio* Beiträge 11. Berlin, 2006.

Moeller, W. O., "The Riot of AD 59 at Pompeii," *Historia* 19 (1970), 84–95.

Montague, W., *The Delights of Holland*. London, 1696.

Moran, A. P., *Sport and Exercise Psychology: A Critical Introduction*. London, 2004.

Morgan, M. G., "Three Non-Roman Blood Sports," *CQ* 25 (1975), 117–22.

Mosci Sassi, M. G., *Il linguaggio gladiatorio*. Bologna, 1992.

Moscovici, S., *The Age of the Crowd: A Historical Treatise on Mass Psychology*. Cambridge, 1985.

Mouratidis, J., "On the Origin of the Gladiatorial Games," *Nikephoros* 9 (1996), 111–34.

Mrozek, S., *Les distributions d'argent et de nourriture dans les villes italiennes du Haut-Empire romain*, Collection Latomus 198. Brussels, 1987.

Müller, S., *Das Volk der Athleten: Untersuchungen zur Ideologie und Kritik des Sports in der griechisch-römischen Antike.* Trier, 1995.

Murphy, P., *Football on Trial: Spectator Violence and Development in the Football World.* London, 1990.

Murray, O. (ed.), *Sympotica: A Symposium on the Symposium.* Oxford, 1990.

Musurillo, H., *The Acts of Pagan Martyrs: Introduction, Texts and Translations* (Acta Alexandrinorum). Oxford, 1954.

    The Acts of the Christian Martyrs. Oxford, 1972.

Nardoni, D., *I Gladiatori romani.* Rome, 1989.

Nelson, T. D., *The Psychology of Prejudice*, 2nd edn. Boston, MA, 2006.

Nelson, T. D. (ed.), *Handbook of Prejudice, Stereotyping, and Discrimination.* New York, 2009.

Newby, Z., "Greek Athletics as Roman Spectacle: The Mosaics from Ostia and Rome," *PBSR* 70 (2002), 177–203.

    Greek Athletics in the Roman World: Victory and Virtue. Oxford, 2005.

Nisbett, R. E., *The Geography of Thought: How Asians and Westerners Think Differently . . . and Why.* New York, 2003.

Noel, J. G., D. L. Wann, and N. R. Branscombe, "Peripheral Ingroup Membership Status and Public Negativity toward Outgroups," *Journal of Personality and Social Psychology* 68 (1995), 127–37.

Nossov, K., *Gladiator: Rome's Bloody Spectacle.* Oxford, 2009.

Noy, D., *Foreigners at Rome: Citizens and Strangers.* London, 2000.

Oakley, S. P., *A Commentary on Livy, Books VI–X.* Oxford, 1997.

Ober, J., "The Athenian Revolution of 508/7 BC: Violence, Authority, and the Origins of Democracy," in L. Kurke and C. Dougherty (eds.), *Cultural Poetics in Archaic Greece* (Cambridge, 1993), 215–32 (= Ober, *The Athenian Revolution*, 32–52).

    The Athenian Revolution. Princeton, 1996.

Orr, H. A., "Darwinian Storytelling," *New York Review of Books* (Feb. 27, 2003).

Painter, S., *William Marshall.* Baltimore, 1933.

Paladino, I., *Fratres arvales: storia di un collegio sacerdotale romano.* Rome, 1988.

Pappas, N. T, C. P. McKenry, and B. S. Catlett, "Athlete Aggression on the Rink and off the Ice: Athlete Violence and Aggression in Hockey and Interpersonal Relationships," *Men and Masculinities* 6 (2004), 291–312.

Parker, H., "Crucially Funny or Tranio on the Couch: The *Servus Callidus* and Jokes about Torture," *TAPA* 119 (1989), 233–46.

Parker, H. N., "The Observed of all Observers: Spectacle, Applause, and Cultural Poetics in the Roman Theater Audience," in Bergmann and Kondoleon (eds.), *Art of Ancient Spectacle*, 163–79.

Parkin, T. G., *Demography and Roman Society.* Baltimore, 1992.

    Old Age in the Roman World: A Cultural and Social History. Baltimore, 2002.

Parlasca, K., *Die Römischen Mosaiken in Deutschland.* Berlin, 1959.

Pasoli, A., *Acta Fratrum Arvalium*. Bologna, 1950.

Patch, R. W., "Culture, Community, and 'Rebellion' in the Yucatec Maya Uprising of 1761," in S. Schroeder (ed.), *Native Resistance and the Pax Colonial in New Spain* (Lincoln, NE, 1998), 67–83.

Patterson, O., *Slavery and Social Death: A Comparative Study*. Cambridge, MA, 1982.

Paulson, R., *Representations of the Revolution (1789–1820)*. New Haven, 1983.

Paulus, P. B. (ed.), *Basic Group Processes*. New York, 1983.

Peachin, M. (ed.), *Aspects of Friendship in the Graeco-Roman World, JRA* Supplementary Series 43. Portsmouth, RI, 2001.

Pearson, J., *Arena: The Story of the Colosseum*. New York, 1973.

Perry, B. E., *Aesopica*. Urbana, 1952.

Petermandl, W., "Zuschauer der Geschichte: Ein Internet-Archiv zum Publikum im Altertum," *Nikephoros* 19 (2006), 45–56.

Peters, E., *Torture*. Oxford, 1985.

Petitot, M., *Collection des mémoires relatifs à l'histoire de France*, 130 vols. Paris, 1819–1829.

Pettigrew, T. F., "The Ultimate Attribution Error: Extending Allport's Cognitive Analysis of Prejudice," *Personality and Social Psychology Bulletin* 5 (1979), 461–76.

Phillips, D. and D. Pritchard (eds.), *Sport and Festival in the Ancient Greek World*. Swansea, 2003.

Pilhofer, S., *Romanisierung in Kilikien? Das Zeugnis der Inschrriften*. Munich, 2006.

Pinker, S., *The Language Instinct: The New Science of Language and Mind*. New York, 1994.

  How the Mind Works. New York, 1997.

  The Blank Slate: The Modern Denial of Human Nature. New York, 2002.

  The Stuff of Thought: Languages as a Window into Human Nature. New York, 2007.

Plass, P., *The Game of Death in Ancient Rome: Arena Sport and Political Suicide*. Madison, 1995.

Pleket, H. W., "Mass-Sport and Local Infrastructure in the Greek Cities of Roman Asia Minor," *Stadion* 24 (1998), 151–72.

Poliakoff, M. B., "Deaths in the Pan-Hellenic Games: Addenda and Corrigenda," *AJP* 107 (1986), 400–2.

  Combat Sports in The Ancient World: Competition, Violence, and Culture. New Haven, 1987.

Pomonariev, N. I., "Sport and Show," *International Review of Sport Sociology* 11.1 (1980), 73–9.

Potter, D., "Martyrdom as Spectacle," in R. Scodel (ed.), *Theater and Society in the Classical World* (Ann Arbor, 1993), 53–88.

  "Performance, Power and Justice in the High Empire," in Slater (ed.), *Roman Theater and Society*, 129–60.

Potter, D. S., "Gladiators and Blood Sport," in M. M. Winkler (ed.), *Gladiator: Film and History* (Oxford, 2004), 73–87.

"Spectacle," in D. S. Potter (ed.), *The Blackwell Companion to the Roman World* (Oxford, 2006), 385–408.

"Entertainers in the Roman Empire," in Potter and Mattingly (eds.), *Life, Death, and Entertainment*, 280–349.

Potter, D. S., and D. J. Mattingly (eds.), *Life, Death, and Entertainment in the Roman Empire* 2nd edn. Ann Arbor, 2010.

Potter, W. J., *On Media Violence*. Thousand Oaks, 1999.

The 11 Myths of Media Violence. Thousand Oaks, 2003.

Prayag Mela Research Group, "Living the Magh Mela at Prayag: Collective Identity, Collective Experience, and the Impact of Participation in a Mass Event," *Psychological Studies* 52 (2007), 293–301.

Pritchard, J. B., *Ancient Near Eastern Texts Relating to the Old Testament*, 3rd edn. Princeton, 1969.

Purcell, N., "The *Apparitores*: A Study in Social Mobility," *PBSR* 51 (1983), 125–73.

Racine, J., *Britannicus, Phaedra, Athaliah*, trans. C. H. Sisson. Oxford, 1987.

Ranke, K., "Androklus und der Löwe," in K. Ranke (ed.), *Enzyklopädie des Märchens: Handwörterbuch zur historischen und vergleichenden Erzählforschung*, 12 vols. (Berlin, 1977–present), vol. 1, 501–8.

Rawson, B., "Family Life among the Lower Classes at Rome in the First Two Centuries of the Empire," *CP* 61 (1966), 71–83.

Rawson, E., "*Discrimina Ordinum*: The *Lex Julia Theatralis*," *PBSR* 55 (1987), 83–114 (= Rawson, *Roman Culture and Society*, 508–45).

Roman Culture and Society. Oxford, 1991.

Reddy, W. M., *The Navigation of Feeling: A Framework for the History of Emotions*. Cambridge, 2001.

Redford, D. B. (ed.), *The Oxford Encyclopedia of Ancient Egypt*, 3 vols. Oxford, 2001.

Redmond, J. (ed.), *Violence in Drama*. Cambridge, 1991.

Reicher, S., "The Psychology of Crowd Dynamics," in Hogg and Tinsdale (eds.), *Group Processes*, 182–208.

Reicher, S. D., "The Determination of Collective Behaviour," in H. Tajfel (ed.), *Social Identity and Intergroup Relations* (Cambridge, 1982), 41–83.

"'The Battle of Westminster:' Developing the Social Identity Model of Crowd Behaviour in Order to Explain the Initiation and Development of Collective Conflict," *European Journal of Social Psychology* 26 (1996), 115–34.

"The Context of Social Psychology: Domination, Resistance, and Change," *Political Psychology* 25 (2004), 40–62.

"Rethinking the Paradigm of Prejudice," *South African Journal of Psychology* 37 (2007), 820–34.

The Crowd. Cambridge, forthcoming.

Reicher S. D., and S. A. Haslam, "Social Psychology, Science, and Surveillance: Understanding *The Experiment*," *Social Psychology Review* 5 (2002), 7–17.

"On the Agency of Individuals and Groups: Lessons from the BBC Prison Study," in T. Postmes and J. Jetten (eds.), *Individuality and the Group: Advances in Social Identity* (London, 2006), 237–57.

"Beyond Help: A Social Psychology of Collective Solidarity and Social Cohesion," in S. Stürmer and M. Snyder (eds.), *The Psychology of Prosocial Behavior: Group Processes, Intergroup Relations and Helping* (Chichester, 2010), 289–310.

Reicher, S., S. A. Haslam, and R. Rath, "Making a Virtue of Evil: A Five-Step Social Identity Model of the Development of Collective Hate," *Social and Personality Psychology Compass* 2/3 (2008), 1313–44.

Reicher, S., R. M. Levine, and E. Gordijn, "More on Deindividuation, Power Relations between Groups and the Expression of Social Identity: Three Studies on the Effects of Visibility on the In-Group," *British Journal of Social Psychology* 37 (1998), 15–41.

Reicher, S. D., and J. Potter, "Pyschological Theory as Intergroup Perspective: A Comparative Analysis of 'Scientific' and 'Lay' Accounts of Crowd Events," *Human Relations* 38 (1985), 167–89.

Reicher, S. D., C. Cassidy, N. Hopkins, and M. Levine, "Saving Bulgaria's Jews: An Analysis of Social Identity and the Mobilisation of Social Solidarity," *European Journal of Social Psychology* 36 (2006), 49–72.

Reinhold, M., "Usurpation of Status and Status Symbols in the Roman Empire," *Historia* 20 (1971), 275–302 (= Reinhold, *Studies in Classical History and Society*, 25–44).

"Human Nature as Cause in Ancient Historiography," in J. W. Eadie and J. Ober (ed.), *The Craft of the Ancient Historian: Essays in Honor of Chester G. Starr* (Lanham, 1985), 21–40 (= Reinhold, *Studies in Classical History and Society*, 45–53).

Studies in Classical History and Society. Oxford, 2002.

Rejal, D., *Torture and Democracy.* Princeton, 2007.

Retzleff, A., and A. M. Mjely, "Seat Inscriptions in the Odeum at Gerasa (Jerash)," *BASOR* 332 (2004), 37–47.

Revell, L., *Roman Imperialism and Local Identities.* Cambridge, 2009.

Reynolds, J. M., *Aphrodisias and Rome.* London, 1982.

Reynolds, R. W., "Criticism of Individuals in Roman Popular Comedy," *CQ* 37 (1943), 37–45.

Richardson, L., "The *Retiarius Tunicatus* of Suetonius, Juvenal and Petronius," *AJP* 110 (1989), 589–94.

Richey, W. and D. Robinson (eds.), *William Wordsworth and Samuel Taylor Coleridge: Lyrical Ballads and Related Writings.* Boston, MA, 2002.

Richter, D. K., *The Ordeal of the Longhouse: The Peoples of the Iroquois League in the Era of European Colonization.* Chapel Hill, 1992.

Riess, W., *Apuleius und die Räuber: Ein Beitrag zur historischen Kriminalitätsforschung.* Stuttgart, 2001.

"Die historische Entwicklung der Römischen Folter – und Hinrichtungspraxis in Kulturvergleichender Perspektive," *Historia* 51 (2002), 206–26.

Ritti, T. and S. Yilmaz, *Gladiatori e venationes a Hierapolis di Frigia*, Atti della Accademia Nazionale dei Lincei, serie 9, volume 10, fascicolo 4. Rome, 1998.

Rives, J., "Human Sacrifice among Pagans and Christians," *JRS* 85 (1995), 65–85.

Rizzolatti, G. and L. Craighero, "The Mirror-Neuron System," *Annual Review of Neuroscience* 27 (2004), 169–92.

Rizzolatti, G. and M. Fabbri-Destro, "The Mirror Neuron System," in G. G. Bernston and J. T. Cacioppo (eds.), *Handbook of Neuroscience for the Behavioral Sciences*, 2 vols. (Hoboken, 2009), vol. i, 337–57.

Rizzolatti, G. and C. Sinigaglia, *Mirrors in the Brain: How Our Minds Share Actions and Emotions*, trans. F. Anderson. Oxford, 2008.

Robert, L., *Les gladiateurs dans l'Orient grec*. Paris, 1940; reprint Amsterdam, 1971. *Hellenica VIII*. Paris, 1950.

Robinson, W. P. (ed.), *Social Groups and Identities: Developing the Legacy of Henri Tajfel*. Boston, MA, 1996.

Rokeach, M., *The Open and Closed Mind*. New York, 1960.

Rose, P., "Spectators and Spectator Comfort in Roman Entertainment Buildings: A Study in Functional Design," *PBSR* 73 (2005), 99–130.

Rose, S. (ed.), *From Brains to Consciousness? Essays on the New Sciences of the Mind*. Princeton, 1999.

Rosenblum, M., *Luxorius: A Latin Poet among the Vandals*. New York, 1961.

Roth, R. E. (ed.), *Roman by Integration: Dimensions of Group Identity in Material Culture and Text*, *JRA* Supplementary Series 66, Portsmouth, RI, 2007.

Roueché, C., "Acclamations in the Later Roman Empire: New Evidence from Aphrodisias," *JRS* 74 (1984), 181–99.
Aphrodisias in Late Antiquity. London, 1989.
Performers and Partisans at Aphrodisias in the Roman and Late Roman Periods. London, 1993.

Roughley, N. (ed.), *Being Humans: Anthropological Universality and Particularity in Transdisciplinary Perspectives*. Berlin, 2000.

Rouland, N., *Pouvoir politique et dépendance personnelle dans l'antiquité romaine: Genèse et rôle des rapports de clientèle*, Collection Latomus 166. Brussels, 1979.

Rowell, H. T., "The Gladiator Petraites and the Date of the Satyricon," *TAPA* 89 (1958), 12–24.

Royer, K., "The Body in Parts: Reading the Execution Ritual in Late Medieval England," *Historical Reflections/Reflexions Historiques* 29 (2003), 319–39.

Ruff, J. R., *Violence in Early Modern Europe, 1500–1800*. Cambridge, 2001.

Ruggiero, G., "Constructing Civic Morality, Deconstructing the Body: Civic Rituals of Punishment in Renaissance Venice," in J. Chiffoleu, L. Martines, and A.P. Bagliani (eds.), *Riti e rituali nelle società medievali* (Spoleto, 1994), 175–90.

Russell, G. W., "Psychological Issues in Sports Aggression," in Goldstein (ed.), *Sports Violence*, 157–81.
The Social Psychology of Sport. New York, 1993.

Ryan, P. T., *The Last Public Execution in America*. Kentucky, 1992. Available at www.geocities.com/lastpublichang/ (accessed March 3, 2010).

Sabbatini Tumolesi, P., *Gladiatorum Paria: Annunci di spettacoli gladiatorii a Pompei*. Rome, 1980.

Sabin, P., "The Face of Roman Battle," *JRS* 90 (2000), 1–17.

Sadchev, I. and R. Y. Bourhis, "Social Categorization and Power Differentials in Group Relations," *European Journal of Social Psychology* 15 (1985), 415–34.

"Status Differentials and Intergroup Behaviour," *European Journal of Social Psychology* 17 (1987), 277–93.

Saggs, H. W. F., "Assyrian Warfare in the Sargonid Period," *Iraq* 25 (1963), 145–54.

Sahagún, Bernardino de, *General History of the Things of New Spain*, 2nd edn., 13 vols. Santa Fe, 1969–82; originally published *c.* 1540–85.

Salisbury, J. E., *Perpetua's Passion: The Death and Memory of a Young Roman Woman*. London, 1997.

Sallares, R., *Malaria and Rome: A History of Malaria in Ancient Italy*. Oxford, 2002.

Saller, R. P., "Anecdotes as Historical Evidence for the Principate," *Greece and Rome* 27 (1980), 69–83.

Personal Patronage under the Early Empire. Cambridge, 1982.

Patriarchy, Property and Death in the Roman Family. Cambridge, 1994.

"The Hierarchical Household in Roman Society: A Study of Domestic Slavery," in M. L. Bush (ed.), *Serfdom and Slavery: Studies in Legal Bondage* (New York, 1996), 112–29.

Saller, R. P. and B. D. Shaw, "Tombstones and Family Relations in the Principate: Civilians, Soldiers, and Slaves," *JRS* 74 (1984), 124–56.

Salomonson, J. W., Voluptatem Spectandi Non Perdat Sed Mutet: *Observations sur l'Iconographie du martyre en Afrique Romaine*. Amsterdam, 1979.

Sanford, N., "The Roots of Prejudice: Emotional Dynamics," in Watson (ed.), *Psychology and Rage*, 57–75.

Sansone, D., *Greek Athletics and the Genesis of Sport*. Berkeley, 1988.

Sapolsky, B. S. and F. Molitor, "Content Trends in Contemporary Horror Films," in Weaver and Tamborini (eds.), *Horror Films*, 33–48.

Schäfer, D., "Frauen in der Arena," in H. Bellen and H. Heinen (eds.), *Fünfzig Jahre Forschungen zur antiken Sklaverei an der Mainzer Akademie, 1950–2000: Miscellanea zum Jubiläum*, Forschungen zur antiken Sklaverei 35 (Stuttgart, 2001), 243–68.

Schama, S., *Citizens: A Chronicle of the French Revolution*. New York, 1989.

Schechter, H., *Savage Pastimes: A Cultural History of Violent Entertainment*. New York, 2005.

Scheid, J., *Le collège des frères arvales: étude prosopographique du recrutement (69–304)*. Rome, 1990.

Romulus et ses frères: le collège arvale modèle du culte public dans la Rome des empereurs, BEFAR 275. Rome, 1990.

Recherches archéologiques à la Magliana: Commentarii Fratrum Arvalium qui Supersunt: les copies épigraphiques des protocoles annuels de la confrérie arvale. Rome, 1998.

Scheidel, W., "Slavery and the Shackled Mind: On Fortune-telling and Slave Mentality in the Graeco-Roman World," *AHB* 7.3 (1993), 107–14.

Death on the Nile: Disease and the Demography of Roman Egypt, Mnemosyne Suppl. 228. Leiden, 2001.

"Germs for Rome," in Edwards and Woolf (eds.), *Rome the Cosmopolis*, 158–76.

Scheidel, W. (ed.), *Debating Roman Demography*, Mnemosyne Suppl. 211. Leiden, 2001.

Schild, W., "History of Crime and Punishment," in C. Hinkeldey (ed.), *Criminal Justice through the Ages: From Divine Judgement to Modern German Legislation* (Rothenburg ob der Tauber, 1993), 99–173.

Schnurr, C., (1992) "The *Lex Julia Theatralis* of Augustus: Some Remarks on Seating Problems in Theatre, Amphitheatre, and Circus," *Liverpool Classical Monthly* 17.10 (Dec.), 147–60.

Schumacher, L., *Sklaverei in der Antike: Alltag und Schicksal der Unfreien*. Munich, 2001.

Schwartz, J. M. and S. Begley, *The Mind and the Brain: Neuroplasticity and the Power of Mental Force*. New York, 2002.

Scobie, A., "Slums, Sanitation, and Mortality in the Roman World," *Klio* 68 (1986), 399–433.

"Spectator Security and Comfort at Gladiatorial Games," *Nikephoros* 1 (1988), 191–243.

Sharpe, J. A., "'Last Dying Speeches': Religion, Ideology and Public Execution in Seventeenth-Century England," *Past and Present* 107 (1985), 144–67.

Shaw, B. D., "'Eaters of Flesh and Drinkers of Milk': The Ancient Mediterranean Ideology of the Pastoral Nomad," *AncSoc* 13–14 (1982–3), 5–31.

"Among the Believers," *EchCl* 28 (1984), 453–79.

"Bandits in the Roman Empire," *Past and Present* 102 (1984), 3–52.

"The Passion of Perpetua," *Past and Present* 115 (1987), 3–45.

"Body/Power/Identity: The Passion of the Martyrs," *Journal of Early Christian Studies* 4.3 (1996), 269–312.

"Seasons of Death: Aspects of Mortality in Imperial Rome," *JRS* 86 (1996), 100–38.

Shay, J., *Achilles in Vietnam: Combat Trauma and the Undoing of Character*. New York, 1994.

Odysseus in America: Combat Trauma and the Trials of Homecoming. New York, 2002.

Shelton, J.-A., "Elephants, Pompey, and the Reports of Popular Displeasure in 55 BC," in S. N. Byrne and E. P. Cueva (eds.), Veritatis Amicitiaeque Causa: *Essays in Honor of Anna Lydia Motto and John R. Clark* (Wauconda, 1999), 231–71.

Shepherd, J. M., "Murders of Passion, Execution Delays, and the Deterrence of Capital Punishment," *Journal of Legal Studies* 33 (2004), 283–322.

Sherif, M., *Group Conflict and Co-operation: Their Social Psychology*. London, 1966.

Sherif, M., O. J. Harvey, B. J. White, W. R. Hood, and C. W. Sherif, *Intergroup Conflict and Cooperation: The Robbers Cave Experiment*. Norman, 1961.

Sherwin-White, A. N., *Racial Prejudice in Ancient Rome*. Cambridge, 1967.

Shore, B., "Human Diversity and Human Nature: The Life and Times of a False Dichotomy," in Roughley (ed.), *Being Humans*, 81–103.

Shulman, J. L. and W. G. Bowen, *The Game of Life: College Sports and Educational Values*. Princeton, 2001.

Sidanius, J. and F. Pratto, *Social Dominance: An Intergroup Theory of Social Hierarchy and Oppression*. Cambridge, 1999.

Simpson, C. J., "Musicians and the Arena: Dancers and the Hippodrome," *Latomus* 59 (2000), 633–39.

Sinha, A. K., and O. P. Upadhaya, "Change and Persistence in the Stereotypes of University Students toward Different Ethnic Groups during the Sino-Indian Border Dispute," *Journal of Social Psychology* 52 (1960), 225–31.

Slater, W. J., "Pantomime Riots," *CA* 13 (1994), 120–44.

Slater, W. J. (ed.), *Dining in a Classical Context*. Ann Arbor, 1991.

(ed.), *Roman Theater and Society*. Ann Arbor, 1996.

Sloan, L. R., "The Motives of Sports Fans," in Goldstein (ed.), *Sports, Games, and Play*, 175–240.

Slovenko, R. and J. A. Knight (eds.), *Motivations in Play, Games, and Sports*. Springfield, 1967.

Small, D. B., "Social Correlations to the Greek Cavea in the Roman Period," in S. Macready and F. H. Thompson (eds.), *Roman Architecture in the Greek World* (London, 1987), 85–93.

Smith, G. J., B. Patterson, T. Williams, and J. Hogg, "A Profile of the Deeply Committed Sports Fan," *Arena Review* 5.2 (1981), 26–44.

Smith, M. S., *Petronius: Cena Trimalchionis*. Oxford, 1975.

Smith, P. B., and M. H. Bond, *Social Psychology across Cultures: Analysis and Perspectives*, 2nd edn. Boston, MA, 1999.

Sparks, G. G. and C. W. Sparks, "Violence, Mayhem, and Horror," in D. Zillmann and P. Vorderer (eds.), *Media Entertainment: The Psychology of Its Appeal* (Mahwah, 2000), 73–91.

"The Effects of Media Violence," in Bryant and Zillmann (eds.), *Media Effects*, 269–85.

Spears, R. C., P. J. Oakes, N. Ellemers, and S. A. Haslam (eds.), *The Social Psychology of Stereotyping and Group Life*. Oxford, 1997.

Spierenburg, P. C., *The Spectacle of Suffering: Executions and the Evolution of Repression from a Preindustrial Metropolis to the European Experience*. Cambridge, 1984.

Men and Violence : Gender, Honor, and Rituals in Modern Europe and America. Columbus, 1998.

Staab, G., "Zu den neuen Gladiatorenmonumenten aus Stratonikeia in Karien," *ZPE* 161 (2007), 35–44.

Starn, O., C. I. Degregori, and R. Kirk (eds.), *The Peru Reader*. Durham, NC, 1995.

Stearns, C. Z. and P. N. Stearns, *Anger: The Struggle for Emotional Control in America's History*. Chicago, 1986.

Stein, A., *Die römische Ritterstand: Ein Beitrag zur Sozial- und Personengeschichte des römischen Reiches*. Munich, 1927.

Stuart, J. and D. McK. Malcolm (eds.), *The Diary of Henry Francis Fynn*. Pieter-maritzburg, 1950.

Stuart, K., *Defiled Trades and Social Outcasts: Honor and Ritual Pollution in Early Modern Germany*. Cambridge, 1999.

Sugden, J. and A. Tomlinson (eds.), *Power Games: A Critical Sociology of Sport*. London, 2002.

Swanson, J. E., *Brain Architecture: Understanding the Basic Plan*. Oxford, 2003.

Syme, R., *The Roman Revolution*. Oxford, 1939.

Szmatka, J., M. Lovaglia, and K. Wysienska (eds.), *The Growth of Social Knowledge: Theory, Simulation, and Empirical Research in Group Processes*. Westport, 2002.

Tajfel, H. (ed.), *Differentiation between Social Groups: Studies in the Social Psychology of Intergroup Relations*. London, 1978.

"The Achievement of Group Differentiation," in Tajfel (ed.), *Differentiation between Social Groups*, 77–98.

"The Roots of Prejudice: Cognitive Aspects," in Watson (ed.), *Psychology and Rage*, 76–95.

Tajfel, H., C. Flament, M. Billig, and P. Bundy, "Social Categorization and Intergroup Behaviour," *European Journal of Social Psychology* 11 (1971), 149–78.

Thackeray, W. M., "Going to See a Man Hanged," *Fraser's Magazine* 22 (Aug. 1840), 150–8.

Thompson, E. P., "The Moral Economy of the English Crowd in the Eighteenth Century," *Past and Present* 50 (1971), 76–136.

Thompson, L. A., *Romans and Blacks*. London, 1989.

Thompson, L. L., "The Martyrdom of Polycarp: Death in the Roman Games," *Jrel* 82 (2002), 27–52.

Thuillier, J.-P., *Le sport dans la Rome antique*. Paris, 1996.

Tolnay, S. E. and E. M. Beck, *A Festival of Violence: An Analysis of Southern Lynchings, 1882–1930*. Urbana, 1995.

Toner, J. P., *Leisure and Ancient Rome*. Cambridge, 1995.

Rethinking Roman History. Cambridge, 2002.

Torr, J. D. (ed.), *Is Media Violence a Problem?* San Diego, 2002.

Townend, G. B., "Calpurnius Siculus and the Munus Neronis," *JRS* 70 (1980), 166–74.

Toynbee, J. M. C., *Animals in Roman Life and Art*. London, 1973; reprint Baltimore, 1986.

Treggiari, S. M., *Roman Freedmen during the Late Republic*. Oxford, 1969.

"Domestic Staff at Rome in the Julio-Claudian Period, 27 B.C. to A.D. 68," *Histoire Sociale/Social History* 6 (1973), 241–55.

Trend, D., *The Myth of Media Violence: A Critical Introduction*. Oxford, 2007.

Tuck, S., "*De Arte Gladiatoria*: Recovering Gladiatorial Tactics from Artistic Sources," Paper delivered at the AIA Annual Meeting 2005. Abstract accessible online at www.archaeological.org/webinfo.php?page=10248&searchtype=

abstract&ytable=2005&sessionid=4F&paperid=189 (accessed March 4, 2010).

Tuck, S. L., "Spectacle and Ideology in the Relief Decorations of the Anfiteatro Campano at Capua," *JRA* 20 (2007), 255–72.

"Scheduling Spectacle: Factors Contributing to the Dates of Pompeian Munera," *CJ* 104 (2008), 123–43.

Turner, J. C., *Rediscovering the Social Group: A Self-Categorizaton Theory*. Oxford, 1987.

"Some Current Issues in Research on Social Identity and Self-Categorization Theories," in N. Ellemers, R. Spears, and B. Doosje (eds.), *Social Identity: Context, Commitment, Content* (Oxford, 1999), 6–34.

Twain, M., *A Tramp Abroad*, 2 vols. Hartford, 1880.

Tyldesley, J. A., *Judgement of the Pharaoh: Crime and Punishment in Ancient Egypt*. London, 2000.

US Federal Trade Commission Reports: *Marketing Violent Entertainment to Children*. Washington, DC, 2000–2.

Van Den Berg, C., "The *Pulvinar* in Roman Culture," *TAPA* 138 (2008), 239–73.

van Dülmen, R., *Theatre of Horror: Crime and Punishment in Early Modern Germany*. Cambridge, 1990.

van Nijf, O. M., *The Civic World of Professional Associations in the Roman East*. Amsterdam, 1997.

van Raalte, J. L. and B. W. Brewer (eds.), *Exploring Sport and Exercise Psychology*, 2nd edn. Washington, DC, 2002.

Vanderbroeck, P. J. J., *Popular Leadership and Collective Behavior in the Late Roman Republic (ca. 80–50 BC)*. Amsterdam, 1987.

Vanderwolf, C. H., *An Odyssey Through the Brain, Behavior and the Mind*. Norwell, 2003.

Vasaly, A., *Representations: Images of the World in Ciceronian Oratory*. Berkeley, 1993.

Vescio, T. K., S. J. Gervais, L. Heiphetz, and B. Bloodhart, "The Stereotypic Behaviors of the Powerful and their Effect on the Relatively Powerless," in T. D. Nelson (ed.), *Handbook of Prejudice, Stereotyping, and Discrimination* (New York, 2009), 247–65.

Veyne, P., *Le pain et le cirque: sociologie historique d'un pluralisme politique*. Paris, 1976.

Ville, G., *La gladiature en Occident des origines à la Mort de Domitien*, BEFAR 245. Rome, 1981.

Vismara, C., *Il supplizio come spettacolo*. Rome, 1990.

Vogt, J., *Kulturwelt und Barbaren: Zum Menschheitsbild der spätantiken Gesellschaft*. Wiesbaden, 1967.

von Boeslager, D.,"Das Gladiatorenmosaik in Köln und seine Restaurierung im 19. Jahrhundert," *KölnJb* 20 (1987), 111–28.

von Ungern-Sternberg, J., "Die Einführung spezieller Sitze für die Senatoren bei den Spielen (194 v. Chr.)," *Chiron* 5 (1975), 157–63.

Wallace-Hadrill, A. (ed.), *Patronage in Ancient Society*. London, 1989.

Wallin, N. L., B. Merker, and S. Brown (eds.), *The Origins of Music*. Cambridge, MA, 2000.

Walton, S., *A Natural History of Human Emotions*. New York, 2005.

Wann, D. L., M. J. Melnick, G. W. Russell, and D. G. Pease, *Sport Fans: The Psychology and Social Impact of Spectators*. London, 2001.

Ward-Perkins, J. B. and J. M. C. Toynbee, "The Hunting Baths at Leptis Magna," *Archaeologia* 93 (1949), 165–95.

Watson, P. (ed.), *Psychology and Rage*. New Brunswick, 2007.

Weaver, J. B. and R. Tamborini (eds.), *Horror Films: Current Research on Audience Preferences and Reactions*. Mahwah, 1996.

Weaver, P. R. C., *Familia Caesaris: A Social Study of the Emperor's Freedmen and Slaves*. Cambridge, 1972.

"Reconstructing Lower-Class Roman Families," in S. Dixon (ed.), *Childhood, Class and Kin in the Roman World* (London, 2001), 101–14.

Weddle, D., *If they Move, Kill 'Em: The Life and Times of Sam Peckinpah*. New York, 1994.

Weeber, K.-W., *Panem et Circenses: Massenunterhaltung als Politik im antiken Rom*. Mainz, 1994.

Weiler, I., *Der Sport bei den Völkern der Alten Welt*, 2nd edn. Darmstadt, 1988.

Weiler, I., and H. Grassl (eds.), *Soziale Randgruppen und Aussenseiter im Altertum: Referate vom Symposion "Soziale Randgruppen und Antike Sozialpolitik" in Graz (21. bis 23. September 1987)*. Graz, 1988.

Weinberg, R. S. and D. Gould, *Foundations of Sport and Exercise Psychology*, 3rd edn. Champaign, 2003.

Weiss, P., *Sport: A Philosophical Inquiry*. Carbondale, 1969.

Welch, K., "The Roman Arena in Late-Republican Italy: A New Interpretation," *JRA* 7 (1994), 59–80.

"The Stadium at Aphrodisias," *AJA* 102 (1998), 547–69.

"Greek Stadia and Roman Spectacles: Asia, Athens and the Tomb of Herodes Atticus," *JRA* 11 (1998), 117–45.

"Negotiating Roman Spectacle Architecture in the Greek World: Athens and Corinth," in Bergmann and Kondoleon (eds.), *Art of Ancient Spectacle*, 125–45.

Welch, K. E., *The Roman Amphitheatre from its Origins to the Colosseum*. Cambridge, 2007.

Westermann, W. L., *The Slave Systems of Greek and Roman Antiquity*. Philadelphia, 1955.

Wiedemann, T., "Between Men and Beasts: Barbarians in Ammianus Marcellinus," in I. Moxon, J. D. Smart, and A. J. Woodman (eds.), *Past Perspectives: Studies in Greek and Roman Historical Writing* (Cambridge, 1985), 189–229.

Emperors and Gladiators. London, 1992.

Wiedemann, T. (ed.), *Greek and Roman Slavery*. London, 1981.

Wierzbicka, A., *Emotions across Languages and Cultures: Diversity and Universals*. Cambridge, 1999.

Wiles, D., "Aristotle's Poetics and Ancient Dramatic Theory," in M. McDonald and J. M. Walton (eds.), *The Cambridge Companion to Greek and Roman Theatre* (Cambridge, 2007), 92–107.

Winter, J. G., *Life and Letters in the Papyri*. Ann Arbor, 1933.

Wiseman, T. P., *Catullus and His World: A Reappraisal*. Cambridge, 1985.

Wistrand, M., *Entertainment and Violence in Ancient Rome: The Attitudes of Roman Writers of the First Century* AD. Göteborg, 1992.

Woolf, G., "Food, Poverty and Patronage: The Significance of the Epigraphy of the Roman Alimentary Schemes in Early Imperial Italy," *PBSR* 45 (1990), 197–228.

   Becoming Roman: The Origins of Provincial Civilization in Gaul. Cambridge, 1998.

Worchel, S. and D. Coutant, "It Takes Two to Tango: Group Identity to Individual Identity within the Framework of Group Development," in Hogg and Tindale (eds.), *Group Processes*, 461–81.

Wuilleumier, P. and A. Audin, *Les médallions d'applique gallo-romains de la Vallée du Rhône*. Paris, 1952.

Wylie, D., *Savage Delight: White Myths of Shaka*. Pietermaritzburg, 2000.

Wynn, T. G., *The Evolution of Spatial Competence*. Urbana, 1989.

Yavetz, Z., "The Living Conditions of the Urban Plebs in Republican Rome," *Latomus* 17 (1958), 500–517 (= R. Seager, *The Crisis of the Roman Republic* [Cambridge, 1969], 162–79).

Yegül, F., *Bathing in the Roman World*. Cambridge, 2010.

Zanna, M. P. and J. M. Olson (eds.), *The Psychology of Prejudice*. Hillsdale, 1994.

Zarate, M. A., B. Garcia, A. A. Garza, and R. Hitlan, "Cultural Threat and Perceived Realistic Group Conflict as Predictors of Attitudes toward Mexican Immigrants," *Journal of Experimental Social Psychology* 40 (2004), 99–105.

Zillmann, D., "The Experimental Exploration of Gratifications from Media Entertainment," in K. E. Rosengren, L. A. Wenner, and P. Palmgreen (eds.), *Media Gratifications Research: Current Perspectives* (Beverly Hills, 1985), 225–39.

   "Television Viewing and Physiological Arousal," in Bryant and Zillmann (eds.), *Responding to the Screen*, 103–33.

   "The Logic of Suspense and Mystery," in Bryant and Zillmann (eds.), *Responding to the Screen*, 281–303.

   "Mechanisms of Emotional Involvement with Drama," *Poetics* 23 (1994), 33–51.

   "The Psychology of the Appeal of Portrayals of Violence," in Goldstein (ed.), *Why We Watch*, 179–211.

   "Basal Morality in Drama Appreciation," in I. Bondebjerg (ed.), *Moving Images, Culture, and the Mind* (Luton, 2000), 53–63.

Zillmann, D. and J. R. Cantor, "A Disposition Theory of Humour and Mirth," in A. J. Chapman and H. C. Foot (eds.), *Humour and Laughter: Theory and Applications* (London, 1976), 93–115.

Zillmann, D. and R. Gibson, "Evolution of the Horror Genre," in Weaver and Tamborini (eds.), *Horror Films*, 15–31.

Zillmann, D. and S. Knobloch, "Emotional Reactions to Narratives about the Fortunes of Personae in the News Theater," *Poetics* 29 (2001), 189–206.

Zillmann, D. and J. B. Weaver, "Viewer's Moral Sanction of Retribution in the Appreciation of Dramatic Represenations," *Journal of Experimental Social Psychology* 11 (1975), 572–82.

"Gender-Socialization Theory of Reactions to Horror," in Weaver and Tamborini (eds.), *Horror Films*, 81–101.

Zillmann, D., J. Bryant, and B. S. Sapolsky, "Enjoyment from Sports Spectatorship," in Goldstein (ed.), *Sports, Games, and Play*, 241–78.

Zillmann, D., K. Taylor, and K. Lewis, "News as Nonfiction Theater: How Dispositions toward the Public Cast of Characters Affect Reactions," *Journal of Broadcasting and Electronic Media* 42 (1998), 153–69.

Zillmann, D., J. B. Weaver, N. Mundorf, and C. F. Aust, "Effects of an Opposite-gender Companion's Affect to Horror on Distress, Delight, and Attraction," *Journal of Personality and Social Psychology* 51 (1986), 586–94.

Zimbardo, P. G., *The Lucifer Effect: Understanding How Good People Turn Evil.* New York, 2007.

Zimbardo, P. G., C. Maslach, and C. Haney, "Reflections on the Stanford Prison Experiment: Genesis, Transformations, Consequences," in T. Blass (ed.), *Obedience to Authority: Current Perspectives on the Milgram Paradigm* (Mahwah, 2000), 193–237.

Zuckerman, M., *Sensation Seeking: Beyond the Optimal Level of Arousal.* Hillsdale, 1979.

"Sensation Seeking and the Taste for Vicarious Horror," in Weaver and Tamborini (eds.), *Horror Films*, 147–60.

Index